INTERNATIONAL ECONOMIC LAW SERIES

General Editor: John H. Jackson

REGULATORY COMPETITION AND ECONOMIC INTEGRATION

Comparative Perspectives

Regulatory Competition and Economic Integration

Comparative Perspectives

Edited by

DANIEL C. ESTY

and

DAMIEN GERADIN

OXFORD
UNIVERSITY PRESS

This book has been printed digitally and produced in a standard specification in order to ensure its continuing availability

OXFORD
UNIVERSITY PRESS

Great Clarendon Street, Oxford OX2 6DP

Oxford University Press is a department of the University of Oxford.
It furthers the University's objective of excellence in research, scholarship, and education by publishing worldwide in

Oxford New York

Auckland Bangkok Buenos Aires Cape Town Chennai
Dar es Salaam Delhi Hong Kong Istanbul Karachi Kolkata
Kuala Lumpur Madrid Melbourne Mexico City Mumbai Nairobi
São Paulo Shanghai Taipei Tokyo Toronto

Oxford is a registered trade mark of Oxford University Press in the UK and in certain other countries

Published in the United States by Oxford University Press Inc., New York

Reprinted 2004

ISBN 0-19-829905-2

To Elizabeth, Sarah, Thomas,
Jonathan, Mercedes, Ana
and Emma—who help
to regulate the competition
of life

DCE
DG

General Editor's Preface

Oxford Univesity Press is very pleased to publish this distinguished work of scholarship and with it to introduce a new series of books dealing with subjects of international economic law. It is indeed fitting that such a book series begin with the subject of this publication—regulatory competition—because this subject is one which is truly central to current governmental responses to many problems of "globalization" which are perplexing government officials and policy makers at all levels, as well as non-government persons with similar interests in private enterprises or non-profit organizations.

Much has been written about globalization. Likewise much has been written about "regulatory competition". But not all that has been written about either topic has contributed to the analysis and thinking needed to assist the formulation of intelligent policy about these topics (to indulge in a bit of understatement). The popular media and the various specially interested policy advocates often detract from the clear thinking needed for the understanding of these subjects and the development of ways to cope with the challenges they present.

"Regulatory competition" refers inter alia to situations where different governments approach a regulatory problem (often a problem involving economic activity) in manners substantially different. As the subjects and titles of the various chapters in this book suggest, the economic activity involved can vary enormously—covering taxation, labor standards, investment regulation, banking, insurance, etc. The regulatory approaches of different governments can create tensions between governments and different societies. If one government concludes that a strict and high level of regulation is appropriate to protect its citizens from oppression of economic power or from fraudulent activities, that government may, in the context of global interdependence and especially with factors that are mobile, find its policy objectives frustrated when other governments and societies conclude that very minimal or lax regulation is appropriate and may indeed give the latter societies some "competitive advantage" in the global marketplace. Sometimes the phrase used for this is "race to the bottom."

The other side of this coin is the view persuasively put forward by some important thinkers that excessive government regulation is damaging to the best use of world resources and inhibits economic progress for societies and the whole world. The Prisoners' dilemma comes to mind. In such cases, such thinkers sometimes applaud "regulatory competition" by which the global market puts pressure on governments to diminish their heavy hand of regulation. Sometimes a phrase used in this context is "race to the top", i.e. a race to deregulate or to more extensively rely on market forces to achieve the policy goals governments want to maximise for their constituents.

It may be that there is no true solution to the dilemmas implied by the previous two paragraphs—wide-ranging and raging academic exchanges have been manifested for decades, and such societies as the United States and the European Union have apparently been on the opposite sides of some of these issues in connection with solutions such as regulatory harmonization which are urged upon them. However, surely it is important to try to better understand the forces at play and how they operate in different societal and institutional contexts. Thus we can see the central importance of this debate to the world we now live in with the revolution that has occurred for both transportation and communication which in turn has created an apparently perilous world economy that lacks adequate human institutions to cope with some of the dangers such as those that created the recent so-called "Asian financial crisis", and the harm it did to millions of families around the world.

This book clearly "moves the marker" in the right direction towards greater understanding. It does this partly by an ingenious structure of comparative analysis: across economic experiences (e.g. US, EU, WTO, etc.), across regulatory subject areas (e.g. environment, labor, banking, corporate law), and bringing to bear different disciplinary approaches (law, business, political science, and economics.) It does not offer the "simple overwhelming solution" so often sought but more often elusive, but it creates for us modes of thinking about these problems and applications of those approaches which will, I think, "stick to our ribs" as we struggle for the greater understanding needed to reduce some of the risks now prevailing in a risky world.

The subject of this book thus stands with those topics which are the core of the very broad landscape of "international economic law." And that brings me to an introduction of this new Oxford University Press endeavor to address that landscape with a series of books, of which this book is the first. I personally, as editorial advisor invited by OUP for this series, am delighted to launch the series with this work. We look forward to an impressive and distinguished series of books, some solo-authored, others created by teamwork such as this book, which are designed to face the risks and dangers of the "globalized" and interdependent world. These risks and dangers are truly roiling the waters of government practice and theories, and of every level of modern life from that of the individual family to the broadest reaches of multilateral international institutions, and the relationships among the various levels which often are described by using opaque and inflammatory or simplistic or ambiguous words such as "sovereignty", or "bureaucracy" rather than going through the tough slogging processes of analytical thinking needed to truly understand. Our goal for this book series is to undertake the tough slogging and hopefully thus to contribute to the understanding so many people need.

John H. Jackson
Washington DC

Acknowledgements

This volume represents a deeply collaborative effort not just between the editors but among all those who wrote chapters and a great number of others as well. The essays presented arose out of an October 1999 Conference at the Yale Law School. That event, cosponsored by the Yale Law School and the University of Liège stimulated considerable thinking about how regulatory competition plays out in various settings and helped many of the contributors to this conference to refine their analysis and arguments. Without the support of Dean Anthony Kronman of Yale and Professor Paul Demaret at Liège, this project could not have been launched, never mind successfully completed.

In many respects, the godfather of the project is Professor John Jackson at Georgetown Law School. His interest in understanding how national-level debates over regulatory competition, harmonization, federalism, and subsidiarity within the United States and the European Union might inform each other and the emerging structure of international economic law was a driving force behind this entire project. We are very pleased to be the first book in Professor Jackson's new Oxford University Press series on international economic law.

We have been very fortunate to work with an outstanding group of authors from both sides of the Atlantic. Given that the essence of this project was comparative work, we might well have found ourselves facing great difficulties given the range of topics, disciplines, and academic traditions that we were seeking to merge. Instead, we have had an extremely good experience working across cultures and disciplines and are very pleased with the results that we present here. We are deeply grateful for the contributions of Mark Barenberg, Lucian Bebchuk, Brian Bercusson, William Bratton, David Charny, Simon Deakin, Paul Demaret, Kirsten Engel, Susan Rose-Ackerman, Michael Faure, Allen Ferrell, Eleanor Fox, Inge Govaere, Gérard Hertig, Jonathan Macey, Joseph McCahery, Richard Revesz, Daniel Shaviro, Joel Trachtman, and David Vogel.

With great sadness, we note that one of the leading scholars in the regulatory competition field and one of the significant contributors to our project, David Charny of Harvard Law School, died as this volume was going to press. We are appreciative of his role in our initiative and the broader academic debate. We will miss his vibrant voice, but we are confident that his chapter in this volume adds to his enduring scholarly mark.

This book would not exist but for several extraordinary research assistants. Both Amy Marx and Chanel Reedy did far more than track down footnotes and missing facts. Both contributed significantly to the editorial process and to the structure and flow of this volume. Elizabeth Jenkins also played a major role with many long hours devoted to the construction of the bibliography, which we see as a significant research tool.

Marge Camera has our undying gratitude for her many contributions to this book and the broader project. She organized the conference which led to this volume. She typed and retyped our own contributions many times over.

We have been fortunate to have the support of an extraordinary team at Oxford University Press. John Louth has been a joy to work with and Mick Belson has made the editorial process go very smoothly.

We received funding for this endeavour from both the Yale Law School and from the Poles d'Attraction Inter-universitaire, a research project initiated by the Belgian State, Prime Minister's Office, Science Policy Programming. In addition, our efforts have been supported by the Global Environment and Trade Study and its funders including the Ford Foundation and the MacArthur Foundation.

Contents

List of Contributors xi

Introduction xvii
Daniel C. Esty and Damien Geradin

I Introduction to Regulatory Competition Theory

1 Federalism and Regulation: Some Generalizations 3
Richard Revesz

2 Regulatory Co-Opetition 30
Daniel C. Esty and Damien Geradin

II Regulatory Competition Theory in the US System

3 Some Observations Concerning Multijurisdictional Tax Competition 49
Daniel Shaviro

4 Federalism and Takeover Law: The Race to Protect Managers from Takeovers 68
Lucian Arye Bebchuk and Allen Ferrell

5 Regulatory Competition in the US Federal System: Banking and Financial Services 95
Jonathan R. Macey

6 Labour Federalism in the United States: Lessons for Coordinated Decentralization in Supranational Regimes 111
Mark Barenberg

7 Environmental Federalism in the United States: The Risks of Devolution 135
Kirsten Engel and Susan Rose-Ackerman

III Regulatory Competition Theory in the EU Context

8 Fiscal Federalism, Jurisdictional Competition, and Tax Coordination: Translating Theory to Policy in the European Union 157
William Bratton and Joseph McCahery

9 Regulatory Competition versus Harmonization in European Company Law 190
Simon Deakin

10 Regulatory Competition for EU Financial Services 218
Gérard Hertig

11 Regulatory Competition in the EU System: Labour 241
Brian Bercusson

12 Regulatory Competition vs Harmonization in EU Environmental Law 263
Michael Faure

IV Regulatory Competition at the Global Scale

13 Regulatory Competition and Regulatory Jurisdiction in International Securities Regulation 289
Joel P. Trachtman

14 Regulatory Competition and the Global Coordination of Labour Standards 311
David Charny

15 Environmental Regulation and Economic Integration 330
David Vogel

16 Antitrust Law on a Global Scale: Races Up, Down, and Sideways 348
Eleanor M. Fox

17 The TRIPS Agreement: A Response to Global Regulatory Competition or an Exercise in Global Regulatory Coercion? 364
Inge Govaere and Paul Demaret

Bibliography 382
Index 421

List of Contributors

Mark Barenberg is Professor of Law at Columbia University, specializing in labor, international, and constitutional law. He has taught these subjects, as well as international economics, economic development, and labor relations, at the Universities of Harvard, Yale, Cologne, Tokyo, and Beijing, and the European University Institute.

Lucian Arye Bebchuk is the William J. Friedman and Alicia Townsend Friedman Professor of Law, Economics, and Finance at the Harvard Law School. He is also a Fellow of the American Academy of Arts and Sciences, a Research Associate of the National Bureau of Economic Research, and a frequent visitor to Tel-Aviv University. He has written extensively on a broad range of subjects at the intersection of law and economics, especially in the areas of corporate law and law and finance. Trained in both economics and law, Professor Bebchuk holds a BA in Mathematics and Economics from the University of Haifa, an LL B from the University of Tel-Aviv, an MA and PhD from the Harvard Economics Department, and an LL M and SJD from the Harvard Law School.

Brian Bercusson was Professor of European Law at the University of Manchester from 1994–2000. He now holds the Chair in European Social and Labour Law at King's College, University of London. In 2001–2002, he will be Herman Phleger Visiting Professor of Law at Stanford Law School. Since January 1997, he has also been Guest Professor at the Swedish National Institute for Working Life in Stockholm. He is Director of the European Law Unit of Thompsons, Solicitors, London, and a consultant to NETLEX, the European Trade Union Confederation's network of trade union legal experts. He co-ordinates a Research Group on Transnational Trade Union Rights for the European Trade Union Institute in Brussels.

William W. Bratton is Samuel Tyler Research Professor of Law at the George Washington University School of Law. Prior to joining the George Washington law faculty in 1999, Professor Bratton was the Kaiser Professor of Law and Director of the Heyman Center on Corporate Governance at Cardozo Law School, and Professor of Law and Governor Woodrow Wilson Scholar at Rutgers School of Law, Newark. Professor Bratton has published articles on a variety of subjects in corporate law and law and economics. He is co-editor of the leading American legal textbook on corporate finance and an Oxford University Press collection of essays on regulatory competition.

David Charny was the David Berg Professor of Law at Harvard Law School prior to his death in August of 2000. He joined the Harvard faculty in 1984 and became Professor of Law in 1991, and the David Berg Professor of Law in 1999. His research interests concerned comparative aspects of corporate law, employment law, health-care regulation, and public choice theory. Professor Charny received the BA summa cum laude, with exceptional distinction, from Yale University, and the JD magna cum laude from Harvard Law School. He served as law clerk to Judge Malcolm R. Wilkey of the US Court of Appeals for the DC Circuit and the late Supreme Court Justice Lewis F. Powell, Jr.

Simon Deakin is Reader in Economic Law at the University of Cambridge. He specialises in the economics of law, with particular reference to corporate governance, labour markets, and competition policy and has published articles on these subjects. Since 1994 he has been research director of the Corporate Governance programme at the ESRC Centre for Business Research in Cambridge. He is the joint editor of the collections *Contracts, Competition and Cooperation* (with J. Michie)(1997) and *Enterprise and Community* (with A. Hughes) (1997).

Paul Demaret is Professor of Law at the University of Liège, where he holds the Jean Monnet Chair in European Economic Law, and is also the Director of the Institut d'Études Juridiques Européennes. Professor Demaret is, additionally, the Director of Legal Studies at the College of Europe, Bruges. His publications are mainly in the field of European Community law and International Trade Law. Professor Demaret holds a doctorate in law from University of Liège, an LL M from Columbia University, and a JSD from UC Berkeley.

Kirsten H. Engel is an associate professor of law at Tulane Law School. Professor Engel is on leave during the 2000–2001 academic year to serve as Acting Chief of the Environmental Protection Division of the Massachusetts Office of Attorney General. She joined the Tulane Law faculty from positions in the Office of General Counsel of the US Environmental Protection Agency and with Sierra Club Legal Defense Fund. Professor Engel has published numerous articles on environmental federalism, constitutional law and resource protection, brownfields redevelopment, and environmental justice issues. She is a graduate of Brown University and Northwestern University School of Law.

Daniel C. Esty is a professor of environmental law and policy at the Yale Law School and the Yale School of Forestry and Environmental Studies. He is also Director of the Yale Center for Environmental Law and Policy and Associate Dean of the Yale School of Forestry and Environmental Studies. A former US Environmental Protection Agency Official, Professor Esty is the author or editor of five books and numerous articles on environmental policy issues and the relationships between the environment and trade, security, competitiveness, international institutions, and development including: *Thinking Ecologically: The Next Generation of Environmental Policy* (ed. with M. Chertow) (1997) and *Sustaining the Asia Pacific Miracle: Environmental Protection and Economic Integration* (with A. Dua) (1997).

Michael G. Faure has been professor of comparative and international environmental law at the law faculty of Maastricht University since 1991. He is also academic director of the Maastricht European Institute for Transnational Legal Research and academic director of the Ius Commune research school. He has published several books and articles in the field of criminal environmental law, liability and insurance and economic analysis of accidents. He studied law in Antwerp and criminology in Ghent and obtained a Master of Laws from the University of Chicago Law School.

Allen Ferrell is an assistant professor of law at Harvard Law School. His areas of interests include regulatory competition, security market regulation, and market microstructure. He holds a BA and MA in philosophy from Brown University, a JD from Harvard Law School and is working on his PhD in economics at MIT. Following graduation from law school, he clerked for Judge Silberman of the United States Court of Appeals for the DC Circuit and Justice Kennedy on the Supreme Court of the United States.

Eleanor M. Fox is the Walter J. Derenberg Professor of Trade Regulation at New York University School of Law. She was a partner and is now of counsel at the New York law firm Simpson Thacher & Bartlett. From 1997 to 2000, she served as a member of the International Competition Policy Advisory Committee of the United States Department of Justice. Her books include an antitrust casebook, a European Union casebook, a merger treatise, and an analysis of competition policy in Central Europe (all co-authored).

Damien Geradin is an associate professor of Law at the University of Liège and a Professor at the College of Europe in Bruges. He also held visiting appointments at King's College London, the University of Paris II, Yale Law School, and UCLA School of Law. During the 2000–2001 academic year, he will be a European Visiting Professor at the University of Peking, China. His research interests include European, international and comparative economic law. He holds a PhD in law from Cambridge University and was a Fulbright Research scholar at Yale Law School.

Inge Govaere is professor of European Law at the University of Ghent and a visiting professor at the Legal Studies Department of the College of Europe of Bruges and Natolin. She has published widely on issues of intellectual property rights in both the European and international context. She is author of inter alia *The Use and Abuse of Intellectual Property Rights in EC Law* (Sweet & Maxwell)(1996).

Gérard Hertig is Professor of Law at the Swiss Institute of Technology at Zurich where he is responsible for the post-graduate program on intellectual property. His areas of research include banking and capital market law, corporate law, competition law and intellectual property. His recent publications include: *Western Europe's*

Corporate Governance Dilemma, in Baums/Hopt/Horn (eds.); *Corporations, Capital Markets and Business in the Law* (2000); and *Comparative Corporate Governance* (1998). He has a doctorate in jurisprudence from the University of Geneva Law School and a masters in comparative jurisprudence (MCJ) from the University of Texas at Austin Law School.

Jonathan R. Macey is the J. DuPratt White Professor of Law and Director of the John M. Olin Program in Law and Economics at Cornell Law School. He is a member of the Legal Advisory Board of the New York Stock Exchange and an honorary Fellow of the Society for Advanced Legal Studies. He has published articles on law and economics. He earned his BA (cum laude) from Harvard, and his JD from Yale Law School, where he was Article and Book Review editor of the Yale Law Journal.

Joseph A. McCahery is Associate Professor of Law at Tilburg University Faculty of Law. He also teaches at the Leiden University Faculty of Law. He was a judicial clerk for the Honorable Nathaniel R. Jones of the US Court of Appeals for the Sixth Circuit. He is co-author of *Corporate Governance: An International Perspective* (2000). He is co-editor of *Venture Capital and the Valuation of IT Business* (forthcoming 2001); *Convergence and Diversity in Corporate Governance Regimes and Capital Markets* (Oxford University Press, 2001); *International Regulatory Competition and Coordination* (Oxford University Press, 1997); *Corporate Control and Accountability* (Oxford University Press, 1993). His research has focused on corporate governance, the regulation of securities markets, and regulatory competition.

Susan Rose-Ackerman is Henry R. Luce Professor of Law and Political Science, Yale University, and Co-director of the Law School's Center for Law, Economics, and Public Policy. She is author of a number of books including *Corruption and Government Causes, Consequences and Reform* (1999), *Controlling Environmental Policy The Limits of Public Law in Germany and the United States* (1995); and *Rethinking the Progressive Agenda: The Reform of the American Regulatory State* (1992). Her research interests include comparative regulatory law and policy, the political economy of corruption, public policy and administrative law, and law and economics. She holds a PhD in economics from Yale University and has held fellowships from the Guggenheim Foundation and the Fulbright Commission.

Richard L. Revesz is a Professor of Law at New York University School of Law, where he directs the Program on Environmental Regulation. He has written extensively about environmental law and policy, particularly on issues of federalism, the use of cost–benefit analysis, the role of courts, the design of liability rules, and the choice of regulatory instruments. Among other professional activities, Professor Revesz is a member of the Science Advisory Board of the US Environmental Protection Agency and a director of the American Law and Economics Association.

Daniel Shaviro is Professor of Law at New York University Law School. His work examines tax policy and public finance issues from an economic and political science perspective, with attention as well to distributive justice and the present tax system's institutional and administrative details. His recent books include: *Do Deficits Matter?* (1997), *When Rules Change An Economic and Political Analysis of Transition Relief in Retroactivity* (2000), and *Making Sense of Social Security Reform* (2000). He has also written recent articles about endowment taxation, the tax rules for American multinationals, and effective marginal tax rates on low-income households.

Joel P. Trachtman is Professor of International Law and interim Dean at the Fletcher School of Law and Diplomacy at Tufts University where he teaches courses in the fields of international economics and business law. His research interests are in international trade, international business regulation, international finance regulation and legal aspects of international economic integration. Professor Trachtman has written numerous articles in scholarly journals and contributions to books on these topics. He graduated from Harvard Law School, where he served as editor in chief of the Harvard International Law Journal.

David Vogel is a professor at the Haas School of Business and in the Department of Political Science at the University of California, Berkeley. He has written extensively on business-government relations and environmental policy in the United States, Europe and internationally. Vogel is the author of six books including *Trading Up: Consumer and Environmental Regulation in a Global Economy* and *Benefits or Barriers: Regulation in Transatlantic Trade*. He has been editor of the California Management Review since 1981. Professor Vogel holds a BA from Queens College, City University of New York and a PhD in politics from Princeton University.

Introduction

DANIEL C. ESTY AND DAMIEN GERADIN

As the twenty-first century dawns, a number of broad political, social, and economic trends promise to restructure the landscape in which governments operate, particularly as regulatory authorities. First, the push toward open markets and higher degrees of international economic interdependence seems inexorable, despite an occasional bump in the policy path. Governments across the world continue to pursue trade and investment liberalization initiatives at both regional and multilateral levels. Second, the role of government has diminished markedly in most countries, as traditional modes of operation are challenged and new approaches to regulation emerge. Third, the market economy stands triumphant, reinforcing the trend toward freer trade and a diminished role for government. This volume examines the intertwining of these trends and their impact on contemporary regulatory reform debates.

In particular, the volume's seventeen chapters explore a critical set of questions that arise in the context of economic integration. Should trade liberalization and economic integration between states or nations be accompanied by a degree of regulatory cooperation or coordination? Or should states or nations remain free to maintain their own approaches to economic, social, and environmental issues? The former strategy, promoting a degree of regulatory harmonization, aims to minimize market failures caused by interjurisdictional spillovers (such as pollution that flows across political boundaries) and strategic standard setting that might trigger a welfare-reducing regulatory 'race toward the bottom' as jurisdictions seek to advance the competitiveness of their industries through lax regulation. The latter approach, encouraging regulatory competition, sees a benefit in variations in approaches and standards across jurisdictions as a mechanism for testing and refining alternative policies, disciplining overreaching governments, and creating incentives for bureaucratic efficiency.

The issue underlying these questions can also be seen as a debate over the proper locus of governmental authority. Indeed, while the forces of globalization and economic interdependence promote centralization, important counterpressures exist, pushing for a more decentralized approach to policy making. In the United States, this debate often turns on the hotly contested concept of *federalism*. For most of the twentieth century, power and regulatory responsibility shifted inexorably from the states to Washington. But, over the past two decades, 'new federalists' have argued for a reallocation of regulatory authority from the federal government back to the states and even to local governments. As former US House Speaker Newt Gingrich, one of the leading architects of the devolution movement, suggests: 'We must replace our centralized, micromanaged, Washington-based bureaucracy with a dramatically decentralized system more appropriate to a continent-wide country' (Gingrich 1985: 9).

A parallel academic debate mirrors this political struggle. Richard Revesz (1992), for example, suggests that not only does geographic diversity argue for decentralized regulatory approaches, but that a set of horizontally arrayed governmental entities competing in the regulatory realm—creating, in effect, a market in 'locational rights' for businesses and even citizens—enhances social welfare. In Europe, similar political and intellectual battles are being waged over the principle of *subsidiarity*, with many commentators interpreting this concept as establishing a presumption against centralization. A new front has recently broken out in this 'jurisdictional' war over the activities of the World Trade Organization (WTO), particularly as the WTO's quasi-regulatory functions have come under attack.

Theory cuts in both directions across this centralization–decentralization debate. The logic of decentralized governmental activity has an intuitive appeal and a significant intellectual pedigree (Olson 1965; Oates 1972; Stewart 1977; Bhagwati and Hudec 1996). It tracks geographic and political diversity, accommodates the divergence of values across societies, and fulfils the civic republican ideal of keeping government close to the people whose lives are affected by the choices made. But a strong countercurrent exists. For more than 100 years beginning in the late nineteenth century in the United States, over the last half of the twentieth century within the European Union, and in recent decades at the global scale, initiatives to harmonize regulatory standards have emerged, designed to foster a 'national market' in the United States, a European 'common market', and a 'global' marketplace respectively. These centralized structures rest on the premise that as economic integration proceeds, divergent regulatory strategies and approaches across jurisdictions can become a major source of trade tension. Differences in emissions standards, labelling requirements, and attitudes toward public health risks can dramatically shape market access for foreign producers. Where a nation's regulatory choices are out of step with its trade partners, the standards imposed on imported goods can create an obstacle to freer trade.

Those contending political, economic, structural, and social claims make for a complicated calculus of regulatory optimization. Unpacking the arguments for greater harmonization of governmental activities and the competing logic of a structure that promotes interjurisdictional regulatory competition is a central focus of this volume.

Both supporters of increased harmonization and regulatory competition theorists argue that their approaches will make markets work more efficiently and improve social welfare in the context of economic integration. Given that the policy implications of these two theories—one arguing for some degree of centralization and the other for decentralization of governmental activity—pull in opposite directions, at first blush it appears that one or the other approach must be wrong. Ultimately, as the chapters that follow demonstrate, this dichotomy need not be so sharp. But there remains an undeniable degree of tension between the two perspectives. At one end are those who would like to see stronger overarching authorities to mitigate the market failures that arise from interjurisdictional externalities.

At the other are those who desire a greater degree of devolution to facilitate inter-jurisdictional regulatory competition that will maximize the incentives for narrowly tailored and efficient governmental market interventions.

The political and policy stakes are high. If the regulatory competition theorists win the day, the European Union's ongoing programme of harmonization through EU-wide regulatory directives would have to be deemed misguided. If, however, the regulatory competition argument does not deliver as promised, then the policy thrust in the United States toward greater decentralization would need to be called into question. In addition, this debate has important implications for the structure of the international trading regime. Whether and to what extent the WTO should seek to discipline national regulatory activities goes to the heart of recent high-profile clashes between advocates of increased trade liberalization and their opponents who object to stronger global-scale economic management.

THE MOVE TOWARDS CENTRALIZATION

In a world without trade and with limited capital mobility, divergent regulatory standards across jurisdictions present no real worry. Each nation or state can have its own regulatory requirements, with little effect on neighbouring countries or states. But as cross-border trade grows, the differences in regulatory regimes become noticeable, and they may emerge as an obstacle to trade liberalization.

Two distinct sets of tensions arise, representing two separate rationales for a degree of harmonization. First, to the extent that *product* standards differ, exporters may find their goods prohibited from certain markets or subject to expensive relabelling, repackaging, retesting, or other restructuring. For example, European wine makers hoping to sell their wares in the United States must label their bottles according to US requirements, which do not track EU rules. Likewise, US beef exporters face divergent (and, in effect, prohibitive) European standards with regard to the acceptable level of residual hormones in their product. Some theorists (Vogel 1995; Sykes 1995) argue that, with regard to product standards, market pressures will tend to produce an optimal degree of harmonization since governments have a strong incentive—lower prices, greater selection, etc.—to allow their consumers access to imported goods so long as basic health and safety requirements are met. But many trade experts remain concerned that product standards can present significant non-tariff barriers to trade liberalization.

The second issue arises from differences in *production processes and methods* (PPMs). Where PPM standards diverge, the issue is not market access but rather competitiveness effects. More fundamentally, the debate centres on what constitutes a legitimate basis for comparative advantage. Where divergent PPM standards arise from differences in circumstances—such as geography, climate, resource endowments, population densities, and income levels—attempts to 'level the playing field' will be counterproductive and reduce the potential gains from trade. But where the standards selected fail to internalize transboundary externalities (such as cross-border pollution) or are set strategically (without regard to public preferences), the marketplace advantage obtained may not be legitimate. In such cases, a degree of regulatory harmonization may be welfare-enhancing.

The federalization of environmental standards in the United States, for example, was driven in large measure by concerns about low-standard states obtaining an unfair advantage in the national marketplace. Notably, Senator Edmund Muskie felt that the paper producers in his home state of Maine were being disadvantaged because they faced competition from producers in the northwestern United States where environmental requirements were more lax. Given the mobility of companies and factories, there exists a general fear in the political domain that jurisdictions with high regulatory standards will find it difficult to maintain these standards in the face of threats from their industries to move to low-standard jurisdictions to escape the regulatory burdens that they might otherwise face. This threat of industrial migration may trigger a 'race toward the bottom' in regulatory stringency as the high-standard jurisdictions revise their rules in order to avoid inflicting competitive disadvantages on their corporations. The 'race' dynamic arises where jurisdiction B responds to the lowering of standards in jurisdiction A by lowering its own standards, perhaps inducing jurisdiction A to further relax its rules and requirements. Whether such a competitive dynamic occurs and whether it is likely to drive regulatory standards to *suboptimal* levels is a central point of dispute between regulatory competition theorists and those who favour regulatory cooperation and harmonization of standards across jurisdictions.

Although unequivocal empirical evidence to support fears of a race toward the bottom does not exist (Jaffe *et al.* 1995), the political logic remains very real—and the anecdotal evidence of 'political drag' arising from competitiveness concerns is significant (Esty 1994). Indeed, the federalization of US laws over the course of the twentieth century arose, in many cases, to ensure that a common standard would be applied across all of the US states. Antitrust laws were set up on a national basis in the nineteenth century, federal labour laws emerged in the 1930s, and a broad array of federal environmental laws were adopted in the 1970s and 1980s. Other areas of regulatory activity within the United States have been less centralized. Banking, for example, operates under a 'dual system' of both state and federal control. Corporation law, in further contrast, has remained largely under state authority.

From a theoretical perspective, where the issue to be addressed involves inter-jurisdictional spillovers or externalities, the case for governmental intervention at an overarching level is strong (Baumol and Oates 1988). More broadly, whenever there exists a risk of market failure, governmental intervention at a scale that is sufficient to address the market failure may be welfare-enhancing. In fact, the logic of collective action (Olson 1965) requires a degree of centralized cooperation or control so as to ensure that a Prisoners' Dilemma dynamic does not undermine collaborative efforts to address shared problems. Where, however, the externalities are purely economic, there exists a debate over whether the transboundary impacts are merely pecuniary (Revesz 1992) or potentially welfare-reducing (Esty 1996), and thus over whether centralized standard-setting makes sense. From an EU point of view, the harmonization imperative—to minimize non-tariff barriers to trade, and prevent divergent regulatory standards from creating 'distortions' of competition—has been overwhelming and has led to sweeping efforts within the European Union to establish common regulatory requirements in many areas of regulation.

THE MOVE AWAY FROM CENTRALIZATION: THE REGULATORY COMPETITION THEORY

While harmonization might be undertaken to address failures that would reduce social welfare, regulatory competition theorists note that governmental intervention often creates its own burdens and inefficiencies. In particular, they note that, to the extent that governments regulate in a suboptimal fashion, industry, and the public more generally, may be saddled with unnecessary costs. Thus, as soon as governments act to check a market failure, questions must be raised about whether the cure is more harmful than the disease—and whether 'government failure' proves to be a more serious problem than the original market failure. Attentive to this prospect, regulatory competition advocates note that incentives for efficient regulation can be created by establishing a market in locational rights that provides businesses (and citizens) with opportunities to resist poorly designed regulation and even to exit from inefficient or high-cost jurisdictions. Thus, while the first generation of scholars to work on the problem of divergent standards across jurisdictions identified harmonization as the way to combat market failures and to mitigate the risk of a regulatory race to the bottom, second-generation scholars argue that, far from unleashing a welfare-reducing deregulatory dynamic, interjurisdictional regulatory competition pressures governments to perform efficiently and effectively.

Regulatory competition theory builds on Charles Tiebout's seminal 1956 article suggesting that decentralized governance, with horizontally arrayed jurisdictions competing to attract residents on the basis of differing tax and benefits structures, would generate increased social welfare and produce a Pareto-superior outcome. The essence of the theory derives from the fact that circumstances will vary from place to place and that individuals and companies will vary in their preferences about the optimal mix of public goods and taxes. By providing these decision makers with multiple locational options, reflecting a range of public goods and taxes, Tiebout (1956) suggests that each business or resident can choose an individually suitable mix. Other theorists have extended Tiebout's analysis. William Fischel (1975) applies Tiebout's regulatory competition model to the environmental realm, concluding that having jurisdictions with various degrees of pollution control and accompanying charges can produce improved social welfare. Wallace Oates and Robert Schwab (1988) relax some of the assumptions on which Tiebout and Fischel depend. They conclude that, so long as governments act rationally and set a tax rate of zero on capital, welfare-maximizing regulatory policies can be achieved in the context of interjurisdictional competition. Other theorists have noted that the question of social welfare gains from regulatory competition remains highly contextual (Esty 1999b; Klevorick 1996; Wilson 1996).

In recent decades, a broad base of regulatory competition literature applying the Tiebout theory in various regulatory realms has emerged. William Cary (1974) argues that state-to-state variations in corporate law might trigger a drive by company executives to reincorporate in the state (Delaware) that best protects management, even if this protection were to come at the expense of shareholder value. Ralph Winter (1977) disputes this suggestion and observes that market forces are likely to constrain managers. He notes that executives who sought to protect themselves at the expense of advancing shareholder interests would likely make their company a target for takeovers. Roberta Romano (1985) carries this argument one step further. She suggests that we should see law as a 'product' and that the market for locational rights can work to promote efficiency in the corporation law domain. Lucian Bebchuk (1992), however, revives Cary's critique of state competition and argues that such competition is likely to fail, due to problems of managerial opportunism and externalities, with respect to certain identifiable issues in corporate law. A similar debate has taken place in the context of bank regulation. Henry Butler and Jonathan Macey (1988) observe that, because bank regulation is not a purely local public good, welfare-reducing interstate competition may occur as bank regulators relax their regulatory vigilance, knowing that Federal Deposit Insurance Corporation (FDIC) protection spreads the cost of bank failures across the entire country. Focusing on the environmental realm, Revesz (1992) argues that interjurisdictional competition should be presumed to be efficient and likely to generate enhanced social welfare.

THIRD-GENERATION SCHOLARSHIP: AN EMERGING SYNTHESIS

While acknowledging that diversity in geographic circumstances and preferences argues for variations in regulatory approaches, recent scholarship has shifted from sweeping presumptions to more nuanced theory. Several scholars have begun to spell out with some precision when regulatory competition is likely to be welfare-enhancing. John Wilson (1996), Daniel Esty (1996), Kirsten Engel (1997), and William Bratton and Joseph McCahery (1997) argue that enhanced regulatory competition may not always lead to improved social welfare. In the face of structural failures in the design of regulatory systems (where the scope of the regulating authority does not match the range of the cost bearers and beneficiaries of the regulation), public choice failures, or technical shortcomings in the execution of regulatory policies, the benefits of interjurisdictional competition cannot be presumed. While acknowledging that efforts to address market failures that arise from interjurisdictional spillovers may be taken too far, and that regulatory interventions are often poorly designed and inefficient, third-generation scholars suggest that regulatory competition, designed to create incentives to avoid governmental failures, may also not work as hypothesized.

What becomes critical is to understand the nature of the particular market and the regulatory regime that is in place. Whether the regulatory competition will generate social welfare benefits thus can be seen as a function of:

- the scope of uninternalized externalities;
- whether the information base of the particular 'market' is sufficient for competition or incomplete in ways that undermine competitive practices;
- the capacity of citizens and companies to obtain and to understand information that is relevant to their choices and options;
- the underlying mobility of both companies and people;
- the existence of regulatory economies of scale;
- the geographic heterogeneity of the issue at hand;
- the degree of public choice distortion that affects decision making; and
- how close to perfect competition the market in locational rights seems to be or whether there exists Prisoners' Dilemma-driven strategic behaviour in standard setting.

This volume seeks to add to this third-generation literature and to spell out in greater detail, through the use of a set of case studies, when regulatory competition is likely to be welfare enhancing and when some degree of harmonization of standards might be superior. In reconciling these competing perspectives, the following chapters span three comparative dimensions: regulatory arenas (environment, banking, corporate law, labour, tax, intellectual property, and antitrust); models of economic integration (from highly integrated systems such as the United States, to somewhat less integrated systems like the European Union, to emergent systems of integration, such as the World Trade Organization (WTO)); and disciplinary perspectives (law, economics, business, and political science). The starting point is a presumption that the benefits of regulatory competition cannot be taken for granted. In some circumstances competitive pressures may be welfare-enhancing, but in other cases the same pressures will prove to be welfare-reducing. Comparative analysis may, however, provide leverage in thinking through when positive results might be expected and when more negative outcomes are likely to emerge.

A clear goal emerges from the volume as a whole: regulatory systems should be set up with enough interjurisdictional cooperation (or harmonization) to ensure that transboundary externalities and other market failures are addressed, but with a sufficient degree of regulatory competition to prevent the resulting governmental structure from becoming an untamed, overreaching, or inefficient Leviathan. How this cooperation–competition balance is struck will depend, as the chapters that follow demonstrate, on the particular circumstances of the regulatory situation and the economic integration experience.

ISSUE COVERAGE

This volume is broken down into four parts. Part I provides an introduction to regulatory competition theory. Part II looks at the theory as applied across several regulatory domains within the US federal system. Part III examines the regulatory competition-versus-harmonization debate in the EU context. Part IV offers some preliminary analysis aimed at thinking through how regulatory competition might apply at a global scale.

In the opening chapter, Richard Revesz casts doubts on the validity of the various rationales—fears of races to the bottom in standard setting, existence of externalities, and public choice distortions—that are generally used to justify adoption of harmonized federal standards in the environmental field. He argues that there is a strong mismatch between what federal environmental regulation ought to do and what it in fact does. The current regime, he adds, is both overinclusive, needlessly trumping the legitimate preferences of the states, and underinclusive, leaving uncorrected serious environmental pathologies for which federal intervention is necessary. Revesz goes on to suggest that a careful analysis of federalism and environmental regulation in the United States might be instructive for those seeking to design regulatory regimes in Europe and at the global scale through the WTO. In particular, he sees in the US experience evidence that a strategy of harmonization would be undesirable for the European Union. Harmonization will not provide the level playing field that EU policy makers seek. On the contrary, it will distort competition by unduly favouring certain member states. Revesz further argues that the race-to-the-bottom concept as used in the areas of environmental protection, corporate law, banking regulation, and economic redistribution policy making describes distinct types of problems. Nevertheless, he identifies important policy implications that may be derived from the environmental experience. Notably, he concludes that under models of perfect competition interstate interactions should be welfare enhancing, but under models of imperfect competition interstate competition will lead to overregulation in certain instances and underregulation in others.

In Chapter 2, Daniel Esty and Damien Geradin argue that both the race *toward* the bottom and regulatory competition theories are overstated from a descriptive point of view and unsatisfactory from a normative one. They observe that the world is diverse and complex, and that regulatory theory must reflect and parallel this reality. Esty and Geradin therefore propose that optimal governance requires a flexible mix of competition and cooperation between governmental actors as well as between governmental actors and non-governmental actors. They call their competing model 'regulatory co-opetition'.

In Chapter 3, Daniel Shaviro opens the second part of the book, focused on the US experience, with an analysis of interjurisdictional tax competition. He casts the question as one of fiscal federalism and notes that, in most cases, the choice between principles of regulatory harmonization and competition turns on the optimal scale of provision for public goods. But Shaviro argues that taxation, unlike pollution control policy, is not a public good that might have, in principle, a scale of optimal provision. He notes that taxation is a way of paying for public goods with varying scales of optimal and actual provision, thus suggesting that no single scale will be optimal for the pursuit of all its aims. In addition, he argues that the prospect of a race to the bottom in source taxation of the income from mobile capital need not be a major concern from the standpoint of distribution policy unless one is otherwise strongly committed to an income tax or believes that in practice consumption taxes are unlikely to match the redistributive impact of income taxes.

In Chapter 4, Lucian Bebchuk and Allen Ferrell analyse certain shortcomings of interjurisdictional competition in the US corporate law system. In particular, they demonstrate that, with respect to takeovers, states have incentives to produce rules that excessively protect incumbent managers. The development of state takeover law in the last three decades, they argue, is consistent with their theory. States have provided managers with wider and more open-ended latitude to engage in defensive tactics than endorsed even by the commentators most favourable to the use of such tactics. Furthermore, states have elected, even though they could have done otherwise, to impose anti-takeover protection on shareholders who did not appear to favour them in a way that left shareholders with little choice or say. Finally, Bebchuk and Ferrell point out that proponents of regulatory competition in the corporate law realm have difficulty in reconciling their views with the evolution of state takeover law.

Jonathan Macey examines in Chapter 5 the role of federalism in the US banking and financial services sectors. He illustrates that in these sectors regulation is an exogenous event that can change the extraterritorial effects associated with an economic activity. Accordingly, it is not the intrinsic nature of the industry that determines whether regulation should be carried out at the local level or at the federal level. Rather, the level of government that assumes the risks associated with regulation should also be responsible for regulation. In practice, Macey maintains, since states have assumed the contingent liabilities associated with regulating (and insuring) the insurance industry, they should also be the primary regulators for that activity. In contrast, since the federal government has largely assumed the risks associated with regulating (and insuring) the banking industry, it should be the primary regulator of that industry. Macey adds that there might be benefits to extending the system of interjurisdictional competition that exists for corporate charters to the regulation of securities.

In Chapter 6, Mark Barenberg analyses the issue of harmonization versus competition in the context of labour rights. He stresses that the US domestic law context varies considerably from the economic integration of contemporary Europe or the world more broadly. He reasons that legal encouragement of collective bargaining and other core labour rights are, in fact, an element of income redistribution policy, which argues against having this realm serve as a forum for interjurisdictional competition. Barenberg concludes, however, that the normative question of how much harmonization or competition to promote cannot be answered without further inquiry into contested substantive values underlying the debate, such as the structure of democracy, the vision of distributive justice, the scope of human rights, and notions of social well-being.

In Chapter 7, Kirsten Engel and Susan Rose-Ackerman propose that devolution poses significant risks in the US environmental domain and thus that regulatory competition is not likely to be welfare enhancing in this realm. Their view contrasts with much of the recent academic literature (Macey 1990; Oates 1998; Revesz 1992), which argues that decentralized environmental regulation may be welfare enhancing. Engel and Rose-Ackerman particularly criticize the strong version of claims for devolution in both policy making and implementation, suggesting that decentralized regulation may result in significant environmental degradation and impose non-trivial social costs even when the underlying environmental problems have no interstate impact.

Part III of this Volume examines regulatory competition in the EU context. The chapters, addressing a range of regulatory domains, find important contrasts between the US and European regulatory experiences.

In Chapter 8, William Bratton and Joseph McCahery examine tax harmonization versus competition in the European Union. They reject the proposition that the principle of subsidiarity demands a decentralized tax system. They observe that the two leading theoretical models, fiscal federalism and jurisdictional competition, point in opposite directions. Fiscal federalism finds significant risks of allocative inefficiency from devolved tax regimes, while jurisdictional competition generates a strong presumption in favour of decentralization. Empirical evidence, they conclude, offers the only clear solution to the dilemma posed. Policy choices must derive from particularized appraisals of the costs and benefits of both competition and coordination. Against this background, they evaluate the EU Code of Conduct on Business Taxation, a tax coordination initiative which identifies and prohibits a zone of government activities that are perceived to distort competition among the member states with respect to the taxation of capital. They contend that the Code may be vulnerable to challenge because its breadth makes its connection to an empirically verified set of justifying conditions tenuous. But they also identify a possible justification for the Code. Specifically, while the empirical evidence is thin, it appears that significant externalities exist in the tax policy domain within the European Union, a problem that will likely intensify as member state economies become more tightly integrated.

Simon Deakin explains in Chapter 9 why jurisdictional competition in the corporate law realm is so limited within the European Union. He notes that the *siège réel* ('real seat') doctrine limits the degree to which a company can choose where to incorporate and, therefore, which corporation law will be applicable to it. He adds that even if the *siège réel* doctrine were to be weakened as a result of a recent decision from the European Court of Justice, the conditions under which reincorporation could serve as the basis for competition between member states' legal systems do not yet exist in Europe. Deakin sees little chance of US-style regulatory competition emerging in the European Union's realm of corporate law. He also shows how several aspects of corporate law have been progressively harmonized by EU legislation. He praises the merits of the technique of 'reflexive harmonization', which permits an ongoing degree of diversity at the level of national legal systems while simultaneously facilitating evolution toward common approaches centred on an emerging set of transnational norms.

In Chapter 10, Gérard Hertig disentangles the strands of regulatory control that affect the European financial services industry. In theory, a financial intermediary that has been approved in one member state where minimum standards are in place holds a so-called 'European passport' and should be able to provide cross-border financial services without being regulated by other member states. Hertig argues that the emergence of regulatory competition depends on—and does not undermine—the presence of a single market. But he points out that, somewhat ironically, until supervision of financial intermediaries is perceived as being quite effective, vibrant interjurisdictional competition cannot emerge. The European passport will facilitate regulatory competition without creating significant risks of cross-border activities leading to a welfare-reducing race toward the bottom, says Hertig. On the contrary, some member states may decide to opt for particularly stringent standards to attract firms that want to signal to investors that they are willing to comply with demanding quality standards (triggering a 'race to the top').

Brian Bercusson discusses the harmonization-versus-competition debate as applied to the EU labour market in Chapter 11. Regulatory competition in this context has become politically charged, as some officials fear that low standards in certain member states have resulted in 'social dumping' and are disrupting European economic integration. As a result, there has been growing pressure for EU-wide harmonized social and labour standards that would minimize the variation in indirect labour costs for all enterprises across the European Union. In so doing, this harmonization would reduce, if not eliminate, competitive advantages based on differences in labour standards. A counter-argument, however, has emerged in favour of retention of national competence over social policy in general, and labour standards in particular, on the theory that interjurisdictional competition might be welfare-enhancing. Bercusson notes that the end results may be similar, since both EU-wide standards designed to address social dumping and the dynamic of 'social regime competition' will lead to reduced policy control at the national level, either explicitly as national standards are displaced by EU standards or implicitly as regulatory competition forces national governments to respond to pressures in the marketplace.

In Chapter 12, Michael Faure provides a critical look at some aspects of the harmonization of environmental law in the European Union. While recognizing that transboundary externalities demand a degree of centralized regulation, Faure rejects traditional European reliance on the view that harmonization of process standards is necessary to prevent 'distortions of competition' between member states. The internal market, he comments, does not require total equality in the conditions of competition. Nevertheless, Faure acknowledges that there may be an argument in favour of harmonization based on the desire to promote uniform environmental quality within the European Union. But this objective, he argues, should be achieved through the adoption of EU-wide ambient quality standards, not rigidly harmonized regulatory regimes. Common standards would require member states to achieve a certain level of environmental protection, but leave them free to tailor the actual emissions reductions to local geographical and political circumstances. Ambient standards would, in fact, permit differentiated emission limits depending on the existing level of pollution within particular member states. Faure observes, however, that most EU environmental directives seek to impose uniform emission limits across member states to 'level the playing field'. Taking a public choice perspective, Faure contends that adoption of harmonized emission limit values is the result of lobbying efforts from producers in areas that are already heavily regulated and that have incentives to extend their strict (national) regulations to the EU level. Faure concludes that some EU environmental directives seek to achieve misguided policy objectives through inappropriate policy instruments.

Part IV of this volume examines the prospects for welfare gains through regulatory competition at the global scale. The analyses advanced have potentially significant implications for the unfolding structure of the international trade regime.

In Chapter 13, Joel Trachtman assesses the benefits and limits of competition in the context of international securities regulation. Trachtman rejects the presumption that regulatory competition generates benefits in this domain. He explains that a variety of parameters must be examined to determine whether a degree of competition will be welfare-enhancing. He remarks, furthermore, that a number of the factors are incommensurable and involve interpersonal comparisons of utility that will not yield unique outcomes. Trachtman concludes that regulatory competition is not the real issue. The fundamental challenge lies in designing an appropriate structure of governmental authority and jurisdiction.

In Chapter 14, David Charny examines the implications of regulatory competition in the global labour market. He observes that the presumption that centralized labour standards will raise labour costs should not be accepted uncritically. Charny notes that a pervasive mismatch exists between the distortions caused by regulatory competition in the global marketplace and the governmental capacities of international labour institutions. But he concludes that a more focused and stronger set of global labour standards would still not address the critical issues that emerge in the labour context because of the wide range of work cultures around the world. He suggests, moreover, that the construction of effective redistributive and social insurance schemes centred on global-scale labour regulations would require substantial transfer payments between jurisdictions, a policy element that is hard to imagine under the current regime of national sovereignty.

David Vogel takes up the question of environmental regulation in the context of international economic integration in Chapter 15. According to Vogel, fears that economic competition will lead to a regulatory race toward the bottom are largely unwarranted. Instead, he submits that economic openness and capital mobility have often encouraged nations to enact higher product standards than they would have done in the absence of increased economic interdependence, triggering a 'race to the top'. Contrary to the claims of those who blame economic globalization for weakening environmental standards in poorer countries, Vogel concludes that the 'greening' of developing nations is reduced or impeded to the extent that they fail to become integrated in the world economy.

In Chapter 16, Eleanor Fox analyses regulatory competition among nations with respect to antitrust or competition law. She argues that states or nations do not compete in any central way in the realm of competition law. Unlike many other types of regulations, competition rules (US-style) do not normally impose costs on market players: by removing market imperfections, they tend to reduce costs. European Union-style rules may impose costs, and US style rules may be a modest salutary pressure on the European Union. There is observable competition, however, between the United States and the European Union in seeking to expand the geographic scope of their competition laws. The real problem is not competition toward the bottom but lack of a vision from the top, in view of the fact that global mandates transcend nations. For certain global problems at the intersection of trade and competition, Fox argues, the WTO is the most appropriate forum.

In Chapter 17, Inge Govaere and Paul Demaret analyse the Agreement on Trade-Related Aspects of Intellectual Property Rights (TRIPS), annexed to the 1994 WTO Agreement. They note that the TRIPS Agreement raises the question of whether worldwide regulation of intellectual property rights is justified. Govaere and Demaret argue that the rationale of the TRIPS Agreement is not to eliminate competition between nations, but rather to equalize the conditions under which firms produce and supply goods and services based on new technologies or incorporate new forms of expression or data. They conclude that the TRIPS Agreement is not about regulatory competition, cooperation, or co-opetition, since these strategies presuppose a respect of sovereignty of states participating in the regulatory process.

The analyses and arguments advanced make one thing clear: there is no simple answer to the question of whether regulatory competition or regulatory cooperation promotes efficiency and enhances welfare. Instead, a particularized inquiry into the specific regulatory domain is required. This conclusion reinforces the need for further 'third-generation' scholarship that examines these circumstances in a careful, systematic, and rigorous way.

PART I

Introduction to Regulatory Competition Theory

1
Federalism and Regulation: Some Generalizations

RICHARD L. REVESZ*

Since the early 1990s, the legal academic literature has paid a great deal of attention to how responsibility over environmental regulation in the United States should be allocated between the federal government and the states. One purpose of this chapter, to which I turn in Part I, is to defend the approach for the analysis of this issue that I have developed in a series of prior articles (Revesz 1997c; 1997e; 1996; 1992).

A second goal of the chapter is to suggest how the analysis of federalism and environmental regulation in the United States can cast light on other questions that are of central concern to the contributors to this volume. Part II deals with the allocation of responsibility over environmental regulation in other systems of economic integration, particularly the European Union. Part III discusses the treatment of environmental matters in international trade disputes. Finally, Part IV turns its attention to other areas of government intervention, such as corporate law, banking, and programmes of economic redistribution.

I. FEDERALISM AND ENVIRONMENTAL REGULATION IN THE UNITED STATES

Traditionally, the two justifications most prominently offered in the academic literature and the legislative arena for vesting responsibility for environmental regulation at the federal level have focused on the existence of a 'race to the bottom' and of interstate externalities. The race-to-the-bottom rationale for federal environmental regulation posits that states, in an effort to induce geographically mobile firms to locate within their jurisdictions, will offer them suboptimally lax environmental standards so as to benefit from additional jobs and tax revenues. In an article published in 1992, I cast doubt on the validity of the race-to-the-bottom rationale as an across-the-board argument for justifying federal intervention (1992).

The problem of interstate externalities arises because a state that sends pollution to another state obtains the labour and fiscal benefits of the economic activity that generates the pollution but does not suffer the full costs of the activity. In an article published in 1996, I showed how the federal environmental statutes had been ineffective in constraining interstate externalities in a desirable manner (1996).

More recently, advocates of federal regulation have devoted considerable attention to the public choice rationale for federal intervention (1997a: 558–61). The

* The Filomen D'Agostino and Max E. Greenberg Research Fund at the New York University School of Law provided financial assistance.

public choice rationale maintains that federal regulation is necessary because state political processes lead to the systematic underprotection of environmental quality. Relative to the federal government, the claim goes, pro-environmental interests are underrepresented and/or anti-environmental interests are overrepresented at the state level. My criticism of this view, on which I am currently working, is previewed in this chapter.

The race-to-the-bottom justification

When states compete for mobile industry through their environmental standards, they are essentially competing for the sale of a good: the right to locate within their jurisdictions (1997c: 99–107). This market, like all markets, might be characterized by either conditions of perfect competition or imperfect competition. Perhaps the most effective way to dispel the idea that interstate competition for industry would inevitably lead to suboptimally lax environmental standards in the absence of federal intervention is through the analysis of the two leading models of the effects of interstate competition on environmental regulation. They show that under conditions of perfect competition the state environmental regulations would be optimal, and that under conditions of imperfect competition they could either be overly stringent or overly lax.

This theoretical inquiry therefore contradicts the claim of race-to-the-bottom advocates that, left to their own devices, states would systematically underregulate. The claim would therefore have to be supported empirically, but convincing empirical support is lacking as well. So far, the weight of the evidence points in the opposite direction (though this situation could change over time).

Theoretical models

The most influential economic model of the effects of interstate competition on the choice of environmental standards—a model of perfect competition—shows that interjurisdictional competition leads to the maximization of social welfare, rather than to a race to the bottom (Oates and Schwab 1988). In this model, Wallace Oates and Robert Schwab posit jurisdictions that compete for mobile capital through the choice of taxes and environmental standards. A higher capital stock benefits residents in the form of higher wages, but hurts them as a result of the foregone tax revenues and lower environmental quality needed to attract the capital.

Each jurisdiction makes two policy decisions: it sets a tax rate on capital and an environmental standard. Professors Oates and Schwab show that competitive jurisdictions will set a net tax rate on capital of zero (the rate that exactly covers the cost of public services provided to the capital, such as police and fire protection). In turn, competitive jurisdictions will set an environmental standard that is defined by equating the willingness to pay for an additional unit of environmental quality with the corresponding change in wages. Oates and Schwab show that these choices of tax rates and environmental standards are socially optimal.

In the absence of perfect competition, game-theoretic interactions among the states could lead to underregulation absent federal intervention. In such cases, federal minimum standards would be desirable. But it is equally plausible that in other instances the reverse would be true: that the game-theoretic interactions among the states would lead to overregulation absent federal intervention. In such cases, federal regulation would be desirable as well, but in such cases federal *maximum* standards would be called for. Accordingly, there is no compelling race-to-the-bottom justification for across-the-board federal minimum standards, which are the cornerstone of federal environmental law.

The most extensive analyses of effects of imperfect competition among the states show that either overregulation or underregulation could result (Markusen, Morey, and Olewiler 1995; 1993). These studies relax the assumption of constant returns to scale in the production functions of firms, which is a necessary condition for perfect competition and a cornerstone of the Oates and Schwab model. Instead, they consider the effects of state regulation on an industry that exhibits increasing returns to scale, a condition associated with imperfect competition. The studies show that, depending on the levels of firm-specific costs, plant-specific costs, and transportation costs, interstate competition can produce either suboptimally lax or suboptimally stringent levels of pollution.

Similarly, if a firm has market power enabling it to affect prices, it will be able to extract a suboptimally lax standard, but if a state has market power, the reverse would be true (Revesz 1992: 1241–2; 1997b: 104–5). In summary, just as there are game-theoretic situations in which interstate competition produces environmental underregulation, there are other plausible scenarios under which the result is overregulation.

Moreover, even if states systematically enacted suboptimally lax environmental standards, federal environmental regulation would not necessarily improve the situation. If states cannot compete over environmental regulation because it has been federalized, they will compete along other regulatory dimensions, leading to suboptimally lax standards in other areas, or along the fiscal dimension, leading to the underprovision of public goods. Thus the reduction in social welfare implicit in race-to-the-bottom arguments would not be eliminated merely by federalizing environmental regulation: the federalization of all regulatory and fiscal decisions would be necessary to solve the problem.

Similarly, there is a concern that absent federal regulation, firms could capture rents created, for example, by locational advantages that otherwise would accrue to the states. But if environmental regulation is federalized, the rents could be captured with respect to another component of costs: only complete centralization would address the problem (Engel and Rose-Ackerman, Ch. 7).

Empirical Studies

The validity of race-to-the-bottom arguments for federal environmental regulation therefore cannot be resolved on theoretical grounds alone: one needs to resort to empirical analysis. An extensive set of empirical evidence shows that the stringency of environmental regulation does not have a statistically significant effect on plant location decisions (Bartik 1989; 1988a; Friedman *et al.* 1992; Levinson 1996; McConnell and Schwab 1990), thereby refuting a critical linchpin of the standard race-to-the-bottom claim.

Moreover, even empirical evidence showing that firms move away from, or do not locate in, jurisdictions with comparatively more stringent environmental standards would not necessarily lend support to race-to-the-bottom claims. Empirical studies of firm mobility measure only what states lose as a result of comparatively more stringent environmental standards; they do not measure the corresponding gains that might result from better environmental quality. A state that makes its environmental standards more stringent and thereby loses industry may well increase its social welfare (because the environmental gains are greater than the losses in jobs and taxes). But it follows, *a fortiori*, that evidence that the stringency of environmental standards does not push industry away severely undercuts the standard race-to-the-bottom claims.

More generally, an extensive review of the empirical economic literature on the effects of environmental regulation finds little evidence to support the hypothesis that environmental regulation has a large adverse effect on economic growth or on other measures of competitiveness (Jaffe *et al.* 1995: 150–8).[1] Recent studies have reinforced this conclusion, finding that environmental regulation does not reduce labour demand (Berman and Bui 1997), and does not impair productivity (1998).

These findings are not surprising given that, for all but the most heavily polluting industries, the costs of complying with environmental regulation are a small proportion of the total costs of production—an average of 2 per cent according to a US Environmental Protection Agency (EPA) estimate (Jaffe *et al.* 1995: 158). It follows that the difference in production costs between jurisdictions with relatively more stringent and relatively less stringent environmental standards is even less. Moreover, there is evidence that large national or multinational firms build their plants to meet the standard of the most stringent jurisdiction in which they have production facilities; thus, they do not benefit from lower costs of environmental regulation when they operate in jurisdictions with laxer standards (Jaffe *et al.* 1995).

One study that partially supports the opposite conclusion concerning the impact of environmental regulation on economic performance finds, for heavily polluting industries, a growth rate in the number of plants located in attainment areas (which meet the US Clean Air Act's National Ambient Air Quality Standards) relative to non-attainment areas (Becker and Henderson 1997; Henderson 1996: 800, 802, 808). But this study does not cast much light on the analysis of the effects of state standards of different stringency. Indeed, in non-attainment areas, new sources not only need to meet a more stringent emission standard—LAER (Lowest Achievable

[1] The authors, however, do not find support for the hypothesis, generally attributed to Michael Porter and David Vogel, that environmental regulation stimulates growth and competitiveness (154).

Emission Rate)—but must also purchase offsets from existing sources, so that the aggregate pollution in the jurisdiction decreases in spite of the location of the new source (42 U.S.C. § 7503 (1994)). The study does not attempt to ascertain how much of the locational impact is due to the more stringent standard and how much is due to the offset requirement.

One commentator, Professor Kirsten Engel (1997: 279), makes an ingenious argument based on a survey of state regulators purporting to show that 'a substantial minority of states relax their environmental standards in order to attract industrial firms'. The majority of respondents, however, indicated that they would not engage in competitive action in response to a firm's threat to exit the jurisdiction.

Professor Engel argues that if '(1) states compete for industry by lowering environmental standards [relying on her survey], but (2) industry location is substantially unaffected by this competition [relying on the existing empirical evidence discussed above], it logically follows that (3) states' welfare will be reduced because there will be no economic gain to compensate for the environmental quality losses' (279). Addressing this claim in a prior article, I noted that making environmental standards more lax is not necessarily undesirable from a social welfare perspective (1997a). If, for example, a state believes that it has market power and therefore sets a baseline that is suboptimally stringent, a relaxation of the environmental standards would increase social welfare.

In a more recent article, Professor Engel, together with Scott Saleska (1998), attempts to respond to this challenge. On the basis of further empirical examination, they claim that states willing to 'compete' with other states by making their environmental standards less stringent in order not to lose industry do not obtain gains in economic performance. Such gains would accrue, they maintain, if competition were desirable (66–7). The authors recognize, however, that states with relatively weak economies could be more likely to compete for industry by making environmental standards less stringent. Even if the economies of these states improved as a result of such action, they may remain weak compared to those of states with strong economies that did not compete for industry in this manner (71).

The authors purport to control for this possibility by means of multiple regression analysis. What needs to be done, however, is to simultaneously determine whether states with weaker economies are more likely to compete for industry and whether such competition improves their economic performance relative to what it would otherwise be (72–3). The authors do not perform such a two-step analysis or appropriately control for the most important factors—such as labour productivity, business climate, or unemployment—that can affect a state's economic performance.

The interstate externality justification

The presence of interstate externalities provides a compelling argument for federal regulation under conditions in which Coasian bargaining is unlikely to occur (Revesz 1996). Particularly with respect to air pollution, transaction costs are likely to be sufficiently high to prevent the formation of interstate compacts. It is difficult for such compacts to emerge in the absence of a clearly defined baseline concerning when upwind states have the right to send pollution downwind, and in the absence of generally accepted mathematical models for translating a source's emissions into a quantity of ambient air quality degradation at all the places at which the emissions affect ambient air quality. Moreover, for different pollution sources, the range of affected states will vary; this shifting membership among the participants at the bargaining table makes less likely the emergence of conditions favouring cooperation (2375 and n. 123).

Nonetheless, the fact that interstate externalities provide a compelling justification for intervention does not mean that all federal environmental regulation can be justified on these grounds. For environmental problems such as the control of drinking water quality, there are virtually no interstate pollution externalities; the effects are almost exclusively local. Even with respect to problems for which there are interstate externalities, such as air pollution, the rationale calls only for a response well targeted to the problem, such as a limit on the amount of pollution that can cross state lines, rather than across-the-board federal regulation.

Indeed, the environmental statutes have been an ineffective response to the problem of interstate externalities. For example, the core of the US Clean Air Act—the statute designed to deal with the pollution that gives rise to the most serious problems of interstate externalities—consists of a series of federally prescribed ambient standards and emission standards.[2] The federal emission standards do not effectively combat the problem of interstate externalities because they do not regulate the number of sources within a state or the location of the sources. Similarly, the various federal ambient air quality standards are not well targeted to address the problem of interstate externalities. They are overinclusive because they require a state to restrict pollution that has only in-state consequences. But they are also underinclusive because a state could meet the applicable ambient standards but nonetheless export a great deal of pollution to downwind states (through tall stacks or location near the interstate border). In fact, a state might meet its ambient standards precisely because it exports a large proportion of its pollution.

In fact, in some ways the federal environmental statutes have exacerbated, rather than ameliorated, the problem of interstate externalities. Again, in the context of the US Clean Air Act, the federal ambient standards give states an incentive to encourage sources within their jurisdiction to use taller stacks (or to locate close to downwind borders). In this way, states can externalize not only the health and environmental effects of the pollution but also the regulatory costs of complying with the federal ambient standards. Thus, not surprisingly, the use of tall stacks expanded considerably after the passage of the Clean Air Act in 1970. In 1970, only

[2] 42 U.S.C. § 7409 (1994) sets out national ambient air quality standards. Section 7411 sets out emission standards for new sources. Ambient standards prescribe maximum permissible concentrations of pollutants in air, but do not directly constrain the behaviour of individual polluters. Emission standards, in contrast, impose enforceable limitations on individual sources.

two stacks in the United States were higher than 500 feet. By 1985, more than 180 stacks were higher than 500 feet and 23 were higher than 1,000 feet. While this method of externalizing pollution is now less of a problem as a result of stack height regulations that followed the 1977 Amendments to the Clean Air Act, tall stacks remain a means by which excessive pollution can be sent to downwind states (Revesz 1996: 2353).

The one environmental programme specifically designed to deal with an interstate externality problem has been the acid rain provisions of the 1990 Amendments to the Clean Air Act, which established a marketable permit scheme in sulphur dioxide emissions. The aggregate decrease in emissions over time is likely to reduce the problem of acid rain in the Northeast, but the fact that trading takes place in a single national market interferes with a desirable allocation of the permits between upwind and downwind sources (2359–60).

There is, moreover, one provision under the Clean Air Act that is specifically designed to combat interstate externalities by creating a mechanism under which downwind states can seek to enjoin excessive upwind pollution (42 U.S.C. §§ 7410 (D), 7426 (1994)). It is particularly ironic that no downwind state has ever succeeded under this provision. In summary, while we should have federal environmental statutes that control interstate externalities, relatively little of the current federal statutory scheme can be justified on these grounds.

The public choice justification

Advocates of federal regulation on public choice grounds cannot simply say that state political processes undervalue the benefits of environmental regulation, or overvalue the corresponding costs. Federal regulation is justifiable only if the outcome at the federal level is socially more desirable, either because there is less underregulation or because any overregulation leads to smaller social welfare losses. There are several reasons for being sceptical about the soundness of a general claim of this sort.

The logic of collective action

The public choice mechanism that makes it possible for federal regulation to correct for underregulation at the state level is far from self-evident (Revesz 1997e: 558–61). For example, Professor Daniel Esty states that '[a]t the centralized level, environmental groups find it easier to reach critical mass and thereby to compete on more equal footing with industrial interests' (1996: 650 n. 302). He adds that '[t]he difficulty of mobilizing the public in many separate jurisdictions is well established' (650–1).

In fact, however, the logic of collective action might suggest the opposite. The cost of organizing on a larger scale magnifies the free-rider problems faced by environmental groups. Moreover, because environmental concerns vary throughout the country, there will be a loss in the homogeneity of the environmental interests when they are aggregated at the federal level, thereby further complicating the organizational problems. For example, environmentalists in Massachusetts may care primarily about air quality whereas environmentalists in Colorado may rank limitations on logging on public lands as most important. Other things being equal, state-based environmental groups seeking, respectively, better air quality in Massachusetts and more protection of public lands in Colorado are therefore likely to be more effective than a national environmental group seeking, at the federal level, better environmental quality with respect to both of these attributes.

In contrast, the situation is likely to be different for industry groups. For many environmental problems, an important portion of the regulated community consists of firms with nationwide operations. For such firms, operating at the federal level poses no additional free-rider problems or loss of homogeneity.

The relevant question is whether the additional problems faced by environmental groups at the federal level are outweighed by benefits arising from the fact that the clash of interest groups takes place before a single legislature, a single administrative agency, and, in part, as a result of the exclusive venue of the D.C. Circuit over important environmental statutes, in a single court (Revesz 1997a).

For example, if one assumed that, beyond a certain threshold, additional resources do not increase a group's probability of being successful in the political process, and if this threshold at the federal level is sufficiently lower than the sum of the corresponding thresholds at the state level, it may be that environmental groups would not be disadvantaged at the federal level even if they were disadvantaged in the states. In this case, the economies of scale of operating at the federal level would more than outweigh the increased free-rider problems.

The assumptions behind such a model, however, are not particularly plausible. The threshold concept might properly describe certain costs associated with effective participation in the regulatory process. For example, with respect to the regulation of a particular carcinogen, each group might need to hire a scientist to review the regulator's risk assessment. It may well be the case that a certain minimum will secure the services of a competent scientist and that devoting additional resources to the problem would be of little, if any, use. Thus, for costs of this type, the marginal benefit of additional expenditures is zero, or close to zero, regardless of the other party's expenditures.

The structure of other costs, however, is likely to be quite different. For example, with respect to access to the legislative process, a standard public choice account is that the highest bidder prevails (Peltzman 1976; Stigler 1971). Thus the benefit that a party receives from its expenditures is a function of the expenditures of the other party. Unless the costs of this type are quite small, the economies of scale of operating at the federal level are unlikely to outweigh the additional free-rider problems.

Plausible public choice accounts of environmental regulation

Given the standard public choice argument for federal environmental regulation, it is not clear why the problems observed at the state level would not be replicated at the federal level (Revesz 1997e: 542–3). The logic of collective action would suggest that the large number of citizen-breathers, each with a relatively small stake in the outcome of a particular standard-setting proceeding, will be overwhelmed in the political process by concentrated industrial interests with a large stake in the outcome. But this problem could occur at the federal level as well as at the state level. In fact, the logic of collective action makes it difficult to explain why there is any federal regulation at all.

As a result, the plausible public choice explanations of environmental regulation proceed along different lines altogether. Indeed, an extensive public choice literature suggests that the impetus for environmental regulation sometimes comes, implicitly or explicitly, from the regulated firms themselves, which can obtain rents and barriers to entry that give them an advantage over their competitors (Keohane, Revesz, and Stavins 1998; Maloney and McCormick 1982). At other times, the advocates are particular regions of the country, which hope to obtain a comparative advantage with respect to other regions (Pashigian 1985). When the relevant interactions are seen in this manner, the case for federal regulation on public choice grounds is considerably weakened.

It is important to stress that the purpose of this discussion is not to argue that public choice explanations for environmental regulation are persuasive, or that they are better than other explanations (Farber 1992). Rather, the claim here is that if public choice justifications are credible at all, they are credible in the context of interactions among interest groups that are quite different from the model pitting industrial polluters against breathers. Public choice claims for federal environmental regulation are weak precisely because they are based on such a model.

State regulatory actions

Public choice arguments for federal environmental regulation appear to rest to some extent on two types of empirical claims concerning the nature of state regulatory actions: that states ignored environmental problems before 1970, when the major federal statutes began to be enacted, and that states continue to be less concerned about environmental problems than is the federal government.

The pre-1970 situation

Before evaluating the situation in 1970, it is important to stress that the deck was stacked against state regulation. As noted below, there is a compelling argument for federal involvement in the provision of the scientific information concerning the adverse health and environmental effects of various pollutants. There are large economies of scale in the production of information of this sort: in fact, there is simply no plausible reason for this task to be performed by each of the states. Before

1970, the federal government did comparatively little in this area (and probably continues to underinvest in it even today). It would thus not be surprising if the states, lacking an appropriate scientific basis for regulating, did little on the regulatory front.

But even so, the view that the states were ignoring environmental problems until 1970 is not correct. For example, several empirical studies show, quite clearly, that during the 1960s, without federal prodding, states were making considerable strides with respect to the control of air pollution. In particular, the concentrations of important air pollutants were falling at significant rates and the number of states, counties, and municipalities with regulatory programmes to control air pollution was increasing rapidly (Crandall 1983: 16–22; Goklany 1998a; 1998b: 12; Portney 1990: 28–9, 50–1; Stern 1982).

Most strikingly, sulphur dioxide concentrations appear to have fallen by 11.3 per cent per year between 1964 and 1971 (before the presence of an active federal role with respect to air pollution control) but only 4.6 per cent per year in the 1970s (in the era of federal regulation). Similarly, the concentrations of total suspended particulates fell by 2.3 per cent per year between 1960 and 1971 but by only 0.6 per cent per year from 1972 to 1980 (Crandall 1983: 19). In a study conducted for the Brookings Institution, Robert Crandall thus concludes that 'these data suggest that pollution reduction was more effective in the 1960s, before there was a serious federal policy dealing with stationary sources, than since the 1970 Clean Air Act amendments' (19).

The leading account of the genesis of federal environmental regulation, which focuses on the passage of the Clean Air Act, is consistent with this evidence. This study argues that the Clean Air Act of 1970 was a response to industry pressure for federal intervention as a means of discouraging states from setting *more stringent* (and disuniform) standards (Elliott, Ackerman, and Millian 1985).

The current situation

A full analysis of what states are currently doing with respect to environmental regulation cannot be undertaken here, but a few examples are nonetheless instructive. As a threshold matter, however, a note of caution is in order. It could well be misleading to point to the existence of state environmental statutes as evidence of environmental concern because it may be that the statutes are merely symbolic and are not being enforced. But in the brief case studies presented below, the state programmes did in fact result in actual environmental improvements.

Moreover, care must be taken to ensure that the examples of state intervention are not federally compelled. Thus the programmes discussed below differ from state regulatory actions, such as the preparation of State Implementation Plans (SIPs) under the Clean Air Act, which are performed under federal command.

The claim here is not that every state is being active in the environmental regulatory arena. The citizens of some states may have preferences for laxer environmental regulation than the federal regulatory level and may therefore not have any reason to voluntarily adopt additional environmental programmes. But it is relevant that a significant number of states are adopting innovative forms of regulation and imposing costs of in-state firms. A brief discussion of state involvement with respect to five important environmental issues follows.

Automobile emission standards

The Clean Air Act contemplates two possible sets of automobile standards: the federal standards and the more stringent California standards. The Act gives states the freedom to choose the California standards if they wish (42 U.S.C. § 7507 (1994)).

In 1991, the twelve Northeastern states that were members of the Ozone Transport Commission (OTC) established under the Act agreed to do so. Massachusetts and New York were the first states to adopt the standards, but their action provoked legal challenges that ultimately proved unsuccessful. Nonetheless, to put their desired standards on a firmer legal footing, the OTC members asked the EPA to require them to adopt the California standards. Ultimately, this process resulted in a voluntary agreement between the automobile manufacturers and the Northeastern states for a set of automobile emission standards that are more stringent than the federal standards. These new standards are now in effect in most of the Northeastern states, and will go into effect nationally in model year 2001 (63 Fed Reg 11, 374 (1998); Fern 1998).

Hazardous waste regulation

The federal Superfund statute has devoted the bulk of its attention to the approximately 1200 sites that are on the National Priorities List (NPL) (Environmental Law Institute 1998: 3). The federal approach has essentially ignored thousands of hazardous waste sites around the country, some of which pose serious risks to health and the environment.

Over the last decade, the states have resolutely moved in to fill the vacuum. All fifty states have now enacted state Superfund programmes. Moreover, as part of these programmes, some states maintain clean-up funds, raised by means of state taxation, to pay for clean-ups at sites at which responsible parties with sufficient solvency cannot be found (Environmental Law Institute 1998). The state programmes have been an effective mechanism for obtaining clean-ups and have recently been the subject of a report by the US General Accounting Office (GAO), which is seeking to determine what lessons the federal government can derive from the experience of the states (General Accounting Office 1998; Guerrero 1999).

One area in which states have taken a definite lead is with respect to the redevelopment of so-called brownfield sites. These sites are typically abandoned former industrial sites in urban areas. They tend to escape the EPA's interest and attention because they are not sufficiently contaminated to qualify for listing under the NPL. Nonetheless, these abandoned sites provide many inner cities with much-needed opportunities for economic development and give rise to environmental justice problems. The sustained actions of several states in sponsoring and facilitating brownfields redevelopment is now leading the EPA to consider playing more of a role in this area.

States have also acted in innovative ways with respect to land transfer statutes. Under the federal Superfund programme, there is no requirement for a clean-up to take place at the time that commercial real estate is transferred. Although both the seller and the buyer are typically liable in the event of a subsequent clean-up (42 U.S.C. §§ 9601 (35), 9707(a) (1994)), many sites that change hands never come to the attention of regulators. A majority of states now require that either clean-ups, commitments to undertake clean-ups, or detailed disclosures take place contemporaneously with real estate transfers. A recent survey indicated that thirty-one states now have some form of property transfer provision, up from six in 1995 (Environmental Law Institute 1998: 36).

Non-hazardous solid waste regulation

The federal government has done very little with respect to the control of non-hazardous solid waste. In the last ten years, municipalities have undertaken considerable efforts to decrease the volume of waste generated, primarily in the form of residential curbside recycling programmes and volume-based pricing of solid waste disposal services.

For example, in 1988 there were approximately 1,000 curbside recycling programmes in the United States; the number of such programmes had reached about 5,000 in 1992 and about 9,000 in 1996. Similarly, whereas in the late 1980s there were only a few dozen volume-based pricing programmes, by 1996 there were 3,600, covering close to 10 per cent of the population of the United States (Jenkins *et al.* 1999). The pressure for recycling and for the reduction of the volume of waste generated has come almost exclusively from outside the federal government.

States have also taken the lead with respect to a variety of other matters. A 1995 survey found that ten states had bottle bills, and that these states are responsible for 95 per cent of the recycled plastic in the United States (Depaolo 1995: 881). Similarly, forty-five states had legislation requiring state agencies to purchase goods made from a minimum percentage of recycled materials, or requiring such agencies to use a minimum portion of their budget to purchase products made from recycled materials (887).

State environmental protection acts

The National Environmental Protection Act (NEPA) requires the preparation of environmental impact statements for any project involving 'major *Federal* actions significantly affecting the quality of the human environment' (42 U.S.C. § 433(c) (1994) (emphasis added)). In the absence of federal actions, such as federal funding or permitting, NEPA does not impose any obligations, and thus does not reach state actions that might pose environmental harms. In most states, however, environmental impact statements must be prepared in such situations as a matter of state law. A recent study suggests that twenty-eight states have now imposed such requirements (Caldwell 1998: 227). As a result, a larger range of projects require the preparation of environmental impact statements: the state programmes have a direct effect on projects for which there is state involvement but no federal involvement.

Moreover, as a result of the Supreme Court's decision in *Strycker's Bay Neighborhood Council* v. *Karlen* (44 U.S. 223 (1980)), the federal NEPA statute is essentially limited to a procedural requirement, which is satisfied if an appropriate environmental impact statement is prepared. Under this interpretation, NEPA has no independent substantive component. Thus, for example, there is no requirement for a project to mitigate its adverse environmental consequences. In contrast, the state statutes of the District of Columbia and at least four states have substantive elements (Cal. Pub. Resources Code § 21002.1; D.C. Code § 6-981; Mass. Gen. L. ch. 30, § 61; Minn. Stat. § 116D.02; N.Y. Envtl. Conserv. L. § 8-0109). While some courts have interpreted these substantive provisions in a restrictive manner (*Laurel Heights Improvement Ass'n* v. *Regents of the Univ. of California*, 764 P.2d 278, 283 (Cal. 1988)), others have given them full effect (*Jackson* v. *New York State Urban Dev. Corp.*, 494 N.E.2d 429, 434–35 (N.Y. 1986)). As a result, environmental projects involving both federal and state action might fail a challenge under state law even if they survive a challenge under federal law.

Wetlands protection

A number of states are beginning to take an active role with respect to wetlands protection. For example, in 1987, Maryland, Virginia, Pennsylvania, and the District of Columbia signed the Chesapeake Bay Wetlands Policy, which set a goal of achieving 'a net resource gain in wetlands acreage and function over existing conditions' (Grasso 1996). The agreement also called for reducing by 40 per cent the amount of nutrients flowing into the Bay by the year 2000. This agreement led to the Tidal Wetland Program and Nontidal Wetland Program, administered by the Maryland Department of Natural Resources; the Tidal Wetlands Program and Submerged Lands Program, administered by the Virginia Marine Resources Commission; and the Dam Safety and Waterway Management Program, administered by the Pennsylvania Department of Environmental Resources. A recent empirical study suggests that these programmes have had a salutary effect (Grasso 1996). Similarly, an empirical study has shown that wetlands loss in Massachusetts has slowed considerably since the passage in 1991 of the state Wetlands Protection Act (Payne 1998).

Toward a desirable federal policy: a regulatory mismatch

The preceding discussion shows why the three principal justifications for federal intervention do not serve as across-the-board arguments justifying federal regulation. This chapter is not the place to work out the details of a desirable federal role with respect to environmental regulation. To add some concreteness to the discussion it is useful, however, to briefly describe the areas in which federal intervention can correct the various pathologies that otherwise would result (Revesz 1997e).

Interstate externalities

The preceding discussion has focused on pollution externalities, principally air pollution crossing state lines, and shown why the existence of such externalities provides a compelling reason for federal regulation. Other externalities that merit federal regulation arise with respect to different environmental problems. For example, to the extent that certain endangered species are located in a particular state, the costs of protection are largely concentrated in that state. The benefits of preservation, however, accrue nationally, or, for that matter, globally.

Similarly, out-of-state citizens place value on the existence of certain natural resources—even resources that they never plan to use. Such existence, or non-use, values provide a powerful justification for federal control over exceptional natural resources such as national parks.

Economies of scale

Advocates of federal regulation often maintain, though without much empirical support, that centralization has strong economies of scale advantages. The economies of scale argument is most plausible in the early stages of the regulatory process, particularly with respect to the determination of the adverse effects of particular pollutants through risk assessment. Indeed, there is little reason for this determination to be replicated by each state.

The force of the rationale, however, is far less compelling at the standard-setting phase. At this stage, not only are the savings from eliminating duplication of efforts likely to be much lower, but centralization will have serious social costs as a result of the difficulty of setting standards that are responsive to the preferences and physical conditions of different regions.

Uniformity

As previously discussed, federal environmental standards are generally minimum standards. The states remain free to impose more stringent standards if they wish. Some standards that apply to pesticides and mobile sources such as automobiles (7 U.S.C. § 136v (b) (1994) (pesticides); 42 U.S.C. § 7416 (1994) (mobile sources)), however, are both floors and ceilings: they pre-empt both more stringent and less stringent state standards. Uniformity of this sort can be desirable for products with significant economies of scale in production. In such cases, disparate regulation would break up the national market for the product and be costly in terms of foregone economies of scale.

The benefits of uniformity, however, are less compelling in the case of process standards, which govern the environmental consequences of the manner in which goods are produced rather than the consequences of the products themselves.

Indeed, unlike the case of dissimilar product standards, there can be a well functioning common market regardless of the process standards governing the manufacture of the products traded in the market.

Protection of minimum levels of public health

There is a powerful notion, informed in part by constitutional considerations, that a federal polity should ensure to all its citizens a minimum level of environmental protection. At some level, this justification is compelling: a minimum level of health ought to count as a basic human right, in the same manner as minimum levels of education, housing, or access to employment. There are two major problems, however, with justifying federal environmental regulation in this manner. First, federal environmental regulation generally seeks to limit the risk of exposure to particular pollutants or from particular sources, rather than limiting aggregate levels of environmental risk. As a result, such regulation is both overinclusive (it regulates more than that which has a claim to quasi-constitutional legitimacy) and underinclusive (it makes no effort to determine aggregate exposure levels, thereby not ensuring that all individuals are in fact above the minimum). Second, because environmental risks are only one component of health risks, it is difficult to understand why the federal government should have such a pre-eminent role in environmental regulation when it does relatively little with respect to the provision of general health care. In fact, investments in preventive measures such as immunization or prenatal care would have a far larger impact on health than investments in environmental regulation. Thus the justification for federal regulation based on the need to guarantee a minimum level of health calls for a radically different form of regulation than that currently in effect: one that focuses on aggregate environmental health risks and the interactions between environmental health risks and other health risks.

Summary

This discussion reveals a significant mismatch between what federal regulation does and what it ought to do. Similarly, there is a wide chasm between the race-to-the-bottom, interstate externality, and public choice justification, which typically are invoked as all-purpose arguments to justify any kind of federal intervention, and the more targeted arguments that provide a sound basis for federal intervention.

II. IMPLICATIONS FOR THE EUROPEAN UNION

The legal issues concerning centralized environmental regulation are framed somewhat differently in the European Union than in the United States (Revesz 1997c: 1338–41). The presence of interjurisdictional externalities has played a role in justifying centralized intervention in the European Union, as it has in the United States (Stewart 1992; Van den Bergh, Faure, and Lefevere 1996). By relying predominantly on ambient standards and emission standards as the primary tools of environmental policy, the European Union's efforts to control interstate externalities are subject to the same criticisms as the federal environmental statutes in the United States.

The other prominent justification offered in the European context for centralized regulation is that harmonization of environmental laws promotes the establishment of a common market (Haagsma 1989: 355; Lomas 1988: 511); this justification has not been nearly as prominent in federalism debates in the United States.

The harmonization rationale has some force in the case of product standards. A product cannot trade freely throughout a common market if states within the market can exclude it on environmental or health and safety grounds. Indeed, before the Single European Act in 1987 and the Maastricht Treaty in 1992 explicitly recognized environmental and health and safety protection as Community goals, the harmonization rationale embodied in Article 100 of the Treaty of Rome provided the basis for an extensive body of regulation in these areas.

Harmonization arguments have, however, also been invoked to justify the vesting of centralized responsibility over process standards, such as environmental ambient and emissions standards. There are several serious problems with extending the argument in this manner.

First, as long as product standards are harmonized, there can be a well functioning common market regardless of the stringency of the process standards governing the products' manufacture. Thus, more accurately, the argument must call for the harmonization of the products' production costs, so as to deny a comparative advantage to states with lax environmental standards.

The second problem, however, is that the costs of complying with environmental regulation, or, for that matter, the costs of complying with any regulation, are only one component of the total costs of production. Other components include a state's investments in infrastructure, health care, and education, as well as its wages, labour productivity, and access to raw materials. These factors, which can have a significant effect on production costs, are unlikely to be (or are incapable of being) the subject of the European Union's harmonization efforts. Thus, rather than eliminating cost differences, the harmonization of environmental standards has the effect of conferring a competitive advantage on states with lower non-harmonizable components of costs.

Third, the harmonization argument cannot be used, as it has been in the European Union, to justify both uniform ambient standards and uniform emissions standards. A centralized regulatory regime consisting of only uniform ambient standards, which permits the states to allocate the pollution control burden among existing and new sources in any way they see fit, would confer a competitive advantage on the states with the smaller industrial base. Indeed, states with lower pollution output could offer their sources less stringent emissions standards without violating the ambient standards. The addition of centralized emissions standards moderates this comparative advantage but does not wholly eliminate it. Highly industrialized states, where the centralized ambient standards constrain further growth, would be unable to attract new sources without imposing additional costs on existing sources.

In the light of these weaknesses, it is not surprising that recent European scholarship has sought to recharacterize the quest for harmonization in race-to-the-bottom terms. Commentators have argued, as have race-to-the-bottom advocates in the United States, that the goal of centralized intervention is to protect states from the pressure to impose suboptimally lax environmental standards as a means of attracting jobs and tax revenues (Kramer 1995; Van den Bergh, Faure, and Lefevere 1996). But, obviously, the analytical shortcomings of the race-to-the-bottom rationale for centralized environmental regulation are not confined to one side of the Atlantic.

The legal status of the debates concerning the strength of the rationales for centralized environmental regulation is also different in the European Union and the United States. In the United States, the choice between federal and state regulation (except when state regulation is coupled with trade restrictions) is, for the most part, a matter of policy. The constitutional constraints are extremely weak, even after the Supreme Court's decisions in *New York* v. *United States* (505 U.S. 144 (1992)) (holding that Congress may not require states to enact or administer a federal programme), *United States* v. *Lopez* (115 S.Ct. 1624 (1995)) (holding, for the first time in over fifty years, that Congress exceeded its authority under the Commerce Clause), and *Printz* v. *United States* (117 S.Ct. 2365 (1997)) (holding that Congress may not compel state officers to execute federal laws).

In the European Union, in contrast, the subsidiarity principle adopted in the Maastricht Treaty in 1992 permits action at the federal level 'only and insofar as the objectives of the proposed action cannot be sufficiently achieved by the Member States and can therefore, by reason of the scale or effects of the proposed action, be better achieved by the Community' (EC Treaty, Art. 36).[3] Thus, in the European Union, the subsidiarity principle constitutionalizes the inquiry concerning the level of government at which responsibility for environmental regulation should be allocated. Although commentators are divided about the likely role of the European Court of Justice in enforcing the subsidiarity principle, some believe that the principle is fully justiciable.[4] As a result, the debates concerning the proper allocation of authority over environmental regulation currently being waged primarily on the

[3] A similar principle had applied exclusively to environmental regulation, between 1986 and 1992, under Article 130r(4) of the Single European Act 1986. For discussion of the application of the subsidiarity principle to environmental law, see Brinkhorst (1993); Van den Bergh, Faure, and Lefevere (1996); and Wils (1994).

[4] Commentators are divided about the role of the European Court of Justice in subsidiarity inquiries. Lenaerts (1994) argues that the Court could merely require reasons for federal action; Toth (1994) argues that the subsidiarity principle raises political questions; and Steiner (1994) argues that the subsidiarity principle is fully justiciable.

US side of the Atlantic may well acquire an even greater salience in the European Union.

Moreover, the subsidiarity principle may affect the substantive nature of the federalism inquiry. In the European Union, the subsidiarity principle could be read as giving rise to a presumption for decentralization grounded in positive law. In contrast, in the United States, any argument in favour of such a presumption must rest on policy grounds, as no constitutional provision, statute, regulation, or judicial decision speaks to this question.

III. IMPLICATIONS FOR THE INTERNATIONAL COMMUNITY

In the international community, the issues concerning the interactions between environmental regulation and systems of economic integration are different than in federal systems (Revesz 1997c: 1332–5, 1341–5). First, in the international community, there is only weak capacity for centralized environmental standard setting and virtually no capacity for centralized environmental enforcement. Second, the differences in wealth and economic development are far more salient in the international community than in federal systems. Third, environmental conditions in some countries are sufficiently dire to give rise to concerns that basic human rights are being violated.[5]

As a result of the lack of a viable system of environmental standard setting and enforcement, there are stronger arguments in the international community than in federal systems for allowing countries to impose environmentally based trade restrictions. Even where centralized regulation might be preferable, for example as a result of interjurisdictional externalities, state regulation coupled with trade measures might be the best available outcome if centralized regulation is not feasible, or if it is not feasible in an enforceable manner.

The different treatment of process standards in federal systems and in the international community is therefore not surprising. In both the United States and the European Union, state-imposed trade restrictions have been coupled with product standards but not with process standards (Stewart 1992: 1342). Instead, environmental regulation with respect to processes has been the domain of the federal government. There is little justification for allowing a state to impose a process standard designed to change the environmental behaviour of another state when a centralized authority can do so directly.

In contrast, process standards have been coupled with trade restrictions in the international community—the United States' restrictions on the import of certain tuna products at issue in the *Tuna-Dolphin* case is probably the best known exam-

[5] One might also worry about whether certain countries have the capacity (and sufficiently well functioning governments) to address environmental matters. But because sovereignty plays a far more central role in the international arena than in federal systems, it would be more difficult at the international level to invoke this public choice concern to displace decentralized authority.

ple (United States: Restrictions on Imports of Tuna, GATT B.I.S.D., 39th Supp. (1993), at 155). Even though the Secretariat of the General Agreement on Tariffs and Trade (GATT), the World Trade Organization's (WTO) predecessor, took a sceptical view with respect to the permissibility of such measures,[6] the issue continues to draw the body's attention (WTO Secretariat 1996: 2–10, 39–42). The recent *Shrimp-Turtle* decision may herald a more favourable reception on the part of the WTO to the enforcement of process standards by means of trade restrictions (United States: Import Restrictions of Certain Shrimp and Shrimp Products, 1998 WL 720123 (WTO) (report of the Appellate Body)). In any event, in the coming years, this issue will be the subject of intense scrutiny in the context of the work of the WTO's Committee on Trade and the Environment.

The second important difference between the systems of the United States and the European Union on the one hand and the international community on the other arises as a result of the more extreme differences in wealth and levels of economic development in the international community. This factor, coupled with the lack of a viable, widespread system for economic redistribution in the international community, implies that the distributional consequences of each policy ought to play a far more salient role in evaluating their relative desirability.

For example, in a federal system of relatively homogeneous states, it might be desirable to adopt policies that lead to the maximization of social welfare without undue concern about how the costs and benefits of such policies are distributed across different geographic subdivisions. Indeed, federal governments regulate in many areas, and the distributional consequences may well even out across programmes. Thus it may not be sensible to compromise the social welfare properties of each programme in order to achieve a better programme-specific distribution. Moreover, even if such evening out of the aggregate distributional consequences does not occur, it is likely to be more desirable to redistribute through a system of taxes and subsidies than by compromising the efficiency of the various regulatory programmes. The situation is different in the international community, with its larger differences in wealth and economic development, and lesser opportunities for redistribution.

Third, because a sufficiently egregious disregard for human health and the environment can be equated with a violation of basic human rights, the use of trade restrictions might be seen as a desirable mechanism for combating such violations. The example of child labour is somewhat analogous.

The following taxonomy seeks to provide a useful way to begin the analysis of when trade measures (either restrictions or sanctions) would be a desirable way of combating overly lax process standards in exporting countries. The emphasis here is on what would be desirable policy; other contributors to this volume are far

[6] The GATT Secretariat (1992: 37, 50) wrote, 'In principle, it is not possible under GATT's rules to make access to one's own market dependent on the domestic environmental policies or practices of the exporting country'.

better able to analyse what the treaty language would actually allow under current interpretations.

The first element of this taxonomy is defined by reference to the geographic scope of the physical effects of the pollution that gives rise to a call for the trade measure. Six situations are relevant: (1) purely domestic effects in the exporting country; (2) physical spillovers into the importing country; (3) physical spillovers into third countries; (4) impairment of existence values in the importing country; (5) impairment of existence values in third countries; and (6) effects on the global commons.

In the first situation—if the effects of the pollution are confined to the exporting country—trade measures are hardest to justify. Producers in the importing country may be upset that one factor of production is cheap in the exporting country, but restrictions imposed for this reason are unlikely to be welfare enhancing. Moreover, given that the costs of production have many non-harmonizable components, such as wages, labour productivity, infrastructure, and educational systems, it is not clear why a single factor should be singled out for special treatment. Finally, just because the exporting country might subject its people to less desirable health and environmental conditions than does the importing country does not necessarily imply that a violation of a basic human right has occurred.[7]

In the second situation—the case of physical spillovers—trade measures might be the only way for the importing country to protect itself. In the United States, the permissibility of such restrictions is sometimes determined by comparing the welfare gains in the importing state with the corresponding welfare losses in the exporting state (Revesz 1996: 2405–8). In the international community, however, the distributional concerns discussed above should complicate the inquiry.

In the third situation—where the physical spillovers affect third countries—the importing country's trade measure might nonetheless increase the global social welfare. Because the importing country is not affected by the pollution, however, one might be concerned that the asserted environmental reason for the restriction is a mere subterfuge, masking a protectionist motivation.

With respect to the fourth and fifth situations, there is no analytical reason for treating existence values, also sometimes known as non-use values, differently from physical spillovers. Citizens of the importing country might suffer a real loss in utility from learning about the destruction of a valuable natural resource abroad, even if they never planned to visit it. The claims of citizens of wealthy countries for trade measures to protect their existence values might not seem particularly sympathetic if the costs fall on citizens of far poorer countries, whose very livelihood might be at stake. Moreover, the controversy surrounding the use of the contingent valuation methodology, which is used to value existence values, makes problematic any attempt to weigh the interests of the various jurisdictions (Portney 1994). As a

[7] If conditions are sufficiently dire to give rise to such a violation, however, there might be an independent ground for action on the part of the importing country.

result, trade measures motivated by the impairment of existence values are likely to be viewed as less legitimate than trade measures motivated by physical spillovers.

Finally, with respect to impacts on the global commons, in some cases trade measures will be expressly permitted by international treaties (Revesz 1997d). Such treaties, however, often take a long time to negotiate (and an even longer time to result in the imposition of specific obligations). In the interim, unilateral trade measures may well be the best available way to protect the global commons.

The second element of the classification system is defined by reference to how the environmental standards in the exporting and importing countries compare to those that would maximize social welfare in the respective jurisdictions. The relevant categories are set out in Table 1.

Table 1. Comparison of the Stringency of Environmental Standards in Countries A (Exporting) and B (Importing)

		B		
		Laxer than optimal	Optimal	More stringent than optimal
A	Laxer than optimal	a	b	c
	Optimal	d	e	f
	More stringent than optimal	g	h	i

To illustrate this table by means of an example, consider the following situation, which is consistent with the box labelled '*g*'. In *A*, the exporting country, the actual standard is 10 parts per million (ppm) of a pollutant, whereas its optimal standard is 12 ppm; thus *A*'s actual standard is more stringent than its optimal standard. In turn, in *B*, the importing country, the actual standard is 8 ppm (more stringent than *A*'s actual standard) but its optimal standard is 6 ppm; thus *B*'s standard is less stringent than its optimal standard.

Should *B*'s use of trade measures be appropriate merely because its standards are more stringent than *A*'s? Such an approach was embodied in the proposed International Pollution Deterrence Act (S. 984, 102d Cong. (1991)), which would have authorized the imposition of countervailing duties equal to the amount that the foreign firm would have to expend in order to comply with the US standards. Similarly, US Vice President Al Gore (1992: 343) wrote, while he was still a Senator, 'Just as government subsidies of a particular industry are sometimes considered unfair under the trade laws, weak and ineffectual enforcement of pollution control measures should also be included in the definition of unfair trading practices'.

The problem with this approach is that it would authorize the erection of trade barriers even when the disparity in the environmental standards is justified by differences in the preferences for environmental protection, differences in the costs of pollution control, and differences in the extent to which pollution produces adverse health and environmental effects in the two countries.

Alternatively, should trade measures be appropriate only in situations *a*, *b*, and *c*, in which *A*'s standards are laxer than optimal? Such an approach would recognize the reasons why it is desirable for different countries to have different levels of environmental protection.

Or should *B* be barred from using trade measures in situations *a*, *d*, and *g* because its own standards are laxer than optimal, even though *A*'s are laxer still? Such an approach would create incentives for *B* to adopt socially desirable standards.

In situations *c*, *f*, and *i*, where *B*'s standards are more stringent than optimal, should *B* be permitted to use trade measures only if its optimal standards are more stringent than *A*'s standards? An affirmative answer might be predicated on the undesirability of allowing *B* to penalize other countries as a result of its own public choice problems that lead it to adopt suboptimally stringent standards.

A full analysis of this issue cannot be undertaken here. It ought to be clear, however, that trade measures ought not to be permitted merely because the importing country has more stringent environmental standards than the exporting country.

IV. IMPLICATIONS FOR OTHER REGULATORY CONTEXTS

The race-to-the-bottom label has been applied in a wide variety of regulatory contexts (Revesz 1992: 1247–53). My focus here is to show how these contexts are analytically distinct—an issue that has not received the attention of the relevant literatures. As a result, for example, how one comes out on the existence of a race to the bottom over environmental regulation should say virtually nothing about the analysis of the so-called races to the bottom caused by interstate competition over corporate and banking charters, and over programmes of economic redistribution. My analysis with respect to environmental problems, however, applies more generally whenever states impose costs on the physical assets of mobile firms to promote the welfare of their citizens.

Competition over corporate charters: principal–agent problems

In the corporate area, the problem alleged by race-to-the-bottom advocates is the principal–agent problem that arises between managers and shareholders when managers make decisions about where to incorporate. The claim is that managers, who effectively are the decision makers on this issue, will choose states of incorporation that maximize their interests at the expense of those of their company's shareholders.[8] The corporate literature does not, however, generally point to any problems

[8] The competing positions are set out by Cary (1974), who posits a race to the bottom, and Winter (1977), who explains why markets prevent managerial rent seeking. The more recent literature includes Bebchuk (1992), Macey and Miller (1987), and Romano (1987b; 1985).

caused by the competition for corporate charters among the states themselves; the problem, instead, is internal to the decision-making structure of the firms (Ayres 1995). In contrast, race-to-the-bottom arguments in the environmental area do not refer to any principal–agent problems between managers and shareholders in deciding where to locate a plant (or to any other internal decision-making problems of firms deciding where to locate their plants).[9] Instead, the focus is on a posited prisoner's dilemma in the relationship among the states themselves.

The two literatures can be classified by reference to the two-by-two matrix in Table 2. It shows that the defects to be corrected by federal regulation can arise in the locational decision-making process of private actors or in the competitive process among states. Race-to-the-bottom advocates in the corporate literature fit into Box 2: they believe that locational decisions are defective but that the competitive process among the states is not.[10] Race-to-the-bottom advocates in the environmental literature fit into Box 3: they believe that the competitive process among the states is defective but that locational decisions of private actors are not. Thus the two literatures do not deal with analogous issues.

Table 2. Environmental and Corporate Races to the Bottom

		Interstate Competitive Process	
		Defective	Not defective
Firm decision-making process	Defective	Box 1	Box 2: Corporate Race
	Not Defective	Box 3: Environmental race	Box 4

Competition over bank charters: interstate externalities

Henry Butler and Jonathan Macey (1988: 715) argue that state chartering of banks gives rise to a 'destructive "race to the bottom"'. They maintain that the major cause for this race is that the Federal Deposit Insurance Corporation (FDIC) charges banks a deposit insurance premium that is independent of the bank's risk of default (680, 714).

For two distinct reasons, states then have an incentive to set suboptimally lax regulatory regimes. First, a state seeking to attract banks, and thereby obtain

[9] Other commentators, however, have suggested that such problems exist (Czamanski and Fogel 1985).

[10] Competition among the states can exacerbate the principal–agent problem by increasing the opportunity for managerial enrichment. Nonetheless, if the principal–agent problem could be corrected, interstate competition would not have undesirable effects.

chartering fees and legal business, will offer the regulatory regime most attractive to bank shareholders (or managers[11]), who will naturally prefer to make risk choices that are unconstrained by a regulatory regime.

Second, a state seeking to promote the interests of in-state depositors will also provide a lax regulatory regime. If the bank can engage in riskier activities, it may pay depositors higher interest rates. If the risky projects fail, the depositors are protected by FDIC insurance. Thus depositors capture the benefits of higher risk but do not bear any of the costs. In any event, given the possibility of making deposits across state lines, depositors would bank in the state that offered the laxest provisions, independent of their state of residence.[12]

The undesirable effects in both instances are caused by the presence of an interstate externality. Bank shareholders and depositors capture the benefits of increased risk, but the corresponding cost is borne by the FDIC, and, indirectly, by the nation's taxpayers. While some of these taxpayers will be residents of the state that adopted the suboptimally lax regulatory structure, most will not.

In the environmental context, I showed why race-to-the-bottom justifications for federal regulation should be seen as distinct from externality-based justifications. I thus use the term 'race to the bottom' in the environmental area to refer exclusively to the destructiveness of interstate competition for industry that is alleged to occur even in the absence of interstate pollution externalities. The banking literature, in contrast, uses the race-to-the-bottom label to refer to a problem that would be corrected by eliminating the interstate externality, for example through the imposition by the FDIC of risk-adjusted rates (Butler and Macey 1988: 715).

The distinction between the problems addressed in the two literatures is illustrated in Table 3. The table shows that the defects to be corrected by federal regulation can arise from interstate externalities or from the competitive process among states. Banking race-to-the-bottom advocates fit into Box 2: they believe that there are interstate externalities but that the competitive process among the states is not otherwise flawed. The environmental race to the bottom, as distinguished from the problem of interstate pollution externalities, fits into Box 3. These literatures therefore do not deal with analogous issues, even though they both invoke the race-to-the-bottom label.

Competition over programmes of economic redistribution: mobility of individuals

The standard account of the effects of interstate competition over programmes of economic redistribution, principally welfare programmes, focuses heavily on the

[11] In principle, the divergence between the interests of shareholders and managers that preoccupies the corporate law literature could also affect bank chartering decisions.

[12] The problem, under either formulation, is different from the alleged race to the bottom that arises from the existence of a choice between federal and state chartering (Scott 1977: 13). For a view that this competition is beneficial, see Fischel, Rosenfield, and Stillman (1987: 335).

Table 3: Environmental and Banking Races to the Bottom

		Interstate Competitive Process	
		Defective	Not defective
Interstate externality	Present	Box 1	Box 2: Banking race
	Absent	Box 3: Environmental race	Box 4

mobility of individuals across jurisdictions. The idea is that wealthy individuals, who would bear the burden of paying the bulk of the cost of economic redistribution, would move to jurisdictions with low taxes, and consequently low welfare payments. In turn, welfare beneficiaries would move to jurisdictions that imposed high taxes in order to finance generous programmes. But in the end the jurisdiction with the high tax rates would lose all its wealthy individuals, its tax base would be destroyed, and there would be no funds with which to pay the welfare recipients (Cashin 1999; LeBoeuf 1994; Peterson 1995). This phenomenon has been described in race-to-the-bottom terms (Alstott 1996: 452; Calabresi 1998: 1019; Mashaw and Calsyn 1996: 321; Ulen 1998b: 935–6).[13]

In the environmental context, in contrast, the asserted race to the bottom occurs in the absence of the mobility of individuals, and the standard models in the area generally assume that individuals are immobile.[14] The defect in the competitive processes necessary to support race-to-the-bottom claims is independent of the mobility of individuals. Table 4 shows the analytical differences between the two contexts.

Generalizing from the environmental experience

The environmental, corporate, banking, and redistribution races to the bottom deal, respectively, with the following distinct types of problems: (1) defects in the interstate competitive process; (2) divergence of interests over locational decisions between principals and their agents; (3) interstate externalities; and (4) mobility of individuals. Little is gained, and a great deal of analytical clarity is lost by attaching the race-to-the-bottom label to these four disparate problems.

[13] Interestingly, preliminary studies of the impact of the recent devolution of responsibility over welfare programmes do not present a clear picture consistent with race-to-the-bottom claims (Brueckner 1998: 19–35; Holahan *et al.* 1998: 51–8; Riedinger 1999: 69–70).

[14] This is the case with the Oates and Schwab (1988) and the Markusen, Morey, and Olewiler (1995; 1993) models described above. In a companion, unpublished paper, Oates and Schwab (1987) show that interstate competition over environmental standards leads to the maximization of social welfare even if individuals are mobile.

Table 4. Environmental and Redistribution Races to the Bottom

		Interstate Competitive Process	
		Defective	Not defective
Mobility of individuals	Present	Box 1	Box 2: Redistribution race
	Absent	Box 3: Environmental race	Box 4

There are ways, however, in which one can generalize from the environmental analysis. The assessment of race-to-the-bottom arguments in the environmental context is relevant whenever states impose costs on the physical assets of mobile plants, through regulatory programmes or through taxes, in order to promote the interests of their citizens. From the preceding analysis of environmental regulation, one would expect that under models of perfect competition the interstate interactions would be welfare enhancing, and that under models of imperfect competition the result of the interstate competition would be overregulation in certain instances and underregulation in others.

CONCLUSION

This chapter attempts to explain why the race-to-the-bottom, interstate externality, and public choice arguments for federal environmental protection, as traditionally discussed in the legal academic literature and in the political process, cannot bear the weight placed on them. They cannot credibly be used to justify across-the-board federal environmental regulation on the ground that states would otherwise underregulate.

At the same time, however, there is a serious mismatch between what federal environmental regulation ought to do and what it in fact does. The current regime is both overinclusive, needlessly trumping the legitimate preferences of the states, and underinclusive, leaving uncorrected serious pathologies for which federal intervention is necessary.

The analysis of federalism issues in the context of the United States sheds considerable light on the treatment of these matters in the European Union. In particular, the strong push toward harmonization in the European context is undesirable. Moreover, harmonization will not provide the level playing field that its supporters so fervently seek. In fact, the effect of harmonization is to advantage countries that already have stringent environmental standards. Moreover, the whole notion of a level playing field is essentially unattainable and, if attained, would go a long way toward destroying the very comparative advantage that makes trade (and, to a large extent, European integration) desirable.

The chapter also has implications for the treatment of environmental matters in international trade disputes. It explains why trade measures might be a desirable means of punishing certain countries with suboptimally lax environmental standards. It also stresses, however, why it would not be desirable to permit such trade measures merely because the importing country has environmental standards that are more stringent than those of the exporting country.

The chapter ends with a discussion of why the so-called races to the bottom in the environmental, corporate, banking, and economic redistribution areas are all analytically distinct. Thus, the conclusions that one reaches with respect to one of these areas have essentially no implications for how one views the other areas.

2

Regulatory Co-Opetition

DANIEL C. ESTY AND DAMIEN GERADIN

For the last two decades, academics have debated the merits of 'regulatory competition' versus the 'harmonization' of standards. This debate has now spilled over into policy circles in the United States, within Europe, and at the international level. Schematically, the discussion has become polarized around two camps. On one side stands a line of argument—especially popular in the 1970s and early 1980s—that calls for the harmonization of regulations so as to facilitate open markets, minimize non-tariff barriers between jurisdictions, and prevent competitiveness-driven, welfare-reducing underregulation (the so-called 'race toward the bottom') (Stewart 1977). This view served to justify a large expansion of federal legislation (and institutions) in the United States in the areas of environmental regulation, consumer protection, health and safety, and labour protection. Similar fears of trade distortions and races to the bottom led to the implementation of sweeping harmonization programmes and thus considerable expansion of centralized legislation in the European Union (Dashwood 1983). To a lesser extent, harmonization or 'regulatory convergence' strategies have also been undertaken at the international level through bilateral or multilateral trade agreements (Geradin 1997a).

More recently, however, the race-toward-the-bottom rationale for centrally adopted legislation has been dismissed by scholars who praise the virtues of regulatory competition (Oates and Schwab 1988; Revesz 1992; Romano 1985). Drawing an analogy between product markets and competition among jurisdictions in standard setting, they argue that regulatory competition leads to the adoption of standards of varying stringency that efficiently match the needs and desires of each jurisdiction. To the extent that there is a race, it generates welfare *gains*. The policy implications of regulatory competition theory, which has gained considerable currency among academics and policy makers in recent years, are significant. Notably, if regulatory competition theorists are correct, then a great number of federal/central regulatory programmes should be dismantled and regulatory powers should be decentralized.[1] Applied to the international sphere, the regulatory

[1] The regulatory competition model has had a major impact on the federalism debate in the United States. The regulatory competition-based argument for decentralized governance has been applied by its proponents to regulatory areas as diverse as corporation (Romano 1985; Winter 1977), securities (Romano 1998), antitrust (Easterbrook 1983), banking (Butler and Macey 1988), environmental (Revesz 1992), and product safety (Rice 1985) law. The regulatory competition model has also crossed the Atlantic and become a source of reference for those searching to define the scope of the obscure principle of 'subsidiarity' (Faure 1998; Hertig 1994; Van den Bergh 1994b). European Union-based regulatory competition theorists argue that, contrary to the ambitious policy of regulatory harmonization that has been pursued for several decades by the European Commission, decentralized regulation

competition approach could also act as a brake on further efforts to promote regulatory integration among nations (Bhagwati and Hudec 1996).

In this chapter, we argue that both race-toward-the-bottom and regulatory competition theories—and the resulting centralization and decentralization strategies that they imply—are overstated from a descriptive point of view and unsatisfactory from a normative one. The world is diverse and complex. Regulatory theory should reflect and parallel this diversity and complexity. We argue therefore that optimal governance requires a flexible mix of competition and cooperation between governmental actors, as well as between governmental and non-governmental actors. We call our approach 'regulatory co-opetition'.[2]

This chapter is divided into three parts. Part I provides a critical overview of competition theory, which today represents the dominant academic thinking about regulatory structure (Bratton and McCahery 1997). We recognize the merits of regulatory competition, but see the prevailing theory as incomplete and unnuanced. Our fundamental critique is two-fold. First, we argue that in many instances the 'locational rights' market created by competition among regulators fails and that some form of cooperation between and among jurisdictions is required to prevent inefficient outcomes. Thus, contrary to the position defended by most regulatory competition theorists, we conclude that, in the real world as opposed to the world of theory (and building on observations from the United States and the European Union), the welfare-enhancing effects of decentralization cannot be presumed. Second, we argue that standard regulatory competition theory posits too limited a mechanism for exerting real competitive pressure on governmental actors (Esty 1998). Competition between horizontally arrayed jurisdictions represents only one of the forms of pressure that disciplines state actors and drives governmental efficiency. Competition between governmental actors at different levels of power (such as state versus federal officials), between stakeholders within a single governmental unit (such as the US Environmental Protection Agency (EPA) versus the US Department of Energy (DOE)), or between government decision makers and non-governmental organizations (NGOs) may also prove valuable (Esty 1999b). In fact, these multiple dimensions of competition, combined with mechanisms of cooperation, seem likely to enhance regulatory efficacy and efficiency more than simple interjurisdictional horizontal competition.

Part II develops regulatory co-opetition as an alternative model. This theory builds on the view that the best regulatory systems require a mix of competition and cooperation across various levels of government, within the branches or

should be the rule and centralization the exception. Regulatory competition theory has begun to penetrate academic discussions in the area of international law (Trachtman 1993), as authors use this model to praise the virtues of regulatory heterogeneity in areas such as environmental law (Klevorick 1996) and international finance (Bernard 1996; Choi and Guzman 1997).

[2] We borrow the concept of 'co-opetition' from Adam Brandenburg and Barry Nalebuff's recent book (1996) of the same name. The book explains that the optimal strategy for business is often a mix of competitive and cooperative actions.

departments of a government, and between regulators and non-governmental actors. Regulatory co-opetition thus has three main dimensions: (1) *inter*governmental (reflecting the dynamics of competition and cooperation *among* governments, both horizontally and vertically arrayed); (2) *intra*governmental (arising from the give-and-take between departments and officials *within* governments); and (3) *extra*governmental (driven by the simultaneously *cooperative* and *competitive* relations between governmental and non-governmental actors).

Part III offers a brief summary and our conclusions. We argue, in particular, that the diversity of the regulatory challenges that governments face and the complexity of the world in which we live demands regulatory strategies that are pluralistic, not simplistic. Sometimes regulatory competition will prove to be advantageous; in other cases, some form of collaboration will produce superior results. More often, a combination of competition and cooperation will be optimal.

I. REGULATORY COMPETITION: A CRITICAL OVERVIEW

Part I introduces a simplified overview of the current status of the regulatory competition debate. Section A analyses the basic features of the regulatory competition model, as well as its main implications. Section B comprises our critique of that model and our effort to begin to identify the variables that determine whether competition, cooperation, or co-opetition will generate the best results in particular circumstances.

The model and its implications

The concept of regulatory competition can be traced to Charles Tiebout's 1956 article arguing that a decentralized governmental system, with horizontally arrayed jurisdictions competing to attract residents on the basis of differing tax and benefit structures, produces efficient outcomes (Tiebout 1956). Taken literally, Tiebout's model has policy implications for only a limited class of government activities (McCahery *et al.* 1996). It addresses the production of 'public goods', or goods and services produced by public authorities for which people are willing to pay taxes, including police and fire protection, primary education, roads, and sewers. An expanded concept of public goods, however, would include regulation—such as environmental or health and safety standards—and thus broadens the policy implications of the theory. Under this expanded view, governments are suppliers of legal structures and products. Like producers of any other good, these actors could and should be disciplined by market forces. Competitive pressures, so the theory goes, force governments to produce their regulatory products at competitive 'prices' (so that the benefits of governmental intervention exceed the costs) on pain of losing their customers, in this case citizens or businesses (Easterbrook 1983). The normative strength of the theory lies in the hope that competition will stimulate experimentation, innovation, and product differentiation in regulation, as in markets for products (Calabresi 1995). The process of refining the product (regulatory requirements and approaches) to meet consumer (societal) desires thus leads to the adoption of more efficient laws and enhances social welfare. From a public choice standpoint, competition forces regulators and their collaborators in industry to abandon the manipulation of regulatory mechanisms for private gain ('capture') and to adopt decisions more in line with the preferences of their citizens (Mashaw 1997; McCubbins *et al.* 1987).

The implications of this analysis on the question of the appropriate level of governance are clear and broad. For regulatory competition theorists, centralized systems of standard setting should be seen as regulatory cartels which, like any other form of collusion between competitors, inhibit the operation of the market, raise prices, and reduce economic efficiency. Such intervention should therefore be eliminated or narrowed to the greatest extent possible.[3] Fundamentally, regulatory competition theory generates a strong presumption in favour of governmental action on a decentralized basis (Revesz 1992).

Limitations of the model

Market failure

The virtues of regulatory competition derive from the forces generated by a functioning and competitive market for legal products. There are, however, a host of reasons to believe that this market rarely operates in the manner envisioned by regulatory competition optimists and is, in fact, often marked by market failures, notably a lack of adequate (never mind *perfect*) information (Esty 1999b). Because the market for locational rights is relatively *imperfect*, untrammelled regulatory competition cannot be counted on to produce optimal outcomes. While these market shortcomings are not universally or uniformly present, their real world frequency makes a strong presumption in favour of decentralized governance or high expectations from simple strategies of regulatory competition unwise.

Externalities

Externalities represent a primary cause of failure in locational rights markets. The inefficiency of markets where private and social costs diverge has long been understood (Pigou 1918), and the extension of this principle in the public goods context to circumstances where a harm (or benefit) to be regulated falls outside the jurisdiction of the regulating authorities has nearly as long a history (Baumol and Oates 1988). If regulators ignore impacts beyond their own jurisdictions, the standards they set will be systematically suboptimal (too low if they overlook

[3] If faithfully applied, the regulatory competition model would suggest that global free trade agreements are also unnecessary, since localities should adopt optimal trade policies on their own. Yet in the WTO arena, regulatory competition advocates recognize market failures of the kind discussed below. For a discussion of this apparent contradiction, see Farber (1997b).

transboundary regulatory benefits and too high if they disregard transboundary regulatory costs). A variety of such uninternalized externalities threatens market failure and allocative inefficiency with regard to decentralized regulation.

Externalities can be found in many realms, but particularly plague certain regulatory domains, such as environmental protection (Stewart 1992; Wils 1994). The classic externality is a *physical* pollution spillover, such as air emissions blowing across political boundaries. For many years, for example, Britain did not control sulphur emissions from its power plants because most of the adverse effects were felt in Scandinavia or elsewhere (Lomas 1988). Given the prevailing winds, Britain did not suffer especially from acid rain, but its air pollution standards were suboptimal from an overarching perspective because they failed to internalize the costs of the pollution that fell beyond British borders. A similar acid rain dynamic exists between the United States and Canada as well as between China and Japan.

Externalities can also be of a *psychological* nature. When Brazil allows the destruction of its tropical forests because its citizens desire economic growth more than rainforest protection, people in other countries may be greatly distressed by the disappearance of rare species or the loss of ecosystems that support biodiversity. These emotional harms are real, and when not factored into the Brazilian regulatory calculus, could be argued to be a market failure.[4]

Externalities may also be *economic*.[5] Weak enforcement of antitrust rules or intellectual property rights in one nation may have a negative impact on the profits of foreign-based producers whose products are thereby squeezed out of the market. To the extent that these spillover effects are not based on market-clearing effects, but rather driven by strategic behaviour, suboptimal results must be anticipated.

To avoid welfare losses and market distortions, such externalities must be corrected through some form of interjurisdictional collective action. The theoretical logic behind the need for regulatory collaboration at an overarching level in the face of transboundary externalities is not much disputed, even by regulatory competition advocates (Revesz 1992). What remains contested is the pervasiveness and scale of such market-disrupting externalities. We believe that the degree of uninternalized externalities may, in fact, vary widely from one field of regulation to the next—with important implications for how much relative emphasis can be placed on regulatory competition.

Successful acid rain abatement, for instance, requires broad-scale governmental intervention and a healthy measure of interjurisdictional cooperation, while regulation of toxic waste sites (localized harms) benefits from increased regulatory competition and decentralized decision making. Similarly, the state-based regulation of bank charters (in a world in which the Federal Deposit Insurance Corporation

[4] While the welfare losses outside Brazil are real, the question is: do those who are disturbed by rainforest destruction have a *right* to object (Esty 1996)?

[5] There is an ongoing debate, which we will not delve into here, about whether economic externalities are 'real' or merely pecuniary (Esty 1996; Revesz 1992).

(FDIC) spreads risk across state lines) invites a race toward the bottom (Butler and Macey 1988), while competition in corporate charter rules, where significant spillovers are not present, seems likely to be welfare enhancing (Romano 1987b).

Imperfect information

A second cause of market failure undermining the potential gains from regulatory competition derives from information deficiencies. For markets to work efficiently, the buyers must have 'perfect' information, which, in the context of regulatory competition, means sufficient data to determine whether the government is delivering an appropriate level of regulation and doing so in a cost-effective manner. The buyers (businesses and citizens) must also be fully informed about the alternative regulatory packages offered by competing jurisdictions, and they must be aware of the options they have to exit or move.

This information may not be readily accessible. Some aspects of the requisite data will be relatively easy to obtain and to compare so long as the competing jurisdictions share the same language and legal traditions. For instance, a US company may well be able to identify—generally with the help of specialized lawyers—state laws and regulatory burdens that might apply to its operations as it contemplates building a new factory somewhere in the United States. The same information gathering will prove more difficult, however, in the European Union—or among other groups of independent nations—because of the greater cultural and regulatory heterogeneity of their component entities. In addition, information costs will often be prohibitive when the buyer is not a firm but an individual trying to determine where to live, when the scope of the inquiry covers a large number of regulatory variables (environment, health, safety, tax burden, support services, etc.) or when the options encompass many jurisdictions.

The likelihood of information-deficiency-induced market failures also mounts in some regulatory realms because of the high level of underlying uncertainty about regulatory costs and benefits (Esty 1999b). Thus, while average citizens may be able to judge whether the roads that a town provides are adequate, they will not be well positioned to determine whether the degree of air pollution protection provided by a particular jurisdiction matches their needs.

In sum, where the regulatory cost/benefit calculus is relatively clear, certain, and visible, regulatory competition will be more likely to yield welfare benefits. But, in realms where the costs or benefits of governmental intervention are more obscure, operation of the market in locational rights may not enhance social welfare.

Lack of mobility

The lack of mobility of market participants may also lead to regulatory market failure. For regulatory competition to work, 'buyers' of standards and the legal regimes that support them must be able to move to the jurisdiction that offers the package of costs and benefits that most closely matches their own needs and values. But the assumption of perfect mobility may not reflect reality.

The Tieboutian vision of 'people voting with their feet' bears little resemblance to the real world. Cultural barriers and tradition affect mobility. In Europe, for example, the vast majority of people live all of their lives in their countries, and even towns, of origin (Van den Bergh 1994b). The elasticity of population migration as a function of policy variability appears, in fact, to be rather low. In the case of businesses, market requirements and regulatory barriers dramatically constrain mobility. Many companies serve local markets or have large amounts of capital tied up in immovable assets. Thus threats to migrate are often empty. Moreover, legal regimes can hinder mobility. The ability of European firms to move (by 'rechartering') to other member states has been impeded, moreover, by the 'real seat' doctrine—the rule that the law governing the corporation is that of its actual seat of business, not simply that of a state in which it has filed appropriate chapters or keeps a mailing address (Charny 1991). Experts agree that application of this doctrine in most member states has been a key factor preventing the famous Delaware incorporation phenomenon from occurring in Europe (Kohl 1996; Kübler 1996).

Economies of scale and transaction cost savings

Economic theory teaches that if economies of scale are important, a single supplier may be more efficient than several competing suppliers. When regulatory economies of scale are present, centralized standard-setting procedures may thus be more efficient than regulatory competition.[6]

Some aspects of regulation are more technically complicated or analysis-intensive, making them susceptible to economies of scale that might overwhelm any benefits from multiple jurisdictions competing with diverse regulatory approaches. Some elements of regulation, moreover, are driven heavily by 'facts' that do not vary geographically—such as the safe level of human exposure to carcinogens—rather than by divergent circumstances and values. It may make sense, therefore, for bank regulation to be decentralized across the fifty US federal states or fifteen EU member states. But having each US state or EU member state undertake the exhaustive and expensive analysis necessary to set its own pesticide residue tolerances makes less sense.

Absent centralized functions, independent regulators will either duplicate each other's analytic work or engage in time-consuming and complex negotiations over the division of technical labour. Moreover, the poorer the jurisdiction, the more likely it is that its regulators will lack basic technical capacity and the resources necessary to do a competent and analytically rigorous job. Likewise, the smaller the regulating entity, the more likely it is to suffer from a lack of scientific, technical, and analytic economies of scale. This reasoning does not mean that all food safety

[6] Industry sectors where large economies of scale can be achieved (e.g. electricity production and transmission) are generally considered to be 'natural monopolies' (Kahn 1970). Similarly, areas where important regulatory economies of scale can be achieved may be considered to be 'natural legal monopolies'.

or air and water pollution standards should be set (or implemented) by central authorities. It simply suggests that at least *some* regulatory functions will be more efficiently carried out on a centralized basis while other activities will likely be more appropriately handled by decentralized governmental bodies (Esty 1996).

Collective action—or high degrees of regulatory cooperation—will likewise be more efficient than regulatory competition when interjurisdictional trade is significant and cross-border regulatory transaction costs are high. For instance, inconsistent safety standards for internationally traded goods will generate substantial costs for producers and may even discourage them from exporting their products. Producers may need to spend vast sums on lawyers to spell out the particularized rules of each jurisdiction and then further amounts to tailor their products to local market requirements (Sykes 1995; 1999). Even the most minor regulatory differences can have considerable economic implications. In such circumstances, it is generally recognized that the convergence of standards or some form of mutual recognition policy will be desirable.[7]

Public choice and political failures

The regulatory competition theory presumes that regulators know the interests of their constituents and act upon them (Revesz 1992). If, however, special interests manipulate the standard setting process or other public choice failures distort the regulatory options available to businesses and citizens, the market for locational rights will not function efficiently (Esty 1996). Much of the recent debate over the value of regulatory competition turns on how pervasive public choice failures are presumed to be. Where regulators pursue the interests of the citizenry in good faith, the market for locational rights will function more smoothly. Where democracy is absent, poor regulatory results should also be anticipated (Dua and Esty 1997).

Prisoners' dilemma dynamics and strategic behaviour

Just as public choice failures may undermine regulatory competition, the market for locational rights breaks down to the extent that competing regulators operate not as 'price takers' but as strategic actors in a prisoners' dilemma standard setting game. That the prisoners' dilemma dynamic in circumstances of economic interdependence can trigger suboptimal regulatory outcomes resulting in welfare losses has long been understood (Stewart 1977). As has been noted, fears of a race toward the bottom represent one of the central underpinnings of US federal regulation, and it has played some role in the 'federalization' of European law. The perils of race-toward-the-bottom strategic behaviour—known in the trade world as

[7] Esty and Geradin (1998) explain that 'harmonization' need not imply absolutely uniform standards. Alternative forms of harmonization or regulatory 'convergence' may permit some degree of standardization without the concomitant efficiency losses that single standards which do not match local needs generate. Harmonization debates themselves often entail competition over whose standards should be adopted. And agreement on a common standard need not bring an end to regulatory competition. Many forms of harmonization are flexible and open enough to allow continued debate over, and refinement of, the standards selected (Slot 1996).

'beggar thy neighbour' behaviour—is also a standard argument used by those desiring the establishment of comprehensive environmental or labour protection regimes at the regional or international level (Charnovitz 1992; Langille 1997).

Regulation competition theorists have recently questioned the logic of the fear of a race toward the bottom (Revesz 1992). Others have argued that there is little evidence that competitiveness-driven strategies of deregulation arise in practice (Jaffee *et al.* 1995; Klevorick 1996; Low and Yeats 1992). But the comfort drawn from the dearth of empirical evidence of welfare-reducing races does not mitigate the powerful logic of the theory of comparative advantage, which argues that there will be industrial migration to low-standard jurisdictions.[8] Recent empirical studies from the environmental field suggest that low standards do, in fact, lure industry (Mani and Wheeler 1999; van Beers and van den Bergh 1997). There is, moreover, ample anecdotal evidence that competitiveness-driven 'political drag' or 'regulatory chill' creates a strategic dynamic that can make it difficult, and in some circumstances impossible, for governments to move towards optimum levels of regulation in the environmental domain (Esty and Geradin 1997). Similarly, the fear that generous social welfare policies and labour rights regimes negatively affect competitiveness has led a number of governments, especially in Europe, to be hesitant about continuing their welfare policies (Rodrik 1997). The breadth of this 'political drag' phenomenon remains, however, a matter of debate.

Our critique of regulatory competition theory and the observation that the market dynamics necessary to produce welfare gains may be present only in limited circumstances should not be seen as an argument in favour of across-the-board harmonization of standards. We simply conclude that just as the benefits of centralization should not be presumed, nor should any generalization in favour of decentralized governance be made. As we discuss in Part II below, what is needed is a multi-tier regulatory regime that gives policy makers access to both centralized and decentralized structures depending on the characteristics of the particular regulatory issue.

Too narrow a set of competitors

The second aspect of our critique of the Tieboutian or neo-Tieboutian models of regulatory competition centres on the fact that they represent far too limited a mechanism for exerting real competitive pressure. Competition between horizontally arrayed jurisdictions represents only one of the ways in which government officials might be disciplined. Other sources of competition, involving a larger set of competitors, should be envisaged.

First, traditional regulatory competition theory tends to overlook the fact that the structure of federalism is inherently competitive. Dividing power among local, state, and federal (and increasingly, international) authorities generates competing

[8] For example, Lawrence Summers's (in)famous World Bank internal memorandum leaked to the press explained that it is economically efficient to encourage migration of dirty industries to less developed nations (The Economist 1992).

policy perspectives. If decision processes at one level of government are suboptimal or distorted by bureaucratic sloth, special interest lobbying, corruption, elite domination, self-serving politicians, or simply inadequate information and analytic limitations, these shortcomings can be highlighted and perhaps even redressed by having parallel decision-making processes operating at higher or lower levels of government (Esty 1999b). If, for instance, state environmental regulators overlook the polluting activities of a particular factory (perhaps because its owners have made significant campaign contributions to the governor), the presence of local officials who demand action or of regulatory oversight from federal authorities can ensure that appropriate environmental protection policies are pursued.

The same logic applies to the presence of governance structures above the nation-state. The Organization for Economic Cooperation and Development (OECD) provides a measure of competitive pressure in this regard. The OECD's widely publicized periodic 'national reviews' of its member countries in a variety of regulatory areas often reveal policy weaknesses. OECD 'guidelines' and information-sharing activities serve, moreover, as benchmarks for policy makers. Similarly, the World Trade Organization (WTO) and other regional trade organizations provide a useful source of discipline against protectionist governmental trade policies (Hudec 1990).

Another form of policy-making discipline that gets short shrift from many regulatory competition theorists is the competition that exists between the various branches or departments of a government. As Breton argues, government actors are inherently competitive (1996). In many policy areas, government departments will struggle to push their own agendas. In the United States, for example, the EPA and the DOE compete vigorously over the design of climate change strategies. These two governmental entities approach the greenhouse gas emissions problem from very different starting points; they bring to the issue quite different bureaucratic strengths; and they draw support and information from highly divergent constituencies. A similar form of welfare-enhancing rivalry can be observed in the EU structure, where Directorate Generals often advance competing strategies to address a common policy issue. The recent struggle between the Directorate General for Industry (DG III) and the Directorate General for Consumer Protection (DG XXIV) over the necessity of banning certain cancer-causing chemicals from toys used by young children provides a good example of this phenomenon (Environment Watch 1999).

Finally, competitive pressures will also be generated by NGOs (Esty 1998). In the intellectual marketplace, it is often NGOs who most aggressively offer alternative data or information, competing analysis, and new policy options. In the United States, the work of the Environmental Defense Fund (EDF) to develop the tradeable SO_2 permit system that is now embodied in the 1990 US Clean Air Act provides an example of NGO-based policy ideas driving the regulatory process. At the international level, the work being carried out by a number of NGOs to convince the WTO and its members to integrate environmental and labour concerns into the multilateral trading system offers another illustration of the vitality of NGO policy-making activity as a mechanism for improving governance.

We thus believe that, in contrast with Tieboutian models of regulatory competition which focus on horizontal competition between jurisdictions, governmental performance can be and should be sharpened by multiple sources of policy development and pressure—playing out at both horizontal and vertical levels and involving both state and non-state actors. Our model of co-opetition further diverges from traditional regulatory competition insofar as we argue that optimal regulatory outcomes cannot be achieved through *competitive* pressures alone. The regulatory process will almost always benefit from a degree of *cooperation* among governmental actors and between government officials and non-governmental actors. This collaboration may occur in the form of shared mechanisms for issue spotting, joint information gathering or data exchange, divided or collaborative research and analytic work, technology or policy transfers, and a division of labour in policy implementation and evaluation (Freeman 1997). Such cooperation often generates economies of scale, permits an efficient degree of division of labour, and allows for the governance structure to extract the benefits of both centralized and decentralized processes.

II. THE ALTERNATIVE MODEL: REGULATORY CO-OPETITION

Regulatory co-opetition plays out, as we noted above, at different levels and involves several types of actors. Three forms of regulatory co-opetition can be distinguished: (1) *inter*governmental; (2) *intra*governmental; and (3) *extra*governmental.

Intergovernmental regulatory co-opetition

We use this term to refer to the dynamics of competition and cooperation taking place *among* governments. This model of co-opetition has both *horizontal* and *vertical* dimensions. A dynamic of co-opetition can take place among or between governmental actors at the *same jurisdictional level* (for example, across the US federal states or EU member states) or between governmental actors at *different jurisdictional levels* (for example, between US federal and state authorities or the European Union and member states).

The main difference between the *horizontal* dimension of intergovernmental co-opetition and Tieboutian models of regulatory competition is that, while both models recognize the virtues of competition among state actors, the former model also recognizes that the regulatory process may, in certain circumstances, benefit from collaboration among horizontally arrayed governments. As illustrated by the US and EU systems, such cooperation can take the form of harmonized standards, mutual recognition procedures, or—at a lower level on the 'integration' scale—exchanges of data, information, and policy experience.

A dynamic of horizontal co-opetition can also be beneficial at the global level. The twentieth century was marked by rigorous economic competition between the United States and Europe, and this interplay had an impact on domestic regulatory policies. Major regulatory reforms within these blocks have often been stimulated by competitive pressures, especially the fear of deteriorating competitiveness. For instance, the opening to competition of the telecommunications and energy markets in Europe was in large measure based on the view that such markets were much less efficient than the deregulated US markets and that this inefficiency threatened the competitiveness of European industry generally (European Commission 1987). Absent such competitive pressures, the grip of telecommunications and energy state monopolies on the European economy would probably have remained largely intact. Conversely, many US regulatory experts argue that the sometimes excessively stringent and often inefficient US environmental regulation and liability rules harm the competitiveness of the US economy. They urge the US government to adopt more flexible and less costly regulatory approaches, such as European-style environmental contracting (Stewart 1993).

The United States and the European Union increasingly collaborate on a range of regulatory issues in an effort to remove non-tariff barriers and thus to facilitate trade. For instance, bilateral regulatory harmonization and mutual recognition efforts have been undertaken by the United States and the European Union in the context of the New Transatlantic Agenda (Krenzler and Schomaker 1996). The two blocks have agreed to consult each other in the early stages of drafting regulations and to rely to a greater extent on each other's technical resources and expertise (Joint Statement of US–EU Summit 1997). Recent global mergers such as Boeing/McDonnell Douglas, Worldcom/MCI, and Daimler/Chrysler have also illustrated the growing level of cooperation between the US Department of Justice and the European Commission on antitrust matters (Melamed 1998; Schaub 1998).

Some degree of regulatory cooperation is also taking place on a multilateral basis. Although differences in levels of development, geographic circumstances, technical competence, and risk preferences make collaborative standard setting and enforcement difficult, a measure of regulatory harmonization has, nevertheless, been achieved under the auspices of the WTO. This process is most advanced in the intellectual property (Ullrich 1995) and telecommunications (Bronckers and Larouche 1997) arenas. Pressure is now mounting for the adoption of multilateral rules on competition policy as well (Petersmann 1996; Mattoo and Subramanian 1997). To some extent, regulatory harmonization and cooperation efforts have also been undertaken by a variety of organizations (including the International Labour Organization (ILO), International Organization for Standardization (ISO), OECD, and Codex Alimentarius) in the areas of labour (Charnovitz 1987), chemical testing (Esty 1994), food safety (Bredahl and Forsythe 1989), and banking standards (Herring and Litan 1995). In the environmental field, little regulatory convergence has been achieved due to the weakness of the United Nations Environment

Program (UNEP), the opposition of developing countries, and hesitancy (fear of downwards harmonization) among some environmental groups (Esty and Geradin 1997).

The dynamics of co-opetition among governmental actors also has a *vertical* dimension. As has been noted above, federalism, with its division of power among federal, state, and local authorities, is inherently competitive. Inefficiencies or incapacity at one level of government will often be corrected by intervention at the other levels. For instance, the almost complete absence of governmental environmental activity in Europe's southern member states was corrected by regulatory intervention at the EU level. Similarly, the expansion of US federal intervention in the environmental field in the 1970s was, in part, due to the failure of existing state regimes to adequately protect the environment (Kraft and Vig 1990).

On the other hand, failures on the part of the federal authorities to carry out their duties, or the risk that centralized governance structures may be subject to 'capture', contributes to the case for some degree of decentralization. The perceived ineffectiveness of the Europe-wide effort at ecolabelling led to calls for more environmental control to be left to the member states. As a result, the European Commission has proposed a broad-scale restructuring of the current EU ecolabelling regime (International Environment Report 1999). The competitive pressure created by a federal structure with several levels of government—each level searching to extend or maintain its scope of power and influence—supports a system of 'checks and balances' that forces each level to strengthen its regulatory performance.

As useful as the tension of regulatory competition can be, we believe that good governance often requires a simultaneous degree of cooperation across different levels of government. In the United States, a fair amount of federal regulation, notably environmental programmes, depends in whole or in part on state implementation. Other examples of the value of cooperation abound. In fact, the shared regulatory responsibility between the federal and state levels of government is so central to the US governance structure that the system is often referred to as 'cooperative federalism' (Mott 1990). In many ways, the EU relies on the same model, with a significant element (perhaps even more so than in the American system) of cooperation between federal/central and member state authorities (Geradin 1997b).

We see a growing role for *vertical* competition. Not only has the capacity of state and local authorities improved dramatically in recent years (Esty 1999b), but the sophistication of international institutions is rising steadily. Today, many regulatory issues are examined at local, state/provincial, federal/national, regional, and/or global levels. As in the case of a federal structure, the existence of several levels of regulatory activity puts pressure on governmental actors to carry out their tasks effectively and efficiently.

The strength of the competitive pressure varies from one regulatory domain to the next. Some tiers in this hierarchy remain generally too weak to add much value.

Local decision making continues to be plagued by technical and analytic incapacity in many places, and many international institutions are too weak to impose real pressure on their member nations. Nairobi-based UNEP, for instance, fails to play much of a role in environmental regulation because it has failed to retain a first-rate staff, develop significant analytic capacities, generate a base of political support, or attract adequate financial and technical resources. In contrast, the trade rules and disciplines imposed by the WTO represent an important barrier to the adoption of protectionist or otherwise trade-restrictive national policies. Clearly, building sufficiently strong international governance structures that enhance the system of 'checks and balances' and contribute to the competitive regulatory dynamic represents one of the greatest challenges facing the world community in the context of growing economic interdependence.

Intragovernmental regulatory co-opetition

We use this term to refer to the dynamics of competition and cooperation taking place *within* governments. Governments are complex structures composed of different branches (legislative, executive, and judiciary), and these branches are themselves often composed of multiple components. These pieces of the governmental 'puzzle' will often contend for power, influence, and intellectual leadership (Breton 1996; Trebilcock and Howse 1998).

The competition may be *intrabranch*, especially within a multi-ministry executive. The struggle between the US EPA and the DOE over the design of air pollution control strategies, or the conflict between two European Commission Directorate Generals over the opportunity to ban certain chemicals from baby toys discussed above, are classic illustrations of intragovernmental competition. This dynamic strengthens the regulatory process by forcing the regulators to come up with innovative and analytically serious proposals and to justify their approaches against the alternatives proposed by others. This give-and-take also depends on the presence of cooperative mechanisms—information sharing, assignment of primary drafting responsibilities, and coordinated implementation—to prevent the rivalry between such bodies from degenerating and resulting in duplication of work, regulatory diseconomies of scale, or even decision-making stalemates.

A dynamic of co-opetition can also be observed among the branches of governments. Courts generally have the power to strike down unconstitutional laws. They thus represent a barrier against the most blatant legislative abuses. Conversely, in some instances, legislative intervention may also be used to correct the distortions created by inconsistent court decisions. A form of competition can therefore be observed between the judiciary and the legislature.[9] In some cases, the

[9] As pointed out by Ogus, competition may also take place between different court systems with overlapping jurisdictions. For instance, the struggle between the Chancery Courts and the Common Law rivals had a significant impact on the development of legal principles in the United Kingdom (Ogus 1999).

executive or judicial branches take the heat for stalemated legislatures. In the 1970s and 1980s, for instance, the European Court of Justice facilitated the free movement of goods with a series of decisions (the so-called *Cassis de Dijon* jurisprudence) declaring that a product that is lawfully produced and marketed in one member state must be admitted in another member state, except where the latter can refer to 'essential requirements' (Gormley 1985). This principle of mutual recognition was designed to compensate for the legislative inaction of the Council of Ministers which, due to the rule of unanimity voting, was unable to achieve its programme of product standards harmonization.

In representative democracies, furthermore, there are regular contests for power (including competition for control of the regulatory apparatus) in the form of voting.[10] Governments adopting inefficient or ineffective regulatory regimes thus risk being driven out of power. Given the relative lack of mobility of citizens, we see the lively tensions of intragovernmental rivalry as a more serious kind of competitive pressure than the hypothetical risk of exit that lies at the heart of Tieboutian models of regulatory competition. And, of course, while political parties compete for power, they must also cooperate between elections in the governing process. Bipartisan support will often be needed for constitutional or other major regulatory reforms.

Extragovernmental regulatory co-opetition

We use this term to refer to the dynamics of competition and cooperation taking place between governmental and non-governmental actors. Co-opetition between governmental and non-governmental actors promises to sharpen governmental performance by unleashing NGOs to act as intellectual competitors in the policy-making domain (Esty 1998). In many cases, NGOs are better positioned to compete with regulators than are other governmental officials. They are entrepreneurial and move to new issues quickly, and operate in a fiercely competitive marketplace for media and public attention as well as fundraising resources. These pressures create a strong incentive to come up with creative solutions to environmental problems and to 'sell' their solutions to the public and in the appropriate governmental arena.

Non-governmental organizations, operating in a 'cooperative mode' *vis-à-vis* governments, can also contribute significantly to optimizing the functioning of policy-making processes. They often supply observations, data, and information that help build the analytic foundation for decision making. They also serve as conduits for information flows to and from citizens. This 'connectivity' looms especially large when policy is being made at highly centralized levels. For instance, in the WTO's famous *Shrimp/Turtle* case, NGOs helped make the WTO dispute

[10] To some extent, political parties competing for power can be compared to firms engaged in competitive bidding for a monopolistic franchise power to provide a service, the competition serving to ensure that the firm offering the most efficient prices and services will be selected (Ogus 1999).

panel aware of the environmental interest—both as a scientific matter and as a matter of public sentiment—in protecting the endangered sea turtles that were dying in the nets of Thai shrimp fishermen. Beyond bringing critical information 'up' to decision makers, such NGO participation in the regulatory process also permits the involved groups to disseminate information 'down' to the disaggregated public, helping citizens to understand decisions made by distant officials.

Industry associations also impose competitive pressures on governments. Like citizens' groups, they will often aggressively come up with relevant data and information, competing analyses, and new policy options. In the area of climate change, for instance, thirty of Britain's largest companies and industry associations have announced their intention to start a pilot emissions trading system (International Environment Reporter 1999). The main objective of this initiative is to demonstrate to the British government that emissions trading is a more efficient and less costly means of reducing CO_2 emissions than energy taxation schemes.

Proponents of regulatory competition may contend that co-opetition leads to increased regulatory 'capture' by interest groups and, thus, reduced governmental transparency and accountability. Pitting environmental NGOs, industry associations, and other interests against each other, however, works to flesh out viable policies, induce investment in the creation of policy analysis and other valuable information, and generate countervailing forces that provide a 'watchdog' mechanism and therefore a check on 'capture'. It could also be argued that competing NGOs and industry associations simply create a cacophony of voices that ultimately cancel each other out. But this vision would be too simplistic. Good governance is not a zero-sum game. Competition between groups for governmental attention forces these entities to generate useful and credible material and to develop 'winning' proposals. This dynamic ensures that government officials will be able to choose among a large set of policy options and hear well-honed arguments where difficult choices must be made.

The benefits of cooperation between governmental and industry actors should also not be overlooked. In the European Union, for instance, the European Commission and the Association of European Automobile Manufacturers (ACEA), acting in co-opetition mode, have addressed the issue of climate change. After joint research efforts designed to identify policy solutions to the CO_2 emissions problem (the so-called Auto-Oil programme), the Commission and the ACEA negotiated and adopted an agreement whereby the ACEA commits itself to achieving an average per vehicle emissions target of 140 g CO_2/km by 2008—in other words, a cut of 25 per cent compared with 1990 levels. Such voluntary agreements are often useful alternatives to binding regulation. They lower the costs of reaching agreement and help provide quick and effective solutions to complex policy issues (Rehbinder 1997).

Cooperation between industry associations and governmental actors can also be observed at the global level. The Transatlantic Business Dialogue (TABD), built on US and EU industry associations, has been one of the driving forces behind the

US–EU regulatory cooperation efforts discussed above (Stern 1997). The TABD provides intellectual support to these efforts by identifying the areas where cooperation would be beneficial to US and EU businesses and by proposing various sets of policy options. One should also note that industry provides essential technical support to the work of the ISO, the objective of which is the adoption of harmonized technical standards for products.

III. SUMMARY AND CONCLUSIONS

Regulatory competition theory makes a critical point: market forces and the tensions they generate provide an important set of incentives for creativity, innovation, efficiency, and forbearance among regulators. But simplistic Tieboutian models of horizontally arrayed governments competing for citizens and factories neither describe the full potential for competition-driven regulatory discipline nor paint a convincing picture of how to squeeze optimal results out of governmental processes.

More importantly, the results to be achieved by traditional regulatory competition will vary depending on the context. Where the market for regulatory results (or locational rights) closely resembles perfect competition, stronger and more constructive (welfare-maximizing) pressures can be anticipated from Tieboutian competition. While we may favour a presumption of competition, exceptions must be made where this market fails, due to uninternalized externalities, information limitations, public choice failures, or strategic behaviour in standard setting.

Given real-world experience, which suggests that some degree of market failure will almost always be present, regulatory co-opetition represents a better model for achieving optimal governance. Harnessing intergovernmental, intragovernmental, and extragovernmental competitive pressures and simultaneously facilitating a degree of cooperation among the various participants in the regulatory process promises systematically improved outcomes. In this diverse and complex world of regulatory challenges, there remains a fair amount of research to be done to identify the variables that determine the optimal mix of competitive and cooperative forces. But we see considerable promise in promoting a degree of 'regulatory ecology' through which different species of regulators and other actors co-exist in relationships that are sometimes competitive and at other times symbiotic.[11]

[11] Thanks to Professor Dan Farber for highlighting this concept.

PART II
Regulatory Competition Theory in the US System

3

Some Observations Concerning Multijurisdictional Tax Competition

DANIEL SHAVIRO*

Should (or when should) separate governments, including sub-units in a federal system, be encouraged to engage in tax competition rather than harmonizing their tax systems? This is a very different question than, say, whether air pollution policy should emerge through regulatory competition or be harmonized at the national or multinational level. The differences suggest a need for lesser generalization in evaluating tax competition as compared to much other regulatory competition.

The choice between principles of regulatory harmonization and competition presents a standard fiscal federalism question concerning the optimal scale of provision for public goods. Harmonization effectively creates a larger-scale decision maker in the subject area that is being harmonized, whether it is imposed by separate sovereigns' agreement or by a higher-level unit of government in a federal system. But taxation, unlike clean air, is not a public good that might in principle have a scale of optimal provision.[1] It is a way of paying for public goods with varying scales of optimal and actual provision. Or, if we rely on official classifications, taxes are a subset of government rules identified by form, not economic content. Government rules can be used to advance a vast and overlapping array of allocative and distributional aims, whether officially called taxes, government spending, or regulation (Shaviro 1997: 411–14), and no one scale is generally best for pursuing all of the aims.

It should therefore be clear that no particular scale for prescribing tax rules is correct across the board or from all standpoints. Accordingly, given a particular set of jurisdictions that must decide how to coordinate their tax rules, neither tax competition nor harmonization is likely to be preferable across the board. Therefore, an overview of the kind offered here must start by considering the general issues raised by regulatory competition. We can then, after a brief tax policy review, consider how these issues play out in different tax settings.

* I am grateful to Reuven Avi-Yonah, Daniel C. Esty, James R. Hines, Richard Revesz, and Julie Roin for comments on an earlier draft.

[1] On the issue of environmental regulation, Esty (1999b) explains, 'For each particular [environmental] issue there exists an [optimal environmental area] that corresponds to the geographic scope of the costs and benefits of the public good or policy at hand'. Of course, it is possible that different air pollutants would have different geographical ranges of effect.

I. BACKGROUND TO THE CHOICE BETWEEN REGULATORY COMPETITION AND VOLUNTARY OR MANDATORY HARMONIZATION

Economic and policy discussion often assume a single national government, presiding over a closed economy. From a normative standpoint, the government's ability to coerce makes it potentially an instrument for addressing various collective action problems such as holdout, prisoners' dilemmas, and adverse selection. Think of its providing such public goods as national defence, police protection, and a legal system that sufficiently defines and protects property rights to make possible a productive exchange economy. Or consider its redistributing wealth from high-endowment to low-endowment individuals, thus potentially increasing everyone's expected utility from behind a veil of ignorance concerning the distribution of endowment (Shaviro 2000a; 2000b). To the extent that, by overcoming collective action problems through coercion, the government brings about actual or ex ante Pareto improvements—alternatives that cover everything a utilitarian would want it to do—we could describe its essential role as one of economizing on transaction costs. After all, without transaction costs all Pareto improvements would presumably take place, including ex ante improvements if we imagine transactions behind the veil.

The analogy to Coase's theory of the firm (1990), in which contractual precommitment replaces ongoing exchange to reduce transaction costs, is quite close. However, the use of coercion by a government with a monopoly on force differs importantly from the use of contract by a firm in a competitive economy. Government actors may face different incentives than the individuals who direct the activities of private firms, and the government's monopoly position may matter. Using coercion to solve collective action problems may have disappointing results either because those problems are simply transmuted into those of collective political action in a democracy, or because the coercion is misdirected from a normative standpoint and becomes itself a problem.

Fiscal federalism, or the economic analysis of multiple levels of government, potentially changes the inquiry in a fundamental way. To be sure, merely examining the optimal scale of provision for a given public good may raise no more than the question of how large each monopolist should be. Yet once we follow Tiebout's (1956) famous lead and remember that people, goods, and capital can to some extent move between jurisdictions, we may begin to see governments, if sufficiently small-scale geographically, as potentially a lot like competitive private firms. Subject to their own internal public choice dynamics, the governments may end up competing for residents and investment in much the same way that firms compete for customers, workers, and investors. This can lead to a 'race to the bottom' with respect to conditions that would tend to drive away residents or investors whose presence is desired. Whether such a race is good or bad from a social welfare standpoint depends on what is being driven to the bottom—for example, sheer waste in service provision on the one hand, or efforts at inducing efficient cost internalization by polluters on the other (Revesz, Ch. 1). Or, more specifically, the race's desirability depends on whether movement towards the bottom brings the variable condition closer to or further from its optimal level.

Where regulatory competition is undesirable, mandatory harmonization, or that imposed by a higher-level government with authority to override the decisions made by smaller sub-units, will naturally come to mind as an alternative.[2] Yet, in some settings, we may observe voluntary harmonization, or that resulting from independent governments' decision to collude rather than compete in their choice of rules. Intergovernmental transaction costs determine whether such collusion is feasible, while intrajurisdictional or political transaction costs (including those that hypothetically impede transactions behind the veil) help determine whether it has good or bad effects. Voluntary harmonization resembles regulatory competition in that it arises without higher-level coercion of the governments that cooperate, but it resembles mandatory harmonization in its end result (the establishment of a larger-scale government cartel that imposes uniform or at least similar rules). Intermediate though it may be, I will generally group voluntary harmonization with the mandatory variety, on the view that the end result is what counts.

In sum, under conditions of mobility, regulatory and other competition between jurisdictions can address problems of misdirected coercion, but potentially at the cost of reviving collective action problems. From this perspective, the decision to employ mandatory harmonization is a lot like the decision, in the setting of a national government presiding over a closed economy, to employ a government rather than a market response to collective action problems. The relative merits of regulatory competition and voluntary harmonization depend on what forms of cooperation different jurisdictions are inclined to select through their political processes and find sustainable despite their own collective action problems as separate actors.

Taxation and efficiency

A second important preliminary step involves reviewing some basic tax policy ideas. A government that is providing public goods cannot charge user fees given the goods' non-excludability, and thus must finance its operations by coercing payments ('taxes') that are unrelated at the margin to the value of the benefits being offered. Even if government services are worth every penny of tax that you pay for them, you do not get more at the margin by paying an extra penny. Taxes in this sense—I exclude Pigovian taxes, such as a well-calibrated pollution tax—therefore may drive a wedge between individual actors' interests and aggregate social welfare. Since my tax payments are purely a cost to me, albeit a zero-sum transfer from

[2] A further possibility is mandatory disharmonization, or that imposed by the high-level decision maker rather than being set through regulatory competition.

the collective standpoint, I may prefer incurring 99 cents' worth of deadweight loss to paying a one-dollar tax. Given this fundamental problem, the usual efficiency aim in tax policy is simply to do as little harm to incentives as possible, rather than (as with some regulation) trying to correct them.

A lump sum tax, such as a uniform head tax, that is invariant to all taxpayer decisions achieves the nirvana, from a tax efficiency standpoint, of leaving incentives unchanged. Yet once all feasible lump sum taxes are ruled out on distributional grounds that we might rationalize roughly in terms of endowment, the remaining plausible tax instruments all rely on imperfect proxies for endowment that taxpayers can affect through their decisions. Consider, for example, taxes on labour earnings, market consumption, income, wealth, or inheritance. Each of these taxes burdens decisions, such as to work or save, that may be socially innocuous or even beneficial.

While all of the major taxes therefore cause inefficiency, as a rough rule of thumb they tend to do the least harm if they at least apply uniformly to the broad categories (such as income or consumption) that they burden. For example, even if we disfavour all market consumption relative to leisure, we need not also distort choices within market consumption.[3] For taxes levied in different jurisdictions, this uniformity aim suggests following the principle of *locational neutrality*, which holds that 'it is optimal that the tax levied, [such as] on a given amount of profit or a given taxpayer, not vary according to the location of any property or persons' (Shaviro 1993: 9).[4] At the limit, this principle might suggest that all interacting jurisdictions should harmonize their taxes in all respects.

From a different starting point, however, one can argue just as strongly for tax competition rather than tax harmonization. Above all, the Tiebout model suggests the possibility of a desirable race to the bottom between jurisdictions in wasting or expropriating (that is redistributing without a good social welfare justification) tax revenues if the jurisdictions must compete with each other to attract mobile entrants. A related Tiebout argument would suggest that tax competition permits jurisdictions to specialize in catering to diverse consumer preferences or local needs, such as by collectively offering a choice between high-tax, high-service and low-tax, low-service options.

[3] The case for uniform income or consumption taxation is weakened by Ramsey's (1927) famous finding that tax rates on commodities should vary inversely with their elasticity. However, more recent work in public economics shows that an optimal non-linear income tax (in effect, a tax applying identically to all commodities except leisure) is not improved by adding in narrower commodity taxes if people's consumption preferences are weakly separable into all goods considered together and leisure (Atkinson and Stiglitz 1976: 68). Even if one is sceptical about the separability assumption (which fails to the extent that different consumption items are leisure complements or substitutes), political economy considerations may suggest urging legislatures to aim for uniformity (Shaviro 2000c).

[4] This conclusion is conditioned on defining taxes, as in the text above, as not Pigovian and unrelated at the margin to the cost or value of the government services that are being provided. Second-best problems may limit the appeal of locational neutrality in taxation—for example, in cases where tax disparities would offset other undesirable locational disparities (such as those resulting from undesirable regulatory variation).

One reason for the tension between the locational neutrality and Tiebout arguments is that they emphasize different margins of decision. Insofar as entry into a government's area of jurisdiction is a prerequisite both to benefiting from its services and to being subject to its taxes, the government can mitigate the public goods problem by treating its overall tax package for residents as a kind of user fee. Hence the appeal of tax competition if we consider the classic Tiebout example of a jurisdiction that finances public schools for all resident children through a real property tax, and that is competing with similar neighbouring jurisdictions that have their own real property taxes and public school systems (Hamilton 1975).

Yet the same example helps underscore the case for tax harmonization if we change our focus a little. Suppose that real property taxes are not well correlated with the number of children in a household who are using the jurisdiction's schools, so that the real property tax is not akin to a user fee. Unless there are relevant differences between regions within the jurisdiction, locational neutrality suggests that real property tax rates should be uniform throughout it. Thus we might want to harmonize jurisdiction-wide assessment methods if it turned out that, for no good reason, tax assessors in the Northeast were coming up with systematically higher valuations for homes of a given value than assessors in the Southwest. Such harmonization might reduce tax distortions insofar as people who could not leave the jurisdiction were deciding where to live in it and how much to invest in their homes.[5]

Clearly, then, the local schools example provides across-the-board support neither for competition nor for harmonization. The claim that one principle or the other is generally preferable becomes more dubious still once we recognize that in most real world examples the scale of provision of a public good will not dovetail so neatly with jurisdictional borders.[6]

In a Panglossian world that was governed by Pareto and ex ante Pareto principles and featured zero transaction costs, governments would simply choose the optimal blend of harmonization and competition across the spectrum of their interactions, leaving little to worry about. After all, any efficiency gain creates surplus that could in principle be divided to leave everyone better off.[7] Of course, we live in no such world. As shown in Part I, however, we can think of the problems that lead to inferior outcomes in transaction cost terms. Among those to keep especially in mind are political transaction costs, such as the defects in political choice that may affect how governments choose to compete or cooperate. Examples may include the differences in competing groups' organizational abilities that give rise to interest group politics, problems of information that create exploitable fiscal illusion among

[5] A line of argument akin to that for uniform commodity taxes might support shifting from this system to one in which the harmonization of assessment methods effectively lowered the distortive tax on home ownership in the Northeast and raised it in the Southwest.

[6] In the above example, all that makes schooling a jurisdiction-wide public good is the legal rule that all resident children and no others can attend.

[7] Note that desirable progressive redistribution is, by definition, efficient in the ex ante sense, although the word 'efficiency' is often given a narrower construction.

voters, and difficulties in observing government decision makers who may be inclined to engage in empire-building or other self-aggrandizement.

In the rest of this chapter, I turn to some commonly arising particulars of tax interaction between jurisdictions. As we will see, in some settings, tax competition seems likely to be harmful; in others, beneficial; and in still others, the assessment depends on one's other tax policy views. I divide the issues I consider into two headings: tariff-like problems of disfavouring outside or multijurisdictional production, and consequences of taxpayer or input mobility.

II. 'TARIFF' PROBLEMS OF DISFAVOURING OUTSIDE OR MULTIJURISDICTIONAL PRODUCTION

The case for tax harmonization in the form of eliminating tariffs

We can start with the example that, for economists since Adam Smith, has been the paradigmatic case of socially wasteful tax interaction between separate jurisdictions. When there is trade across jurisdictional boundaries, each jurisdiction may conceivably be inclined to impose tariffs burdening imports. This is generally inefficient; it results in deadweight loss by inducing consumers to substitute locally produced goods for those that they would have preferred if not for the differential tax treatment. Gains from trade across jurisdictional boundaries by people with different areas of comparative advantage are therefore lost. A tariff does not even benefit the taxing jurisdiction on balance—consumers' losses exceed local producers' gains by reason of the deadweight loss—unless the jurisdiction has market power as a monopsonist that the tariff, by organizing local consumers in a cartel, enables it to extract.[8] Tariffs that on balance harm the jurisdictions imposing them presumably bespeak political transaction costs of some kind (as further discussed below). And even 'optimal tariffs' that advance the taxing jurisdiction's interests by exploiting monopsony power are inferior from a global standpoint to the hypothetical zero-transaction-cost solution of simply extracting a lump-sum payment from outside producers in exchange for not exercising monopsony power.

Familiar though this line of reasoning may be, several points about its relationship to fiscal federalism are worth mentioning. First, the opportunity to create gains through trade without being impeded by tariffs is a kind of public good, the scale of provision for which is the entire trading area. Allowing each jurisdiction to set its own rules for taxing outside production, rather than setting a uniform policy for the entire area, invites adverse spillover. Even if a jurisdiction loses overall by imposing tariffs, it does not internalize all of the harm. Prospective trading partners outside the jurisdiction lose as well.

[8] If the monopsonist's market power is such that the tariff cannot be passed on to customers within its jurisdiction through a price increase, then the tariff is akin to a mandatory price rebate, collected by the government on behalf of the customers and other residents.

Second, spillover is neither sufficient nor necessary to produce inefficient tax barriers to trade across jurisdictional boundaries. One could imagine each jurisdiction being sufficiently enlightened about its own self-interest to eschew all tariffs in non-monopsony cases, without regard to what any other jurisdiction did. Or one could imagine a centralized decision maker offering each region's producers protection against outside competition. The motivation might be that of a cartel that agrees to carve up territory among its members. Or this equilibrium might arise more haphazardly as the decision maker acceded to one localized interest group demand after another.

Third, the evils of tariffs do not ineluctably result from tax competition as such. They are not for the most part a way of attracting entry into the taxing jurisdiction, but rather of cordoning it off from the world economy.[9] In addition, there is no unique competitive equilibrium with respect to tariffs. One could imagine jurisdictions getting into trade wars where they respond to each other's tariffs by escalating their own. Or they might instead negotiate mutual and offsetting tariff reduction. Or they might all be politically satisfied with a stable arrangement whereby tariffs protect powerful entrenched producer groups throughout the trading area.

Nonetheless, tax harmonization has significant advantages as a device for reducing tariffs. Consider that the optimal tax regime from a global standpoint is one in which everyone has the same tax policy in this regard: no tariffs. The virtues of this uniform policy reflect the case for locational neutrality, which suggests that the locus of production relative to consumption should have no effect on tax liability, notwithstanding the admitted inefficiency of taxing market consumption in general.[10]

In addition, even though in theory small-scale governments might eschew tariffs and a central authority might impose them, in practice they seem clearly associated with having multiple taxing authorities who decide on their tax rules independently. This largely reflects the spillover problem. If adversely affected parties outside a jurisdiction lack political influence, then only local consumers, who may tend to be poorly organized, are left to oppose a given tariff from the inside. Enlarging the jurisdiction that effectively sets tax policy may increase the political influence of producers who would lose from particular tariffs, and also reduce the

[9] To be sure, a tariff that is levied by a jurisdiction with monopsony power may attract investment by persuading outside companies to avoid it by producing locally. Consider Japanese car producers in the 1980s and 1990s, who moved production to the United States in response to US import restrictions. Viewed optimistically from a purely US perspective, one might see this as benefiting the United States either because it got to collect income tax revenues from Japanese owners with respect to more of their car production, or because their US capital investment had positive local externalities. Either claim may require assuming US monopsony power, but such an assumption could be plausible, given the size of our consumer market and sunk costs in the automobile industry.

[10] The efficiency argument for eliminating production distortions with respect to a given commodity is less uncertain than that for taxing different commodities (but not leisure) at the same rate (Diamond and Mirrlees 1971).

transaction costs involved in securing general agreement to move towards a policy of reciprocal forbearance.

Enlarging the jurisdiction need not mean adopting mandatory as opposed to voluntary harmonization. International trade agreements between independent sovereigns have in fact resulted over the last fifty years in greatly reduced tariff barriers. Such agreements have, however, relied heavily on the larger-scale institutional back-up (through standard-form agreements and specific mechanisms for resolving disputes) provided by the General Agreement on Tariffs and Trade (GATT) and the World Trade Organization (WTO). Strong-arming of developing countries by the World Bank and the International Monetary Fund has also played a significant role.

The discussion thus far has been purely in terms of tariffs on imports. A similar analysis can apply, however, to customs duties on exports. Burdening exports has similar effects to burdening imports because the two are ultimately traded for each other. In many cases, export duties may be less popular politically than tariffs due to the political power of the producer groups that might bear the transition loss from increasing them unexpectedly. (And indeed disputes more commonly arise over export subsidies, which benefit the same local producer constituencies as tariffs.) Yet there is a plausible scenario in which spillover problems make export duties politically appealing. This is the case where local voters perceive the duties as permitting tax exportation, or the shifting of local tax burdens to outsiders such as worldwide consumers or corporate shareholders.[11]

Tariff equivalents and analogues

Even if tariffs and similar levies ought to be eliminated, as the previous section suggested, how do we identify them? Formally, a tariff might be defined as a special excise tax on imported goods. Yet the critical end result of burdening imported goods relative to those produced inside a given jurisdiction does not require using this form. Taxes of apparently general application can have similar results, as can targeted spending (such as building infrastructure to aid local businesses but not their foreign competitors) along with a variety of policies that are denominated as regulatory.

For a simple tax illustration, consider how state governments tax national businesses on their income. Income that is generated through synergistic interactions between operations in different states may not have a clear geographic source. To determine what income is within their reach, states generally measure a business's national income and then apportion an arbitrarily determined portion of it to themselves. Most states use a three-factor formula that turns on the percentages of

[11] A good example is provided by the high severance taxes that states such as Alaska, Montana, and Wyoming levy on the extraction of oil and coal that is almost entirely exported. Ironically, this results only in perceived, not actual, tax exportation if, as seems likely, these states lack market power in worldwide energy markets (Shaviro 1993: 20, 74–5).

the business's national property, payroll, and sales that are found in-state. However, states use different versions of the formula, often giving greater weight to the factors that favour a high apportionment. For example, 'market' states often give extra weight to the sales factor (Shaviro 1993: 28). The result may be that a national business has more than 100 per cent of its income apportioned to the various states. This may cause the national business to be taxed at a higher effective rate in the aggregate than separate businesses in the various states if—perhaps a big if—it cannot sufficiently exploit any interstate income-shifting opportunities that permit it to relocate taxable income in low-rate states.[12] Where national businesses are disadvantaged, the result is not exactly equivalent to a tariff, in that the burden falls on being a multi-state business rather than on producing goods in one state for consumption in another. Yet such a result similarly distorts production decisions (here, whether to operate as a multi-state business)[13] and may, as a political matter, be attributable to spillover. Local businesses may seek to disfavour their national rivals, or local voters may believe that they can export tax burdens to out-of-state shareholders.[14]

The use of such devices in lieu of explicit tariffs to disfavour outside production or multijurisdictional presence does not alter the basic applicability of the previous analysis. Accordingly, tax harmonization has an advantage whenever tax diversity potentially disfavours outside producers or those who operate in multiple jurisdictions relative to domestic or single-jurisdiction producers. When taxes of general application are involved, however, something more may be going on than just the imposition of a locationally distortive levy. Thus, rather than assume tax harmonization is the best approach overall, we generally must compare its advantages in eliminating tariff-like levies to any offsetting advantages of tax competition.

[12] Shifting of taxable income to low-rate states may make multijurisdictional presence a tax benefit on balance even if more than 100 per cent of a company's income ends up being taxed. In illustration, suppose that Company A has $100 of taxable income in State X, which imposes a 10 per cent corporate income tax, while Company B has $100 of taxable income in State Y, which imposes a 5 per cent corporate income tax. Their combined tax bill is therefore $15 ($10 on Company A and $5 on Company B). Suppose that they merged into Company AB and their total earnings remained $200, but that the tax result, given the state apportionment formulae, was that X now claimed $50 of taxable income while Y claimed $160 of taxable income. The two states together would include more than 100 per cent of AB's income ($210 rather than $200), but its tax liability would have declined to $13 ($5 in State X and $8 in State Y). AB would therefore benefit on balance from its multijurisdictional presence.

[13] To be sure, even if all states used the same apportionment formula it would distort production decisions, by inducing them to locate their property, payroll, and sales in low-tax rather than high-tax states (Gordon and Wilson 1986).

[14] The main alternative to apportionment, generally followed in the international setting, is to allocate taxable income between jurisdictions by specifying the transfer price that one arm of a commonly owned business supposedly would have charged another had they dealt at arm's length across jurisdictional boundaries. Like apportionment, this approach can be used to disfavour multijurisdictional businesses by taxing them on more than 100 per cent of their worldwide income. Mansori and Weichenrieder (1999) urge harmonization of governments' transfer pricing regulations to forestall a 'non-cooperative equilibrium characterized by the double taxation of corporate profits, and consequently by a depressed level of international trade'. Once again, however, multijurisdictional presence can, on balance, be a tax benefit even if more than 100 per cent of income is taxed, since businesses can use it to shift income from high-tax to low-tax jurisdictions.

Harmonization in practice to eliminate undue general tax burdens on outside or multijurisdictional business

Achieving desirable tax harmonization in the treatment of multijurisdictional compared to single-jurisdictional businesses requires choosing both political institutions and underlying principles. From an institutional standpoint, perhaps the most obvious approach is mandatory harmonization, such as the approach to defending national markets against protectionism by the states. While Congress can always override state taxes that burden outside or multi-state businesses, perhaps more important in practice has been the negative or dormant Commerce Clause, invoked by the federal courts to overturn state legislation that discriminates against interstate commerce.

Supreme Court decisions under the dormant Commerce Clause have been widely condemned for their incoherence, inconsistency, undue formalism, and unpredictability (Currie 1985: 234; Eule 1982).[15] Most commentators agree, however, that having the Court on hand to exercise this harmonizing authority does more good than harm (Shaviro 1993: 68–77; Schoettle 1991; Regan 1986). Perhaps more important than any instance in which the Court struck down a discriminatory tax is the 'dog that doesn't bark' phenomenon of discouraging enactments that would be vulnerable under the dormant Commerce Clause. As for Congress's harmonizing authority under the Commerce Clause, in the area of state and local taxation, it has not seen fit to invade in any repeated or substantial way the authority of state and local governments. Thus its power to impose mandatory harmonization seems not to have significantly reduced state-level tax competition and diversity, except insofar as nationalizing various government functions under the shield of the Commerce Clause shifts entire tax-and-spending packages to the federal level.

The international arena helps to show that mandatory harmonization is not the only potentially effective kind. Paralleling the recent decades of relative success in tariff abatement, international taxation has generally avoided anything approaching the level of tax disadvantage to global businesses that would result if each government with a claim of jurisdiction sought duplicatively to tax such businesses' entire worldwide income. Formally, the main mechanism for such harmonization is a web of more than 1,500 bilateral tax treaties that provide complicated rules for coordinating the claims of 'source' countries where income is earned and 'residence' countries where business owners are found. However, rather than emerging spontaneously without broader harmonizing institutions, these treaties generally follow, in their broad outlines, a set of model treaties first developed in the 1920s through intensive multilateral negotiations under the auspices of the

[15] See also *Northwestern States Portland Cement Co.* v. *Minnesota*, 358 U.A. 450, 457 (1959) in which the Court itself termed its decisions a 'quagmire' that 'leaves much room for controversy and confusion and little in the way of precise guides to the States in the exercise of their indispensable power of taxation'.

International Chamber of Commerce and the League of Nations (Graetz and O'Hear 1997). The global setting of these agreements lowered transaction costs for individual countries to agree on specific terms of mutual forbearance. In addition, to businesses that were anxious to avoid double taxation, the global institutions offered a forum at once more favourable than national politics and yet able to be leveraged into such politics through the argument: this is what everyone else is doing; you'd better join the club.

At both the federal and international levels, the scope of harmonization efforts and their placement along the spectrum from voluntary to mandatory are to some extent disputed. In the United States, Justices Antonin Scalia and Clarence Thomas denounce the dormant Commerce Clause as historically illegitimate and urge, apparently as a first step towards abandonment, that its reach be limited to state and local taxes that 'facially' discriminate against outsiders (*Oklahoma Tax Comm'n* v. *Jefferson Lines, Inc.*, 514 175, 200 (1997)). The international setting has witnessed various efforts to expand binding higher-level review (such as through arbitration or the WTO) of income tax and other rules that are deemed discriminatory. Success has mainly been limited to the level of regional organizations such as the European Economic Community (EEC).

The tentative argument of this Part has been that, from where we currently stand at both the federal and international levels, the scope and the mandatory character of the harmonization achieved to date with respect to moderating tariff-like burdens ought if anything to be expanded, not curtailed. A possible suggestion that I have made in the past is requiring all state and local governments to use the same formula for apportioning domestic source income, and perhaps even the same definition of the income tax base, thus confining their income tax competition to rates (Shaviro 1993: 97–104). My argument relied in part on sceptical views of political choice and the value of diversity in income tax bases, along with concern about the compliance costs to national businesses of conforming to multiple income tax rules. Only Congress could implement such a proposal, since it goes well beyond the plausible exercise by the courts of their authority to strike down discrimination against interstate commerce.

III. CONSEQUENCES OF TAXATION AND MOBILITY

Part II emphasized a margin of decision—entry into a jurisdiction to produce or sell goods—where small-scale governments may have monopsony power, or flawed incentives that reflect the interaction between interest group politics and spillover. This Part shifts the focus to a margin where governments have less market power, and where their incentives are closer to those of a private business that competes vigorously if it must, but is also prepared to collude if it can. The topic here is taxpayer mobility, or the differentially distributed power to leave a jurisdiction if the tax price relative to the value of benefits provided grows too high. My conclusions here will be more contingent on factors distinct from fiscal federalism, and also at times more sympathetic to tax competition, than those in the previous Part.

Public goods and Tiebout competition

Taxpayers' locational decisions have important financial implications for governments. Residing in a jurisdiction or engaging in economic activity there may increase the local government's revenues disproportionately to the marginal effect, if any, on its cost of providing goods and services. Put in terms of the theory of clubs, jurisdictions often fall short of the optimal size where 'the marginal decrease in [average tax levels that an additional entrant would make possible] just equals the per person marginal increase in congestion costs' (Rosen 1999: 474).[16]

Taxpayer mobility, or the power to exercise locational choice between competing jurisdictions, can therefore align the interests of governments with those of taxpayers in the manner of Adam Smith's invisible hand. Governments must please mobile taxpayers, or at least make the best available offer, in order to attract them. However, just as businesses need not please customers as assiduously if they can form cartels to limit supply, so governments use tax harmonization to loosen their competitive constraints. Once exit from the reach of their harmonized rules has become impossible, only internal political dynamics can limit their power to coerce and expropriate as they choose.

This, of course, is the Tiebout side of the choice between harmonization and competition. To take the other side, one might reply that even coercion and a dollop of expropriation have their place. Suppose initially that an important public good of global scope—say, defending the world against nuclear terrorists—was completely non-excludable, even territorially, and that taxpayers were subject to no locational frictions (they could move immediately across jurisdictional boundaries at zero cost). The equilibrium would be that no government could supply it, even if everyone valued it. Any government that wanted to supply the good would have to increase its taxes to pay for doing so, and in the absence of locational frictions this would drive everyone away.

Taken too literally, this scenario would be as overheated as one that jumped immediately from tax harmonization to unlimited expropriation, but it similarly makes a broader point. Taxation responds, through coercion, to a collective action problem in supplying public goods. Thus the fact that harmonization makes taxes more effectively coercive cannot be the end of the matter unless we know that the coercion would otherwise be too great. Giving greater scope to market forces through tax competition is not necessarily desirable if taxation is itself a response to market failure. One needs to examine what sort of race to the bottom (for exam-

[16] The theory of clubs concerns voluntary associations of people who band together to share a benefit that can be limited to club members but is a public good as to the members (Sandler and Tschirhart 1980).

ple, in wasting tax revenues or making would-be free riders pay for public goods) mobility is inducing in a particular case.

Taxation of capital and other mobile factors of production

Suppose we have two individuals or productive inputs that are identical except that one is more mobile than the other. To simplify the example, assume also that competing tax jurisdictions offer everyone the same services, which they produce at the same cost, but can choose different ways of allocating tax burdens between taxpayers whose persons or property are subject to their jurisdiction. Under these circumstances (or even under more complicated real-world circumstances), we would expect the less mobile individual or input to bear greater tax burdens than the one that was more mobile.

In one sense, this differential is likely to be inefficient, or else efficient purely by happenstance. Mobile inputs are tax-preferred relative to others, and individuals have a tax incentive to enhance their personal mobility,[17] because tax payments are a pure cost to the taxpayer, albeit a transfer societally. Nonetheless, if for some reason mobile inputs and individuals would otherwise have been overtaxed relative to others, efficiency may be fortuitously enhanced. In addition, tax competition might permit mobility desirably to reduce overall tax levels even if the effects of differences in mobility were regrettable.

While many allocative choices might be affected by the tax consequences of differential mobility, the distinction most noted in the literature lies between income from capital and income from labour. The greater mobility of capital is widely recognized—I can shift where I invest more easily than where I work—and capital flight might even ultimately make capital income taxation impossible unless enough jurisdictions colluded in eliminating this race to the bottom. Many commentators find this prospect a cause for alarm, noting also that, as a practical matter, a cross-border investor's country of residence may be unable to measure her capital income even if it is legally taxable there, thus requiring the source country to collect the tax if it is to be collected at all (Avi-Yonah 2000).

One possible response to this concern, however, is to ask: So what? The issues raised by reducing or eliminating capital income taxes can be divided into those of efficiency and distribution. Starting with efficiency, a tax on capital income burdens saving (and thus future consumption) relative to immediate consumption. Economists mainly find that eliminating this distortion through a shift to consumption taxation would enhance efficiency (Auerbach 1996), although the analysis is complicated by the fact that labour supply would continue to be tax-distorted. The efficiency conclusion is strengthened by the observation that all existing capital

[17] For simplicity, I assume here that differences in individuals' mobility result purely from their decisions, such as in selecting tastes and developing skills. For differences in mobility that are innate or otherwise beyond individual control, the questions raised by tax-favouring it go to distribution, and thus are pertinent to efficiency only in the ex ante sense mentioned in Part II.

income taxes have significant inter-asset biases, which would be eliminated by taxing all capital income at a zero rate (arguably the most politically and administratively feasible uniform rate). The usual main concern, however, goes to distribution. People who we might for convenience call 'the wealthy' (even if our distributional measure relies on endowment or lifetime income) tend to have a higher proportion of capital income to labour income than other people. Thus exempting capital income implies a less progressive system than taxing it if all else remains the same. Some might even fear that the proverbial coupon-clipper, who lives entirely off portfolio saving, can avoid taxation altogether if capital income is tax-exempt. However, these common views require significant modification.

An initial response is that not all else need remain the same. A consumption tax with progressive rates need not fall short of an income tax in its redistributive impact, although the nominal rates may need to be a bit more graduated. Thus income taxation is not in general more progressive than consumption taxation unless administrative or political economy differences tend to make it so in practice.

In addition, concern that the cross-border coupon-clipper will pay no tax either is mistaken or rests on a particular administrative feature of certain taxes that we observe in practice, rather than depending on the decision to burden saving through an income tax. In the economic literature, it is a truism that a wage tax and a consumption tax are equivalent if we define 'wages' to include all returns to labour, including whatever enables one to generate infra-marginal returns. The two taxes may differ as to when tax is paid—upon earning or upon spending—but not as to the present value of tax liability. Postponing the payment of tax until consumption occurs merely provides deferral at market interest. An income tax is equivalent as well, except that it adds a distinct tax on the risk-free return to waiting (Shaviro 2000c: 171–4). Thus, if we observe a cross-border coupon-clipper paying no income tax this year, the earnings that funded the investment should have been taxed in the past under a wage tax methodology (which all existing income taxes employ), and/or should be taxed in the future under a consumption tax methodology (which retail sales and value-added taxes employ).

A view of the cross-border coupon-clipper as wholly untaxed is therefore erroneous under any sophisticated present-value analysis, unless it rests on a gap in wage or consumption tax collection. Such collection may indeed be impeded by the difficulty of observing cross-border transactions. Consider the growing controversy over taxing internet sales, or the longstanding problem of collecting local sales and use taxes on mail order sales. These are not problems of capital income taxation as such, however; they are problems of business-level collection of taxes (of any variety) where that would otherwise be the preferred methodology.

In sum, therefore, there is no analytical reason why a race to the bottom in capital income taxation must reduce efficiency or undermine distributional objectives. Indeed, it seems likely to enhance the former, and to leave the opportunity set for the latter little changed although conceivably reducing the progressivity that is achieved in practice for administrative or political economy reasons. Given the controversiality in the literature of the choice between income and consumption taxation, perhaps it is best just to say that, while tax competition promotes and harmonization deters a race to the bottom in capital income taxation, what one should think of this race depends on tax policy views that are independent of the fiscal federalism analysis in this chapter.

Progressive and other redistribution

Whether or not capital income taxation vitally affects distributional policy, the extent of individuals' mobility plainly does. In the fiscal federalism literature, it is a truism that progressive redistribution should be addressed at the national level. The basic idea is that if, say, New York City tries to take money from the rich and give it to the poor, the rich will tend to leave and the poor to enter, potentially making the redistributive programme fiscally unsustainable. Leaving the United States, however, is considerably harder for most Americans than leaving New York City. Accordingly, if international mobility is limited, the United States can pursue progressive redistribution with considerably less concern about adverse selection.[18] Sufficient international mobility might make progressive redistribution unsustainable even at the national level, thus requiring some degree of international tax harmonization if it is to be pursued effectively. And perhaps this point is already being reached between countries, such as the member states of the European Union, between which there is high mobility.

Under an ex ante Pareto view of redistribution from high-endowment to low-endowment individuals as potentially increasing everyone's expected utility from behind a veil of ignorance concerning the distribution of endowment, this might be seen as a straightforward public goods problem in which coercion can help to overcome transaction costs. The public good is insurance against endowment risk, and it ought to be provided universally if we push the argument for insurance behind the veil to its limit. Yet readers need not adopt this perhaps controversial way of viewing distributional policy in order to accept the conclusion: if we like worldwide progressive distribution, not just in principle but as practised, then we should welcome international tax harmonization in taxation of the rich versus the poor. The race to the bottom here, in the amount of redistribution to which mobile, well-off individuals are subjected (or from which mobile, poorly-off individuals are allowed to benefit), may well pose significant challenges to distributional policy in the twenty-first century.

Suppose, however, that we instead view progressive redistribution (at least at the level at which a harmonized global tax system would provide it) as undesirable. Or

[18] On the difficulties states may face in pursuing redistributive policies, Robert Moffitt (1992) agrees that variations in welfare benefits in the United States significantly affect residential decisions. Similarly, Martin Feldstein and Marian Valliant (1994) point out that states' ability to redistribute income is impaired by the responsiveness of before-tax wages to changes in states' marginal tax rates.

suppose that in practice we expect governments to follow bad distributional policies (such as enriching local despots) if exit is not available to restrain their expropriative urges. This may suggest preferring tax competition to harmonization, despite the absence of any change in the analysis of how mobility works.

Tax havens and holidays

Perhaps the hottest current topic in international tax competition is what one might call discrimination in favour of outside commerce—governments' occasional predilection to offer outside businesses or passive investors more favourable tax terms than those available to the locals (Avi-Yonah 2000; Organization for Economic Cooperation and Development: 1998a). This is also a hot topic inside the United States, where states or localities have at times competed for new factories, professional sports franchises, and the like (Appleborne 1993; Passell 1998). For convenience, we can use the term 'tax haven' to refer to a jurisdiction that offers outside investors favourable tax rates on financial investment such as portfolio interest, and 'tax holiday' to refer to offering them favourable tax rates on marginal real investment such as building a new factory.[19]

Anxious governments that view the offering of tax havens and holidays as 'harmful tax competition' threatening their own revenues have sought international agreements not to offer them.[20] Such efforts at defensive cartelization are only to be expected, although this does not tell us whether the efforts are good or bad given the need for cartelization to finance public goods. Many commentators applaud these efforts to discourage tax havens and holidays, based in part on distributional concerns that I have suggested here may rest on exaggerating the significance of capital income taxation (Avi-Yonah 2000). A few commentators have taken a different tack, noting the possible relationship between at least some varieties of such tax competition and desirable Tiebout processes (Roin 2000).

This is an issue where the various lines of analysis in this chapter really collide. Consider the following natural extensions of what has been said so far.

First, tax havens and holidays reduce locational neutrality by making locational decisions ever more tax-driven. Indeed, they violate both of the more limited neutrality principles that usually drive international tax analysis. Given that locational neutrality is violated whenever two jurisdictions have different tax rates, commentators often speak of the choice between capital export neutrality (Tax Investor X, who lives in Country A, at the same rate whether she invests in Country A or

[19] In some cases, a holiday jurisdiction may generally have high tax rates relative to the jurisdictions with which it is competing for mobile investment. In such a case, a time-limited tax holiday may merely serve to mitigate its tax disadvantage in attracting international business, rather than to place it squarely ahead.

[20] The European Union, for example, recently adopted a non-binding 'code of conduct' on business taxation, seeking to freeze and gradually roll back the granting of tax concessions to outside businesses. The OECD (1998a) has likewise sought to discourage what it views as harmful tax competition, such as offering concessions to mobile new investment.

Country B) and capital import neutrality (Tax Investor X and Investor Y, who lives in Country B, at the same rate when they invest in the same country). Tax havens and holidays in Country B violate both principles, by giving Investor X a rate that is lower than both the rate she gets in Country A *and* the rate Investor Y gets in Country B.[21]

Second, similarly, tax holidays increase the undesirable incentive for real investment to take forms that can benefit from mobility and thus demand holiday treatment, and may distort trade by, in effect, providing negative tariffs.

Third, on the other hand, tax holidays permit a kind of price competition between jurisdictions that want to attract real investment from the outside. They may therefore in effect facilitate the flow of resources to the highest-valuing user—a process that we often assume is efficient (Roin 2000).

Fourth, the internal political choice problems that suggest being hostile to tariffs are not as clearly present here. We no longer have the scenario of local businesses using their organizational advantage to exploit local consumers. While we might substitute the scenario of an outside company unduly influencing local officials to agree to the exploitation of local taxpayers (who pay for the holiday if the investment would have been made in any event), the new scenario may not be credible in cases where the holiday receives substantial political attention. In such cases, local taxpayers may believe, perhaps even rightly, that the investment would not otherwise have been made and will benefit their economy even if the company pays no tax.

Fifth, perhaps, however—reverting to the anti-tax competition side—other flaws in domestic political choice might lead the holiday jurisdiction to make a bad choice from the standpoint of its own interest. Local voters may be inclined to overrate the effect of tax holidays on job creation by confusing the number of jobs provided in a new factory with the actual increase (if any) in local employment at equilibrium. Politicians who have high discount rates because their terms in office are limited may be unduly inclined to give away future revenues for the current political payoff that they may get by delivering highly visible new factories and resulting jobs.

Sixth, the spillover problem resulting from tax havens and holidays that favour outside commerce is different and arguably less grave than that resulting from tariffs that disfavour it. Outside businesses are being benefited rather than harmed. To be sure, outside governments may be losing revenue. Yet one could argue from a Tiebout perspective against treating this externality as of comparable significance.

[21] To be sure, the number of principles violated need not matter. Concern should perhaps focus on capital export neutrality, which may affect efficiency more than capital import neutrality since people are generally less mobile than capital. (Violations of capital export neutrality provide an incentive to change where one invests, while violations of capital import neutrality provide an incentive to change where one lives.) Capital import neutrality may also induce the 'wrong' people to save, as in the case where X saves in lieu of Y despite having a higher discount rate because Country A's tax rate on saving is lower than that in Country B, but this has limited significance for efficiency if (as some evidence suggests) the compensated tax-elasticity of saving is low.

Economists generally agree that we should not be swayed by the competitive harm to, say, a retailer when a store with better prices opens next door.[22] The analogy between competition by shops and by taxing jurisdictions is apt to the extent that the public goods a jurisdiction provides are limited to those present in it.

Seventh, despite the Tiebout argument, the spillover problem when other jurisdictions lose tax revenues cannot be entirely dismissed. Consider the common case where an investor's country of residence sets out to tax her worldwide income, including portfolio interest, subject to a limited foreign tax credit for taxes paid on foreign source income. Whatever its rules say, however, the residence jurisdiction cannot tax unreported income that it cannot find. Suppose further that the haven jurisdiction in which the investor places her portfolio resists information disclosure to the residence country about the investor's holdings there (again, a common scenario). This makes the haven country a kind of accommodation party that offers, presumably for a modest fee, to aid illegal tax evasion in the residence country. This impedes the residence country's efforts to allocate the cost of public goods among its residents as they collectively prefer. This may be good cause for complaint even if it could have chosen a graduated consumption tax that was approximately as redistributive as its attempted worldwide income tax.

Eighth, tax holidays present a different, and probably less serious, version of the same problem. Since business activity tends to be more observable than how an individual's portfolio is invested, the problem of outright evasion is largely transmuted into one of transfer pricing (used to misallocate income to the holiday jurisdiction) that jurisdictions may find easier to address through tax audits than the non-reporting of portfolio income.

Ninth, if residence countries really taxed residents in full on their worldwide income, subject only to strictly limited foreign tax credits, haven and holiday jurisdictions would merely be surrendering revenue to those countries, other than in cases of evasion and aggressive transfer pricing. Investors would not be attracted by the prospect of merely substituting extra domestic taxes for the taxes avoided abroad. Often, therefore, the holiday jurisdictions must count on some such feature of the residence country's tax system as deferral for foreign source business income until it is repatriated, or perhaps cross-crediting (the use of extra foreign tax credits from high-tax jurisdictions to offset taxes on income earned in low-tax jurisdictions). In such cases, the critique that holiday jurisdictions are acting as accommodation parties to the practice of tax evasion loses its force, and residence country tax law change is the obvious response.[23]

[22] The argument could be put in terms of potential Pareto improvement if, say, the lower price results from lower operating costs or the elimination of local monopoly profit.

[23] In some cases, foreign tax credit rules may cause non-haven jurisdictions to benefit from the availability of tax havens and holidays to their investors. Suppose, for example, that investors use transfer pricing to shift foreign taxable income from Germany to the Bahamas. Even if the investors pay less tax overall, they may pay more tax to the United States than previously by reason of the reduction in their foreign tax credits. On this point, James R. Hines and Eric Rice (1994) conclude that the Treasury probably gains revenue, on balance, from the availability of offshore tax havens.

Tenth, such changes in residence countries' tax laws may have social costs of their own. Consider the armies of tax lawyers that international businesses often must consult simply to comply with the ever more baroque international tax rules that respond to tax planning opportunities such as cross-crediting.

On the whole, it is hard to reach a confident judgement about the tax competition engaged in by haven and holiday jurisdictions, notwithstanding the full-throated cries against them that one hears in some circles (Avi-Yonah 2000; Organization for Economic Cooperation and Development: 1998a). Whether they are undesirable on balance or not, some of the preceding analysis suggests that the case for imposing harmonization is stronger with respect to passive-investment related tax havens than business-related tax holidays. Yet havens may be harder than holidays for cartelizing governments to limit. They require offering only a credible promise that investments will be secure and confidential, without regard to the attractiveness in a given area of real business investment. And they may not be as subject to being bid down by market forces as the investment response to them increases.

CONCLUSION

Is tax competition good or bad? At that level of generality, one might as well ask whether government is good or bad. The questions turn on similar issues of transaction cost that affect the desirability of using coercion to address collective action problems.

By focusing the analysis a bit more, we can start to derive meaningful conclusions. Harmonization, for example, may be desirable as a device for minimizing the imposition of tariffs and similar tax disadvantages on imports and multijurisdictional production. Such harmonization can, however, to an extent emerge voluntarily (albeit perhaps requiring the help of large-scale coordinating institutions), rather than necessarily requiring coercive imposition by a higher level of government. Still, both within the United States and internationally, further progress may be desirable in reducing tariff-like barriers through harmonization—for example, by encouraging or requiring the use of uniform income tax bases and rules for allocating income between jurisdictions.

Taxpayer and capital mobility have mixed implications for the choice between tax competition and harmonization. We may be glad that taxpayers can limit undesirable expropriation through the power to exit, while at the same time being concerned about the possible effect on progressivity and about the efficiency consequences of creating tax incentives to be mobile. The prospect of a race to the bottom in capital income taxation need not be a major concern, however, unless one is otherwise strongly committed to an income tax or believes that in practice consumption taxes are unlikely to match the redistributive impact of income taxes.

4

Federalism and Takeover Law: The Race to Protect Managers from Takeovers

LUCIAN ARYE BEBCHUK AND ALLEN FERRELL*

Twenty-five years ago, William Cary (1974) published his most lasting contribution to corporate law: his Yale Law Journal article entitled 'Federalism and Corporate Law: Reflections upon Delaware'—one of the most well-known and widely cited articles in corporate law (Shapiro 1991: 1462). In the article, he argued that Delaware's reliance on revenues generated from corporate charters had led it to favour corporate managers in crafting its corporate code. Cary believed that managers, often at the expense of shareholders, enjoyed unjustifiably lax constraints with regard to issues ranging from fiduciary obligations to a parent's treatment of a corporate subsidiary. To stop this harmful 'race to the bottom', Cary proposed that Congress adopt 'federal standards of corporate responsibility' (1974: 701).

Cary's sceptical view of state competition has not been widely accepted by corporate law scholars. Indeed, scholars since Cary have largely taken a favourable view of state competition for corporate charters. Ralph Winter (1977), in an influential critique of Cary's position, argued that state competition for corporate charters leads to a 'race to the top' as a result of market constraints on managers' behaviour. Frank Easterbrook and Daniel Fischel have endorsed and developed Winter's contention that state competition benefits shareholders (Easterbrook 1984; Easterbrook and Fischel 1991; Easterbrook and Fischel 1983; Fischel 1982). Roberta Romano (1998; 1993a; 1987b) has similarly argued that state competition ensures that corporate law maximizes shareholder wealth. Indeed, Professor Romano labels the federalist structure of corporate law 'the genius of American Corporate Law' (1993b).

Several years ago, one of us pursued the route suggested by Cary and developed an analysis of the problems produced by state competition (Bebchuk 1992). That analysis suggested that, with respect to a set of important corporate issues, state

* This chapter is a slightly revised version of our article with the same title published, as part of the Symposium on the Legacy of William Cary, in 99 Colum. L. Rev. 1165, 1168 (1999) (also available for downloading from www.law.harvard.edu/faculty/bebchuk). For their valuable comments, we wish to thank Victor Brudney, John Coates, Jesse Fried, Andrew Guzman, Marcel Kahan, Mark Ramseyer, Michael Whinchop, and participants at the Symposium on the Legacy of William Cary and at the Conference on Regulatory Competition and Economic Perspectives, Yale Law School. We also wish to thank the John M. Olin Center for Law, Economics and Business at Harvard Law School for its financial support.

competition is unlikely to serve shareholder wealth maximization.[1] Rather, the analysis suggested that states might have an incentive to provide rules that are preferred by managers and controllers—and that on these issues the rules preferred by managers and controllers may well be different from what is beneficial to shareholders.

Building on that analysis, we continue in this chapter to examine the contention, articulated by Cary, that there are serious problems with state competition. Our analysis suggests that state competition suffers from important structural problems, and that competition among states is therefore likely to produce troubling results with respect to some critical aspects of corporate law. Cary carefully examined several corporate law issues, such as proxy contests, de facto mergers, fairness in parent–subsidiary transactions, and directors' duty of care, all hot issues in the 1960s. We will discuss the issues involved in the state competition debate through the lens of takeover regulation, perhaps the most important issue in corporate law in the last two decades.[2] We use takeover law as a case study of the shortcomings of state competition.

Our analysis is organized as follows. Part I will argue that there are strong theoretical reasons to believe that states will have incentives to produce a body of takeover law that excessively protects incumbent managers and restricts hostile takeovers. Because managers play a key role in incorporation decisions, states (especially ones with a large number of already incorporated companies, such as Delaware) will give substantial weight to satisfying managers' preferences. To be sure, in some areas of corporate law, because managers' and shareholders' interests are sufficiently aligned due to various market forces, the rules that managers would like states to adopt are those that maximize shareholder value. But, we argue, in the area of takeovers, this is unlikely to be the case. Because of the value that managers might place on their independence, they may prefer rules that excessively restrict takeovers, notwithstanding that such rules might somewhat reduce share value and make it somewhat more difficult for them to acquire other companies when they wear the acquirer's hat.

Part II analyses the development of state takeover law and argues that it is consistent with the above theoretical analysis. States have developed a substantial body of rules, including both anti-takeover statutes and judicial decisions permitting the use of defensive tactics, that make takeovers more difficult. We suggest that these

[1] Moreover, state competition for corporate charters might lead to inefficiencies when the interests of not only shareholders but also third parties are implicated by a legal rule (Bebchuk 1992: 1485–95). The present discussion will focus on shareholder wealth.

[2] A parallel debate has been taking place concerning competition among jurisdictions in the international sphere. Some commentators believe that this form of competition is generally beneficial, (Choi and Guzman 1998; 1997; Romano 1998). Others predict harmful effects resulting from such competition (M. Fox 1997). While this chapter focuses on competition among states, the analysis also has implications for international competition among jurisdictions. For reasons explained by Bebchuk (1992: 1507–8), international competition and state competition have similar structural problems. Thus the implication of our analysis is that international competition would not work well with regard to rules governing takeovers.

rules are quite likely to excessively protect managers. To start with, we show that the extent to which these rules restrict takeovers has little support in the policy literature on takeovers. States' relentless effort to come up with new anti-takeover statutes seems to be motivated more by a desire to make takeovers more difficult than by an attempt to address in a cost-effective way some valid policy concerns. And the latitude that states have given to defensive tactics has surpassed what even the strongest supporters of defensive tactics have advocated. Furthermore, states have provided managers with more anti-takeover protections than shareholders seemed to have been willing to give them. Finally, and perhaps most importantly, states have elected to proceed in a way that imposed anti-takeover protections without giving shareholders much choice or say.

Our analysis of Delaware takeover law highlights the fact that its rules governing defensive tactics seem to be characterized by unnecessary ambiguity and unpredictability, resulting in frequent litigation. While this aspect of Delaware law benefits the interests of the Delaware bar, which might be of importance to Delaware, it is difficult to see how shareholders are benefited by the excessive unpredictability and vagueness of its rules. Finally, our analysis of state takeover law ends in a comparison of it to the body of takeover law produced by the British City Code, which is the product of self-regulation by a body that might well have stronger incentives to care about shareholder interests than do states. In sharp contrast to state takeover law, the British City Code severely restricts defensive tactics by incumbents, restricts bidders only to an extent that seems to serve some valid policy concerns, and overall regulates takeovers through rules that are much clearer and more predictable in application.

Part III discusses the inability of state competition advocates to square their position with their own view that state takeover law, including that of Delaware, excessively protects incumbent managers and excessively discourages bidders. Indeed, some of the fiercest critics of impediments to takeovers, which are as much a product of state competition for corporate charters as any other aspect of corporate law, are also the leading state competition advocates. We conclude by expressing our belief that state competition advocates would be well advised to reconsider their position. Pro-state competition scholars' own criticisms of state takeover law, many of which we share, demand no less.

I. THE THEORY OF TAKEOVER LAW UNDER STATE COMPETITION

As one of us has argued, state competition might have virtues with respect to some corporate law questions, but performs badly with respect to others (Bebchuk 1992). According to that analysis, the issues with respect to which state competition will work poorly are: (1) issues that are 'significantly redistributive' (in that their effect on managers' or controlling shareholders' private interests is not insignificant relative to their effect on shareholder value); (2) issues that directly affect the strength of market discipline; and (3) issues that implicate the interests of not only shareholders and managers but also third parties. In this chapter, we will focus our attention on one very important area of corporate law: the rules governing takeovers. The argument will be that states have an incentive to design takeover law that is more restrictive on bidders and more protective of managers than is in shareholders' interests.

The importance of managers

A state's takeover law will apply to companies incorporated in that state which become takeover targets. These companies have, almost by definition, sufficient dispersion of shares such that managers have some measure of de facto control.

Let us begin by explaining why states, in particular Delaware, will care about managers' preferences. The reason for this is simple: managers play a pivotal role in determining whether a company reincorporates to another state.[3] If a state wishes to maximize the number of companies that are incorporated there—the starting assumption of the 'race to the top'/'race to the bottom' debate—the state will take an interest in both initial incorporation decisions and subsequent reincorporation decisions.

Consider Delaware, which has a very large number of companies already incorporated there. It is critically important to Delaware's continued success, and any state in a similar situation, that it retains companies already chartered there. The potential loss by Delaware of chartered companies through reincorporation, for any given period of time, is greater than the potential gain from initial incorporations. While the number of initial incorporations in any given year is likely to be fairly limited, the number of companies that Delaware could potentially lose through reincorporation—that is, the companies already chartered there—is significant. Moreover, Delaware will not only be interested in preventing its companies from reincorporating to another state, but inducing companies chartered elsewhere to move to Delaware.[4] For these reasons, it would not be surprising if Delaware's corporate law catered, to a significant extent, to the preferences of managers, whatever those preferences may be.

Indeed, the incentive of states which do not have a large number of chartered companies to provide shareholder wealth-maximizing rules, when these harm managerial interests, is not nearly as strong as one might think. First of all, by providing rules preferred by shareholders the state will place itself at a disadvantage in

[3] A company cannot reincorporate without the company's managers deciding to bring a reincorporation proposal to a shareholder vote (Clark 1986: § 10.2.4). Moreover, managers in companies with widely dispersed ownership of shares can have significant influence over the outcome of a shareholder vote through control of the voting process.

[4] Delaware has been very successful in the market for reincorporations. Roberta Romano (1985: 265–78) has found that 82 per cent of all reincorporating companies between 1960 and 1982 switched to Delaware. Similarly, Demetrio Kaouris (1995: 1011) found that out of 255 surveyed companies that changed their corporate domicile between 1982 and 1994, 89 per cent reincorporated to Delaware.

the market for reincorporations with respect to the companies that are currently chartered there and to those that might otherwise consider reincorporating to that state.

But would not a state that provided rules beneficial to shareholders attract more initial incorporations as a result? Not necessarily. It is questionable the extent to which companies initially incorporating in a state with shareholder wealth-maximizing rules, when those rules differ from the ones preferred by managers, would benefit from them in the form of a higher price for securities sold in an initial public offering. Buyers of securities in a company initially incorporated in such a state might anticipate that if the state ever did enjoy a significant number of chartered companies, it would then have a powerful incentive, much as Delaware does, to craft its law so as to satisfy managerial preferences. Even if the state were judged unlikely to make such a mid-stream change in its law, a similar shareholder wealth-decreasing result might nevertheless be anticipated due to the ability of managers to reincorporate the company, at a later point in time, in a state that does have rules to the liking of the managers.

But merely concluding that states, and in particular Delaware, care a great deal about managers' preferences does not by itself imply that managers' and shareholders' interests are likely to systematically diverge. This was perhaps the most underdeveloped aspect of Cary's position. Pro-state competition scholars are quick to argue that state competition for corporate charters works well because, due to market incentives, managers want to do what is in the interests of shareholders (Easterbrook and Fischel 1991; Romano 1993b; Winter 1977). Below we explain why these market incentives may often be insufficient to induce managers to prefer takeover rules that are more restrictive than what would be optimal for shareholders.

Managers' preferred takeover law

Market incentives

At first glance, one might reason as follows: since managers want to keep their jobs and independence, they will surely want to prevent any takeover that does not receive their approval. It is not possible to jump to this conclusion, however, because managers also care about share value, for several widely noted reasons. Moreover, to the extent that restrictive takeover law would reduce shareholder value, they might prefer a state that opts for a more permissive approach.

Among the potential reasons why managers might have a strong interest in maximizing share value, we address two of the main ones. First, unnecessarily low share value can lead to an increased likelihood of takeover. The greater the difference between a share's value and what it could be worth if managers were acting in shareholders' interests, the more profitable, *ceteris paribus*, a takeover will be, and hence the more likely it is that one will occur. Second, managers' compensation and wealth are often tied, at least to a certain extent, to a share's price through share options and share holdings. Insofar as managers are shareholders themselves, they will have an incentive to make decisions that reflect the interests of shareholders.

As will be explained, however, these two market constraints are unlikely to be sufficient, in a number of cases, to cause managers to prefer a permissive takeover legal regime.

The effect of restrictive takeover law on managers' interests

As noted, pro-state competition theorists argue that the threat of a takeover will cause managers to seek the legal arrangement that would be beneficial to shareholders. The argument is roughly as follows. Suppose there are two legal arrangements and one produces higher shareholder value compared with the other. In that case, managers will prefer the regime which maximizes shareholder value, because that arrangement also reduces the probability of a takeover. Higher share value makes takeovers more costly and, as a result, less likely.

But let us further suppose that, of the two regimes, A is the optimal takeover regime from the perspective of shareholders while B is a somewhat more restrictive arrangement. Since A is the optimal arrangement, share value would be, by definition, lower under regime B. But that does not necessarily mean that the likelihood of a takeover would be increased by B. To be sure, with a lower share value, a takeover at the same price would be more profitable. But if B makes it sufficiently more difficult to do a takeover, then the likelihood of a hostile takeover would be smaller despite the lower share price.

It is important to note that making a hostile takeover more difficult overall can benefit managers in two ways. First, they might be able to use the protective arrangement to prevent a takeover altogether—a valuable option since they could then retain all the private benefits of control that come with independence (including not losing their jobs). Alternatively, they can use their increased ability to resist takeovers so as to benefit themselves in any takeover, perhaps by maximizing the side payments they receive from an acquirer in a negotiated acquisition.

However, one might raise the interest of managers in increasing share value because of their stock options and stock holdings. But the two effects mentioned above which are potentially quite important to managers, can easily dominate this interest. Consider managers who now have, say, 3 per cent of the company's stock and enjoy substantial private benefits of control.[5] If a legal arrangement would substantially reduce the likelihood of their losing these private benefits of control, then that might well be more important to them than avoiding some reduction in the value of their existing holdings.[6]

[5] The correlation between managerial pay and performance has been found to be weak (Jensen and Murphy 1990a; 1990b).

[6] Melvin Eisenberg (1989: 1510) concluded that managerial interests are strongest when managers' jobs are implicated, thereby creating an incentive for states to adopt rules that enable managers to keep their positions.

Managers' interests in acquiring other companies

Thus far, we have explained why managers of a Delaware company might prefer that, if their company were to become a target, they enjoy the protection of a legal regime that restricted takeovers more than is optimal from the perspective of shareholders. But it might be said that this does not imply that they would prefer Delaware to have rules that inefficiently restricted takeovers, for such rules would apply to them regardless of whether their company becomes a target. Such rules may also apply to companies that they will want to acquire in the future. One might posit that this creates a countervailing consideration (Romano 1993b: 59–60). Because managers can be on both sides of a takeover, so to speak, they will not favour a takeover law that is too restrictive.

But this symmetry does not exist. For several reasons, managers of a Delaware company will likely care more about how Delaware's takeover rules would affect them should their company become a target than they would about the impact of Delaware's takeover law should they wish to acquire other companies.

First of all, while Delaware law would surely affect them if they become an acquisition target, it may or may not affect them should they want to acquire another company. It will affect them if they want to buy another company that is incorporated in Delaware with dispersed ownership, but it will not affect them if they go after a company with a controlling shareholder, a company that is closely held, or a company with dispersed ownership that is incorporated elsewhere.[7]

Second, even assuming that Delaware takeover law would apply each time they go after a target, there is an asymmetry in the stakes to managers. It might very well be extremely important to them to retain their own positions and private benefits of control—here the personal stakes of managers could be quite substantial. In contrast, it is unlikely to be as important to them to weaken the power of the managers of a company with dispersed ownership which they might wish to acquire. Their personal interests are not implicated to anywhere near the same degree; at most they will have to choose different acquisition targets or pay a higher acquisition price (including any side payments to the target's managers). This asymmetry is evidenced by the fact that corporations are the primary lobby responsible for the passage of anti-takeover legislation (Carney 1998: 749–50; Romano 1987a: 121–227), even though this legislation will presumably impede their own future acquisitions of corporations falling within the legislation's ambit.

Conclusion

The bottom line of the preceding analysis is that states competing for corporate charters—and in particular Delaware, which is presumably striving to maintain its

[7] In other words, a manager's decision as to where to (re)incorporate has no effect on the takeover law governing potential acquisitions. Foregoing (re)incorporation in a state with anti-takeover defences does not increase the probability that a potential target will do the same.

dominant role in this market—have an incentive to provide a body of law that makes takeovers more difficult regardless of whether this is in the interests of shareholders. We now take a look at Delaware's takeover law and reflect on whether it is consistent with our theoretical conclusions.

II. REFLECTIONS ON STATE TAKEOVER LAW

We start with a qualification: this Part does not constitute a full analysis and evaluation of the development of state takeover law in the last twenty-five years. This would be too large an undertaking—the literature on takeovers is voluminous. What we do is to offer a set of observations on the body of takeover law that Delaware and other states have produced. Our observations are consistent with the preceding theoretical analysis, which indicated that state competition is unlikely to produce a body of takeover law that is optimal from the viewpoint of shareholders.

The pro-management tilt of state takeover law

How states worked to make takeovers more difficult

States have worked hard, and quite successfully, to make takeovers more difficult. State takeover law consists of a substantial body of rules—both statutory and judge-made—that significantly impedes hostile takeovers and shields incumbent managers. The fruits of these efforts are reflected in both rules governing bidders and those governing the use of defensive tactics. As we will explain, it is the rules concerning defensive tactics that have erected the most important impediments. But we will also analyse the rules restricting the activity of bidders, both for the sake of completeness and because they also reflect, though less dramatically, the tendency of states to substantially restrict takeovers.

Rules restricting bidders

One popular way among states of protecting managers from unwanted takeovers is restricting what bidders are able to do. While the Securities Exchange Act of 1934[8] and the Securities Act of 1933[9] regulate various aspects of tender offers, the most important source of restrictions on the activities of bidders have come, by and large, from state anti-takeover legislation. Over a twenty-five-year period, there have been several waves of state anti-takeover statutes, easily making the passage of anti-takeover legislation one of the top priorities of states in the corporate law area. Numerous states over the years have enacted anti-takeover statutes, imposing a bewildering array of requirements on bidders.

[8] The Williams Act amendments to the Securities Exchange Act of 1934 impose various disclosure and procedural requirements on cash tender offers.

[9] If a portion of the consideration for the target company is securities of the bidder, the Securities Act of 1933 will often be applicable.

The first state takeover statute was enacted by Virginia in 1968 (Takeover Bid Disclosure Act, Va. Code §§ 13.1-528, 13.1-541). Over the next thirteen years, thirty-six states followed Virginia's lead (Romano 1985: 234). These statutes often imposed disclosure requirements on bidders as well as—more burdensomely—requiring administrative approval for a bid to proceed. After the constitutionality of the first wave of statutes was seriously called into question (*Edgar* v. *MITE Corp.*, 457 U.S. 624 (1981)), states enacted a new set of anti-takeover statutes.

So-called second-generation anti-takeover statutes spread rapidly.[10] There were several types of second-generation anti-takeover statutes. 'Control share acquisition' statutes typically require a shareholder vote approving an 'acquisition of control' by a party. Other states adopted 'fair price' statutes which prohibit a 'second-step' merger[11] between the bidder and the target company unless a supermajority shareholder vote approves the merger or the bidder provides a 'fair price', as defined by the statute, for the remaining shares. In a somewhat similar vein, states also adopted 'redemption rights' statutes, which provide minority shareholders with the right to sell to the bidder shares for their 'fair value', again a price determined by statute. Some states, including Delaware, adopted a 'business combination' statute prohibiting bidders from engaging in certain business combinations with an acquired company for a specified period of time (Choper *et al.* 1995: 1054–7). Thirty-seven states adopted second-generation anti-takeover statutes within a mere eight years of the *MITE* decision (Carney 1998: 752–3). The hard work of states ultimately paid off. They had fashioned anti-takeover statutes that were likely to pass constitutional muster.[12]

However, the states were still not satisfied. Yet another type of anti-takeover statute, the so-called 'constituency statute', has become popular among states. The focus of these statutes, however, is somewhat different from the others. They are concerned with what target management can legally do in frustrating an unwanted bid, not on what bidders can do. It is to this central issue that we now turn.

Rules governing defensive tactics

The most important impediment to takeovers today is the wide latitude given to managers to engage in defensive tactics, especially the ability to hide behind a poison pill.[13] Perhaps the most critical development creating this managerial power

[10] While we refer to five different types of statutes as second-generation statutes, it is worth pointing out for purposes of clarity that some commentators have divided these statutes into several different generations.

[11] A 'second-step' merger is a merger between a corporation and a shareholder holding a significant percentage of the corporation's stock.

[12] *CTS Corp.* v. *Dynamics Corp.*, 481 U.S. 69 (1987), upheld Indiana's second-generation anti-takeover statute against a dormant Commerce Clause challenge.

[13] The Chief Economist for the Securities and Exchange Commission (1986: 1, 6–7) defined a poison pill as:

> [A]ny financial device that when triggered by a particular action (e.g. merging a target's assets or acquiring more than some specified amount of the target's common stock), results in one or a combination of the following:

cont./

was the approval by the Delaware courts of poison pills put in place by management.[14] After it became clear that managers had the power to erect poison pill defences, the key question became (and continues to be): when would managers be forced to dismantle them in a takeover contest? Delaware law has gradually evolved so as to allow directors, consistent with their fiduciary obligations to shareholders, to 'just say no' to potential bidders *with* their poison pill defences in place.

Many states have adopted 'constituency statutes' that enable directors to consider the interests of non-shareholder constituencies, such as employees and local communities, in exercising their authority.[15] Arguably, this provides managers with an even greater ability to formulate a legally acceptable reason not to dismantle a poison pill or to refrain from whatever other defence manoeuvres they might wish to engage in. It is worth noting that even though Delaware does not have a 'constituency statute', its case law has long permitted managers, in evaluating and responding to a hostile takeover, to consider its 'impact on "constituencies" other than shareholders (that is, creditors, customers, employees, and perhaps even the community generally' (*Unocal*, 493 A.2d at 955; *Time* v. *Paramount*, 571 A.2d 1140, 1153 (Del. 1990)).

The corporate fortress

Considering the cumulative effect of the restrictions states have placed on the activities of bidders as well as managers' ability to erect and maintain anti-takeover defences, especially the poison pill, it is obvious to even the most casual observer that managers have substantial power to block takeovers. Companies are today surrounded by high walls that can be very costly for bidders to breach against a determined target management. As a result of these legal developments, the impact on the operation of the market for corporate control has been far-reaching.

As one would expect, states have varied somewhat in how far they have gone in this direction. As pro-state competition scholars have emphasized, Delaware, despite offering managers substantial protection against unwanted acquisitions, has not fortified the corporate castle as much as other states have. But for our purposes,

a. the acquirer is forced to purchase securities from the shareholders of the target firm at prices equal to or exceeding their market value
b. security holders of the target firm gain rights to exchange stock of the target firm for a combination of cash and securities from the target firm exceeding that of the surrendered stock (acquirer is generally excluded from this exchange)
c. the security holders of the target firm gain rights to purchase securities from the target firm at prices below market value (acquirer is generally excluded)
d. the acquirer must sell securities of the acquiring entity at prices below market value to security holders of the target firm
e. the acquirer loses substantial voting power of his or her shares relative to other security holders of the target firm.

[14] The use of the poison pill to ward off a potential bidder was first approved by the Delaware Supreme Court in *Moran* v. *Household Int'l, Inc.*, 500 A.2d 1346 (Del. 1985), a case which we will discuss later in this chapter.

[15] Thirty-one states have adopted 'constituency statutes' since 1986 (Choper *et al.* 1995: 1057).

what is important is not the differences among states, which are, on the whole, small compared to the long road toward restricting takeovers that almost all states have travelled. What is important is the aggregate product of state competition and how that differs from the body of rules that would maximize shareholder wealth. Accordingly, we now offer some observations on why the impediments to takeovers that states have so vigorously created are excessive.

The weak policy basis for state anti-takeover law

Being academics, we start with the observation that the powerful anti-takeover position taken by Delaware does not appear to have a strong basis in the extensive literature examining the desirability of different types of takeover regulation from the perspective of shareholders. Before proceeding, we want to emphasize that this is just one observation and not the basis for our view that Delaware has gone too far. Of course, the best arrangement could, in fact, be one that receives little support in academic circles. Even if powerful anti-takeover protections are justified, we will argue below that they should have been afforded to managers in a manner much different than they were. But a natural place to begin the analysis is to see how Delaware's anti-takeover position has fared in policy debates.

Rules restricting bidders

In this section, we will examine the policy basis for the arrangements introduced by state anti-takeover statutes. As we have seen, while these statutes have made takeovers more difficult, their impeding effect is likely less than that of the rules governing defensive tactics. Our problem with takeover statutes, however, is not so much with the magnitude of the difficulties they pose for takeovers. Instead, as explained below, our problem is that these statutes seemed to have been created to a large extent for the purpose of making takeovers more difficult rather than to address legitimate policy concerns.

We start with the observation that states have consistently come up with very different types of anti-takeover statutes, focusing on various issues and using different techniques. When a particular type of statute was found to be constitutionally suspect or to provide little impediment to takeovers, states simply went back to the drawing board and adopted another type of statute. The first generation focused on the tender offer process, a similar focus to that of the Williams Act. When the constitutionality of these statutes was called into question in *MITE*, states simply went back to the drawing board having in mind that a statute regulating a company's internal affairs would likely be permissible under the decision's rationale. They then tried to use this opening to impede takeovers, without interfering in the takeover process directly, by altering the powers that an acquirer would have following a takeover. When various second-generation statutes—many of which, as explained below, have a plausible policy rationale—were upheld against constitutional challenges but did not seem to pose a substantial impediment to tender offers that shareholders would want to accept, states went back to work. They came up with a new and different set of statutes. The one common denominator to all the anti-takeover statutes is that they all seek, in one way or another, to make takeovers more difficult.

As has already been mentioned, for some second-generation statutes one could at least find a legitimate policy rationale: the need to address the pressure-to-tender problem that shareholders sometimes confront when considering a tender offer. The pressure-to-tender problem results from shareholders' incentive to tender their shares to a bidder out of fear of ending up with low-value minority shares in the event that other shareholders tender and the offer succeeds. Shareholders will have this incentive even if they all reach the conclusion that their shares would be worth more if the tender offer did not succeed (Bebchuk 1985; 1987; Brudney and Chirelstein 1974: 336–7).

One type of second-generation statute that some states adopted, referred to earlier, is the 'control share acquisition' statute. This statute could conceivably be justified as addressing the pressure-to-tender problem as it required shareholders to vote on whether a bidder can acquire control of a company. Such a vote might prevent a coercive offer from proceeding and, thus, benefit shareholders.[16] This type of statute provides shareholders with direct input as to whether an acquisition should proceed. In sharp contrast, many of the more formidable defensive tactics, as we shall see, are so potent precisely because they prevent shareholders from ever deciding for themselves the merits of a tender offer.

Another type of second-generation statute that addressed the pressure to tender problem is the 'redemption rights' statute. This statute typically ensures that the post-tender offer value of minority shares will not fall below the offer price. This again would eliminate the pressure to tender. Tender offers that shareholders do not find attractive would not be able to succeed through a bidder exploiting a shareholder's pressure to tender for fear of being stuck with less valuable minority shares.

So it is fair to say that many second-generation anti-takeover statutes responded to a concern that the literature had identified as important. One might have thought that states would rest content with their 'control share acquisition' or 'redemption rights' statutes. To the extent that the pressure-to-tender problem was effectively addressed by these statutes, the only tender offers that would be able to succeed are the ones shareholders want. Moreover, while these second-generation statutes would arguably frustrate all offers that shareholders would not want to succeed, they probably would not substantially deter offers that shareholders would want to take (Gilson and Black 1995: 553–8). But states did not stop here. Tellingly, states continued to add more restrictions on bidders which do not seem designed to address specific concerns over the operation of the takeover process.

[16] In *CTS Corp.* v. *Dynamics Corp. of America*, 481 U.S. 69 (1987), the US Supreme Court explains, 'By allowing [ ] shareholders to vote as a group, [Indiana's control share acquisition statute] protects them from the coercive aspects of some tender offers'.

Take, for example, the 'business combination' statutes. Delaware has one (Del. Gen. Corp. Law § 203), along with thirty other states (Choper *et al.* 1995). These statutes typically restrict a successful bidder's ability to engage in a wide range of transactions with an acquired company, such as mergers, liquidations, sales of assets, and stock issuances. These statutes might also prevent some takeovers which shareholders would want. They could conceivably reduce the potential efficiency gains resulting from the bidder acquiring control to the extent that those gains would require, say, effecting a merger between the bidder and the target.

Some observers argue that the costs imposed on bidders by Delaware's 'business combination' statute, and similar statutes, are not all that large and thus, by themselves, should not greatly curtail takeovers (Gilson and Black 1995: 558–73). But our point does not depend on how large the costs are. Assuming that just having fewer hostile takeovers is not an end in itself, these statutes are not an effective instrument for addressing any valid concern. The only justification that could be given for these statutes is that, by defending minority shares in the aftermath of a takeover, they prevent coercion and unequal treatment of shareholders. A 'control share acquisition' statute or a 'redemption rights' statute would clearly be superior in accomplishing these goals. A state could fulfil these goals in a complete way without preventing efficient takeovers. In contrast, 'business combination' statutes carry the potential cost of preventing some desirable acquisition offers.

Reviewing what states have done legislatively in restricting bidders causes one to suspect that states really care about making takeovers more difficult rather than merely eliminating particular distortions in the takeover process. This impression is powerfully reinforced by looking at state rules governing defensive tactics. We now turn to this subject.

Rules governing defensive tactics

The use of defensive tactics by managers raises an obvious conflict of interest problem. There is no question that allowing managerial discretion to use defensive tactics entails costs. This has led some commentators to support a ban on defensive tactics. While other commentators have supported the use of some tactics to address particular threats and distortions, they did not want managers, given the severe conflict of interest problem, to be granted an open-ended licence. But this is the direction in which state laws have moved.

The discussion in this section will focus on the most powerful impediment to takeovers—the ability of managers, at least in a wide range of circumstances, to 'just say no' to potential bidders while keeping in place a poison pill defence. There can be no question that the use of defensive tactics by managers presents a serious problem, because of the inherent conflict of interest faced by them in the takeover context. After all, managers' private interests, including their very jobs, are directly implicated. There is always the danger that managers will oppose a shareholder value-enhancing offer in order to maintain their corporation's independence. As the Delaware Supreme Court has repeatedly emphasized, there is always the 'omnipresent specter that a board may be acting primarily in its own interests, in a takeover' (*Unocal Corp.* v. *Misa Petroleum Co.*, 493 A.2d 946, 954–55 (Del. 1985)).

There is a large body of literature that argues that managers should be completely prohibited from engaging in defensive tactics—a literature which includes contributions by leading advocates of state competition (Easterbrook and Fischel 1981; Gilson 1981; Romano 1992). Those who oppose defensive tactics do not ignore the possibility that abusive takeover tactics might result in a bad takeover outcome. For example, there is the concern, discussed earlier, that shareholders will be pressured to tender due to the fear of being left holding minority shares with a value lower than the bid price (Bebchuk 1985). But those who oppose defensive tactics can point to legal arrangements that would address such problems. The pressure to tender problem, for example, can often be resolved by having a shareholder vote on a tender offer. There is no need, on this view, to use the costly remedy of giving managers the power to use defensive tactics and, thus, to have some veto power over acquisitions.

While both of us share the above view, some commentators favour giving managers power to use defensive tactics in order to address abusive takeover tactics. For instance, Reinier Kraakman and Ronald Gilson, in trying to explain and rationalize Delaware's early cases applying *Unocal*'s proportionality test, suggested that defensive tactics, including retaining the pill in the face of a hostile tender offer, should pass judicial review insofar as they address two particular threats: so-called structural and substantive coercion (Gilson and Kraakman 1989). They argued that a pill should be retained only if either: (1) the offer is structured in a coercive way, or (2) the managers can demonstrate (by, say, relying on an investment banker's opinion) that the independent value of the target significantly exceeds the offer consideration. The point worth emphasizing is that even commentators who endorse the use of defensive tactics to address abusive takeovers do not wish managers to have an open-ended, unlimited power to 'just say no'.

It is interesting to note that even Martin Lipton, inventor of the poison pill and champion of takeover defences, writing in the 1980s, did not go so far as to argue that managers should always have the ability to frustrate hostile tender offers. In a 1987 article, Lipton justified defensive tactics by pointing to a list of particular takeover abuses, each of which he discusses at length (Lipton 1987). He does not at any point argue that managers should be allowed to 'just say no' when the identified abuses are not present.

But the Delaware courts have left the reasoning of all these commentators, even those sympathetic to some types of defensive tactics, far behind, instead endorsing a much more expansive licence for managerial use of poison pills and 'just say no' (Grundfest 1993). This was done in stages. Initially, Delaware law seemed to be willing to allow tactics only in response to particular well-defined threats. But later on, without much in terms of providing explicit justification, Delaware went well beyond this.

The first seminal Delaware cases, decided in the mid-1980s, which dealt with managers' ability to use defensive tactics to defeat hostile tender offers, were *Unocal Corporation* v. *Mesa Petroleum Co.* (493 A.2d 946 (Del. 1985)) and *Moran* v. *Household International, Inc.* (500 A.2d 1346 (Del. 1985)). In both cases, the Delaware Supreme Court was careful to both examine the particular threat to shareholders that would have existed without managerial use of the defensive tactic in question and whether the defensive tactic that was used addressed that particular threat. Only then did the Court conclude that the use of the defensive tactic was appropriate. In *Unocal*, the Delaware Supreme Court reviewed a selective self-tender offer by a target corporation that was being offered as a way of defeating a hostile tender offer. In explaining why the target management had not violated their fiduciary duties to shareholders, the Court repeatedly emphasized the fact that the board reasonably believed that the hostile tender offer was a 'grossly inadequate two-tier coercive tender offer' and that the self-tender offer was 'reasonably related to the threats posed' (493 A.2d at 956, 958). In *Moran*, the Delaware Supreme Court approved the use of another defensive tactic by managers: the erection of a poison pill defence. The Court relied on the fact that the plan was mild and would therefore not deter bidders. Rather, the poison pill at issue merely provided reasonable protection against a coercive two-tier tender offer (500 A.2d at 357). Moreover, the Court pointed out that once a bidder did arrive on the scene, a decision not to dismantle the pill at that time would be reviewable by the Delaware judiciary.

After these decisions, the Chancery Court began to develop a jurisprudence limiting the use of defensive tactics so as to protect shareholders not only from coercive hostile tender offers but also from managerial abuse of these tactics. For example, in *AC Acquisitions Corporation* v. *Anderson, Clayton & Co.* (519 A.2d 103 (Del. Ch. 1986)), the Chancery Court concluded that the target board's selective self-tender offer was itself coercive and, therefore, not reasonable. The Chancery Court followed this up with its decision in *City Capital Associates* v. *Interco Inc.* (551 A.2d 787 (Del. Ch. 1988)). There, the court forced a target board to redeem its poison pill in the face of a non-coercive tender offer that the board believed was too low.[17] Indeed, in the course of its analysis, the court approvingly cited Gilson and Kraakman's interpretation of the *Unocal* standard (796 n. 8). Later that same year, the Delaware Chancery Court in another case forced a target board to redeem its poison pill in the face of a non-coercive tender offer (*Grand Metropolitan Public Limited Co.* v. *The Pillsbury Co.*, 1988–1989 Transfer Binder, Fed. Sec. L. Rep. (CCH) 94,104 (Del. Ch. 1988)). Unfortunately, this searching inquiry of manage-

[17] The Chancery Court forcefully explained that '[t]o acknowledge that directors may employ the recent innovation of "poison pills" to deprive shareholders of the ability effectively to choose to accept a noncoercive offer . . . would, it seems to me, be so inconsistent with widely shared notions of appropriate corporate governance as to threaten to diminish the legitimacy and authority of our corporation law' (*City Capital Assoc.* v. *Interco*, 551 A.2d at 799–800).

rial use of defensive tactics, and whether shareholders were being well served by them, was not to last.

Perhaps the key turning point in creating a much more expansive licence for managerial use of defensive tactics was the Delaware Supreme Court's decision several years later in *Paramount* v. *Time* (571 A.2d 1140 (Del. 1990)) wherein the Court went out of its way to explicitly disavow the approach of the Chancery Court in *Interco*. The Delaware Supreme Court stressed that the all-cash, all-shares tender offer for Time by Paramount threatened the target management's business plan (here, merging with Warner)—a threat it found to be legally cognizable. In contrast to what one might have thought from *Unocal* and *Moran*, and the Chancery Court cases building on their analysis, the *Time* Court made very clear that the use of defensive tactics is not limited to situations where the tender offer is coercive—which Paramount's offer clearly was not—or when management has particular, defensible reasons to believe the offer is inadequate. The potential discretion this line of reasoning provides to managers is sweeping.

Until this decision, Delaware was arguably in line with those commentators, such as Professors Kraakman and Gilson, who endorsed defensive tactics in response to particular, well-defined threats. Beginning with *Paramount* v. *Time*, Delaware courts have, however, increasingly tolerated, although this is not much acknowledged, the open-ended use by managers of defensive tactics far more drastic than the one at issue in *Moran*, without requiring, in any meaningful way, a demonstration of structural or substantive coercion.[18]

This important leap was made by the Delaware courts without much justification. This development also had little support in the literature, at that time or since. Now it is always possible that Delaware law, notwithstanding the lack of articulated policy justifications, is in fact the legal regime that is beneficial to shareholders and reflects what shareholders want. In the end, what is important is not what some academics believe, but what actually serves the interests of shareholders.

And this brings us to our next two critical observations: that Delaware, as well as other states, has adopted stronger anti-takeover protections than those shareholders at the time were willing to voluntarily provide; and that states have imposed these arrangements on shareholders in a way that left them with little choice or say.

States granted to managers what shareholders were not willing to give

It is worthwhile to stress that impediments to takeovers, to the extent that they are favoured by shareholders, can be adopted through charter provisions. In the late 1970s and early 1980s, managers did indeed push for various anti-takeover charter

[18] In *Unitrin, Inc.* v. *American Corp.*, 651 A.2d 1361 (Del. 1995), for instance, the Delaware Supreme Court upheld a target corporation's repurchase of its stock, which was designed to defeat a hostile tender offer. The Court pointed out that the bidder could always conduct a proxy contest. This analysis seemed to give short shrift to the interests of shareholders in having the ability to agree to the terms of the competing tender offer and the difficulty of conducting a successful proxy contest.

amendments (Gilson 1982). But it became increasingly clear that informed shareholders were willing to vote only for 'mild' anti-takeover arrangements—ones aimed at addressing the pressure-to-tender problem but not going much beyond this (826–7).

Already in the 1980s, Roberta Romano described how managers were successful in gaining anti-takeover protections from states more severe than those they could receive from shareholders (1987a: 129–30, 147–8). If this was true then, it has become even more so since. The protections from takeovers which managers have been afforded by states have only grown stronger.

States imposed anti-takeover rules on shareholders

States could have taken the approach of making it easier for companies to have takeover protections should shareholders approve. This approach would likely have pleased state competition advocates, who often place great emphasis on the importance of permitting shareholders to choose the legal regime that governs the corporation in which they invest. States, however, have almost universally shunned this approach.

In the takeover context, shareholders did not appear interested or willing to restrict takeovers much beyond arrangements needed for eliminating the pressure to tender. Despite this, Delaware, along with other states, imposed its anti-takeover arrangements on shareholders ex post in a way that left them little choice.

The imposition of legislative anti-takeover protections

Consider the anti-takeover statute adopted by Delaware (8 Del. Code § 203).[19] Tellingly, Delaware did not follow its earlier approach concerning limitations on directors' liability. In the aftermath of *Smith* v. *Von Gorkom* (488 A.2d. 858 (Del. 1985)), Delaware changed its corporate code so as to allow companies to adopt charter provisions that limit directors' liability.[20] In contrast, shareholders were not given the option of adopting the anti-takeover protections contained in Delaware's 'business combination' statute by approving a charter provision to that effect. Instead, the Delaware statute afforded managers these protections unless the corporation opted *out* of it by charter amendment. Why did Delaware adopt opt-in limitations on liability but opt-out limitations on takeovers?

The difference between opt-in and opt-out is of critical significance. This is because a charter amendment must be brought to a shareholder vote. As a result, shareholders cannot opt out of the Delaware statute unless the directors want this to happen.[21] And since managers generally prefer to have anti-takeover protection,

[19] Delaware's anti-takeover statute, with certain exemptions, bars an acquirer from conducting a second-step merger with the target for a period of three years after the target's acquisition.

[20] 8 Del. Code § 102(b)(7) permits the certificate of incorporation to contain 'a provision eliminating or limiting the personal liability of a director to the corporation or its stockholders for monetary damages for breach of . . . [duty of care]'.

[21] Del. Code § 242(b) sets out that shareholders cannot propose charter amendments on their own.

there is no reason for them to opt out. In short, the Delaware takeover statute has followed an enabling approach for the *managers*, not the shareholders—it is the managers who can have an anti-takeover arrangement if they want it (which they generally do).[22]

Most states have adopted a similar approach in deciding not to condition legislative anti-takeover protections on shareholder consent.[23] Indeed, some states do not even allow for opting out of their takeover statute (such as Wisconsin's anti-takeover statute, which Judge Easterbrook confronted in *Amanda Acquisition Corporation* v. *Universal Foods Corporation*, 877 F.2d 496 (7th Cir.)). But practically, the difference between permitting opting out and not permitting it is usually not all that significant. As long as managers control the opting-out process, we are often going to have the anti-takeover arrangement preferred by managers regardless of shareholders' interests.

The imposition of poison pills

The introduction of more and more potent poison pills, and their approval by Delaware courts and the courts of other states, has changed the landscape of takeovers. Poison pills have altered fundamentally the allocation of power between managers and shareholders.

What poison pills did was to use the formal power that managers have to issue securities. This power was originally given to facilitate the raising of capital.[24] The creators of the poison pill, however, used this power to design securities not with a view to raising capital but rather with the sole purpose of preventing acquisitions managers' wish to block it.

There is no question that the introduction of poison pills in the 1980s could not have been anticipated in the 1970s, 1960s, or 1950s. It took huge managerial demand for anti-takeover protection, coupled with the creative legal ingenuity of Martin Lipton and his colleagues, for poison pills to be invented and implemented on a widespread basis. Shareholders buying shares in Delaware companies earlier on simply could not have anticipated poison pills and the reallocation of power that they would cause.

And a drastic reallocation it is indeed. As long as they are not redeemed by managers, poison pills typically prevent shareholders from having access to an offer. For

[22] Professor Romano's suggestion that the opting-out structure of Delaware's takeover law saves on the transaction costs that would be incurred by forcing corporations to opt in (Romano 1987b: 729) is a fairly insignificant consideration in the light of the harm resulting from the increased ability of managers to thwart value-maximizing takeovers at the expense of shareholders.

[23] Carney (1998: 752) describes as the very purpose of state anti-takeover statutes the provision of 'takeover defenses without the necessity of [a shareholder] vote'.

[24] 8 Del. Code § 157 states that:

> Subject to any provisions in the certificate of incorporation, every corporation may create and issue, whether or not in connection with the issue and sale of any shares of stock or other securities of the corporation, rights or options entitling the holders thereof to purchase from the corporation any shares of its capital stock of any class or classes, such rights or options to be evidenced by or in such instrument or instruments as shall be approved by the board of directors.

this reason, they have had a dramatic effect on the takeover picture and the division of power between shareholders and managers.

Our point here is not that this reallocation is necessarily bad. Let us grant for a moment that it might be beneficial to shareholders. The important point is that this was a major reallocation, which had not been anticipated earlier. If states wanted to ensure that this was in shareholders' interests and not just in managers' interests, they would have required this reallocation of power to first enjoy shareholder consent.

Shareholder consent could have been required in any number of ways. Courts developing the doctrines governing the use of the poison pill could have required, given the inherent conflict of interest, that pills be ratified by the shareholders either right away or within a certain period of time. Or a court could have required managers to redeem a pill when shareholders express a clear preference for them to do so—say, by tendering *en masse* to a non-coercive bid. Or, at the minimum, courts could, in such circumstances, have required the managers to carry a heavier burden of demonstrating in a meaningful way the benefits of maintaining the pill. Similarly, state corporate statutes could have been amended to condition the use of poison pills on the adoption of a charter provision allowing managers to do so.

But this is not what Delaware and other states have done. Delaware has imposed on the shareholders of Delaware corporations an arrangement whereby managers enjoy a much greater level of protection from takeovers than they had before without requiring shareholders' consent or giving them some practical way of getting out of an undesired arrangement.

This is all consistent with the mid-stream problem discussed in Part I. Delaware cares a great deal not only about new incorporations but also about maintaining the large stock of companies it currently has. Managers play a crucial role in how successful Delaware is in maintaining its current position. The need to satisfy the preferences of managers of existing chartered corporations has proved to be an important force in the development of Delaware's law.

The pro-uncertainty tilt of Delaware anti-takeover law

Besides predicting that states will tend to adopt corporate rules whose substantive content benefits shareholders, the pro-state competition position also entails that these rules would likely be formulated in a way that similarly maximizes shareholder wealth. Roberta Romano, one of the strongest supporters of state competition, suggested in her earlier writings that one of the advantages of Delaware law is its certainty and predictability (1985: 273–9, 280–1; 1987b: 720–5). It is important to realize that this dimension is not the same as where the law stands substantively. For example, a body of law can restrict takeovers greatly in either a predictable or fuzzy way. And similarly, if the law is permissive, this can again be done in a predictable or fuzzy way. That is, one dimension is roughly where the line is drawn, and the other dimension is how clearly that line is drawn.

Other things being equal, predictability is desirable. It reduces uncertainty and the amount of litigation. It is for these reasons that Romano viewed it as a virtue and suggested that Delaware law's certainty and predictability has enabled it to remain dominant in the competition for corporate charters despite widespread copying of Delaware law by other states (1985: 226). The problem, however, is that Delaware law does not enjoy this virtue of predictability and certainty. Delaware courts have consistently filled Delaware jurisprudence with principles that are open-ended and unclear (Coates 1999; Kamar 1998: 1913–23). The principles throughout Delaware law contain terms which call for a case-specific assessment by the court. Moreover, there is always some room for the Chancery Court's equitable intervention. Any plaintiff's lawyer knows that it would be difficult to attack successfully a freezeout or to get a derivative suit to pass the test formulated in *Aronson* v. *Lewis* (473 A.2d. 805 (Del. 1984)). But the outcome is never certain.

There are reasons to believe that this is no accident. Delaware might purposely be maintaining a legal regime that encourages litigation (Branson 1990; Macey and Miller 1987; Kamar 1998). Delaware's corporate lawyers, an important interest group in Delaware, benefit from more, rather than less, litigation. Thus, regardless of where Delaware law stands substantively, Delaware has an incentive and, consequently, the tendency to draw the line in a way that is more fuzzy and litigation-inducing than would be good for shareholders.

The pro-uncertainty tilt of Delaware's takeover law is as apparent as it is in other areas. Delaware could have given managers a great deal of power to 'just say no' while circumscribing very clearly the boundaries of what managers can and cannot do. But no—Delaware has chosen to do it in a way that leaves a fair amount of uncertainty as to where exactly the line is drawn.[25] Characteristically of Delaware, the court's requirement of a very case-specific investigation always keeps the door open, at least a little, to judicial intervention.[26] It is no coincidence how frequently takeovers result in litigation.

Comparison to the British City Code

We would like to end our observations on state takeover law by comparing it to the regulatory arrangement created by Britain's City Code on Takeovers and Mergers (Begg 1991). British regulation of takeovers is interesting because it is basically in the hands of the Panel on Takeovers and Mergers, a non-governmental body which administers and revises the City Code. The City Code and its implementation is an example of a system of regulation that is not imposed from the outside by a detached governmental body but rather by a group that has strong

[25] In *Unocal Corp.* v. *Mesa Petroleum Co.*, 493 A.2d 946 (Del. 1985), and *Revlon, Inc.* v. *McAndrews & Forbes Holdings, Inc.*, 506 A.2d 173 (Del. 1986), the Court emphasized the need to conduct a very case-specific investigation to determine whether a manager acted improperly in rebuffing a takeover attempt.

[26] In *Unitrin, Inc.* v. *American Gen. Corp.*, 651 A.2d 1361, 1374 (Del. 1995), the court described the Unocal test as a 'flexible paradigm that jurists can apply to the myriad of "fact scenarios" that confront corporate boards'.

connections to interested parties. The chair of the panel is chosen by the Bank of England, with other members representing such groups as the insurance industry, pension funds, investment banks, clearing houses, British industry, and the London Stock Exchange (DeMott 1983: 954).

The British City Code contains a body of arrangements that is very different from US state takeover law when measured along the two dimensions focused on earlier—the extent to which regulatory arrangements protect managers, and the extent to which they generate confusion and litigation due to a lack of clarity.

On the first dimension, the City Code differs sharply from US state takeover law on managerial defensive tactics. In particular, the Code contains a sweeping prohibition on defensive tactics unless shareholder consent is obtained. General Principle seven of the City Code states:

> At no time after a bona fide offer has been communicated to the board of the offeree company, or after the board of the offeree company has reason to believe that a bona fide offer might be imminent, may *any action* be taken by the board of the offeree company in relation to the affairs of the company, without the approval of the shareholders in general meeting, which could effectively result in any bona fide offer being frustrated or in the shareholders being denied an opportunity to decide on its merits. (Begg 1991: A7.4) (emphasis added)

This general prohibition is reflected in Rule 21 of the City Code, which specifically prohibits a target board from engaging in a list of certain defensive tactics without shareholder approval[27]—a list which the Panel has made clear is not exhaustive.[28]

It is not the case that the City Code ignores the problems that takeovers might pose. To prevent the possible pressure to tender problem, the Code provides that, if an offer is successful, non-tendering shareholders will get a second opportunity to tender (Begg 1991: A7.14–A7.15), much like state 'redemption rights' statutes. But given that it is possible to enable shareholders to make an undistorted choice by having such an arrangement, the Code does not leave any room for defensive tactics.

Turning to the certainty/uncertainty dimension, the British regulatory arrangement seems to provide more certainty and less room for litigation than those under US state law. The clear prohibition on the use of defensive tactics contained in the

[27] Under Rule 21, a target board may not unilaterally:

. . .

B. issue any authorized but unissued shares;
C. issue or grant options in respect of any unissued shares;
D. create or issue, or permit the creation or issue of, any securities carrying rights of conversion into or subscription for shares;
E. sell, dispose of or acquire, or agree to sell, dispose of or acquire, assets of a material amount;
F. enter into contracts otherwise than in the ordinary course of business. (Begg 1991: A7.22)

[28] In Consolidated Gold Fields PLC (Takeover Panel, 9 May 1989: 14) it was concluded that the commencement of litigation against the bidder by a target board was 'frustrating action' in violation of General Principle 7.

City Code is one such example. It is not a 'flexible' balancing test tailor-made for endless litigation.[29] Indeed, a major concern of the Panel on Takeovers and Mergers, as well as others involved in London's financial markets, is that the European Union might pass takeover regulation that will enable targets to engage in strategic takeover litigation so common in the United States and so rare in Great Britain (*Financial Times* 1997).

The reasons why the Code went in such a different direction might lie in the different incentives its designers had from those who crafted US state takeover law. Presumably those responsible for the City Code gave less weight to managerial interests because of the close connection at least some of them had with the interests of shareholders. Moreover, corporate managers operating in a federal system such as the United States have significantly more influence, as they can reward states that cater to their interests and punish those that do not through their incorporation and reincorporation decisions.

The British regulatory system is an example of a national system of regulation that both addresses possible defects in the takeover process and ensures that shareholders, not management, have the ultimate say on whether a takeover proceeds. It accomplishes this without the degree of uncertainty and pervasive takeover litigation that characterizes US state takeover regulation. The British experience suggests that the federalist structure of corporate law might not be as powerful a force for desirable corporate rules as some pro-state competition advocates contend.

III. TAKEOVER LAW AND THE SUPPORTERS OF STATE COMPETITION

So far we have argued that state takeover law is consistent with the theory of state competition, outlined in Part I, which views such competition as problematic. We now make our point in another way—by showing how supporters of state competition are unable to square their position on state competition with their views on the type of takeover regulation that maximizes shareholder value.

As will become clear, the leading advocates of state competition are also vigorous supporters of a robust market for corporate control. As a result, there is a deep tension in their views. We begin by analysing the reasoning of four prominent proponents of state competition and how they try to reconcile their respective positions on state competition and takeovers. Then we will argue that their attempts at reconciling these two positions are unconvincing. We suggest that a more productive path would be for them to reconsider their position on state competition in the light of their own arguments concerning the substantial benefits takeovers can create for shareholders.

[29] Another example is the Code's rigid timetable for the completion of a tender offer. A takeover bid must be completed in no more than 102 days.

The dilemma facing supporters of state competition

The most prominent supporters of state competition—Ralph Winter, Frank Easterbrook, Daniel Fischel, and Roberta Romano—also simultaneously advocate a legal regime that facilitates, rather than frustrates, takeovers. The hostility of state law to takeovers therefore poses a serious problem. What would explain the poor record of states in the takeover area without undermining their general position on state competition? Assessing how successful they are in reconciling their facially inconsistent positions will go a long way towards determining how convincing their views are on the desirability of state competition. Accordingly, we will examine these pro-state competition scholars' arguments.

Ralph Winter

Ralph Winter (1977: 256) formulated the classic response to Cary's contention that state competition results in a 'race for the bottom' that harms shareholders. He built his critique on the observation that a corporation chartered in a state with an inefficient corporate code will have a lower rate of return on investment as a result (1989: 1526). Companies with sub-par rates of return will have greater difficulty raising capital (1977: 257), have less success in the product market, and be more likely to be the target of a takeover (264–6). The consequences of inferior returns created by inefficient corporate rules reduce managers' private benefits of control, including their job security. Managers accordingly have a strong incentive to ensure that the legal regime governing the operations of their corporation results in shareholders receiving the greatest possible return on their investment. In other words, in Winter's view, managers will maximize shareholder value out of self-interest.

At the same time, however, Winter expressed his general belief that a regime that facilitated takeovers maximized corporate profits (288). Profit maximization is obviously what shareholders, as residual claimants, typically want. Not surprisingly, he was critical of state anti-takeover statutes and, indeed, attributed part of the high cost of takeovers to the comparatively regulatory light-handed federal law (Williams Act, 15 U.S.C. §§ 78m(d)–(e), 78 n(d)–(f)) regulating tender offers. There was much for Winter to object to. Some 'first-generation' state anti-takeover statutes went so far as to prevent acquisitions of companies which had their principal place of business in the state unless a state official approved it.

In explaining how existing state anti-takeover law, which he disapproved of based on its effect on shareholder wealth, was consistent with his defence of state competition, Winter made several points—points that, as we shall see, have often been repeated by others. He stressed that Delaware's anti-takeover statute, by far the most important state statute on the subject, was relatively innocuous (289). More importantly, Winter claimed that whether federal regulation was appropriate in the takeover context was an issue 'quite different' from the arguments raised by Cary (270). Since existing state anti-takeover statutes typically had extraterritorial application—they applied to companies even if they were not chartered in the state—these laws, accordingly, implicated a 'chartering issue in only a peripheral sense' (289). Indeed, Winter believed that the extraterritorial features of anti-takeover statutes substantiated his basic contention that states competing for corporate charters have strong incentives to provide efficient corporate rules.

This last explanation, based on state anti-takeover statutes' extraterritorial application, is obviously inadequate to explain the reaction of states to the Supreme Court's decision in *MITE* (457 U.S. 627 1981), which called into serious question the constitutionality of these statutes. After this decision, the vast majority of states, including Delaware, quickly passed new anti-takeover legislation that was confined to companies chartered in the state. State anti-takeover law, as a result, can no longer be cabined from the rest of state corporate law in the way that Winter suggested. On the other hand, his other two arguments—that state anti-takeover law somehow raised different issues than other aspects of corporate law, and the reliance on Delaware's regulatory light touch—are ones that remain popular to this day with pro-state competition scholars.

Frank Easterbrook and Daniel Fischel

Frank Easterbrook and Daniel Fischel are also strong, even passionate, believers in state competition for corporate charters. Thus, in their academic work, they presume that doctrines produced by state competition are efficient (1983: 398). However, like Winter, they are vigorous supporters of takeovers and, as a result, strongly oppose the use of any and all defensive tactics by target management (1981), because regulation that allows managers to impede takeovers is unjustified and socially wasteful.

The inconsistency in their position is even more obvious than was the case with Winter. Easterbrook and Fischel have consistently argued, over a period of some fifteen years in numerous articles, that state competition generally produces efficient corporate rules (Easterbrook 1984; Easterbrook and Fischel 1983; 1991; Fischel 1982). Yet on this important issue state competition produces the opposite of what they strongly believe are desirable legal arrangements. To their credit, they candidly acknowledge the problem state anti-takeover legislation creates for their position, describing it as 'embarrassing' (Easterbrook and Fischel 1991: 221). The dilemma they face is painfully reflected in *Amanda Acquisition Corporation* v. *Universal Foods Corporation* (877 F.2d 496 (7th Cir. 1989)) where Judge Easterbrook, while considering the constitutionality of a state anti-takeover statute, forthrightly acknowledged the tension between his belief in both state competition and the folly of anti-takeover regulation.

However, Easterbrook and Fischel, at the end of the day, are only willing to concede that state anti-takeover regulation reveals that state competition is not perfect. State competition, they argue, creates efficient rules over a period of time. We must be patient and recognize that the 'long run takes time to arrive' (507). They identify the shortcoming in state competition, at least in the short run, with respect to takeover legislation as this: states that adopt anti-takeover laws are not penalized as much as perhaps they should be by competition from other states as investors will realize that any state can pass anti-takeover legislation mid-stream (Easterbrook and Fischel 1991: 222). State anti-takeover law, we are assured, is a 'special', though important, case (212).

Like Winter before them, Easterbrook and Fischel point to Delaware's anti-takeover statute. They stress that it is relatively mild compared to those of other states (222–3). This is used to substantiate the assertion that state competition, even in the takeover context, creates powerful incentives for states to enact efficient regulation.

Roberta Romano

Roberta Romano is another leading supporter of state competition. While avoiding taking a stand on the issue in her initial writings, she now characterizes state competition for corporate charters as the 'genius of American Corporate Law' (1993b: 1). Her belief in state competition is as strong as anyone's. Indeed, she has recently argued that securities law should be recast, based on the American corporate law model, so as to allow competition between chartering jurisdictions (1998).

Also, like Winter, Easterbrook, and Fischel, Romano views legal arrangements enabling managers to erect anti-takeover defences as inefficient. She acknowledges the 'dismal track records of most states in takeover regulation' (1992: 859). Is Romano any more successful in resolving the conflict?

In the course of defending the consistency of her position, Romano emphasizes that Delaware has been slow to adopt anti-takeover legislation, even though it typically has been a leader in most major corporate law reforms. Moreover, its anti-takeover statute is not as draconian as in other states, such as Pennsylvania's disgorgement statute (1993a: 855). Furthermore, Romano spends a great deal of time arguing that, whatever the imperfections of state regulation, any federal takeover law is likely to be worse.

This last defence is hardly a ringing endorsement of state competition. Rather than showing the 'genius' of American corporate law, it is rather an argument that we must live in a highly imperfect world. We find it hard to imagine that Romano, or indeed the other pro-state competition scholars we have discussed, would oppose a hypothetical federal statute that sharply limited the ability of states to restrict takeovers. Whether this is a realistic possibility is beside the point. Support for such a statute would underline the fact that state competition suffers from serious shortcomings. What, if anything, should be done about these shortcomings is another analytical question.

Why supporters of state competition should reconsider

One type of reaction by state competition supporters, as we have seen, views state takeover law as an anomaly, an exception, or an imperfection. This is most explicit in Easterbrook and Fischel's writings. The sentiment here seems to be that even a process that has strong structural reasons to function well can fail from time to time, and these failures do not imply that the process is not a good one.

But it is not clear that one can brush aside takeover law as an anomaly or an isolated failure, and comfortably continue to believe that state competition is such a great process. To start with, takeovers might well have been the most important issue with respect to which state corporate law has had to develop a position in the last twenty years.

If states have produced bad takeover law, this was not a fluke, a one-time isolated mistake. We are talking about a gradual process developing over quite a few years, in many steps and decisions, and with much attention and occupation by state officials along the way. There were several waves of anti-takeover statutes, all representing the persistent attempts by states to place impediments in front of takeovers with little or no support in the academic literature. And as for judicial decisions, this involved not one case, but rather an issue that has been visited and revisited over many years. If state competition has persistently produced bad, even indefensible, results concerning the most important corporate issue of recent times, how can we be confident that it performs well elsewhere?

All this means is that it is hard to brush this away as an anomalous exception and continue to think that state competition can reliably produce good results. Easterbrook and Fischel's explanation of why states have adopted inefficient takeover legislation—the fact that these were mid-stream legislative changes—is in no way limited to takeovers. Mid-stream changes are possible with respect to any legal rule, not just takeover regulation, that managers might wish to change. Moreover, mid-stream changes are not only possible through a state changing its corporate code, due, say, to campaign contributions, but by a corporation reincorporating to another state as well.

Another common reaction by supporters of state competition is to point out that Delaware has not been as extreme as some other states in its anti-takeover statute. This is true. But through case law, and in particular the approval of the poison pill, Delaware has erected formidable barriers to takeovers. Delaware's anti-takeover position has had, as it typically does, a central and very influential role. The use of poison pills is now very widespread. The debate is over the body of law produced by state competition. And while states differ somewhat in the extent to which they restrict takeovers, they all by and large go much further in that direction than Winter, Easterbrook, Fischel, and Romano would approve of.

While the pro-state competition view has a serious problem accounting for existing state takeover law, needing to rely on excuses and anomalies, the view that Cary held, and that we are advocating, has no problem whatsoever explaining this. Our concern with the possible shortcomings of state competition for corporate charters is not only consistent with the state takeover law that we observe but helps explain why state law has evolved in the regrettable direction that it has. By reconsidering their largely unqualified endorsement of state competition, its supporters can both gain a better explanation of why states have adopted restrictive takeover rules and retain their belief in the efficiency of a more permissive legal arrangement.

CONCLUSION

This chapter has sought to highlight the problems involved in state competition for corporate charters. On some important issues, states might have incentives to provide rules that are attractive to managers but not shareholders. Takeover law is one important area in which state competition might well have produced a body of law that excessively restricts takeovers. It is an area in which state competition is likely to fail. There are strong theoretical reasons to expect that state competition will work to produce a body of corporate law that excessively protects incumbent managers. The development of state takeover law, we have argued, is consistent with this view. It should lead the many who offer unqualified support for state competition to reassess their position.

5

Regulatory Competition in the US Federal System: Banking and Financial Services

JONATHAN R. MACEY

In this chapter, I will discuss the concept of federalism in the banking and financial services sectors from the narrow, and rather peculiar, way that the term 'federalism' is used to describe the contemporary federalist system of government in the United States. As I have observed before, federalism generally describes 'the complex relationship between the states and the federal government' (Macey 1990: 265). In principle, federalism 'restricts economic policymaking via limits on the discretion of government' (Weingast 1995: 3; Oates 1972; Tiebout 1956: 416–24). A properly functioning system of federalism appears to be highly correlated with economic success. As Barry Weingast (1995: 3) has observed, for much of the world's history over the past 300 years 'the richest nation on earth has had a federalist structure'.[1]

What the US system calls a federalist system, however, is hardly a federalist system at all. True federalist systems, as William Riker (1964) observes, are identified by two core characteristics. First, such systems have two (or more) levels of government ruling 'the same land and people'. Second, in such systems, each of the respective levels of government must have an autonomous, clearly defined scope of authority, so that each level of government operates with autonomy in its own sphere of political authority.

One of the principal advantages of a properly functioning federal system is that it better permits the costs and benefits associated with government regulation to be internalized or 'matched' more effectively (Butler and Macey 1996: 25). The idea is that where the costs of a particular economic or regulatory activity are confined to a limited area, then the government that is closest in scope to that area should regulate.

Here it is important to note that regulatory power should not necessarily track regulatory effects. In fact, often (as is the case with jurisdictional competition for corporate charters in the United States), regulation should not follow regulatory effects. For example, the regulatory effects of Delaware's corporate laws clearly are extraterritorial. However, it is efficient for Delaware to regulate corporate chartering because that state internalizes the costs and benefits generated by its production

[1] Citing, as examples, the Netherlands from the late sixteenth to the mid-seventeenth century, England from the early eighteenth to the mid-nineteenth century, and the United States from the nineteenth to the late twentieth century.

of corporate laws quite directly. The costs and benefits would not be as well internalized if regulatory authority were shifted to some other entity, such as the federal government. Thus regulatory authority should flow to the governmental unit that internalizes the costs and benefits associated with regulation regardless of where the effects of the regulation are internalized within the state.

This chapter seeks to make three points about federalism. Part I observes that the United States does not, in fact, have a true federalist system with respect to the regulation of banking and financial services. Regulatory authority is allocated on the basis of political power, not on the basis of constitutional principle. Part II makes the point that the government can *control* the allocation of costs and benefits associated with regulation by how it allocates regulatory authority. Part III applies the analysis here to the important area of stock exchange regulation. I argue that jurisdictional competition would work for stock exchanges as it works for corporate law. The US Securities and Exchange Commission (SEC) should, therefore, relinquish its regulatory control over stock exchanges, alternative trading systems, and the Intermarket Trading System, and allow the several states to regulate in this area. But it won't.

I. FEDERALISM IN THE UNITED STATES

At first glance, the United States appears to have a federalist system with respect to its laws governing banking and financial services. For example, the United States has a dual banking system. Banks can seek charters either from the Comptroller of the Currency at the national level or from any of the fifty-odd state banking supervisors at the state level (Macey and Miller 1997). The registration of securities and the continuous disclosure system for issuers, along with the anti-fraud provisions of the securities laws and the regulation of market professionals, all are carried out at the federal level (Romano 1998: 2361). But corporate governance is relegated to state law, and 'investors commit their funds to corporate directors on the understanding that . . . state law will govern the internal affairs of corporations' (*Sante Fe Indus.* v. *Green*, 430 US 462 (1975)); (*Cort* v. *Ash*, 422 US 66, 84 (1975)).

Thus, from a distance, the United States appears to have a complex, highly textured, regulatory system with respect to the delivery of banking and financial services regulation. However, the US system does not meet the minimum requirements for a federalist system articulated by William Riker and described above. Specifically, while the US system of government at both the state and the federal level satisfies the requirement that there be two levels of governmental rule over the same land and people, it fails to satisfy the requirement that each level be autonomous within its own sphere of political authority.

Under well-settled principles of US constitutional jurisprudence, the federal government has broad authority to displace local rules (Economist 1985: 1721; Van Alstyne 1985: 21). In particular, long-standing interpretations of the Supremacy

(Article VI)[2] and Commerce (Article I, § 8)[3] Clauses of the Constitution permit the federal government to displace local rules whenever it so chooses. Whatever modest limits there may be over the federal government's power in certain areas, there is absolutely no question that the central government has the power to pass laws that pre-empt state law.

The only limitation to federal power is that federal regulatory agencies still lack the power to unilaterally pre-empt state law. This principle is reflected in the landmark case, *Business Roundtable* v. *Securities and Exchange Commission* (905 F.2d 406 (D.C. Cir. 1990)), in which a US federal court denied the SEC the right to regulate the internal corporate governance of US corporations.

The legal battle in *Business Roundtable* v. *SEC* began with a decision taken in 1984 by General Motors (GM), a venerable New York Stock Exchange (NYSE) corporation, to change its capital structure by issuing a second class of common stock. This second class of GM common stock would have one-half vote per share, while the original class of GM stock had one vote per share. GM's proposed new class of common stock would have produced a capital structure which violated the rules of the NYSE that required listed companies to provide one vote per share of common stock.

For competitive reasons, the NYSE elected not to delist GM. Delisting would only have resulted in GM's shares being traded on the rival National Market System of the National Association of Securities Dealers. The NYSE did not want to enforce its rules at the risk of losing the listing fees and trading commissions of one of its most valuable customers. Instead, the NYSE asked the SEC for permission to change its one-share-one-vote rule.

The SEC declined to approve the NYSE's proposal. Instead, it ultimately substituted its own rule, SEC Rule 19c-4, which barred both national securities exchanges (like the NYSE) and national securities associations (like the NASD) from listing stock of a corporation that takes any corporate action 'with the effect of nullifying, restricting or disparately reducing the per share voting rights of [existing common shareholders]' (Voting Rights Listing Standards; Disenfranchisement Rule, 53 Fed. Reg. 26,376, 26,394 (1988)). The SEC's rule would have prohibited voting dilution of the kind that GM was proposing, even where approved by shareholder vote of the corporation.

In this important litigation, the SEC took the position that it had broad discretion to regulate the internal corporate governance of US firms. The DC Circuit Court of Appeals took a different view, finding that the SEC's attempt at rule-making in the area of shareholder voting 'would . . . overturn or at least impinge severely on the tradition of state regulation of corporate law' (*Business Roundtable*, 905 F.2d at 412).

[2] 'This Constitution, and the laws of the United States . . . shall be the supreme law of the land . . . anything in the constitution or laws of any state to the contrary notwithstanding.'

[3] '[T]he Congress shall have power . . . [t]o regulate commerce with foreign nations and among the several states, and with the Indian tribes.'

Thus, after *Business Roundtable* v. *SEC*, it is clear that there is at least one constraint on the power of the federal government to regulate the internal corporate governance of firms. However, this constraint is on regulatory agencies only. True, if Congress wanted to pre-empt state corporate law, it would have to be quite clear about what it was doing. But there is no question about the fact that the Commerce Clause gives Congress the power to displace the current US system of state regulation of internal corporate governance and thereby to eradicate the current system of jurisdictional competition for corporate charters. State law can only govern the internal affairs of corporations as long as Congress acquiesces in this allocation of governmental power (*Sante Fe Indus.*, 430 US at 479).[4]

As I have observed before, the United States does not have a true federalist system with respect to the provision of the legal rules concerning financial services law and banking because the states are not independent political actors (Macey 1990: 265). States have no autonomous sphere of power in which they can operate free of the spectre of being overridden by the central government.

This peculiar state of affairs raises a number of interesting questions. First, one must wonder why the federal government would ever cede regulatory authority to the states over an area as important as corporate law. After all, if the provision of regulation, as well as regulatory forbearance, are sources of political power—and they are—then why would the federal government ever give states this power? Similarly, under what circumstances should we expect to observe the federal government ceding regulatory authority to the states? And finally, one wonders what costs and benefits are associated with the current system: is there anything to recommend it from a normative perspective?

The answer to the first question, which concerns why the federal government would ever cede its power to the states, is simple. From the perspective of the political interests of federal regulators, power will be allocated to the states whenever the (political) benefits of delegating power are greater than the (political) costs. In the United States, at least for the moment, it seems that the benefits of giving the states power over such things as abortion policy and corporate governance outweigh the costs.

Turning to the second question, it should in fact be possible to specify, at least to some extent, the circumstances under which we would predict legislative power being allocated to the states. Generally speaking, state regulation will supplant regulation at the federal level under three conditions: (1) when a particular state (like Delaware) has developed a body of regulation that comprises a valuable capital asset and federal regulation would dissipate the value of that asset; (2) when the political-support maximizing outcome varies markedly from area to area due to the existence of spatial monopolies, variegated local political optima, and variations in voter preferences across regions (as is the case with local zoning laws); and (3)

[4] [E]xcept where federal law expressly requires, state law will govern the internal affairs of the corporation.'

where Congress can avoid potentially damaging political opposition from special-interest groups by allocating the responsibility for a particularly controversial issue to state and local governments (as is the case with the issue of abortion) (Macey 1990: 258).

In other words, the US form of federalism should properly be viewed as just another branch of administrative law. The same kinds of political factors that inform Congress's decision about whether to delegate a particular policy issue to a regulatory agency of the issue will also inform its decision whether to allocate a particular policy issue to the states or to retain control over the issue for itself. Of course, this is not the system that the founders of the US constitutional system wanted to create. The founders 'had a high regard for the autonomous existence of the states and intended the Constitution to guarantee this autonomy' (McConnell 1987: 1486). They intended a system of dual sovereignty. They did not get one, at least with respect to any issues that touch upon matters of commercial importance, as the law of banking, financial services, and corporations clearly does.

Finally, from a normative perspective, one might defend the US federalist system with the observation that a semblance of federalism is better than none at all. After all, with respect to corporate law, for example, the states have, to a large extent, retained their traditional regulatory powers. This has resulted in a robust jurisdictional competition for corporate charters among the states, which, in turn, has produced a dynamic and responsive set of corporate laws, without any sacrifice of the virtues of uniformity (Romano 1985: 225).

On the other hand, as Roberta Romano has shown, the US system of securities regulation is depressingly inefficient from a federalist perspective (Romano 1998: 2361). It would be possible to create a system of securities regulation that duplicates the system of competitive federalism that we observe in corporate law. Under the system proposed by Romano, issuers, who internalize the costs and benefits associated with the legal rules governing their securities offerings, would be able to select the state to which it allocates jurisdiction over all transactions in the issuers' securities. Under such a system, issuers of securities would benefit from the same robust, innovative, and responsive competition that characterizes the US market for corporate charters (Romano 1998: 2361).

In other words, from a normative perspective, the US system sometimes generates bad results. However, the above discussion was not meant to suggest that the right result is *always* regulation at the local level. In fact, as Henry Butler and I have observed elsewhere (1988: 677), in the field of banking regulation, the best policy outcomes will generally be obtained by taking regulatory authority away from the states and allocating it to the federal government. Similarly, in the case of insurance, there are situations in which regulation at the federal level may be necessary to protect competition (Macey and Miller 1993). A prime example of this is where states attempt to impose fees on insurance companies which attempt to exit from a state that imposes inefficient regulations, or prevent companies from implementing pricing policies that cope effectively with moral hazard problems.

II. GOVERNMENT CONTROL OVER THE COSTS AND BENEFITS OF REGULATION

The point of the above discussion has been to show that there is no clear a priori answer to the question of which level of government should have regulatory authority over a particular issue. Rather, regulatory authority should track economic effect. Where the economic effects of an activity are national or international, then regulation is best conducted at the national or international level. However, it will inevitably be the case that regulators will attempt to expand the size and scope of their bureaucratic turf by claiming that the bounds of a particular economic activity match their own regulatory jurisdiction. This much is well known (Niskanen 1971).

However, what is less well known is that, over a wide range of issues, particularly in the field of economic regulation, government regulation itself will determine the boundaries of a particular economic activity. Thus, while previous writing in the field of regulatory theory suggests that regulation should follow economic activity to the end of its impact and no further (Olson 1969; Posner 1982; Tullock 1969), here I show that, over a wide range of issues, the regulator can determine the actual scope of economic activity. When this happens, of course, then the government's claims about the presence or absence of extraterritorial effects associated with a particular activity become a sort of self-fulfilling prophecy.

The point here can be illustrated by looking at the allocation of regulatory authority in the United States over banking and insurance. Both the insurance industries and the banking industry are very heavily regulated. Regulatory responsibility over insurance companies is the subject of state regulation, while regulatory authority over banks is, primarily and increasingly[5] (though not exclusively), the subject of state regulation.

Students of federalism sometimes fail to observe that in the financial services area regulation follows contingent liability. Whichever level of government bears the contingent liability for the failure of a financial institution must have regulatory authority over that institution. For example, state regulators of insurance companies have established regulatory safety and soundness rules, minimum capital requirements for insurance companies, as well as state-managed and funded guaranty programmes. These regulatory systems restrict the types of assets in which an insurance company can invest, and have a wide range of regulatory weapons at their disposal to deal with insurance companies that are identified as having financial problems. These sanctions range from increased audits and 'jaw-boning' in minor cases at the lower end of the continuum, to formal orders requiring the insurance company to improve its financial condition by increasing its capital lev-

[5] For example, state regulatory authority to regulate such important issues as the bank capital and reserve requirements has been displaced. More recently, the states' ability to prevent the geographic expansion of banks through acquisitions by bank holding companies has been removed.

els or restructuring its investments in the middle range, to placing the institutions in conservatorship, receivership, or liquidation at the upper end of the continuum.

Similarly, with respect to capital levels, authority to determine an insurance company's level of capital and surplus is the responsibility of the insurance commissioner in the state where the company is domiciled (Macey and Miller 1993: 86). Beyond that, other states may decline to permit an insurance company to write policies in their state if its capital and surplus are not considered sufficient to provide adequate protection for policyholders.

Most importantly, for our purposes, is the fact that every state has established a regulatory system, roughly analogous to the better-known funds administered at the federal level by the Federal Deposit Insurance Corporation (FDIC). These funds cover policyholders in every state who purchase homeowners', automobile, and other property and casualty insurance policies (Gastel 1990: 81'). Beyond this coverage, virtually every state in the United States has guaranty funds that cover for policies written by life and health insurance companies. And, of course, most states have workers' compensation funds. Many of these programmes are, in fact, 'guaranty funds' in name only. Unlike the programmes administered by the FDIC, the states do not have permanent funds already in place in case a local insurance company experiences financial distress or insolvency. Rather, other insurance companies that participate in the programme will be assessed to cover payments to policyholders where the assets of the policyholders' own insurance company are not sufficient to cover such losses.

When one looks at the US insurance industry, it is clear that—contrary to extant theories of federalism—the regulatory structure of the industry, rather than the scope of the economic activity itself, establishes the appropriate scope of the externalities associated with insurance. Having established that the several states, rather than the federal government, bear the contingent risks and liabilities associated with insurance company insolvencies, it then becomes clear that the states should bear the regulatory responsibility for the safety and soundness of such institutions. If the federal government wants to assume regulatory responsibility for the insurance industry, it must assume the regulatory risks as well.

Where insurance provides an example of a situation in which the states have succeeded in staking out a claim to regulate a particular economic activity, banking provides an example of how regulation at the state level can be engineered to justify regulation at the federal level. It is well known that the United States operates, at least ostensibly, under a 'dual banking' system in which both the states and the federal government have the power to grant bank charters. Some have argued that the regulatory competition inherent in this dual state and federal system of chartering produces more flexible and efficient legal rules (Scott 1977). However, in my own joint work with Henry Butler (1988), we maintain that the theoretical ideal of the dual banking system is fundamentally at odds with the reality of the US system of federally sponsored, federally insured deposit insurance. Simply put, in 1933, when the federal system of deposit insurance was put into place, the states' justification for regulating the safety and soundness of banks disappeared entirely.

In fact, federal deposit insurance poses a clear moral hazard for state regulators. This moral hazard exists because the costs of lax state safety and soundness regulation are allocated among the fifty states, while the benefits of such lax regulation are enjoyed disproportionately within the state where the bank is located. The costs of lax state safety and soundness regulation come in the form of higher assessments on banks and taxpayers to pay for the higher incidence of bank failures that accompanies such lax regulation. The benefits of lax regulation come in the form of more relaxed lending policies and lower lending rates due to lower regulatory compliance costs. In other words, if left unchecked, having a federal system of deposit insurance, coupled with a state-based system of safety and soundness regulation, would result in a system in which state banking supervisors were free to conduct their own, home-grown, expansionary monetary policy at the expense of the federal fisc.

There is some evidence, particularly in the Southwest United States, that this sort of thing occurred during the 1980s. Specifically, insolvent banks were allowed to remain open long after they should have been closed from a safety and soundness perspective. By permitting such banks to remain open, state regulators increased the ultimate costs associated with resolving these insolvencies. However, these local regulators also succeeded in preventing distressed loans from being called in in a timely fashion, thereby postponing the foreclosure of mortgages and the closing of borrowers' businesses. This forbearance gave such borrowers the opportunity to take greater risks in order to try to restore their businesses to solvency, and also postponed layoffs and other politically unpopular exigencies. And, of course, federal deposit insurance permitted the state regulators to 'externalize' the costs associated with their forbearance strategy onto those supporting the federal deposit insurance scheme.

Consistent with these observations, the history of the dual banking system since 1933 has been a steady, relentless march towards federal regulation of all aspects of banking related to safety and soundness. This, of course, means that there has been a steady march towards federal pre-emption in all important aspects of banking regulation. These areas include the regulation of minimum capital requirements for banks, the regulation of reserve requirements for deposits, and the allocation of regulatory authority over the bank closure decision. All of these areas once were subject to the regulatory jurisdiction of state banking regulators, but federal law now controls all of these issues.

Even in areas only tangentially related to safety and soundness concerns, such as geographic expansion of banks, the dual state–federal banking system has not produced enviable results. States have systematically tried to restrict branching, and expansion via automatic teller machines (ATMs), when it has been in the interests of local banking interests to do so (*Bank One Utah Nat. Assoc.* v. *Guttau* 190 F.3d 844 (8th Cir. 1999)). For example, the state of Iowa recently attempted to enforce a statute preventing a Utah-based national bank from installing ATMs in retail stores in Iowa, including Sears Roebuck & Co. The Iowa Superintendent of Banking based his decision on a provision of Iowa law barring ATM operations by out-of-state banks that do not have in-state offices. The US Court of Appeals for the Eighth Circuit reversed the decision, finding that 1996 amendments to the National Banking Act clarified the fact that ATMs are not branches, and that state laws attempting to regulate the ATMs of federal banks had been pre-empted.

To summarize the argument to this point, in the financial services industry, it is not the intrinsic nature of the industry that determines whether regulation should be carried out at the local or the national level. Rather, the level of government that assumes the risks associated with regulation will also, inevitably, assume the responsibility for regulation. And, despite the considerable appeal of local regulation, in a federal system one must always be watchful of protectionism and other parochial attempts to capture local benefits from regulation while externalizing the costs of such regulation.

One might argue that many of the problems described here could be solved through deregulation. In particular, strong arguments can be made that the government should not be in the business of providing guarantees for insurance companies or banks at either the federal or the state level. The social costs of such insurance are high. Such insurance policies create significant moral hazards. It is argued that if the government got out of the business, consumers would be more careful about which companies they selected as their insurance carriers. Moreover, repealing these state guaranty schemes (and not replacing them with insurance at the federal level) would protect the states against the potentially catastrophic losses associated with the failure of a major insurance carrier. It would also eliminate the need for the costly and burdensome regulations now imposed on the banking industry in order to protect state governments against their massive contingent liabilities. However, both the states and the insurance industry have significant investments in the current regulatory scheme, and change of any kind is highly unlikely.

More importantly, there are political consequences associated with regulation. For politicians, permitting the failure of a major insurance company would be very costly from a political perspective. Having assumed regulatory and supervisory responsibility for the insurance industry in the eyes of the public, permitting large-scale failures within the industry would reflect very badly on the competence of the administration under whose jurisdiction such failures occurred. In other words, as a matter of *real politik*, once the government is seen to have assumed responsibility over a particular economic activity, such as insurance or banking, then widespread losses by the customers (taxpayers) become very costly politically.

Thus far, this chapter has provided two additional ways to look at US federalism. Traditionally, from a normative perspective, federalism has been viewed as a mechanism for coping with the challenges posed by externalities. The most obvious example of this is the case of pollution, particularly water and air pollution, which in many cases extends beyond the boundaries of a particular state. Here national solutions at the federal level are called for, so that economic actors in one state are not permitted to externalize the costs of their activities on the citizens of other states. Similarly, of course, where the effects of a particular economic activity are confined within a single state, regulatory authority over that state should be confined to that state. By keeping regulation over local matters confined to the local level, regulatory responses will be more efficient both because such responses can be better tailored to local preferences and because local conditions can be taken into account to arrive at lower-cost solutions.

However, despite these rather obvious normative insights about how regulatory authority ought to be allocated between the federal government and the states, we see that, as a practical matter, the pattern of regulation that we actually observe does not resemble the normative, theoretical, ideal. Local matters are increasingly regulated by the federal government. Moreover, we see situations, such as the jurisdictional competition for corporate charters, in which local regulation of a matter (corporate law) with striking extraterritorial national effects is best regulated by states because the states internalize the costs and benefits associated with their own regulatory schemes (Romano 1985).

Adding to our understanding of US federalism, I wish to observe first that government can create and define the appropriate contours of regulation by the very act of regulating. As shown above in the context of local (state) regulation of the insurance industry, by establishing guaranty funds at the state level, states have established for themselves regulatory authority over insurance companies because the existence of these guaranty schemes means that the costs associated with the failure of an insurance company are now internalized within the state in which the insurance agency is established.

Second, it is clear that states can also lay claim to having regulatory authority over particular issues by creating political expectations that these issues are their responsibility. In other words, states can stake a claim to having regulatory authority over a particular area by taking actions far short of actually setting themselves up with contingent liability by establishing a state guaranty fund for customers of a particular industry. In the case of insurance, for example, the establishment of minimum capital rules and a system of safety and soundness regulation may create the expectation of government protection and supervision in the minds of the public. This, in turn, will mean that the political costs associated with bad outcomes in the face of such regulation will be internalized locally.

This observation about political accountability appears to hold generally. The point can easily be illustrated by comparing the regulatory systems in the United States and the European Union. For example, in the United States, regulatory authority over nuclear power plants is vested with an agency of the federal government, the US Nuclear Regulatory Commission (NRC). The NRC is an independent agency established by the US Congress under the Energy Reorganization Act of 1974 'to ensure adequate protection of the public health and safety, the common defense and security, and the environment in the use of nuclear materials in the United States. The NRC's scope of responsibility includes regulation of—commercial nuclear power reactors; nonpower research, test, and training reactors fuel cycle facilities; medical, academic, and industrial uses of nuclear materials; the transport, storage, and disposal of nuclear materials and waste' (http://www.nrc.gov/NRC/about.html).

By contrast, in the European Union, individual member states have the authority to license and monitor the nuclear reactors within their borders. This means that, despite the obvious extraterritorial effects that would be associated with an event at a European nuclear reactor site, from both a practical as well as a moral perspective, the awesome responsibility for regulating nuclear power facilities is allocated to the individual member states where such facilities are located.[6]

III. THE PROPER SCOPE OF REGULATORY AUTHORITY OVER STOCK EXCHANGES

The above discussion has touched on three types of heavily regulated activities: insurance, banking, and the provision of nuclear power. As argued above, in each of these areas, there is a very strong sense that citizens in a democracy are entitled to protection from the risks of harm associated with each of these economic endeavours. Whether it is desirable from a normative perspective that people have these expectations is beside the point. Rightly or wrongly, this set of expectations must be taken into account when policy choices are made, because in a democracy the careers of regulators and politicians will depend on whether citizens' expectations with respect to these issues have been met or exceeded. This reality indicates that, at times, second-best decisions will be necessary. For example, while eliminating deposit insurance for bank deposits might be a good idea in a perfect world, in the real world deposit insurance can be defended because it sets a limit or upper bound on people's expectations about what they will receive in the case of bank insolvency. In other words, deposit insurance can best be justified on the grounds that it places a ceiling on the government's commitment to bail out depositors. Absent such insurance, political pressure is likely to cause government officials to bail out all depositors, regardless of size, in order to maintain public confidence in the banking system. In other words, deposit insurance can be justified because it 'enables a democratic government to make a credible commitment . . . ex ante that limits the amount of the government's exposure to the amount of the guarantee' (Macey and Miller 1995).

However, this argument does not appear to obtain to the case of the regulation of stock exchanges and electronic trading systems. Unlike people who live in the

[6] There is some regulation at the European level, such as the requirement in Articles 2 and 3 of the Council Directive 85/337/EEC for an Environmental Impact Statement before decommissioning a nuclear facility. However, regulatory supervision, as well as the basic decisions about commissioning and decommissioning power plants, is left to the regulatory discretion of the individual member states (Complaint of Sydkraft AB for Itself and as the Owner of Barsebäck Kraft AB, 20 August 1999).

shadow of a nuclear power plant, or deposit money in a cheque account at a US bank, or buy homeowners' insurance, people who invest in the stock market have no particular expectation that the government will protect them from loss. It is well known that the SEC, which regulates the securities markets, does not guarantee investor losses, even in the case of fraud. Thus the expectations-driven allocation of regulatory authority described in this chapter does not appear to obtain with respect to the regulation of exchanges and alternative trading systems.

Moreover, there is strong reason to believe that local provision of stock exchange rules would produce the same positive results as local provision of corporate law rules. Just as issuers have a strong incentive to locate in states with efficient corporate law rules in order to lower transaction costs, so too do issuers have incentives to locate their trading activity to venues where the costs of trading are low. And, as is the case with jurisdictional competition for corporate charters, there are significant potential benefits to states that produce efficient trading rules for investors.

In a recent and highly influential article on securities regulation, Professor Romano (1998: 2361) has argued vigorously and persuasively in favour of extending jurisdictional competition for corporate charters to cover the registration of securities, corporations' continuous disclosure obligations, and the anti-fraud provisions associated with such registration and ongoing disclosure. However, Romano stops short of advocating such a system for securities exchanges, claiming that the benefits of regulatory competition would be 'far more attenuated for exchanges than for issuers' since exchanges are able to compete effectively now.

Professor Romano's assertion that the benefits from regulatory competition in the areas of disclosure and other issuer-related matters are greater than the benefits from regulatory competition among exchanges is undoubtedly correct. The waste associated with the current system of mandatory disclosure is enormous. However, it is important to recognize the extent to which the SEC uses its regulatory authority over stock exchanges to stifle competition and to promote uniform rules, like fixed commission schedules, that stifle competition by effectively cartelizing the industry (Phillips and Zecher 1981: 53–89; Romano 1998: 2371). The price collusion among traders in stocks quoted on the NASD's National Market System (the 'odd-eighth quote' imbroglio) was not investigated by the SEC until two finance professors identified this anti-competitive practice in an article in an academic journal (Christie and Schultz 1994). An embarrassed SEC censured the NASD two years later (*In re National Assoc. of Sec. Dealers, Inc.*, Exchange Act Release No. 37,538 (1996)).

More importantly, it is quite clear that the already vigorous competition among exchanges and other trading venues is becoming even more intense. The SEC recently adopted new regulations that permit alternative trading systems (ATSs) to register as national securities exchanges. Prior to these new regulations, the SEC permitted such systems to register as broker-dealers, and limited exchange status to firms that permitted members a voice in the operation and management of the system.

Under recently enacted SEC Rule 3b-16, an exchange is now defined as any 'organization, association or group of persons that: (1) brings together the orders of multiple buyers and sellers; (2) uses established, non-discretionary methods under which such orders interact with each other; and (3) the buyers and sellers entering such orders agree to the terms of trade' (Securities Exchange Act Release No. 40760 (1998); 63 Fed. Reg. 70843 (1998); Securities Exchange Act Rule 3b-16). The SEC now characterizes as an exchange not only those firms that hold themselves out as maintaining a continuous two-sided market and regularly executing orders at quoted prices, but also trading systems that permit buyers and sellers to interact among themselves pursuant to prescribed sets of rules, protocols, and procedures. Thus an automated trading system that permits subscribers to buy or sell securities on the basis of an offer or a bid posted on a computer system, a system that accepts unpriced orders for securities and executes them on the base of a price obtained from another market, or obtained by looking at an index, interest rate, or other variable (such as the weighted average trading price for the security on a specific date),[7] as well as auction pricing systems, would be considered an exchange under the SECs new rules.

Trading systems characterized as exchanges are subject to a variety of rules that did not apply when such systems were regulated as broker-dealer firms. These obligations include self-regulatory responsibilities such as the responsibility for enforcement of participants' compliance with the federal securities laws, and the 'fair' representation of various constituencies in the exchange's corporate governance (including the requirement that trading systems that are characterized as exchanges have at least one 'public' member).

In addition, trading systems that are characterized as exchanges will no longer be able to permit institutional investors who are not registered broker-dealer firms to become members or direct participants in their systems. This rule cannot be supported or understood on any basis other than as a naked attempt to benefit the broker-dealer cartel by barring such institutional investors from trading directly by forcing them to use broker-dealer firms as intermediaries. In fact, the SEC does allow 'give-up' arrangements in which broker-dealer firms that are exchange members provide institutional members with access to proprietary trading systems in exchange for order flow.

It is sometimes thought that the basic problem with the current regulation of trading systems is that issuers do not have control over trading in their own securities, much less over trading in the derivative instruments whose prices are derived from their securities (Amihud and Mendelson 1996). Over a wide range of policy issues, the preferences of issuers will diverge from the preferences of exchanges and other participants in secondary market trading. This is because issuers will want to be able to make a credible commitment to purchasers that secondary-market

[7] The POSIT (Portfolio System for Institutional Traders) system is an example of the type of system that I am attempting to describe here.

trading costs will be kept low. Issuers able to make such credible commitments will enjoy lower capital costs. By contrast, participants in secondary markets have strong incentives to profit by keeping trading costs (such as wide bid-asked spreads and high commissions) high, since such high trading costs translate into higher profits for secondary market participants.

The reason why removing regulatory responsibility from the SEC and transferring it to the states would be a good idea is because the SEC's natural constituency is the investment banking and trading community, rather than issuers. In fact, there is some evidence that the SEC has been captured by the trading community, and is therefore unlikely to produce the exchange rules that are best for investors (Haddock and Macey 1987). And it is well known that the SEC regularly consults privately with top investment bankers and other securities industry officials before proposing rule changes that affect the trading in issuers' securities. Recently, for example, press reports revealed that the chairmen of Goldman Sachs Group, Inc., Merrill Lynch & Co., and Morgan Stanley Dean Witter and Co. were all privately consulted and all received advance copies of SEC Chairman Arthur Levitt's recent policy proposals concerning major changes to the rules related to secondary securities trading (Wall Street Journal 1999). There is no evidence that the SEC is similarly attentive to the policy preferences of issuers, despite the clear conflicts between the preferences of such issuers and those of investment bankers.

Courts have been similarly inattentive to the property rights of issuers. In *Golden Nugget, Inc.* v. *AMEX*, 828 F.2d 586 (9th Cir. 1987), for example, an issuer, whose shares were listed on the New York Stock Exchange, sued to block trading in options on its stock by the American Stock Exchange and the Options Clearing Corporation without its consent. The US Court of Appeals for the Ninth Circuit rejected the argument that property rights over trading privileges in a corporation's stock and in derivatives whose value is derived from the value of that stock should be allocated to the issuer.

The SEC's regulatory responsibility over exchanges and secondary market trading, and judicial rulings such as the one in *Golden Nugget*, undermine the ability of issuers to fulfil their fiduciary duties to maximize shareholder value, because they prevent issuers from crafting the trading rules and from selecting the trading venues that best enhance liquidity for investors. At the moment, regulatory authority is vested in an administrative agency and a constellation of self-regulatory organizations whose incentives are to keep transaction costs high. Indeed, these groups see as profits what issuers and traders view as transaction costs.

Thus, like Romano's argument that corporations should be able to select their securities regulator from among the fifty states, I believe that corporations should also be able to specify for themselves where their securities should be traded and which securities laws (state or federal) should apply to such trading.

It is important to recognize the limits of the proposal being made here. The proposal is limited to allocating to issuers and to states regulatory authority over trading venues and trading rules. There are significant economies of scale associated with monitoring the anti-fraud rules, anti-manipulation rules, and, particularly, the rules against insider trading. These economies of scale in enforcement suggest that monitoring of trading activities and the regulation of market professionals should remain centralized. It is not at all clear that the current system, in which US equities are increasingly being traded in multiple venues, makes enforcement of trading rules more difficult. Indeed, there are clear benefits as well as costs associated with this system. The benefits come in the form of vigorous price competition and intense incentives to innovate technologically in order to offer the best possible trading system from a technical point of view.

However, while multi-venue trading fosters competition, it also generates costs, which come in the form of fragmentation and free-riding. For some firms, the benefits of competition outweigh the costs. For such firms, multi-venue trading systems will be preferred to single-venue ones. For others, the costs of fragmentation and free-riding associated with multi-venue trading will outweigh the benefits. Such firms should be able to confine their trading to a single forum. At the moment, firms are unable to do this. Currently, regional exchanges have the right to act unilaterally to obtain trading privileges in securities that are listed on other securities exchanges, regardless of whether the issuer or the exchange on which the security is listed objects (15 U.S.C. § 781(f)).[8] While this rule may serve the interests of increasing trading liquidity by fostering competition among traders in the stock of certain firms, it may reduce liquidity where the costs of fragmentation outweigh the benefits of competition among rival market-makers.

Perhaps most important is the fact that increased competition and new technologies are causing rapid and dramatic changes in the securities markets. Regulation is stifling innovation. Competition among states and issuers would improve the situation by creating strong incentives to innovate.

CONCLUSION

The financial services industry in the United States is subjected to a highly complex, widely variegated system of regulation. Starting at the bottom, insurance companies are regulated at the state level. Banks are regulated at both the state and the national level. Over time, however, the national component of the regulatory mix has systematically displaced the local component, particularly in areas touching on banks' safety and soundness. The securities industry is regulated at the federal level, although a vestige of state-level regulation survived the Depression-era Securities Acts.

Current normative theories of federalism posit that regulation should track externalities. The assumption of such theories is that the presence or absence of

[8] Eliminating the requirement that SEC approval be obtained before unlisted trading privileges are granted.

extraterritorial effects is endogenous to a particular economic activity. In this chapter, I have argued that regulation is an exogenous event that can change the extraterritorial effects associated with an economic activity. Thus for many activities, such as insurance and banking, it is not the intrinsic nature of the industry that determines whether regulation should be carried out at the local or the national level. Rather, the level of government that assumes the risks associated with regulation will also, inevitably, assume the responsibility for regulation. Thus, since state governments have assumed the contingent liabilities associated with regulating (and insuring) the insurance industry, then the states should be the primary regulators for that activity. By contrast, since the federal government has assumed the risks associated with regulating (and insuring) the banking industry, it should be the primary regulator of the nation's banks.

Moreover, I have argued that, over time, the public has developed clear, precisely contoured expectations with respect to the government's responsibilities in certain areas, such as banking, insurance, and the control of the risks associated with the generation of nuclear power. Regardless of efficiency arguments in favour of deregulation, in a democracy politicians ignore citizens' well-settled expectations at their peril.

However, unlike the situation in the banking and insurance industries, there are no such well-entrenched expectations about the role of government in the area of securities regulation. Securities trading operates on a much more *laissez-faire* foundation. This chapter endorses Roberta Romano's proposal to extend the same system of jurisdictional competition for corporate charters that exists for corporate governance to the registration of securities, corporations' continuous disclosure obligations, and the anti-fraud provisions associated with such registration. However, Romano has described the benefits associated with regulatory competition among exchanges as 'attenuated' (Romano 1998: 2371). I think that Romano may have underestimated the salutary effects of the increased competition among exchanges and ATSs that would come from removing regulatory authority from the SEC and allocating it to the states and to issuers. For this reason, I favour extending her proposal to cover exchanges as well, subject to the caveat that the monitoring of fraud and the regulation of market professionals be centralized due to the likely presence of significant economies of scale in enforcement in these areas.

6

Labour Federalism in the United States: Lessons for Coordinated Decentralization in Supranational Regimes

MARK BARENBERG*

United States domestic law—like the domestic law of many other federal nation-states—has for decades rested on the settled principle that core labour rights, enforced by the central government, are fundamental constituents of a multi-state common market. The US Supreme Court and the US Congress have explicitly embraced the idea that substandard labour conditions are a form of illegitimate subsidy to low-wage employers and that the federal government is therefore justified in prohibiting interstate traffic in goods produced under such conditions (*West Coast Hotel* v. *Parrish*, 300 U.S. 379 (1937); *NLRB* v. *Jones & Loughlin Steel Co.*, 301 U.S. 1 (1937); *United States* v. *Darby*, 312 U.S. 100 (1941)). Over three or four decades beginning in the mid-1930s, that idea animated the relatively successful implementation of a federal policy enforcing core labour rights. In the last third of the twentieth century, while that formal policy commitment and its regulatory shell persisted, its actual implementation faded away (Gross 1995).

Whether core labour rights can and should be integrated into supranational rules of economic governance even as a formal matter, however, remains a hotly contested policy question. The labour side agreement of the North American Free Trade Agreement (NAFTA) has proved more robust than its detractors initially supposed, but still too weak to satisfy US labour unions sufficiently to blunt their opposition to further economic integration in the Western Hemisphere. By contrast, the European Union, from the Tripartite Employment Conferences of the 1970s to the Treaty of Amsterdam of 1998, has pursued an incremental, iterative process of coordinating member states' labour and employment policies (Goetschy 1999). Nonetheless, the EU social dialogue remains distinctly subordinate to the already advanced project of building an 'economic constitution' through the integration of markets in goods, services, and finance and through the harmonization of monetary and fiscal policy on a Europe-wide basis. At the Seattle Ministerial Meeting of the World Trade Organization (WTO) in November 1999, of course, the controversy over linking core labour rights to trading rules proved a serious obstacle to the launch of a new round of negotiations on global economic liberalization. Ministers representing the governments of low-wage countries emphatically rejected the idea, embedded in the US jurisprudence of domestic 'labour

* Thanks, for their helpful feedback and discussion, to Brian Bercusson, David Charny, Dan Esty, Rob Howse, Chuck Sabel, and Kathy Stone.

federalism', that substandard labour conditions may constitute an unfair trade practice.

The rise and demise of multi-state harmonization of core labour rights in US domestic law occurred in a political and economic environment markedly different from that of the projects of economic integration in contemporary Europe, North America, the Western Hemisphere, and the world. The theory of regulatory competition suggests, nonetheless, that there may be sufficient commonalities in the dynamics of multi-state systems, at least when modelled at a sufficiently broad level, to make comparative analysis of domestic federal regimes a worthwhile exercise for shedding light on some of the contested questions of policy at the regional and global levels.

Indeed, this chapter contends that the twentieth-century path of US labour federalism points to politico-economic processes that need greater emphasis than previously given in broad-gauged, deductive models of regulatory competition, whether applied at the domestic or multinational level. I draw these lessons from a survey of the US regulatory institutions aimed at federal redistribution of income and wealth, by means of legal encouragement of collective bargaining. A comprehensive picture of federal redistribution through legal regulation of workplace governance, labour markets, and factor returns would include many additional branches of employment law, social insurance, tax and transfer policies, macroeconomic policy, and so on. This chapter's focus on federal rights of collective bargaining is nonetheless a particularly appropriate starting point, for at least two reasons.

First, the current debate over international labour standards is itself focused on whether the fundamental right of worker association (that is, collective organizing and bargaining) should be codified in regional and global trade regimes. Second, the story of federalized rights of collective bargaining seems especially relevant in light of the contemporary interest in centralized regulatory regimes that facilitate decentralized ordering through negotiation and deliberation—through regulatory competition *and* coordination—among public and private entities.[1] Indeed, collective bargaining—regulated by federal public institutions, but implemented through a mix of adversarial bargaining and deliberative problem-solving by private actors at local, industry, regional, national, or even supranational levels—is in many ways the legal-institutional forerunner of such regimes. In the European Union, supranational collective agreements, 'social dialogue' between European-wide union and employer confederations, and EU-supported regional employment pacts remain today among the most interesting

[1] Conceptualization of these regimes ranges from the theories of 'co-opetition' and 'reflexive regulation', both represented in contributions to this volume (Esty and Geradin, Ch. 2; Deakin, Ch. 9), to the theories of 'comitology' (Evans 1998) and 'democratic experimentalism' (Barenberg 1994; Dorf and Sabel 1998). The remainder of this chapter uses the term 'coordinated decentralization' to denote this family of regimes.

examples of centrally coordinated, yet locally divergent, multi-tier architectures (Bercusson, Ch. 11; Goetschy 1999).[2]

Using the experience of US labour federalism as a springboard, this chapter offers five broad lessons for the design of a supranational architecture for the enforcement of core labour rights through coordinated decentralization. First, a key dynamic of regulatory regimes aimed at redistributive goals is the 'endogeneity of interest groups'. That is, regulatory rules for large-scale redistribution promise to alter the relative power of interest groups, even while those groups act strategically to alter the substance and enforcement of the regulatory rules. Particularly in regimes of coordinated decentralization, the specific institutional design will generate self-reinforcing cycles which either strengthen redistributive regulation and concurrently strengthen the interest groups benefited thereby, or weaken redistributive regulation while strengthening the interest groups that would otherwise suffer from redistribution.

Second, the trajectory of such self-reinforcing cycles depends heavily on the path-dependent 'mechanisms of coordination' that span the central and local tiers of the regulatory regime. These mechanisms constitute the institutional infrastructure of communication, deliberation, and bargaining that determines whether 'coordination' among regulatory actors will yield collaborative upward races or collusive downward races. In US labour federalism, these institutions include political parties, labour and business federations, multi-state corporate and financial organizations, the multi-tier administrative organs formally charged with enforcement of labour rights, as well as innumerable other public and private entities. At the supranational level, the relevant institutions of coordination include the obvious analogues of these domestic mechanisms, as well as private international non-governmental organizations (NGOs), public international bodies such as the International Labour Organization (ILO), WTO, and international financial institutions, and unilateral trans-state instruments such as trade sanctions and financial leverage deployed by the United States and the European Union.

Third, redistribution by means of coordinated decentralization of core labour rights poses a more specific challenge to the design of such mechanisms of coordination. Because core labour rights include rights of association in civil society, the regime must 'bootstrap' local regulatory participation (the exercise of substantive civil rights of association) and central regulatory representation (the exercise of procedural democratic rights of association). The challenge for institutional design—domestic or supranational—is to enable those central and decentralized actors already committed to associational rights to 'discipline' or 'incentivize' those actors not so committed, and to disable the reverse process—toward the ultimate goal of diminishing rather than widening any prevailing 'democracy deficits' at the central or local levels.

[2] Note that Simon Deakin's chapter in this volume presents the EU Directive on European Works Councils as a paradigm of 'reflexive regulation' (Deakin, Ch. 9).

Fourth, the US experience reveals that the normative problem of whether core labour rights should be enforced at the central or local level in multi-state systems cannot be resolved by simple notions of 'sovereign self-determination'. Rather, answering that normative question inevitably requires debate over contested substantive values of democracy, distributive justice, deontological rights, social well-being, and the like.

Finally, the US experience shows that this difficult normative inquiry is made even more complex and uncertain, in light of as yet unresolved theoretical and empirical debates about the sources of economic growth and organizational innovation in the contemporary period.

These lessons from the experience of US labour federalism are set out in Part III of this chapter. Part I first introduces the conceptual project of designing multi-tier institutions that are based on coordinated decentralization. Part II then provides a brief summary of the institutions of US labour federalism, and of their empirical rise and fall in the twentieth century, in order to provide points of reference for Part III's analysis of the lessons for supranational regimes enforcing core labour rights.

I. THE CONCEPTUAL PROBLEM: WHICH MECHANISMS OF COORDINATION AMONG PUBLIC AND PRIVATE ACTORS WILL ENCOURAGE UPWARD RACES IN REDISTRIBUTIVE PROGRAMMES?

The basic normative question posed by the theory of regulatory competition is familiar: when is central (federal) regulation superior to regulation at the local (multiple-state) level? In most areas of regulation, 'superiority' is defined as maximization of aggregate welfare, typically measured by maximization of monetary wealth. In US labour law, however, the normative superiority of the regulatory regime is measured by its achievement of two explicit legislative purposes other than wealth maximization. Those two purposes are, in labour and capital markets, redistribution of income from investors to workers; and, in workplace governance, redistribution of decision-making power from the exclusive control of collective representatives of investors (managers) to joint determination with collective representatives of workers (unions) (Barenberg 1993).

In the most pristine models of regulatory competition, local sovereigns compete among themselves by offering alternative packages of taxation and regulatory programmes to more or less mobile 'consumers' of those packages. The 'consumers' are households and businesses, or providers of labour and capital (factors of production). The normative question is: will regulation through centralized collective action prove superior—against the yardsticks of wealth maximization, redistribution, or other relevant regulatory purposes—to the decentralized 'market for regulation'? The pristine models of regulatory competition assume that action at the federal level takes the form of vertical public imposition—that is, centralized collective action that harmonizes or uniformly pre-empts regulation by local sovereigns—while regulation at the local level entails horizontal, wholly uncoordinated public and private action by local sovereigns and private households and businesses responding to the price, output, and quality of the regulatory 'product'.

The more elaborate models of 'regulatory co-opetition', 'reflexive regulation', 'comitology', and 'democratic experimentalism', to the contrary, assume that *coordinated* action can take more complex forms than centralized harmonization.[3] These models highlight the ways in which private and sovereign actors may communicate, bargain, and cooperate both horizontally and vertically. Federal regulation, in turn, is not exclusively a matter of central harmonization of substantive rules and central enforcement of those rules, but may take the form of central coordination of divergent local standards and enforcement mechanisms. At the same time, federal regulation is not limited to central *diktat* directed at local sovereigns or private actors, but may entail ongoing exchange of information, mutual monitoring, experimentation with and revision of regulatory mechanisms, and collaborative goal setting among complex coalitions of public and private entities at multiple tiers and across territorial boundaries.

It is important to note that the pristine versions of regulatory competition by no means rule out such complex patterns of coordinated action. Indeed, a fundamental question in standard Coasian analysis is whether centralized regulation is rendered unnecessary by communication and bargaining among those parties who may be hurt or helped by externalities produced when actors exercise their background legal entitlements. Coasian bargaining is therefore one way to conceptualize the kind of coordinated action among public and private entities that is given greater emphasis in such theories as co-opetition, reflexivity, comitology, and experimentalism. The latter theories, however, have the advantage of explicitly opening the black box containing the mechanisms of coordinated action.

By 'mechanisms of coordinated action', I mean: (1) the specific institutional environment that allocates opportunities, incentives, and resources for communication, bargaining, and deliberation among the relevant public and private parties, (2) the inherited cultures—the preferences structures and cognitive maps—that influence whether the parties' communication and bargaining will yield superior outcomes (welfare enhancement, egalitarian redistribution, or achievement of other regulatory goals) or inferior outcomes (collusive rent-seeking, maldistribution, or subversion of other regulatory goals); and (3) the ways in which these institutional and cultural environments, *over time, encourage or discourage learning and innovation* that may enhance regulatory capacities to achieve superior outcomes and improve democratic processes for determining regulatory goals.[4] Taken together, these mechanisms comprise the institutional architecture that determines whether

[3] See above, note 1.

[4] The twin emphases on innovation of both regulatory means and ends and on democratic participation in regimes of coordinated decentralization are especially strong in theories of 'democratic experimentalism' (Barenberg 1994; Cohen and Sabel 1998; Sabel 1995).

regulatory competition and coordination will encourage upward or downward regulatory races, and whether the regulatory process will promote or diminish democratic participation and representation.

What, then, can the history of US labour federalism teach us about the institutional architecture that may encourage democratic regulatory races toward the top rather than undemocratic races toward the bottom in coordinated, decentralized regimes (top and bottom defined by the posited goal of redistributing income and decision-making power from investors to workers)?

II. EMPIRICAL POINTS OF REFERENCE: FIVE PHASES OF US LABOUR FEDERALISM

As points of reference for the conceptual analysis in Part III, this Part sets out five phases in the development of US labour federalism in the twentieth century.

Before the 1930s, US constitutional law prohibited affirmative regulatory protection of collective bargaining rights at either the federal or state level (Forbath 1991). The courts ruled, under the doctrine of substantive due process, that such state protection amounted to an interference with the liberty of contract of both employers and employees. This does not mean that labour relations were unregulated or unchanging before the 1930s. Rather, the distributive contest between employer and employee was regulated by the states' common law rules of contract, property, and tort, and by state and federal rules of fair competition and antitrust. The 1932 Norris–LaGuardia Act marked the successful culmination of a decades-long campaign to exempt labour union activity from federal court injunctions under the antitrust laws. Labour unions might lawfully organize and strike, while employers retained their common law privilege to discharge and blacklist union activists and strikers. Hence this first phase can be called the period of 'voluntaristic' collective bargaining. The law authorized each side to use a wide range of self-help weapons to achieve or stave off collectivized 'relational contracts' in the labour market.

In the second phase, 1933–40, the New Deal introduced the current policy of uniform federal encouragement of collective bargaining for purposes of class redistribution and 'industrial democracy' (Barenberg 1993). This encouragement took the form of legal prohibition of employer reprisal against the exercise of workers' rights collectively to organize, bargain, and strike. Further, the new federal law affirmatively required that employers bargain with any union chosen by the majority of workers in a government-approved bargaining unit. The National Labor Relations Board (NLRB) and the federal courts fleshed out these rules and deployed coercive sanctions to enforce them—at least after 1937, when the Supreme Court, reversing its jurisprudence of substantive due process, first ruled that the federal and state legislatures were constitutionally permitted to change common law rules of contract and property for redistributive purposes (*NLRB* v. *Jones & Laughlin Steel Co.*, 301 U.S. 1 (1937)). From the point of view of contemporary global trade law, the

Court's reasoning is significant. Before 1937, the Court characterized minimum labour rights and standards as an illegitimate interference with the competitive market, interference which effectively required employers to 'subsidize' employees and the community (*Adkins* v. *Children's Hospital*, 261 U.S. 525 (1923)). After 1937, the Court turned that terminology upside down and adopted the theory that workers and the community paid a 'subsidy' to employers who maintained substandard labour conditions (*West Coast Hotel* v. *Parrish*, 300 U.S. 379 (1937)). The Court thereby recognized low labour standards as an unfair trade practice, subject to regulation precisely through Congressional exercise of its power to regulate interstate commerce. This conceptualization, which remains firmly lodged in the jurisprudence of US labour federalism, is the precise theory rejected by contemporary opponents of linkage between international trade and labour rules.

The New Deal labour policy both responded to and galvanized employee support for industrial unionism. Nonetheless, it was only during World War II—the third phase of US labour federalism—that unions embraced a sufficiently large portion of the industrial workforce to pose the possibility that the US unions would become the kind of encompassing organizations that underpinned the national or sectoral 'social dialogues' and 'neocorporatism' of postwar European social democracy, later raised to the level of formal EU policy. The spread of unionism in World War II resulted from direct government intervention aimed at uninterrupted economic mobilization for the war effort, and from the indirect strengthening of workers' bargaining power in the overheated wartime labour market (Atleson 1998; Lichtenstein 1982).

The fourth phase—roughly 1945–68—was marked by the unions' failure to achieve the promise of formal neocorporatist bargaining based on comprehensive union organization of the national workforce. The arrested, fragile equilibrium in the nation's political economy can be characterized as a kind of 'informal neocorporatism'. Unions spanned a major, but still partial, segment of the workforce. Terms and conditions of employment were informally synchronized across employers and industries, and labour costs were limited to productivity gains, by means of 'pattern bargaining' rather than by formal nationwide or sectoral pacts (Piore and Sabel 1984). The three principal setbacks to the achievement of formal neocorporatism were the defeat of the Congress of Industrial Organization's (CIO) immediate postwar campaign to organize the non-union Southern economy (Griffith 1988); the Cold War backlash against and outright dismantling of the American Federation of Labor and Congress of Industrial Organizations' (AFL-CIO) militant wing of 'mobilizing unionism' (Halpern 1988); and, after 1960, the AFL-CIO's dual failure, inside the workplace, to organize the influx of women and others in the new service economy, and, outside the workplace, to sustain a multipolar liberal alliance with the diverse new anti-war, civil rights, feminist, and environmental movements (Davis 1986; Goldfield 1997).

The last quarter-century, the final phase, has witnessed the steady erosion of labour unionism by reason of the flow of capital out of the unionized sector and into non-union plants and regions, and the concurrent triumph of a non-union, 'human resources' managerial strategy over the unionized 'industrial relations' model of the wartime and immediate postwar periods (Jacoby 1997; Kochan, Katz, and McKersie 1986). In the legal arena, this phase marked the de facto defeat of the New Deal policy of redistribution through centralized enforcement of collective bargaining rights, and the de jure ascendancy of direct regulation of the individual employment relation through a patchwork of state and federal anti-discrimination law, occupational health and safety law, wrongful discharge law, and so on (Weiler 1990). In the political economy, these trends contributed to the 'flexibilized' job creation, increased inequality of earnings, and erosion of employment security that, for good and ill, distinguished the US labour market at the end of the century (Osterman 1999).

III. LESSONS FROM US LABOUR FEDERALISM

In the historical sequence outlined in the previous section, US labour federalism in the twentieth century witnessed both a third of a century (1935–68) of relatively successful federal harmonization of collective bargaining rights and a subsequent, equally long period in which centralized regulation failed—success defined both by the degree of effective federal protection of pro-union workers against employer reprisals, and by the degree of achievement of the ultimate New Deal policy objective of promoting high levels of unionization and collective bargaining. Both the success and failure offer lessons for multi-state regulatory competition and cooperation.

Endogeneity of interest groups in a central regime facilitating decentralized class redistribution

In formal law, the federalized commitment to redistributive collective bargaining has, since the 1930s, fully pre-empted state and local regulation or deregulation of industrial relations (*Machinists Lodge 76* v. *Wisconsin Employment Relations Comm'n*, 427 U.S. 132 (1976); *San Diego Bldg. Trades Council* v. *Garmon*, 359 U.S. 236 (1959)). Nonetheless, fulfilment of that commitment was ultimately undermined by decentralized competition and coordination. There are, of course, many variables, legal and extra-legal, that explain that outcome, and their relative weight is empirically contested. Certain salient features of the federal regulatory programme itself, however, are plainly significant and carry lessons for other multi-state regimes. In the 1930s and 1940s—the heyday of mass production and unrest among newly homogenized workforces amidst the political and economic upheaval of the Great Depression and the War—these features were pragmatically well suited to the goal of encouraging collective bargaining. In the decades that followed—as capital mobility, corporate flexibility, and domestic and international product-market competition increased exponentially—these same features promoted the self-destruction of harmonized national regulation.

The first regulatory feature is a legislative quirk stemming from the particular 'founding moment' of the National Labor Relations Act (NLRA). The drafters of the 1935 NLRA had every expectation that the Act would yield a nationwide system of collective bargaining—a comprehensive system of corporatist partnership between management and labour, rising from below, to replace the corporatist industrial codes of the 1933 National Industrial Recovery Act (NIRA), imposed from the top down, which the Supreme Court had struck out on constitutional grounds. Their optimism grew from their eyewitness observation and mediation of a tidal wave of labour uprisings stretching across the country in the summer of 1934. And yet they codified a seemingly odd means to the end of comprehensive national bargaining. Workers would initially unionize by choosing representatives on a company by company basis, or plant by plant, or even department by department or job category by job category. That is, the NLRA required that the NLRB designate 'bargaining units' no broader in scope than a single company. The NLRB could not designate bargaining units at the regional, industry, or national level, nor did it have the authority to order 'extension' of the 'most representative' collective contracts across regions or industries, as provided in the regulatory regimes of many other countries.[5]

We now know that the drafters' expectation that workers nationwide would freely, on a unit-by-unit basis, select union representation by locals affiliated with national unions of the American Federation of Labor (AFL) or Congress of Industrial Organizations (CIO) would not be fulfilled. The wave of pro-union uprisings was not sustained. The drafters did not anticipate the sustained aggressiveness of employers' anti-union campaigns in the face of federal legislation promising workers the right freely to designate their bargaining representative. At least, they did not anticipate that the NLRB would, at least after the 1950s, lack the regulatory capacity and will sufficient to enforce that right against such employer interference (Gross 1995), and so they did not foresee that the economic logic of adversarial unit-by-unit organizing campaigns would actually create incentives for

[5] The drafters felt it necessary for the NLRB to designate the scope of bargaining units, because the regulatory system of a majority-selected collective representative presupposed an identifiable electorate of workers. The scheme of majority choice under government supervision, in turn, was simply the drafters' pragmatic response to the problem they faced in mediating strike after strike in 1934. Employers had refused to acknowledge that their workforce in fact supported the 'outside' union which demanded to bargain, rather than the 'inside' or company-authorized unions, or no union at all.

But why did the legislation mandate decentralized units no broader than individual companies? The reason was simple. In the actual disputes that the drafters had mediated across the country, the local-union affiliates of national unions were demanding to negotiate collective agreements at the company or plant level. (For discussions of the historical reasons why unions in the United States demanded initial recognition and negotiation at the company or plant level, as opposed to the level of regional, industry, or national employer associations, as in many European countries, see Barenberg (1993), Rogers (1990), and Bok (1971). Employers and unions did not contest the scope of the bargaining unit. The only dispute facing government mediators was whether the outside union had the support of a majority of workers in the undisputed unit (Barenberg 1991; Handler 1974).

individual employers and local unions to wage pitched battles.[6] Such pitched battles became routine. There is good reason to believe that, in the absence of intimidating anti-union campaigns or in the presence of federal facilitation of industry- or nationwide bargaining, unionization would have penetrated far more deeply and sustained itself far more enduringly in the post-1960s US political economy (Barenberg 1994; Rogers 1990; Weiler 1983).

A second self-destructive feature of the NLRA regime is closely related to the first. The regime not only requires that workers affirmatively choose to unionize, unit by unit, it also allows investors, with relative ease, to divest from unionized plants and companies and reinvest in non-union ones. More importantly, it allows companies wholly to escape unionization by investing retained earnings or other newly acquired capital in new non-union facilities rather than existing unionized facilities. This was the primary—and relatively invisible—mode of long-term de-unionization in the postwar period (Jacoby 1997; Kochan, Katz, and McKersie 1986). This phenomenon—together with management's strategic duplication and dispersal of important production facilities in order to prevent strikes at one plant from crippling multi-plant, company-wide production—helps account for the fact that the United States exhibits the most dispersed industrial geography of any national economy.

A third feature of the New Deal labour regime that contributed to its de facto failure is its dependence on the mutual reinforcement of organized labour's continuing strength in workplaces and in politics. Stated conversely, the regulatory regime was vulnerable to a downward spiral in which a weakening of unionization of workplaces would lead to a weakening of unions' political power, which would lead to further weakening of unionization of workplaces, and so on.

The causal link from weaker unions to weaker political power is obvious enough.[7] The causal feedback link from weaker political power to weaker unionization is based on the fact that the NLRA provided for presidential appointment of the members of the NLRB and Congressional allocation of its level of enforcement resources—as well as the fact that Congress, of course, may constitutionally amend or threaten to amend the substantive rules and enforcement procedures of the NLRB. The language of the NLRA gave ample room for NLRB discretion in shaping substantive labour rights and enforcement procedures, either dramatically in favour of unionization or dramatically against it. The historical record strongly confirms the operation of the circular relation: weaker unionization in the work-

[6] The logic is familiar. Individual employers threatened with unionization face the potential competitive disadvantage of higher labour costs compared with employers not yet unionized or employers able to resist unionization. The drafters of the NLRA, of course, understood this logic, but assumed the problem would not arise in a world in which workers overwhelmingly preferred unionization and in which they could freely register that preference in the light of the (mistakenly) anticipated effective NLRB deterrence of 'hard fights' by intimidating employers.

[7] A primary, explicit purpose of the NLRA was to promote not only workers' voice and bargaining power in the workplace but also the political empowerment of working people, in order to strengthen political democracy by creating a countervailing power against corporate influence.

place → weaker political power of organized labour → increasingly pro-management interpretation, enforcement, and amendment of the NLRA → weaker unionization in the workplace (Gross 1995).

These three elements of regulatory implosion have their analogues in potential dynamics of regulatory competition and cooperation in the contemporary global multi-state system. The decentralization of bargaining units within the United States is paralleled by the balkanization of low-wage, national sovereigns in the global regime. In the United States, local workforces compete for capital that lawfully moves, or threatens to move, across the boundaries of bargaining units in search of non-union labour. At the global level, national and subnational workforces analogously compete for capital that may lawfully move across the boundaries of nation-states, export-processing zones, and transnational production chains.

Concurrently, if long-term domestic stabilization of collective bargaining depends on a self-reinforcing cycle between ongoing unionization in the workplace and labour's continuing political power to ensure uniform enforcement of organizing rights, the analogous potential for a reverse cycle is manifest globally. That is, as capital moves to labour-repressive nation-states and regions, the political weight of low-wage, non-union nation-states, export-processing zones, and mobile investors—global interest groups likely to oppose aggressive supranational enforcement of labour rights—increases in international fora. Hence the incapacity of low-wage countries to break the *synchronic* collective-action problem of interstate competition for mobile capital may reinforce the *diachronic* weakness of supranational political processes that could otherwise mitigate that problem.

On both the domestic and global levels, then, we see a dynamic of regulatory competition that predictably plays a relatively stronger role in regulatory regimes aimed at redistribution, as distinguished from those aimed at wealth-maximization. This phenomenon might be called the *endogeneity of interest groups*—that is, legal rules aimed at large-scale redistribution self-consciously attempt to alter the balance of economic, and therefore political, power among contending social groups. Interest groups threatened by such rules, of course, will predictably exert political pressure to weaken their enforcement or alter them in their favour. Interest groups aided by such rules will attempt the opposite. In light of the endogeneity of interest groups, we can expect to see self-reinforcing cycles that either weaken redistributive rules while politically strengthening their interest-group opponents, on the one hand, or strengthen redistributive rules while fortifying the political power of their interest-group beneficiaries, on the other.

The simple lesson from US labour federalism—especially when compared to European regimes which harmonized labour rights through nationwide or industry-wide rather than decentralized bargaining units (Bok 1971; Rogers 1990)—is that a *diachronic* redistributive upward cycle of core labour rights and public-choice realignment is likely to be impeded by a supranational regime that lacks a mechanism of *synchronic* coordination to overcome competition for capital among national and subnational workforces.

Suppose the workers, managers, and governments of every low-wage country would prefer not to compete by repressing core labour rights. Each country may nonetheless rationally represent to the international community that it prefers not to be held to internationally recognized core labour standards—in the absence of some pre-existing or proposed institutional mechanism that credibly guarantees coordinated action among low-wage countries, or that credibly guarantees to low-wage countries that supranational bodies will even-handedly and synchronically enforce core labour rights in all low-wage (and high-wage) countries. Low-wage countries may well be sceptical of the sufficiency of such guarantees, when supranational bodies are dominated by high-wage countries whose labour-rights policies with respect to any particular low-wage country may be buffeted by many geopolitical and public-choice distortions. The scepticism of low-wage countries may be compounded by the manifest difficulty in uniformly and fairly measuring compliance with core labour rights across economies with very different national institutions of labour relations, levels of labour productivity, and other criteria potentially relevant to contextual application and interpretation of such abstractly worded rights.

The challenge, then, is to design supranational institutions that adequately promise synchronic, even-handed enforcement of clear but flexible and fair specifications of core labour rights. The experience of US federalism sheds some further light on the 'mechanisms of regulatory coordination' which are likely to be important elements of a 'coordinated, decentralized' architecture that embodies these design features.

Mechanisms of Coordination in Decentralized Regulation—Collaborative Upward Races or Collusive Downward Races?

The rise and fall of centrally coordinated but decentrally implemented collective bargaining depended, in the United States, on the path-dependent design and internal political conflicts of several multi-tier institutions that spanned the federal, state, and local governments. These institutions include political parties, national labour federations, and the nationwide hierarchies of multi-state corporations and financial institutions. The empirical importance of these institutions suggests that theories of regulatory competition and coordination must carefully attend to the 'public-choice' dynamics inside such private 'federal systems' and their interactions (coordination and competition) with one another as well as with public federal systems.

The New Deal coalition of regionally diverse and often clashing interest groups—institutionalized in the national Democratic Party—proved critical to both the success of federally harmonized labour rights and the subsequent de facto collapse of that regulatory project. The party structure's contribution to the period of success is well illustrated in the successful strike against General Motors (GM) in 1936–37. That strike, the most important of the twentieth century, achieved the key breakthrough in mass industrial unionism and opened the door to widespread unionization and collective pattern-bargaining—characterized above as 'informal neocorporatism'—throughout the economy's manufacturing core. The strike would have failed had it not been for the New Deal's consummation of the 'Al Smith Revolution' which, for the first time, brought the nation's new immigrant workforces into active party politics (Barenberg 1993). The strike itself took the form of a sit-down or factory occupation and therefore constituted illegal trespass under Michigan state property law. Yet neither the state nor federal government was willing to enforce the court injunction awarded to GM against the strike (Fine 1969). For the first time in the nation's history, a pro-labour political party controlled the levers of both the federal and state executive police powers, which for decades previously had been routinely deployed to break such strikes. President Roosevelt and Michigan Governor Frank Murphy, an ardent labourite (and later Supreme Court Justice), declined to use state coercion against the strikers.

In the case of the GM sit-down strike, the Democratic Party was a key 'mechanism of coordination' that mediated the process of 'interest group endogeneity' discussed in the previous section. The Democratic Party acted as a horizontal and vertical channel of coordination among private interest groups and public entities, state and federal, in support of a redistributive race toward the top and, in the process, strengthened those very interest groups supporting continuing redistribution.

The coordinating mechanism of the Democratic Party, however, subsequently proved incapable of sustaining this 'collaborative upward race'. Indeed, in the postwar years, the Party's coordinating function ultimately consolidated a 'collusive downward race' in US labour federalism, by reason of the peculiar path-dependent coalition at the Party's base. The national Democratic Party spanned not only unionized ethnics and urban liberals of the industrialized Northern states, but non-union, white segregationist regimes of the Southern agrarian states (Bensel 1984). In the South, the commitment of local and state-level Democratic Party machines to racial segregation and low-wage economic development was manifest in the aggressive legal and extra-legal denial of core rights of association exercised on behalf of either racial equality or collective bargaining (Honey 1993). After the failure of Roosevelt's effort to purge the Democratic Party of its Southern racialist wing in the 1938 election, the national Party presided over a policy of collusion with local Southern élites who de facto denied workers' de jure federal labour rights. (Davis 1986; Honey 1993).

A key turning point was the dismal failure of the CIO's postwar campaign to organize the newly industrializing, non-union strongholds of the Southern states. The failure of so-called 'Operation Dixie' rested on the interaction of the internal politics of the Democratic Party with the equally path-dependent internal structure of the national labour federations. The divisive conflicts between the old craft unions of the AFL and the new industrial unions of the CIO, and between anti-communists and the radical left in both federations, is a long and complicated story.

The historical outcome relevant to this chapter—that those internal divisions crippled the CIO's Southern campaign almost from the start—is amply supported by the empirical record (Honey 1993; Zieger 1995). The mutual reinforcement of the divisions within the labour federations and those within the national Democratic Party structure is also well documented (Davis 1986).

In sum, the internal structure and historical path of coordinating mechanisms—parties, labour federations, and multi-state corporations and financial institutions—first yielded a collaborative upward race in enforcement of labour rights, and subsequently a collusive downward race. The concrete result was the temporary consolidation of harmonized collective bargaining in Northern manufacturing and the maintenance of Southern industry as a union-free zone. In light of the synchronic competition among decentralized bargaining units and the diachronic endogeneity of interest groups, discussed above, the future opportunity and incentive for capital to move to a reliably non-union sector was secured.

Are there intermediary coordinating institutions at the global or regional level that are functional analogues of US political parties, labour federations, and multi-state corporate and financial institutions? In the public sphere, the obvious analogues include many supranational organizations that span high- and low-wage countries (for example, ILO, WTO, International Monetary Fund (IMF), International Bank for Reconstruction and Development (IBRD), etc.); social clauses in regional regimes (for example, NAFTA's labour side agreement, the European Union's social provisions, MERCOSUR (the Southern Common Market) social committee, etc.); bilateral and unilateral mechanisms through which low-wage countries' access to rich countries' consumers and investors is conditioned on compliance with core labour rights (for example, in US trade law, Section 301 of the Trade Act, the Generalized System of Preferences, etc.). In the private sphere, the analogues are more direct: multinational corporations and banks; global, regional, and sectoral federations, and secretariats of labour unions; networks of NGOs aggregating and pressing the interests of workers and business; and the recent proliferation of foundations that engage in pooled monitoring of corporate codes of conduct (for example, in the United States, the Fair Labor Association and the Council on Economic Priorities' SA8000 Program; in Europe, the Clean Clothes Campaign and the Ethical Trading Initiative).

To map the institutional structure, internal politics, and interaction of these coordinating mechanisms—with a view to proposing comprehensive institutional reforms that would encourage an upward race in global compliance with core labour rights—is too large an inquiry to undertake in this chapter. Nonetheless, the comparative experiences of US and European labour federalism indicate some broad directions that inquiry might usefully pursue. The rise and fall of the New Deal harmonization of labour rights suggests the relevance of a question central to the theory of economic segmentation or 'dualism', particularly in the well-developed theory of labour-market segmentation: are particular coordinating mechanisms, prevailing or proposed, better adapted to facilitate the Northern economic vanguard's 'pulling up' the labour rights of the Southern rearguard, or instead to facilitate the Southern rearguard's 'dragging down' the labour rights of the Northern vanguard? (Castaneda 1996; Unger and Cui 1994). The analogous question addressed to the European Union is this: Are the coordinating mechanisms of the European Union—including the dialogue among the quasi-public European-wide 'social partners'—likely to pull the low-wage member states and regions up to the labour standards of the powerhouse economies of Germany, France, Italy, and the United Kingdom, or vice versa?

We now have sufficient empirical evidence from specific areas of European social policy to conclude that 'pulling upward' is a realistic outcome—if the institutional infrastructure is favourable. For example, in occupational health and safety, in vocational training, and perhaps in regional employment policy, EU standards are the product of central deliberations which formulate—and of centralized incentives for member states to adopt—European-wide 'best practices' that often, indeed, exceed the prevailing standards of any single member state. Even the weak standards of the labour side agreement of NAFTA—which require only that the three member states 'effectively enforce' their existing domestic standards—have shown that such a supranational regime has the potential effectively to 'leverage upward' the rules and procedures of member states' labour-rights enforcement (Compa 1995). That potential is great, in light of the substantively very strong, but administratively very under-enforced, codes of worker rights on the books in the United States and Mexico. Again, the capacity for the economic vanguard to pull up the rearguard is institutionalized through central coordination which implements disciplined comparison of the performance of laggard states with the best enforcement practices of other member states (the United States and Mexico relative to Canada; Mexico relative to Canada and the United States).

Bootstrapping central and local rights of association: the interdependence of substantive and procedural rights in labour federalism

The experience of the United States points to another challenge for enforcing labour rights through a federal regime committed to coordinated decentralization. Call this the challenge of 'bootstrapping procedural and substantive rights of association'. A key substantive goal of labour federalism, of course, is protection of the core right of association among workers. At the same time, the legitimacy of the institutions which proclaim, interpret, and enforce that substantive right turns in large part on the degree to which they embody democratic procedures, including participatory mechanisms at the local level and representative mechanisms at the central level. Civic-associational activity such as labour organizing, in turn, is a precondition of democratic local participation and central representation.

The interdependence of procedural and substantive rights of association is illustrated vividly in the United States by the pervasive state and local suppression of core labour rights, especially in the South, before and after the New Deal. As mentioned above, state and local officials, aligned with local business élites, deployed legal and extra-legal police powers in coercive counter-campaigns against labour organizers; and such opposition of Southern élites to interracial union organizing reflected a commitment not only to maintaining a racial caste system[8] but also to a strategy of economic development and social privilege based on low-wage labour.[9]

These local élites were politically entrenched through one-party, rotten-borough regimes which denied democratic rights to associate and to vote not only to African-Americans but to much of the white workforce as well, via property qualifications, poll taxes, and raw coercion (Davis 1986; Honey 1993). The local denial of democratic rights of political association, as sketched above, was transmitted upward through the Democratic Party—in which Northern unionists and urban liberals embraced Southern political machines—thereby creating a deficit in the democratic legitimacy of federal political institutions as well (Bensel 1984).

The federal democracy deficit, in turn, mutually reinforced the denial of core labour rights at the local level. In the critical twenty-five years after enactment of the NLRA, the Roosevelt, Truman, and Eisenhower Administrations permitted the widespread exercise of state and local police power contrary to the federal policy of harmonized labour rights. Effective enforcement of those rights would have required a wholesale federal assault on the Southern political machines that resisted civic association on behalf of labour rights and racial equality—a task postponed until the civil rights revolution of the 1960s.[10]

[8] State and company officials, together with large segments of the white workforce, were active in the para-police activities of the Ku Klux Klan (Zieger 1995).

[9] As discussed below, Southern élites were not monolithically committed to the low-wage strategy.

[10] The successful unionization of General Motors in early 1936, as we have seen, turned on the refusal of the New Deal executives—at the level of both the federal and Michigan state governments—to apply direct force against the sit-down strikers. Equally important, though less visible in the historiography of US labour law, is the fact that throughout the New Deal period other state and local governments continued to deploy their militia and police in frequently lawless strikebreaking, most vividly in the defeat of the national textile workers' strike of 1934 and the repression of the Steel Workers Organizing Committee in late 1937. In 1935, seventy-three strikes faced militiamen deployed by twenty state governors, a majority of whom headed Democratic state administrations.

Roosevelt had not only failed in his meek attempt to realign the party by cleansing it of Southern conservatives in the 1938 elections. Instead, liberal Democrats wholly lost control of Congress to an alliance of Southern Democrats and Republicans. Thereafter, the Democratic coalition rested on the uneasy compromise, described above, between Northern urban liberals and unionists, on the one hand, and Southern anti-union conservatives, on the other.

The Party would not launch a frontal attack on the Southern élites' commitment to racial hierarchy and to a non-union, low-wage economic structure. In return, the Southern élites helped maintain the Democratic Party's national power and tolerated moderate bureaucratic centralization in areas that did not threaten their local hegemony. A common commitment to wartime and Cold War aims provided the coalition with some degree of affirmative cohesion. The domestic ideological campaigns of the Cold War also indirectly sustained the strange alliance by inducing the union movement to dismantle the strong leftist wing that sought an immediate interracial, democratic dissolution of the Southern power structure—a task, and a challenge to the New Deal alliance, that was left to the civil rights movement of later decades.

Not surprisingly, then, one continuous faultline of political stress and adjustment in this bipolar alliance—apart from the issues of civil rights and core labour rights—was the question of stronger

The European experience confirms both that the problem of 'bootstrapping rights of association' is a general one and that the particular regulatory response to that problem depends heavily on background political institutions. In the European Union, the interdependence of procedural and substantive rights of association is embedded in, and strongly inflected by, the distinctive democratic institutions of neocorporatism. Under classic neocorporatism, of course, parliamentary politics are overlaid by tripartite bargaining among the peak organizations of labour, business, and government. That is, democracy grounded on representation of the general citizenry co-exists with democracy grounded on functional or group representation. The legitimacy of the neocorporatist regime therefore depends on the democratic legitimacy of the functional organizations of labour and business, the so-called 'social partners'.

In both domestic and European-wide institutions, this central problem of political legitimacy is reflected in a variety of legal doctrines which evaluate the 'representativity' of the organizations that are designated as social partners. The 1990s witnessed an attempt to 'bootstrap' the recognized social partners at the level of the member states into legitimately representative social partners at the European level. Professor Bercusson's contribution to this volume describes precisely the kind of political and legal *legerdemain* one would expect in a process captured by the paradoxical metaphor of bootstrapping—the EC adroitly playing off the Inter-Governmental Conference against the European employers associations; the artful decision by the European Court of First Instance in the *UEAPME* case, addressing a challenge to the representivity of the EU social partners (Bercusson, Ch. 11).

At the global level, the interdependence of procedural and substantive rights of association is illustrated in some of the most pressing questions of supranational governance. The Seattle protests against the undemocratic structure of the WTO, for example, were met by some trade ministers' argument that the WTO's intergovernmental agreements in fact have greater procedural legitimacy than the social and environmental clauses formulated and urged by unelected NGOs purporting to represent transnational civil society. Meanwhile, the delegates of low-wage countries, in opposing international enforcement of labour rights, claimed to represent the interests of Third-World workers, even while a surprising number of Third-World labour movements allied themselves with Northern NGOs and unions against their own governments' delegates, whose democratic legitimacy is not always manifest, to put it mildly.

national wage and hour standards and deeper unemployment insurance cushions favoured by Northern Democrats and disfavoured by Southern Democrats (Bensel 1984; Blaustein, Cohen, and Haber 1993). The politics of national labour market policy retreated from class-redistributive strategies that entailed regional conflict—such as effective harmonization of collective bargaining rights, raising the nationwide 'social wage', or full employment through industrial planning or aggressive macroeconomic policy. The Democratic Party coalition instead compromised on a 'labour market policy' that deployed such devices as devolution to the states of authority to set differential levels in welfare benefits and unemployment compensation; the Taft-Hartley Amendment permitting state legislation that derogated from the union security provisions of the NLRA; and 'job creation' by pork-barrel distributions of federal funds for state infrastructure and military investment (Weir 1992).

Recent debates surrounding the ILO present a second example of the interdependence of procedural and substantive rights of association at the global level. The ILO's substantive norms are increasingly thrown into question by that organization's tripartite structure, an inheritance from the heyday of social democracy. As in the EU's Social Dialogue, deliberations or deals among the pre-designated interests of labour, business, and government are only as legitimate as the representatives who purport to speak on behalf of the social groups affected by global labour and social rules. Can labour and business federations adequately address the concerns of the unemployed and of the vast workforces in non-unionized, informal sectors of poor and rich economies? Even more challenging: on such crucial matters of social ordering as, for example, the relation between work and family, do labour unions and businesses—to the exclusion of, say, women's organizations or religious groups—have the sole legitimate claim to formulate binding norms?[11] These questions challenge the New Deal and the neocorporatist presumption that governance structures based on fixed economic interests—those of labour and capital—are enduringly legitimate in the face of social problems that affect multiple groups whose 'interests' are fluid and may only crystallize in the process of deliberation itself.

Against the backdrop of democracy deficits at global and nation-state levels, a supranational regime of 'coordinated decentralization' must therefore embody some solution to four broad challenges of institutional design. First, deliberative or administrative bodies at the central level must implement norms that assess the representivity of the public and private entities that participate in coordinating mechanisms, which include the central bodies themselves. Second, the supranational regime must implement norms that determine which decentralized interests and social groupings shall be so represented. Third, the regime must implement norms that determine how these decentralized actors shall participate in interpreting, monitoring, and enforcing compliance with rights of labour association 'on the ground'—the participative processes that Professor Sabel calls 'learning by monitoring' (Sabel 1995). Fourth, as to all three sets of constitutive norms, the supranational regime must choose among norms that range along a spectrum from the more substantive to the more procedural. That is, the regime might apply specific criteria of representivity, of relevant affected interests, and of local participatory compliance, or it might instead establish general, second-order frameworks for deliberation about those criteria, which, at least initially, would be more general and fluid than the constitutive norms of traditional regulatory regimes. Second-order frameworks and fluid interest-definition are likely to prove more appropriate to an institutional architecture intended to encourage genuine decentralized experimentation and 'reflexivity' among central and local actors (Barenberg 1994; Dorf and Sabel 1998).

[11] The same question arises at the level of regional or national integration. Suppose European-wide women's or religious organizations were to challenge the 'representativity' of the European labour and business federations in EU rule-making in matters of childcare, parental leave, flexi-time and the like.

Linkage of trade and labour: the unavoidability of normative debate about distributive justice

The discussion above, at two different points, rested on unstated normative premises. The discussion in the second section of Part III assumed that, when collective-action problems in multi-state systems block individual states from realizing their sovereign preferences for higher labour standards, central coordination on behalf of core labour rights is called for. The discussion in the third section of Part III assumed that, when there is a clash between the preferences of democratic and undemocratic sovereigns, the former should prevail.

The stylized facts of US labour federalism again provide a useful starting point for analysis of these controversial assumptions. Put schematically, the Northern states' sovereign preference to enforce core labour rights clashed with the Southern states' preference to follow a non-union, low-wage development strategy. The second section of Part III presented one seemingly value-neutral ground for the conclusion that the former preferences should override the latter: that is, if we assume that all low-wage states would prefer to follow a high-wage, unionized path but are deterred by interstate competition, then coordinated action that unblocks that path does not require a controversial choice between alternative sovereign preferences.

But assume that one or more Southern states holds a sovereign preference for a developmental strategy based on the comparative advantage of low, non-union wages—as some 'Southern' nation-states today pursue in global competition. There are at least three possible arguments for a federalized regime of core labour rights, whether or not implemented through coordinated decentralization. The first is an argument from democracy. Even if the US federal institutions in the 1950s and 1960s themselves exhibited a democracy deficit—the very deficit which underlaid the political choice of de facto non-enforcement of core labour rights—the formal federal commitment to core labour rights carried greater democratic and constitutional legitimacy than the preference by renegade Southern states, whose relatively undemocratic political machines were dominated by anti-redistributive élites, to resist those rights.

Of course, there is a crucial disanalogy between the US federal commitment to enforce core labour rights in its Southern states and any hypothesized supranational commitment to enforce such rights in the Southern nation-states. The legitimacy of US federal pre-emption of Southern state preferences rests in part on the fact that the several states are constituents of an overarching, national democratic constitutional order. In the intergovernmental agreements that constitute, say, the WTO, there is no such presumptively legitimate principle giving precedence to democratic preference formation at either the supranational or nation-state levels.

This disanalogy can be countered, however, by two normative arguments. The first argument points to the codification of core labour rights by supranational deliberative bodies which have greater democratic legitimacy than the intergovernmental bargaining forum of the WTO. Specifically, the ILO's recent

Declaration of Fundamental Labour Rights (1998)—proclaimed after deliberation and supermajority vote by its tripartite, representative governing body—is formally binding on all ILO member states. This combination of the formally binding ILO commitment to core labour rights and the veto-power over effective enforcement of such rights by individual nation-states in the non-majoritarian processes of the WTO evinces some parallel, however rough, with the obstruction of federal labour rights by Southern political machines in the United States. The second argument simply rejects the positivist premise that global normative commitments are limited either to existing intergovernmental agreements or even to existing majoritarian votes among representatives of states with widely varying degrees of democratic legitimacy. If one instead gives priority to normative principles of democracy over positivist principles of sovereignty, then the relative degree of democracy in the decision-making processes that yield sovereign preferences for or against core labour rights of association becomes relevant and perhaps decisive.[12]

This last argument points toward an even deeper flaw in the presumption that supranational bodies should respect the sovereign preferences of nation-states which opt to repress core labour rights (or, stated less tendentiously, which opt for the comparative advantage of non-union wages). If that preference in fact imposes a significant competitive cost on nation-states that prefer to comply with core labour rights, then the behaviour of the labour-repressive nation-states has the spillover effect of limiting the policy options open to the latter. As Coase famously pointed out, in the context of economic spillovers there is no value-neutral way to decide whether to assign an entitlement to the actor whose preference-maximizing behaviour 'produces' the spillover or instead to the actor whose preference-maximizing behaviour is constrained by the spillover. Applied to the question of enforcing labour rights across nation-states, this logic suggests that giving priority to the sovereign preference to repress labour rights over the sovereign preference to enforce those rights when the two substantially clash—as posited by some officials of developing countries—is an unavoidably normative choice. Of course, the conclusion that core labour rights should be internationally enforced does not immediately follow. Coase's argument, remember, is that there is no presumption favouring the preferences of either the 'source' or the 'recipient' of a spillover.[13]

If, then, the choice to protect labour-repressive policies is grounded in an argument from sovereignty, that argument begs the question. We are faced with the clash between the policy preferences of two sovereigns. If the choice to immunize the labour-repressive policies is grounded in an argument from comparative advan-

[12] Thanks to Robert Howse for helping me clarify this point.

[13] Coase's theory, of course, offered an affirmative theory for assigning legal entitlements—based on the norm of wealth maximization. While that particular norm could be deployed to allocate the entitlement to repress or enforce core labour rights, the analysis in this chapter assumes that core labour rights rest exclusively on deontological, democratic, and distributive norms, as is true of the legislative purpose behind labour rights enforcement in US labour federalism. For a thorough analysis of international labour rights from the point of view of both wealth maximization and redistribution, see Professor Charny's contribution to this volume (Charny, Ch. 14).

tage, that argument too begs the question. 'Comparative advantage' can only be defined by a baseline of property and contract entitlements, which cannot be assigned in a value-neutral way. Stated conversely, any set of market rules that constitute the 'comparative advantage' of nation-states unavoidably codifies a vision of fundamental entitlements and a particular distributive outcome that must be justified or defended by considerations of distributive justice. Positing a set of international market rules that permit nation-states and employers to penalize workers who exercise core rights of association is no less a normative choice than positing a set of rules that enforces such 'fundamental human rights'.[14] There is no neutral, pre-political definition of 'comparative advantage', just as there is no neutral, pre-political prioritization of clashing sovereign preferences.

Thus, in addressing the question of whether core labour rights should be enforced across multiple sovereigns, there is no avoiding thorough normative debate over the weight of sovereign self-determination as a value; the relative normative weight of different modes of direct and indirect interstate interaction that directly or indirectly constrain such sovereign self-determination (most relevantly: (1) economic competition among states that repress and states that enforce core labour rights, and (2) economic sanctions against states that repress core labour rights); and the relative weight of values that may compete with sovereign self-determination, such as democracy, deontological human rights, distributive justice, welfare maximization, and so on.

At the level of domestic federalism, these questions are difficult enough. At the international level, they take on the added complexities of cross-border justice. Do US consumers, individually or collectively, have the right or responsibility to exercise their purchasing power in the name of overseas human rights or of democracy abroad? As a matter of distributive justice, how is reduction of inequality across social strata to be weighed against reduction of inequality across nation-states and regions (Kapstein 1999; Sen 1999; Rawls 1999)?

The experience of US labour federalism points to a final descriptive inquiry that may make these normative questions less pressing or, to the contrary, even more complex and urgent.

A threshold descriptive question: the theory and endogeneity of economic growth and economic organization

The normative questions posed in the previous section, as well as the questions of institutional design mooted previously, take for granted the descriptive proposition that investors will divert mobile capital from nation-states that enforce labour rights to nation-states that repress labour rights. More precisely, they take for granted the proposition that the officials of nation-states—particularly low-wage nation-states—believe, and act on the belief, that capital will so flow.

[14] The argument from human rights on behalf of international enforcement of core labour rights is well made by Robert Howse (1999).

This descriptive claim is both crucial and contested. Empirically, the claim is broadly true of officials in the Southern states of the United States in the era of mass production. It is worth noting, however, that even in that context, the low-wage, labour-repressive strategy was not monolithically endorsed by local and state élites. There were élite factions, however outnumbered, who saw a long-term local advantage in attracting high-wage jobs requiring greater investments in human capital, even in sectors, such as automobile manufacturing, in which unionization was virtually inescapable (Honey 1993). But the low-wage path was the line of least disruption to settled social hierarchies, so much so that some localities actively discouraged investment by high-wage employers, unionized or not, who threatened to dislodge local wage scales.

Neoclassical economic theory predicts that capital will indeed flow to regions and countries that have relatively lower capital/labour ratios and lower unit labour costs, until factor returns and capital/labour ratios are equalized across borders (Ehrenberg 1994). The 'New Growth Theory' maintains, to the contrary, that capital may be attracted to nations, regions, and cities that have greater accumulations of public infrastructure, private capital (especially in producer services), and public and private human capital. There is substantial empirical evidence that these 'agglomeration effects' predicted by the New Growth Theory may outweigh the factor-price incentives of neoclassical growth theory, at least across a substantial range of service and industrial sectors (Ellison and Glaeser 1994; Head *et al.* 1994; Katz and Shapiro 1994). Such agglomeration effects may be reinforced by organizational trends identified in various theories and empirical studies of the 'New Organization'. According to these studies, the total-quality protocols and internal labour-auditing standards of value-adding, high-performance organizations are transmitted to low-wage countries through multinational corporations and global production chains. In the name of production disciplines, quality control, worker morale, or brand reputation, these protocols and standards may weigh against heavy-handed repression or exploitation of labour (Sabel, O'Rourke, and Fung 1999).

Note that the competing theories of economic growth and optimal economic organization may well be self-fulfilling or, again, 'endogenous' to the dynamics of the regulatory architecture. If, for example, investors internalize a cognitive map that includes the New Growth Theory—or if they expect that the financial community as a whole will invest in ways predicted by that theory—then they are more likely to allocate their mobile capital toward pre-existing agglomerations, thereby fulfilling that theory's prediction. A regulatory architecture that blocked the 'low road' of competition through squeezing labour and other social costs might encourage an epistemic cascade favouring investment strategies based on such economies of agglomeration.

The normative implication of the New Growth and New Organization theories and supporting empirical evidence is by no means straightforward. If mobile capital is indeed attracted to regions with already high technological, skill, labour, and social standards, this may indeed mitigate the feared 'race to the bottom' that motivates the call for supranational enforcement of labour rights. For those who give great normative weight to global equality, however, that fear may be replaced by another—the fear of heightened global polarization as capital-rich regions get richer still. Attempts to enforce global labour rights—without providing concurrent incentives for movement of physical and human capital to low-wage, low-productivity regions—may amount to pushing on a policy string.

Fortunately for 'cosmopolitan liberals' who favour egalitarian redistribution both across borders, on the one hand, and among classes in both rich and poor nation-states, on the other, this theoretical and empirical debate may not affect the policy prescription. Whether existing flows of capital go to poorer, labour-repressive countries or instead to richer, labour-protective countries, the cosmopolitan liberal is likely to support additional incentives for public and private investment in the poorest regions, combined with synchronic enforcement of core labour rights. The latter ensures that investment flows do not disproportionately benefit investors through higher profit/wage ratios, but rather provide non-trivial wage gains to workers drawn from vast, elastic supplies of unemployed labour. Core labour rights may afford such workforces the collective bargaining power to ensure that wages rise with productivity. It is true that neoclassical economic theory predicts that wages will 'naturally' rise in tandem with labour productivity in individualized labour markets, without the need for the enhanced bargaining power provided by workers' capacity to threaten collectively to withhold their labour (via the union's strike weapon). But in the actual context of dualist economies with large reservoirs of unemployed workers, this result is not inevitable or even likely in the absence of special institutional infrastructure for supporting wages in the economy's developing sector (Mead 1990; Rothstein 1996).

On the other hand, the potentially complex empirical and normative implications of the New Growth and New Organization theories have only just begun to unfold. If, for example, the reality of agglomeration effects is joined with local officials' perception of regional first-mover advantages, as some preliminary evidence suggests, then the fear of races toward the bottom may be self-fulfilling. That is, officials of low-wage nation-states may race to repress regulatory standards in order to attract the pioneer capital that will jump-start the anticipated winner-take-all chain reaction caused by subsequent, self-reinforcing agglomeration effects. Unfortunately, there is some preliminary evidence from US federalism—in the recent era characterized by locally and sectorally variable levels of collective bargaining and of other social protections—that local and state governments are competitively motivated to offer regulatory relaxation precisely in this fashion, resulting in nationwide detriments to welfare and equity (Head *et al.* 1994).

CONCLUSION

Even these broad-brush lessons drawn from the experience of US labour federalism amply reveal the complexity of the normative and descriptive questions that must be addressed before policy analysts can confidently defend or oppose institutional blueprints for international enforcement of labour rights. Such inquiries have barely begun to scratch the surface. The very uncertainty and complexity of the policy questions, however, suggest that the optimal institutional architecture should be biased toward decentralized, participatory experimentation in the substantive specification and procedural enforcement of core labour rights, combined with central deliberation and incentives for encouraging an upward race toward the best practices that emerge from such local or regional innovation. That is, the family of 'coordinated, decentralized' regimes is likely to provide the optimal architecture for fleshing out, enforcing, and evaluating the normative desirability of core labour rights, which are still a highly abstract idea with uncertain consequences.

7

Environmental Federalism in the United States: The Risks of Devolution

KIRSTEN ENGEL AND SUSAN ROSE-ACKERMAN*

Federalism in the United States is currently characterized by two recent developments: the federal government is devolving regulatory policy making and enforcement to the states, and the federal courts are challenging long-held views of federal power. Both developments have important and problematic implications for environmental policy. Although there are indeed benefits from state involvement in environmental affairs, the current decentralizing trends should not obscure the risks associated with too great a reliance on lower-level governments.

Even the staunchest proponents of states' rights recognize the need for federal regulation when pollution crosses state lines. Air and water pollution are obvious examples where federal statutes force the states to internalize the externalities of economic activity (Merrill 1997: 933; Revesz 1996: 2346; Stewart 1977: 1216). Nevertheless, even for air and water pollution, the actual implementation of the federal law can be left to the states under federal supervision. When this occurs, the federal government should balance the benefits of giving states flexibility against the risks that states will favour local interests over national pollution goals.

Some environmental problems, however, only have local impacts. For these, the extent of the pollution problem is no greater than the extent of the political boundaries. Democratic ideals as well as economic efficiency seem to suggest that decision making should rest with state and local governments for such problems as noise, local parks, and waste dumps that do not leak into interstate waterways (Butler and Macey 1996; Oates 1998). A number of federal laws deal with such ostensibly local environmental problems (Safe Drinking Water Act, 42 U.S.C. §§ 300f to 300j-26; Resource Conservation and Recovery Act, 42 U.S.C. §§ 6901 to 6992k). Some legal commentators, critical of the status quo, advocate a reduction of the federal role in these areas (Butler and Macey 1996; Revesz 1992; Stewart 1993). In cases where repeal of the federal law appears unlikely, these scholars recommend that the sanctioning of violations be left to state and local regulatory authorities who are knowledgeable about local conditions and who, presumably, have the most to lose from non-compliance.

In this chapter, we criticize the strong version of claims for devolution of both policy making and implementation. Extensive devolution to state and local

* We wish to thank Scott Saleska and Joshua Sarnoff for their helpful comments on earlier drafts.

governments may entail significant environmental and social costs even when the underlying environmental problems have no interstate impacts.

We discuss the appropriate role of the federal government under two contrasting assumptions concerning the representative nature of state government. First, we assume that state governments do a good job of representing the interests of their citizens. Second, we consider the role of the central government when state government officials poorly reflect the underlying long-term interests of their constituents. We ask whether the justifications for centralized regulation are altered when state governments are not adequately representative. We then apply our framework to recent attempts by the US Environmental Protection Agency (EPA) to devolve policy-making and enforcement powers to the states as well as recent federalism decisions by the US Supreme Court. We conclude that some of these developments may retard, rather than enhance, the development of sound economic policy, and may lead to the imposition of significant social and environmental costs.[1]

I. REPRESENTATIVE STATE GOVERNMENTS

First, we assume that state officials trade off economic growth and environmental quality in accord with the wishes of citizens residing within their jurisdictions. Nevertheless, the federal government has a policy-making and implementation role, even with respect to environmental problems lacking interjurisdictional effects, if: (1) states lack sufficient incentives to provide public goods, such as scientific or economic research, that would improve their decision-making capability; (2) economies of scale make divergent standards enacted by individual states costly; (3) states or local governments are engaged in destructive competitive interactions like those captured by game-theoretic models such as the classic 'prisoners' dilemma'; or (4) state choices of different policy tools produce inefficiencies.

Providing public goods and realizing economies of scale

The first two arguments are quite uncontroversial, and we deal with them quickly. First, in highly technical areas such as the environment, the federal government can provide the public good of information. Although many states may benefit from better information, no state may have an incentive to provide this information on its own (Dwyer 1995: 1222). Thus one role for the federal government is to overcome this free-rider problem by doing the research itself.[2]

[1] We are primarily concerned here with efficiency justifications for environmental regulation and thus omit discussion of other arguments for federal environmental regulation, such as the claim that federal regulation is necessary to realize individual rights to minimum environmental quality. For a broader view, see Engel (1997: 288) and Merrill (1994: 486).

[2] Many provisions of US federal environmental law require exactly that (Clean Air Act § 108, 42 U.S.C. § 7408; Clean Water Act § 304(a), 33 U.S.C. § 1314(a)).

Second, federal action may be justified if the costs of diverse local rules outweigh the benefits. Uniform national regulation may produce economies of scale of production and distribution for firms selling nationally. For example, federal laws that set uniform emission standards for new vehicles and uniform consumer safety warnings on nationally distributed chemical products are sometimes justified on these grounds.[3] Federal pre-emption may also reduce search costs, and produce a more stable and predictable legal framework for business investment.[4] Mixed systems may sometimes make sense when federal product standards can be supplemented by local restrictions on use. Thus a federal standard on the noise produced by motorcycles could be combined with local rules limiting night-time use and restricting the places where noise can be produced.

Preventing a regulatory 'race to the bottom'

One rationale for federal environmental regulation holds that state governments will engage in a welfare reducing 'race to the bottom' in environmental standard setting and enforcement for the purposes of attracting and retaining mobile industries (Davis and Lester 1989; Esty 1996; Engel 1997; Saleska and Engel 1998; Sarnoff 1997; Stewart 1977; Swire 1996; Revesz 1992). The problem of destructive interstate competition between the US states has been extensively discussed in the context of state business taxes and investment aids.[5] Its application to environmental policy is more recent. According to this rationale, failures in the market for the location of industrial firms are similar to the market failure illustrated by the classic 'prisoners' dilemma' of non-cooperative game theory. Hence, much like the prisoners in the story, states will pursue individually rational decisions that nevertheless lead to the adoption of suboptimal environmental standards. Pre-emptive federal standards are understood to be the solution to this problem because they provide a minimum level of environmental quality and hence limit interstate competition.[6] The same logic applies to federal enforcement guidelines that accompany

[3] Under the federal Clean Air Act, Congress has pre-empted all state vehicle emission standards other than those identical to California's vehicle emission standards (which are more stringent than the federal standards) (42 U.S.C. §§ 7507, 7543). The Federal Insecticide, Fungicide and Rodenticide Act pre-empts state requirements for labelling and packaging 'in addition to or different from' those required by federal regulation (7 U.S.C. § 136).

[4] For example, the US chemical industry has actively supported uniformity in a number of regulatory areas. The chemical industry joined with the Occupational Safety and Health Administration in support of uniform national labelling standards (Mashaw and Rose-Ackerman 1984). Under the Resource Conservation and Recovery Act, the Chemical Manufacturers Association favoured uniform federal standards (Schnapf 1982).

[5] The majority of commentators have concluded that because state tax incentives and other subsidies play a comparatively minor role in an industry's location decision, they are essentially unnecessary expenditures. Hence states' continued practice of offering such incentives depletes government revenue sources and erodes the level of government services (Hellerstein 1986: 1036; Pomp 1987: 395; Spindler and Forrester 1993: 36; Wolkoff 1992: 343).

[6] Richard Revesz argues that: (1) it is equally plausible that game-theoretic interactions between the states similar to the prisoners' dilemma dynamic could lead to suboptimally stringent environmental

the devolution of implementing authority to the states under any type of environmental statute.

Some commentators argue that interjurisdictional competition over environmental standards is likely to be efficient when cross-border externalities do not exist (Farber 1986: 413; Revesz 1992: 1242–7). Communities trade off environmental cleanliness against jobs in a way that reflects the differing preferences of residents of each community. The formal models that produce efficient interjurisdictional competition assume a simple representative system where all citizens in a single jurisdiction are either identical or have preferences along a single dimension so that majority rule produces consistent results. Competition between jurisdictions for business location eliminates monopoly profits and prevents state governments from capturing such rents to satisfy their citizens.[7] The most important feature of these models is the lack of economic rents or excess profits in equilibrium. Thus under perfect competition, interjurisdictional differences simply reflect differences in community preferences.

But, of course, these strong competitive assumptions do not hold in the real world. As a consequence, a prisoners' dilemma may operate such that individually rational actions produce a result that is worse for state governments overall (Engel 1997: 302–5; Mashaw and Rose-Ackerman 1984: 117–18, 122–32; Revesz 1992: 1213–27; Rose-Ackerman 1992: 166–70). To see how this can happen, consider a case where economic rents or excess profits exist. Even when governments have a simple representative character, both firms and state governments may engage in a strategic search for rents so long as the market for location rights is not perfectly competitive. Interjurisdictional competition favours relatively mobile groups (Gey 1989–90). Business firms that can invest in any state gain relative to immobile citizens. Firms with little fixed capital or ones that can threaten to go out of business also have a political advantage over both ordinary voters and solvent firms with high levels of fixed capital. Governments may try to outdo each other in offering

standards; and (2) in the absence of interstate competition, states are likely to adopt suboptimally stringent environmental standards. In either case, Revesz argues that the appropriate federal solution is not minimum standards of environmental quality, but either federal maximum environmental standards (under (1)), or, presumably, no federal regulation at all. Empirical data presented by Kirsten Engel and Scott Saleska tend to refute both of Revesz's theories (Engel 1997: 315–51; Saleska and Engel 1998: 63–74).

[7] The recent theoretical articles are summarized in Revesz (1992). The most sophisticated is Oates and Schwab (1988: 335–42), but the efficiency result obtains in only one of the models they present. In the Oates and Schwab model, each town sets a tax on capital and a ratio of emissions to labour in production. Capital is mobile and labour is not. Firms operate in a competitive market and earn zero profits in equilibrium. Individuals within each community have identical utility functions defined over consumption and pollution/labour ratio. The treatment of pollution is clearly a simplification since one would expect people, in fact, to care about the total level of pollution in the town, not its ratio to labour. Communities seek to maximize the utility of residents. The resulting equilibrium is efficient, with the capital tax equal to zero in every town and pollution standards reflecting the residents' marginal trade-off of higher incomes against lower pollution/labour ratios. Importantly, Oates and Schwab go on to consider cases where efficiency does not prevail. If taxes on capital are constrained to be greater than zero, if bureaucrats value large budgets, or if a non-homogeneous community uses majority rule to make decisions, the result in each of these three cases is unlikely to be efficient (342–9).

low levels of environmental regulation or weak implementation to attract business (Markusen, Morey, and Olewiler 1995; 1993). Thus state and local officials may support federal laws limiting their ability to compete with each other. Because states will also have an incentive to undercut each other at the implementation stage, state officials may also support federal enforcement efforts.

The empirical evidence on this contested issue is suggestive, though far from definitive. In a previous article, Engel (1997: 337–47) argued that the empirical evidence refuted the proposition that state competition is efficiency-enhancing and is consistent with the claim that interstate competition for industry results in a welfare-reducing race to the bottom. Engel's evidence consisted of: (1) a survey of state environmental regulators showing that a substantial minority were willing to relax their state's environmental standards out of a conviction that lax standards were important to attracting and retaining industries (337–47, 377–98); and (2) numerous econometric studies showing that the stringency of state environmental standards is unimportant in industry-location decisions.[8] Engel argues that if states compete for industry by relaxing environmental standards, but industry location is substantially unaffected by this competition, then interstate competition will result in a lessening of state welfare because the states fail to gain economic benefits to offset their environmental quality losses (1997: 351–4). Officials in some states appear to make deals that are hard to justify on efficiency grounds and that sometimes produce arguments for federal pre-emption to limit the bargaining power of national business firms.

This evidence is difficult to interpret because, beginning in approximately 1970, Congress enacted a series of environment laws which either impose pre-emptive national minimum environmental quality standards[9] or subject state standards to a federal approval process that can sometimes breed conformity.[10] As a result, one

[8] Engel's survey of state environmental regulators found that a significant minority of the state regulators surveyed claimed that concern over their ability to attract or retain industries contributed to the state levying smaller or lighter civil or criminal penalties for environmental violations (31 per cent), or dropping the enforcement action altogether (17 per cent) (1997: 341, 381). As to the second claim, US evidence suggests that interjurisdictional differences in policy are not a major determinant of firm location because interstate differences in pollution control costs constitute a relatively small share of industrial siting costs. In her article, Engel summarizes the recent evidence and presents the results of her own survey of state environmental regulators. See also Bartik (1988b: 32–3), Duerksen (1983: 56–71), McConnell and Schwab (1991), and Levinson (1996).

[9] Section 109 of the Clean Air Act (42 U.S.C. § 7409) imposes federal maximum concentrations for various conventional air pollutants. Section 111 of the Clean Air Act (42 U.S.C. § 7411) requires national compliance with federal best available air pollution control technology performance standards by major industrial facilities; and Section 301 of the Clean Water Act (42 U.S.C. § 1321) requires major categories of water pollution dischargers to conform with performance standards based upon varying levels of best available technology.

[10] For example, under § 303(a) of the Clean Water Act, states establish water quality standards that both determine the 'use' of the water (e.g. fishing, swimming, irrigation) and determine the allowable concentration of pollution that will ensure attainment of the use (33 U.S.C. § 1313(a)). However, the EPA must approve the state's standards, and, if it does not, it is required to promulgate federal quality standards for the state (§ 304(c)). The degree of uniformity produced by such 'federal approval' provisions has tended to shift with the philosophy of the political administration in office. During the late

cannot observe what would happen in a fully decentralized system. Furthermore, observations today can provide only limited insight into possible past strategic behaviour by states and industries and hence interstate competition over environmental standards (currently disallowed by federal law) could have an important effect upon firm location but just not under current conditions. Even if the consequence of this competition were interstate uniformity, this might well be the result of mobile firms striking hard bargains.

Current federal law has not entirely eliminated the states' ability to adopt varying levels of environmental quality. First, the federal framework of environmental laws contains significant gaps, which states are free to exploit to attract or retain mobile industries. For example, the federal government does not regulate the often highly toxic wastes generated through oil drilling and production, leaving states free to create an environment friendly to the oil industry through lax regulation of oilfield wastes (42 U.S.C. § 6921; 53 Fed. Reg. 25,446, 25,447 (1988)).[11] Second, gaps in the substantive coverage of the regulations, as well as the flexibility permitted by the federal regulations, give states room for variation even for environmental problems subject to federal regulation (General Accounting Office 1996; Flatt 1997).[12] However, the variation permitted within the current framework does not appear to be generating benefits for the states. Labour market conditions and geographical location are the key influences on firm location, outweighing environmental regulations (Engel 1997).

State choice of implementing mechanism

So far, we have focused on variations in the level of environmental standards and the conditions under which decentralized state choices are likely to produce efficient outcomes. In addition, interstate variations in implementing mechanisms

1970s, this philosophy was less deferential to states' arguments for variation from suggested federal guidelines and resulted in greater uniformity in state standards. See, for example, *Mississippi Commission on Natural Resources* v. *Costle* (625 F.2d 1269 (5th Cir. 1980)), which reviews the EPA's disapproval of Mississippi water quality standards, which varied from suggested EPA guidelines. The more recent states-rights philosophy prevalent in the Clinton Administration has resulted in the EPA's approval of greater variation in state water quality standards. See, for example, *Natural Resources Defense Council* v. *EPA* (16 F.3d 1395 (4th Cir. 1993)), which reviews the EPA's approval of a Virginia and Maryland dioxin standard 1,000 times more lenient than the EPA's recommended criteria.

[11] 42 U.S.C. § 6921 postpones regulation of oilfield drilling wastes pending further study by the EPA, and 53 Fed. Reg. 25,446, 25,447 (1988) sets out the EPA's decision to continue to exempt oilfield waste from federal regulation.

[12] In its report, the General Accounting Office (GAO) found that significant differences existed between states in the stringency of the controls they imposed upon industrial discharges of five toxic metals to surface waters. This was despite the fact that state discretion is restricted by a federal permit programme often criticized for imposing uniform standards upon industry: the National Pollution Discharge Elimination System (NPDES). The GAO found that the differences were attributable to 'differences in surface waters across the country and because of flexibility in the implementation of the pollutant discharge programme provided for in the Clean Water Act and the EPA's regulations'. As a result of this flexibility, the GAO found that states varied in the numeric standards they imposed and even whether they imposed any standards at all—some states required only monitoring of the toxic metals.

could also trigger inefficiencies that may sometimes justify federal intervention (Rose-Ackerman 1994: 1592–5). Our argument is an extension of the discussion of the prisoners' dilemma, but we make it separately to highlight a neglected feature of the debate.[13]

Some methods of achieving environmental goals are widely viewed as more efficient than others. For example, if a state has fixed a discharge goal, tradeable pollution rights are more efficient than requiring all firms to achieve the same level of percentage removal. A tradeable rights scheme allows firms to treat to varying levels and hence distributes the costs of treatment efficiently over dischargers with different marginal cost curves. In equilibrium, the marginal cost of treatment is equalized across all firms, but the levels of percentage removal differ. Of course, a perfectly informed regulatory agency could mimic the results of a tradeable rights scheme, but to do so it would need to have detailed cost information from all dischargers. Lacking such information, command-and-control regimes frequently rely on simple rules of thumb such as equal percentage removal.

Now consider what might happen in a decentralized federal system where states can select which implementing mechanism to use. Suppose that two states have identical environmental goals but select different enforcement tools. One issues a fixed number of tradeable rights, and the other sets equal percentage treatment levels. Suppose that a new firm is trying to decide where to locate. In the first community, it must purchase rights from existing holders as part of the cost of entry. In the second, it must remove a fixed percentage of its pollution. In the first state, pollution levels remain fixed and the price of rights increases. In the second state, pollution levels increase unless the state responds by increasing the required percentage removal for all firms. Suppose that a particular firm would remove the same percentage of its waste in either state. So long as other factors are equal, the firm prefers to locate in the command-and-control state because it does not have to bear the costs of buying rights. Even if the command-and-control state always adjusts the overall percentage removal levels whenever entry or expansion occurs, the firm may still prefer this state. The only firms that prefer the state with tradeable rights are those that would purchase a large quantity of rights because they have very high treatment costs. Of course, land values in the states could adjust to take account of these differences in regulatory regimes, and command-and-control states can increase the required levels of removal to compensate for entry. However, the basic point remains. If one state charges firms for their discharges and another does not, this will distort location choices.

One way around this problem would be for the federal government to require every state to announce an overall discharge target and then permit states to administer the target by fees, tradeable permits, or command and control. Then new entrants would be forbidden from breaking the target and would have to negotiate

[13] Most theoretical work on interjurisdictional competition assumes that the basic policy tool has been fixed a priori. Jurisdictions are only free to decide on its level (Oates and Schwab 1988: 336).

with existing firms to buy their way into the state. A tradeable rights mechanism provides an automatic mechanism for doing this. Other forms of regulation would need extra structures to handle entry. For example, in the command-and-control case, state administrators might assign discharge quotas to existing firms based on their raw pollution loads. Federal regulators could require the states to permit new entrants to purchase rights from existing firms.

Absent such federal intervention, states that choose command-and-control regulation are likely to attract more entry than those using market-based schemes simply because the command-and-control states are not charging for pollution discharges. Although states can design mechanisms to counteract this tendency, they seem complex and politically unrealistic, and they may be of questionable constitutionality (*South Dakota* v. *Dole*, 483 U.S. 203 (1987). Thus devolution to the states seems a poor way to test new implementation ideas that impose differential costs on firms.[14] Observers will not learn anything about the value of market-based instruments, and interstate variation in tools will generate an inefficient pattern of entry into polluting industries. Thus when policy making is devolved to the states, the federal government may need to limit states' choices of implementing mechanisms even if it permits them to decide on the level of environmental benefits.

II. PUBLIC CHOICE CONSIDERATIONS

Public officials are not mere functionaries implementing the clearly articulated and well-informed preferences of citizens. Instead, the self-interest of politicians may sometimes diverge from that of their constituents. We discuss two possibilities. First, politicians may become allies of business firms against the interests of a state's citizens in return for outright bribes or more subtle promises of campaign funds or future employment. Second, politicians' re-election motives can produce distorted incentives under some conditions. In either case, reliance upon the policy choices of state politicians can result in inefficient environmental decisions. These inefficiencies can arise either when the federal government has withdrawn entirely from a regulatory area or when it has taken a hands-off attitude toward state-level implementation of a federal law.

Government capture

Smaller governments are frequently more subject to capture by narrow interests than larger governments, and the interests of industry are often more narrowly focused and better articulated than the diffuse interests of the general citizenry. In

[14] For a sceptical view of the claimed benefits of federalism as a way to test the value of innovation, see Rose-Ackerman (1980).

the case of environmental protection, local environmental groups are often subject to crippling free-rider problems (Olson 1965). State or provincial governments may limit interstate commerce to protect local businesses and line their own pockets in return for favours granted to firms (Regan 1986: 1122).[15] State governments may be under the control of narrow elites that use the apparatus of government for personal gain. Although competition between jurisdictions for investment resources limits corrupt possibilities, it does not eliminate them. The very smallness and intimacy of local jurisdictions may make corrupt relations possible (Rodden and Rose-Ackerman 1997: 1538). Indeed, the most corrupt and patronage ridden governments seem to be at the local level in many countries, including the United States. The close cooperation between public authorities and private interests limits partisan politics and the supervision it provides (Rose-Ackerman 1999: 149–51).

Distorted re-election motives

Even if there is no outright corruption of state or local officials, there may be a divergence between a politician's interests and the interests of the citizenry at large. Scott Saleska and Kirsten Engel (1998: 74–84) offer such an explanation for the environmental concessions granted to firms.[16] According to them, a politician's grant of concessions to a potential entrant is individually rational when two conditions hold. First, the public is convinced that concessions are important to firm location decisions or, at worst, is uncertain as to their efficacy. Second, the politician reaps the largest positive political payoff when it offers a firm an incentive and the firm actually does locate in-state. He or she suffers only a small negative political payoff if a firm that is offered a concession still chooses to locate out-of-state (because officials are given credit for doing everything possible). If a firm that is denied a concession locates in-state anyway, the politician will be unable to take credit for the siting. If a firm denied a concession sites elsewhere, the politician is blamed for being insufficiently aggressive. In this last situation, politicians will be unable to defend themselves convincingly by pointing to statistical studies showing that environmental concessions are rarely decisive in firm location decisions. Thus even if citizens have fairly strong environmental values, so long as they are also concerned about jobs and are ignorant of the true importance of concessions, officials have an incentive to provide inefficiently large concessions.

[15] In the United States, jurisprudence under the dormant Commerce Clause provides examples of economic protectionism by state governments. *Wyoming* v. *Oklahoma* (112 S.Ct. 789, 800 (1992)) invalidated, as purposefully protectionist, a state statute requiring that 10 per cent of the coal burned by in-state utilities originates from Oklahoma mines, and *New Energy Co. of Indiana* v. *Limbach* (486 U.S. 269, 274, 278–81 (1988)) invalidated, as purposefully protectionist, an Ohio tax credit for ethanol produced in Ohio.

[16] Saleska and Engel's explanation is an elaboration and adaptation of an example presented by Harold Wolman (1988: 25–6) which he uses to explain the seeming irrationality of states' continued practice of offering industry economic development incentives, despite empirical data indicating that such incentives are of low value in attracting industry.

Implications

Public choice problems at the state and local level support a stronger regulatory role for the national government only if the national government is less vulnerable to these problems. This issue has not been resolved empirically, but it appears that state and local governments may be especially vulnerable to capture by narrow interests.

Capture by industry can be avoided if the political influence of environmental interests counter-balances industry interests. Environmental organizations may be more influential at the national level, where such groups can use the national media to motivate voters and hence reduce the problem of free-riders (Esty 1996: 650–1).[17] Some scholars also argue that federal interest group excesses tend to trigger a corrective backlash, while state and local environmental policy manipulation often goes unnoticed. Furthermore, the technical complexity of many environmental problems favours interest groups that can back up their demands with expertise, a characteristic that also favours better-funded national environmental groups as opposed to local organizations.

Federal regulation may counteract unrepresentative state environmental policy making caused by distorted re-election motives. Although federal politicians and regulators may be as adept as any in obtaining tax loopholes or sweetheart deals for their favourite home-state industries, the comprehensive nature of most federal environmental standards provides less opportunity for federal politicians to favour their own state.[18] Hence federal politicians seem less likely to be susceptible to the perverse matrix of incentives that may lead state politicians to offer concessions to industrial firms that result in reduced welfare for the state as a whole (Saleska and Engel 1998: 83–4).[19]

In contrast, the competitive federalism literature argues that the 'exit' threat of mobile industries (that is, their threat to relocate elsewhere) enhances the representative nature of government by limiting public officials' ability to extract excessive rents from mobile capital owners (Weingast 1995: 5). This argument is sometimes used to support calls for placing regulatory authority over economic matters in the hands of lower levels of government, on the grounds that they are vulnerable to exit threats while the national government is not.

Despite its superficial attractiveness, the 'exit threat' remedy takes a narrow view of the public choice problem and is unrealistic from the standpoint of real-world politics. Calls for decentralized regulation on the basis of enhancing the 'exit' threat of mobile industry supposes that the most important problem is the overreaching

[17] Revesz (1997e: 558–61), on the other hand, argues that the costs of organizing on the larger scale of national politics may magnify the free-rider problem faced by environmental groups, rather than ameliorate it.

[18] Ackerman and Hassler (1981) argue to the contrary.

[19] Saleska and Engel note, however, that national decision makers may be subject to the same type of perverse incentives *vis-à-vis* competition with other nations for the siting of an international firm within the United States.

rent-seeking behaviour of government which imposes extortionary taxes upon capital through excessively stringent regulations. But that is only part of the story. The 'exit' threat cannot remedy unrepresentative regulation arising out of the excessive market power of mobile capital *vis-à-vis* state governments (Engel 1997). Furthermore, even if the main problem is overreaching government regulators, the 'exit' argument ignores the possibility that elected leaders may face electoral incentives to ignore the threats of mobile industry and make pacts with coalitions of less mobile constituents (Rodden and Rose-Ackerman 1997: 1533–46).

III. APPLICATION TO UNITED STATES POLICIES

Our framework suggests that federal–state cooperation in environmental law and policy can be valuable, but it also implies that state implementation of federal statutes requires continued federal supervision. At present, budgetary restrictions at the federal level are such that most federal environmental laws are implemented by the states rather than the national government (General Accounting Office 1995: 1:1). Furthermore, there are indications that the system of federal supervision of state implementation and enforcement—never very popular with state governments (Steinzor 1999)—is being retooled in a manner that reduces federal authority. The federal government has recently supported a number of decentralization initiatives aimed at increasing the discretion of states to implement federal environmental laws, and the federal courts are providing states with greater immunity from lawsuits that seek to compel their compliance with federal mandates. Given the impediments to efficient state environmental regulation that we have identified, these developments are a cause for concern.

Devolution of programmes

The implementation of most federal environmental laws is mainly carried out by state governments under a variety of intergovernmental arrangements. These arrangements include: (a) federal mandates, where Congress orders states to promulgate regulations or implement federal laws (Lead Contamination and Control Act of 1988, 42 U.S.C. § 300j-24(c); Emergency Planning and Community Right-to-Know Act, 42 U.S.C. § 11001 (a));[20] (b) programme delegation, where the EPA permits states to apply for and receive authority to implement and enforce federal law (Clean Air Act § 502, 42 U.S.C. § 7661a; Resources Conservation and Recovery Act § 3006, 42 U.S.C. § 6926; Clean Water Act §§ 402(b), 404(g), 33

[20] Examples of legislation where Congress has used the 'direct order' approach include the Lead Contamination Control Act of 1988, which requires that states provide a 'remedial action program' for the removal of lead contamination from school drinking water systems, and the Emergency Planning and Community Right-to-Know Act, which requires the governor of each state to either establish an emergency response commission or to personally act as the commission.

U.S.C. §§ 1342(b), § 1344(g));[21] and (c) 'cross-cutting requirements', where Congress applies federal requirements to state and local government entities in the same manner as they apply to private persons and businesses (Light 1998: 799–807). Recent Supreme Court decisions make transfers through federal mandates problematic since they interpret the Tenth Amendment as prohibiting the federal government from forcing states to enact legislation or to enforce federal laws (*New York* v. *United States*, 505 U.S. 144 (1990); *Printz* v. *United States* 117 S.Ct. 2365 (1997)).[22] Thus, of the three, programme delegation is the dominant method of transferring implementation authority to the states.

Under the programme delegation model, Congress authorizes the EPA to delegate to a state all implementation and enforcement tasks related to a federal statute so long as the state demonstrates that it has the resources and legal authority to promulgate regulations as stringent as the federal standards and to pursue the same enforcement measures (Clean Water Act, 33 U.S.C. § 1342).[23] Once a programme is delegated, it normally operates 'in lieu' of the federal regulations (although the federal law remains in effect), and the state implements the programme as a matter of state law. The EPA cannot exercise implementation or enforcement powers under federal law unless there is evidence that the state programme is failing to meet the requirements of the delegation. Delegation is thus a bargain between the states and the EPA under which the EPA agrees to leave the day-to-day administration of the programme to the states in exchange for the state's agreement to implement the federal programme effectively (Light 1998: 806).

The effective implementation of one government's goals and priorities by another obviously demands a system of supervision. With respect to programme delegations, that supervision traditionally takes the form of detailed work plans drawn up by the EPA. According to these plans, states agree to accomplish Congress's statutory mandates as well as other programme-building tasks according to statutory deadlines and the EPA's priority ranking of the various chores. States are given grant moneys to permit them to implement each task or group of tasks.[24]

Studies show that states are currently having a hard time meeting federal obligations under delegated programmes (General Accounting Office 1995: 2:3). Nevertheless, the states have recently fought for and won significant concessions

[21] The Clean Air Act § 502 provides for delegation of air permits for major sources from the EPA to states; the Resource Conservation and Recovery Act § 3006 provides the same with respect to permits for hazardous waste treatment, storage, and disposal facilities; the Clean Water Act § 402(b) provides the same with respect to permits for water pollution discharges; and § 404(g) provides the same with respect to permits for the deposit of dredge and fill in navigable waters.

[22] *Printz* v. *United States* invalidated provisions of the Brady Gun Act because they required state officers to expend state resources on enforcing a federal statute; and *New York* v. *United States* invalidated provisions of a federal radioactive waste disposal law because they forced states to either enact state legislation in conformity with federal requirements or take title to the waste itself.

[23] The Clean Water Act specifies the conditions under which the NPDES permit programme may be delegated to states.

[24] Telephone interview with Art Horowitz, Office of Enforcement and Compliance, US EPA (12 August 1999).

that limit federal supervision. For instance, a 1995 agreement between the EPA and a coalition of state environmental administrators increased state flexibility and reduced federal supervision. As a result, 'Performance Partnership Agreements' have replaced work plans, and the federal government now provides lump sum grants instead of line-item grants.[25] The new agreements differ vastly in detail and content, with some omitting nearly all references to how and when the state will perform federal statutory mandates under the delegated programme.[26] This new approach gives states the discretion and the financial resources to perform federal statutory mandates in a manner that accords with their own state-level priorities. However, where those state priorities are at odds with federal regulatory priorities because of limitations in state regulatory systems (for example, state 'capture' or destructive interstate competition), this looser approach could result in harmful reductions in environmental quality. Even if interstate differences could, in principle, reflect differences in citizen preferences, variations that arise from states' freedom to set implementation priorities under federal law seem a problematic way to reflect these differences.

Devolution of enforcement

A second set of possibly harmful developments concerns enforcement. First, when the EPA has delegated programme implementation, it faces challenges to the continued authority and capacity of the federal government to enforce environmental regulations. Second, some states are replacing traditional enforcement tools with novel and untested methods of questionable efficacy.

The sheer number of facilities subject to environmental regulation, together with the in-depth knowledge of regulated entities possessed by lower levels of government, means that most enforcement activities should be carried out by state rather than federal agencies. Indeed, over 90 per cent of environmental inspections are performed by the states (Kuehn 1996: 2381). Nevertheless, recent studies reveal a widespread decline in state environmental enforcement activities, ranging from inspections to monitoring to the filing of administrative and judicial actions against significant violators (US Environmental Protection Agency, Office of Inspector General 1999a; 1998a; 1998b; 1998c; 1997a). Many states, such as Virginia and Pennsylvania, are failing to bring enforcement actions against significant violators, or responding to such violations with weak sanctions (Cushman 1997; 1996; US Environmental Protection Agency, Office of Inspector General 1999b; 1997b).

[25] As of April 1997, twenty-seven states had signed Performance Partnership Agreements with EPA regional offices, while thirty-seven states had entered into separate Performance Partnership Grant Agreements (Steinzor 1999).

[26] Telephone interview with Professor Rena Steinzor, University of Maryland School of Law (2 September 1999); telephone interview with Chuck Kent, US EPA, Office of Reinvention (3 September 1999). See also US Environmental Protection Agency Partnership (April 1998).

In some states, declines in traditional enforcement (levying of civil and criminal fines and sanctions) have been replaced with compliance assistance and 'cooperative' enforcement measures. Of such measures, one common type exempts from penalties violations discovered by companies during the course of a routine environmental audit. Under these audit immunity laws, companies who report a violation discovered in the course of an environmental audit may not be assessed an administrative or civil penalty for violations identified during the course of the audit and corrected soon thereafter (National Association of Attorneys General 1997). In some states, environmental audit reports, as well as other information or reports generated by the audit, are not admissible into evidence or subject to disclosure in legal proceedings.

The spread of cooperative enforcement mechanisms is troubling because there currently exists little empirical basis for state claims that cooperative mechanisms are more effective in achieving compliance. Indeed, what empirical data do exist appear to point in the opposite direction. For instance, a recent study by the National Conference of State Legislatures of the auditing practices of 988 manufacturing facilities found no statistically significant difference between the number or frequency of audits conducted by firms located in states with audit privilege and immunity laws or policies and states without such laws or policies (Morandi 1998).[27] If 'cooperative' enforcement mechanisms are less effective than traditional enforcement and, as discussed above, many states are neglecting traditional enforcement activities, devolution of enforcement authority to the states is currently exacting high social and environmental costs.

A federal role in overseeing state enforcement activities and in pursuing independent federal enforcement actions even in states with delegated enforcement authority can play an important role in achieving effective compliance with environmental laws. States may be reluctant to, or incapable of, effective enforcement where: (1) enforcement actions are subject to economies of scale; (2) state officials are using their enforcement discretion to engage in a welfare-reducing race to the bottom in environmental quality; (3) state agencies have been 'captured' by regulated industries; and (4) state officials have demonstrated an unwillingness to bring enforcement actions against their own agencies or local governments. Moreover, even where states are eager to enforce environmental laws, they may be aided in their efforts by the polluters' fear of 'the gorilla in the closet'—possible federal enforcement action (Kuehn 1996; Ringquist 1993; Stanfield 1984).

Endorsement of a federal enforcement presence should not ignore the problems that a dual system of enforcement can create. The exercise of federal enforcement

[27] Interestingly, more companies reported conducting audits in states with no audit law or policy than in states with audit privilege or immunity laws or policies, though the difference was not statistically significant. Furthermore, whether or not a firm was located in a state with an auditing law or policy had no effect upon whether or not firms disclosed violations discovered during an audit to environmental regulators. Facility operators reported that their primary motivation for conducting an audit was to avoid the discovery of a violation by a government inspector, thus confirming the superiority of traditional enforcement tools over new state initiatives (Dana 1996: 972 n.13; Morandi 1998).

powers may undermine state enforcement efforts. Firms may be reluctant to cooperate with the state if the federal government is likely to sue over the same violation. It can also lead to wasteful duplication of effort, for both industry and government agencies.[28] Because it may also *strengthen* state efforts due to the 'gorilla in the closet' phenomenon, however, and because it is an important environmental safeguard in cases of 'captured' state governments, a credible federal enforcement presence should be maintained even in states with delegated enforcement authority.

Nevertheless, recent developments are undermining the federal government's ability to carry out this supervisory role with respect to state environmental enforcement. Recent reports document widespread inadequacies in the EPA's record of overseeing state enforcement programmes (US Environmental Protection Agency, Office of Inspector General 1999a; 1998a; 1998b; 1998c; 1997a). This is perhaps not surprising, given cuts in the EPA's enforcement budget (Environmental Reporter 1996) and Congress's occasional restriction upon agency expenditure of funds on certain enforcement priorities (Environment Reporter 1995).

Furthermore, the EPA's legal authority to bring an enforcement action in a state with delegated enforcement authority is now being questioned. Recently, a federal appeals court forbade the EPA from 'overfiling' a state enforcement action in a delegated state under the nation's hazardous waste disposal law, the Resource Conservation and Recovery Act (*Harmon Ind., Inc.* v. *Browner*, 191 F.3d 894 (1999)).[29] Overfiling means that the EPA, usually seeking a much more substantial penalty, files an enforcement action after the state has already concluded an enforcement action against the same violator for the same violations. If this decision is extended to other statutory contexts, it will discourage the EPA from ensuring that state enforcement efforts are sufficiently vigorous. Federal environmental statutes authorize the EPA to withdraw programme delegation in states that are failing to conduct adequate enforcement and implementation (Clean Water Act § 4026, 33 U.S.C. § 1342 (c)).[30] However, because this is not a realistic response either to a single case of a state that has failed to bring an enforcement action

[28] It might also be argued that federal enforcement deprives states of the ability to use their enforcement discretion to tailor the stringency of federal environmental laws. We reject this argument, however, on the grounds that the process of establishing standards of environmental quality that match citizen preferences should be implemented through the standard-setting process, as opposed to the enforcement process. This is because the standard-setting process, whether performed by state legislators or state bureaucrats, is generally more democratic than the enforcement process, and agency exercise of enforcement discretion is generally shielded from public scrutiny or judicial review (*Heckler* v. *Chaney*, 470 U.S. 821 (1984)).

[29] Also in *In re: Zoo Med Laboratories, Inc.*, 1999 WL 637242 (E.P.A.), EPA pesticide enforcement claims filed subsequent to settlement between defendant manufacturer and delegated state were barred by *res judicata*.

[30] The Clean Water Act § 402(c) authorized the EPA to withdraw delegation of a state water pollution permit programme upon finding that the state was failing to administer the programme in accordance with the Act.

(*NRDC* v. *EPA*, 859 F.2d 156, 181 (D.C. Cir. 1998))[31] or to a situation of widespread state failure to enforce (General Accounting Office 1995: 2:3:1),[32] the EPA is limited to asserting its enforcement authority in discrete cases by 'overfiling' a state action.

Constitutional law

Recent Supreme Court decisions make it much more difficult to hold states liable for violating federal environmental laws. By interpreting state sovereign immunity broadly, the Supreme Court has essentially left the decision of whether or not to comply with federal laws up to the states themselves. Given the expanding role of state governments in environmental regulation and the diminishing role of the national government, this trend has negative implications for efficient environmental regulation because it will be extremely difficult to hold states accountable for implementing or obeying federal regulations.

In nearly all federal environmental laws, Congress has used its power to regulate under the Commerce Clause to authorize private parties to sue states for non-compliance with federal regulation. Congress presupposes that states can be sued for violating a federal law in their capacity as an owner or operator of a polluting facility. For example, under the federal Superfund law, any 'person' may sue another 'person' for the costs of cleaning up a site where hazardous waste has been deposited (Comprehensive Environmental Response Compensation and Liability Act § 107, 42 U.S.C. § 9607). Because 'persons' include both individuals and states (§ 9601 (21)), Superfund authorizes private parties to sue a state to recover clean-up damages. Also, nearly all federal environmental laws provide for citizens to file suit against states for violation of an emission standard or an order (Clean Air Act § 304, 42 U.S.C. § 7604).

Under a series of recent Supreme Court decisions, however, states can claim immunity from Superfund cost-recovery actions as well as citizen suits seeking state compliance with federal environmental regulations. Starting in 1997, the Supreme Court has dealt repeated blows to the ability of citizens to use the courts to compel state compliance with federal law. First, in *Seminole Tribe of Florida* v. *Florida* (517 U.S. 44, 72–73 (1996)), the Court held that federal legislation enacted pursuant to the Commerce Clause cannot abrogate state sovereign immunity to suits filed by citizens in federal court. The Court subsequently applied the same limita-

[31] *NRDC* v. *EPA* characterizes withdrawal of a delegation as being 'so drastic that EPA cannot be expected to use it except in egregious cases'. It is not clear that the EPA has ever followed through with the withdrawal of a state programme that it initiated, though the agency has taken back delegated programmes that states have 'returned' to the EPA. The EPA initiated the process of withdrawing the 'primacy', or enforcement-led status, of Alaska, California, Colorado, Hawaii, Kansas, Maine, South Dakota, and Washington, but never finalized the action (General Accounting Office 1995: 2:3:1).

[32] The GAO quotes EPA officials in three different regional offices as stating that, were the agency to withdraw a delegated programme, it would not have sufficient resources to implement more than a 'bare bones' programme.

tion to lawsuits filed against states in a state court. In the recent case of *Alden* v. *Maine* (119 S.Ct. 2240 (1999)), the Supreme Court broadly construed states' sovereign immunity to hold that Congress lacks the power under Article I to waive states' immunity from suits filed in state court.

As a result of these decisions, there are very few options left for holding states accountable for compliance with federal environmental law. First, and most obviously, states can always waive their immunity to suit in state court or, under the Eleventh Amendment, in federal court. However, the likelihood that states will do so expressly is small and another recent Eleventh Amendment decision, *College Savings Bank* v. *Florida Prepaid Postsecondary Education Expense Board* (119 S.Ct. 2219, 2225–31 (1999), prevents courts from finding that states 'constructively' waived their immunity through their participation in various forms of activity, including commercial activity. Second, Congress can still subject states to suit in federal court when it legislates under the Fourteenth Amendment to protect persons from deprivation of liberty or property, as opposed to legislating under Article I. However, it may prove difficult to argue that federal statutes that broadly protect human health and the environment are enacted by Congress to protect liberty and private property, and, in any case, another of the Court's recent sovereign immunity decisions severely narrows the type of legislation falling within this exception (*Florida Prepaid Postsecondary Education Expense Board* v. *College Savings Bank* 119 S.Ct. 2199 (1999)).[33] Third, citizens may still file for prospective injunctive relief against state officials in federal court under the judicially created fiction that the lawsuit is against the official, and not the state (*Ex Parte Young*, 209 U.S. 123 (1908)),[34] though *Seminole Tribe* has significantly narrowed the circumstances in which this doctrine now applies.[35] Moreover, the doctrine is of little help where the federal statutory right at issue is the payment of monetary damages, rather than injunctive relief. For example, a lower federal court has applied the recent decision to restrict the ability of a private party to sue a state for the recovery of environmental clean-up costs under Superfund where the state owned the source of the hazardous substance releases (*Burnette* v. *Carothers*, 192 F.3d 52, 59 (2d. Cir. 1999)). Fourth, the federal government could try conditioning federal grants or even state programme delegation upon a state's waiver of its sovereign immunity, though it is possible that the Court would find this condition 'unduly coercive' (*South*

[33] *Florida Prepaid Postsecondary Education Expense Board* v. *College Savings Bank*, holds that because Congress's enforcement power against states under § 5 of the Fourteenth Amendment is remedial, to hold that an act of Congress waives states' Eleventh Amendment immunity to suit in federal court, Congress must, in enacting the act, identify a pattern of state abuse of liberty and property interests outlawed by the act.

[34] *Ex Parte Young* allows for federal jurisdiction over a suit against a state official when that suit seeks only prospective injunctive relief in order to 'end a continuing violation of federal law'. *Idaho* v. *Coeur d'Alene Tribe of Idaho* holds that suits against a state based upon *Ex Parte Young* survive the Court's decision in *Seminole Tribe*.

[35] Through *Seminole Tribe*, the *Ex Parte Young* doctrine has become unavailable where Congress has provided for a detailed remedial scheme that does not contemplate a federal lawsuit against a state official.

Carolina v. *Dole*, 483 U.S. 203 (1987)). Finally, although these recent decisions do not affect the authority of the federal government to file an enforcement action against a state, the federal government faces a variety of disincentives to filing such suits, including the fact that it relies heavily upon states to implement environmental laws.

The recent Supreme Court decisions on state sovereign immunity, as well as the other recent developments at the EPA and in the states, indicate a basic shift in policy. States are obtaining greater authority to implement and enforce environmental laws, and the EPA and citizens have fewer ways to hold states accountable for compliance with federal environmental laws and for the accomplishment of the federal objectives of delegated programmes. Although such discretion may increase diversity in environmental problem-solving, such diversity may come at the cost of environmental quality.[36]

CONCLUSIONS

We have highlighted the risks of devolving environmental policy making and implementation to the states. These risks, of course, do not imply that devolution is never called for. Some problems are truly confined within state and local boundaries and may not generate any destructive interstate competition. In other cases, the accountability of state and local governments to their constituents may indeed be higher than that of federal politicians and bureaucrats. Nevertheless, a blanket endorsement of devolution is unwarranted once one takes account of the problems we highlight. Our overview of the current state of federal enforcement pro-

[36] In contrast to the federalism cases discussed in the text, the Supreme Court has been very strict with the states under the Commerce Clause in cases that involve the interstate shipment of waste (Rose-Ackerman 1994: 1600–1). These rulings might discourage states from implementing an environmental standard through a tradeable right mechanism (Engel 1999). For example, in return for removing regulatory strictures on electric power, several states require energy retailers to include a minimum percentage of renewable power. The most efficient way to implement this mandate is to make the obligations tradeable. Once the obligations are tradeable and move in interstate commerce, however, the renewable subsidy can flow out of the state, spreading the benefits of renewable energy (for example, cleaner air) widely, but localizing the subsidy cost in the originating state. Faced with this prospect, a state may impose barriers against trades in energy credits into or out of its jurisdiction. Under the Supreme Court's jurisprudence, however, states are prohibited from discriminating against interstate commerce on the basis of the geographic origin of a good or service subject to trade. Hence the Commerce Clause could eliminate a state's incentive to use tradeable renewable energy credits to meet its renewable energy mandate. If state regulators are simply concerned with a global increase in the use of renewable energy sources to save scarce supplies of oil or gas, they too will be indifferent to where the renewable power is generated. However, if the state instead wishes to encourage renewable energy sources in-state, that goal is undermined by out-of-state trades. Of course, one might suppose that, like the air pollution permits discussed above, renewable energy credits could be defined to include only power produced in-state. But because such a limitation may favour in-state over out-of-state producers of wind and solar power, it might raise Commerce Clause objections. A state may be able to argue successfully in court that the restriction serves a valid state purpose. If not, federal regulation may be warranted because of the state's inability to remove the constitutional impediment itself.

grammes and constitutional law doctrine suggests some worrying trends in environmental law that may weaken many valuable features of existing federal statutes. Especially when federal statutes fulfil national goals, excessive devolution can undermine the statutory purpose. But we have shown that even when the environmental impacts are localized, a federal presence will often be justified to overcome the negative impacts of interstate competition and the narrow interests of state and local politicians. Devolution and decentralization should not be taken as obviously desirable principles in the environmental area but should be subject to a sceptical assessment in light of the potential for opportunistic behaviour that can undermine public control of government.

PART III

Regulatory Competition Theory in the EU Context

8

Fiscal Federalism, Jurisdictional Competition and Tax Coordination: Translating Theory to Policy in the European Union

WILLIAM BRATTON AND JOSEPH MCCAHERY*

Economic theory is often said to provide a basis for setting presumptions to help allocate regulatory authority in federal systems. Less is said about its operation as a basis for rebutting presumptions respecting allocations of authority in federations, the matter we take up in this chapter. The presumption in question is the European Union's (EU's) subsidiarity principle. The case for rebuttal concerns the Code of Conduct on Business Taxation (the Code), a tax coordination initiative that identifies and prohibits a zone of distortionary competition among the member states respecting taxation of capital. The Code is presently pending before the European Council as part of a larger package of tax measures. Its evaluation under subsidiarity raises three questions: (1) Whether subsidiarity's decentralization presumption implies a further presumption favouring tax competition; (2) Whether the subsidiarity's decentralization presumption can be overcome by a purely theoretical showing of distortionary effects of tax competition; and (3) Whether, if empirical evidence of distortionary effects is required, the coordination legislation in question must address the empirically established distortion with adjudicative particularity. We reach a firm answer only as to question (1): subsidiarity does not favour tax competition, remaining neutral on the subject. We find ourselves unable to answer questions (2) and (3) with technocratic surety. The strength of both the decentralization presumption and the rebuttal case depends on political risks and opportunities specific to the situation, as well as economic factors. In the case of the Code, the risks turn out to be low, permitting the presumption to be rebutted by a strong theoretical case on a patchy empirical record.

As we work through these questions we address further questions about the nature and strength of, first, the presumption favouring decentralization bound up in the subsidiarity principle, and, second, the presumption favouring decentralization lying at the core of the economics of fiscal federalism. The subsidiarity principle, set out in paragraph 2 of Article 3b [5] of the Treaty on European Union, concerns subject matter as to which the European Union and its member states share competences (Dehousse 1994: 110). It imposes a burden of proof to justify

* The authors would like to thank Peter Essers, Tom Heukels, Hugh Jacobson, Gerard Meussen, and Sacha Prechal for their comments and suggestions on an earlier draft of this chapter.

action by the higher level of government (Demaret 1996: 19), seeking to ensure, first, that EU action taken in lieu of member state action is justified, and, second, that any authority thereby accorded to the European Union is limited to the minimum necessary to achieve the articulated objective. As such, subsidiarity is not a principle of decentralization even as it incorporates a presumption in decentralization's favour. It is instead a principle that guides the upward and downward allocation of regulatory authority within the federation (Cass 1992: 1107).

The subsidiarity principle bears a close, familial resemblance to a basic assertion of the theory of fiscal federalism. Fiscal federalism has in turn been suggested, appropriately in our view, as a source of normative content for subsidiarity (Van den Bergh 1996: 363; Inman and Rubinfeld 1994: 147). Like subsidiarity, this economic theory sets a rebuttable presumption in favour of decentralization. The presumption follows from the decentralization theorem of Wallace Oates (1972: 54): absent either cost savings from centralized provision of a local public good or interjurisdictional externalities, local provision of locally efficient levels of public goods will always cause welfare to be at least as high as or higher than would be the case under central provision at a single, uniform level. The insight is that, all other things being equal, heterogeneous citizen preferences are more likely to be satisfied through the state and local provision of public goods and services; citizens can match preferences with public goods packages by sorting themselves among different jurisdictions. But all other things are not always equal. Central government remains better situated to perform the macroeconomic stabilization function, to redistribute wealth, and to provide national public goods, such as defence (Oates 1999: 1121).

The internalization of economic externalities within the federation also tends to be a central function under fiscal federalism theory (Inman and Rubinfeld 1997b: 45). Significantly, the operative concept of externality is fiscal rather than physical, as in torts contexts, and encompasses any distortion of economic behaviour stemming from state and local regulation or public goods provision. Room for debate about the conditions necessary to rebut the decentralization presumption expands accordingly. This is particularly likely to be the case respecting taxation, as to which an extensive theoretical literature describes possibilities for horizontal externalities and other distortionary effects among states in federations. The tax competition to which the Code is directed shows up on the list of distortions, rebutting the decentralization presumption at a theoretical level.

A complicating factor shows up, however, at this stage in the analysis of tax coordination. Jurisdictional competition theory also comes to bear to strengthen fiscal federalism's presumption favouring decentralization. In the tax competition context, this theory combines the insights of two famous models: the Tiebout (1956) model of competition among localities and the public choice model of the Leviathan state (Brennan and Buchanan 1980). The two combine to assert that decentralization respecting taxation not only enhances chances for preference matching but provides a useful protective device in a world where public officials are self-seeking maximizers who, left to their own devices, maximize the size of the state rather than the welfare of its citizens. Centralization invites the appearance of a Leviathan state—a big government that just gets bigger. Decentralized regulation, taxation, and public service provision ameliorate that problem by triggering inter-state competition for capital and citizens. Competition constrains government excess and keeps taxes low.

We emerge with conflicting theoretical signals. Fiscal federalism's descriptions of allocative inefficiencies from state and local taxation operate at cross-purposes with jurisdictional competition theory's strong commendation of decentralization. The former line of economic analysis addresses one set of problems to suggest a weak decentralization presumption respecting taxation, while the latter line of economics addresses a different set of problems to suggest a strong presumption. Empirical evidence holds out the only clear solution to the dilemma posed. If a tradeoff must be made, then the choice lies in a particular appraisal of the costs and benefits of both competition and coordination respecting taxation.

We evaluate the Code within the foregoing framework. Considered as an exercise in legislative drafting, it emerges as vulnerable to challenge. This is not because tax competition causes no externalities, but because the Code is so broadly drafted that its connection to an empirically verified set of justifying conditions becomes tenuous. It is easy to show that fiscal federalism has modelled a possible distortion and thereby creates a tax coordination issue for the European Union. Verifying the distortion's existence is much harder, and the empirical showings in the Code's legislative history are thin. Tailoring a self-executing corrective is harder still, and may not even be possible at all.

We nonetheless assert that subsidiarity's decentralization presumption has been overcome in the entire circumstances of the case. In a world that holds out no perfect correctives, overinclusive drafting may be defensible on rough cost–benefit grounds. That rough determination also includes scrutiny of the benefits claimed under jurisdictional competition theory. Here we find a thicker empirical literature but no more persuasive empirical proof. The Code, moreover, is 'soft law' carrying no mandate and is proposed for voluntary acceptance by the member states. It thereby holds out a minimal risk of perverse effects. Its non-mandatory status responds to political frictions. So far as taxation is concerned, the European Union continues to operate in a cooperative rather than majority-rule framework. Tax mandates must be agreed upon unanimously by representatives of the member states. Cooperation has failed to emerge to facilitate significant tax coordination heretofore, even though economic theory predicts that cooperation holds out significant possibilities for welfare improvement in this context. The persistent non-cooperation helps to justify the Code under subsidiarity. The pattern makes it clear that tax coordination, as opposed to taxation, does not lie within member state competence. Even in a Coasian bargaining situation such as this, central government institutions and actors play critical roles in setting the agenda, regulating the bargaining process, and negotiating the final outcome. We conclude that, on balance, the Code is justified.

We also conclude that subsidiarity's decentralization presumption does not imply a presumption favouring tax competition. Here we think that fiscal federalism, taken as theory, suffices to establish the point. It suggests that the list of legitimate central government functions lengthens even as a minimal federation like the European Union successfully brings about economic integration by opening national borders to the free movement of people, commodities, and capital. As member state economies become less heterogeneous and economic interconnections between them increase in number and depth, member state economic policies, particularly taxing and spending policies, cause more fiscal externalities. The theory also describes allocative inefficiencies in competitive tax systems, particularly with respect to corporate income and commodity taxes, and highlights negative distributional consequences of tax competition (Kirchgaessner and Pomerehne 1996: 351–2). Coordinative initiatives directed to the elimination of resulting inefficiencies in resource allocations hold a legitimate place on the European Union's agenda.

Part I sets out basic precepts of fiscal federalism and jurisdictional competition, depicting them as related branches of a larger economics. It then lays out a series of fiscal federalism assertions affording a theoretical justification for tax coordination in the European Union. Part II goes on to set out the terms and process context of the Code. Part III evaluates the Code under fiscal federalism, showing that, despite some questionable drafting, it is defensible as a policy matter and easily qualifies under subsidiarity. Part IV is a conclusion.

I. LESSONS OF FISCAL FEDERALISM FOR DIRECT TAXATION AND WEALTH DISTRIBUTION

Two lines of economics, jurisdictional competition and fiscal federalism, come to bear on tax coordination issues in the European Union. They appear on first inspection to diverge neatly into an oppositional dialectic, with jurisdictional competition signalling negatively on central intervention and fiscal federalism signalling positively. This Part looks at the structural relationship of these two lines of analysis, showing that the opposition is not fundamental. They give different signals because they explore different strategies for solving different problems. Fiscal federalism studies a class of phenomena which literally is assumed away in jurisdictional competition theory, even as both theories hold significant assumptions in common. Transposed back to the world of policy, both theories at best offer loose projections of possible gains in welfare. Instead of dialectically opposite choices, we get factors to be traded off as facts are gathered and judgements are made. For the present context, we get cautionary lessons instead of firm policy prescriptions, more particularly: (1) a subsidiarity claim that relies on the economics of jurisdictional competition but makes no reference to distortions from interstate externalities is incomplete as a matter of economic theory; (2) given such distortions, central government intervention against member state-level tax competition can be justified in theory; and (3) such distortions cannot be presumed; they must be shown.

This Part goes on to present a sequence of fiscal federalism assertions that leads to a theoretical justification for tax coordination in the European Union. The sequence begins with the proposition that citizens in democracies have a preference for wealth redistribution by government. Next comes an assertion that this function should be allocated to the central government. The decentralization presumption is overcome here because, given citizen mobility, local governments will redistribute at a level lower than their residents prefer. Indeed, given a fully integrated labour market, state-level redistribution is in theory pointless because worker migration will cause wages to rise and fall so as to eliminate any state-level redistributive effects. But this will not be the case where, as in Europe, labour is not yet fully mobile across the federation. Another problem arises instead, due to the fact that capital has become mobile across the European Union's open borders even as labour has tended to remain within national borders. The mobility differential can result in two distortions, given tax competition: (1) public goods may be underprovided, and (2) other tax bases may be overtaxed to take up the slack.

Taxation, allocative efficiency, and jurisdictional competition

We begin this section with some fundamental precepts of jurisdictional competition and tax economics. The story continues with fiscal federalism in the following section.

Classic jurisdictional competition theory aspires to the first-best result of universal preference satisfaction in a federal context. In so doing it assumes, *inter alia*, that people and capital have perfect mobility between and among jurisdictions. It follows that those who dislike a given jurisdiction's regulatory menu can and do leave to find a more suitable jurisdiction. It also assumes that government actors have high-powered incentives to attract (and retain) people and capital to their jurisdictions. The two assumptions combine into an assertion: the threat of outward migration and the desire to attract new people and capital forces government actors to regulate in the public interest. The interaction between citizen migration and government response amounts to a market mechanism that solves the problem of interest-group capture of regulation, provided that regulatory authority is vested at junior levels of government.

In the first-best federation thus hypothesized, taxation and public goods provision meet the Samuelson (1954: 387–8) condition—that is, the sum of each person's willingness to pay for another unit of a public good for her marginal benefit equals the cost of producing that additional unit (Wilson 1996: 397). For that to be the case, all costs and benefits must be restricted to the providing jurisdiction. Classic jurisdictional competition models sustained this first-best result by making two further assumptions. First, there were no cross-border externalities or spillovers. Second, each jurisdiction had an efficient, non-distortionary tax regime built exclusively on a residential head tax. With a head tax, there could be no inter-jurisdictional tax spillovers, and, given the assumption of perfect mobility and a further assumption of unlimited supply of member states, no state could be positioned to export its tax burden (Inman and Rubinfeld 1996: 315). It followed, given all of the above, that interstate tax competition should be encouraged—it would enhance welfare by forcing state governments to lower tax rates, constraining the self-serving activities of politicians, and limiting efficiency losses that politicians could otherwise cause (McLure 1986).

The theory's first-best aspirations encounter significant frictions in the transition to real-world policy, however. One problem concerns its assumption of a non-distortionary tax regime. Economics teaches that the only tax that induces no inefficiency is a lump-sum tax—a tax whose yield is independent of taxpayers' behaviour and whose sole effect is to decrease the taxpayer's income. The only taxes that actually fit this bill are taxes on unimproved land and head taxes on individuals. All other taxes, direct and indirect, cause deadweight losses by distorting economic choices (Stiglitz 1988: 478–9). Indirect taxes, such as customs duties, turnover taxes, and excises, distort the optimal allocation of resources by driving a wedge between producer and consumer prices. Direct taxes, such as income taxes, drive a wedge between the wage paid and the wage received (Frey and Eichenberger 1996). The distortions become even more pronounced when the same good or activity is taxed at different rates or pursuant to different principles in different jurisdictions, as tends to be the case with cross-border trade. At a broad theoretical level, then, harmonization arguably would move taxation in the European Union in an efficient direction by reducing behavioural distortions stemming from variations in national tax regimes.

This advice implies no prediction of real-world movement to the first best, however. Tax economics is very much a second-best inquiry because optimal, non-distortionary tax systems do not occur in the real world. In the case of the European Union, politics, along with prospects for countervailing gains from tax competition, loom large as explanations for this failure to move decisively toward the first best in respect of distortions stemming from tax disharmony. The explanatory focus shifts for distortions arising within the tax systems of given nation-states. Here redistributive objectives figure prominently, particularly in respect of the allocative inefficiencies that stem from progressive direct taxes. A first-best tax regime comprised of only lump-sum direct taxes constrains the scope of wealth redistribution. By hypothesis, widespread progressive taxation and accompanying tax-generated inefficiencies bespeak a citizen preference for wealth redistribution (Stiglitz 1988: 479–80). Models in public economics reflect this hypothesis in various ways. In some models the redistributing government is conceived as a benevolent maximizer of the preferences of actors who favour equality. Alternatively, a model may assume that the wealthy share the wealth because they want to maximize social welfare; sharing maximizes welfare because the poor place a higher value on the marginal dollar (Kaplow 1996: 472–3). As a further alternative, self-interest can be worked into a description of democratic redistribution. Redistribution's positive effects on community life can be conceived as local public goods (478). Or a regime of redistributive taxing and spending can be presented in a model where the utility function is that of the median voter, and the median voter has below-average income (Boadway, Marchand, and Vigneault 1998: 476).

Fiscal externalities

The classic jurisdictional competition models have been superseded in fiscal federalism by tax competition models that discard the first-best template. The newer models continue to share significant assumptions with the classic models, however. Like the classic models, they assume that state officials have incentives to compete, although now tax dollars rather than citizens are the sought-after commodity. These models also often presuppose mobile citizens and capital and mobile consumption across state borders. But they both relax the classic models' assumption of no externalities and non-distortionary taxation and situate the competitive mechanism in a world of myopic government actors. They then predict what happens when governments make cost–benefit decisions respecting public goods provision that fail to consider secondary effects, in some cases effects internal to the taxing state and in other cases external (Scotchmer 1994: 115). The predicted result is often economic distortion, a problem that can be aggravated when governments compete for factors of production or capital.

The basic model comes from Gordon (1983). It assumes a two-tier federal structure in which residents reside in one state and sell their factor inputs and purchase goods and services throughout the federation. State governments hire factor inputs to produce goods and services and meet their revenue needs by taxing factors and goods and services. Social welfare is defined as an aggregate of: (1) the social welfare function for all types of people across states; (2) after-tax prices for goods, services, and factors; (3) public goods provision; and (4) a state-by-state congestion factor tied to prevailing price levels. Taxes may be residence-based or source-based—that is, they are either based on the residence of the taxpayer or based on the sources of transactions, whether the place of employment or the point of purchase of goods and services. Each state sets its own tax rate, constrained by a requirement that it balance its budget. In addition, the state government must satisfy the re-election demands of local citizens—the model specifies a political objective function sensitive to the political power wielded by groups in state politics. The maximization of the political objective function determines the state's tax rates, subject to the budget constraint. Households and factors are mobile across jurisdictions. Finally, each state government is assumed to be myopic respecting the allocative effects of its tax rates on tax rates in other states and on relocation decisions of citizens (577).

The model shows that where an island jurisdiction could set an optimal tax rate, interstate effects prevent a state in a federation from so doing, leading to suboptimally low provision of public goods. Five types of distortive effects are described: tax exportation, regressivity, 'not-in-my-backyard' tax devices, tax spillovers, and 'beggar-thy-neighbour' tax competition. Central government, modelled as a benevolent maximizer, can improve on the inefficient results: if it has full information and enough independent tax instruments available and can commit to its tax policies, it can always eliminate suboptimal state-level results and replicate the optimum that would obtain for a unitary system by fashioning a pattern of corrective taxes and subsidies (Keen 1998: 457). More generally, on these assumptions, any fiscal outcome that can obtain under a highly devolved structure can be replicated by a central authority. The reverse is not the case, however (Cremer and Pestieau 1996: 753–4).

There results an economics that describes productivity-based allocations of authority in federal systems, balancing enhanced chances for preference satisfaction at the state and local level against central-level internalization of externalities (Johnson 1988). The presumption favouring the junior level still operates, but not because a market mechanism is thought automatically to cause local officials to match citizen preferences. The presumption instead follows from the more modest assertion of the decentralization theorem. All other things being equal, heterogeneous citizen preferences are more likely to be satisfied if public goods and services are provided at the state and local level. All other things are not equal, however, when an externality appears (Inman and Rubinfeld 1997b: 45).

A general prediction for the European Union is implicit: more and more of the problems identified in the balancing model can be expected to crop up as economic integration becomes tighter. Highly integrated markets are those most prone to fiscal externalities: the more movement across borders, the greater the likelihood of inadvertent spillovers.

Competition, regressivity, and mobility differentials

Classic regulatory competition theory and subsequent fiscal federalism share another important proposition: competition inhibits wealth redistribution at the state and local level. Assume that citizens and capital are fully mobile and that local governments fund themselves by taxing real estate. A locality that raises its taxes in order to redistribute will see out-migration of the rich and in-migration of the poor and consequent erosion of its tax base. A rich locality, even assuming no possibility of redistributive social welfare spending therein, will still have an incentive to deter the in-migration of the poor. This is because the poor own less real estate per capita and thus will pay less per capita for the same package of education, police and fire protection, parks, and other public goods enjoyed by the rich. More generally, given full mobility, a decentralized federation can be expected to redistribute at a level lower than that preferred by its citizens, assuming the preference. The greater a state or locality's preference for redistribution, the higher the cost to it of participation in the federation. There follows a second shared proposition of public economics: redistribution in a federation must be effected at the central government level (Boadway, Marchand, and Vigneault 1998: 474; Stiglitz 1998: 640).

This is a discomfiting result for advocates of tax competition. Centralization of an important spending function implies significant centralization of the taxing function. Centralized taxation in turn reduces the zone within which different types of citizens can sort themselves among different jurisdictions with different tax regimes tailored to their particular preferences. With sorting, those with similar tastes regarding redistribution gather in given jurisdictions, implying a higher aggregate level of preference satisfaction for the federation as a whole than would obtain with an overall median voter result (Pauly 1973). Sorting also permits taxpayer migration to limit the power of rapacious state governments to extract rents. To the extent that redistribution is centrally managed, then, the Leviathan state arguably is unconstrained (McLure 1986).

At this point the issue seems to be joined in the oppositional framework: one line of analysis favours centralization and more redistribution, while the other favours decentralization and less redistribution. But the story does not end here. A responsive line of work questions the extent to which sorting works out as predicted. Preference matching respecting levels of redistribution at the state level may not be feasible in a federal system containing a common labour market. The sorting models assume exogenously fixed incomes. Once that assumption is relaxed, but still assuming that citizens are mobile, a given state's redistributive policy will have external effects. The low-tax state will get in-migration of citizens looking for higher after-tax income. Wages in these states will fall as the pool of employees increases. At the same time, the pool of potential employees in the high-tax states will shrink, causing pre-tax wages to rise. When equilibrium is reached, real after-tax incomes will be equal across the states (Feldstein and Wrobel 1998: 370). Migration thus will have undone any redistributive effect in the high-tax state. Moreover, in equilibrium, the level of redistribution emerges as lower than that otherwise preferred by the citizens of a redistributing state. Finally, depending on more particular assumptions, the emerging allocation of labour may be inefficient (Wildasin 1991).

In theory, a fully informed central government can stave off this distortionary, fiscally induced migration and achieve a first-best outcome with a package of lump sum taxes and matching grants. In the first-best allocation, the net marginal benefit of an input of labour should be zero in each state. Thus an efficient allocation of labour requires equalization of wages and transfers across the states (Raff and Wilson 1997: 414). This can be achieved if the states pay lump-sum taxes to the central government and receive grants in return. The amount of the grant increases with the level of poverty in the state's population, so that the grants serve to transfer wealth from the rich states to the poor ones. Once the supplemental income grant to the poor is equal across states, further migration will cause wages to become equalized. Only one problem remains. To eliminate migration, the transfers to the poor must be equal across the federation. As a result, the state with a weaker internal preference for redistribution gains the windfall of a matching grant larger than the transfer it would effect if left to its own devices (Cremer and Pestieau 1996: 752).

It must be questioned whether migration equilibria actually eliminate the effects of state-level redistribution. In the real world, mobility is costly and tax and public goods packages are not fully transparent, slowing the convergence of wages across regions and inhibiting the correction mechanism (Bratton and McCahery 1997). The author of the leading model acknowledges this problem and suggests that the long-run case for migratory correction is stronger than the short-run case (Wildasin 1991: 767–8). But we note a recent empirical showing of short-term wage/tax corrections in the United States (Feldstein and Wrobel 1998: 373). For the United States, then, the upshot of this economics is that, even if wages do not fully adjust for state tax differentials, some adjustment does occur; accordingly, redistributive initiatives and funding should continue to be the primary, if not exclusive, function of the central government.[1] The open question concerns the preferred explanation for the puzzling persistence of significant state-level redistributive programmes (Feldstein and Wrobel 1998: 371; Kaplow 1996: 472–9).

For the European Union, the issue is different. Interstate labour mobility is less frequent in Europe because the costs are more significant. Quantitatively significant internal migration has, of course, occurred in Europe in the past (Wildasin 1991: 771–2).[2] Moreover, a new class of highly mobile individuals has appeared recently, including well-educated entry-level employees and employees of multinationals. The European Union's opening of the borders invites a projection that this class will increase in size (Keen 1993: 17). But for most Europeans the costs of learning a new language and abandoning the national community of one's birth loom larger than the benefits of a new job in another EU member state. It follows that in- and out-migration of workers does not significantly deter redistribution by the member states, at least not yet. For the present and immediate future, the factor of production that takes significant advantage of Europe's open borders is capital. This does not mean to say that capital has achieved full mobility within the European Union. National borders remain relevant to European investors, for transnational information asymmetries and other frictions persist (Gordon and Bovenberg 1996). But firms investing in Europe have clearly been taking advantage of its expanded menu of locational alternatives. Liquid investment capital does move from market to market. Even sunk capital may be affected: the present value of the income stream that a firm expects from costs sunk in a present facility can easily be less than the present value of the income stream from a facility performing the same function at a new location, at a saving in the costs of wages and taxes.

The mobility differential implies that the European Union's opening of borders has redistributive effects. Given competitive states, mobile capital will tend to be

[1] For example, three-quarters of welfare spending is federally funded (Kaplow 1996: 473).

[2] We note also that even in the European Union some classes of people—the young, the highly skilled, the retired—will migrate in larger numbers (Cremer and Pestieau 1996: 750).

undertaxed. Indeed, given full capital mobility, fiscal federalism makes a prediction about asymmetric capital tax competition: it will be optimal for small countries to exempt capital from taxation completely (Bucovetsky 1991; and Bucovetsky and Wilson 1991), and, as a result, capital taxes will fall across the board (Persson and Tabellini 1991). Even where capital is not fully mobile, it can still prove to be difficult to tax. Marginal mobility may be all that is necessary to prompt fiscal competition. When Germany recently introduced a step up in tax on interest, DM 100 billion left the country forthwith, quickly causing the withdrawal of the proposal (Sinn 1998). Undertaxation of capital can mean underprovision of public goods, the burden of which may fall differentially as between rich and poor. Undertaxation of capital due to mobility can also mean overtaxation of other sources, particularly labour to the extent that it lacks comparable mobility (Zodrow and Mieszkowski 1986). During the past twenty years, in fact, the relative importance of tax on labour has increased in most Organization for Economic Cooperation and Development (OECD) countries, even in those where labour tax rates have fallen in absolute terms (Koskela and Schob 1998: 2).

Additional distortionary effects of differential mobility and concomitant possibilities of distortions within the European Union have been projected. Assume that domestic economic shocks are imperfectly coordinated across a federation. The federation's opening of borders thereby benefits risk-averse capitalists, who can now move their capital in response to shocks and minimize the impact of shocks in advance by diversifying geographically. Where labour is less mobile, this capital movement carries a negative externality. As capital moves in response to shocks, workers, who are also risk-averse but unable similarly to diversify their risk, experience heightened wage fluctuations. A state seeking to correct the externality might subsidize the workers, funding the subsidy with a capital tax. But of course, with a high level of capital mobility, that corrective will be unavailable (Rodrik and van Ypersele 1999b). Thus capital market liberalization can have secondary redistributive effects even as it makes it harder to promulgate reverse redistributive corrections (9).

The result that states ameliorate the capital mobility problem by limiting their taxation of mobile capital and shifting the burden elsewhere has an analogue in fiscal federalism theory. States *should* in theory limit taxation of mobile capital because fiscally induced capital movement implies locational inefficiencies. States can ameliorate the problem by shifting to benefit taxation of mobile units of capital; that is, the units should only pay for the benefits of locally provided public goods that they actually receive (Oates 1996). This does not, however, imply that capital should only pay taxes in respect of benefits received. Rather, it implies that non-benefit taxation of capital should be carried out at a higher level of government, where, coincidentally, significant redistributive programmes also must be located (1125). But this solution to the problem of fiscally induced capital mobility is not available to Europe. The European Union has no taxing power and the member states continue to bear most of the redistributive burden.

Summary

From the fiscal federalism perspective, cross-border migration may or may not be value-creating. Sometimes it is, as where productivity differences lead to wage differences. But other migration leads to inefficient resource allocation, as where state fiscal policies induce the movement. Tax competition, labelled a positive phenomenon under jurisdictional competition theory, emerges as a distortion. The reversal has important implications for the European Union. Prior to the formation of the European Community, the uncoordinated European states manifested their competitive aggression in tariffs, the ultimate tax competition vehicle. Now that tactic is constrained by the European Union's legal institutions. But the motivating national economic aggression does not necessarily disappear with economic integration. It may persist in different forms that utilize other components of the tax system. Ireland presents a famous case of successful tax aggression, with its effective corporate tax rate of 12 per cent, the European Union's lowest, and accompanying success in attracting new capital (Bucovetsky 1998).

From the perspective of the jurisdictional competition paradigm, Ireland is an innovative entrepreneur, the success of which helps to bring down tax rates across the European Union. Fiscal federalism emphasizes a different part of the picture, pointing out that some other taxpayer, perhaps a working person in a member state other than Ireland, may be left holding the bag. From the fiscal federalism perspective, Ireland's behaviour could give rise to an opportunity for collective gain from harmonization, or, indeed, could even signal the desirability of central taxation (Keen 1993: 16–17). But note also that these assertions imply empirical questions. They also suggest a tradeoff between central constraint and member state discretion, which in turn means political questions. In the Part that follows, we show how all of these factors have come to bear in the context of EU tax coordination initiatives.

II. TAX COORDINATION IN THE EUROPEAN UNION

Taxation coordination in the European Union raises the same substantive choice posed by the economics: preference satisfaction at the member state level or centralized direction for the elimination of distortions resulting from myopic member state policy. Tax coordination also implicates a basic process choice between cooperative or majority-rule federalism. The European Union remains in a cooperative mode respecting taxation, having excepted it from the regime of qualified majority voting (QMV) at the Council of Ministers ('the Council') (Bendar *et al.* 1996; Golub 1999). The process constraint looms large in the history of the European Union's tax initiatives, with coordinative failure having been the most frequent result. Movement to QMV could break this pattern, provided that the larger member states could agree on a substantive strategy. But QMV on taxation is not a present agenda item, although it remains a subject of discussion (Tucker 1999). Meanwhile, the proposed Code of Conduct of Business Taxation explores a new strategy for achieving agreement in the cooperative framework, placing a modest substantive agenda within a voluntary 'soft law' process framework. The framework's capacity to bring concrete results in the member states' tax codes is not yet proven. But the political results so far suggest a possible cooperative break with a non-cooperative past. Meanwhile, the motive force behind the Code stems from a bureaucratic alliance. Here the European Commission ('the Commission') works in tandem with the member states' finance ministries to win the simultaneous assents of the heads of government, acting as the European Council.[3]

From harmonization to coordination

The European Community Treaty looks toward a level economic playing field (Article 2 [2]). National tax systems can impede this goal in numerous ways: by imposing fiscal burdens on movement of goods, services, or capital across borders; by treating domestic and imported goods and services or residents and non-residents differently; by double taxing foreign source income (Terra and Wattel 1997: 1); or by distorting economic behaviour through other differentials as to rate or treatment. Elimination of these impediments has held a constant place on EC and EU agendas. But basic questions and choices remain open respecting the regulatory strategy to be followed.

Top-to-bottom tax standardization, including centrally mandated tax rates, suggests itself as a means to realize the Treaty's goal as a matter of simple logic. Until the late 1980s, it was the approach favoured by actors within the EC (Radaelli 1996: 407–8). But the member states proved disinclined to give up sovereignty on tax matters (Owens 1993: 40–1). In addition, tax competition theory came into circulation to provide an opposing point of view. It claimed to provide not only preference matching, but the least cost means to the end of harmonization of tax rates and provisions. To see how EU tax systems might thus converge on a market-driven rather than centrally mandated basis (Radaelli 1996: 407), assume free movement of goods, people, and capital and two neighbouring member states with comparable levels of economic opportunity, infrastructure, social security, and public services. If the states diverge in their tax burdens, then economic activity will move to the lower-tax state, forcing the higher-tax state to bring down its rates (Terra and Wattel 1992: 2). This opposition argument made its mark. The Commission dropped its grandiose harmonization proposals and shifted to specific and limited proposals respecting double taxation and cross-border trade and investment.

[3] Article 103 [Article 99] of the Maastricht Treaty accords fiscal power to the heads of state meeting as the European Council; the agenda comes from the Council of Ministers.

Now the European Union articulates tax policy under the rubric of 'coordination', a shift that reflects the appearance of the subsidiarity principle. At the same time, the Commission has remained committed to a goal of tax neutrality (as opposed to harmonization *per se*).[4] Under this approach harmonization may remain legitimate as a remedy given a showing of a market- or politically driven distortion of economic choice (Radaelli 1996: 407–9). In effect, the European Union's door is open for case-by-case application of the fiscal federalism paradigm.

Indirect taxes

Most of the European Union's coordination efforts have been directed to indirect taxation—customs duties, turnover taxes, and excises—toward the end of ensuring that producers compete across national borders solely on the basis of production cost, with no ancillary benefits or detriments stemming from tariffs or other national levies. The constitutional bases for this lie in Articles 95 [90] and 99 [93] of the Treaty. Article 95(1) prohibits discriminatory indirect taxes, but without mandating that the member states adopt any particular form of internal taxation.[5] It requires only that the system of indirect taxation adopted is applied without discrimination to similar imported products. Article 99 provides the basis for harmonizing customs duties (Case 21/79, *Commission* v. *Italy*, 1980 ECR 1).[6]

The 'destination principle' has guided implementation of these authorizations. Under this, traded commodities and capital flows should be taxed by national systems only on the basis of the destination. With goods and services, this destination principle means that the tax follows from the consumer's residence. Value added tax (VAT), imposed at the destination, has been the focal point for coordination. In the 1980s the Commission unsuccessfully proposed VAT rate ranges with upper limits. Now it proposes minimum rates only (Janeba and Peters 1999: 93). But it mostly just proposes. By its own statement, there has been very little progress toward harmonization of the terms or rates of the VAT regimes of the member states.

Direct taxes: the Code of Conduct and the Directive on Taxation of Interest

The European Union draws its authority to deal with direct taxes—taxes on personal, corporate, and capital income—from the general harmonization clause of

[4] Kirchgaessner and Pomerehne (1996: 351–2) charge that despite the change of course away from harmonization, EC policy makers continue to believe that there should be a uniform tax system.

[5] Article 95(2) [90(2)] deals with indirect tax protection of products which, without being similar within the meaning of Article 95(1) [90(1)], are nevertheless in competition, directly or indirectly, with products of the importing countries.

[6] Indirect discrimination also is regulated under Article 95(1) [90(1)] (Case 112/84, *Humboldt* v. *Directeur des Services Fiscaux*, 1985 ECR 1367 [1986]). It should be noted, however, that the European Court of Justice recognizes objective justifications where the national policy is acceptable from the EC's perspective, even if it tends to benefit domestic traders more than importers (Case 140/79, *Chemical Farmaceutici* v. *DAF SpA* [1981] ECR 1).

Article 100 [94]. They have been an area of secondary emphasis within EU tax policy. This is not surprising: VAT and excise taxes are more immediately implicated by the opening of borders. Moreover, political resistance to harmonization is keener with direct taxes. To see why, assume that the European Union were to succeed in fully harmonizing direct taxes in addition to VAT and excise taxes. As a result, the member states would be left with policy control over less than one-third of their revenues. The neutral-sounding goal of harmonization would thereby materially inhibit national discretion over fiscal policy and social programmes (Owens 1993: 40–1). Accordingly, no one anticipates significant concessions of member state sovereignty respecting direct taxes (Terra and Wattel 1997: 3).

At the same time, there is an oft-told distortionary tax competition story respecting direct taxes in the European Union. The member states use both residence- and source-based taxes for income derived from capital. The residence-based taxes are personal income tax on income from interest and dividends and corporate tax on retained earnings; the source-based taxes apply to income from investments at the place where it accrues (Keen 1993: 27). Rates on source-based taxes on capital have declined over the past two decades, following the worldwide trend. The rate arguably evidences tax competition. The competition has broken out because capital mobility has increased, stimulated in Europe by the European Union's successful opening of the borders (Netherlands Ministry of Finance 1999: 14, Table 3). The member states drop their rates to hold onto the capital they have and attract new capital. Their tax bases erode as a result. As a further result, administrators in both the European Union and in many member states have continued to argue that coordination of some sort is necessary to help the member states protect their existing tax bases.

Initiatives prior to 1997

Despite the foregoing argument's large number of adherents, initiatives respecting direct taxation have seen little success. The Commission made its first communication on the subject in 1967 (CEC 1967). In 1975, it proposed harmonization of corporate tax and withholding taxes on dividends. But it adopted no proposals before 1990 and then went forward only on discrete matters respecting the taxation of mergers (European Commission 1990a) and parent–subsidiary income (European Commission 1990b). Around the same time, it withdrew its broader harmonization proposals. It did so, said the Commission, in the name of the subsidiarity principle: member states would set their own corporate tax rates unless distortions necessitated EC intervention (CEC 1990). At the same time, the Commission appointed an expert committee to look into the possibility that capital tax differentials had just such a distortionary effect and to assess whether tax competition could be expected to eliminate those distortions. Distortions were reported back and a number of recommendations made, including minimum and maximum tax rates. But the initiative came to nothing (CEC 1992).

The issue did not go away, however. A new tax coordination initiative, launched by Commissioner Mario Monti, resulted in a report in 1996 ('the Monti Report') (CEC 1996). The Monti Report found no problem of fiscal erosion: over fifteen years, total taxes and social security revenues had remained in a constant or slightly increasing percentage of GNP. But the relative burden shifted nevertheless: between 1980 and 1993 the tax rate on employed labour had grown by one-fifth while those on self-employed labour and capital had decreased by one-tenth. Differential mobility was suggested as the explanation: labour was less mobile than capital and thus bore the brunt. More generally, while liberalization of financial markets had brought more efficient resource allocation and had lowered the cost of capital, it had widened the scope for strategic tax planning and tax evasion (3–4). Member states had made up for lost revenues by stepping up tax on personal incomes. To alleviate the problem of excessive tax on labour, the Monti Report suggested a step up in the VAT rate. True to the past pattern, VAT was not increased. But a group composed of representatives of the member states' finance ministers, themselves organized as the Economy and Finance Council (ECOFIN), was formed to look into the development of a policy on mobile tax bases.

The Code of Conduct on Business Taxation

The group reported back with the code of Conduct on Business Taxation (CEC 1997a), which was accepted by the ECOFIN Council in 1997 (ECOFIN 1998a). Technically, the Code is a resolution of the ECOFIN Council that the Commission has subsequently commended to the member states for adoption. The member states, thus invited to accept the Code voluntary by their heads of government meeting as the European Council (CEC 1997a: Annex 1, C) later placed the Code on a common agenda with more controversial tax measures so as to delay final consideration (SN 2000/00, ADD 1). If and when the European Council finally assents to the Code, it will remain 'soft law' that does not bind the member states (Snyder 1994: 197). It nevertheless marks a process advance for the tax coordination movement. By proceeding softly where harder approaches have failed, at least it will have garnered agreement in principle.

It also embodies a legislative drafting strategy that makes a substantive advance. The Code targets 'potentially harmful' tax measures (PHTMs) on business—regulations and administrative practices as well as code provisions—which are 'unfairly' competitive by virtue of 'a significant effect on the location of business activity' (CEC 1997a: Annex 1, C). The defining characteristic is a 'significantly more effective level of taxation, including zero taxation, than that which generally applies in the Member State in question'. Supplemental identifying factors include: (1) tax benefits available only to non-residents or otherwise cordoned off (or 'ring-fenced') from the domestic market and national tax system; (2) tax benefits available absent real economic activity; (3) determinations of profit levels for transactions within corporate groups departing from principles agreed upon by the Organization for Economic Cooperation and Development (OECD); and (4) tax provisions lacking transparency, including covert relaxation of rules at the administrative level (Annex 1, D; Pinto 1998b: 394). An adopting member state commits itself to refrain from introducing new PHTMs and to re-examine existing laws and practices to identify existing PHTMs for elimination within two years (CEC 1997a: Annex 1, E–F).

What this voluntary undertaking will mean in terms of actual legislation, whether or not within two years, remains a question. The Commission's explanatory communication speaks in terms of an invitation to member states 'to commit themselves at a political level' (para. 9). Enforcement of non-binding commitments at such a 'political level' presumably could present a significant practical problem, even assuming that each member state assents at the European Council. The non-binding format invites cheating by legislatures or executives seeking short-term political benefits from new capital investment, along with foot-dragging respecting the rollback of existing PHTMs. A member state might very well assent to the Code on a 'cheap talk' basis: one suspects it is easier for a government to sign on to a generally phrased, prohibitive, but not 'legally binding' code than it is for the same government to roll back a given tax break or to refrain from promulgating a new tax break (and making ancillary deals with benefited interest groups). Member states with a history of successful tax competition, such as Ireland, Luxembourg, and the Netherlands, have particularly strong incentives to delay or avoid compliance.

The Code, anticipating these problems, looks to mutual monitoring to encourage the 'political' commitment's actualization in member state legislative action. The assenting state undertakes to make its tax system transparent by informing the others about present or prospective PHTMs (Annex 1, G). Of course, a member state about to enact a PHTM might not be expected to publicize the fact to other member states. Accordingly, the Code provides for a supervisory group made up of delegates designated by the signatory finance ministries ('the Group'). The Group accepts complaints respecting member state tax measures, reviewing their status as PHTMs (Annex 1, I). Also, a member state with a concern about another member state's taxation activity may request information about the measure in question and an opportunity to discuss and comment on it at the Group (Annex 1, H). The Group reports to the ECOFIN Council, which has the option of publishing its findings (Annex 1, I). The Code's 'political' enforcement mechanism reaches its end at this point. Meanwhile, the Group, organized under the chairmanship of Dawn Primarolo, Paymaster General of the United Kingdom, has been active. In December 1998 it presented an initial report which identified at least eighty-five PHTMs across the member states (Pinto 1998b: 396–406).

It should also be noted that 'soft law' can have the hard edge of precedent. The Commission, acting under Articles 4 [7] and 155 [211] of the Treaty, often creates soft law in the process of negotiating the effectiveness of EC law. Such pronouncements appear in the form of interpretive guidelines, and, despite their non-binding status, can be used as a source of legal reasoning. The European Court of Justice has, particularly in the case of Commission recommendations, taken this into account when deciding disputes (Klabbers 1994; Wellens and Borchardt 1989).

Finally, we note that the actors responsible for the Code are developing an accompanying 'hard law' stick (Besley and Seabright 1999: 23–5; CEC 1997a: Annex 1, L). Here they draw on the state aid provisions of Articles 92 to 94 [87 to 89] of the Treaty. These provisions are part of the Treaty's competition rules and have the force of law. They seek to restrict member state competition through subsidy of business and have been held by the European Court of Justice to apply to indirect subsidies such as tax breaks (Case 102/87, *France* v. *Commission*, 1988 ECR 4067). It follows that where a PHTM amounts to state aid, a Commission enforcement action against the member state in the European Court of Justice is possible. The Code mentions this possibility, and the Commission has been laying groundwork for an enforcement experiment. It has issued a Notice—a soft law interpretive guideline—under the Code that sets forth general criteria to determine whether tax assistance constitutes state aid within the meaning of the Treaty (European Commission 1998a). The criteria identify tax measures which: (1) confer an advantage relieving recipients from a normal tax burden, such as a reduction in tax base, total or partial reduction in the amount of tax by exemption, credit, deferral, rescheduling or cancellation; (2) grant the advantage by state or state resource, including a regional or local body; (3) impact on competition and trade between member states; and (4) specifically protect certain undertakings or the production of specified goods. Mario Monti, now the European Commissioner for Competition, states that the Commission will flesh out the meaning of these criteria by applying them among the PHTMs already collected by the Group. Says Monti: '[I]t would be premature to state at this time whether the competition rules have been breached . . . [But] I am firmly convinced of the synergy between the right against harmful tax competition and rigorous enforcement of the competition rules' (KPMG 1999).

The Directive on Minimum Effective Taxation of Interest Income

In 1998, the ECOFIN Council followed the Code with a Draft Directive to Ensure a Minimum of Effective Taxation of Savings Income in the Form of Interest Payments within the Community ('the Draft Directive') (ECOFIN 1998b). The Draft Directive has been highly controversial and has come to dominate the EU's tax agenda. Consideration of the Code, which occupies a subordinate place on the agenda, has been repeatedly delayed pending solution of political problems raised by the Draft Directive.

The Draft Directive's aim is to limit the evasion of capital tax by individuals who invest in member states or third countries where there is no taxation (such as Luxembourg). It would apply to financial institutions that carry out business in the European Union and make payments of interest directly to beneficial owners who are individual and resident, for tax purposes, in member states different from the member states in which the paying institution carries on business. The member states are given a choice of two conforming approaches: the member state would either levy a withholding tax of 20 per cent on the interest paid by subject financial institutions to non-residents from within its territory, or it would impose an obligation on the financial institution last in the payment chain before the investor to report the amount of the payment to the payee's state of residence. The Draft Directive, as a directive, would have the force of law. Unsurprisingly, it has proved more controversial than the Code.

Critics contend that the proposed withholding tax would stimulate further capital flight to countries beyond the European Union's frontiers, at least absent cooperation with these countries. More particularly, Eurobonds, which are currently tax-free, would be subject to the 20 per cent withholding tax. This has led the British government to threaten to veto the Directive. Britain asserts that the withholding would trigger the bonds' built-in tax gross-up provisions. The resulting administrative costs, borne by the bonds' paying agents, would ultimately mean higher costs of capital for the bonds' issuers. This would force the 2 trillion pound market to migrate out of London to an offshore location, such as Zurich (Economist 1999: 25).

Britain's objections continued despite an earlier and unsuccessful attempt at a compromise. An early proposal flatly exempted Eurobonds, only to prompt intervention by the European Parliament, which rejected it by 421 to 78 votes. Britain advanced an alternative proposal which exempts most Eurobond payments. Lobbying groups from the British financial sector seek to keep Britain on this course. Luxembourg and Austria then joined Britain, objecting to any directive that does not guarantee enactment of similar measures in countries outside the European Union and dependent territories like the Channel Islands.

The Council of Ministers agreed to a compromise at Feira in June 2000. This preserves the option of withholding tax or information exchange (SN 2000/00 ADD 1), but by itself assures no real-world results, since it is conditioned on the adoption, by 31 December 2002, of equivalent arrangements in all member state dependent or associated territories and in non-EU jurisdictions like Switzerland, Liechtenstein, Monaco, Andorra, and San Marino. The agreement implicates changes in the bank secrecy laws of Austria and Luxembourg and includes a sunset clause allowing each to operate a withholding tax regime during a seven-year transition to the information exchange system. Finally, the Feira agreement provides that '[w]ork shall be pursued . . . with a view to reaching agreement . . . according to a parallel timetable' for the Code and other agenda items.

III. EVALUATING THE CODE UNDER FISCAL FEDERALISM

The Code emerges with incomplete economic support due to an overinclusive definition of distortionary tax competition and a thin supporting empirical case.

But the Code remains defensible nonetheless. Its definition, although broad, is not comprehensive and leaves open avenues for competitive tax setting. The empirical evidence, while thin, certainly is supportive, suggesting the presence of significant externalities within the European Union, a problem likely to intensify as member state economies become more tightly integrated. In addition, the Code operates in an open-ended process framework that leaves tax-competitive member states significant opportunities not only to defend their suspect legislation but to refuse to comply altogether. Thus the Code holds out little threat of perverse effects. Indeed, the level of concrete legislative response remains to be seen. Even if that response is disappointing, the Code has a juridical effect, reducing the possibility that subsidiarity could be interpreted to include a presumption favouring tax competition. At this level, fiscal federalism provides strong support.

Politics and process

The Code and the Draft Directive follow different strategies toward the common goal of unanimously-approved tax legislation. The contrast teaches a lesson about prospects for achieving coordination by means of Coasian bargaining in the European Union's cooperative federal framework (Scharpf 1997).

With the Draft Directive we get a textbook example of the frictions that impair bargaining over tax mandates. Its objective is uncontroversial: cross-border tax evasion by rich depositors and bondholders has little to commend itself from a public policy point of view. The Commission, moreover, took care to build flexibility into the Draft Directive. Viewing the proposal in the abstract, then, a unanimous vote at the Council would seem feasible. Such a vote might even occur in the teeth of a credible threat of capital flight: as between capital within the European Union that evades taxes and capital outside the European Union that evades taxes, there is little difference from a revenue-raising point of view. The problem is that the negative economic effects of the flight of some of this capital fall differentially on the member state that provides the venue for the capital's market. Deep institutional conflicts over the Draft Directive mirror this policy conflict. On the one hand, popular sentiment against tax evaders has caused the European Parliament to intervene in the legislative process so as to block exemption of Eurobonds. On the other hand, Britain, responding to pressures from its domestic interest groups, threatens to use its veto at the Council to block a popular tax compliance initiative. The Commission plays the role of mediator (Moravcsik 1999: 278).

In theory, a cooperative result ought to follow from this bargaining between and among the Council, the Commission, the European Parliament, and the member states. As a tax enforcement measure, the Draft Directive implies not only a welfare gain but a welfare gain that will register concretely in the member states' treasuries. The bargaining institutions thus ought to be able to find a way to allocate the gain, compensating the losers, Britain and Luxembourg, and making everyone better off. The European Union's federal institutions do not, however, possess the powers of an ideal Coasian deal manager. The European Union draws its revenues from a small and specific collection of sources, getting a percentage of the VAT collected by the member states, a transfer of a percentage of each state's gross domestic product, and certain customs duties and agricultural levies, with all of the revenues being collected by the member states and amounting to no more than 5 per cent of their total spending (Inman and Rubinfeld 1994: 151). Accordingly, spending does not play a significant role as an EU policy instrument (Terra and Wattel 1997: 3). In the present context, therefore, even if the amount of the tax compliance gain could plausibly be estimated in advance, the Commission would be disabled from serving as an allocative conduit. The gains go directly to the member states, necessitating a multilateral gain-sharing contract. Such an arrangement presumably implicates administrative problems and possibilities for defection. The Commission, meanwhile, emerges in a weakened position in backroom bargaining, making tradeoffs across its agenda as a whole rather than direct fiscal accommodations. Moreover, even assuming a more pliable fiscal infrastructure, strategic behaviour could prevent an agreement's emergence (Inman and Rubinfeld 1997b: 48–9). In the present case, for example, interest group pressures could retard British acceptance of an otherwise institutionally acceptable tradeoff.

The Code of Conduct for Business Taxation provides a contrast if only because it overcame its first set of hurdles quickly, avoided the Council completely, and could yet garner formal member state assent without inciting significant controversy. The possibility of success should be attributed to the absence of a mandate binding the member states, which have persistently objected to such conventionally packaged tax directives (CEC 1997a: para. 6). The Commission's process strategy and process control should also be cited.

Under this alternative strategy the Commission once again serves as the first mover in a multi-stage negotiation process. Here also EU and member state institutions bargain. The context thus differs from other soft law-making situations where the Commission articulates policy views without having to negotiate with other institutions (Jachtenfuch 1995). But the soft law context also changes the bargaining stakes. The absence of a mandate and the limitation of the subject matter to business taxes enhance chances for success. Furthermore, the parties at the first stage of approval—representatives of finance ministries—are particularly likely to be in sympathy with the Commission's coordinative objective. Strategic considerations also show up in the legislation that results from the first round: the Code reflects a manifest concern for ease of application even though it only carries soft law status. The Commission, having stage-managed the Code's appearance, turns it over to the member states in the form of an invitation. At the same time, the Commission's allies in the finance ministries operate as an interpretative committee that further defines the stakes by identifying target PHTMs. One suspects that political considerations could come to bear in this selection process. Finally, and at a late stage, the Commission makes a mild threat, its notice regarding state aid raising a spectre of enforcement actions respecting an unspecified subset of PHTMs.

To what will the European Council be assenting, given the absence of a mandate? The Code itself makes no guaranty of tangible legislative results. While it does contemplate formal rulings of non-compliance by the group, there are only two enumerated consequences. One is publicity by the Commission, and the other is a possible Commission enforcement action against any PHTMs deemed to fall within its state aid criteria. Only in the latter case does soft law, used as a sword, become hard law.

Apart from these consequences, what does the Code accomplish? There is at a minimum an agreement in principle among the Commission, the finance ministries, and the member states' governments to the core idea expressed in the definition of a PHTM. The potential value of that agreement can be variously described. In game theoretic terms, this is a non-cooperative fact pattern characterized by multiple equilibria (Cremer and Pestieau 1996: 751). Capital tax rates have not yet converged in the European Union, despite jurisdictional competition theory's prediction. As of 1996, five member states had corporate rates between 35 and 40 per cent; three states had higher rates; and seven states had lower rates. Nine states had rates falling into a wider band of 33 to 41 per cent (Netherlands Ministry of Finance 1999). Nothing guarantees the persistence of this status quo. Future rounds of non-cooperative competitive tax cutting are a distinct possibility. The Code's definition (and its ongoing articulation by the Group) supplies a focal point around which the member states can coordinate their legislative activities in an uncertain environment, making widespread competitive tax cutting a less likely outcome. The member state inclined toward cooperation gets a point of reference for ordering its conduct, and, indeed, a stronger basis by staying in a cooperative mode as it makes tax policy. The Code gives it an information source to which to turn to ascertain the status of cooperative initiatives in other states. Given this connection, it can cooperate with diminished fear that it does so in isolation, assured of a sucker payoff. This does not of course mean that the non-cooperative state changes course. But that state's situation has changed too. The Code makes the non-cooperative state a defector in a world of repeat players. This enhances the possibility of political retribution by cooperating states.

Alternatively, the PHTM definition can be seen as an expression of a norm against tax competition, and the consenting member states as manifesting acceptance of the norm. The hope is that the norm becomes internalized over time, making it more difficult for a member state to choose to deviate. The ongoing process of normative assimilation is coordinated by the Group, whose members are, as designees of finance ministries, highly likely to have internalized the norm ex ante. By putting the true believers at the centre of the information-gathering and application process, the Code increases the chance that the norm, rather than lawyerly logic, guides the exercise of articulating the Code's meaning.

Whether the Code manifests coordinative logic or normative entrepreneurship, continued bargaining can be expected to figure into its operation, perhaps determining whether or not it results in concrete legislative revisions. If tax coordination is economically justified, it is not because it makes the pie bigger for the member state group as a whole. Yet even the most cooperatively-minded member state would be ill-advised to coordinate voluntarily without an eye to the particulars of the arrangements for sharing the gain. A member state inclined toward non-cooperation and enjoying the benefits of capital inflows from a competitive tax regime would be even more acutely concerned about gain-sharing. As it contemplates the costs and benefits of switching to cooperation, this state presumably demands a give-back (Keen 1993: 17; Radaelli 1996: 414). The Code contemplates such trading without specifying potential sources of consideration (CEC 1997a: para. 13).

Substance

The Code's process approach serves double duty as its substantive defence. Whatever the Code's imperfections, its voluntary aspect minimizes the capacity for substantive harm. Should it lead to tangible legislative results, the implication is that the member states widely concur with the principle that tax competition has perverse effects. That principle in turn is defensible in economic theory, which holds that fiscally induced movement causes allocative inefficiencies. Meanwhile, the Code's framework allows any costs or other perverse effects to be put on the table for inspection. The process framework bears on the subsidiarity case: given the history, tax coordination clearly is a central competence; at the same time, the magnitude of federal intrusion is minimized with a soft law initiative.

The European Union, in short, has little to lose here, given political barriers to mandatory legislation. But, because the Code amounts to an important legislative precedent respecting transnational tax coordination, it still should be inspected for substantive soundness, as if it carried a mandate.

The Code, fiscal federalism, and subsidiarity

Read broadly, fiscal federalism justifies the Code. The theory asserts that in a world with suboptimal taxes, any cross-border movement motivated by fiscal concerns rather than pure productivity concerns is a distortionary event. The Code targets just such movement in its PHTM definition. But a problem becomes apparent when we take this broad reading a step further. Fiscal federalism also teaches that, given open borders and cross-border transactions, all tax differentials that impede or influence the movement of goods and services are distortionary. This amounts to an economic justification for across-the-board harmonization, an approach rejected under subsidiarity.

A question accordingly arises about the code: even though its *per se* rule respecting tax rates is justifiable under the broad reading of fiscal federalism, it can be questioned from a subsidiarity point of view for overbreadth. The PHTM definition, instead of conditioning legislative coordination on a showing of a distortion, presumes distortion on a showing that a particular business tax embodies a downward shift from the member states' overall business rate level, a case which strengthens to the extent that the measure carves out a special class of tax beneficiaries. The definition no doubt is crafted for easy application in the real world. But it is not clear that a downward shift in a given tax rate on business need necessarily entail a distortionary effect (Pinto 1998b: 394–5; Ellis 1999: 79). Assume, for example, that the highest taxing member state strategically drops selected rates, matching those of the next highest taxing state, but that no new capital migrates there in response. The failed strategy has no external effect and thus is benign from an economic point of view. Indeed, it could even reflect salutary domestic developments respecting tax policy. Competitive distortions need not follow even if we change the facts and drop the rate below that of several other states. Business relocation decisions follow from a number of factors. If the member state's trading and labour markets and regulatory and social environments are not otherwise attractive, the tax lure does not work. Contrariwise, tax rates need not be the primary cause of in-migration. Yet, because the lower rate could conceivably induce movement, it 'may affect in a significant way the location of business activity in the Community' within the meaning of the Code (CEC 1997a: Annex 1, paragraph A).

Even if the foregoing hypothetical case can be dismissed as *de minimis*, there still arise questions of degree. A range of more particular distortions can follow from tax preferences. Preferences can cause diversion of financial and investment flows; they can cause tax burdens to shift; they can discourage tax compliance and make tax collection more costly; and they can cause domestic taxing and spending to take a shape not preferred by the voters (OECD 1998a: 16). Some tax provisions will cause more harm than others, depending on all the facts. Since subsidiarity appears to contemplate tax rate variation and a residuum of member state discretion, a coordination regime insensitive to these matters of degree could be suspect.

Fiscal federalism theory, read more narrowly, signals a strategy more sensitive to these matters of degree. Its policy application changes accordingly. We see the narrow reading in the analytical structure of the Monti Report, the study that preceded the Code. First it identifies and verifies a distortionary effect of competition on member state tax systems—the externality bound up in the upward shirt in the tax rate on labour and the downward shift in the rate on capital tax. Only then does it look at coordination strategies. In other words, under subsidiarity, coordination should be directed at demonstrated rather than presumed externalities, spillovers, or other distortions of economic behaviour.

The narrow approach solves the subsidiarity problem, only to run into problems of verification. Here the economic literature provides little assistance. There is a paucity of empirical work on tax externalities (Auerbach 1997). The best available evidence to support the Code concerns the capital/labour rate distortion. Yet this provides at best an incomplete basis for verification. Consider the statistic deemed to verify it in the Monti Report: across a thirteen-year period rates on employed labour had grown by one-fifth while rates on capital had decreased by one-tenth. To use this verifying statistic as the justification for a constraint on capital taxation in a given state is to make a series of empirical assertions. More particularly, selective business tax cuts are distortionary because: (1) they are pitched to capital that has greater mobility than labour; (2) that movement causes erosion in states' tax bases; and (3) those states have made up the difference by increasing tax on the less mobile taxpayer. The question is whether the cited drop in capital tax rates proves the occurrence or likely occurrence of the whole three-step scenario. Consider some additional facts: all OECD countries have tended to decrease their corporate tax rates over the last two decades (Edwards and Keen 1996: 114); at the same time, corporate and capital tax rates have not converged internationally. Ideological shifts might be pointed to as the primary cause just as plausibly as, or perhaps more plausibly than, tax competition. Moreover, even as those rates fell in the 1980s, the percentage of corporate tax did not decrease as a percentage of gross domestic product or of total revenues because the corporate rate base was expanding. This suggests that factors other than competition might be at work respecting the increase in rates on labour. A causal connection between competition and the increase of rates on labour still is suggested, of course. Indeed, it has been shown that between 1973 and 1990 taxes on labour went up faster in OECD countries with leftist parties in power (Heylen 1995). This suggests that pressure from mobile capital does cause governments to hold or reduce rates despite themselves, taxing their own political allies in order to maintain social programmes. On the other hand, whatever the ideology of the party in power, cross-border tax competition need not necessarily be a part of the simultaneous decrease of capital tax and increase of labour tax. The capital/labour rate scenario plausibly can be accounted for on a standard public choice basis: even as ideology shifted in its favour, business became more effective as a domestic lobbying force in countries across the world, with a concomitant decline in labour's political influence. On this scenario, the shifting tax burden does not implicate anything resembling the competitive process described in the jurisdictional competition paradigm.

Let us assume that if the Code's drafters were to be asked to verify the existence of distortions related to business tax rates in the European Union (no verification is offered in their report), they would proffer the capital/labour rate differential. At this point another problem would arise. The fit between the Code as drafted and the solution of the problem bound up in the capital/labour rate differential is at best approximate. The Code does not necessarily apply so as to call for correction in every case where capital mobility has a causal connection to a capital/labour rate differential. For example, labour could be the target of a disproportionate tax increase whether or not a given state's business tax has been subject to selective rate cutting falling into the PHTM definition. The fact of differential mobility could cause the tax on labour to go up even as business taxes remain constant.

Alternatively, assume that: (1) all member states have the same corporate tax rate; (2) a first-mover state drops its corporate tax rate 10 per cent; (3) all other member states follow suit within a short period; and (4) no other tax rates change because all economies are in a state of expansion and tax returns are generally increasing. Here, at the end of the day, each member state's corporate rate remains out of line with its other business rates and thus each state's corporate tax can be questioned as a PHTM. But there would be a counter-argument that the application of the Code is inappropriate in view of its stated purpose: the competitive round of follow-the-leader having been completed across the states, the fall in the rate would not induce any capital movement. At the same time, the across-the-board drop creates a possibility of a disproportionate increase in the rate on another taxpayer, such as labour, in the event that one or more of the states needs to raise more revenues.

The Code and jurisdictional competition

For a tax competition advocate, the problem with the Code and its open-ended process lies in the chance for success. Despite the Code's voluntary aspect, much about it looks suspect from this perspective. For example, the responsibility for normative experiments respecting taxation should not be accorded to the member states' collective finance ministers, the interest group most likely to favour stepped-up taxing and spending. Instead, tax policy should be made by government actors in the course of responding to problems stemming from taxpayer mobility. Nor should declining corporate tax rates be considered a policy problem. With corporate tax bases, erosion due to competition should be seen as not a bad thing. By causing rates to drop, competition instead serves as the means to the end of long-term investment and higher living standards (Rodrik 1997). Finally, if tax rates rise due to widespread acceptance of a cooperative norm, governments will be encouraged further to indulge an inherent tendency to overtax and overspend.

Restating the fiscal federalism justification

Three counterpoints can be made in the Code's defence: (1) the Code is also underinclusive and as objectionable to opponents of tax competition as it is to proponents; (2) jurisdictional competition claims have their own verification problems and intrinsic infirmities; and (3) the European Union is not constitutionally equipped to accommodate legislative solutions to tax competition problems that draw directly on the recommendations of fiscal federalism, narrowly read.

The Code is under- as well as overinclusive, and does not prevent tax competition. A member state can continue to take a competitive posture by lowering its business tax rates across the board, benefiting existing businesses as well as new entrants. No doubt tax competition on such a basis would be more difficult to effect as a technical, political, and fiscal matter. But, if the predictions of jurisdictional competition theory have any validity, competitive forces should still operate on this aggregate basis in the long run. Compare at this point a description of 'good' or 'acceptable' tax competition appearing in the OECD's recent report (1998a: 15–16) on the subject. This emphasizes that a state should not be prevented from lowering business taxes in order to enhance the competitiveness of domestic business (15–16). Presumably a state can pursue such a goal under the Code, so long as it introduces no differentials triggering the PHTM definition. There would appear to be no way, however, to prevent such a domestically motivated competitive tax regime from inducing cross-border movement, provided the rates were sufficiently low.

Cross-border competition along these lines may already be appearing in the European Union. Consider new corporate tax legislation announced by Ireland in response to the Code. Ireland ex ante possesses the archetypical PHTM with its split rate of 10 per cent for firms located in the Dublin Financial Centre and 32 per cent for other companies. It plans to shift to a new single 12.5 per cent rate for all companies by the end of 2002, with the standard rate of 32 per cent being gradually reduced annually until then (Young 1999). Whether or not Ireland will be in compliance given these adjustments may depend on whether they encompass all Irish 'business taxes' within the meaning of the Code. But one thing is clear: Ireland intends to remain corporate tax-competitive. We also note a potential negative spillover effect from its adjustment to comply with the Code: if Ireland's across-the-board extension of its 12.5 per cent rate means a revenue loss, increases in its other sources of direct taxation could result. On this scenario, the Code, in attempting to lessen the distortion of fiscally induced capital movement, encourages distortionary rate adjustments within a given member state. But perhaps distortion within a member state should not be cognizable for policy purposes where it stems from the member state's commitment to tax competition. Any domestic victims presumably have a local political voice along with a chance to share the benefits of new investment induced by the low capital tax rate.

Verification and the benefits of tax competition

The probative shortcomings of the evidence of the labour–corporate tax distortion become less salient when considered in the context of the wider body of empirical studies of jurisdictional competition. Jurisdictional competition scenarios are famously difficult to verify empirically (Dowding, John, and Biggs 1994). The many studies are descriptive and shed little light on the normative question as to whether or not jurisdictional competition is efficient (Oates 1999: 1137). The descriptive studies also fall well short of clear proof that the market mechanism predicted in the theory exists in the real world. Results are stronger on the demand side than the supply side. Citizen sorting across different jurisdictions with different public goods packages is indeed well verified. When such a showing is tied to a showing of citizen satisfaction with tax levels and public goods provision, we do get an implication of a constraint on government. But we do not get confirmation of entrepreneurial incentives and competitive responses in government actors tied to citizen and factor mobility. As an example, consider Kirchgaessner and

Pomerehne's recent attempt (1996: 354) to verify the existence of tax competition within the Swiss Confederation. No direct evidence, such as a rate shift followed (or not followed) by cross-border migration, presented itself. So Kirchgaessner and Pomerehne instead tested for tax competition indirectly by regressing the dispersion of the wealth across the cantons against three factors: tax rates, earnings opportunities, and area attractiveness. Tax rates were found to have a small but statistically significant negative effect on the presence of rich people. But the other two factors had much more significant positive effects: it seems that economic opportunity and locational amenities more manifestly attract rich people (354, 357, 359). The results strongly suggest that the rich avoid taxes and tend to gravitate to low-tax localities. As such the results are consistent with the possible presence of tax competition. But they do not come close to proving that tax competition shapes the cantons' tax regimes because they tell us nothing about the relationship between the migration of rich people and the behaviour of the government actors in the target jurisdictions. Once again the slate is clean for a plausible public choice story that includes no tax competition: rich people gravitate to cantons with economic opportunities and amenities and, once there, influence the tax rates.

To generalize, it is not safe to assume the existence of the benefits predicted by tax competition proponents. We have asserted elsewhere that claims for benefits from jurisdictional competition should be subject to a suitability test. More particularly, a claim that competitive benefits redound, presently or prospectively, from the vesting of regulatory authority at junior level will be more plausible where: (1) the regulation is unbundled; (2) the regulation implicates no substantial interconnections with other jurisdictions or with later consumers; (3) all actors affected by the regulation are highly mobile; (4) all actors are well informed; and (5) competitive pressures registered by all actors affected by the regulation determine its content (Bratton and McCahery 1997: 262–3). To the extent that one or more of these variables does not obtain, the case for competitive benefits weakens. We have also argued that a proponent with a strong claim should be able to describe a causal connection between the mechanism of competition and the claimed beneficial outcome, showing the impact on the alignment of interest group politics and other factors that influence regulatory outcomes in the competing jurisdictions (263).

Corporate tax competition clearly passes only test (1). But, notably, its unbundled aspect is also a factor picked up in the PHTM definition, and could just as easily have distortionary effects as beneficial effects. Test (4) probably also is passed, as least so far as it concerns tax competition's beneficiaries. But it fails tests (2), (3), and (5), since it has external effects, differential mobility obtains, and it is not clear that those whose interests are impaired, such as labour and other taxpayers, get to register competing pressures in the political arena.

These problems would be mitigated if the tax competition proponent could show countervailing benefits. With such a showing, the competition/coordination issue becomes a matter of making a tradeoff. Three benefits are claimed for tax competition: (1) through sorting, it increases the likelihood that citizen preferences match tax regimes; (2) it helps contain the size of government and makes government actors more responsive by reducing the tax base; and (3) it can reduce reliance on particular distortionary taxes. None of these three come to bear unequivocally to assist the case in the European Union.

As to benefit (1), it seems plausible, given the capital/labour mobility differential, to assume that citizen preference matching through voting with the feet is not yet a widespread phenomenon in Europe (Oates 1999: 1124). The benefits lie instead on the side of capital: capital tax competition helps firms and equityholders match a preference for avoiding taxes. Taken by itself, however, this particular preference match does not provide a proxy for welfare enhancement for society as a whole.

Benefit (2), containment of government size, could obtain in Europe. There is no question that governments can extract surpluses from their taxpayers in a second-best world in which agendas matter and voters lack mobility. But this possibility, taken by itself, does not justify tax competition. First, as we have seen, tax competition does not automatically cause government size to be contained. The burden lifted from capital may merely be shifted to a less mobile revenue source. Second, even where no shifting occurs, containment is a benefit only to the extent that the member state's citizens are dissatisfied with the government's performance. Prima facie, we see no reason to assume that member states' taxing and spending programmes lie outside the range of preferences of their median voters. Indeed, openness to foreign trade has been shown to be a statistically significant predictor of expansion of government consumption. This apparently follows from larger doses of external risk attending open borders and a voter preference for social insurance (Rodrik 1997). It may or may not follow that a given member state government grows due to the advent of the single European market. But it certainly does follow that Leviathan tendencies among the member states should be demonstrated rather than assumed (Bergstrom *et al.* 1988). Third, assuming the presence of Leviathans in the member state group, it is by no means clear that tax competition is the best available means of control. The literature sets out a long menu of ways to hardwire constitutions so as to limit the power to tax and the incentive to spend (Brennan and Buchanan 1980: 62–9, 142–4). Indeed, the European Monetary Union Treaty entails a loss of monetary policy autonomy for member state signatories, limiting, among other things, the scope for borrowing against temporary shocks (Obstfeld 1999). Whether these constraints will hold or be undermined by political actors remains a controversial question. Meanwhile, scattershot effects of tax competition do not promise significantly to improve the fiscal picture.

Benefit (3) obtains if the tax constrained by competition is distortionary. Such a charge can plausibly be laid against capital taxes. Capital taxes arguably inhibit investment and a consequent burden shift could mean employment of a less distortionary tax device. Also, when capital is taxed even as government borrows, the pain of paying the cost of present government expenditure is shifted to future taxpayers, exacerbating government's tendency to increase in size (Brennan and

Buchanan 1980: 107–8). On the other hand, a tax on already accumulated capital is not distortionary (Gordon 1985), provided that the taxing state can make a credible advance commitment to a stable tax policy (Persson and Tabellini 1994). To this we add the point that the very capital movement that tax competition theory presupposes and encourages is intrinsically distortionary under fiscal federalism theory. In sum, then, a capital tax competition claim of movement toward a less distortionary regime needs to be demonstrated with particularity in a second-best framework.

European Union taxing power and asymmetric information

Even though the Code's substantive approach is flawed as a matter of fiscal federalism, it may be the best available approach because the superior regulatory strategy suggested by a narrow reading of the economics is not feasible for the European Union.

The Code seeks to correct a problem of distortionary taxation by constraining the member states' legislative and fiscal discretion. Fiscal federalism models contemplate a different corrective approach. The central government instead identifies externalities that stem from myopic member state activity and follows up by imposing Pigovian taxes. If, for example, the use of a low tax rate to attract capital from another member state is distortionary, then the central government should induce the externality's internalization by taxing each unit of capital attracted (Piketty 1996: 6). As a second example, reconsider the solution to the labour market distortion that results from state-level wealth redistribution. The central government levies lump sum taxes and redistributes them as grants to the states to subsidize poor workers, with the levels of grants keyed to the states' levels of poverty. The European Union would not be equipped to play the Pigovian role in either case, for it has no direct, open-ended taxing power. As noted above, the European Union draws limited resources from specific sources collected by the member states and taxation is not an EU policy instrument. Legislative and other regulatory harmonization is the only means available to capture the gain from coordination. In theory, this need not necessarily be a problem. Mandates take their place with taxes and subsidies on the menu of corrections that fiscal federalism holds out to central government. The mandate's terms can of course affect the impact point of the costs of correction (Inman and Rubinfeld 1997b: 46–7 and n. 6). Significantly, in the present context, the costs of a central mandate respecting tax rates fall on the tax-competitive state (and its customers), the same place at which they fall with the Pigovian tax in the first example.

We also note that it is not at all clear that first-best corrections would be achievable even if EU-level corrective taxation was a practical possibility. Empirical problems interpose themselves. To see this, return to the examples in the preceding paragraph. In the first case, the correcting central government has to verify the number of units of capital attracted to the low-tax jurisdiction. Unfortunately, information about such movement may be decentralized and none of the actors immediately involved will have an incentive to reveal it (Piketty 1996: 7). Similar problems of asymmetric information would come up respecting the equalizing grants in the second example. Recall that there the grants' purpose is to equalize income and to undo the labour market effects of state-level redistribution. Presumably, basic facts about the states' redistributive policies and programmes will be verifiable. But more information may be needed. Tastes for redistribution may vary across states; ability to pay may vary depending on production functions in each state. The states will have a disincentive to disclose this information if it will have the effect of lowering the amount of the grant received back from the central government. Adverse selection through underdisclosure would be the result. So might underinvestment—the states could fail to make investments or bureaucratic efforts with a view to enhancing the payout stream of their equalization grants (Raff and Wilson 1997: 408).

This analysis shows us that the first-best adjustments the theory commends may be difficult to effect. Of course, it remains an open question whether or not the particular information problems identified in these models present significant barriers to central government action in the real world. We suspect that they more closely describe the European Union's situation than they describe federal–state relations in the United States. In the United States, with its higher degree of integration and enormous federal-level infrastructure for welfare provision and taxation, the zone of information advantage for state governments could very well be immaterial for present purposes. Since EU institutions operate more at second hand so far as information is concerned, there is at least cause for further inquiry.

IV. CONCLUSION

The foregoing asymmetric information approach sounds a note of caution respecting the strictness of standards brought to bear in evaluating tax coordination initiatives under subsidiarity's decentralization presumption. A theoretically questionable initiative like the Code may survive rough cost–benefit scrutiny due to the very lack of a plausible alternative. Depending on the gravity of the problem addressed, the benefits could easily outweigh the perverse effects (Alesina and Wacziarg 1999). But questions remain respecting the values to be compared in the rough. How does one weigh the benefit of discouraging fiscal externalities versus the cost of constraining the member states' policy?

Edwards and Keen (1996) pose an answer to this question in a model that assumes that government actors prefer to maximize their own welfare through excessive taxing and spending but that citizen utility constrains their excesses, whether due to re-election concerns or a qualified sense of public responsibility. In Edwards and Keen's set-up, the government actor in a unitary system equates her marginal rate of substitution between wasteful expenditures and citizen utility to the marginal price she pays to raise citizen utility by foregoing wasteful public expenditure. In a federation, tax competition will prevent state officials from reaching this point. But at the same time, the competition could cause government to become too small—public goods provision could be less than that preferred by median voters. So the question is whether tax coordination among the states in the federation will be welfare-enhancing. To the extent that coordination succeeds, the welfare of government actors obviously is enhanced. The citizens may or may not be better off: the increased taxes cause a reduction in their private consumption. But there can be a positive income effect if the citizens' utility gain from additional public goods produced with the new taxes is greater than the cost of foregone consumption. Meanwhile, the constrained government actor will indeed devote the new taxes to public goods calculated to increase citizen satisfaction, but will produce only just enough public goods to leave public utility unchanged net of the tax increase. Any excess will be wasted expenditures that satisfy the official. There is also a relative price effect: as more public goods are provided, the citizens' marginal valuation of goods decreases. This makes it less expensive in terms of foregone public utility for the official to divert revenues to her own purposes. The outcome lies in the balance between the income effect and the relative price effect—the marginal cost to the official of buying welfare for the citizen. Coordination is beneficial if the official's income elasticity of demand for public utility enhancement is stronger than her marginal propensity to waste revenues (117–25).

This presentation gives us a formula that yields quantified policy results for tax coordination in Europe only if we accept its mechanism of government constraint in all particulars. But we still emerge with a sharper sense of how to apply fiscal federalism in policy making. Reading Edwards and Keen broadly, tax coordination can make sense provided a specific spending goal has been specified ex ante. Only with a specified goal do we have a basis for evaluating the coordination initiative. In the model the goal is public goods provision. In another situation—today's European Union, for example—the goal might be elimination of a horizontal externality. Coordination for its own sake, in contrast, suggests a Leviathan behaviour pattern. Thus expanded, Edwards and Keen's public choice model reinforces and parallels the policy advice offered by fiscal federalism models that assume a benevolent sovereign. In Edwards and Keen, coordination serves the single objective of increasing the tax base; welfare is enhanced if the states have a good use for the money. Elsewhere in fiscal federalism, central intervention presupposes identification of a distortion; correction of the distortion enhances welfare.

Fiscal federalism thus warns of tradeoffs and bids that facts be gathered, less toward the end of a 100 per cent guaranteed first-best policy than to assist in the application of its precepts as presumptions. With the Code we have a very strong theoretical prediction of distortion in respect of competition of taxes on capital, along with some evidence of it. We also have legislation which, while imperfect, is targeted to a limited class of distortionary tax provisions. On the contrary side, we have the prediction of benefits from tax competition theory. But that prediction also turns out to be subject to qualifications. There is, moreover, no particular evidence of competitive benefits in the European Union, except for persons in the labour market in places like Dublin and Luxembourg.

We conclude that subsidiarity is satisfied. Indeed, with the matter in this posture it is reasonable to place the burden to show a cognizable opportunity cost on the tax competition proponent. But the decision maker ultimately must proceed under uncertainty, with the potential for perverse effects varying with the process context. With the Code's soft law framework, that potential is acceptably low.

9

Regulatory Competition versus Harmonization in European Company Law

SIMON DEAKIN*

European company law exemplifies the limited extent to which harmonizing measures have led to greater uniformity in the private and commercial laws of the EU member states. Although important Directives have been adopted in relation to a number of areas, including accounting requirements and rules relating to the maintenance of share capital, taken together they fall a long way short of establishing a systematic code relating to the formation and governance of companies. Numerous initiatives in the field of company law currently remain in a state of suspended animation; these include proposals for a model European company statute, standardized rules for public companies, and a framework for the regulation of takeover bids.

This looks like good news for advocates of greater regulatory competition in the European Union: diversity in the laws of the individual member states has survived attempts at harmonization, making it possible for member states to experiment in their search for efficient and workable rules of company law, as seems to be the case in the United States. However, the other side of member state autonomy is the absence of an effective market for incorporations in the European Union. The possibility of a market for incorporations has been blocked, in part, by the operation of national-level rules of the conflicts of laws which limit the degree to which a company can choose its applicable law—the so-called *siège réel* doctrine. National-level laws also differ widely in their attitude towards the movement of companies from one jurisdiction to another, that is to say, their reincorporation across jurisdictional boundaries. The draft Fourteenth Directive, which aimed to provide a common solution to the issue of reincorporation, has in effect been abandoned, at least for the time being. For these reasons, the mechanisms of corporate entry and exit which, in the US context, have brought the corporate law systems of the states directly into competition with one another simply do not exist within the European Union.

There are signs that this picture of relative stability may not last. The catalyst for change has been the *Centros* decision of the European Court of Justice (Case

* I am most grateful for comments from Mads Andenas, John Armour, Brian Cheffins, and participants in the Conference on Regulatory Competition and Economic Integration: Comparative Perspectives, organized by the Regulation and Competitiveness project at Yale University in cooperation with the Institut d'Etudes Juridiques Européennes of the University of Liège, at Yale Law School. I bear sole responsibility for the views expressed.

C–212/97 *Centros Ltd.* v. *Erhvervs-og Selkabsstryrelsen*, [1999] ECR I–1459), which, in the views of some commentators, promises (or threatens) to undermine the *siège réel* doctrine by characterizing it as an obstacle to freedom of establishment under the EC Treaty. As we shall see further below, the *Centros* case, in itself, is unlikely to lead to the end of the *siège réel* doctrine. However, whatever its precise legal scope turns out to be, the *Centros* case has certainly reignited debate on the merits and demerits of a Delaware-style resolution to the current impasse in the European company law programme.

Two related questions arise at this point. The first is concerned with the likely effects of increasing regulatory competition on the company law systems of the member states. Would diversity be preserved and possibly even strengthened, or would regulatory competition lead to de facto uniformity as laws converged around a stable set of solutions to the tradeoffs between the rights of shareholders and other parties which are implicit in company law regimes? The second question is concerned with the efficiency implications of choosing regulatory competition on the basis of a market for incorporations. In so far as we can identify the kinds of changes in company law systems which regulatory competition of this kind would be likely to induce, would the result be efficiency-enhancing? It is arguable that regulatory competition would lead to the removal of inefficient legal rules which, until now, have been insulated from change by the absence of a market for incorporations. On the other hand, there is a view that freedom of incorporation will put in jeopardy certain mandatory laws which may have efficiency-enhancing effects. Here, the debate over harmonization intersects with arguments concerning the nature and effects of laws which seek to balance the rights of shareholders with those of other stakeholder groups, in particular employees. Laws of this kind currently operate in several member states.

Providing answers to these questions is inherently problematic. Studies of regulatory competition in the United States disclose a number of possible explanations of the nature and effects of the rise of Delaware as the primary state of incorporation for larger and public companies. These include the race-to-the-bottom hypothesis (Cary 1974); the contrary idea of the efficient selection of rules through competition (Easterbrook and Fischel 1991; Romano 1993b); and institutional explanations which stress the role of interest-group activity, lock-in, and path dependence (Macey and Miller 1997; Roe 1993). From a European perspective, it is difficult to get a clear message from the US experience which would be relevant in the different market and institutional environment of the European Union.

To make progress on this issue, some rethinking on the relationship between competition and harmonization may be required. United States debates draw a contrast between those areas of law which are left up to competition between states on the one hand and those which are governed by the federal legislature as a 'monopoly regulator' on the other (Romano 1998). In the European context, on the other hand, it is possible to see how harmonization may complement and even encourage the process of evolutionary adaptation in laws at state level. Certain types of 'reflexive harmonization' may in the end be the most effective guarantor of diversity between national systems, and hence of experimentation in regulatory design. By contrast, unregulated competition between jurisdictions could well eliminate the most significant differences between them, *but* without any guarantee that the system which eventually prevailed would be the most efficient. The apparently paradoxical conclusion, then, is that the harmonization of company law may represent the best chance of capturing beneficial aspects of regulatory competition, in terms of evolutionary adaptation, within the framework of the single market.

This argument is developed below in the following way. Part I provides some context by outlining the development of EU company law to date and its relationship to the company law systems of the member states. General reference is made to those Treaty provisions which are concerned with company law and to directives and regulations in this area. In Part II, the focus shifts to the *Centros* case and to the potential effects of a market for incorporations inside the European Union. The concept of reflexive harmonization is then analysed, and its implications are considered in the context of two issues of central importance within contemporary debates, namely employee participation and the conduct of takeover bids. Part III argues that the experience of European company law has wider lessons for harmonization within the European Union and, more generally, for the way in which the process of regulatory competition is understood.

I. AN OVERVIEW OF EUROPEAN COMPANY LAW

The place of company law in the legal order of the European Union

European Union company law has its roots in provisions of the EC Treaty protecting freedom of establishment. Article 43 of the EC Treaty (ex Article 52) provides:

> [R]estrictions on the freedom of establishment of nationals of a Member State in the territory of another Member State shall be prohibited. Such prohibition shall also apply to restrictions on the setting up of agencies, branches or subsidiaries by nationals of any Member State established in the territory of any Member State.
>
> Freedom of establishment shall include the right to take up and pursue activities as self-employed persons and to set up and manage undertakings, in particular companies and firms within the meaning of the second paragraph of Article 48, under the conditions laid down for its own nationals by the law of the country where such establishment is effected . . .

For this purpose, Article 48 (ex Article 58) provides:

> Companies or firms formed in accordance with the law of a Member State and having their registered office, central administration or principal place of business within the Community shall, for the purposes of [the chapter on freedom of establishment], be treated in the same way as natural persons who are nationals of Member States.

'Companies or firms' means companies or firms constituted under civil or commercial law, including cooperative societies, and other legal persons governed by public or private law, save for those which are non-profit-making.

The power to introduce harmonizing measures in the field of company law is essentially ancillary to these rights of free movement for companies. Under Article 44(2)(g) (ex Article 54(3)(g)), the Council can adopt directives aimed at 'coordinating to the necessary extent the safeguards which, for the protection of the interests of members and others, are required by member states of companies and firms . . . with a view to making such safeguards equivalent throughout the Community'. In other words, some degree of parity or equivalence in the laws protecting shareholders and 'others'—the latter term could include a range of stakeholder groups (Villiers 1998: 19)—was deemed by the Treaty's drafters to be necessary in order to remove disincentives to the movement of companies from one member state to another.

During the early development of the Community's company law programme, the case for harmonization echoed the claims made at around the same time by the 'race-to-the-bottom' school in the United States (Cary 1974). Thus Clive Schmitthoff's assessment, in 1973, was that, without harmonization, standards of shareholder and creditor protection within the European Union would be eroded. In order to avoid a repeat of Delaware, harmonization, in his view, should aim for the 'virtual unification of national company laws' (1973: 9). Although this view can be reconciled with the principle of freedom of establishment, on the grounds that 'unharmonized national safeguards may make establishment too burdensome or even impossible' (Villiers 1998: 19; Wolff 1993: 22), it arguably goes further than necessary in order to achieve the goal of equivalence or parity between member states. Rather, Schmitthoff's argument saw Community-level intervention as having a substantive policy goal, namely the preservation of regulations conferring protections on various corporate constituencies, which, it was feared, a Delaware-style effect might otherwise erode.

It was partly this spirit of protective regulation which, along with the goal of ensuring freedom of establishment, motivated the early company law directives, the so-called first-generation directives, which were heavily prescriptive in their approach (Edwards 1999; Villiers 1998: 29). The First Directive, adopted in 1968, laid down certain core minimum standards for both public and private companies and for limited partnerships relating to disclosure of basic information concerning the company's constitution and statutes. It also set standards for state laws concerning the validity of obligations entered into by the company with third parties, and the bases for the nullity of a company. The Second Directive, adopted in 1976, laid down a number of basic requirements for public companies, including the obligation to have a minimum paid-up share capital as well as rules relating to the maintenance of capital.

This early emphasis on uniformity and prescription soon gave way, however, to more flexible approaches which placed greater stress on member state autonomy.

Charlotte Villiers (1998) describes the successive waves of measures as second-, third-, and fourth-generation directives. Characteristic second-generation measures were the so-called accounting directives, the Fourth (1978), Seventh (1983), and Eighth (1984). These laid down basic accounting and audit standards in the form of a set of options which essentially represented the predominant approaches which were then in operation in various member states.

The third-generation directives reflected the 'new approach' to harmonization which the Commission instituted around the time of the passage of the Single European Act in 1986 and the initiation of the single market programmes. The 'new approach' began in the context of product standard harmonization, where it established a principle that Community intervention should be limited to the harmonization of essential safety-related requirements. It also established the 'reference to standards' approach, under which it was presumed that a product which conformed with a standard set by a European-level body, or, failing that, with the relevant national standard, also complied with EC law (Armstrong and Bulmer 1998: 152). Company law was one of the other areas in which this decentralizing approach was applied. Hence the Twelfth Directive on single-member private companies (1989), which was adopted in pursuance of the Community's goal of promoting the growth of small and medium-sized enterprises, explicitly left a range of regulatory issues concerning disclosure of information and creditor protection to be decided at member state level.

Fourth-generation measures took the process a stage further by adopting a 'framework' model for directives. This again favoured the articulation of general principles or standards rather than the promulgation of rigidly prescriptive rules. However, new techniques were also involved. The aim was to achieve policy goals by linking regulatory interventions to the activities and processes of autonomous rule-making bodies, such as industry-level associations and self-governing professional organizations in the financial sector. The draft Thirteenth Directive on Takeover Bids (last amended in 1997) exemplifies this approach, in particular in the scope it provides for its general principles to be implemented through local-level action by self-regulatory bodies (such as, in the UK context, the City Panel on Takeovers and Mergers, which is an entity formed by organizations and professional associations in the finance sector rather than a body emanating from the state).

The 'flexibilization' of directives did not, however, make it any easier to reach agreement on some of the key proposals for company law harmonization which were being discussed at this time. The draft Fifth Directive was first proposed in 1972; further versions appeared in 1982 and 1988, and amendments were most recently made in 1991. This draft Directive essentially laid out a model set of regulations for the governance of public companies. Large parts of the draft were relatively uncontentious. However, the proposal essentially foundered on the issues of board structure and employee representation, thereby suffering the same fate as the so-called Vredeling draft Directive of the mid-1970s, which would have introduced forms of employee participation in management decision making into transnational companies. The original draft of the Fifth Directive provided for a two-tier board structure with employee representation on the supervisory board, more or less along the lines of the German co-determination system. This was later amended to allow for the possibility of a unitary board, but still with a basic requirement of employee representation either at board level or through a consultative council. But these provisions still proved unacceptable to a number of member states, including Britain.

Disagreement on the question of employee representation has also been the main reason for the failure of proposals for a model European Company Statute. The idea of a model constitution for transnational European companies goes back to the earliest days of the Community, and some versions even pre-date the Treaty of Rome of 1957. The first concrete proposal was made by the Commission in 1970; the most recent dates from 1996. The present proposal is for a Regulation which would provide for a European public company, a *Societas Europea* (SE), to be established through a number of different mechanisms, most of which require the involvement of two or more companies which are governed by the laws of at least two member states. Significant features of the model constitution include the requirement for a minimum paid-up share capital (currently 120,000 euros); the identification of the company's registered office, which must be in the territory of the European Union, with its central administration (an application of the *siège réel* principle); and a range of options on board structure, including two-tier and unitary boards of various kinds. The Regulation is currently attached to a directive which makes provision for employee representation. As with the draft Fifth Directive, a number of options are made available, ranging from employee membership of a supervisory or a unitary board, the establishment of a consultative council, and a collective agreement setting out the basis for employee participation. The draft SE Directive would also impose certain minimum requirements of information and consultation with regard to employees.

The impasse on the issue of employee representation has been overcome to a certain extent by the adoption in 1994 of the Directive on European Works Councils ('EWC Directive'). This Directive adopts a labour law solution to the issue of information and consultation, by requiring transnational companies above a certain size to enter into negotiations with employee representatives for the establishment of a framework for information and consultation. In the event of the failure of negotiations, a default procedure is imposed by law. The passage of the EWC Directive does not solve all the problems associated with the SE proposal, since it does not touch on the question of board structure and membership. The relationship of the EWC Directive to the wider company law harmonization programme is analysed in further detail below.

Diversity in the company law systems of the member states

It can be seen from the preceding discussion that progress on harmonization has stalled, above all, on the question of how to treat stakeholder groups, in particular employees. This failure is a reflection of the divide which exists, at the level of the laws of the member states, between 'insider' and 'outsider' systems of corporate governance (Mayer 1997). Within 'insider' systems such as those of Germany and France, share ownership tends to be concentrated in the hands of family groups or held in large blocks by other corporations, thereby giving rise to cross-ownership of shares between companies. Hostile takeovers are extremely rare, with the result that there is only a minimal or embryonic market for corporate control. In some insider systems, although not all, these conditions are reflected in board structure. Germany has the most articulated and deeply embedded system of stakeholder participation in corporate decision making. Two-tier boards of the kind which exist in Germany for public companies, in addition to providing for formal representation of the interests of a wide range of stakeholders, also offer continuity and a degree of entrenchment for managerial teams.

By contrast, in 'outsider' systems, the predominant mode of ownership in public companies is through the holdings of institutional investors, who strive to diversify their holdings in order to minimize risk and so frequently lack strong ties to particular companies. The interests of shareholders in an active market for corporate control are defended by takeover codes which limit the scope for defensive actions by target managements. A number of other rules, in particular those relating to disclosure of investment information and the prohibition of insider dealing, aim to maintain a high degree of stock market liquidity. Employee representation operates (if at all) through collective bargaining and similar arrangements which lie strictly outside the framework of company law. This is broadly descriptive of the British system which, in most respects, more closely resembles that of the United States than it does those of its fellow EU member states.

It is not surprising that, following the first enlargement of the EC in 1973 to include Britain, Denmark, and Ireland, there was strong resistance to the attempt in the first version of the draft Fifth Directive to impose a system based on the German model of 'insider governance'. The emergence of more flexible regulatory techniques in subsequent drafts can be seen as indicating an acceptance of diversity. However, the more recent impasse over the European Company Statute shows that this has not been enough to resolve the debate. The failure to agree now turns on whether it is appropriate to address the issue of stakeholder representation through company law at all.

This, again, is a basic point of divergence in the company law systems of the member states. As just explained, the British system, with very few exceptions, sees stakeholder rights as mainly lying outside the framework of company law, which is predominantly concerned with the position of shareholders and, to a lesser extent, creditors. An important feature of some 'insider systems', of which Germany represents the best example, is not simply that they recognize certain claims of non-shareholder stakeholders which go unrecognized in outsider systems, but that they do so in such a way as to incorporate stakeholder voice directly into the processes of governance and control within companies. The most important illustration of this, as we have already seen, is the involvement of the representatives of employees and in some cases other stakeholders, such as local government and environmental interests, on the supervisory boards of public companies. Other features of stakeholder voice in Germany, such as the system of employee representation through works councils, do not operate at the level of company law as such; in the manner of the EWC Directive, they operate through the mechanisms of labour law. However, it is the close linkages between company law and labour law which are important here; in the German context, co-determination and the two-tier board are best viewed as closely interlocking elements of a single system of stakeholder representation.

In the context of directors' duties, the furthest English company law can go by way of recognition of the interests of non-shareholder stakeholders is the idea of 'enlightened shareholder value'. In other words, directors may act out of concern for other stakeholder groups if, by so doing, they believe that they will maximize the value of the business and thereby meet shareholders' interests (which for this purpose may mean their longer-term interests). This is quite different from the civil law idea that the company has an interest 'in itself' (Teubner 1994) which serves as a means of reconciling the different perspectives of a number of stakeholder groups, none of which is entitled to priority. In the words of the Viénot Report (1995: 91) on corporate governance in France:

> In Anglo-Saxon countries the emphasis is for the most part placed on the objective of maximising share values, whilst on the European continent and France in particular the emphasis is placed more on the human assets and resources of the company . . . Human resources can be defined as the overriding interest of the corporate body itself, in other words the company considered as an autonomous economic agent, pursuing its own aims as distinct from those of its shareholders, its employees, its creditors including the tax authorities, and of its suppliers and customers; rather, it corresponds to their general, common interest, which is that of ensuring the survival and prosperity of the company.

Hence the French and other 'insider' systems of company law essentially see the business enterprise as having an *organizational* dimension which rests on the contributions made by a number of stakeholder groups, and not simply a *financial* dimension which describes the contribution of the shareholders. This divergence of approach operates at a fundamental conceptual level, so that even the terms used to define the business enterprise in legal terms are not precisely analogous. The English law concept of the 'company', for example, refers to the essentially financial relationship between managers and investors; there is no equivalent to those concepts which recognize the enterprise's organizational dimension, such as the French *entreprise* or German *unternehmen*.

The *siège réel* principle, which identifies the company's registered office with its central management or administration rather than with its chosen place of incorporation, is part of the same organizational orientation to the legal conceptualization of the business enterprise. The recent challenge to the *siège réel* principle is therefore also, unavoidably, a challenge to the stakeholder model of company law which has evolved in a number of EU member states. The *Centros* case has brought the debate full circle, back to the concerns of the early 1970s with the race to the bottom. We turn next to a closer analysis of the *Centros* decision and its implications.

II. NEGATIVE HARMONIZATION AND COURT-LED DEREGULATION: THE IMPLICATIONS OF *CENTROS*

The meaning of negative harmonization

The *Centros* case can be seen as an example of 'negative harmonization'. This occurs when state-level rules are struck down by the courts on the grounds of their incompatibility with the principles of free movement and undistorted competition within the internal market of the European Community. Since these principles have the status of fundamental rights under the EC Treaty, they are capable of having direct effect in national legal orders in such a way as to confer rights on individual parties. Moreover, thanks to the doctrine of the supremacy of EC law, they take priority over national provisions in the event of a conflict.

Following its landmark decision in the *Cassis de Dijon* case (Case 120/78 *Rewe-Zentral AG* v. *Bundesmonoplverwaltung für Brantweinn* [1979] ECR 649), the European Court of Justice has massively expanded its jurisdiction in this area, with the result that rules in a range of areas concerning product regulation, environmental protection, and labour standards have been called into question. The technique used by the Court has been to bring an ever wider body of rules and regulations under the scope of its review while at the same time expanding, through its case law, the range of potential excuses or justifications which member states can put forward in defence of the rules which are under attack. Broad, effects-based tests have been used to determine when regulatory laws can be deemed to interfere with the circulation of economic resources within the internal market, and a wide meaning has been accorded to certain key concepts (such as the notion of 'undertaking') within the Treaty's competition policy provisions. Some limitations on the reach of this technique have been set, most importantly as a result of the Court's decision in the *Keck* and *Mithouard* cases (Joined Cases C–267/91 and C–268/91 *Keck* and *Mithouard* [1993] ECR–I 6097), but the general direction of the case law since the late 1970s is not in doubt (Deakin 1996).

As a result of its intervention, the Court has placed itself in a pivotal position to influence the pace and direction of legal integration on matters of economic and social regulation. The Court's intervention has tended, in practice, to favour deregulation. Where the Court rules that a particular body of regulation—such as the law governing retail opening hours—is contrary to the principle of free movement, for example, the effect is to induce a form of 'levelling down' between the member states. However, this is not at all the same thing as saying that the Court has set out to encourage interjurisdictional competition. On the contrary, by invoking rules aimed at protecting the integrity of the internal market, the Court has often limited the autonomy of member states and thereby restricted the scope for differentiation and experimentation at the state level.

Member states can nevertheless draft laws which achieve the purpose originally intended for the regulation in question, but do so in a way which is compatible with the Treaty. This is possible in practice since the Court very rarely strikes down laws on the grounds that they are *per se* illegal—it tends instead to operate a version of the 'rule of reason'. This has the effect that the measure in question may be upheld if, first of all, it seeks to achieve an aim which is regarded as legitimate in this context. The *Cassis de Dijon* case established that the Court could develop categories of legitimate justifications for regulatory policy through its own case law (the so-called 'mandatory requirements' doctrine) in addition to those provided by the Treaty in Article 30 (ex Art. 36). The second broad requirement is that the particular measure can be shown to be 'proportionate' to the aim being pursued. While there are various versions of the proportionality test, it essentially requires that the measure should be effective in achieving the substantive goal which is being sought, while at the same time interfering as little as possible with the operation of the internal market.

To that extent, a significant space for member state autonomy is preserved. Nevertheless, the effect of a Court ruling is often to undermine national-level legislation in a particular area of social and economic regulation. It may be impossible to predict with any certainty how the balancing of factors which is inherent in the proportionality test will work out. Legislation may be formally valid but in practice a dead letter during the period between the first formal challenge to the Court and the final resolution of the issue, as occurred in the case of UK Sunday trading legislation in the early 1990s (Barnard 1994).

There is another sense in which 'negative harmonization' may restrict interjurisdictional competition rather than enhancing it. The Court cannot intervene to strike down state-level rules under the *Cassis de Dijon* doctrine if there is an EC Directive or Regulation on the matter in question (assuming that the latter is, itself, compatible with the wider terms of the Treaty). Where such regulation is absent, the Court's intervention is often read as an invitation for the EC legislature to act, and so put the matter beyond doubt. This does not always happen, since obtaining the agreement of the member states may be problematic, even when qualified majority voting is allowed. However, the point is that the *Cassis de Dijon* doctrine is completely compatible with the legislature's intervention to take the issue in question 'out of competition'. The Court's approach is ultimately founded on the logic of legal integration, not that of regulatory competition.

The uncertain implications of *Centros* for the *siège réel* doctrine

The *Centros* case illustrates the tenuous place which the idea of regulatory competition currently occupies in the EU legal order. At first sight, *Centros* appears to improve the chances of a market for incorporations developing, by casting doubt on the *siège réel* doctrine. At present, EU member states are divided in the approach they take to determining the applicable law of corporate constitutions. The United Kingdom, along with Ireland, the Netherlands, and Denmark, operates a 'state of incorporation' rule, according to which the applicable law is that of the state in which the company is incorporated or registered. The effect of the incorporation approach is that the applicable law is a matter of choice for managers of the company or, in the final analysis, for its shareholders; a company can carry on business in one member state while being incorporated in another. The company laws of the state of incorporation will prevail.

This is in contrast to the position in member states which operate the so-called 'real seat' or *siège réel* doctrine. The effects of the *siège réel* doctrine are complex and differ from one state to another, and according to the context which is being considered. Essentially, however, it means that courts will regard the applicable law as that of the member state in which the company has its main centre of operations—its head office or principal place of business. If the company in question has incorporated elsewhere, a number of consequences may then follow. In some instances, the effect will be to deny certain advantages of corporate form to the shareholders; in others, the law of the state in which the company has its head office will be applied over that of the state of incorporation. In either event, the effect of the *siège réel* doctrine is to limit freedom of incorporation; in that sense, it obstructs the emergence of a 'Delaware effect', since one aspect of that is the principle that entities can be incorporated in a state where they have no physical or other business presence.

The legality of the *siège réel* doctrine under EU law has often been called into question (Mortimer 1996), but the issue has gained new prominence as a result of the Court's decision in *Centros*, which was delivered in March 1999 (Case C–212/97 *Centros Ltd.* v. *Erhvervs-og Selskabsstryelsen*, [1999] ECR I–1459). In this case, two Danish citizens incorporated in the United Kingdom a private company named Centros Ltd, of which they were the sole shareholders. One of the two shareholders then applied to have a 'branch' of the company registered in Denmark for the purposes of carrying on business there. A 'branch', for this purpose, refers not to a subsidiary company but simply to a business or trading presence in one country of a company which is registered in another country. The Danish legislation on branches is in line with the Eleventh Company Law Directive, which requires member states to have legislation providing for the registration of branches on the grounds that this is necessary to protect third parties who deal with the company through its branches.

At the time of the registration request, Centros Ltd had never traded in the United Kingdom. The Danish Registrar of Companies refused to register the branch as requested, on the grounds that what the company was trying to do was not to register a branch but, rather, its principal business establishment. The Registrar took the view that by incorporating in the United Kingdom, which has no minimum capital requirement for private companies, and subsequently seeking to carry on business in Denmark through a branch, the company's owners were seeking to evade the Danish minimum capital requirements which are designed to protect third party creditors and minimize the risk of fraud.

The Court ruled that the refusal to accede to the registration request was contrary to the right of freedom of establishment under Article 43 (ex Art. 52) of the Treaty, read with Articles 46 (ex 56) and 48 (ex 58). It held, firstly, that there was a potential infringement of freedom of establishment in any case where 'it is the practice of a Member State, in certain circumstances, to refuse to register a branch of a company having its registered office in another Member State'. This was because:

> The provisions of the Treaty on freedom of establishment are intended specifically to enable companies formed in accordance with the law of a Member State and having their registered office, central administration or principal place of business within the Community to pursue activities in the Member States through an agency, branch or subsidiary.
>
> That being so, the fact that a national of a Member State who wishes to set up a company chooses to form it in the Member State whose rules of company law seem to him the least restrictive and to set up branches in other Member States cannot, by itself, constitute an abuse of the right of establishment. The right to form a company in accordance with the law of a Member State and to set up branches in other Member States is inherent in the exercise, in a single market, of the freedom of establishment guaranteed by the Treaty. (paras. 26–7)

The Court then went on to consider whether the Danish government could show that the refusal to register was justifiable in the circumstances. This involves a consideration of whether there was some countervailing policy objective behind the Danish practice and whether, in the particular circumstances of this case, the proportionality test could be said to be satisfied. The Danish government argued that the Registrar's action was intended to maintain Danish law's minimum capital requirement for the formation of private companies. The purpose of this law was:

> [F]irst to reinforce the financial soundness of those companies in order to protect public creditors against the risk of seeing the public debts owing to them become irrecoverable since, unlike private creditors, they cannot secure these debts by means of guarantees and, second, and more generally, to protect all creditors, public and private, by anticipating the risk of fraudulent bankruptcy due to the insolvency of companies whose initial capitalisation was inadequate. (para. 32)

In many ways, this was the crux of the case, and the most ambiguous and problematic aspect of the Court's judgment. The Court ruled that the justification offered was inadequate since, in the first place, 'the practice in question is not such as to attain the objective of protecting creditors which it purports to pursue since, if the company concerned had conducted business in the United Kingdom, its branch would have been registered in Denmark, even though Danish creditors might have been equally exposed to risk' (para. 35). In other words, the Registrar's decision failed the proportionality test since it was inconsistent—the vital factor in his refusal was, it seems, the failure of the company to trade in the United Kingdom, but this was immaterial to the protection of creditors since they would have been no better off if the company had previously traded and, as a result, had been able to get its branch registered in Denmark.

A major difficulty in determining the implications of *Centros* for the *siège réel* doctrine lies in the complexity of Danish law on the status of that doctrine. In most respects, Danish law follows the incorporation rule, and not that of the *siège réel*. Hence there was no possibility, under Danish law, of the registration of Centros in the United Kingdom itself being invalid. In essence, then, the Court decided that it was inconsistent, under the proportionality test, for the Registrar to refuse to register the branch of a company *which, in all other respects, was treated as a validly formed entity*. It is therefore quite possible to give *Centros* a narrow reading which does not touch on the validity of the *siège réel* doctrine.

However, the Court's dicta on the scope of the freedom of establishment principle, quoted above, do have clear implications for the *siège réel* doctrine. These dicta can be read as saying that the validity of an incorporation in one member state cannot be called into question in another solely on the grounds that the principal business presence or central administration of the company concerned is not located in the state in which it is incorporated. Admittedly, since the *siège réel* doctrine was not clearly before the Court, this interpretation cannot be relied on with any certainty. Had the issue been clearly raised, other governments would have made submissions to the Court, and it is possible that the Court would have held that the doctrine was not incompatible with freedom of establishment. However, after *Centros* it is more, rather than less, arguable that the *siège réel* doctrine does pose a barrier to freedom of establishment, in which case everything will turn on the question of justification. This would be consistent with the Court's practice over the years since *Cassis de Dijon*, which, as we have seen, has been to expand its jurisdiction to review state-level rules against the criteria of market access and transparency, while allowing states considerable leeway through the proportionality test.

However, in *Centros*, the application of the proportionality test shows how problematic the process of review by the courts can be. In addition to the argument which we have already considered, and which was specific to the 'inconsistency' which the Court perceived to exist in Danish practice, it considered two others which are of wider significance for the survival of creditor protection devices. It held, firstly, that 'contrary to the arguments of the Danish authorities, it is possible to adopt measures which are less restrictive, or which interfere less with fundamental freedoms, by, for example, making it possible in law for public creditors to obtain the necessary guarantees' (para. 37). Secondly, it argued that the Danish authorities were not precluded from coming to an agreement with their British counterparts for dealing with any cases where genuine fraud on the part of company founders could be established; but this had not been shown to be the case here.

Neither of these arguments is particularly convincing as grounds for rejecting the use of minimum capital requirements to protect creditors. A minimum capital requirement may be thought of as a means of ensuring that a certain level of capital is maintained within the company, so that, to that extent, the normal rules of priority in insolvency are observed and the rights of creditors are protected. It may therefore offset negative externalities arising from the abuse of incorporation by under-capitalized firms. It is arguable that a rule of this kind may cause more harm than good, for example by setting up excessive barriers to entry (Easterbrook and Fischel 1991: 60–2). It may also be the case that a minimum capital requirement is not a particularly efficient means of achieving creditor protection, by comparison with other methods which would interfere less with freedom of establishment (Armour 1999). However, this is not a matter which can be resolved without evidence of the kind which cannot easily be collected and evaluated by a court. In fact, the Court did not even consider the argument in the terms in which most academic writers have addressed it; its focus on the rights of public creditors and on fraud scarcely exhaust the possible arguments which could have been made in defence of the measure.

This kind of open-textured, policy-orientated issue would seem, on its face, to be the kind of question which can be addressed much more effectively through the legislative process. The efficiency of minimum capital requirements could be assessed through a deeper consideration of the relevant evidence. The effect of the reasoning in the *Centros* case, as in similar decisions flowing from the Court's approach to the freedom of movement provisions of the Treaty, is to bypass the legislature altogether.

The prospects of a market for incorporations in the European Union

Given the uncertainty which surrounds the application of the proportionality test in the context of freedom of establishment, it would seem to be premature to argue that the *Centros* case necessarily implies the end of the *siège réel* doctrine. There are other respects, too, in which the European Union's institutional environment is ill-suited to a market for incorporations. Even systems which follow the state of incorporation approach, such as the United Kingdom, would not be in a good position to replicate Delaware's success in establishing itself as the leading state of incorporation. Delaware has established its position by attracting *reincorporations* from existing businesses set up in other states. Initial incorporations have formed only a small part of its stock of companies. In contrast to Delaware, UK company law is not fully receptive to reincorporations. The effect of English conflict of law rules is that a company which has been incorporated in one member state cannot be reincorporated in another unless both jurisdictions permit this (which may not be the case under the *siège réel* doctrine, as we have just seen) (Cheffins 1997: 427).

The problem can be avoided by transferring the business of the company to a company set up in the United Kingdom especially for that purpose. However, there is no mechanism specifically designed to facilitate cross-border mergers of this kind. It seems that existing mechanisms, such as a scheme of arrangement under sections 425–7 of the Companies Act 1985, are not appropriate since they involve complex and expensive procedures whose effects, moreover, may be unclear in so far as they involve a merger between companies from different jurisdictions (428).

The end of the *siège réel* doctrine would thus be only the first step in the emergence of a market for incorporations. As Brian Cheffins argues, the right elements would have to be in place on both the 'demand' and 'supply' sides. In the US context, he argues that 'Delaware's success demonstrates that managers of larger corporations find it worthwhile to pay the legal expenses and filing fees associated with switching jurisdictions' (431). In the context of the European Union, similarly, the willingness of some German and Danish firms to reincorporate outside their home states in order to avoid minimum capital requirements is evidence of pent-up demand.

On the supply side, member states would have to alter their laws to make reincorporation more feasible. Incentives to customize company law regimes to the needs of business owners and managers may exist in the form of tax revenues from incorporation and registration. However, Delaware's position in this respect is highly unusual. Around 20 per cent of the total tax revenue of the state is derived from a combination of incorporation fees, fees for amendments to corporate charters and by-laws, and an annual franchise tax. The state lacks other major sources of income in part because it has very little indigenous industry and a small population. It is the high proportion of incorporation taxes in relation to the overall tax take which provides judges and legislators in Delaware with an incentive to respond to business needs and which, in turn, gives managers and owners confidence that the state will continue to be responsive to new needs (Romano 1993b). It follows that the Delaware effect would not be so easily replicated in the context of state jurisdictions which did not rely to such a high degree on revenues from incorporation. For this reason, there is some reason to doubt whether an EU Delaware could emerge among the member states, few of which would be in a position to become dependent upon company registrations as a source of tax income (a closer analogy might be with statelets such as Liechtenstein which are currently outside the European Union).

The nature of the underlying forces tending towards the emergence of interjurisdictional competition are also affected by the way in which reincorporations, in the EU context, would be affected by other regulatory controls over business activity. Regulations imposed upon businesses by labour law, as well as tax obligations, tend to apply on a territorial basis, rather than following the law of the company's domicile (Deakin 1996). Similarly, many aspects of securities law tend to follow the law of the country in which the transaction takes place, rather than the country in which the company is incorporated (Amihud and Mendelson 1996;

Licht 1998).[1] The application of insolvency procedures is subject to highly complex rules on conflicts of laws as well as to a number of local-level jurisdictional effects. Because of all these factors, it may make little difference in terms of the company's overall regulatory burden where it is *incorporated*; what may matter more is where it carries on its productive activities (in the case of employment law and tax law) or where its shares are traded (in the case of securities law). Demand-side pressures for a company-friendly company law may, to that extent, be overwhelmed by other cost considerations.

Conversely, the gains to a member stated which is able to attract incorporations from businesses carried on outside its own jurisdiction could well be limited. It might be the case, for example, that the fiscal benefits to the state in question would be minimal if the company's profits were taxed elsewhere. This argument would not apply if the territorial application of labour laws and tax laws could be attacked under Article 43 (ex Art. 52) of the Treaty. In the past the European Court of Justice has taken the view that the principle of territoriality can still be applied in both cases notwithstanding the existence of the freedom of establishment principle (Case C–113/89 *Rush Portuguesa Ltd.* v. *Office Nationale d'Immigration* [1990] ECR 1417 (on labour law); Case 81/87 *R.* v. *HM Treasury and Commissioners of the Inland Revenue, ex parte Daily Mail and General Trust plc* [1998] ECR 5483 (on tax law); Davies 1995; Deakin 1996; Mortimer 1996), but this could change as the Court's case law evolves.

Nevertheless, many of the same factors have been present in the US experience, but have not prevented a market for incorporations developing there. In part, this is because of the role played by the legal and accounting professions, who are most probably the principal beneficiaries from the market for incorporation, in maintaining Delaware's pre-eminent position as the state of choice for incorporation (Roe 1993). It has been argued that the British professions, as well as the judiciary and the regulatory authorities, would be in a similar position to 'make incorporating under British law an appealing proposition' if the right legal and institutional environment were to be put in place (Cheffins 1997: 443).

The possibility that it might at some stage in the foreseeable future become UK government policy to encourage reincorporations from other member states certainly cannot be ruled out. The Company Law Review currently being undertaken under the auspices of a steering group set up by the Department of Trade and Industry has noted that UK company law is perceived in some quarters to be more 'business friendly' (Company Law Review Steering Group 1999: 96) than the company law regimes of most other EU member states, and contrasts the 'relative structural and institutional flexibility' of UK company law with 'countries [such as] Germany, with inflexible mandatory rules on capital structure and forms of employee participation and split boards, presenting major problems for companies

[1] On arguments for and against the creation of jurisdictional competition in securities law, see Choi and Guzman (1998; 1997) and Romano (1998).

unfamiliar with such systems' (97). The Steering Group also regards the need to supply a 'business-friendly' company law as one issue to be taken into account in the process of company law reform. Research commissioned by the Steering Group for its 1999 Consultation Document found that 'irritants' of UK company law noted by inward investors included the capital maintenance rules, rules relating to directors' loans, difficulties with moving corporate domicile into and out of the UK jurisdiction, and the requirements of the localization of the register of members in Britain. At the same time, the Consultation Document recognized that measures perceived as 'irritants' by managers might be seen as protective by shareholders, creditors, and employees.

This brings us to the fundamental issue of what the economic consequences would be of the initiation of Delaware-type regulatory competition within the European Union.

The possible consequences of interjurisdictional competition over company law within the European Union

Discussion of the potential effects of interjurisdictional competition in the European Union is bound to be somewhat speculative. Nevertheless, an active debate has begun to develop on this subject. Cheffins argues that the United Kingdom would benefit from being in a position to establish itself as the pre-eminent state of incorporation. Tax revenues from incorporations would not be comparable to those raised by Delaware. The registration fee for UK incorporations has fallen in recent years, and it is unlikely to be raised significantly in the near future since government policy has sought to avoid any disincentive for small firm start-ups (Freedman and Godwin 1994; Hicks, Drury, and Smallcombe 1995). There would nevertheless be benefits for UK lawyers and accountants and an expansion of employment in related areas of services.

As Cheffins notes, the question of 'whether a market for incorporations would undermine the development of a distinctive European identity', while it might be expected to influence EU-level policy makers, is not a question which is easily susceptible to economic analysis (1997: 45). It is more meaningful to ask what the costs and benefits of the process would be to particular groups (shareholders, creditors, and employees) and whether the overall result would be an improvement in the responsiveness of company law to the needs of companies.

The question of whether shareholders would benefit from competition between jurisdictions depends in part on how far shareholders can bring influence to bear on the incorporation decision. In the US context, it would seem that shareholders in public companies are rarely involved directly in the incorporation decision, in large part because, under Delaware company law, a resolution on incorporation can only be tabled with the agreement of the directors (Bebchuk and Ferrell 1999). By contrast, it seems highly likely that UK institutional investors would be able to exercise some influence over management on a question of this kind. Regular communications take place, outside the framework of general meetings, between the institutions and senior managers of listed companies. Even where shareholders could not influence managerial decision making directly, indirect pressure through the capital markets (in the form of the reaction of share prices to managerial behaviour) could be expected to bring influence to bear. In general, the degree of institutional shareholder influence over corporate governance in Britain is very high, as indicated by the production of strongly pro-shareholder regulations in the area of takeovers (Deakin and Slinger 1997) and board structure (Deakin and Hughes 1999). Managers would therefore have a number of direct and indirect incentives to avoid decisions which were seen as clearly contrary to shareholders' interests.

Given the likelihood that shareholders could influence incorporation decisions to some extent, a more difficult issue relates to whether creditors and employees would be adversely affected by jurisdictional competition. The *Centros* case illustrates how creditors might be affected: if companies had the right to move between jurisdictions at will, they would be able to avoid otherwise mandatory state laws which were designed for the protection of creditors such as, in this case, a minimum capital requirement. In the same way, they could choose whether to observe mandatory laws relating to employee participation or co-determination rights, in so far as the application of such laws was a function of the legal domicile of the company as opposed to its physical or economic presence on the territory of a particular jurisdiction. As noted above, the principle of territoriality tends to determine the application of most labour law rights, rather than the domicile of the company. This is not always the case, however. The German rules on stakeholder membership of supervisory boards relate to the corporate form or legal entity through which an organization is constituted, and not just to its physical or business presence. Moreover, EU law may one day take a more critical view of the territoriality principle in labour law.

The mere possibility that co-determination laws, for example, could be avoided through reincorporation might induce states to repeal them. States could act in a self-interested way to remove mandatory laws if, by doing so, they thought they could attract more incorporations or retain those which they had: '[S]tates competing to attract incorporations will have an incentive to focus on the interests of managers and shareholders and to ignore the interests of third parties not involved in incorporation decisions' (Bebchuk 1992: 1441). It seems plausible, then, that a market for incorporations would lead to a reduction in mandatory laws of all kinds, and to an increase in permissive or 'default' rules which leave companies free to bargain around them. This could occur even if little or no movement of companies actually took place, as long as states could rationally take the view that companies would not submit to a mandatory regime which they did not perceive as being in their interests when they could choose between that system and a more permissive one elsewhere.

To determine whether such a result would be desirable, we have to consider whether mandatory laws are likely to be efficient or not. Many commentators have argued that creditors rarely need mandatory protection, since they are often in a good position to bargain for whatever protection they require (Cheffins 1997; Easterbrook and Fischel 1991; Posner 1976). It is also argued that mandatory laws for employee participation are unlikely to be efficient (Cheffins 1997), although the opposite case has been put (Rogers and Streeck 1994). For employees, the efficiency case for regulation depends in part on the existence of externalities such as 'reverse free-rider effects' which deter individual firms from offering contracts which would otherwise be optimal (Freeman and Lazear 1994).

In the European context, the longevity and stability of systems which incorporate stakeholder voice into corporate governance processes suggests that, while such arrangements may not be ideal in all circumstances, they may possess a 'survival value' which is not reconcilable with the view that they are fundamentally inefficient. It is true that these systems have not been subjected to direct competition through the threat of corporate exit in the manner of the United States. However, they have been subject to less direct but, in the long term, highly significant constraints, in the form of product-market competition and other economic pressures on governments and law-makers to maintain effective conditions for business organization. Moreover, given the degree of diversity which exists between systems, it is likely that there is some degree of matching of the rules and practices of company law to local conditions. Path dependence may also be expected to play a role, in the sense that increasing returns to particular institutional forms lead, if anything, to further divergence between systems over time rather than to convergence. These suggestions are reflected in research which compared corporate governance practices in large British and German companies. The study found:

> [T]here is no 'one best' system of corporate governance. Rather, the two systems have different comparative advantages. The British corporate governance system better supports companies in sectors where there is a need to move quickly into and out of new markets and in which there is need for great flexibility in the use of employees. The German system, by contrast, better supports companies in sectors that require long-term commitments and investments by employees, suppliers and other 'stakeholders'. (Vitols *et al.* 1997: 35)

The crucial determinants of the respective 'comparative advantages' which companies enjoy are the differences in the organization of capital markets, the rules of company law, and the forms of employee participation in the two countries; these are reflected in the different ways in which corporate governance practice has evolved in response to issues of agency costs, delegation, and stakeholder participation. For example, the German two-tier board system, with its emphasis on stakeholder involvement, enables large-scale restructurings to be handled on the basis of consensus. Moderate shareholder pressure, in contrast to the more intense scrutiny of British capital markets, enables strategic, long-term planning to be put in place and implemented. The British system, which concentrates managerial decision-making power in the hands of the board and the chief executive, possesses a 'major advantage' in terms of the speed with which decisions can be taken and implemented, but runs a greater risk of strategic mistakes being made by top management. On the basis of this analysis, the authors of this study argue that, even with the growing internationalization of investment flows, the two systems are unlikely to converge: '[C]hange can better be characterized as incremental adaptation rather than the wholesale adoption or replacement of corporate governance systems' (36).

The US experience suggests that regulatory competition in company law leads, over time, to a fairly high level of convergence between states, with the dominant model being one in which mandatory rules are the exception: '[S]tate charter competition has . . . produced substantial uniformity across state codes, preserving variety in its enabling approach to rules, an approach that permits firms to customize their charters' (Romano 1998: 2394). Although it would seem that many mandatory rules can be found in the Delaware company law regimes (Coffee 1989; Eisenberg 1989), there has been a recent tendency to change mandatory rules into default rules, as in the case of the opt-out with regard to the director's duty of care (Alva 1990). The minimalist regime of shareholder protection contained in Delaware's Limited Liability Company Statute also points to a movement away from mandatory rules (Cohen 1998).

The suggestion, then, is that in the US context regulatory competition has led to a system in which company laws are comparatively uniform in content, but where they are also highly permissive. This enables companies to adjust to particular conditions through amendments to the basic default rules supplied by the legal system, although it is not clear just how far this is translated into variety in the terms of corporate constitutions. In the European Union, on the other hand, divergence operates at the level of the law itself, with legal systems making greater use of mandatory rules. This has led, in its turn, to diversity of corporate governance practices between (rather than within) legal systems. It is not obvious that one approach should be preferred to the other on efficiency grounds. It seems likely that rules which provide for stakeholder involvement can only be made effective through mandatory regulation of some kind, which might not survive the introduction of a US-style market for incorporations within the European Union. On this basis, we should expect to look for alternative mechanisms for change within the European systems to those provided, in the United States, by regulatory competition. With this in mind, we now turn to a closer examination of the role which harmonization has played in stimulating reforms within the laws of the member states.

III. REFLEXIVE HARMONIZATION AND STAKEHOLDER REPRESENTATION

An outline of the theory of reflexive harmonization

A number of economic justifications may be offered for harmonizing legislation in the field of company law (Bebchuk 1992; Charny 1994: 365–402). A case can be made for company legislation to establish a core of uniform rules which, because of network externality effects, may save on the transaction costs of company formation and thereby promote cross-border capital mobility. In respect of creditor and employee protection, as we have seen, harmonized rules may be necessary to avoid a race to the bottom. It is sometimes argued that where directives set basic standards in this way, they do so in order to establish a parity of costs or a level playing field upon competing firms; this kind of justification can be found in some of the earlier company law directives. However, it is doubtful whether this aim can be achieved using the regulatory techniques currently available to the Community legislator, or even whether it is desirable to do so. In the related field of labour law, most directives set basic or minimum standards as a 'floor of rights' which member states must not derogate from, but upon which they may improve by setting superior standards (Deakin and Wilkinson 1994). These directives, then, can be thought of as implicitly encouraging a 'race to the top', while ruling out less socially desirable forms of competitive federalism.

The process by which states may observe and emulate practices in jurisdictions to which they are closely related by trade and by institutional connections is more akin to the concept of 'co-evolution' than to that of regulatory competition. Co-evolution assumes that a variety of diverse systems can co-exist within an environment, each one retaining its viability (Teubner 1993: 52). By contrast, the idea of regulatory competition implies convergence around a single, efficient system which wins out through the competitive process. By placing limits on competition, harmonization may aim to preserve the autonomy and diversity of national legal systems, while at the same time seeking to 'steer' or channel the process of evolutionary adaptation of rules at the state level.

This idea is borrowed from theories of reflexive law which represent an attempt to move beyond a straightforward dichotomy between, on the one hand, 'instrumentalist' theories of regulation and, on the other, 'deregulatory' theories which argue for the removal of all external regulatory controls (Deakin and Hughes 1999; Rogowski and Wilthagen 1994; Teubner 1993). The problem with instrumentalism, in this context, is the capacity of self-regulating social and economic systems to resist external regulatory interference, in the process frustrating the policy objectives of intervention and undermining the legitimacy of the regulatory process. This phenomenon, well known from studies of regulation at the state level, can also be seen in numerous cases of the ineffective translation of directives and other transnational legal instruments into national legal systems. The problem with deregulatory approaches is the excessively optimistic, even Panglossian, view which they hold of self-regulating systems such as those of the market. In the light of evidence that regulatory competition produces rules which, from the viewpoint of economic theory, are far from optimal (Bebchuk and Ferrell 1999), these theories have to fall back on somewhat unconvincing appeals to the 'long-run' benefits of market-based solutions (Easterbrook and Fischel 1991: 222).

The essence of reflexive law is the acknowledgement that regulatory interventions are most likely to be successful when they seek to achieve their ends not by direct prescription but by inducing 'second-order effects' on the part of social actors. In other words, this approach aims to 'couple' external regulation with self-regulatory processes. Reflexive law therefore has a *procedural orientation.* What this means, in the context of economic regulation, is that the preferred mode of intervention is for the law to underpin and encourage autonomous processes of adjustment, in particular by supporting mechanisms of group representation and participation, rather than to intervene by imposing particular distributive outcomes. This type of approach finds a concrete manifestation in legislation which seeks, in various ways, to devolve or confer rule-making powers to self-regulatory processes. Examples are laws which allow collective bargaining by trade unions and employers to make qualified exceptions to limits on working time or similar labour standards (Deakin and Wilkinson 1994) or which confer statutory authority on the rules drawn up by professional associations for the conduct of financial transactions (Black 1997).

A procedural orientation also implies an important difference in the way in which the law responds to market failures or externalities from the way in which it is normally represented in the law and economics literature. Reflexive regulation does not seek to 'perfect' the market, in the sense of reproducing the outcome which parties would have arrived at in the absence of transaction costs (the so-called 'hypothetical bargaining' standard). This is partly because it is understood that information problems facing courts and legislatures make the process of identifying an 'optimal' bargaining solution extremely hazardous. It is also because of a perception that the essence of competition is that it is a process of discovery or adaptation, rather than the achievement of optimal states or distributions.

In the context we are considering here, this implies a particular role for the transnational harmonization of laws. The purpose of harmonization would not be to substitute for state-level regulation; hence the transnational standard would not operate to 'occupy the field' in the manner of a 'monopoly regulator' as, it is suggested, is often the case with US federal regulation (for example, in the field of securities regulation (Romano 1998)). Rather, transnational standards would seek to promote diverse, local-level approaches to regulatory problems by creating a space for autonomous solutions to emerge when, because of market failures, they would not otherwise do so. This may involve what some regard as a restriction of competition, in the sense of ruling out certain options which could be associated with a 'race to the bottom', while leaving others open. As we have seen, this is a familiar technique in labour law, where directives mostly set basic labour standards as a 'floor of rights', allowing member states to improve on these provisions but, on the whole, preventing 'downwards' derogations.

At the intersection of labour law and company law, the EWC Directive (Directive 94/95) is a good illustration of these techniques of reflexive law. As previously explained, the Directive does not set out directly to impose any particular model of employee representation, in marked contrast to the techniques tried out unsuccessfully in the context of the Vredeling proposals and the draft Fifth Directive. What the EWC Directive does is to provide the transnational companies coming under its scope[2] with an incentive to enter into negotiations with employee representatives for the establishment of a works council or a similar mechanism for information and consultation. The incentive is provided in the form of a default procedure which applies in the event of the failure of negotiations. However, employers have a number of opportunities to avoid this outcome. First, employers who agreed on an information and consultation procedure of their own with their employees and implemented it before the Directive came into force are effectively exempted from the provisions of the Directive (or of the national-level law implementing it). Second, employers who fail to do this may nevertheless escape the default procedure by arriving at an agreement with a 'special negotiating body' of employees within three years of negotiations beginning.

The Directive operates, then, through a 'penalty default' rule (Ayres and Gertner 1989; Deakin and Hughes 1999)—in other words, a fallback provision which induces a more powerfully placed or better-informed party (here the employer) to enter into a bargaining process when it otherwise would lack an incentive to do so. The justification for the Directive derives from the failure on the part of the member states to put in place similar mechanisms to deal with the particular issue of information and consultation in transnational companies. The Directive can therefore be seen as a response to a coordination failure at the level of the states. However, it takes effect not by imposing a uniform solution but by encouraging *both* member states, through their laws, *and* companies themselves, through negotiations with employee representatives, to develop local-level solutions.

This procedural orientation also influenced the Davignon Report of the Group of Experts set up to analyse systems of worker involvement, which reported in May 1997 ('European Systems of Worker Involvement, with Regard to the European Company Statute and Other Pending Proposals', Report to DG 5, Brussels, 1997). The Report suggested that one way of making progress on the European Company Statute proposal would be to encourage negotiations over the form of employee participation prior to the establishment of an SE. Agreement has still not been reached in the Council, in part because of a failure to reach consensus on the 'default procedure' which would be applied in the event of a failure by the parties to agree. However, it seems likely that, if the deadlock on the European Company Statute is to be broken at all, a procedural solution is the way forward.

[2] The Directive applies to 'Community-scale undertakings', which are undertakings with at least 1,000 employees in the European Union as a whole and 150 employees in at least two member states; a similar definition applies to group undertakings operating at the Community level. For an overview of the Directive's provisions, see Deakin and Morris (1998). For a valuable discussion of the Directive in the context of a wider argument in favour of using EU-level interventions to maintain national and subnational diversity, see Streeck (1999).

It may be suggested, then, that reflexive harmonization operates to induce individual states to enter into a 'race to the top' when they would have otherwise had an incentive to do nothing (the 'reverse free-rider' effect) or to compete on the basis of the withdrawal of protective standards (the 'race to the bottom'). This is done by giving states a number of options for implementation as well as by allowing for the possibility that existing self-regulatory mechanisms can be used to comply with EU-wide standards. In these ways, far from suppressing regulatory innovation, harmonization aims to stimulate it.

Tensions between market integration and stakeholder representation: the case of takeover regulation

This is not to suggest that the process of reflexive harmonization is a straightforward one. On the contrary, it is a highly controversial technique. It is called into question, on the one hand, by those who argue for a more comprehensive, centrally driven approach to the fusion of legal systems. On the other, there are those who stress the merits of market integration, driven by the free movement and competition policy provisions of the Treaty. These tensions are exemplified in the long-running debate over the draft Thirteenth Directive on the Regulation of Takeover Bids. The history of the draft Thirteenth Directive also offers an interesting comparison with US experience.

As noted above, hostile takeovers are a rarity in most EU member states. The major exception is Britain, where a combination of corporate governance practices, certain rules of company law, and the City Code on Takeovers and Mergers, the product of self-regulation in the financial sector, have combined to produce a vigorous market for corporate control. Defensive tactics by target boards are virtually ruled out once a bid starts by the rules of the Takeover Code, while shareholder pressure has successfully resisted the introduction of poison pills and similar devices in corporate constitutions of the kind which were used to deflect hostile bids in the United States in the 1980s (Deakin and Slinger 1997).

Much of the US (and British) debate takes it as given that an active market for corporate control generates gains for shareholders on average, as well as inducing greater managerial efficiency, even though evidence for this proposition is, to say the least, mixed (Mueller and Sirower 1998). The continental European debate tends to focus on the negative implications of hostile bids for stakeholder relations. This focus is not surprising, given the existence of alternative mechanisms within 'insider systems' for holding the management of public companies accountable, such as cross-shareholdings, the close involvement of banks in monitoring, and the operations of supervisory boards. The draft Thirteenth Directive cuts across this debate by proposing, in effect, an extension of the shareholder-protection mechanisms of the UK Takeover Code to the other member states. These would include the outlawing of most bid-frustrating tactics by target boards; requirements for the target board to obtain neutral financial advice on the merits of a bid; and the imposition of various duties on bidders, including an obligation of equal treatment with regard to shareholders of the target, thereby ruling out most types of 'coercive' bids.

Opposition to the Thirteenth Directive has come from two main sources. On the one hand, the City Panel on Takeovers and Mergers has resisted it on the grounds that its own relatively informal procedures would be put in jeopardy by any transfer of authority for regulating bids to the courts and/or the European Commission. In response to this objection, the latest version of the Directive allows member states to implement its provisions by way of delegation to a self-regulatory body such as the City Panel. The other set of objections has been raised through the European Parliament, and relates to the weakness of those parts of the Directive which aim to confer a degree of protection on non-shareholder stakeholders.

The current draft of the Thirteenth Directive requires the board of a target company to 'act in the interests of all the company, including employment' when responding to a bid (*Official Journal of the European Communities* C 378, 13.12.97). Similarly, section 309 of the UK Companies Act 1985 requires directors to take the interests of the company's employees into account when discharging their duties to the company. This provision, despite its superficiality to certain 'third-generation' stakeholder statutes in the United States, has had little or no effect in terms of protecting employee interests during a bid. Employees have no standing to bring an action for breach of directors' duties by the target board, and section 309 is overshadowed in any event by provisions of the Takeover Code which place directors under a series of specific obligations to ensure that shareholders receive disinterested advice about whether the bid is in their interests (Deakin and Slinger 1997).

A more concrete measure of stakeholder protection which has been proposed from time to time in the protracted debate over the draft Thirteenth Directive is to require both the bidder and the target companies to engage in a process of consultation with employee representatives during the course of the bid. Rule 24.1 of the Takeover Code merely requires the bidder company to state its intentions with regard to future relations with employees. Offer documents issued by bidders under the rules of the Code nearly always contain a statement to the effect that existing rights of employees will be fully respected. This says nothing more than that the bidder company will respect the company's prior legal obligations to its employees; it has become a formality, which is represented in offer documentation by use of a standard 'boilerplate' formula (Slinger and Deakin 1999).

If managements were required to consult with employee representatives in the course of the bid, this could substantially affect the relative balance of power and influence of shareholders and other stakeholder groups. Such information and consultation rights already exist under EU law in respect of decisions for collective redundancies (The Trade Union and Labour Relations (Consolidation) Act 1992; Directive 75/129 on Collective Redundancies) and corporate reorganizations effected through a business transfer (The Transfer of Undertakings (Protection of Employment) Regulations 1981, implementing EC Directive 77/187 (the

'Acquired Rights Directive')). To consult employee representatives, in this context, means to do so with a view to making an agreement (Deakin and Morris 1998: 786–8). However, the existing consultation rights do not extend to changes of control by a transfer of shares, as is the case with a takeover bid.[3] The anomaly persists, since in recent drafts of the Thirteenth Directive concerns about the possibility of lengthy and costly disruptions to bids led to the deletion of any references to employees' consultation rights, as opposed to lesser rights to receive information. The draft Directive currently follows the lead of Rule 24.1 of the UK Takeover Code, which, as we have seen, merely requires bidders to state their intentions with regard to the future treatment of employees (*Official Journal of the European Communities* 1997, C 378, 13.12.97).[4]

This is not the occasion to revisit the debate about whether the market for corporate control always and everywhere operates, as its proponents insist, in the interests of economic efficiency. For present purposes, the interest of the draft Thirteenth Directive lies in the very different way in which this question has been approached in the European and US contexts. In the United States, legal restrictions on hostile takeovers emerged in the 1990s through the process of regulatory competition between states. There is considerable disagreement among corporate law scholars as to the significance of Delaware's adoption of certain elements of the third-generation model of stakeholder statutes. Do the Delaware amendments reflect only a minimal move in favour of stakeholder protection (Romano 1998) or a more serious breach in the market for corporate control, with serious implications for the protection of shareholder value (Bebchuk and Ferrell 1999)? If the latter, does this indicate that the process of interjurisdictional competition is capable of producing inefficient results, on the basis that state legislatures are unduly susceptible to the claims of corporate managers who are responsible for taking decisions on incorporation and reincorporation? Either way, a solution of a kind to the conflicting pressures associated with the hostile takeover has been arrived at through a process of decentralized adaptation to changing economic and political circumstances.

In the context of the European Union, the same debate has been carried on through a process of negotiation and deliberation over many years. Many of the same interest groups have been involved as in the United States: institutional shareholders, legal and financial professionals, trade unions, and governments at various levels. As the Thirteenth Directive has evolved through various drafts, the price of

[3] There is a provision for there to be annual consultation over merger plans between company representatives and representatives of employees in the Annex to the EWC Directive. However, it is arguable that this provision, on its own, is unlikely to lead to significant employee participation in decision making on mergers (Wheeler 1997).

[4] The background to the proposal is explained in a Commission document (COM (97) 565 final) and in a report by the House of Lords Select Committee on the European Communities (*Takeover Bids*, 13th Report, HL Paper 100, Session 1995–96). In June 1999, the member states agreed on a common position on the latest form of the draft Directive, and it seems highly likely that it will be formally adopted in the near future.

reaching agreement has been the need to accommodate different interests within the framework of a single legal measure; this has resulted in the kind of 'reflexive' harmonization which has become characteristic of the single market programme. But the difficulties of reaching a compromise by this route are clear. The danger is that a clear solution to the conflict between stakeholder rights and the pursuit of market integration will not emerge. Moreover, the process illustrates how vulnerable the process of law-making at EU level is to concerted action by powerfully situated interest groups, and how marginal the role of the European Parliament still is within this process (Villiers 1998). These public-choice dimensions of the European law-making process undoubtedly require further analysis and research, along the lines opened up by similar US studies of the Delaware effect (Roe 1993). What is striking on first impression is how the recent dilution of the employee consultation provisions of the Thirteenth Directive contrasts strongly with the achievement of regulatory competition in producing pro-stakeholder legislation in the US context.

CONCLUSION

The study of European company law has important lessons for our broader understanding of the role of harmonization within the process of legal and economic integration. The form of harmonizing legislation in Europe has moved away from the prescriptive style of the early 1970s, in favour of 'reflexive' regulatory techniques which aim to encourage decentralized forms of self-regulation at the member state level and below. By contrast, the principal alternative to this form of reflexive harmonization—court-led deregulation or 'negative harmonization', initiated by a rigid interpretation of the freedom of establishment provisions of the EC Treaty— would limit the autonomy of member states in the company law field and thereby induce a greater degree of convergence over time. It has been argued in this chapter that if negative harmonization were to be extended in this way, it would be at the expense of those mechanisms of evolutionary adaptation which currently operate within member states. There is therefore no guarantee that a process of negative harmonization would lead to greater efficiency and, indeed, good reason to think that it would not.

In practice, there are limits to what court-led intervention can achieve. The prospects of a Delaware-like effect emerging within the European Union in the foreseeable future would be remote even if the *siège réel* doctrine were to fall as a result of some of the broader interpretations being placed on the ECJ's decision in the *Centros* case. The conditions under which the exit-based mechanism of reincorporation could serve as the basis for competition between legal systems do not yet exist. In order for US-style competitive federalism to emerge within company law, some degree of harmonization of the rules of the conflicts of laws and the practices of the member states relating to incorporation and reincorporation would be required. Thus the question of which issues are appropriate for harmonization, and the techniques which should be used to implement harmonizing measures, cannot be avoided.

From this perspective, a strong case can be made for a form of harmonization which reflects the different traditions of corporate governance within the member states, rather than attempting to erode those distinctions. This implies a procedural orientation to the law, that is to say, one which aims to promote autonomy at the level of self-regulatory systems both below and beyond those of national governments. Such an approach would find its concrete expression in legal measures which promote mechanisms of collective voice and representation. The EWC Directive is one notable recent example of this approach. The draft Thirteenth Directive on takeover bids may prove to be another, although in this case there is arguably a need for the voices of employees and other stakeholders to be represented alongside those of the institutional shareholders and market professionals who currently dominate the framing and operation of takeover codes.

The enduring contribution of European company law to the wider European project is likely to lie in the further elaboration of these techniques of reflexive regulation. European-level harmonization is widely but wrongly seen, by analogy with US federal legislation, as blocking processes of innovation and discovery in state laws, thereby preventing the emergence of efficient regulatory solutions. This chapter has suggested that it may be more meaningful, in the European context at least, to see harmonization as a guarantor of diversity in the laws and practices of the different member states, while also encouraging innovation in forms of self-regulation in the corporate and financial spheres. Co-evolution based on diversity at the level of national legal systems, coupled with encouragement for devolved solutions, represents a more likely path for European company law than the type of convergence around a single, dominant regime which appears to characterize the Delaware effect in the US context.

10

Regulatory Competition for EU Financial Services

GÉRARD HERTIG

The European Union could be caricatured both as a regulatory colossus of world-wide stature and as an entity that is more or less irrelevant in the area of banking and financial services, its choices being dictated by either global international organizations or powerful member states. As always, there are some elements of truth in the caricature. However, it would be wrong to pay too much attention to the regulatory status of the European Union as it is perceived today. In the first place, the European Union has recently undertaken many institutional and regulatory reforms that are only now beginning to have a practical impact. Second, the financial services[1] industry is being fundamentally reshaped, due to the globalization of world trade, technological development, and increased competition.

Given the instability of the current equilibrium, this chapter will adopt an evolutionary approach. Part I will evaluate the current and foreseeable future impact of the EU mutual recognition approach to market access. Having made the free movement of capital a reality by the end of the 1980s, the European Union was able to undertake a regulatory programme to harmonize essential requirements governing the provision of financial services. In theory, once authorized in a member state that has adopted such minimum standards, a firm should be able to provide cross-border financial services without being regulated by other member states ('European passport'). In practice, member states have preserved the power to apply elements of their regulatory framework to cross-border financial services. It follows that a single financial market has yet to be achieved: firms remain subject to multiple regulatory regimes, which inevitably makes transaction costs higher than they need be. However, it is quite difficult to quantify how far the European passport facilitates or has failed to facilitate the cross-border provision of financial services. Market integration does not depend solely on the elimination of regulatory barriers, it is also a function of other important components such as technological infrastructure, competition, taxes, etc. In addition, it takes time for regulatory reform to have a practical impact on the provision of cross-border services.

The second section of Part I will therefore attempt to forecast that impact by analysing the implications of regulatory reforms for regulatory competition. Indeed, as the US experience has shown, increased regulatory competition is a clear sign that a single market is in the making. In other words, it is reasonable to assume

[1] Unless banking services are specifically mentioned, references to financial services should be read as including banking services.

that the introduction of the European passport will foster the cross-border provision of financial services if it provides member states with incentives to compete by offering attractive regulatory packages. The creation of such incentives has to be analysed at two levels. On the one hand, member states may be induced to reduce regulatory costs for financial intermediaries by getting closer to minimum standards—engaging in what will be defined here as a race to the bottom, given that underregulation may follow (Bebchuk and Ferrell 1999; Licht 1998; Mayer 1995: 156). On the other hand, member states may be induced to increase regulatory benefits by aiming at integrating 'best practice' standards—engaging in what will be defined here as a race to the top. The analysis will, quite predictably, show that the European passport facilitates regulatory competition, but that remaining barriers to cross-border activities leave limited room for races to the bottom.

However, EU regulatory competition cannot be analysed in terms of a mere race to the bottom or race to the top, especially because attempts to facilitate races may give rise to private-interest issues. Taking due account of the self-interest of regulated entities, member states, and supervisory agencies will help us understand EU regulatory competition (Part II). The first section of Part II will emphasize that the EU mutual recognition approach relies on the private incentives of market participants inasmuch as it permits them to choose a single regulatory regime to govern their activities EU-wide. However, regulated entities are only being offered a true choice if EU minimum standards have not been set too high. Otherwise there will be little diversity among member states, liberal regimes being prohibited and demanding ones adding little to the 'standard' regime. The analysis will show that EU minimum standards cannot be considered high compared to non-EU systems, or to what member states would have done in the absence of EU harmonization.

The second section of Part II will point out that EU regulation also takes account of intra-EU spillovers. The reduction in regulatory barriers to cross-border financial services is of sufficient magnitude to allow for positive externalities, as member states cannot prevent the benefits from their competitive position from spilling over into other member states. There is, moreover, no sign that the European passport permits larger-scale fraud than would have been possible under the former regulatory regimes, nor that it allows a member state to impose higher systemic risks on other member states. It is true that the European passport allows for some free-riding by member states that rely more on non-domestic providers of financial services (their supervisory costs should be lower). However, the resulting asymmetries in the distribution of regulatory costs remain limited, because of EU law obliging host member states to cooperate with home member states.

The final section of Part II will be devoted to public choice issues. It will point out that the most influential interest groups have a growing interest in centralization, which is likely to make regulatory self-interest a significant EU issue. Indeed, major financial intermediaries and exchanges are increasingly lobbying for the further reduction of regulatory barriers to cross-border activities and for the setting of a level playing field as far as supervision is concerned. There is less objection to diversity in national legal regimes as far as smaller/weaker players or company law issues are concerned, but there is a quite significant exception, with respect to consumer protection in the e-commerce area. For further centralization requiring harmonization, the bodies composed of member state regulators in charge of drafting EU regulation will play an essential role. It is not unrealistic to believe that self-interested regulators will be willing and able to push through reforms incorporating some centralization mechanisms, especially as far as supervision is concerned.

One way of evaluating the interaction between the private interests just mentioned and centralization (or regulatory competition) is to evaluate the freedom to choose a legal regime, including the applicable law and the authorities enforcing it (Part III). Under the EU system, there is no room for truly unilateral extraterritorial application of law, especially since the European Court of Justice has the last word regarding jurisdiction. This does not prevent issues typical of regulatory competition from arising. The ability of member states to protect their sovereignty or retaliate against regulatory arbitrage can be tested by evaluating market participants' freedom to express preferences in four areas: contractual framework, incorporation regime, regulation governing issuers, and supervision of financial services providers (Part III, first section). Generally, the EU system allows significant freedom to choose the contractual framework for sophisticated market participants. On the other hand, corporations still face obstacles to reincorporation and their freedom as issuers is a function of the effectiveness of home regulators. Since the same is true of financial intermediaries' freedom to provide services, the degree of freedom allowed to market participants will essentially depend upon the effectiveness of home member state supervision.

In other words, host member states are not likely to allow market participants to opt for a supervisory regime that puts the interests of their constituencies at significant risk. Given that modern financial supervision requires supervisory agencies to successfully hire and retain a large number of specialists, there are signs that both providers of financial services and regulators are willing to trade a certain amount of regulatory diversity against centralized EU supervision of the main financial intermediaries and regulated markets.

The overall conclusion of this chapter is that protectionism remains a significant obstacle to intra-EU regulatory competition. As a result, it is likely that centralized EU supervisory authorities will be established. While it is too early to assess the desirability of such a development, it should favour global regulatory competition by decreasing the likelihood that institutions such as the International Monetary Fund (IMF) will be given a global supervisory role.

I. MARKET INTEGRATION AND COOPERATIVE COMPETITION

The nature and level of EU regulatory competition is evolving in tandem with the maturing of the internal market. Although the single market is still far from being achieved, there is no question that many legal obstacles to the EU-wide provision of financial services have been eliminated. Indeed, regulatory efforts contributed to making the free movement of capital a reality by the late 1980s, and further integration is being achieved by using the well-established EU mutual recognition strategy (Molle 1997: 145–7).

Mutual recognition

Mutual recognition requires both the abolition of trade barriers ('negative integration') and the setting of common minimum standards ('positive integration'). In practical terms, it means that each member state has to grant providers of financial services established in other member states free access to its market, provided that the regulatory framework in the member state(s) of origin offers a minimum level of systemic and investor/creditor protection.

The key issue is obviously if, and to what extent, such protection is provided by the home member state. To avoid lengthy litigation (which might ultimately deter financial intermediaries from making effective use of their freedom), the European Union has adopted a large number of regulations aiming at setting common minimum standards. However, serious harmonization efforts have only been undertaken in the 1980s (Pelkmans 1997: 110)—the original schedule for a mutual recognition regulatory programme having been outlined in the well-known White Paper on completing the European Market (European Commission 1985).

As a result, member states have had to regulate and/or deregulate parts of their financial law framework. On the one hand, member states are generally obliged to subject financial intermediaries and so-called regulated markets (organized securities trading entities that function regularly, enforce minimum standards, and are recognized as such by the home member state) to an authorization procedure before they begin their activities. Authorization requirements vary depending upon the type of services provided (loans, investment services, securities trading, mutual funds, insurance,[2] etc.). However, the regulatory frameworks are similar. Providers of financial services must respect various organizational rules, comply with capital adequacy requirements, adopt specific accounting and disclosure policies, employ experienced managers that are of good repute, and obey or enforce rules of conduct.

On the other hand, providers of financial services benefit from a 'European passport'. The European passport allows them to offer cross-border services or open a branch in a member state other than the home member state without need of additional authorization; it also basically exempts financial intermediaries from host member state supervision and regulation. However, it would be going too far to assert that providers of financial services are now subject to a single set of regulations, namely that of their home member state. Mutual recognition has

[2] Insurance activities will not be the subject of a specific analysis, as their regulation is likely to be significantly overhauled and subjected to requirements comparable to those applicable to other supervised financial intermediaries.

remained imperfect, as host member states have been allowed to keep their regulatory powers in some areas, especially regarding rules of conduct (Hertig 1996).

In other words, there has been a compromise between what can be defined as cooperative and adversarial regulatory competition (Stephan 1999). There is *cooperative* competition because mutual recognition allows financial intermediaries to choose the regulatory regime of one member state (the 'home' member state) and then operate EU-wide under that regime. Member states have agreed that: (1) financial intermediaries can provide financial services on their territory even though they are 'merely' supervised by another member state and (2) they will cooperate with the home member state in such situations, for example by providing information. Both a limited race to the bottom and an unlimited race to the top have thus been facilitated by EU law. Member states whose standards are currently higher than the minimum standards set by EU Directive can safely bring their existing standards closer to the EU minimum level without fear that other member states will be able to impede access to their markets. At the other extreme, member states are now in a better position to adopt and advertise standards more stringent than current regulatory standards—an approach that market participants may favour, because mutual recognition guarantees that financial intermediaries will be able to operate EU-wide under this one 'best practice' regime.

There is *adversarial* competition because member states continue to have the power to apply elements of their regulatory framework to the provision of all financial services within their jurisdiction, whether domestic or cross-border. However, EU law constrains the exercise of this partial monopoly. As the European Court of Justice has made clear, member states, in their host capacity, have jurisdiction only insofar as their regulation is in the general interest, proportionate, non-discriminatory, and does not institute overlapping controls (Case C–384/93, *Alpine Investments BV* v. *Minister van Financien*, 1995 ECR I–1167; Case 205/84, *Commission* v. *Germany*, 1986 ECR 3775).

Impact on market access

The European Union is still an international rather than a federal arrangement. Therefore, market access restrictions have to be analysed separately from regulatory advantages (Sykes 1999: 51). This section will deal with market access restrictions, that is, actual or potential impediments to cross-border financial services that increase the costs of doing business for *foreign* firms. The issue of cost advantages conferred to *indigenous* firms because of regulatory competition (race to the bottom or race to the top) will be analysed in the next section.

So far as I know, no empirical evaluation of the overall impact of the EU mutual recognition approach on the cross-border provision of financial services has yet been made.[3] Nevertheless, it is possible to state that the oft-predicted 'Fortress

[3] In a recent speech, the President of the European Central Bank was compelled to admit that few national statistics serve as accurate guides for trends in the euro zone (T. Barber (1999), 'Monetary Union Seen Resting on Integration' *Financial Times*, 7 September at 2; OECD 1997: 82–3).

Europe' effect has not materialized and that mutual recognition has yet to significantly contribute to the Europeanization of banking and capital markets.

There is no sign that access to EU financial markets has been made more difficult for non-EU financial intermediaries, issuers or investors. Major non-EU banks were already well established in the European Union before the launch of the mutual recognition programme (Hoschka 1993: 19–24), and have an ever-growing role in the European Union. European Union exchanges (or their home member states) cannot afford to erect barriers to entry in the face of US exchanges positioning themselves to attract more foreign listings. For their part, US distributors of mutual funds and global institutional investors are continuously developing their EU activities, sometimes at a frenetic pace. Clearly, factors other than regulatory reform contribute to EU market entries and consolidation, but the latter make the 'Fortress Europe' argument appear rather weak.

At the same time, the pan-European provision of financial services remains limited to specific areas and is difficult to evaluate in those areas where it does take place (Danthine *et al.* 1999: 46–7); in any event, it does not seem to owe much to the European passport.

In the first place, most banking activities, which have traditionally been the dominant European financial services industry (Walter 1999: 450), remain local. There are not many banks that truly operate at the member state level and large-scale entry into other member states remains rare, especially for commercial banking (Danthine *et al.* 1999: 33). For example, in the euro area, entry into foreign markets in 1999 was still less than 10 per cent on average in terms of banking assets (Padoa-Schioppa 1999: 298); similarly, bank loan markets still remain very national (Centeno and Mello 1999). This may change in the near future, as e-banking matures and cross-border banking mergers become more common (European Central Bank 1999: 18–20). However, political opposition has up to now prevented significant EU cross-border banking mergers.[4] Admittedly, European Commission interventions may deter governments from opposing friendly cross-border takeover bids. On the other hand, since it is less obvious that member state intervention restricts free movement of capital in the case of hostile bids, European governments are likely to pursue their efforts to prevent hostile cross-border takeovers from growing at the same rate as domestic ones[5]—helped in this by the maze of domestic laws which, in the absence of harmonization, remain applicable to such takeovers. In addition, despite (or because of) the important intermediary role banks will continue to play in the European Union (Danthine *et al.* 1999: 103; Schmidt, Hackethal, and Tyrell 1999), the monopoly left to member states in the

[4] J. Guyon (1999), 'The Coming Battle of Europe's Banks', *Fortune*, 20 December, at 66–7. On the small number of major cross-border banking mergers, see also Smith (1999: 338) and Dermine (2000).

[5] There were close to seventy hostile deals in Europe in 1999 (compared to between fifteen and thirty-five annually from 1994 to 1998), with a total value of US $400 billion (compared to less than US$ 50 billion per year between 1994 and 1998) (E. Portanger (1999) 'Backers Tout Takeover Defense Role in New Europe', *The Wall Street Journal Europe*, 24 November, at 16; European Central Bank 1999: Annex 2 at 8).

setting of rules of conduct and the adoption of provisions for the liquidation of banks may slow down the Internet-assisted integration process.

Second, while it is true that the introduction of the European passport has made Luxembourg the EU centre for international management and the distribution of investment funds, Luxembourg disappears from the top ten EU major mutual funds centres if account is taken of exports to the EU country from which the fund is promoted (Zurstrassen 1998: 209–10, 227). In other words, the European passport's main function is not to foster cross-border distribution but to permit tax savings by registering funds in Luxembourg rather than in the member state in which they are to be distributed.

Third, to the extent that there are pan-European markets for corporate finance and asset management services, their development pre-dates the European passport (Walter 1988). Actually, in those areas where mutual recognition could have made a difference, the failure to adopt EU minimum standards has prevented the emergence of a single market. This is especially true of pension funds, which have had little incentive to buy cross-border financial services because many member states still impose portfolio restrictions that limit foreign investments. That attitude should change as the introduction of the euro eliminates currency-related restrictions, but the EU record on the liberalization of pension funds (European Commission 1997) casts doubt on the speed of integration in that area.

Fourth, as far as bond and equity markets are concerned, market forces (and somewhat muddled behaviour on the part of national regulators) have made the Eurobond market the preferred international market for the past two decades and, more generally, have contributed to the emergence of European securities markets (Danthine *et al.* 1999: 37–40; Smith and Walter 1997). Further integration will occur due to the introduction of the euro and the explosive expansion of e-trading. For example, the ability to issue bonds denominated in euros has made the tapping of the European market more attractive for many EU companies.[6] Similarly, the euro is credited for mergers and acquisitions (M&A) activity in Europe more than doubling in value in 1999.[7] More generally, surveys among major European banks regularly show that they expect the introduction of the euro to unleash a true cultural revolution in Western Europe, even in financial centres such as the United Kingdom and Switzerland that are not (yet) part of the euro zone (Dermine 1999b: 12; Walter 1999: 448). However, across-the-board use of the euro is yet to come. Moreover, member states' securities regulation is still considered a significant barrier to cross-border trading and investment. Part of the blame is attributed to harmonization gaps in the corporate governance area and, more importantly, to practical shortcomings in EU directives on the mutual recog-

[6] E. Luce (1999), 'Euro Proves Top Currency for Euro', *Financial Times*, 16 December, at 17; M. Sesit (1999), 'Europe May be Weak, But Look at What It's Made Possible', *Wall Street Journal Europe*, 1 December, at 1, 4.

[7] M&A with European companies as the target were worth US$ 1,200 billion, of which half were European cross-border mergers ('The Construction of Europe', *Financial Times*, 1 January 2000 at 26).

nition of prospectuses and listings (Horn 1999). But the discretion of member states in the implementation of EU law is also part of the problem (Lee 1998b: 230–1; Steil 1996a: 131–4).

A good example is provided by the cross-border regulation of trading systems, where the Investment Services Directive (ISD)[8] leaves member states considerable scope for protectionism. The ISD requires host member states to allow a regulated market in another member state to provide cross-border remote access. Nevertheless, host member states may erect barriers to entry, for example by refusing to consider that a foreign regulated market provides appropriate remote access facilities within their jurisdiction (Lee 1998a: 296). Similarly, market participants blame regulatory barriers (at least to some extent) for the fact that EU regulated markets have yet to complete a single EU cross-border merger.

This example also shows that one cannot just rely on the development of Internet-assisted securities trading to eliminate regulatory barriers. Exchanges as we know them may not survive, but it will be easy for member states to adjust the definition of regulated markets to cover e-trading platforms provided by financial intermediaries or issuers. In addition, should trading platforms be set up by entities that are difficult to regulate even if it is assumed that major jurisdictions will cooperate, investors will still call for reputable clearing and settlement systems. This provides member states with a default regulatory target and is one of the reasons why the not very exciting topic of clearing and settlement regulation is moving to centre stage (Giddy, Saunders, and Walter 1996).

To summarize, there is no clear evidence that the European passport has led to the pan-European provision of financial services.[9] However, the passport can be considered an improvement on pre-harmonization days in that it makes home country supervision a recognized principle, eliminates obvious regulatory barriers to cross-border activities such as overlapping capital requirements, and sets the framework for further lowering of barriers to market access (Horn 1999: 155). Thus the somewhat disappointing record of mutual recognition may, to an extent at least, simply reflect the fact that it takes time for the full impact of regulatory reform to materialize (Danthine *et al.* 1999: 45).

Races to the bottom and to the top

The argument that it takes time for mutual recognition to contribute to the pan-European provision of financial services would gain in persuasiveness if it could be verified that EU harmonization has significantly favoured races to the bottom or to the top. As the US experience has shown, increased regulatory competition is a clear sign that a single market is in the making. In other words, if it can be shown

[8] Council Directive 93/22/EEC on investment services in the securities field, OJ L 141/27, 11 June 1993.

[9] For a critical assessment, see D. Shirreff, 'Disgrace at the Heart of Europe', *Euromoney*, October 1999, at 75–8.

that member states now have incentives to offer attractive European passports (by offering regulatory packages that favour cross-border activities), this should be an indication that pan-European provision of financial services is in the making. Indeed, if there are such incentives, the mere possibility that some member states may offer attractive European passports should encourage the main European jurisdictions to engage in liberalization and other market-oriented regulatory reforms required for the completion of an EU single market.

The current persistence of the monopoly power of host member states implies that there is limited room for a race to the bottom. First, to attract non-domestic firms or investors, member states have to respect EU minimum standards. Even assuming that member states are legally allowed to disregard such standards because of loopholes in EU harmonization, doing so may repel both the sell and buy side. Financial intermediaries and issuers (the sell side) will hesitate to incorporate in a jurisdiction that cannot guarantee mutual recognition of its regulatory framework: the cost of engaging in cross-border activities or financing could be significantly increased, as they might also be required to comply with the regulatory framework of all relevant host member states. Non-resident institutional investors (the buy side), for their part, may be prevented by their domestic regulatory framework from investing in a member state with subminimal standards.

Second, it is also risky to set standards that are above the minimum, but only slightly so. European Union regulations leave ample opportunity for punishing a member state that tries to make an aggressive business out of regulatory arbitrage, and securities regulators are likely to 'play games' in a global market (Licht 1999). Let us assume that a member state wants to attract automated trading systems by adopting a generous definition of regulated markets, thus making the European trading passport easier to obtain. Host member states can easily retaliate by using their discretion to decide that: (1) the facilities offered by such automated systems are not 'appropriate' for remote trading, or (2) their investors cannot opt out of the obligation (still allowed by Art. 14 ISD) to use domestic regulated markets. A similar strategy can be adopted against member states that prove lax in supervising credit institutions or investment services firms. Host member states should be able to find ways to use their powers in the rules-of-conduct area to adopt policies which, without being openly disproportionate or discriminatory, would penalize institutions which have adjusted their organization or information systems to the lax policies of the home member state.

It is true that retaliating host member states themselves run the risk of infringing EU law by miscalculating minimum standards or their regulatory powers. However, they may refuse to back down without the intervention of the European Court of Justice. Given the resources and time involved, this prospect may be sufficient to discourage financial intermediaries, issuers or investors from taking advantage of a 'serious' but more deregulated jurisdiction.

The conclusion that there is limited room for a race to the bottom does not mean that the introduction of the European passport has resulted in less rather than more regulatory competition between member states. It is true that the cross-border provision of financial services seems most intense in areas that remain generally unregulated (for example, within the Eurobond market), and that regulatory competition seems most developed with jurisdictions that are not covered by the European passport (for example, between the United Kingdom and the United States).

On the other hand, mutual recognition has forced most member states to liberalize their regulatory requirements. In addition, when it comes to intra-EU regulatory competition, the number of players is limited and they are likely to engage in or favour a race to the top rather than a race to the bottom. For example, the main EU financial centres (London, Frankfurt, and Paris) have no interest in being perceived as having low listing standards in an era where firms are listing on the New York Stock Exchange (NYSE) primarily in order to signal to investors that they are willing to comply with demanding quality standards (Fuerst 1998). Similarly, the two dozen EU financial intermediaries with across-the-board international activities do not want to be perceived to be subject to lax supervision, because of the risk of a costly increase in scrutiny by non-EU supervisors.

Obviously, mutual recognition increases the attractiveness of a race to the top. Previously, even where a home regulatory regime clearly had above-minimum standards, host member states would submit cross-border activities to authorization and supervision. With the European passport, it is a straightforward violation of EU law for host member states to impose their own regulatory regime if the home member state's regime goes well beyond minimum standards. This should prevent host member states from even attempting to play the retaliation game mentioned in connection with the race to the bottom.

The attractiveness of a race to the top could induce member states to overregulate the provision of financial services, especially as the European Union has not set maximum standards. In theory, this seems to be mainly a risk for domestic entities: the discretion of host member states to recognize that cross-border services satisfy minimum standards should not permit them to force overregulation on non-domestic firms. However, this is not a correct conclusion if the EU mutual approach has resulted in a significant increase in the regulatory burden, that is, if EU minimum standards have been set too high.

In short, despite EU limitations, there is somewhat more room for a race to the bottom than under the former regime. In addition, a race to the top has been made more attractive by the European passport. These are indications that the pan-European provision of financial services is in the making, supporting the argument that it takes time for mutual recognition to produce results. However, increased regulatory competition brings new issues: could the higher attractiveness of a race to the top lead to overregulation due to a heavy EU regulatory burden? Could the increased room for a race to the bottom bring member states to act to the detriment of the EU interest? Could regulators take personal advantage of the interest of market participants in regulatory competition?

A partial answer to these questions can be provided by analysing how mutual recognition takes account of the various 'private' interests involved.

II. TAKING ACCOUNT OF 'PRIVATE' INTERESTS

Costs for regulated entities, externalities, and the role of interest groups or self-interested regulators are issues that may be amplified by regulatory competition, but may not be fully reflected by a 'race' analysis (Easterbrook 1994; Revesz 1997b; 1997a). Therefore, this section will assess the impact of the EU regulatory arrangement on regulatory burden and on intra-EU spillovers, as well as take account of specific public choice issues.

Regulatory burden

Regulation brings both costs and benefits to the regulated. Given the choice, market participants will opt for a regulatory regime that minimizes the net regulatory burden, which is the sum of the costs it imposes (for example, because of compliance efforts or transaction restrictions) minus the benefits it offers (for example, a decrease in competition, an increase in reputation, or a lighter lever of supervision in a host jurisdiction) (Levich 1990: 373; Smith and Walter 1997: 172–81).

The EU mutual recognition approach aims at permitting market participants to choose the regulatory regime they prefer. It limits the risk of regulatory competition being fought out in the wrong dimension by reducing the attractiveness of protectionism: member states cannot protect against foreign regulatory regimes that meet minimum standards. It also guarantees a minimum of diversity, both by leaving states some autonomy to set rules of conduct and by allowing them to engage in unrestricted races to the top.[10]

However, this reliance on the private incentives of market participants can only work if EU minimum standards have not been set too high. Should minimum standards be *excessively* high, they are likely to function as EU-wide barriers to entry, protecting established financial intermediaries against new competitors. But even if minimum standards are simply set *too high*, they will translate into overregulation for those markets that could have been governed by lower standards. Even worse, setting minimum standards too high might foster the adoption of uniform regulatory regimes across member states, as diversity is either prohibited (member states cannot adopt liberal regimes) or made less attractive (there is less to gain by racing to the top).

Current EU minimum standards cannot be considered high in relative terms. Compared to the United States or to what full harmonization would have produced, the EU regulatory burden can be considered light (Padoa-Schioppa 1999).

[10] For a less optimistic perspective, see Mayer (1995: 156).

This is mainly because the mutual recognition approach focuses on the opening of markets and on framework, rather than on detailed regulation. However, the cumbersome EU legislative process has also contributed to preventing growth in interventionist EU regulation.

In the near future, the European Commission's most recent regulatory action plan (European Commission 1999), and recurring calls to make the EU legislative process more flexible by delegating it to committees, could lead to an increase in the EU regulatory burden. Nevertheless, the EU system is unlikely to be made any heavier than non-EU systems. The reason is quite straightforward. Given the technical and political influence of global regulatory forums such as the Basle Committee on Banking Supervision, the International Securities Commissions Organization (IOSCO), and the OECD task forces, it has become virtually impossible for the European Union to depart significantly from the regulatory framework these forums have 'recommended'.

The EU financial regulation burden can also be considered light in comparison to the potential costs of regulation by member states if there had been no harmonization at the EU level. Obviously, one can only speculate about regulation in the absence of EU integration, but three specific points can be made.

First, those member states that would have participated in international regulatory competition would also have faced the constraints imposed by global regulatory fora. In other words, they would not have been able to adopt a regulatory framework significantly lighter than that required by current EU minimum standards.

Second, EU harmonization cannot be said to have significantly added to the pre-existing regulatory burden. Admittedly, member states had to pass new legislation because of EU legal developments, but the net effect is likely to have been neutral. In some sectors, activities that were not supervised had to be submitted to authorization, which created obvious (private) regulatory costs. But in other sectors, EU integration prodded member states into adopting reforms that clearly diminished (private) regulatory costs. A good example of the latter development is Italy's recent securitization law, which eliminates costly registration procedures for issuers and allows special-purpose vehicles as an alternative to burdensome off-shore structures.[11]

Third, it may even be that EU harmonization is actually decreasing the regulatory burden thanks to economies of scale, especially for financial intermediaries which were already providing services in more than one member state. Insofar as they operate through branches, their supervisory fees should decrease (since they no longer need a licence from host member states) and their overall lobbying costs may be reduced as the regulatory process becomes more centralized.

In conclusion, regulated entities have not had to pay the price of a higher regulatory burden in order to get the European passport. A degree of regulatory

[11] Y. Hassany (1999), 'Italian Securitization Boosts Banks', *Wall Street Journal Europe*, 6 September, at 25.

diversity remains possible, leaving some scope for private incentives and ensuring that the choice of regulatory regime is more than perfunctory.

Intra-EU spillovers

European Union regulation deals with interjurisdictional externalities in various ways. Most obviously, mutual recognition reduces the ability of a member state with a major financial centre to prevent the benefits of its competitive position from spilling over to other member states: the European passport forbids depriving foreign firms of access to a given EU market.

Mutual recognition does not, of course, mean that regulatory barriers to cross-border activities have been eliminated, even in areas where EU harmonization has taken place. As already mentioned, foreign-regulated markets still find it difficult to tap capital in a major financial centre because it is hard to demonstrate the adequacy of their remote-access facilities. Similarly, foreign issuers still incur transaction costs when seeking an additional listing in a major financial centre due to loopholes in the harmonization of the mutual recognition of prospectuses. But whereas remaining regulatory barriers may be sufficient to hamper the internationalization of financial services, they are certainly not high enough to allow a member state to significantly curb positive externalities.

Interjurisdictional externalities are also dealt with through mechanisms aiming at (somewhat) reducing the danger of 'open' borders being exploited for purposes of large-scale fraud. As already mentioned, EU regulation has subjected most financial services to authorization and minimum standards. In addition, following the Bank of Credit and Commerce International (BCCI) débâcle, where authorities in two member states each relied on the other doing the necessary supervision, EU regulations now require the head office of a supervised financial intermediary to be located in the member state of incorporation.[12] At a minimum, it can be said that the European passport does not permit larger-scale fraud than would have been possible under the former regime.

More importantly, the EU regulatory framework also makes it more difficult for member states to engage in strategic behaviour aimed at enjoying the (tax and other) benefits from financial intermediaries incorporating in their jurisdictions, while unloading the costs of higher systemic risk onto other member states. Home member states not only have supervisory responsibility for intermediaries they attract, they are also obliged to follow minimum supervisory standards, including those for consolidated supervision.[13] In addition, host member states still have the power to intervene in their domestic markets, which should help reduce systemic risk (Baltensperger and Dermine 1990: 33).

[12] For a description of the provisions adopted in the wake of the BCCI scandal, see Clarotti (1994: 52–3).

[13] See e.g. Council Directive 92/30/EEC on the supervision of credit institutions on a consolidated basis, OJ L 110/52, 28 April 1992, amended by OJ L 141/1, 11 June 1993.

However, the danger that one member state will externalize costs to other member states is not the only type of spillover considered. European Union regulation also takes into account asymmetries in the distribution of regulatory costs among member states by laying down the foundations of cooperation among national supervisors. A member state cannot free-ride the supervisory efforts of other member states by opening its borders to holders of European passports (the idea being that its supervisory costs as a home member state will decrease because the number of domestic firms will shrink). European Union regulation requires home and host member states to exchange information and coordinate their enforcement efforts in areas where they share regulatory powers. As a matter of fact, member states have acknowledged their mutual dependence by concluding numerous bilateral Memoranda of Understanding on the exchange of information and on reciprocal commitment between financial services supervisors. Clearly, this does not prevent member states with major financial centres from incurring higher supervisory costs than member states with less developed banking and capital markets. On the other hand, it makes free riding more difficult, as there is no way of dispensing with the supervisory apparatus or avoiding at least a proportion of the costs of supervising cross-border activities.

In sum, it is clear that EU regulation takes account of intra-EU spillover effects. This does not necessarily mean that the solutions adopted are efficient. In particular, economies of scale could make it preferable to let member states free-ride the supervisory efforts of large financial centres. Nevertheless, as the analysis of the effectiveness of EU supervision will show (Part III, second section), such free-riding may well cause costs that more than offset its benefits.

Public choice issues

Data regarding the role of interest groups in the development of the EU financial regulatory framework is obviously very difficult to obtain. Therefore, this section will neither attempt to assess the exact role of the various lobbyists in harmonization, nor try to compare their influence at the EU level to what they could have done at member state level. However, it is possible to show that the most influential interest groups will have a growing interest in centralization and that this is likely to make regulatory self-interest a significant EU issue.

Interest groups

Financial intermediaries, exchanges, issuers, and investors alike have incentives to try to influence the scope, content, and enforcement of EU financial regulation in order to foster their private interests.

However, EU financial intermediaries are a rather heterogeneous group. Their individual interests will diverge depending upon the services provided and the local or cross-border nature of their activities. For example, institutions which develop investment banking activities should be more favourable to the opening of markets than plain commercial banks, as the latter have historically enjoyed a greater degree of regulatory protection against foreign competition. Or, to take another example, retail credit institutions may have no interest in EU lobbying activities, believing that they are likely to survive any integration development if they confine themselves to a local market.[14] The steady increase in available financial products and services is likely to further fragment industry interests. It is even possible that individual intermediaries' preferences may prove very volatile, due to constant changes in market structures and the development of Internet-assisted distribution channels.

As a result, it seems probable that only the largest financial intermediaries will have enough financial and strategic influence to continue to lobby effectively at the EU level. Should this be the case, future lobbying efforts will aim at further reducing regulatory barriers to cross-border activities, without an increase in the net regulatory burden. The favoured strategy to that end seems to be to push for further EU harmonization and to level the playing field by ensuring that major financial intermediaries are subjected to more comparable supervision.

Exchanges, for their part, have repeatedly lobbied for EU regulation to incorporate tools allowing member states to limit competition between the trading markets of the European Union (Lee 1998a: 230). Considering that there has as yet been no (completed) cross-border merger of regulated markets, and that existing pan-European trading platforms such as Easdaq (Tirez 1997) are still marginal players, it might seem that exchanges have proved to be a powerful interest group. On the other hand, there is growing evidence that true pan-European trading platforms will soon become common, chiefly owing to technological progress. Further, the current consolidation in the EU financial services industry should eventually lead to significant cross-border mergers.

In this perspective, it is in the interests of major regulated markets to lobby for further diminishment of regulatory barriers to cross-border trading, without an increase in the net regulatory burden. It therefore comes as no surprise that some of the most important EU exchanges are already campaigning for further EU harmonization, and even wish for a central EU supervisory authority[15]—with some encouragement from the legal and economic literature (Danthine *et al.* 1999; Hoppmann 1999; Thieffry 1999).

Issuers, or publicly traded companies, would prefer standards on accounting, reporting, and disclosure to be set at the highest regulatory level possible, which is that of global best practice. They do not particularly want member states to keep regulatory powers over the listing of their shares and bonds, as this is only likely to increase transaction costs. It follows that they are likely to support centralization efforts undertaken by EU exchanges. On the other hand, issuers (that is, their controlling shareholders or managers) seem to favour decentralization in the areas of

[14] See Goldman Sachs industry survey, reported in P. Coudret (1999), 'Une Europe et quelques banques', *Le Temps*, 24 August, at 2–3.

[15] See 'No SEC please, we're European', *The Economist*, 21 August 1999, at 62.

corporate governance and the regulation of takeovers—which is probably why proposed directives in those areas have been blocked for decades.

Finally, large investors and consumers face the usual collective action problems. Up to now, major institutional investors seem to have put more efforts into lobbying at the member state than at the EU level (Baudru and Kechidi 1998). Indeed, they are most interested in corporate governance issues, but it is futile to try to get the European Union to tackle them, given the repeated failures to pass company law directives in that area. Consumer representatives have been quite influential at the EU level, not least because their activism has often suited the European Commission's own agenda. However, consumer protection concerns have until now mainly materialized in the adoption of directives that were of general application or that focused on areas other than financial services.[16] This may be changing, not least because the introduction of the euro has focused attention on the high fees charged for cross-border retail payments and because the Internet is facilitating cross-border trading by small investors. As a matter of fact, the European Commission has announced its intention to further regulate relations between consumers and financial intermediaries (European Commission 1999).

In short, to the extent that they show EU activism, interest groups seem to have little objection to diversity in national legal regimes as far as smaller/weaker players or company law issues are concerned. Controversies are limited to situations where the co-existence of multiple mandatory regimes could impose high transaction costs on cross-border financial activities—the main current debate being about EU directives on e-commerce that aim to protect consumers. On the other hand, major financial intermediaries and exchanges are increasingly lobbying for additional harmonization to further reduce regulatory barriers to their cross-border activities and for a level playing field as far as supervision is concerned.

Self-interested regulators

While one can confidently assert that the resulting regulatory reforms are likely to be tainted by both the industry's and the regulators' self-interest (Boot and Thakor 1993; Kane 1990), it is much more difficult to predict whether any significant reform will take place and which interests will dominate.

Bodies composed of member state regulators, in particular the Banking Advisory Committee and the Forum of European Securities Commissions (FESCO), are likely to have a significant influence on the drafting of EU harmonization regulation aimed at further opening national borders. Obviously, it is not possible for these bodies to act openly to the detriment of the general interest. However, the lack of transparency in their agenda, procedures, and discussions gives member states considerable scope for favouring their own hidden agendas and allows representatives to pursue self- rather than public interest (Baldwin and Cave 1999: 150–79).

[16] See Directive 98/27/EC of the European Parliament and of the Council on injunctions for the protection of consumers interests, OJ L 166/51, 11 June 1998, and the list of directives covered.

In my opinion, given monetary union and Internet developments, it is not very likely that member states will strongly object to further liberalization. Nonetheless, they might well resist the institution of EU supervisory bodies, especially since this is likely to increase the powers of the European Central Bank (ECB). Indeed, Article 105(6) of the Maastricht Treaty instituted a simplified procedure to entrust the ECB with supervisory tasks for the major EU banks, making it the leading candidate for EU banking regulator. Regulators, for their part, are likely to have the opposite incentives.

This is because the further opening of borders is likely to be a complex task if the goal is to provide a level playing field. It may also make enforcement more complicated, which could facilitate abusive practices and tarnish the regulators' reputations. A good example is provided by the mutual and pension fund industry. A recent proposal to liberalize risk-diversification requirements for index-tracker funds has antagonized managers of funds not covered by the proposal, and is considered to encourage excessive risk-taking.[17] On the other hand, the institutionalization of EU supervisory authority for the main EU banks and for (at least some) EU securities markets may provide some regulators with an opportunity to obtain a more prestigious job in the new entity or a promotion within the national supervisory body (Benston 1994: 221). For regulators in smaller member states, it could also be an elegant way to 'kick upstairs' the complex and politically delicate task of regulating major financial intermediaries.

It is not unrealistic to believe that regulators will be able to push through reforms incorporating some centralization mechanisms. First, they can show that they have support from industry, especially from managers—probably the most important constituency when it comes to regulatory competition. Second, mainly due to the EU requiring cooperation among regulators, the latter have developed strong ties across jurisdictions, which facilitates cartel-like behaviour. It is too early to tell whether or not centralization will be a positive development. There are some good arguments in favour of centralized EU supervisors. For example, an EU supervisor should be able to attract higher quality personnel and to better resist individual demands by major EU players, as the latter would no longer be the biggest fish in the pond. The decisive element is the effectiveness of supervision as it currently exists—an issue that is discussed in the next Part.

III. EXPRESSING PREFERENCES FOR A LEGAL REGIME

The interactions between 'private' interests and centralization (or regulatory competition) can also be analysed by evaluating the freedom to choose a legal regime, that is, applicable law and the authorities (agencies or courts) enforcing it. Indeed,

[17] G. Matlock (1999), 'Proposed EU Rule Change for Index-Tracker Funds Draws Flack', *Wall Street Journal Europe*, 6 September, at 24.

the degree of regulatory competition depends on market participants being able to select the legal framework(s) they prefer (Brand 1997).

Under the EU system there is no room for aggressive unilateral extraterritorial application of law. First, under the 'home country control' approach, member states need to cooperate in the supervision of financial intermediaries, which rather limits the attractiveness of a confrontational strategy. Second, there are mandatory EU provisions on jurisdiction[18] and applicable law[19] in commercial matters. Finally, and most importantly, it is the European Court of Justice, not the member state concerned, that has the last word regarding jurisdiction in regulatory matters.

This does not prevent issues typical of both adversarial and cooperative competition from arising. Thus there may be divergences about whether the conduct of a financial intermediary within its home member state produces sufficient effects in another member state to give the latter supervisory jurisdiction. Or, to take a cooperative competition example, there may be divergences when it comes to identifying the home member state of a regulated market or of an issuer.

How well member states can protect their sovereignty or retaliate against regulatory arbitrage can be tested by evaluating market participants' freedom to express preferences in four areas: contractual framework; incorporation regime; regulation of issuers; and supervision of financial services providers (Part III, first section). However, regarding the latter preference, the freedom given to market participants will essentially depend upon the effectiveness of home member state supervision (Part III, second section): Host member states are not likely to allow providers of financial services to opt for a supervisory regime that puts the interests of their constituencies at significant risk.

Applicable law and enforcement

Contractual framework

So long as no consumer protection issue arises, there is extensive freedom to choose applicable law and the enforcement regime, such as arbitration. European Union harmonization has reduced the diversity in the international private law of member states, but this has the advantage of making it more difficult for member states to claim that there are public order reasons for restricting contractual freedom.

On the other hand, when it comes to retail activities or to the suitability of financial products for market participants, contractual freedom is more restricted. In the pre-contractual phase, the right to choose a regime that permits informational comparisons with competing financial instruments is limited by the autonomy member states still have to adopt rules of conduct. More importantly, the right of

[18] 1968 Brussels Convention on jurisdiction and the enforcement of judgments in civil and commercial matters, OJ 299/32, 31 December 1972; Convention on jurisdiction and the enforcement of judgments in civil and commercial matters (Lugano Convention) OJ L 319/9, 5 November 1988.

[19] 1980 Rome Convention on the law applicable to contractual obligations (consolidated version), OJ C 27/34, 26 January 1998.

member states to object to consumers' opting out of their mandatory regime is the subject of much debate, as shown by the controversies created by e-commerce regulatory initiatives or by the reform of the EU's framework for international private law.

It is difficult to evaluate these restrictions on contractual freedom. The European Court of Justice has signalled that consumer protection justifies restricting both the canvassing of consumers and the freedom to escape mandatory provisions (Case 205/84, *Commission* v. *Germany*, 1986 ECR 3775; Cases C–267/91 and C–268/91, *Keck and Mithouard*, 1993 ECR I–6127; Case C–384/93, *Alpine Investments BV* v. *Minister van Financien*, 1995 ECR I–1167). On the other hand, it remains unclear whether member states can forbid opt-out clauses or are merely allowed to force providers of financial services to provide sufficient information about the proposed legal regime (Wernicke 1996: 86–7).

In short, the EU system allows sophisticated market participants significant freedom to choose their contractual framework. The situation is more murky in the consumer/unsophisticated investor area, and as a result market participants are pressing for a clear definition of the professional/sophisticated counterparties and investors who can be allowed to deal unencumbered by consumer protection clauses.

Incorporation

A corporation is basically free to choose its EU country of incorporation. However, some significant obstacles remain. First, the theory of *siège réel* that prevails in the majority of EU jurisdictions brings uncertainty: the validity of the choice of one member state's regulatory regime may be questioned when important company decisions are taken in another member state (Xanthaki 1999).

Second, the cross-border moving of the corporation's registered office to take advantage of another regulatory regime remains an area where free movement is not yet established. This partly reflects the difficulties encountered by harmonization efforts (Special Issue 1999). However, it is also due to the uncharacteristic pusillanimity of the European Court of Justice, most noticeably when it came to interfering with the tax sovereignty of member states. Thus, in the *Daily Mail* case (Case 81/87, *The Queen* v. *H.M. Treasury and Commissioners of Inland Revenue ex parte Daily Mail and General Trust*, 1988 ECR 5483), fears of the political fallout if the United Kingdom were made to suffer from tax undercutting by the Dutch deterred the Court from calling the UK regulatory regime what it was: a clear obstacle to the free movement of persons.

As a result, it is still rather unlikely that a corporation will consider reincorporating in another member state because it prefers the latter's regulatory regime. Nevertheless, recent case law from the European Court of Justice (Case C–212/97, *Centros Ltd* v. *Erhvervs-og Selskabsstyrelsen*, 1999 ECR I–1459) and renewed harmonization efforts to facilitate free movement of companies (Viandier 1998) could lead to an EU 'Delaware effect'. Indeed, recent threats by German corporations have made it clear that cross-border migration is no longer unthinkable, should the regulatory burden become too heavy in one member state (Hammen 1999).

An increased freedom to reincorporate is likely to have an effect on regulatory competition in the financial services area. However, to understand its true impact, we must evaluate the freedom of issuers and financial intermediaries to choose their supervisory regime.

Issuers

Issuers still face difficulties regarding the pan-European offering and listing of securities.

Harmonization has forced member states to adopt the prospectus requirement for the public offering of securities by corporations within their jurisdiction. Yet, despite EU directives on mutual recognition of prospectuses and listings, host member states can still force some degree of compliance with their regulatory regimes. Similarly, takeover bids continue to be regulated by both the home member state of the bidder and the home member state of the target (Schuster 1996: 603).

In other words, EU mutual recognition does not permit a corporation to opt for a securities regime regardless of the country of incorporation, nor does it give the member state of incorporation sole jurisdiction over the corporation's securities. However, the fact that such solutions have been proposed to fight excessive centralization of US securities regulation (Romano 1998) does not mean that there is no EU regulatory competition. On the contrary, Internet developments and the emergence of pan-European online trading platforms are likely to facilitate such competition, especially when it comes to races to the top.

Indeed, host member states are not likely to insist that their regulatory regime must apply when the home member state has adopted best-practice quality standards that go well beyond the minimum. The only practical issue will be the effectiveness of home supervision. In particular, host member states are likely to be sensitive to consumer protection issues and will make sure that unsophisticated investors do not suffer from supervisory failures (Hirsch 1991: 360).

Supervision of financial services providers

As already pointed out, EU financial intermediaries can choose the member state of incorporation, provided their head office is located there—which could make reincorporation quite costly, even ignoring tax issues. The European passport generally permits them to obey a single regulatory regime, the one provided by their home member state. The main exception concerns rules of conduct, where host member states still have autonomous regulatory powers. Given that host regulators tend to be particularly concerned with the protection of small depositors and investors (Dalhuisen 1999: 181), financial intermediaries have been anxious, as in the contractual framework area, to elicit a clear definition of professional/sophisticated counterparties and investors.

Regulated markets, for their part, can provide cross-border remote access, provided the host member state recognizes that the regulated market's facilities are appropriate. It has been mentioned that this apparently innocuous restriction can be used to protect domestic regulated markets. Since the same is true of rules of conduct applicable to financial intermediaries, the extent to which providers of financial services are free to choose the applicable supervisory regime becomes debatable.

In my opinion, despite the room that remains for protectionism, freedom of choice and therefore regulatory competition here again depend essentially on the effectiveness of supervision in the various member states.

Effectiveness of supervision

Generally speaking, host member states will be best placed to justify regulatory barriers if a corporation has opted for a supervisory regime that could put the interests of their constituencies at significant risk. It will be much harder to restrict the cross-border provision of financial services when there is both significant business activity in the home member state and effective supervision by that state.

For this reason, the European Union has adopted minimum standards regarding supervision in the financial services area. But harmonization of supervision is not likely to be sufficient to take care of host member states' concerns. First, modern financial services supervision puts great weight on the adequacy of risk management tools. However, because risk management techniques have become very sophisticated, supervisors have moved away from imposing specific rules in favour of certifying the procedures and tools used by providers of financial services. This development has put great strain on supervisory agencies, as they generally have neither the internal human resources to do their own certification nor the financial resources to hire a large number of specialists.

The European passport has compounded these shortages of human capital. Home member states are now responsible for EU-wide supervision of all authorized providers of financial services. This is only possible with additional manpower or with increased cooperation from host member states. Although EU law lays down the foundations of cooperation among national supervisors, supervisors do not seem able to efficiently assist each other. Indeed, political considerations are forcing supervisory authorities to favour home supervision to the detriment of host cooperation, even though the latter may reduce overall supervisory expenditure.

When issues related to the introduction of the euro and the development of the Internet are tossed in, it is no surprise that both regulators and providers of financial services are willing to trade some regulatory diversity for centralized supervision of the main financial intermediaries and regulated markets. Hence EU central bankers have dropped some not-too-veiled hints as to the desirability of setting up an EU banking supervisor (Louis *et al.* 1995; Padoa-Schioppa 1999). Industry representatives have made much blunter calls for what had long been considered a lost cause—the creation of a European Securities and Exchange Commission (Lee 1996).

In short, free choice of regulatory regime is likely to require further centralization.

IV. PROTECTIONISM, COMPETITION, AND CENTRALIZATION

European Union regulatory competition has not waited for the European passport to be in force to develop. This is partly due to the fact that member states anticipated such development and adjusted their regulatory framework accordingly. Yet these reforms have failed to set a legal framework truly contributing to the pan-European provision of financial services becoming a reality.

To date, the availability of the European passport has not produced this result either. Regulatory barriers to the cross-border provision of financial services remain significant. However, given that member states now have incentives to offer attractive European passports, it can be argued that a single financial market is in the making. In other words, it takes time for mutual recognition to contribute to the pan-European provision of financial services. This does not mean that the European Union will be the theatre of fully fledged regulatory competition: races to the bottom will remain limited due to the need to respect minimum standards.

This reliance on EU minimum standards brings the risk of overregulation. Fortunately, current EU minimum standards cannot be considered high compared to non-EU systems, or to what member states would have done in the absence of EU harmonization. Similarly, adopting minimum standards to reduce barriers to cross-border financial services is not a negative development from an externalities point of view. Member states cannot prevent the benefits from their competitive position from spilling over into other member states. It is also unlikely that member states will take advantage of mutual recognition to unload costs onto other member states.

On the other hand, both major financial intermediaries and regulators have an interest in further harmonization and supervisory centralization. But, contrary to what might be expected, these developments should not restrict the freedom to choose among a diversified set of regulations. It is not unlikely that harmonization will facilitate cross-border activities and therefore regulatory competition. First, it might reduce member states' discretion to adopt measures protective of their domestic industry. Second, creating EU supervisors for the main financial intermediaries and regulated markets would improve the reputation of supervisors overall. Economies of scale and greater power over individual regulated entities should make EU supervisors more effective than national supervisors. In turn, the reduction in the latter's responsibilities would permit more resources to be devoted to the more local areas that remain theirs, increasing their effectiveness. This would give host member states the confidence required to eliminate regulatory barriers to cross-border activities.

Centralization of supervision would also help the European Union to resist some manoeuvring by the IMF (IMF 1998) and other institutions operating at the global financial level to arrogate the responsibility for supervisory regulation (Rogoff 1999). Such institutions necessarily influence the regulatory environment of jurisdictions that require their assistance. As a consequence, it could be perceived as logical to give them a global supervisory role. Unless EU supervisors are established, EU financial intermediaries and regulated markets of worldwide stature are likely to support such an allocation of powers, as it would mean the best possible level playing field. On the other hand, should EU supervisors be established, support for a global supervisor would be significantly reduced and the risk of regulatory competition giving way to a global, monopolistic regulator would remain very small.

11

Regulatory Competition in the EU System: Labour

BRIAN BERCUSSON

In their introduction to a collection of essays on *International Regulatory Competition and Coordination*, the editors identify three 'primary and interrelated concerns . . . in debates about global regulation':

First comes the question of how institutions emerge and evolve in mediating the dynamic of the global marketplace. Secondly, there is a functional policy concern—the problem of the appropriate level for public governance of economic activities. This has long been a question within federal systems, and is now posed at the international level. Thirdly, there is a problem of democratic deficit. This stems from a perception that internalized economic activities are no longer subject to control or facilitation by national governments acting alone, while international structures are institutionally underdeveloped. (Bratton *et al.* 1996: 2)

The collection includes chapters on the European Union (EU) which, according to the editors, 'continues to occupy a central position as a catalyst and a precursor of global institutional developments' (4).

The view of the European Union as a catalyst and precursor in the field of labour regulation may be either an optimistic aspiration or a fearful threat; the reality arguably still falls somewhat short of fulfilling such a role. However, the institutional, functional, and political dimensions of labour regulation in the European Union have been the subjects of my special interest over the past ten years. In this chapter I will address these concerns of the debate on regulatory competition.

I. COMPETING REGULATORY INSTITUTIONS

The history of labour regulation in the European Union is best understood in the context of the evolution of the European Communities in general since their foundation with the European Coal and Steel Community (ECSC) in 1951. Throughout this almost half-century, the EU has experimented with a variety of different legal strategies for the formulation and implementation of labour law and social policy.

The earliest strategy is that which characterized the founding of the ECSC: active labour market policy and labour involvement in regulation. In complete contrast, the following period was characterized by a strategy of neo-liberal *laissez-faire*, reflected in the almost total absence of social policy and labour law provisions in the Treaty of Rome of 1957. This strategy was in turn replaced by an ambitious

Social Action Programme adopted in 1974 which sought to harmonize labour legislation in the common market. The abrupt halt to this strategy caused by the election of a Conservative government in the United Kingdom in 1979 led to a search for a non-legislative strategy in the form of indirect financial instruments and the launching of the European social dialogue in 1985. The 1992 objective of the Single European Market led to pressures for a strategy to achieve a social dimension through fundamental social and economic rights. More recently, the social dialogue strategy has been institutionalized in the Maastricht Protocol and Agreement on Social Policy, now incorporated into the EC Treaty by the Treaty of Amsterdam. Finally, there is the introduction of a new Employment Title in the Treaty of Amsterdam.

What this history shows is the extraordinary range of legal and institutional strategies which have characterized attempts to construct a European labour law, and the struggles that have taken place among the member states, the Community institutions, and organized interest groups, primarily organizations of employers and trade unions, in the course of developing these strategies.

There is not space here for a detailed account of the political, legal, and institutional conflicts which characterized the different phases of labour regulation in the European Union and their attendant strategies (Bercusson 1996: chs 3–6). One episode will be briefly described as illustrating the theme of regulatory competition.

Regulatory competition in the context of the Single European Market programme: 'social dumping'

One review of the economics and politics of regulation divides the last fifty years into three periods characterized by 'regulation' (1945–70), 'transition' (1970–80) when interventionist regimes came under attack, and 'deregulation' (1980–present) (Chang 1997: 724). Labour regulation in the European Community (EC) became a subject for contestation, particularly in the period after the launch in 1985 of the Single European Market programme, to be completed in 1992. The struggle was largely conducted between the representatives of labour and capital (hereafter, 'the social partners') at national and EC level.

The creation of the single European market allows for enterprises heretofore operating in the context of a national market to be exposed to competition with others in other member states. This means that pressure will be exerted on enterprises with high direct wage costs to secure the productivity that will enable them to compete with enterprises elsewhere in the Community with lower wage costs. This aspect of competition, aimed at rewarding productivity, was one of the objectives of the Single European Market programme.

However, national systems of labour law and social protection impose indirect labour costs on enterprises, such as costs of compliance with labour standards and costs of contributing to social protection schemes. Lower labour and social standards in some member states may entail lower indirect labour costs for enterprises in those states. The result is to give enterprises in those countries with lower indirect labour costs a competitive advantage compared with enterprises in member states with higher labour and social standards. This advantage may be offset by other factors which favour enterprises in countries with higher labour and social standards, such as better transport infrastructures or a more highly trained and skilled workforce. Nonetheless, differences in direct and indirect labour costs may constitute a significant competitive edge.

One consequence of such differences has been argued to raise the threat of 'social dumping'. As a result of what has been called 'social policy regime competition' between member states, states will be under pressure to reduce their labour and social standards in order to ease the burden of high indirect wage costs on enterprises (Streeck 1990: 48). Enterprises, particularly multinational enterprises, will be tempted to locate new investments or even relocate existing establishments to countries where lower labour and social standards entail lower indirect labour costs.[1] Two tables illustrate this graphically (European Industrial Relations Review (1993: 18–19).

Table 1. Hourly labour costs in industry in the EC, 1990 in ecus

Country	Labour cost (hourly)
Germany	20.08
Belgium	19.30
Netherlands	17.47
France[a]	15.27
Luxembourg[b]	14.48
Italy[a]	14.24
UK	12.20
Ireland	11.64
Spain	11.30
Greece[b]	5.24
Portugal	3.57

[a] 1989 figures
[b] 1988 figures

Social dumping posited two alternative scenarios for the institutional arrangements of formulation and implementation of EU labour law and social policy. One scenario envisaged the transfer of social policy jurisdiction to the EU level. Harmonized or uniform social and labour standards throughout the Community, established through EU legal measures, would secure the objective of greater equalization of indirect labour costs for all enterprises, and reduce, if not eliminate,

[1] A notorious case was that of the relocation by Hoover of a manufacturing plant in Dijon, France to Cambuslang, Scotland (European Industrial Relations Review, March 1993: 14).

Table 2. The structure of labour costs in industry in the EC, 1990

Country	Direct cost (%)	Of which direct remuneration (%)	Indirect cost (%)	Of which social security (%)
Denmark	96.2	83.1	3.8	3.0
UK	86.8	84.2	13.2	11.5
Luxembourg[a]	82.8	67.4	17.4	16.3
Ireland	82.2	70.5	17.7	14.9
Greece[b]	80.0	61.0	19.0	19.0
Germany[c]	76.3	56.0	23.7	21.5
Spain	74.9	55.3	25.1	24.5
Portugal	74.2	56.0	25.8	21.7
Netherlands	73.3	54.3	26.7	23.2
Italy[d]	70.0	50.3	30.0	26.7
Belgium	69.5	49.1	30.5	28.9
France[e]	68.0	51.4	32.0	28.6

[a] 1989 figures
[b] 1988 figures
[c] 1988 figures
[d] 1988 figures
[e] 1988 figures
Source: Eurostat (1992) 'Labour costs: updating 1989–90', Luxembourg

the threat of unequal standards distorting competition in favour of member states with lower standards. The second scenario favoured the opposite: retention of national competence over social and labour standards, accepting the consequence of direct competition between different member state social regimes.

These two scenarios were obviously linked with wider political strategies concerned with the pace and direction of European integration in general. In that general context of European integration, however, the interesting feature of the two apparently opposing scenarios regarding EU social policy and labour law is that both lead to a loss of member state autonomy in these fields of policy.

The first scenario is explicit about this result: member states relinquish their competence over social policy and labour law in favour of regulation of these areas by harmonized and uniform EU standards. Future developments in these policy areas are thereby left to EU initiatives.

But the second scenario also, though not so explicitly, entails the reduction or elimination of national autonomy in social policy and labour law making. This is because member states considering initiatives in the field of social policy or labour law will be highly conscious of the implications of undertaking such initiatives for enterprises on their national territory. Any initiative which involves compliance costs with labour regulations or social protection measures will impose higher indirect labour costs compared with enterprises in the other member states. This is bound to make it more difficult to obtain internal political consensus for such social legislation. Moreover, the pressure will continue on member states to reduce their social and labour standards to the levels prevailing in countries with competing enterprises.

What both scenarios have in common, therefore, is a policy of 'deregulation' at the national level; either because this is the result of social policy regime competition, or because regulation at the national level is replaced by exercise of regulatory competence in social and labour matters at the EU level.

The dangers posed by 'social dumping' and 'social regime competition' as a result of the 1992 Single European Market programme led to a fierce and protracted political battle between the social partners at the European level.

The strategy of the trade unions at the European level was characterized by Wolfgang Streeck as dictated by a 'political-distributive' logic. This recognized the dangers posed by social dumping in the single market, but also acknowledged the advantages to be reaped by enterprises free to compete without national hindrance. The aim was to achieve a balance between the costs of the social protection necessary to offset the risk of social dumping and the losses to enterprises entailed by this necessary degree of regulation. The strategy, therefore, was one of political regulation at the European level to secure the fair distribution of the benefits of the single market, requiring attention to questions of labour and social standards and implementation mechanisms.

The strategy of employers' organizations was characterized as dictated by an 'economic-productive' logic. The social dimension of the single market was to aim at achieving the maximum productive and competitive efficiency. For firms in the EC, the principal competitive challenge came from outside the EC—mainly the United States and Japan. Enterprises in those countries benefited from significantly lower social and labour standards, a competitive advantage which hindered enterprises in Europe. The social policy of the EC in the new single European market should, therefore, aim at reducing this competitive advantage by eliminating that social and labour regulation which was such a burden on European enterprises. Freed of such a burden, the productive and competitive efficiency of European enterprise would achieve the requisite growth generating the economic benefits for living and working standards. European employers, therefore, had a positive social policy: that of deregulation to allow for the necessary flexibility and competitiveness.

Each of these social policy strategies for the single European market had an accompanying legal strategy. The deregulation strategy put forward by the employers' organizations was based on the assumption that there were to be no common social and labour standards imposed through EC measures. This had the advantage that it would reduce the need for a central regulatory bureaucracy—not required, given the non-interventionist policy. It had the corollary benefits of operating to inhibit social regulation initiatives at the national level, for fear of burdening member state enterprises. Finally, it allowed for regulatory social regime competition, in which member states would compete against each other to lower indirect social and labour costs.

The consequences for labour of such a strategy would have been negative. The benefits of the single European market were, at that stage, purely speculative and highly uncertain. The exclusion of any attempt at social regulation meant that the widely anticipated restructuring of enterprises would be unrestrained. There would be no EC political regulatory regime capable of supporting social protection or labour rights, collective or individual. And the prospect of social dumping would become a reality, with particular threats to social security regimes imposing employer contributions.

The struggle that ensued between these protagonists and their strategies involved not only the social partners but also the Community institutions and the member states, which also had a stake in the outcome. One result was an institutional innovation with profound consequences: the emergence of the European social dialogue.

Institutional regulatory competition: states or social partners

The United Kingdom (UK) government's stance from 1979 in preventing the adoption at the Community level of legislation on labour policy was dictated by its domestic policy. This stance coupled similar 'deregulation' at the domestic level with an equally wholesale policy of exclusion of trade unions. This included both exclusion of trade unions from areas of policy where they had previously been part of tripartite policy-making machinery (such as industrial training and manpower policy) and, more crucially, the reduction and weakening wherever possible of collective bargaining.

It is, therefore, ironic that it was this UK blockage of labour legislation at the EU level which provided the critical impetus to a transformation in legal strategy for social policy and labour law at the EU level: the emergence of dialogue between the social partners at the European level. The doubtless unintended consequence of the UK government policy of decollectivization of industrial relations at the domestic level was the huge advance in collectivization of industrial relations at the European level.

The emergence of the European social dialogue in the mid-1980s was dictated by the conjuncture of the 1985 Single European Market programme being threatened by the UK veto on the development of a parallel social dimension. The crucial initiative was taken by Jacques Delors, the incoming President of the Commission, in January 1985. Following his invitation, the social partners met at the castle of Val Duchesse outside Brussels on 31 January 1985 and agreed to engage in furthering the social dialogue. A second meeting on 12 November 1985 set up two joint working parties, which led to adoption of 'joint opinions' on 6 November 1986, 6 March 1987, and 26 November 1987.[2]

[2] For a contemporary outline of the development of the social dialogue in the Community, see Commission of the European Communities (1988a: Annex 10).

The social dialogue received crucial formal recognition through the insertion into the Treaty of Rome, by the Single European Act 1987, Article 22, of a new Article 118B:

> The Commission shall endeavour to develop the dialogue between management and labour at European level which could, if the two sides consider it desirable, lead to relations based on agreement.

The social dialogue moved to a second phase with a meeting held at the Palais d'Egmont on 12 January 1989, which set up a political steering group. Further working parties were set up and further joint opinions were produced in the years that followed.

As the term 'joint opinions' may indicate, the social partners engaged in the dialogue, and in particular the employers' organizations, were ambivalent about the formal outcomes of the process they were involved in. The employers' organizations could hardly resist the pressures coming from the Commission to participate, and they supported the Single European Market programme on the whole, but that did not imply a commitment to what Article 118B characterized as 'relations based on agreement'.

The development of the 1992 programme carried with it increasing concern with the social consequences of the creation of the Single European Market. The social policy of the EC, as developed over its first thirty years, did not seem adequate to the task.[3] The Val Duchesse 'social dialogue', even reinforced by the provision in Article 118B, did not fulfil the perceived need for the formulation and implementation of a comprehensive social dimension for the 1992 programme.

The negotiations at Maastricht produced the Treaty on European Union (TEU) signed by the member states of the European Community on 7 February 1992. The TEU included a Protocol on Social Policy, and an Agreement, annexed to the Protocol, between eleven member states, with the exception of the UK, also on Social Policy.

The key documents were drafted by the member state holding the Presidency of the Council of Ministers—the Netherlands. But their final form, and most of the substance of the provisions which eventually became the Agreement on Social Policy (ASP) between the eleven member states, were the result of negotiations between the peak organizations of employers (UNICE and CEEP) and of workers (ETUC) at the European level.[4]

These negotiations culminated in the Agreement dated 31 October 1991 between ETUC and UNICE/CEEP on a new draft of Articles 118(4), 118A, and 118B of the Treaty of Rome. With few modifications, this Agreement was adopted

[3] For a contemporary summary of the social policy of the Community during this period, see Commission of the European Communities (1987: 51–62; 1988b: 19–20).

[4] Union des Confédérations de l'Industrie et des Employeurs d'Europe (The Union of Industrial and Employers' Confederations of Europe (UNICE)); Centre Européen de l'Entreprise Publique (The European Centre of Public Enterprises (CEEP)); and Confédération Européenne des Syndicats (The European Trade Union Confederation (ETUC)). Hereafter denominated 'the EU social partners'.

by the eleven member states as the basis for the future labour and social law of the European Union.

Jon Erik Dolvik provides the most detailed account yet published[5] of the negotiations which led up to the agreement of 31 October 1991 between ETUC, UNICE and CEEP, which was the foundation for the Protocol and Agreement on Social Policy of the Treaty on European Union (1997: 189–239).

Dolvik also provides an incisive analysis of what appears to have been the Commission's strategy in February–March 1991 in setting the social policy agenda for the Maastricht summit (194–7). On the one hand, the social partners, but the employers in particular, were threatened with extended use of qualified majority voting (QMV), but simultaneously tempted with the prospect of avoiding legislation by substituting negotiated agreements. On the other hand, member states were to be 'faced with an input from the [European level] social partners that would be difficult to reject' (197):

> By designing its proposal in this way the Commission might mobilize a source of legitimacy which could bolster its case in two ways, through an advanced, double-edged operation. By simultaneously using the risk of QMV being adopted by the IGC [Inter-Governmental Conference negotiating the Maastricht Treaty] to convince employers to agree on the 'negotiate or we will legislate' formula, the latter was, on the other hand, used as a means of convincing member-states to accept extended QMV. In other words, by using 'supranational' resources built up within the social dialogue as a card in intergovernmental bargaining *and* using intergovernmental bargaining as a card in the social dialogue, the Commission (as the only political actor present in both settings) was trying to exploit tensions between intergovernmentalism and supranationalism to construct a new institutional framework of Community social policy.

This early strategy was only successful following further dynamic developments, a process Dolvik characterizes as 'social dialogue negotiations in the shadow of IGC' and, eventually, 'stumbling into the 31 October agreement'.[6]

The outcome of the Maastricht summit is of outstanding importance for the future of Community labour regulation. The implementation of EC labour law through collective bargaining within member states is explicitly recognized. A role for the social partners at the EC level in formulating EC labour law is introduced. The procedure is that of 'bargaining in the shadow of the law'. The social dialogue is delicately timed to take place during the Commission's procedure of consulting the social partners about social policy proposals. This raises complex issues of subsidiarity. If the social partners at the EC level reach agreements, it appears that member states are obliged to implement these agreements within their national legal orders.[7]

[5] There are other accounts not yet published in English. One is Petersen (1995: 89–96).

[6] In addition to analysis, Dolvik provides fascinating details on, for example, the position of the British employers (CBI) and the Swedish and German trade unions (1997: 202–3 and note 125).

[7] For detailed analysis, see Bercusson (1996: 523–70).

II. COMPETING LEVELS OF REGULATION

In the EU context, the issue of competing levels of labour regulation appears in various guises. Of these, perhaps the best known concerns the competition between member states and the EU institutions where both have competence. The applicable principle goes under the title of 'subsidiarity'.

Subsidiarity: EU institutions or member states

The 'subsidiarity' principle was the subject of explicit elaboration in Article 3B (now Article 5) of the EC Treaty agreed at Maastricht:

> The Community shall act within the limits of the powers conferred upon it by this Treaty and of the objectives assigned to it therein.
>
> In the areas which do not fall within its exclusive competence, the Community shall take action, in accordance with the principle of subsidiarity, only if and insofar as the objective of the proposed action cannot be sufficiently achieved by the member states and can therefore, by reason of the scale or effects of the proposed action, be better achieved by the Community.
>
> Any action by the Community shall not go beyond what is necessary to achieve the objectives of this Treaty.

The issue has been made rather more complex by the injection of EC level action involving not EC institutions but the social partners at the EC level. European Community level action can now be undertaken by the social partners as well as by the Commission and the Council.

The principle of subsidiarity only applies when the EC and member states both have competence. The question is which of the two (EC or member states) is to exercise the competence. As defined in Article 5 (ex 3B) of the EC Treaty, there are two conditions for EC action: first, insufficient achievement by member states of the objectives of the proposed action; and, second, better achievement by the Community by reason of the scale or effects of the proposed action.

The issue is to be posed in relative terms: which level is better (as in 'cannot be sufficiently achieved by the member states and can . . . be better achieved by the Community'). The EC could argue member state insufficiency, and the member states could argue that the EC is no better (or worse). This raises the difficult question of which criteria and standards to adopt to assess sufficiency. The allocation of competences depends on a reliable assessment of relative sufficiency. The terms of the assessment are critical; in particular, what is the role of economic or other criteria and standards?

The debate over subsidiarity may be influenced by the European Economic Community logic of economic rather than political (let alone social) union. 'Exclusivity/competences' is the language of legal/political union. 'Efficiency' (sufficiently achieved) and 'scale or effects' are the language of economic union. The ambiguity is apparent in the (slippery) terms in which the debate has been conducted: (political-social) objections to centralization are dressed up in (economic) terminology of efficiency. But economic theory includes political and social considerations to varying extents. The neo-classical school of economics, which underlies the old conception of the European Economic Community, may not be sustainable in the context of the European Union.

Efficiency may have to be weighed against fundamental constitutional principles of member states which include other values.[8] For example, in the specific context of the application of the principle of subsidiarity to the question of who regulates, the social partners at the EU level, or the EC or the member states themselves, the principle of the autonomy of the social partners should be brought into the equation. 'Efficiency' might dictate EC or member state action, but long-standing hegemony of the social partners over certain policy areas may dictate leaving it to management and labour to settle the substance of EC labour policy in that area.[9]

Subsidiarity being a relative test as between levels, if, for example, the social partners are unable to adopt measures as a result of the intransigence of one side, this will be a sign that the competence may be exercised at a different level. Similarly, if the EC is unable to adopt measures due to majority or unanimous voting requirements, competence should be exercised by the social partners at the 'better' level.

There is a further point. The subsidiarity principle has been misconceived as implying an allocation of powers to either a higher or lower level. The test of relative sufficiency indicates that it is not a question of exclusive allocation. Instead, deciding which level is better implies that both have something to contribute. Though one may be better overall, the other may be more advantageous in some respects. The solution might be to use the subsidiarity principle to delineate the respective advantages of each level and promote cooperation between them, rather than assign exclusive jurisdiction to one or the other. Within the relevant field of competence, different levels can coordinate their action. This is a familiar problem in labour law and industrial relations: the relative roles of legislation and collective bargaining in regulating different policy areas.

This ties up with the problems of criteria and standards for efficiency. The allocation of competences, particularly if cooperation/interdependence rather than exclusivity is the objective, depends on a reliable assessment of relative sufficiency, a concept which should be expanded beyond its narrow economic confines. More than ever, it becomes clear that a court of law is ill-equipped to deal with the issue.

The problem of subsidiarity becomes, therefore, one of practical application. What are the procedures and institutional structures appropriate for resolving

[8] For the contention that 'solidarity' provides an equally weighty value in the European legal order, see Bercusson *et al.* (1996: 69–74).

[9] A practical illustration of this principle may underlie the exclusion of competence on the right of association and the right to strike in Article 2(6) of the ASP (now Art. 137(6) EC). There is an argument as to the social partners retaining competence on this issue (Bercusson 1996: 546–8).

conflicts over which level or levels take action?[10] What may be required is a body which could adjudicate, mediate, arbitrate, report, or whatever in an effort to unfreeze any stalemate, and, more importantly, give guidance aimed at coordination of cooperative action at different levels. Labour law and industrial relations dispute resolution machinery in member states provides a reservoir of experience.

Competing with the social partners: horizontal subsidiarity

The ASP's confirmation of the fundamental role of the social partners in the implementation of the social dimension at the EC level is seen by the Commission as:

> [R]ecognition of a dual form of subsidiarity in the social field: on the one hand, subsidiarity regarding regulation at national and Community level; on the other, subsidiarity as regards the choice, at Community level, between the legislative approach and the agreement-based approach. (European Commission 1993a: para. 6(c))

This is said to be 'in conformity with the fundamental principle of subsidiarity enshrined in Article 3B (now Article 5 EC) of the Treaty'.

The European Parliament has emphasized the distinction between horizontal and vertical subsidiarity. Vertical subsidiarity refers to the division of competences between different levels: European and national. Horizontal subsidiarity refers to the division of responsibilities between public authorities and, for example, the social partners at the same level.

The Economic and Social Committee (ECOSOC) was alert to the implied subsumption of both horizontal and vertical subsidiarity under Article 5 (ex 3B). Its opinion emphasized that the criteria specified in Article 5 (ex 3B) refer only to vertical, not horizontal, subsidiarity (ECOSOC 1994).

There is no indication that Article 5 (ex 3B) has any relevance to the application of the principle of horizontal subsidiarity—the choice between action by the social partners or public authorities, at the EC level (ETUC/UNICE/CEEP or EC institutions) or at the member state level (social partners or the member state). The criteria for choosing which set of actors at the same level is appropriate are not necessarily those of Article 5 (ex 3B). This has important implications for applying the principle of horizontal subsidiarity evident in Articles 138 and 139 EC (ex 3 and 4 of the ASP): in deciding whether the EC or the social partners should act.

The ECOSOC was able to provide examples of horizontal subsidiarity from a careful reading of the Protocol and Agreement on Social Policy and the attached

[10] One example of EU versus member state competition over labour regulation is the jurisdictional conflict over free movement of goods affected by transnational industrial action (Case C–265/95, *Commission* v. *France*, [1997] ECR I–6959; European Commission 1998c). Another is the extent to which member states may improve on EU minimum standards of health and safety (Case C–2/97, *Societá italiana petroli SpA (IP)* v. *Borsana Srl*, [1998] ECJ CELEX LEXIS 5925 at *1). Most recently, the question of the anti-trust immunity of collective agreements was the subject of dispute in Case C–67/96, *Albany International BV* v. *Stichting Bedrijfspensionenfonds Textielindustrie* [1999] ECJ CELEX LEXIS 2600 at *1, Opinion of Advocate General Jacobs delivered on 28 January 1999, decision of the European Court of Justice delivered on 21 September 1999.

Declarations. The Declaration on Article 4(2) (now Article 139(2) EC) of the ASP provided an indication of the application of horizontal subsidiarity at the national (member state) level. The member states expressly delegated to collective bargaining the development of the content of EC level agreements and acknowledged no obligation to undertake legislation.[11]

Article 2(4) of the Agreement (now Article 137(2) EC) provides another example of the application of horizontal subsidiarity at the national (member state) level. The implementation of directives at the member state level may be entrusted to management and labour, subject to a guarantee by the member state of the results imposed by the directive.

Similarly, support for different criteria for the application of the principle of horizontal subsidiarity follows from decisions of the European Court.[12] This jurisprudence emphasized that the competence of the social partners, as opposed to the public authorities, to implement EC measures through collective agreements must satisfy certain conditions. The agreements concerned must cover all employees, and must include all the directive's requirements.

The possibility of implementing directives through the actions of the social partners at the national level was confirmed by the Commission in an exchange of letters with the Danish social partners. The Commission recognized the principle that directives relating to labour market matters may be implemented in Denmark through collective agreements without the need for legislation.[13] This principle had been introduced earlier by the Danish Commissioner, Henning Christophersen.

The conclusion is that the principle of horizontal subsidiarity is confirmed by a wide range of institutions at the European level: the Council, the Court of Justice, the Commission, and ECOSOC. However, the criteria for the application of horizontal subsidiarity remain to be elaborated.

Conditional competition: negotiated regulation of multinational enterprises

The Council of Ministers of the EU approved the European Works Councils (EWC) Directive 94/45/EC on 22 September 1994 (European Commission

[11] The Declaration attached to the ASP reads: 'The 11 High Contracting Parties declare that the first of the arrangements for application of the agreements between management and labour at Community level—referred to in Article 4(2)—will consist in developing, by collective bargaining according to the rules of each member state, the content of the agreements, and that consequently this arrangement implies no obligation on the member states to apply the agreements directly or to work out rules for their transposition, nor any obligation to amend national legislation in force to facilitate their implementation.' The legal status of this Declaration has been disputed.

[12] In Case 148/83, *Commission of the European Communities* v. *the Kingdom of Denmark* [1985] ECR 427, para. 8) the European Court of Justice held: 'Member states may leave the implementation of the principle of equal pay in the first instance to representatives of management and labour'. See also Case 235/84, *Commission of the European Communities* v. *the Italian Republic* [1986] ECR 2291.

[13] This exchange of letters took place on 11 May 1993. A similar exchange of letters took place between the Commission and the Swedish government on 29 May 1993.

1994d). This requires the establishment of a European Works Council (EWC) or a procedure in Community-scale undertakings and Community-scale groups of undertakings for the purposes of informing and consulting employees. With a calculated 1,480 multinational enterprises covered, each with a European Works Council comprising up to thirty members, aided by an expert, the Directive has the potential to make a decisive step towards a transnational industrial relations system.

The Directive is characterized by a strategy which is assuming ever greater prominence in European labour regulation: the delegation to the social partners, management and labour, of the competence to negotiate the relevant European labour law standards. Central management and the representatives of the workforce are to negotiate the EWC Agreement.[14] However, the delegation to social partners of the power to make agreements is not complete: it is subjected to a subtle structuring process which shapes the strategies pursued by the social partners.

The subtlety of the Directive's strategy lies in apparently leaving all to the unfettered negotiations of the Special Negotiating Body (SNB) representing the workers and central management. While providing a set of fall-back minimum standards in an Annex, the Directive explicitly allows for the exclusion of these minimum requirements in any agreements reached. Formally, the content of the agreement is not confined by the Annex. But the Annex's subsidiary requirements apply where the SNB and the central management so decide (Article 7 (1)); central management refuses to commence negotiations within six months of a request; or three years elapse after a request without an agreement. In practice, central management will have to offer incentives to persuade the SNB to make an agreement offering less than the subsidiary requirements in the Annex.

On the other side, the employees' representatives on the SNB also are not bound by the Annex. Negotiations can flexibilize Annex requirements, and both sides have an incentive to treat it as the basis for negotiations. The Annex can be seen as a package which could be negotiated and varied, if enough incentives are offered.

In practice, therefore, the structure of negotiations between the SNB and central management is such that the subsidiary requirements in the Annex become the effective threshold for agreements. This happens where the SNB is not willing to settle for less than the subsidiary requirements. The argument is that the Directive provides the framework for a negotiating strategy of the SNB.

[14] The range of issues to be negotiated is impressive: national law applicable, the signatory parties, coverage, EWC composition, numbers and seat allocation, the term of office, functions and procedure, venue, frequency and duration of meetings, financial and material resources, duration of the agreement and the procedure for its renegotiation, issues for information and consultation, experts, confidentiality, select committee, employee-side meetings prior to full EWC meetings, rules on deputies to employee representatives, languages policy and interpretation provided, procedure for agreeing the agenda and joint procedure for drawing up minutes or other record. This list is derived from a review of agreements negotiated under Article 6 of the Directive one year after it came into force (European Works Councils Bulletin, September/October 1997: 12–17).

The Directive does not make this a simple task. The SNB can act by a majority of its members (Article 6(5)). A simple majority on the SNB could, by agreement with central management, determine the composition, functions, procedures, resources, and so on of the EWC apparently in any way the parties wished. It will be up to trade unions from the different countries represented on the SNB to develop cooperative strategies to secure an effective EWC.

Competition in standard setting on working time regulation

Introducing its first proposal for a directive on working time, the Commission explained that it 'intends to propose a groundwork of basic provisions on certain aspects of the organization of working time connected with workers' health and safety at work' (European Commission 1991: para. 2). However, 'other issues mentioned in the action programme in the field of the adaptation of working time should be left to both sides of industry and/or national legislation' (3).

The delicate balance between legislation and collective bargaining was spelled out twice in the Explanatory Memorandum in almost identical terms, once at the beginning and again in its final provisions:

> [G]iven the differences arising from national practices, the subject of working conditions in general falls to varying degrees under the autonomy of both sides of industry who often act in the public authorities' stead and/or complement their action. To take account of these differences and in accordance with the principle of subsidiarity the Commission takes the view that negotiation between the two sides of industry should play its full part within the framework of the proposed measures, provided that it is able to guarantee adherence to the principles set out in the Commission's proposals . . . In other words, it is important in this field to take into consideration the fact that such agreements concluded by management and labour can in principle make a contribution to the application of Community directives, without, however, releasing the member states concerned from the responsibility for attaining the objectives sought via these instruments. (4, para. 3; 16–17, para. 32)

The final text of the Directive included a large number of provisions which made collective bargaining an element in the setting of EC standards on working time. In the final text, the role of collective bargaining in determining some of the EU standards on working time had undergone a significant qualitative change. In the past, it was largely confined to allowing for derogations to prescribed standards.[15] The present Directive also allows for collective agreements themselves to fix or define relevant standards, usually only with the consent of the member state concerned, but, in one exceptional case, with priority over member state legislation (daily rest periods, Article 4).

[15] These remained in Directive 93/104/EC (European Commission 1993b). Article 17(3) allows for general derogations 'by means of collective agreements or agreements concluded between the two sides of industry at national or regional level or, in conformity with the rules laid down by them, by means of collective agreements or agreements concluded between the two sides of industry at a lower level'.

III. COMPETITION FOR LEGITIMACY AMONG INSTITUTIONS AND LEVELS

The Maastricht Treaty on European Union transformed EC labour law by formally 'constitutionalizing' the social dialogue in the Protocol and Agreement on Social Policy (Bercusson 1996: 523–37). Following the UK's opt-in to the ASP, the role of the social dialogue in the making of EC labour law is formally enshrined in the EC Treaty by the Treaty of Amsterdam of June 1997.[16] Almost exactly one year after the Amsterdam summit, the Court of First Instance (CFI) delivered a judgment which highlights the constitutional nature of the integration of social dialogue into the EC Treaty (Case T–135/96, *Union Européenne de l'Artisanat et des Petites et Moyennes Entreprises (UEAPME)* v. *Council of the European Union* [1998] ECR II–2335 (hereafter referred to as *UEAPME*)).

The judgment raises profound issues of the democratic legitimacy of EC labour legislation, the autonomy of the social partners engaged in social dialogue, and the role of litigation as a control mechanism of this legitimacy and autonomy.[17] The case also raises issues of concern to EC lawyers in general, engaged in debates over the democratic deficit of the EC in general, the role of private organizations in EC law-making, and *locus standi* before the European Court of Justice.

In *UEAPME*, an organization representing artisans and small and medium undertakings (SMUs) challenged the legality of the Parental Leave Directive before the CFI (European Commission 1996a). The Parental Leave Directive was the first product of the new social dialogue procedure under the Protocol and Agreement on Social Policy.

The first stage in the new procedure was initiated on 21 January 1995, when the Commission decided 'to consult management and labour on the possible direction of Community action with regard to reconciling working and family life' (*UEAPME*: para. 5). The first stage of the consultation process engaged UEAPME. The CFI judgment recounts that:

> On 6 April 1995, the applicant and some of the other representative associations consulted addressed to the Commission a document stating a common position. The signatories to that document urged the Commission to do everything in its power to ensure that certain important issues and certain representatives of management and labour were not excluded from the negotiations. (*UEAPME*: para. 6)

In June 1995 the Commission initiated the second stage of consultations under Article 3(3) of the ASP (now Article 138(3) EC) and, again, on 5 July 1995, UEAPME and the other associations submitted a statement of a common position. The CFI decision states:

[16] Articles 117–122 of the EC Treaty are renumbered Articles 136–145. The old numbering will be used in this Part, with the new numbers in brackets.

[17] For a discussion of some of these issues, see Bercusson (1999).

On the same date, UNICE, CEEP and the ETUC informed the Commission, in accordance with Article 3(4) of the Agreement (now Article 138(4)EC), of their desire to exercise the option available under Article 4(1) (now Article 139(1)EC) of opening negotiations on parental leave. (*UEAPME*: para. 8)

The EU social partners' negotiations were successful: on 6 November 1995 they agreed a proposal for a framework agreement which was finally concluded on 14 December 1995 and 'submitted to the Commission with the request that it be implemented by a Council decision on a proposal from the Commission, in accordance with Article 4(2) of the ASP (now Article 139(2)EC)' (*UEAPME*: para. 9).

The EU social partners did not involve others in their negotiations. After they had made their proposed agreement, UEAPME formally communicated to the Commission 'its regret at having been unable to take part in the dialogue between management and labour, and submitted its criticisms of the proposed framework agreement' (para. 9).[18] UEAPME, together with other organizations consulted and informed, but not signatories to the agreement, were sent copies of the framework agreement on 20 December 1995, and attended a meeting for information and discussion on 5 January 1996 (*UEAPME*: para. 10). The agreement was incorporated into Directive 96/34, adopted by the Council on 3 June 1996.

On 5 September 1996, UEAPME brought an action under Article 173 (now Article 230) of the EC Treaty for annulment of the Directive.

Challenging social dialogue agreements: democratic legitimacy

The first question was the apparently narrow technical obstacle of the standing of the applicant, UEAPME, under Article 173 (now Article 230 EC):

[I]t is necessary to determine whether, notwithstanding the legislative character of Directive 96/34, the applicant may be regarded as directly and individually concerned by it. (*UEAPME*: para. 68)

The CFI chose to treat this as raising issues of constitutional importance:

In view of the particular features of the procedure which led to the adoption of Directive 96/34 on the basis of Article 4(2) of the Agreement (now Article 139(2) EC), it is also necessary to determine whether any right of the applicant has been infringed as the result of any failure on the part of either the Council or the Commission to fulfil their obligations under that procedure . . . (*UEAPME*: para. 83)

The CFI contrasted the two possible outcomes under the ASP. The first outcome follows from the normal legislative process, and the CFI declared:

[T]he democratic legitimacy of measures adopted by the Council pursuant to Article 2 of the Agreement (now Article 137 EC) derives from the European Parliament's participation in that first procedure.

[18] UEAPME's communications were on 30 November and 13 December 1995.

The second results from the social dialogue. The directive which emerges from the Council embodies the agreement reached by labour and management. Of this, the CFI said:

In contrast, the second procedure, referred to in Articles 3(4) and 4 of the Agreement (now Articles 138(4) and 139 EC), does not provide for the participation of the European Parliament. However, the principle of democracy on which the Union is founded requires—in the absence of the participation of the European Parliament in the legislative process—that the participation of the people be otherwise assured, in this instance through the parties representative of management and labour who concluded the agreement which is endowed by the Council acting on a qualified majority, on a proposal from the Commission, with a legislative foundation at Community level. In order to make sure that requirement is complied with, the Commission and the Council are under a duty to verify that the signatories to the agreement are truly representative. (*UEAPME*: para. 89).

Challenging the social partners: representativity

The most important part of the CFI's decision concerns the parties to any social dialogue agreement. For an agreement to be democratically legitimate, the CFI stipulates that it must be ascertained:

[W]hether, having regard to the content of the agreement in question, the signatories, taken together, are sufficiently representative. (*UEAPME*: para. 90)

Applications under Article 173 (now Article 230 EC) are challenges to a legal measure by a specific party. The nature of the measure challenged and the characteristics of the challenger, conditions to success under Article 173 (230), shaped the CFI's vision of the social dialogue.

Representativity in relation to the specific agreement

The challenge was to a specific directive incorporating a social dialogue framework agreement on parental leave. The CFI insisted that the representativity of the parties is to be measured 'in relation to the content of the agreement' (para. 90), or 'with respect to the substantive scope of the framework agreement' (*UEAPME*: para. 91). It looked, for example, at who exactly were the workers covered by the agreement (*UEAPME*: para. 94). The implication for the social partners is that, for the future, agreements may be democratically legitimate when signed by organizations which are only representative as regards the narrow scope of the agreement concerned.

'Sufficient collective representativity'[19]

This is the key phrase repeatedly used by the CFI to describe the parties to a democratically legitimate agreement. The CFI had to determine whether UEAPME

[19] The official language of the case was French. This phrase first appears in paragraph 90 (and thereafter is repeated in the same formulation) as 'partenaires sociaux signataires . . . ont une representativité cumulée suffisante'. This is translated relatively accurately into English as 'signatories, taken together,

qualified as an applicant under Article 173 (230) as 'directly and individually concerned' by the Directive. The CFI interpreted those words in the context of social dialogue agreements as follows:

> [R]epresentatives of management and labour . . . which were not parties to the agreement, and whose particular representation—again in relation to the content of the agreement—is necessary in order to raise the collective representativity of the signatories to the required level, have the right to prevent the Commission and the Council from implementing the agreement at Community level by means of a legislative instrument . . . they must be regarded as directly and individually concerned by that measure. (*UEAPME*: para. 90)

The implication for the social partners is that, even after the difficult process of social dialogue has resulted in an agreement, EC law allows non-signatories to challenge the validity of directives implementing social dialogue agreements.

The specific formula adopted by the CFI to legitimize EU-level agreements explicitly encapsulates two elements of central importance. First, the requisite degree of representativity is not absolute; it must merely be 'sufficient'. Second, one implication of the CFI's use of the word 'collective' ('cumulée') is that a number of social partner organizations, some concentrated in or confined to only a few member states, could sign an agreement which, cumulatively, achieved the requisite degree of representativity. This appears to conflict with the Commission's understanding of 'representativity', which is that the organizations 'be organized at European level' (Bercusson 1996; 558–62; European Commission 1993a).[20]

Representativity: criteria

While emphasizing the importance of representativity, the CFI was less than clear on the question of criteria. It referred to the criteria set out by the Commission in its Communication of 1993 and seemed to look for evidence of representativity in parties 'having regard to their cross-industry character and the general nature of their mandate' (*UEAPME*: para. 96). Thus, as regards UNICE: '[T]hat body represented undertakings of all sizes in the private sector, which qualified it to represent the SMUs' (*UEAPME*: para. 98).

The CFI acknowledged that the criterion of numbers represented may be taken into consideration; however, 'the number of small and medium enterprises (SMUs) represented respectively by the applicant (UEAPME) and UNICE . . . cannot be regarded as decisive in relation to the content of that agreement' (*UEAPME*: para. 102). The statistics produced by the parties, and quoted by the CFI, demonstrated

are sufficiently representative'. In subsequent paragraphs, however, the phrase is formulated as 'sufficient collective representativity' (para. 94). This translation of 'cumulée' as 'collective' is questionable in failing to highlight a key dimension. Representativity is cumulative in that the signatories (on either side) may, taken separately, not be representative, but, taken together, may achieve the requisite degree of representativity. A better translation of this key concept, it is suggested, would be 'sufficient cumulative representativity'.

[20] The 1993 Communication was reaffirmed by a 1998 Communication (European Commission 1998b: 5).

a degree of uncertainty likely to undermine any reliance on numbers (*UEAPME*: para. 103).

The CFI seemed rather to be satisfied if the interests of the category of SMUs were taken into account. The CFI emphasized 'the argument that UNICE does have a general mandate—to defend the interests of undertakings of whatever kind—by contrast with the more specific mandate of other cross-industry organizations, such as the applicant' (*UEAPME*: para. 99). It cited the text of the agreement, 'which makes it clear that the SMUs were not left out of the negotiations leading to its conclusion' (*UEAPME*: para. 105).

A concept of an organization's 'representativity' based on its claim to represent interests, rather than actual numbers of members, poses problems—even more so, if the evidence for representation of those interests is based on the text of agreements concluded. The question of interest representation in the constitutional context of the EU raises issues going far beyond the summary considerations in the CFI's judgment.

Challenging the social dialogue: autonomy

The ASP established a delicate equilibrium between autonomy of the EU social partners and the role of the Commission, an equilibrium characterized as 'bargaining in the shadow of the law' (Bercusson 1996: 538–52).

The autonomy of the social partners was confirmed by the CFI in rejecting UEAPME's claim to participate in the negotiations leading to the Parental Leave Agreement. The CFI strongly asserted the voluntary nature of the social dialogue under the Maastricht Agreement:

> [I]t is the representatives of management and labour concerned, and not the Commission, which have charge of the negotiation stage properly so called. (*UEAPME*: paras. 78–9)

However, the CFI took the view that this autonomy ceases when the parties wish their agreement to be transformed into an EC legal measure by a decision of the Council and turn to the Commission, 'which thereupon resumes control of the procedure and determines whether it is appropriate to submit a proposal to that effect to the Council' (*UEAPME*: para. 84).

The shadow of the Commission on the social dialogue process is lengthened by the CFI's reinforcing the Commission's power to assess the representativity of the parties to the agreement (*UEAPME*: para. 85). Although apparently post-agreement, this assessment in effect reaches back to the conduct of negotiations, since the social partners' exclusion of other parties from the negotiations may lead the Commission and the Council to reject their agreement as insufficiently representative. The Commission can effectively force the participation of certain parties required for the 'sufficient collective representativity' needed to achieve democratic legitimacy. If these are excluded, the agreement may be successfully challenged by the excluded party.

The impact on the autonomy of the social partners of the CFI's decision is evident in its aftermath. The indications were that UEAPME would appeal from the decision of the CFI to the European Court of Justice. The appeal was dropped. Instead, a 'Proposal for a Cooperation Agreement between UNICE and UEAPME', dated 12 November 1998, outlines 'the modalities of cooperation between UNICE and UEAPME in social dialogue meetings, including negotiations' (Clause 1.2). This includes provisions whereby 'UNICE undertakes to consult UEAPME prior to taking public positions on behalf of the employers group in social dialogue and negotiating meetings' (Clause 3.1) and 'UEAPME representatives fully participate in preparatory meetings of the employers group and in plenary meetings with ETUC' (Clause 3.2).

The shadow of the Commission was further lengthened by the CFI seeming to approve the view expressed in the Commission's Communication that it would consider:

> [T]he representative status of the contracting parties, their mandate and the 'legality' of each clause in the collective agreement in relation to Community law, and the provisions regarding small and medium-sized undertakings set out in Article 2(2). (*UEAPME*: para. 86, quoting para. 39 of the Commission's Communication of 1993)

This opens up new avenues for the Commission to exert influence on the social dialogue process, as the parties negotiate under this scrutiny. The potential for Commission influence expands if the substance of agreements comes under scrutiny in the light of Community law, itself not always predictable. The CFI continued:

> The Council, for its part, is required to verify whether the Commission has fulfilled its obligations under the Agreement, because, if that is not the case, the Council runs the risk of ratifying a procedural irregularity capable of vitiating the measure ultimately adopted by it. (*UEAPME*: para. 87)

The autonomy of the social dialogue process is further compromised if the shadow of Commission scrutiny is enhanced further by the CFI's addition of the Council's and, indeed, the Court's scrutiny. The constitutional sensitivity of such additional supervision was evident in the view expressed by the Legal Service of the Council shortly after the CFI's decision (Legal Service 1998).[21]

The concern of the Council is but a reflection of the concerns of the social partners faced with not one, but three levels of scrutiny: Commission, Council, and Court. Such scrutiny might, and then only might, be justifiable if the process in question is indisputably of a legislative nature, raising issues of constitutional accountability. It is questionable at least whether it is compatible with the autonomy of the social dialogue, which is arguably among the fundamental rights of labour and management recognized in the constitutional traditions of the member

[21] The Legal Service asserted that the degree of control retained by the Court was excessive and its reasoning was damaging to the institutional prerogatives of the Council (Legal Service 1998; para. 25).

states and embodied in ILO Conventions 87 and 98 (Bercusson 1997). Any such infringement of autonomy may be the source of future litigation.

IV. CONCLUSIONS

The *UEAPME* case involves a choice of conceptual frameworks to define the legal nature of the EU social dialogue. In the CFI's view, the EU social dialogue is equated with the EU legislative process; as such, it must attain the equivalent degree of democratic legitimacy. The constitutional implications of this vision are fundamental: it involves a role for the EU institutions in scrutinizing the social partners (representativity), their dialogue (autonomy), and their agreements (legitimacy).

This perspective is historically linked to the origins of the EU social dialogue, which was developed as a consequence of the failure of the legislative process in developing EC labour law (Bercusson 1996: 72–8). The ASP was conceived under the pressure of the constitutional development of a social dimension in the Treaty on European Union. The dynamic of the EU social dialogue, as constructed in the ASP, links social dialogue with the EU legislative process: 'bargaining in the shadow of the law'.

It is quite a different matter, however, to extrapolate from this historical evolution and functional dependence in the development of EC labour law to the assumption of political and legal equivalence of social dialogue and legislative processes, an assumption that the same or similar principles of political legitimacy and legal institutional accountability should apply.[22]

This is to ignore the qualitative difference between the legislative machinery of the EU institutions making EC labour law and the EU social dialogue law-making machinery. The latter has its conceptual roots not exclusively in the political legal traditions of constitutional arrangements but also, indeed mainly, in those of industrial relations. Specifically, the EU social dialogue is perceived as akin to another, transnational, level of collective bargaining superimposed on national systems. This was the image reflected in the first path to implementation of agreements laid out in Article 4(2) of the ASP (now Article 139 (2) EC): articulation with national systems.[23]

[22] As Obradovic concludes

> The overlap between the spheres of responsibilities of the EU institutions and the social partners is so great that it is practically impossible to determine exactly where their respective responsibilities begin and end. As a result, the concept of accountability under the [Social Policy] Agreement is blurred . . . the quest for accountability of the social partners must be conceived, in many respects, as part of the quest for greater overall political accountability in the European Union. (1998: 34).

[23] In a parallel enquiry into the legitimacy of the social dialogue process, Sandra Fredman similarly outlines two models, 'the first relying on an industrial relations model, the second on a model of participatory democracy'. The industrial relations model is said to be plausible, but to have characteristics which make it fundamentally different from collective bargaining: the outcome is more powerful in

In the *UEAPME* decision, the CFI opted for the EU constitutional law paradigm of democratic legitimacy, institutional scrutiny, and judicial review. In looking exclusively to EC law for inspiration in developing a conceptual paradigm for the European social dialogue, the CFI risks divorcing European labour law from national labour law systems, traditionally rooted also in an industrial relations model.

having legislative consequences; and the sanctions available to the parties are weaker than in collective bargaining. Of the participatory democracy model, it is said that it 'makes more sense than a collective bargaining model of the strong influence of social dialogue on legislation'. But it, too, is 'far from unproblematic'. She highlights a problem of the participatory democracy model in 'the extent to which such corporatism appears to side-step other important democratic institutions, particularly Parliament' (1998: 408–11).

12

Regulatory Competition vs Harmonization in EU Environmental Law

MICHAEL FAURE

This chapter addresses a topic which, in a European legal perspective, concerns the subsidiarity principle. In this presentation, the subsidiarity principle is addressed from an economic perspective. The central question of European environmental law from an economic perspective is whether we need harmonization of the conditions of competition (in other words harmonization of environmental standards) to reach the goals of the EC Treaty, as laid down in Article 2. This being essentially an economic question, economic methodology will be used to answer it.

The question merits further research since the traditional approach of European environmental law seems largely to have been based on the idea that a full harmonization of rules and standards is necessary in order to harmonize the marketing conditions. Introduced by the Single European Act for environmental matters, and enlarged to a general principle of community policy by the Maastricht Treaty, the subsidiarity principle now allows for a new and probably more critical approach than has traditionally been taken. The subsidiarity principle at least forces policy makers to think more critically about whether full harmonization of rules and standards is indeed necessary to reach the goals of the Treaty. To answer this question, attention will be paid to the literature regarding the optimal level of regulation within federal systems.[1]

Part I provides a brief insight into the traditional argument of European environmental policy: that conditions of competition should be harmonized. Part II discusses the criteria for (de)centralization. Part III applies this theory to environmental issues. Parts IV and V discuss the consequences of these findings for environmental standard setting, as well as for European environmental policy. Part VI presents a public choice perspective, and Part VII formulates a few concluding remarks.

I. EUROPEAN ENVIRONMENTAL POLICY: HARMONIZATION OF CONDITIONS OF COMPETITION

So far, the European Union has been extremely active with respect to environmental law, issuing directives aimed at the harmonization of emission standards,

[1] This chapter is partially based on earlier research. See Faure (1998), Faure and Lefevere (1994; 1995; 1996), and Van den Bergh, Faure, and Lefevere (1996).

ambient quality standards (also referred to as target standards), and procedural rules.[2] A nice example of an approach in which these objectives are drawn together is the Directive on the Integration of Pollution Prevention and Control of 24 September 1996 ('IPPC Directive') (Backes and Betlem 1999; European Commission 1996b). A (limited) procedural harmonization is reached in this Directive by prescribing the permit as the central instrument to control emissions. Rules are prescribed in order to harmonize emission limit values, as well as target standards (Faure and Lefevere 1996).

The European Commission has set out a variety of reasons for legislative action at the European level with respect to environmental law. Although most directives tend to have different reasons for their adoption (Van den Bergh, Faure and Lefevere 1996: 128–31), the most important for our topic are as follows.

1. The transboundary nature of the environmental problem to be targeted. Several directives refer to the transboundary character of the pollution in order to argue for regulation at the European level. This is the case with, for instance, the directive dealing with the discharge of dangerous substances into the aquatic environment (European Commission 1976b).
2. A second justification for the adoption of EC environmental legislation is precisely the creation of equal conditions of competition. It is argued that harmonizing conditions of competition is necessary for the functioning of the common market. This argument, which is often referred to as the need to create a 'level playing field' for industry in Europe, is not only used in environmental law, but is also advanced to harmonize any kind of legislation within Europe.[3] The directive on discharges of dangerous substances into the aquatic environment, mentioned above, was based on this 'harmonization of conditions of competition' argument. It was argued that disparity between the provisions on discharge may create unequal conditions of competition and thus directly affect the functioning of the common market.[4]
3. A third reason advanced for European action with respect to environmental matters can be called a purely 'ecological' one. There are a number of environmental directives which aim to protect the 'European environmental and cultural heritage and human health'. An example is the Habitats Directive (European Commission 1992b).

[2] For information on the different harmonization techniques used in European environmental law, see Pfander (1996) and Esty and Geradin (1997).

[3] Also, the European Directive on Product Liability of 25 July 1985 was justified on the ground that differing liability rules in the member states would hamper the conditions of competition. The considerations preceding the Directive read: 'Whereas approximation of the laws of the member states concerning the liability of the producer for damage caused by the defectiveness of his products is necessary because the existing divergences may distort competition and affect the movement of goods within the common market' (European Commission 1985a).

[4] The same argument was made concerning other directives as well (Van den Bergh, Faure, and Lefevere 1996: 129).

I will attempt to address the possible meaning of these reasons for legislative action at the European level from an economic point of view. First, however, it should be stressed that we can expect to learn more about the specific reasons for legislative action at the European level now that the subsidiarity principle has been introduced explicitly in the Treaty as a result of the so-called Maastricht Treaty. According to this principle, the 'community shall take action if and only in so far as the objectives of the proposed action cannot be sufficiently achieved by the member states and can, therefore, by reason of the scale or effects of the proposed action, be better achieved by the community' (Article 3B(2)).[5] This formulation has not been changed by the Treaty of Amsterdam.

Part II turns to the economic approach by briefly addressing the question: What does economics generally teach about the necessity of harmonization? The remainder of the chapter will then deal with the question of how Europe has dealt with (environmental) subsidiarity in light of the economic criteria of centralization. These criteria have been addressed in the context of the discussion concerning (de)centralization.

II. STARTING POINTS FOR (DE)CENTRALIZATION IN GENERAL[6]

The Tiebout model

The question whether (environmental) regulation should be promulgated at a centralized (that is, European or federal) level or at a more decentralized (that is, state) level has been addressed in the economics of federalism.[7] The starting point for the analysis is usually the theory of Tiebout about the optimal provision of local public goods (Tiebout 1956: 416–24; Rose-Ackerman 1992: 169–70). Tiebout argued that when people with the same preferences cluster together in communities, competition between local authorities will, under certain restrictive conditions, lead to allocative efficiency. If, for example, citizens in one community have a high preference for sporting facilities and citizens in another community have a preference for opera, the first community will probably construct sporting facilities, whereas the second will probably provide an opera house. If someone living in the second community would prefer sporting facilities instead of the opera house, he could then move to the first community, which apparently provides services that better suit his preferences. The idea is that well-informed citizens will move to the community that provides the local services which are best adapted to their personal preferences. This so-called 'voting with the feet' competition between local

[5] For information on the issue of subsidiarity, see Kimber (1995: 321–6).

[6] This part of the chapter is largely based on the inauguration address of Roger Van den Bergh, in which the economic literature provided criteria for (de)centralization are discussed (1994a; 1994b).

[7] In other words, the question is: What kind of environmental regulation should be set at which level?

authorities will lead citizens to cluster together according to their preferences. In practice, one may notice that different communities do indeed offer a variety of different services. The idea is that the citizen can influence this provision of local public goods either by influencing the decision making (vote) or by moving (exit).

Competing legal orders

The Tiebout model applies not only to community services but also to fiscal decisions (Inman and Rubinfeld 1994; Kirchgässnner and Pommerehne 1993; Oates 1972) and environmental choices (Oates and Schwab 1988). In addition, this idea of citizens moving to the community that provides services which best correspond with their preferences, can also be applied with respect to legal rules. Thus it has been argued by Roger Van den Bergh (1998) that competition between legislators will lead to legal systems competing with each other, and thus providing legislation that corresponds best to the preferences of citizens. Similarly, Ogus has argued that the various law makers in the nation-states will create a competitive market for the supply of law (1999). The idea, therefore, is that in an optimal world citizens will cluster together in states that provide legal rules which correspond to their preferences. Well-informed citizens who may be dissatisfied with the legislation provided, could move (voting with their feet) to the community that provides legislation which corresponds best to their preferences. This idea, assuming that different legal systems offer different legal rules, explains the variety and differences between the legal systems (Van den Bergh 1998: 134). Moreover, it shows that differences between the various legal rules of different countries should not necessarily be judged as negative, as is often the case in Europe today. The idea of competing legal systems can probably best be seen 'in action' in private international law, where actors can choose the legal systems that best suit their needs in a choice of law regime.[8] Frey and Eichenberger have proposed an extreme form of this competition between legal orders by suggesting the emergence of Functional Overlapping Competing Jurisdictions (FOCJ), whereby citizens could choose different governmental unities for different functions of government (Casella and Frey 1992: 639; Frey 1996; Frey and Eichenberger 1996: 335).

Obviously, this system, assuming that competition between legal orders leads to allocative efficiency in the provision of legal rules, works only if certain conditions are met. One condition is that citizens have adequate information on the content of the legal rules provided by the various legislators, in order to be able to make an informed choice. In addition, exit is often costly, so people may stay even if the (legal) regime does not optimally suit their needs.[9] Moreover, a location decision

[8] However, the choice of a particular legal regime may not always be related to the quality of the legal system, for instance, but to the quality of the court or arbitration system. The latter explains, according to Ogus, the popularity of English law in choice of law clauses in contracts (1999: 408).

[9] As Ogus states, there should be no barriers to the freedom of establishment and to the movement of capital (1999: 407).

is obviously made under the influence of a set of criteria, whereby the legal regime may not be decisive.[10] Usually job location and residence are so important that in reality there is little left for people to choose (Rose-Ackerman 1992: 169). Finally, as I will discuss below, this system of competition between legal orders works only if the decisions in one legal order have no external effects on others.

'Bottom up federalism'

In economic literature, this Tiebout model is used to argue that, from an economic point of view, decentralization should be the starting point, since competition between legislators will lead to allocative efficiency. Van den Bergh (1998) uses this theory as well to provide criteria for centralization/decentralization within the European Union. Taking the Tiebout model as a starting point and assuming that competition between decentralized legislators will lead to an optimal provision of legal rules, the central question is: Why centralize? Van den Bergh therefore criticizes a part of the current discussion in the European legal literature that seems to focus on the question of why there should be decentralization (referred to by Van den Bergh as 'top-down federalization'). According to economic theory, that is the wrong question. Starting from Tiebout's model, there is reason to believe in what Van den Bergh calls a 'bottom up federalization', assuming that in principle the local level is optimal, since the local level has the best information on local problems and on the preferences of citizens. Only when there is a good reason should decision making be moved to a higher level.[11] Economic theory has indeed suggested that there may be a variety of reasons why the local level is not best suited to take decisions and where central decision making can lead to more efficient results.

III. CRITERIA FOR CENTRALIZATION OF ENVIRONMENTAL ISSUES[12]

Transboundary character of the externality

The Tiebout argument in favour of competition between local communities obviously works only if the problem to be regulated is indeed merely local. Once it is established that the problem to be regulated has a transboundary character, there may be an economies-of-scale argument to shift powers to a higher legal order that has competence to deal with the externality over a larger territory. This corresponds with the basic insight that if the problem to be regulated crosses the borders

[10] That is one of the reasons why Frey and Eichenberger argue in favour of FOCJ: the choice for one legal or institutional regime should not be exclusive; there may be 'overlapping' jurisdictions depending upon the different functions (1996: 316–18).

[11] A major US supporter of this 'presumption in favour of decentralization' is Revesz.

[12] Much of this Part is based upon Esty (1996: 599); Rose-Ackerman (1995); and Stewart (1977).

of competence of the regulatory authority, the decision making power should be shifted to a higher regulatory level, preferably to an authority that has jurisdiction over a territory large enough to adequately deal with the problem (Esty 1996: 625; Kimber 1995; Ogus 1999: 414; Rose-Ackerman 1992: 164–5). As Susan Rose-Ackerman points out, 'Economic theory provides a straight forward but unrealistic answer to regional pollution problems: draw "optimal" jurisdictional boundaries' (1995: 38).

This argument in favour of centralization could play a role with respect to environmental problems, which are often transboundary.[13] The transboundary character of an externality is, within the European context, obviously an important argument for decision making at the European level. Indeed, many environmental problems cross national borders. A great many of the environmental directives fit into this economic criterion for community action. These include the regulation on the transboundary shipment of waste (European Commission 1993c), as well as many other directives which regulate pollution of a transboundary character.[14]

However, some have warned that the argument that centralized powers are necessary to deal with transboundary problems should not be accepted too easily. Daniel Esty and Damien Geradin have powerfully argued against an 'all or nothing' approach, meaning that it is wrong to focus all powers with the local authorities or to shift all powers to the central level. They have argued that transboundary pollution problems can be dealt with via legal instruments other than centralization, such as instruments that do not involve a change of the national environmental laws of a particular country.[15] One possibility is the external application of (domestic) high-standard country laws. Another is the national enforcement of domestic laws with cross-border monitoring. In other words, the transboundary character of the externality may be an argument for cooperation, but not necessarily for homogeneity of legal rules. However, Esty and Geradin admit that these alternative approaches have serious limitations as well and might not be effective remedies in all cases (1998: 34–5).

Marc Cohen has argued that Coasean bargaining between the polluting and the victim state may lead to negotiated agreements between them (Cohen 1996; Van den Bergh 1999). Therefore, Cohen argues that there is no a priori reason to centralize regulatory decision making (1996: 167–71). There might, however, be several reasons why the ideal solution from Coase's world might not be possible to solve transboundary pollution problems, as in the case of transboundary rivers such

[13] Oates and Schwab (1988) also argue that as long as the effects of pollutants are confined within the borders of the relevant jurisdictions, local authorities will make socially optimal decisions of environmental quality.

[14] This is certainly also the case for Directive 76/464 on the Discharge of Dangerous Substances into the Aquatic Environment (European Commission 1976b). For other examples, see Van den Bergh, Faure, and Lefevere (1996: 131–2).

[15] Esty and Geradin (1997; 1998) provide an interesting overview of the various legal instruments dealing with harmonization and apply this in the NAFTA and European contexts. See also Trebilcock and Howse (1998).

as the Rhine or the Meuse. First, Coase assumes that property rights are clearly defined (Cohen 1996: 168–9). Although there are some indications in international environmental law on this point, it might not be certain whether the legal rule is the right to pollute or the polluter pays. This uncertainty concerning the assignment of property rights might endanger negotiations. Second, adequate information is needed both on the consequences of pollution and on the possible abatement techniques (Cohen 1996: 168). Third, there may be no strategic behaviour. Finally, parties need to be able to enforce a negotiated agreement.

In that respect, the EC framework might have several advantages. The European Community offers an institutional framework that provides legal instruments to enforce an agreement. Moreover, the EC regulatory framework might fix the property rights uncertainty. Also, the fact that member states within the EC framework are repeat players (he who is an injurer today may be a victim tomorrow) may cure the risk of strategic behaviour. If one also looks at the practice of transboundary pollution in Europe, one may argue that the EC approach has achieved far better results than all attempts towards bilateral agreements. For example, EC directives on (transboundary) pollution of waters provided Dutch victims of Belgian pollution of the river Meuse with a powerful tool to force the Belgians to perform pollution abatement (Pâques 1996),[16] a result which probably could never have been achieved through the long-lasting negotiations between the two countries. Thus the European Commission has undoubtedly played an important role as far as providing remedies against transboundary pollution is concerned.

However, Van den Bergh has demonstrated that in certain situations, particularly in the area of private law, European law cannot be considered an effective remedy to the interstate externality problem (1998: 143). In some cases, European law goes further than is needed to cure transboundary externalities; in other cases, less far-reaching legal instruments than total harmonization could be used to remedy the problem (144–5). There is, in other words, always the risk that the cure may be worse than the disease. The first issue relates to the problem that European directives often cover both local and community-wide pollution, without making a distinction between regional and interstate pollution (Van den Bergh 1999: 10). The second point is that in some cases transboundary externalities may also be internalized by national law. The simple fact of transboundary effects is therefore not sufficient to justify European law making (Van den Bergh 1998: 144–5). Nevertheless, there can indeed be cases where one can hold that decentralized legal rule making will not be able to remedy the transboundary externality.

The most important reason for community action with respect to the environment is therefore probably not the often stated argument of the 'harmonization of conditions of competition', but simply the transboundary character of the pollution problem to be regulated. Many of the environmental directives indeed deal with pollution problems that cross the borders of one single member state. These can be

[16] For the case of the river Rhine, see Van Dunné (1991).

justified under this first economic criterion. Obviously, this does not necessarily imply that the contents of every directive on this point have been efficient, nor that the instruments used to cure transboundary pollution have always been optimal. Indeed, in some cases the European Commission considers the transboundary character of a problem as a sufficient justification for centralized rule making without differentiating between local and transboundary pollution.[17] Moreover, a great many of the environmental directives also deal with relatively 'local' problems that do not cross national borders. The question therefore arises whether an economic rationale can be found for European jurisdiction in those cases where the effects of pollutants are confined within the borders of the relevant member states.

'Race to the bottom'

Risk of destructive competition

There may be an economic argument for a regulation of local pollution problems, in that there is a risk that a 'race to the bottom' between countries would emerge to attract foreign investments. As a result of this, prisoners' dilemmas could arise, whereby countries would fail to enact or enforce efficient legislation. Centralization can be advanced as a remedy for these prisoners' dilemmas. This 'race-to-the-bottom' argument could in theory play a role in environmental cases as well (Esty and Geradin 1998: 16–19). It would mean that local governments would compete with lenient environmental legislation to attract industry (Rose-Ackerman 1992: 166–70). The result would be an overall reduction of environmental quality below efficient levels. This should correspond with the traditional game theory result that prisoners' dilemmas create inefficiencies.

This 'race-to-the-bottom' argument, that competition among jurisdictions for economic activity will be 'destructive', follows the European legal argument that the creation of harmonized conditions of competition is necessary to avoid trade distortions. As indicated above, this argument was traditionally used to harmonize legislation of the member states in a variety of areas. Simply stated, the argument is that complying with legislation imposes costs on industry. If legislation is different, then the costs will differ as well and conditions of competition within the common market will not be equal. The argument apparently assumes that total equality of conditions of competition is necessary for the functioning of the common market. 'Levelling the playing field' for European industry remains the central message.

The 'race-to-the-bottom' argument has had several supporters and opponents in US scholarship. Law and economics scholars tend to stress the benefits of competition between states and point at the danger of centralization (Revesz 1992; 1996), whereas some legal scholars tend to profess a stronger belief in the 'race-to-the-bottom' rationale for centralization in environmental matters (Esty and Geradin

[17] Directive 74/464 regulates discharges of dangerous substances into the aquatic environment for both transboundary rivers and local pounds (European Commission 1976b).

1997; 1998). In Europe, these issues are rarely discussed in the context of the 'race to the bottom', but rather in the EC dogma of 'levelling the playing field to avoid distortions of competition'. This somewhat confuses the debate. The 'harmonization-of-conditions-of-competition' argument could either be interpreted narrowly in 'race-to-the-bottom' terms or more broadly as a general argument to harmonize all kinds of rules and standards. The latter is the usual interpretation in Europe.

'Race to the bottom' versus 'common market'

There are, however, some problems with this traditional European argument, which claims that any difference in legislation between the member states might endanger the conditions of competition and therefore justifies harmonization of legal rules. The latter argument seems particularly weak. From an economic point of view, the mere fact that conditions of competition differ does not necessarily create a 'race-to-the-bottom' risk. There can be differences in marketing conditions for a variety of reasons, and if the conditions of competition were indeed totally equal, as the argument assumes, there would also be no trade.

Also, Europe has developed an elaborate set of rules that guarantees, *inter alia*, a free flow of products and services (Articles 28–30 [30–36] of the Treaty) and thus contributes to market integration without needing to harmonize all rules and standards.[18] In this respect, one can think of the case law of the European Court of Justice regarding the free movement of goods versus environmental protection.[19] This shows that the goal of market integration can be achieved via (other) less far reaching instruments than total harmonization (Esty and Geradin 1997: 296–9; Ogus 1994a: 177–9) which can equally remove barriers to trade. Hence one should make a distinction between the political ideal of creating one common market in Europe on the one hand and the (economic) 'race-to-the-bottom' argument on the other hand (Revesz 1997c). This political goal of market integration may, as such, be questioned on economic grounds (Van den Bergh 1999) and may justify the need for rules aimed at a reduction of trade restrictions, such as a harmonization of product standards.[20] The problem in environmental law is that initiatives in that area also aim at a harmonization of process standards to harmonize conditions of competition. That seems questionable on efficiency grounds (Revesz, Ch. 1). Thus, what can be said about this 'harmonization-of-conditions-of-competition' argument either in its 'race-to-the-bottom' or 'common market' version?

From an economic perspective, differences in the conditions of competition only pose a problem if it is clear that environmental costs would be considerably different between the member states and that these differences would lead to the

[18] For information on the potential conflict between free trade and environmental protection, see Esty (1999a).

[19] For an overview of this case law, see Lefevere and Faure (1995) and Trebilcock and Howse (1998: 21–8).

[20] These were the result of directives issued as a consequence of the so-called 'Single Market Initiative' (Vogel 2000).

relocation of firms to the member states with the lowest standards.[21] In that case, the so-called 'race-to-the-bottom' argument, in environmental cases referred to as the 'pollution haven' hypothesis, might be an argument in favour of centralization.[22] The question therefore arises whether there is empirical evidence that states can indeed attract industry by lenient environmental standards.

Empirical evidence of 'pollution havens'

Empirical evidence to uphold this 'race-to-the-bottom' rationale is rather weak. Robert Repetto argues that pollution control costs are only a minor fraction of the total sales of manufacturing industries (1994). Moreover, Jaffee *et al.* (1995) have argued that empirical evidence shows that the effects of environmental regulations are 'either small, statistically insignificant or not robust to tests of model specification'. They maintain that the stringency of environmental regulations might have some effect on new firms in their decision to locate for the first time (Esty and Geradin 1998: 12–15), but that this will not induce existing firms to relocate. They equally argue that other criteria, such as tax levels, public services, and the unionization of the labour force, have a much more significant impact on the location decision than environmental regulation. Recently this empirical evidence has been somewhat contradicted by Yuqing Xing and Charles Kolstad (1995), who have found that the laxity of environmental regulations in a host country is a significant determinant of foreign direct investment by the US chemical industry. The more lax the regulations, the more likely the country is to attract foreign investment, so Xing and Kolstad claim. Although this somewhat weakens the evidence presented by Jaffee *et al.* (1995) as far as the location of new firms outside the United States is concerned, it does not contradict their finding that existing firms will not relocate because of the stringency of environmental regulations (Esty and Geradin 1997: 272).

This material, therefore, debilitates the prisoners' dilemma argument. Moreover, as far as environmental standards are concerned, it is not at all clear that there will be a race to the bottom. Some evidence suggests that member states precisely try to strive for high environmental standards, even if this puts extra costs or burdens on their industry. Some countries may actually be more involved in a 'race to the top' than a 'race to the bottom' (Van den Bergh, Faure and Lefevere 1996: 141–2).[23] One could also wonder whether European law is at all able to remedy a real 'race-to-the-bottom' risk, given the enforcement deficit.

[21] Revesz also argues that, given the weaknesses of the 'harmonization-of-conditions-of-competition' argument, it is not surprising that recent European scholarship has sought to recharacterize the quest for harmonization in race to the bottom terms (Ch.1).

[22] However, Esty and Geradin have rightly pointed out the fact that a whole variety of legal instruments exists which may remedy the problem, whereby the total harmonization of standards would be the most far reaching (1997: 282–94).

[23] Ogus argues that there may be benefits to firms located in a high-standard member state, since they may generate technological advancements and thus competitive advantages; this may explain the 'race to the top' (Ogus 1999: 415; Vogel 1995; Trebilcock and Howse 1998: 13–14).

'Levelling the playing field'

The European argument that markets will be distorted without a harmonization of conditions of competition is not only constantly repeated in a stereotypical way, but its validity is hardly ever questioned. The argument, as it is usually presented in Europe, cannot fit into the economic criteria for centralization, since it suggests that removing any difference in legal systems would be necessary to cure the 'race-to-the-bottom' risk, which is neither supported by economic theory nor by empirical evidence. Even if one took the (political) 'common market' goal as a starting point and environmental regulations were harmonized on that ground, a level playing field still would not be created since differences in, for example, energy sources, access to raw materials, and atmospheric conditions will lead to divergent market conditions (Van den Bergh 1999: 6).

There is, in addition, a strong counter-argument, in that there are many examples showing that economic market integration is possible (without the distortions predicted by the race-to-the-bottom argument) with differentiated legal orders. Public choice scholars have often advanced the Swiss federal model as an example where economic market integration goes hand in hand with differentiated legal systems (Frey 1994: 338–42). It is apparently possible to create a common market without a total harmonization of all legal rules and standards (Revesz, Ch. 1).

Arguments against the 'race-to-the-bottom' rationale for centralized environmental regulation have also been formulated with respect to the US example. Many scholars, and in particular Revesz, have argued that this race-to-the-bottom argument finds no support in existing models of interjurisdictional competition (Elliott, Ackerman, and Millian 1985; Peltzman and Tideman 1972; Revesz 1992: 1996). In addition, Revesz stresses that central standard setting would not be an effective response to the race-to-the-bottom problem, since the local communities concerned would have other means to attract industry if they wish (by relaxing regulatory controls in other areas). Revesz has encountered opposition, especially from Esty (1996), but he has provided a powerful reply to his critics (Revesz 1997e).

These arguments therefore weaken the prisoners' dilemma argument in the field of environmental law both in its 'race-to-the-bottom' form and in the (disguised) way it is presented in the European debate. The European argument—that any difference in legal rules between the member states would endanger market integration and therefore a harmonization of law is needed in order to harmonize conditions of competition[24]—is too general, too unbalanced, and not supported by economic theory. Differences between legal systems of member states may, from an economic point of view, constitute a problem, if this would result in an inefficient race to the bottom. But the empirical evidence available suggests that this may not be a serious risk in the environmental field. Even if differences in the stringency of environmental law exist between member states, this will generally not lead

[24] For support, see the formulation in the preamble to the Products Liability Directive (European Commission 1985a).

companies to relocate to 'pollution havens' within Europe. The least one can argue is that if the European Commission were to use a 'race-to-the-bottom' rationale for centralization, it should prove that without centralization in the specific field a risk of destructive competition would emerge.[25] The debate in Europe has, so far, never focused on that question,[26] since it was always argued that any harmonization of legal rules was necessary to achieve market integration, which obviously confuses the debate.

Reduction of transaction costs?

There may, however, be one final economic argument in favour of harmonization, based on transaction costs reduction.[27] This is often advanced by European legal scholars pleading for harmonization of private law in Europe, and is based upon the argument that differences in legal systems are very complex and only serve Brussels law firms.[28] This argument cannot be examined in detail here.[29] It is obviously too simple to state that a harmonized legal system is always more efficient than differentiated legal rules because of the transaction costs savings inherent in harmonized rules.[30] The argument neglects the fact that there are substantial benefits from differentiation when legislation can be adapted to the preferences of individuals (Mendelsohn 1986: 301). Furthermore, given the differences between the legal systems (and legal cultures) in Europe, the costs of harmonization may be huge, if not prohibitive (Legrand 1997: 111). The crucial question then is whether the possible transaction cost savings of harmonization outweigh the benefits of differentiated legal rules. Yet, there is little empirical evidence to support the statement that transaction costs savings could justify a European harmonization of all kinds of legal rules. Moreover, the transaction cost savings are likely to be relatively small (Van den Bergh 1998: 146–8).

The transaction costs argument could, however, play a role to justify the so-called negative harmonization, which aims at a coordination of, for example, product standards to prevent states from hindering a free flow of products and services (Vogel, Ch. 15). While this type of cooperation between states can reduce transaction costs, it does not necessitate a homogenization of process standards, which is often the goal in environmental law.

[25] In that case there may seriously be a valid argument for an intervention by Brussels. In the US context, consider the remark by Rose-Ackerman, 'If state and local laws seem designed to protect local business rather than reflect genuine differences in tastes across jurisdictions, the federal government should take a hard look to determine the possible interference with interstate commerce' (1992: 173).

[26] Esty and Geradin (1997: 308) argue that the risk of a regulatory race to the bottom for environmental reasons has not been a major issue in the European Community.

[27] For a somewhat related but different argument relating to economies and diseconomies of scale in administration, see Rose-Ackerman (1992: 165–6).

[28] This is one of the arguments made by the Danish scholar Lando in favour of harmonized private law (1993: 473–4).

[29] It is further developed and criticized in a recent paper by Van den Bergh (1998).

[30] Rose-Ackerman argues that uniform federal regulation may reduce search costs and produce a more stable and predictable jurisprudence (1992: 172).

The conclusion is that the economic argument to harmonize environmental rules with respect to problems that are not transboundary is relatively weak. Nevertheless, many European directives (for example, addressing drinking water or bathing water) deal with problems which are not typically transboundary, and for which economic theory does not justify European level involvement. However, can a non-economic argument be advanced for regulation at the European level?

'European heritage'?

'Psychic spillovers'?

Can this argument support environmental protection at the European level? The protection of habitats and entire ecosystems comes to mind. A traditional example is the question whether there should be any European jurisdiction to protect an imaginary turtle that has, say, only one habitat, which is in Greece. The traditional economic argument in such a case would be that since the problem is merely local, the Greek population should decide whether or not to protect the turtle. An attempt in the direction of an economic argument for European competence has been made by Wouter Wils, who classifies the protection of endangered species as justified by the fact that this endangerment causes 'psychic spillovers' (1994: 85–90). The argument then follows that the endangerment of the Greek turtle would also harm the interests of, for example, a Dutch citizen living in Maastricht, who would suffer a psychic spillover from the fact that the Greek turtle would be endangered.[31] According to this view, the externality would be considered transboundary (although the turtle lives only in Greece) and there would, again, be an economic rationale for centralization.[32] Perhaps this argument still holds for turtles or for Italian nature parks, because their well-being also affects other European citizens.[33] But what about a European directive regulating the quality of drinking water in Greece?

Differentiation according to preferences

A European directive regulating the quality of drinking water in Greece seems, at first sight, contrary to basic economic logic. From an economic point of view, the environmental quality to be provided could differ according to differing preferences of citizens (Ogus 1994b: 25–30; 1999: 413). Again from an economic point of view, there is no reason for centralization if the externalities are local and no prisoners' dilemmas exist. This economic argument in favour of differentiation according to the preferences of citizens is not only valid for the question of whether or

[31] However, consider Esty's statement: 'The health of ecosystems to which we have no physical connection may enter directly into our utility calculus' (1996).

[32] Ogus argues that harmonization may be justified if foreigners derive disutility from observing the plight of victims in the offending state (1999: 418).

[33] However, the Greeks should probably be compensated for the extra costs involved in this European habitat protection (Rose-Ackerman 1995: 42–3).

not the Greek turtle should be protected at the European level;[34] it is also valid for the whole body of environmental law, and especially for environmental quality standards. This corresponds with the Tiebout model of competition between legal orders where citizens are free to choose the environmental quality that corresponds optimally with their preferences. The consequence of this economic approach is that it should be for Greece to decide to prefer economic development rather than environmental quality.[35] A consequence of this economic argument whereby citizens choose a level of environmental protection according to their preference should obviously be that the environmental quality would vary according to the individual preferences of citizens. This argument is also used at the normative level in the United States, where there are increasing pleas in favour of standard setting by the states rather than by the federal environmental agency (Schoenbrod 1996: 18–25). This economic argument therefore leads to an environmental federalism in which environmental quality between member states could differ as long as there are no transboundary effects and no 'race-to-the-bottom' risks.[36]

Guaranteeing a basic environmental quality?

There is, however, an important legal or policy argument which could lead to centralization. This has to do with the idea of guaranteeing to all European citizens similar environmental quality. This is sometimes referred to as the protection of the 'European environmental and cultural heritage and human health'. If this argument is accepted at the policy level, it could be used to harmonize environmental quality. However, note that the reason for centralization in such a case would not be the economic need of market integration, but the ecological desire to guarantee all citizens within the European Union a similar, or at least basic, level of environmental quality. The consequence would then be that, contrary to economic logic, it is not the preferences of citizens that would prevail, but the policy desire to provide one basic level of environmental quality in Europe.[37] This corresponds with the point made by Ogus that the preferences of citizens for lower standards at lower costs may sometimes be overruled if it is held that these low standards would infringe widely held perceptions of human rights.[38] In the environmental context,

[34] To be very specific, this chapter is not concerned with the normative question of whether or not the Greek turtle deserves protection. It is concerned only with the question of whether such a decision should be taken in Greece or at the European Community level.

[35] Again, this is not to say that Greece should not protect the environment, but only to argue that, from an economic point of view, this is not a question about which Brussels should be concerned.

[36] However, since firms are in a competitive environment, a member state that chooses to impose a high level of protection (and thus high costs on firms) will have to compensate with lower taxes on wages in order to avoid the exit of business (Rose-Ackerman 1995: 41).

[37] Yet Esty argues in favour of global environmental norms that should represent a behavioural minimum. Revesz's argument is, however, critical towards such an approach.

[38] 'Rights may, in this instance, justifiably "trump" efficiency' (Ogus 1999: 418). Cohen calls for minimum quality standards at a centralized level for reasons of 'equity, justice, or pure paternalism' (1996: 170). Likewise, Stewart states that geographically uniform standards ensure every individual a minimum level of a healthy environment, even though such uniformity is economically inefficient (1977).

this point could take the form of guaranteeing a basic level of environmental quality to all citizens.[39]

Again, I am not arguing at the normative level that this would not be a valid argument for centralization, but it is important to stress that if this argument for centralization is used, it is only for ecological (or policy) reasons, not for economic reasons, that one would strive for harmonization of environmental quality. A problem with this 'European heritage' argument is that it may be valid to defend a European-wide protection of, say, the Colosseum in Rome,[40] but less so to guarantee a minimum environmental quality. In that case it would make more sense to strive for a European-wide minimum level of public health, which is not the case today.

But if this 'European heritage' reason for centralization in order to guarantee to all European citizens a basic level of environmental quality is accepted, there are several consequences. If externalities are merely local and no 'race-to-the-bottom' risks exist, it is hard to find an economic rationale for centralization. At the policy level, truly ecological reasons can be advanced for centralization to guarantee a similar standard of environmental quality throughout the European Union. But then this ecological argument, not the 'harmonization-of-conditions-of-competition' argument, has to be advanced to justify, for example, the guarantee of a minimum level of environmental quality in Greece. In addition, if the idea is accepted that it is for ecological reasons (harmonizing environmental quality in the European Union) that centralization is needed, this has consequences for environmental standard setting.

IV. CONSEQUENCES FOR ENVIRONMENTAL STANDARD SETTING[41]

Introduction

Esty and Geradin have rightly paid attention to the fact that 'centralization' is too general a concept, which may cover a whole variety of legal techniques to achieve a harmonization of rules, standards, or procedures (1998: 39–46). I cannot discuss all the techniques that have been used in Europe so far to construe what is now considered to be the area of 'European environmental law'. I will focus on two types of standards, ambient quality standards and emission standards, to address the issue of which of these should be harmonized at the European level. These are of particular interest because they allow us to consider whether the goal of European action should be (economic) market integration or the guarantee to European

[39] As Kimber states, 'An analogy may be drawn here with human rights. It is arguable that certain minimum standards of environmental protection ought to be achieved by all countries and regions, particularly if one accepts that the environment is the common heritage of us all' (1995: 1690).

[40] At the same time, there is the transboundary ('psychic') spillover which justifies European intervention.

[41] The arguments made in this Part of the chapter have been developed in Faure and Lefevere (1999).

citizens of a basic level of environmental quality. I will argue that the choice between those goals has consequences for the types of standards one wishes to harmonize; moreover, I will argue that the type of harmonization selected by the European Commission so far does not correspond with the policy goal set.

Environmental (ambient) quality standards

If it is a policy decision to guarantee a basic level of environmental quality to all European citizens, irrespective of individual preferences, quality standards should be harmonized. This idea can now often be found in European rhetoric,[42] and this clearly shows the difference between the economic and the legal approach. From an economic perspective, the quality standards could be differentiated, taking into account individual preferences (Ogus 1994a). The European idea of guaranteeing a basic level of environmental quality can be realized only through harmonized quality standards, to which the environmental components in the European Union should, in principle, correspond. These quality standards, also referred to as target standards, should then of course be the standards of an ideal level of environmental quality to be achieved and not merely standards that function as a 'red flag', as has sometimes been the case. Obviously, this assumes that Europe would set powers to monitor whether these quality standards are actually achieved, which is not the case today.

Emission limit values

If it is accepted that in Europe a basic level of environmental quality should be guaranteed through harmonized quality (target) standards, the next step is to ask how these standards can be achieved. The quality standards will be influenced by the specific emissions coming from various sources. However, according to the theory of optimal specificity of legal rules (Ehrlich and Posner 1974; Ogus 1994a; 1994b), the costs of meeting a certain level of environmental protection (in other words, the target) may well vary according to location-specific circumstances (Esty and Geradin 1997; 1998; Faure and Lefevere 1996; Kolstad 1987). In the words of Esty and Geradin, 'Differential standards are more economically efficient than total harmonization because they better match regulatory requirements to localized needs' (1998: 43).

For example, the local conditions in Belgium or Germany may be totally different from those in Portugal or Greece. Hence the emission limit values which are needed to reach a similar environmental quality within the European Union will

[42] For example, the Wild Birds Directive states: 'whereas conservation is aimed at the long-term protection and management of natural resources as an integral part of the heritage of the peoples of Europe' (European Commission 1979). Obviously, the European heritage was not the only justification for the Wild Birds Directive. Since birds tend to fly, the transboundary character of the issue comes into the picture as well (Van den Bergh, Faure, and Lefevere 1996).

have to take these differences into account.[43] The inevitable conclusion is that where the environmental quality (target) to be reached may be uniform, the emission limit values have to vary according to the location-specific circumstances and will therefore be differentiated.[44] An obvious consequence is that firms operating in member states that are less polluted can have less stringent emission limit values and can therefore market their products at lower prices. Thus, they acquire a competitive advantage (Esty and Geradin 1997: 271, 306). Again, this should not be a problem as long as these differences do not pose a 'race-to-the-bottom' risk.[45]

European practice

This approach of harmonized target standards, but differentiated emission limit values, has not been the European policy so far. Indeed, the often mentioned Directive 76/464 attempts to harmonize emission limit values,[46] and even the recent IPPC Directive still explicitly refers to the setting of emission limit values at the community level.[47] This idea of harmonizing emission limit values runs counter to the idea of achieving a uniform environmental quality: harmonized emission limit values will obviously lead to differentiated environmental quality. This was precisely the point made by the United Kingdom during the heavy discussions preceding Directive 76/464 concerning the prevention of water pollution by certain dangerous substances. The United Kingdom therefore pleaded in favour of harmonized ambient quality standards (Esty and Geradin 1997: 305–6).

The conclusion is that the European approach of harmonizing emission limit values on the basis of the 'levelling-the-playing-field' argument runs counter to the idea of achieving one similar environmental quality in Europe and, moreover, is not necessary to facilitate market integration.[48] Hence, as far as environmental

[43] Esty and Geradin rightly argue that an intervention to eliminate differences in standards which reflect natural locational advantages would not be a good policy (1997: 271).

[44] Revesz appropriately states: 'The harmonization argument cannot be used, as it has in the European Union, to justify both uniform ambient standards and uniform emission standards' (Revesz 1997c: 1339–40; 2000: 25).

[45] If there is a 'race-to-the-bottom' risk, interjurisdictional differences will still lead to inefficiencies (Rose-Ackerman 1995: 40–1).

[46] Even though Esty and Geradin (1997: 304) correctly mention that this is merely a minimum harmonization (and member states are allowed to adopt stricter national standards), the preamble to the Directive clearly states that 'levelling the playing field' is the ultimate goal of this Directive: 'Any disparity between the provisions in the discharge of certain dangerous substances into the aquatic environment already applicable or in preparation in the various member states may create unequal conditions of competition and thus directly affect the functioning of the common market' (European Commission 1976b). The 'minimum' harmonization does not solve the problem of member states who argue that even the 'minimum' is too strict and unnecessary to reach the environmental quality, given their specific local conditions.

[47] Article 18 of the IPPC Directive explicitly refers to the possibility of setting Community emission limit values (European Commission 1996b).

[48] In the words of Van den Bergh, 'This alignment of EC environmental policy to the market integration goal diverts the attention away from economic welfare oriented criteria for the diffusion of powers between the European Community and the member states' (Van den Bergh 1999: 5).

policy is concerned, Europe has been 'harmonizing for the wrong reasons' (Faure 1998: 169–75). Probably, to some extent, there is a historical explanation for this. Before the Single European Act introduced in 1987 the ability to issue directives merely for environmental reasons, it was only possible to issue directives 'to harmonize conditions of competition'. Since this was the legal basis for the environmental directives before 1987, it is likely that the Commission simply continued to refer to this 'wrong reason' even when another legal basis was already available.

V. POLICY CONSIDERATIONS FOR EUROPE

Several conclusions can be drawn from this analysis. First, if Europe is concerned with ecological goals and wishes to achieve a uniform level of environmental quality throughout the European Union, it should set harmonized target standards. Europe should, in other words, be interested in the end product: the level of environmental quality to be reached. This also assumes that Europe would receive powerful tools to monitor whether this environmental quality is actually achieved (which is still a major weakness today[49]) and to enforce the target in cases of non-compliance. The fact that it is difficult to monitor the actual quality of the environment may also explain why Europe has long preferred directives containing emission standards whereby the Commission only checked whether there was a correct formal implementation in the legislation of the member states.

Second, in order to reach this uniform level of environmental quality, the emission limit values should be differentiated. This differentiation is efficient as long as the benefits of differentiation outweigh the (administrative) costs.

Third, the conclusion that differentiated emission limit values, taking into account location-specific circumstances, are necessary to achieve uniform environmental quality does not necessarily imply that values should be set by the member states. The member states may have the advantage of better information on location-specific circumstances (Kimber 1995: 1662); on the other hand, it is also conceivable that differentiated emission limit values could be set at the European level. This would be the case if one fears regulatory capture of member states by special interests representing industry. Thus there can be centralization of decision making in Brussels, but not necessarily harmonization of standards. This would amount to a balanced and flexible solution of joint competences. However, this assumes that no serious risk of a 'race to the bottom' exists.

Fourth, some emission limit values can still be European-wide, such as a prohibition on emitting carcinogenic substances, which will always have a strong negative impact on environmental quality. The same can be said for some 'minimum standard' harmonization which may be supported by an assumption of

[49] In Europe, there is no enforcement agency that possesses police powers because this is considered by member states to violate their sovereignty (Kimber 1995: 1685; Ogus 1994a: 212–13; Pfander 1996: 72–5).

homogeneity of preferences (Ogus 1994b; 1999). This point somewhat weakens our critique of European environmental law. Indeed, the rhetoric of 'harmonization of conditions of competition' seems wrong, or at least not reconcilable with the ecological goal of 'guaranteeing a minimum environmental quality'. However, in practice, many directives, such as that on the discharge of dangerous substances into the aquatic environment, deal with a prohibition on emitting carcinogenic substances. Such a prohibition at the European level could well be defended in economic terms under the assumption of the homogeneity of preferences.

Fifth, an obvious consequence of accepting the idea that emission limit values can be differentiated is that values in less polluted member states might be more lenient than in states which are more polluted. The conclusion, therefore, is that if the policy goal is uniform environmental quality, harmonization of conditions of competition should not be the goal. That would then lead to precisely the opposite result because environmental quality would be differentiated.

Sixth, it follows that the idea of harmonization of conditions of competition, as it is pronounced as a goal for European environmental action, is wrong for several reasons. It is wrong for economic reasons, since full harmonization of conditions of competition is not needed to reach the economic goals of the Treaty; and it is equally wrong for ecological reasons, since it does not allow for the goal of uniform environmental quality. The conclusion may only be different if externalities are transboundary or there is a serious risk of a run to pollution havens. However, while these may be the arguments for the harmonization of emission limit values, it should be clear that this may lead to differentiations in environmental quality. In this case, European policy makers will have to make a choice between either 'levelling the playing field' through harmonized emission standards or ecological harmonization of environmental quality. One way to (partially) reconcile these goals is to shift powers to Brussels because of the transboundary character of the externality, but to set differentiated emission limit values (Esty and Geradin 1997: 291). There are examples in the United States as well of federal regulatory programmes that take into account geographical differences (Rose-Ackerman 1992: 165).

VI. A PUBLIC CHOICE PERSPECTIVE

An obviously crucial question is why this model of differentiated emission limit values is not always followed in European legal practice, where one can still note a strong tendency to harmonize emission limit values at the European level. One explanation may be that the European Commission harmonizes emission limit values in cases where externalities are transboundary or a serious 'race-to-the-bottom' risk exists. Then harmonization would fit into the economic reasons for centralization and could be considered 'in the public interest'. Nevertheless, Europe harmonizes emission standards much more generally 'to harmonize marketing conditions' in cases where the economic criteria do not call for centralization. Why? One explanation can obviously be found in the fact that Europe has been harmonizing to 'level the playing field', not merely to remedy a 'race-to-the-bottom' risk. Another reason is found in public choice theory, which focuses on the role of interest groups in legislation (Yandle 1999). Lobbying activities at the European level are extremely strong.[50] Additionally, with respect to environmental standard setting, intensive rent-seeking behaviour by interest groups can be identified.

In this respect, one should note that one important difference between Europe and the United States has to do with the fact that European scholars fear regulatory capture, especially in Brussels, as a result of the lack of transparency of the Brussels bureaucracy. The point made by US scholars that the risk of capture is larger at the state level may be true in the US context, when compared to the open, transparent debate that can take place at the federal level.[51] In Europe, however, industry may be confronted with 'green' non-governmental organizations (NGOs) at the member state level, at least in 'green' member states like Denmark and Germany,[52] whereas those countervailing powers are almost absent in Brussels. Hence one can expect European industry (located in the industrialized but 'green' member states) to engage in serious lobbying efforts, particularly in Brussels.[53]

In certain cases, special interest groups representing industry might, understandably, lobby in favour of a harmonization of European emission limit values (Esty and Geradin 1997: 303). Interest groups in areas that are already heavily regulated may have incentives to extend their strict (national) regulations to the European level, forcing foreign competitors to follow the same strict regulations with which they already comply. The result is that industry will lobby to erect artificial barriers to entry. In addition, green NGOs will be pleased with this lobby and will obviously support the demand to transfer strict national standards into a European standard.[54] Thus industries in heavily regulated (and probably polluted) areas can (supported by green NGOs) force their very stringent emission limit values upon their (southern) competitors, although these member states probably would not need such stringent values if the policy goal were one of reaching a uniform level of environmental quality.

This is precisely what happened with the IPPC Directive. A strong lobbying exercise in favour of emission limit values at the community level was undertaken by German industry (Faure and Lefevere 1996). They argued that industries in

[50] For a discussion of harmonization efforts from a public choice perspective, see Van den Bergh (1998: 129).

[51] However, Rose-Ackerman (1992: 171) argues that in the United States, unlike in Europe, citizens may favour federal intervention, since special interests representing industry would be more powerful at the state and local level than they are nationally.

[52] This may be less the case in the southern countries.

[53] For details, see Faure and Lefevere (1994: 334–42).

[54] These 'alliances' between environmentalists and domestic producers are also discussed by David Vogel in his contribution to this volume (Ch. 15).

other member states should bear the same costs that German producers already had to bear (as a result of strict domestic standards) (Esty and Geradin 1997: 30). Thus it becomes clear that the 'harmonization-of-conditions-of-competition' argument is used by industries in heavily regulated areas to erect barriers to entry. Their competitors from member states with more lenient environmental standards may indeed not have the ability to comply with these more stringent environmental standards. The southern member states (and, once again, the United Kingdom) therefore understandably lobbied in favour of harmonized ambient quality standards with domestic emission limit values (Esty and Geradin 1997: 307). Hence environmental law can be used to limit market entry, and abused to serve private interest goals.

This leads to the conclusion that the 'harmonization-of-conditions-of-competition' argument, as presented in European rhetoric, is problematic, from both the economic and ecological points of view, and in fact serves the interests of industrial groups in heavily regulated areas.[55] It may be in their interests that 'conditions of competition' are actually harmonized.

VII. CONCLUDING REMARKS

In this chapter, I used the economic literature on federalism to provide a critical look at some aspects of the harmonization of environmental law in Europe. In fact, I have only dealt with two specific, but important, aspects of European environmental law. First, I have sought to provide an economic analysis of the traditional European argument that conditions of competition should be harmonized to 'create a level playing field'. This argument is too general to fit into the economic criteria for centralization. The economic literature provides for a balanced answer with respect to the types of subject matter that should be regulated at the centralized or decentralized level. This shows that the questions concerning centralization/harmonization cannot be answered in black or white statements. The European argument of equalization of marketing conditions is apparently difficult to fit into the economic model. This relates to the second point examined in this chapter: what the goal of harmonization of environmental law should be and how this relates to the issue of standard setting. If European environmental policy is, as is sometimes stated, to promote uniform environmental quality within the European Union, this can be reached by setting a harmonized environmental quality, to be enforced by the Commission, but with differentiated emission standards. As I have discussed, some European directives aim at the harmonization of emission standards to 'harmonize conditions of competition'. Although I criticized the

[55] This is not to say that there is no risk of regulatory capture resulting in inefficient standards at the level of the member states. For information on the US context, see Rose-Ackerman (1992: 166, 173). However, in Europe, it is especially the untransparent Brussels bureaucracy that is feared from a public choice perspective.

rhetoric used, I equally indicated that the result (for example, a prohibition on emitting carcinogenic substances) may sometimes be well justified, at least if one takes into account the quality goals set.

Of course, some may reply that the conclusion of the chapter—that some pieces of European action with respect to environmental law do not correspond with the economic model of centralization—should not be surprising. There may have been other, non-economic, reasons for action at the European level with respect to environmental quality. One reason may be the simple fact that the European bureaucracy of the Commission could justify its legitimacy through these environmental directives. The fact that bureaucracies have their own incentives to seek justifications to increase their competences is well known. However, this argument may have been valid in the 1970s when the Commission probably 'needed' environmental directives to justify its existence, but is less valid today now that European powers have substantially increased as a result of the Treaties of Maastricht and Amsterdam. Moreover, the Commission cannot simply neglect the economic criteria of centralization now that 'raising the standard of living and quality of life' has been promoted to one of the goals of the Treaty in Article 2. Economic concepts can certainly be useful in reaching this goal.

It is, moreover, possible that in the future the consensus on European action with respect to the environment might be more in line with the economic approach. In that respect, the Proposal of the Commission for a Council Directive establishing a framework for community action in the field of water policy is quite promising (European Commission 1997b). The focus of this framework directive is indeed to set quality standards at the European level, but to let member states and local authorities decide on the means to achieve these objectives.

To reiterate, this chapter does not deal with the basic normative question concerning the need for environmental regulation. That is undisputed. It is concerned only with the question of the level at which, within a European Union, environmental rules and standards should be set, given different policy goals. It was shown that economic literature can provide important guidance in that respect and that harmonization in fact sometimes serves industry, not ecological interests. One should, however, be somewhat cautious about generalizing the results of US (economic) studies on environmental federalism to the situation in Europe, since there are many differences.[56] One is the lack of transparency at the European level, which explains why some European scholars especially fear regulatory capture in Brussels (Esty 1996: 609–11) more than in member states.[57] Another is that Europe has practically no powers to enforce, for example, European-wide ambient quality standards. This may also explain the reluctance to rely heavily on these. It is obviously easier for the Commission to force member states to impose emission standards where it only checks whether member states

[56] One is obviously the degree of market integration (Van den Bergh 1999: 5).

[57] To the contrary, Rose-Ackerman (1992: 166, 171–3) fears those effects in the US context at the state level.

have enacted legislation which formally complies with the requirements of the directives. But given differences in enforcement strategies, the differences between member states (which were the reason for European intervention in the first place) may well remain after implementation of the directive concerned. This point substantially weakens the justification for European intervention, since in practice it may not always provide the powerful tool either to remedy the 'race to the bottom' or to guarantee a 'harmonization of conditions of competition' (Van den Bergh, Faure, and Lefevere 1996).

The economic literature makes clear that European policy makers should think more thoroughly about the reasons for harmonization, or at least about the rhetoric used to justify such harmonization. More particularly, they should realize that they can either opt for the ecological goal of uniform environmental quality or for the goal of harmonizing emission standards, but not for both at the same time. One now has the impression that the instruments chosen (harmonization of emission standards) do not always correspond with the expressed goals (harmonization of environmental quality). Recently, European legal scholars have realized this insight as well. Bruno De Witte has argued that Europe should now abandon the (wrong) rhetoric about harmonization of conditions of competition and should clearly state that it wants to achieve a minimum level of environmental quality for its citizens (2000).

Equally, it should be examined whether harmonization of process standards is always needed to reach a common market in Europe. Other helpful, but not so far-reaching (less inefficient), instruments may be available. One can think, for example, of a standardization of procedures within environmental law which still remains useful because of the transboundary character of pollution and industrial operations (Esty and Geradin 1997: 293). This can indeed increase transparency, as was intended to be achieved by the IPPC Directive, and can reduce transaction costs. However, such a harmonization should not necessarily be achieved through formal directives but through a search for common principles, using comparative research, to find a *ius commune*.

Accordingly, it should be stressed that economic analysis of federalism provides useful insights concerning the question of centralization, but it does not always provide an answer regarding which of the many possible legal techniques of harmonization should be chosen to deal with a particular problem. The economic notion of centralization is too general to cover all of the legal techniques of harmonization. It therefore certainly merits further research on which of these harmonization techniques is best suited to deal with a particular problem. Moreover, in the economic analysis there are also questions that remain unanswered. One is how the need to centralize decision making in the case of transboundary externalities can be reconciled with the ecological goal of a uniform environmental quality. Another is whether industry in heavily polluted areas may be disadvantaged with more stringent emission standards compared to their competitors in 'cleaner' countries. Some of the questions need further empirical research on, for example, the influence of environmental regulation on industry behaviour. In that respect, Europe should certainly look carefully at the US experience with environmental federalism.[58]

[58] For comparative analyses of environmental federalism in the United States and Europe, see Kimber (1995), Pfander (1996), Rose-Ackerman (1995), and Esty and Geradin (1997; 1998).

PART IV

Regulatory Competition at the Global Scale

13

Regulatory Competition and Regulatory Jurisdiction in International Securities Regulation

JOEL P. TRACHTMAN*

This chapter seeks to assess the limits of competition, and the need for regulation of competition, among jurisdictions in the context of international securities regulation.[1] It looks to the theory of property law, as well as to the Tiebout model, to suggest answers. I argue that it is impossible to generalize about the benefits of competition in regulation, and that a number of factors must be considered (Bratton and McCahery 1997). First, the regulatory competition model, like all models, has particular parameters that must be met in order for it to apply. These parameters cannot be assumed, but must be evaluated in particular cases. Second, the parameters are never completely met, placing us in the realm of the theory of the second best. The theory of the second best suggests that, given that all of the conditions of the fundamental theorem of welfare economics are not satisfied, there can be no assurance that increasing the level of satisfaction of any other conditions—such as enhanced mobility of firms—will yield greater efficiency. The realm of the theory of the second best calls for legislative deliberation rather than judicial or scholarly determination (Ulen 1998a). Third, these factors are incommensurable and involve interpersonal comparison of utility. Therefore again, the design of regulatory competition, like other decisions about regulation, is best left for political determination, informed by scholarly analyses of these factors.

Perhaps more importantly, the focus of public policy analysis (and therefore of this chapter) should not be regulatory competition. Rather, the central issue in international society, as in a federal society, is allocation of jurisdiction (just as the central issue in domestic society is allocation of property, and jurisdiction) (Trachtman 1997; 1996; 1994; 1993). Of course, allocation of property and allocation of jurisdiction are about more than material things, on the one hand, and legal technicalities, on the other hand. Competition, and where we think it will lead, is simply one vector in the decision about allocation of authority. This

* This chapter applies a theoretical perspective developed more fully in a companion article (Trachtman 2000). Thanks for comments and suggestions to Jeffrey Atik, William Bratton, David Charny, Jeffrey Dunoff, Daniel Esty, Damien Geradin, Gerard Hertig, Howell Jackson, Edward Kane, Carsten Kowalczyk, Brian Langille, Joseph McCahery, Roberta Romano, Richard Steinberg, and Paul Vaaler, as well as other conference participants. Errors are mine.

[1] It has been proposed by Professors Choi and Guzman (1998) and Romano (1998) that more competition, facilitated by a less restrictive basis for allocating regulatory jurisdiction, would be desirable. In this case, a less restrictive basis for allocating regulatory jurisdiction would be by reference to the jurisdiction of incorporation of the issuer, or perhaps simply by reference to the choice of the issuer.

chapter attempts to place regulatory competition within a broader analytical framework (Rodden and Rose-Ackerman 1997). It analyses regulatory competition in the context of debates regarding horizontal and vertical allocation of regulatory authority. It also considers issues such as competition, externalities, and economies of scale as vectors in the allocation of regulatory authority.

I. THE THEORY OF REGULATORY COMPETITION AND THE THEORY OF REGULATORY JURISDICTION

Roberta Romano (1998: 2367) argues that the need for regulation does not indicate a need for a monopolist regulator. However, in an important sense, regulators are always monopolists, at least where they apply mandatory regulation. Thus the need for regulation indicates a need for 'monopolist' regulation, and Romano's argument is better interpreted as an argument that the scope of the monopoly should not be excessive. As with private monopolies, we must examine the geographic and product scope of the monopoly enjoyed by regulators—the barriers to entry—in order to determine the contestability of these regulatory markets. Often the relevant choice of law rules (for private and, more saliently, for public law) determine the geographic scope of the monopoly. The real question, then, is what is the temporal, subject matter and geographic scope of monopoly.

Romano proposes 'elimination of the exclusive mandatory character of most of the federal securities laws' (2363). She proposes that both domestic and foreign issuers be permitted to 'opt' into a US state or non-US securities domicile, and thereby avoid application of US federal securities laws. She appears to maintain a requirement that issuers subject their transaction to *some* securities regulation as opposed to a private, contractual regime. This serves to limit the number of options. On the other hand, under Romano's approach, a state, such as the Cayman Islands or Mongolia, would presumably move to the *reductio ad minimum*: imposing no substantive obligations. This would be substantively identical to making regulation completely optional, although Romano argues that her proposal has the advantage of reversibility: issuers and investors could migrate to a state that imposes substantive regulation. However, almost by definition, if investors were able to protect themselves in this way, they would not need regulation in the first place.

Romano's proposal would entail a change in the current choice of law (or prescriptive jurisdiction) approach in securities regulation, from territoriality to an approach modelled on the choice of law approach in US domestic corporate law, the internal affairs rule. The internal affairs rule simply applies the law of the jurisdiction of incorporation to corporate governance, regardless of the place where the shares are purchased, the principal place of business of the issuer, the nationality of the purchaser, or other more substantive connections.

In order to analyse the question of whether and when regulation is optional, we must refer to the question of choice of law, or regulatory jurisdiction. Indeed, the arguments for regulatory competition are really arguments for *increased* regulatory competition by virtue of adjustment of choice of law rules. This adjustment has two components. First, it involves recognition, or exclusive home country control (exclusive of host country control, that is). Second, it calls for a *laissez-faire* approach to determination of the 'home country' for jurisdictional purposes. It may be worth noting here that recognition in the European Union is generally 'managed': essential harmonization is required prior to recognition, and host states retain jurisdiction of various kinds to ensure that foreign regulation remains acceptable (Nicolaidis and Trachtman 2000). This chapter suggests that managed recognition may address some of the serious issues with proposals for increased regulatory competition.

This chapter turns the question of regulatory competition on its head, suggesting that it can only be answered within the context of a broader inquiry into the optimal allocation of regulatory jurisdiction.[2] Of course, the utility of regulatory competition is also *internally* dependent on the question of regulatory jurisdiction, in the form of questions of positive and negative externalities that may limit the utility and domain of the Tiebout model.[3] Relying on more detailed work done in *Regulatory Competition Theory* (Trachtman 2000), this chapter distils from the Tiebout model and property rights theory a set of factors to consider in decisions about allocation of regulatory jurisdiction. It also suggests how these factors might apply to three possible approaches to allocation of jurisdiction in securities regulation.

Before assessing the possibilities for *increased* regulatory competition in the securities field, it should be noted that today there exists substantial scope for international (as opposed to federal) regulatory competition in the field of securities regulation,[4] especially both: (1) because there *is* substantial mobility (although not

[2] Many parameters affect the allocation of regulatory jurisdiction. Within a public choice framework, decentralization is expected to lead to greater responsiveness to citizen preferences and greater innovation in government-provided goods (Bratton and McCahery 1997: 216). From a public interest perspective, internalization of externalities seems important (Trachtman 1994). Choi and Guzman see the achievement of a separating equilibrium as the ideal outcome; as they find that extraterritoriality might interfere with this equilibrium, they reject it (proposing, in order to promote competition, a territoriality test with safe harbour for exchange-based transactions) (1997: 1883). However, it is not clear how they determine that the achievement of a separating equilibrium would be more valuable than the internalization of externalities through 'extraterritoriality'. Furthermore, they do not meet the argument, raised by Breton (1991) and by Bratton and McCahery (1997), among others, that externalities (which could be prevented by 'extraterritoriality') prevent the achievement of any equilibrium at all.

[3] After stating that current empirical evidence is suggestive that competitive local governments can provide an efficient level of congestible (local) public goods, Inman and Rubinfeld (1997a: 86) offer the following caveat:

> What is not assured is the efficient allocation of public goods with significant spillovers. In this case, a subsidy is needed to internalize the externalities. But any such policy to control interjurisdictional spillovers would require the agreement of the competitive city-states. For such agreements we must look to more encompassing political institutions. In Madison's compound republic this is the representative central government.

[4] Romano (1998), on the other hand, states, '[T]here is at present no competitive regime for securities laws'.

as much as the proponents of regulatory competition recommend), and (2) because even without mobility there may be reason to expect regulatory competition. It is argued that mobility is reduced by the 'bundling' effect resulting from the dominant position of the US capital markets: foreign firms cannot avoid the US capital market. However, in order to understand the true effects of this bundling, we must examine barriers to entry or mobility. The rise of the Euro markets in the 1960s shows that even under circumstances of less technical and regulatory mobility, the barriers to entry to dollar markets are surmountable.

Finally, we must recognize the fact of efforts to harmonize disclosure standards on a multilateral level. The International Accounting Standards Committee (IASC) is working on a set of international accounting standards designed to provide the predicate for recognition—for acceptance of financial statements from other jurisdictions. The International Organization of Securities Commissions (IOSCO 1998) is involved in this effort, and is also involved in setting minimum standards for non-financial statement disclosure.[5] To the extent that these efforts are successful, they will provide a basis for recognition, and enhanced mobility.

II. JURISDICTIONAL MOBILITY

It cannot be denied that technical mobility has increased in recent years, especially in a field such as securities regulation. However, technical mobility, allowing persons to effect transactions in multiple territories at low cost, does not necessarily translate into jurisdictional mobility. For jurisdictional mobility depends on constructed rules of regulatory jurisdiction. States are free to modify their rules of regulatory jurisdiction in response to technical mobility (Trachtman 1998). I have suggested elsewhere that states may be expected to do so in order to limit externalities: in order to prevent regulatory arbitrage where the purpose of the arbitrage is to impose an adverse effect on the relevant state (Trachtman 1997). However, technical mobility has certainly increased jurisdictional mobility to some extent, and by doing so has enhanced the conditions for regulatory competition. The sources of technical mobility are not simply enhancements of telecommunications, but also include advances in financial engineering. The use of derivatives and securitization permits private persons to structure their affairs more flexibly, and to move from one jurisdiction to another for varying purposes.

While competition can occur without mobility, greater mobility would certainly contribute to the possibility of competition, as indicated by the Tiebout model. Mobility in the regulatory context is defined by jurisdictional rules.

[5] The Securities and Exchange Commission (SEC) has proposed these standards for public comment ('International Disclosure Standards', 64 F.R. 6261 9 February 1999) (available at http://www.sec.gov/rules/proposed/33-7637.txt)) (Hanks and Nardini 1999).

III. THE TIEBOUT MODEL

Most claims in favour of regulatory competition are based on the Tiebout model, which predicts a Pareto optimal (first best) outcome assuming certain parameters are met. For each application of the Tiebout model to make predictive claims, it is necessary to measure the relevant context against these parameters. Thus, even if one were convinced that regulatory competition has provided benefits in domestic US corporate governance (Romano 1998: n. 76),[6] one would have to show the operative factors there, and explain whether they exist or do not exist in the international securities regulation context.[7] Furthermore, the theory of the second best (Symposium 1998) raises substantial issues regarding the ability of the Tiebout model to tell us anything if all of its parameters are not fully met (which is generally the case).

The Tiebout model has been described and debated in great detail in many important works (1956; Bratton and McCahery 1997), so I will simply sketch it here. The Tiebout model of interjurisdictional competition posits that, subject to the satisfaction of five conditions, competition among small cities for mobile individuals results in the efficient supply of local public goods by those cities. In Table 1, I list the five conditions and suggest why none of them are likely fully to be met.[8]

T4 raises an important difference between fiscal competition—the original focus of the Tiebout model—and regulatory competition as it arises in the securities law context. In the securities law context, proponents of greater competition argue that there is a 'joint' jurisdictional decision made by issuers and investors, investors acting by virtue of their decision to invest. So we must address the ability of investors, as well as issuers, to become informed as to the fiscal attributes of each jurisdiction. Yes, institutional investors are able to assess regulatory regimes. But they may not need the protections of securities regulation in the first place, and private placements under Regulation D, combined with trading among qualified institutional buyers under Rule 144A, exempt transactions with institutional investors from important protections of the US securities laws. If we are to assume that all investors are sophisticated enough to assess the quality of the securities regulation regime, should we not be able to assume that all investors are sophisticated enough not to need securities regulation in the first place? It is not that the argument for regulation is an argument for monopoly of regulation, but that it is, obviously, an argument for minimum levels of regulation.

[6] On the other hand, Bebchuk and Ferrell (1999) argue that, at least in some circumstances, competition among states in the US corporate law system does not yield efficiency. Bebchuk (1992) and Cary (1974) argue the same.

[7] Romano (1998: 2385) places the burden of proof differently: 'There is no reason to expect state competition to operate differently for securities law than it does for corporate law.'

[8] The left column is adapted from Inman and Rubinfeld (1997a). See also Bratton and McCahery (1997).

Table 1. Condition counterindications

T1	Publicly provided goods and services are produced with a congestible technology (there is an optimal size of jurisdiction)	There may not today be an optimal size of jurisdiction for securities regulation that is smaller than the entire world; we examine below the issue of economies of scale
T2	There is a perfectly elastic supply of jurisdictions, each capable of replicating all attractive economic features of its competitors	Requires greater homogeneity of resources than exists in the international setting
T3	Mobility of households among jurisdictions is costless	Mobility of firms to other securities regulation jurisdictions will entail substantial costs, at least of searching and analysing the relevant securities laws
T4	Households are fully informed about the fiscal attributes of each jurisdiction	Serious concerns regarding whether firms or investors are fully informed regarding the attributes of each securities regulation jurisdiction
T5	There are no interjurisdictional externalities	The very existence of securities law—implicating legislative decision that externalities exist—indicates that variations in securities regulation would produce interjurisdictional externalities

IV. THE STRATEGIC PERSPECTIVE ON INTERJURISDICTIONAL COMPETITION

There are substantial concerns as to whether the Tiebout model can result in a stable equilibrium (Bratton and McCahery 1997; Bretton 1991; Gramlich 1987). The stability of intergovernmental competition is separate from its efficiency: an unstable market for regulation might be characterized by 'price wars' or a race to the bottom (Breton 1991: 43). Instability can result from a failure to satisfy condition T2 listed above: where the number of jurisdictions is smaller than that needed to produce a separating equilibrium (Choi and Guzman 1998) in which the population separates into strictly homogeneous groups (Breton 1991: 46). Furthermore, externalities can be a source of instability (51). The international securities law context is rife with possibilities for both positive and negative externalities.

Breton points out that centralization may not be the best way to provide stability, but the *existence* of central authority appears necessary to address problems of instability. One approach to the problem of instability is to empower a central government in more limited ways than full centralization would entail (or to have a central government that otherwise enjoys plenary power commit to exercise its powers in limited ways). The central government may set minimum standards of regulation, as has been done in the European Union's essential harmonization technique. Breton concludes that 'in the area of international competition, it would be impossible to prevent an unstable competitive process from degenerating, unless, in the language of international relations "realists", a hegemonic power undertook to prevent the debacle' (51–2). Hegemony implies control of a system by a single actor within the system, whereas centralization entails concentration of power in a system, without the need for special influence by any particular actor in the system. The difference between centralization and hegemony as regards stability may be too subtle for some of us, but there appears to be no reason in theory why this hegemonic power must be a state; we have seen the European Union emerge as just such a power in Europe, and it might be argued that the World Trade Organization (WTO) or functional organizations such as IOSCO may play such a role.

Within the US federal system, stability is provided by the ability of the federal government to intercede; this is an important distinction between regulatory competition in the US domestic context and regulatory competition in the international context. In the international context, we must build and empower a central authority. The question for the international community is how much authority must it cede to a central 'government' in order to develop satisfactory horizontal competition. Again, this question cannot be answered separately from other questions about the level at which governance should take place, or power should be assigned—from questions of subsidiarity.

V. THE PROPERTY RIGHTS THEORY OF REGULATORY JURISDICTION

While the Tiebout model includes consideration of externalities, it does so only to test the quality of jurisdictional competition, and, as noted above, this parameter is rarely satisfied, and cannot be satisfied in the international securities regulation context. Thus there are substantial reasons to be concerned with externalities. The thesis of this chapter is that policy makers cannot set jurisdictional rules simply to enhance competition, but must consider other factors, including those suggested by property law theory. Even if regulatory competition produces efficient securities laws, this may come at the cost of rules for allocation of regulatory jurisdiction that are inefficient in other respects. These rules may be efficient for the local society, but inefficient from a global standpoint, because they impose costs on other societies greater than the benefits to the local society. For example, there may be economies of scale or commons problems, or transaction costs or strategic problems, that must be addressed in the choice of jurisdictional rule. As Demsetz (1967: 348) writes, 'A primary function of property rights is that of guiding incentives to achieve a greater internalization of externalities' (Papendrou 1994). A primary function of jurisdictional rules is similarly that of shaping incentives to achieve a greater internalization of externalities among political units. On the other hand, transaction cost and strategic considerations may well cause us to decline to internalize in particular cases (Trachtman 1997).

VI. COMPARATIVE INSTITUTIONAL COST–BENEFIT ANALYSIS

As we seek to apply the Tiebout model to international securities regulation, we are definitely operating in the realm of the second best (Bratton and McCahery 1997). However, the Tiebout model contains important insights about the benefits of regulatory competition, which should not be ignored simply because the model itself cannot be applied. Property law theory is suggestive as to jurisdictional rules, but also finally refers to a need for judgement, or commensuration and interpersonal comparison of utility. And property law theory does not formally incorporate concerns for interjurisdictional competition.

However, the concerns of these bodies of theory may be used as a guide to analysis, and their insights incorporated in a comparative cost–benefit analysis of various jurisdictional rules, although we are a long way from anything approaching quantification. Comparative institutional analysis must select particular institutions and develop parameters for comparison. The choice of institution, of course, is quite difficult, as all institutions are imperfect, interconnected, and embedded in broader institutional settings. In *Regulatory Competition Theory* (Trachtman 2000), I distil from the Tiebout model and from property rights theory the following parameters of comparison: (1) discipline of government/avoidance of risk of cartelization/preference revelation; (2) potential innovation; (3) government close to people/customization/consumer choice; (4) economies of scale and network externalities; (5) externalization and commons problems; (6) costs of overlapping and unpredictable application of jurisdiction; and (7) facilitation of transactions in jurisdiction, including creation of organizations, in appropriate cases.

Application to international securities regulation

In this Part, I first analyse the current structure of the international 'market' for securities regulation. Second, I pose three basic jurisdictional structures for evaluation. Third, I suggest how the above comparative parameters might be used to evaluate these jurisdictional structures in connection with international securities regulation.

VII. THE STRUCTURE OF THE INTERNATIONAL MARKET FOR SECURITIES REGULATION

Of particular interest in the context of this chapter is the fact that there is already substantial ambit for competition in the international securities law system, as issuers of, and investors in, securities may with relatively little restriction choose, internationally, the jurisdiction in which they wish to offer or purchase securities. As territoriality is the chief basis for jurisdiction, the choice of location often determines the applicable securities law.

The type of securities regulation with which we are concerned here is transactional in nature: registration, disclosure requirements, and anti-fraud rules in connection with public offerings of securities or securities that trade in public markets. While most states follow a national treatment principle—treating transactions in their markets by foreign issuers as they would treat those by domestic issuers—there are two major types of variations in the exercise of prescriptive jurisdiction. First, US anti-fraud rules have a less clear scope of application than US registration and specific disclosure requirements. The registration and specific disclosure requirements are applied only to 'onshore' transactions as defined under Regulation S, and so comply with the national treatment principle mentioned above (although some may argue that the definition of 'onshore' could be narrowed). The anti-fraud provisions are applied based on both a territorial conduct and territorial effects basis, and so are potentially applicable to offerings that take place offshore, where there is sufficient conduct or effect in the United States (in cases where territorial conduct-based national treatment would not permit prescriptive jurisdiction, either because it does not take account of effects or because it requires a higher threshold of conduct). The scope of this expansion has been narrowed in some recent cases, but remains potentially wide. Second, the United States and Canada, on the one hand, and the European Union, on the other hand, have separately made arrangements for mutual recognition of prospectuses.

Territorial conduct-based national treatment provides substantial ambit for regulatory competition. Issuers dissatisfied with the regulatory requirements in state A may simply effect their transaction in state B, on state B's securities markets, and may engage in additional offerings in the securities markets of states C, D, E, and F.

The US securities laws provide a basic statutory rule that they may not be waived. However, there are circumstances in which the Securities and Exchange Commission (SEC) or the courts, by interpretation, have allowed individuals in effect to waive the application of certain provisions of the securities laws (Regulation S—Rules Governing Offers and Sales Made Outside the United States Without Registration Under the Securities Act of 1933, 17 C.F.R. 230.901–904 (1998)).[9] In fact, in connection with the promulgation of Regulation S, the SEC

[9] As to courts, see the line of cases arising from US customers' agreements to act as Lloyd's Names, and to subject these agreements to English law and courts.

states that '[a]s investors choose their markets, they choose the laws and regulations applicable in such markets' (Securities and Exchange Commission 1990). The SEC has also promulgated Regulation D (private placements) and Rule 144A (trading of privately placed securities) in order to make registration under the Securities Act (but not application of anti-fraud rules) optional for certain types of offerings and sales to certain types of sophisticated investors. At the other end of the spectrum, Rule 12g-3(2)(b) provides an exemption from registration under the Securities Exchange Act for foreign issuers with limited numbers of US security holders, provided they supply the information that they supply in their home jurisdiction. These exemptive rules in effect already provide limited recognition to foreign law, and thus an exception to national treatment.

Nevertheless, we know that the SEC comes under substantial further pressure to relax its regulation further in relation to foreign issuers, including pressure founded on assertions that foreign issuers decline to enter the US capital markets due to the onerous regulatory requirements. So both voice and exit are at work. Romano, and Choi and Guzman, seek to accentuate the impact of exit by recommending the adoption of a rule of recognition of foreign securities regulation, demolishing the barrier to entry that keeps foreign regulators out of the US market. They seek to enhance mobility.

The SEC has generally responded in the negative to pressure to relax its regulation in relation to foreign issuers. It states that it is concerned about fraud being perpetrated in US capital markets. It is also explicitly concerned about the pressure for relaxation of regulation of domestic companies that would follow a decision to relax the application of US regulation to foreign companies.

VIII. THE INSTITUTIONAL STRUCTURE OF THE MARKET FOR SECURITIES REGULATION: FEDERAL SYSTEMS AND THE INTERNATIONAL SYSTEM

Obviously, the US federal system is different from the international system, but how important are these differences to an analysis of the transferability of learning about regulatory competition from one jurisdiction to another (assuming one accepts that there is learning, and assuming one accepts that securities law is sufficiently similar to corporate law)? The main difference is in the general lack of mandatory regulatory authority in the international system. The US Commerce Clause provides wide authority to the federal government to pre-empt state law within the United States by virtue of majority votes in Congress and concurrence of the President. International law may cover a broad range of subjects and could be designed to have direct effect but, except within the European Union, there is little authority for majority voting. Thus it is not clear that there is a reliable way to create the stability necessary for the Tiebout model to operate.

Furthermore, there is far less heterogeneity in corporate law within the United States than in securities law internationally. If the degree of difference of law is taken as a measure of the potential for externalization, this would indicate greater potential externalization, and instability, further limiting the applicability of the Tiebout model.

IX. THE MAXIMAND OF SECURITIES REGULATION

In order to make claims about the utility of regulatory competition, or decentralization, it is necessary first to identify the maximand. Once this maximand and its components are identified, it is possible to suggest how it is affected by regulatory competition. We begin with two problematic assumptions, motivated by public choice analysis: first, that we can identify a discrete maximand for securities regulation, and second, that states seek to maximize aggregate national social welfare.

It is sometimes difficult to distinguish between an argument for greater regulatory choice or competition and an argument for no regulation at all. Given the fact that some duly elected legislatures have enacted securities regulation, the best starting place for an analysis is an assumption that securities regulation serves a social function (Black 1999; Coffee 1984; Easterbrook and Fischel 1984; Kitch 1995). Thus its evisceration by virtue of liberal choice of law rules should not follow from a predilection for regulatory competition. In other words, in addition to examining the appropriate level of regulation, it is necessary to examine the social need for regulation in order to make a persuasive argument about the value of regulatory competition. A much more complete evaluation of the benefits of federal regulation, and of jurisdiction based on sales of securities, or effects, is necessary before discarding these laws. Could it be that federal regulation has been responsible, in part, for the growth in liquidity, size, and efficiency of US capital markets? Is this the dog that did not bark?

Studies of international listings seem to show a positive effect on valuation of shares of foreign issuers cross-listing in the United States, taking on US disclosure and insider trading regulation (Sundaram and Logue 1996: 67).[10] A recent cross-sectional analysis of possible sources of country-based variation in valuation by Sundaram and Logue (83) finds no valuation differences based on the quality of home country financial reporting and disclosure compared to US Generally Accepted Accounting Principles (GAAP):

> We expected that companies listed on comparatively underdeveloped financial markets with differences in governance systems from that of the U.S., or those with poor reporting environments . . . would have enjoyed more beneficial valuation effects from listing in the U.S.

[10] Other studies of stock prices around the time of listing on a US stock exchange (and presumably taking on disclosure obligations under the Securities Exchange Act of 1934) fail to distinguish between *inter alia*, the effects of increased liquidity and the effects of increased disclosure. Foerster and Marolyi (1993: 763) find some positive price effects in advance of Canadian firms listing in the United States. Saudagaran and Biddle (1995: 319) show that firms are more likely to list on foreign stock exchanges with lower financial disclosure levels than their domicile.

This is not the case. Similarly, we expected that companies from countries with well-developed financial markets, with governance systems similar to that of the U.S. [and] strong disclosure requirements . . . would not have substantially enhanced their valuations by cross-listing, but they do.[11]

Sundaram and Logue conclude that the benefits of cross-listing come from the reduction of the adverse effects of international capital market segmentation.[12] However, another interpretation relevant to this chapter is possible. Assuming that there are variations in securities regulation, and that these variations may affect the value of companies subject thereto, this data suggests that investors are unable to respond effectively to such variations. Of course, the regulatory competition prescription depends on the ability of investors to do so.

If the sole goal of securities regulation were investor protection, then an event study (if such a study existed) showing that share prices import the value of moves from low-regulation jurisdictions to high-regulation ones, or vice versa, would leave us sanguine about regulatory competition in international securities regulation. After all, if the goal is investor protection, and investors are able to assess and price variations in securities regulation, there would appear to be little need to protect them from regulatory arbitrage or regulatory competition.

Securities regulation serves broader social goals. Securities law may serve a policy goal of promoting small shareholders at the expense of large shareholders, or promoting market stability and therefore macroeconomic stability in a collective action problem context, and of promoting accuracy of capital allocation (M. Fox 1998: 696).[13] The achievement of these goals of securities law may not be reflected in securities prices. In more formal terms, the private marginal benefit of an issuer's disclosure is likely to be less than the social marginal benefit (Fox undated).

Furthermore, there is a set of substantial arguments that the state charter competition evidence is irrelevant to the international securities law context: state corporate law does little to protect investors, is overshadowed by federal securities law, and is substantially uniform among the states, and so one would not expect a substantial price effect to arise from a change of state corporate law (Coffee 1999: 699).

The main purpose of securities regulation, congruent with protection of the 'market', is the maximization of accuracy in capital allocation net of costs of capital

[11] Sundaram and Logue point out that there may be biases in their sample. During the period they examined, no firms from countries with particularly weak disclosure listed their shares on the New York or US stock exchanges.

[12] Similarly, Smith and Sofianos (1997) find an 11 per cent increase in stock prices after listing, but find that none of their explanatory variables explain this price change. However, Fuerst (1998) argues that managers of high-quality issuers may use high regulatory environments such as the United States as a device for credibly conveying private information regarding the quality of their companies, and are compensated by higher market values.

[13] Fox argues for an issuer nationality basis for regulatory jurisdiction in disclosure regulation, on the basis that this type of recognition will *reduce* pressure on the United States to relax its disclosure requirements. It would reduce pressure from stock exchanges, which could obtain foreign business more easily. Fox does not believe US issuers would apply pressure for a 'level playing field', allowing them to comply with a relaxed disclosure regime if foreign issuers are permitted to do so.

allocation (Kitch 1995: 875; Securities and Exchange Commission 1990).[14] In this public-interest theoretical sense, the capital market is 'planned' to provide a specific kind of social benefit. Accuracy in capital allocation directs investment to the most productive uses, defined in terms of profitability. This is a social benefit, not a mere private benefit. If fraud is perpetrated in, for example, the US capital market, regardless of whether the *fault* rests in a foreign regulatory authority or US regulatory authorities, not only will US investors be hurt but the integrity of, and confidence in, the US capital market will be diminished. This may result in reduced liquidity and prices, raising the cost of capital to issuers. In turn, this has a broad effect in the real economy. Thus externalities are imposed on private investors and on the United States as a whole.

Romano (1998: 2377) notes studies showing a decrease in return variance after the legislation of the Securities Act, but discounts these studies as evidence of the benefits of securities regulation, on the ground that investors are compensated for bearing risk. Yet this decrease in return variance is associated with more accurate price predictions (Seligman 1993: 10), and therefore more accurate financing decisions yielding greater efficiency. It is odd to ignore such welfare benefits.

As shown above, even event studies of securities prices on the occasion of an international transfer from one securities regulation system to another (Meek 1983)[15] would tell us little about whether social benefits are maintained regardless of the applicable securities regulation. Romano relies on event studies relating to corporate law in the US federal context.[16] But the evidence in the international context, relating to capital market benefits, supports the importance of securities regulation: in fact, it supports the claim that, at least in the international context, corporate law and securities regulation are important to maximize social benefits. But it does not support the race-to-the-top claim because it suggests that a substantial part of the benefits will not be captured by individual investors themselves, or by issuers.

This broader social purpose for securities regulation supports the argument that greater regulatory competition may raise concerns, insofar as it indicates substantial externalities. That is, while individual investors may not be concerned about securities regulation, society as a whole may suffer from inappropriate regulation.[17] There is a link between quality of the legal protection of investors and general social welfare. Furthermore, weak legal protection may be durable because it 'may magnify the rent-seeking potential of politicians' (Modigliani and Perotti 1998: 11).

[14] Choi and Guzman (1998: 941 n. 112) disagree.

[15] This study does not address the question of whether acceptance of US disclosure requirements affects market value.

[16] These event studies are not unambiguous in their own context. Licht (1998: 609–35) argues that, due to the 'bundling' of various legal rules in any stock price, it is difficult for markets to 'price' individual legal rules. Dodd and Leftwich (1980), Romano (1985), and Weiss and White (1987) make similar arguments.

[17] Several economists have recently stressed the role of legal protection in capital market development generally (Demirgue-Kent 1998: 2134; La Porta *et al.* 1997; Modigliani and Perotti 1998).

X. THREE ALTERNATIVE JURISDICTIONAL STRUCTURES

There are varying possible rules of prescriptive jurisdiction, including: (1) recognition (apply home country law to activities within the host country), as recommended by Choi and Guzman, and Romano; (2) national treatment (apply host country law to all activities within the territory); and (3) harmonization (agree on uniform substantive law, rendering choice of law irrelevant). These rules will have different ramifications for the ability to externalize and for regulatory competition. I assess each of the above jurisdictional alternatives by evaluating them in relation to the cost and benefit factors referred to above.

XI. ROOTLESS RECOGNITION

Recognition is termed 'portable reciprocity' by Choi and Guzman. Perhaps a better term for this is 'rootless recognition' as reciprocity is not a critical *jurisdictional* feature, and it calls for the recognition of *any* state's law, without examining the connections between the issuer and the chosen state, or whether that state's law fulfils the regulatory goals of the host state. Recognition of home country law would be *exclusive* of the application of host country law.

XII. TERRITORIALITY-BASED NATIONAL TREATMENT

Territoriality-based national treatment is the basic rule in effect in the world today. The obverse of this structure is recognition by other states of the law of the jurisdiction in which the transaction is conducted. Thus this type of recognition has some features in common with the type of recognition discussed above, but is more 'rooted'. It is worth recalling that a regime of national treatment *is* a somewhat competitive market.

XIII. MANAGED RECOGNITION WITH ESSENTIAL HARMONIZATION

The European Union often engages in essential harmonization, as a predicate to mutual recognition, to forge the single market. In negotiating harmonization directives, states recognize that the increased regulatory competition that will result from the proposed mutual recognition will place pressure on their ability to maintain regulation which, by definition, *is otherwise desirable* from a purely local standpoint, having been legislated through presumptively legitimate processes. Before agreeing to mutual recognition, they agree on a minimum level of regulation that will insulate their home regulation from being reduced in unacceptable ways. Furthermore, they exact a *quid pro quo*, both in terms of essential harmonization and in terms of other market liberalization in other areas. Thus the European Union has devised a complex legislative, judicial, and administrative process to manage the choice—or better, the compromise—between regulatory competition and centralization in particular cases, including the following instruments:

1. Judicial examination of equivalence: While there is no structure in the securities law field that would provide for this type of examination today, the WTO Agreement on Technical Barriers to Trade, the WTO Agreement on Sanitary and Phytosanitary Measures, and other international mechanisms provide for such review in other sectors. It is feasible that these disciplines could be extended to the securities law field. The result would be that recognition would only be required where the host state's regulatory goals are met by the home state regulation.
2. Legislative establishment of essential harmonization: IASC and IOSCO efforts amount to 'legislative' establishment of essential harmonization. Unlike in the European Union (since the Single European Act), the international system does not provide for majority voting, and the United States stands as the pivotal, if not the bottleneck, state in these efforts. These kinds of efforts must be regarded with suspicion by proponents of regulatory competition, but they are entitled to lobby for harmonized rules that would leave room for competition in areas where competition provides the most benefits.
3. Maintenance of 'safeguards' that would allow states to address threats to their public policy: EU harmonization and mutual recognition initiatives such as the Second Banking Directive contain provisions that allow host states to act to protect the 'general good'. These provisions provide a safeguard against externalization, at least in more egregious cases.

These devices could be used to determine, in more particular cases relating to particular regulatory systems, and particular regulatory rules, whether competition or coordination is the superior alternative. Indeed, once it is shown that competition is not *always* superior, which this chapter has done, it is for the proponents of unmitigated competition to make an administrative cost or other argument against a more refined system to identify particular circumstances when competition is superior.

XIV. ASSESSING THE THREE JURISDICTIONAL STRUCTURES

Below, I engage in a suggestive evaluation of each of the above jurisdictional regimes from the standpoint of the cost and benefit (Sun and Pelkmans 1995: 82–8) factors developed in *Regulatory Competition Theory* (Trachtman 2000).

XV. DISCIPLINE OF GOVERNMENT AVOIDANCE OF RISK OF CARTELIZATION/ENHANCED PREFERENCE REVELATION

This is the great expected benefit of regulatory competition. From a public choice perspective, one expects greater discipline of government; from a public interest perspective, enhanced preference revelation. On the other hand, from a public interest perspective, competition diminishes the authority of regulators, jeopardizing their ability to maximize the public interest. Furthermore, decentralization itself may make enforcement of regulation more difficult, simply due to the need to coordinate among regulators in a context where regulation differs from jurisdiction to jurisdiction. Although harmonization alone does not ensure regulatory cooperation, it facilitates cooperation, and harmonization may be combined with centralization of supervisory authority.

National treatment, as noted above, also provides some of the benefits of competition. On the other hand, national treatment rules may be viewed as raising some barriers to entry, while a process of essential harmonization toward mutual recognition may be seen as a method of negotiating reduction of these barriers, in exchange for a level of harmonization that will reduce the threat or magnitude of externalization.

XVI. POTENTIAL INNOVATION

The scope for regulatory innovation is equally under rootless recognition and territoriality-based national treatment. However, proponents of regulatory competition would argue that the *incentives* for innovation are stronger under rootless recognition. On the other hand, to the extent that harmonization takes place in combination with recognition, there would be reduced scope for decentralized innovation. However, harmonization would provide greater economies of scale in regulatory analysis and innovation addressing the harmonized regulation, and so it is not clear how this factor would cut.

The possibility of 'intellectual property' piracy might have the effect of suppressing the innovation that is expected by the proponents of increased regulatory competition. Thus, if Thailand incurred great research costs in developing a better system of securities regulation, what impedes Singapore from simply copying the Thai regulatory structure? While there may be first-mover advantages, or the possibility for investment in institutions or commitment strategies, like those that are thought to keep Delaware the market leader, it is by no means clear that they would be successful in other contexts.

XVII. GOVERNMENT CLOSE TO PEOPLE/CUSTOMIZATION/CONSUMER CHOICE

Under the 'government close to the people' parameter, an initial analysis might indicate that only harmonization seems to raise concerns: thus both rootless recognition and territoriality-based treatment are *decentralized* regimes. Consumer choice and customization are greater the more rootless the recognition regime; thus Choi and Guzman's portable reciprocity would provide a higher level of choice, giving regulated persons the opportunity to identify regimes more appropriate to their circumstances. However, rootless recognition gives initial choice to the regulated person, leaving open the question of whether the protected person is making an informed choice: to which people is government close?

Choi and Guzman argue for the value of customization, which they expect to arise by virtue of a separation equilibrium that may result from increased regulatory competition.[18] For example, there is an argument that the United States *benefits* from its higher disclosure standards in international regulatory competition: that the United States is winning a race to the top (Chen 1992). This benefit arises in part from the financing flexibility available to US companies due to the fact that they *already* comply with strict US standards. Of course, the value of customization must be weighed against the value of uniformity.

XVIII. ECONOMIES OF SCALE AND NETWORK EXTERNALITIES

Technical mobility has raised the question: is there a subglobal optimal regulatory area for securities regulation? There appear to be economies of scale in securities regulation, as well as network externalities. Network externalities arise when the value of adopting a certain measure depends on how many others adopt the same measure: standards for telephone systems are a clear example, but prospectus disclosure may have some similar characteristics.

Investors realize benefits from centralization, including greater ease of comparability of disclosure (Geiger 1997; White 1996). This is one of the SEC's greatest concerns, although it is probably true that the costs involved in interpreting diverse disclosure requirements are not great deterrents to institutional investors. The United States already has an important first-mover advantage, and may benefit from network externalities (Choi and Levich 1990: 90–8; Coffee 1999: 694).

Rootless recognition would entail greater costs for investors to identify and evaluate the various relevant regulatory systems—a US investor cannot simply assume that if she purchases securities she will be protected by US federal securities laws (Choi 1998).[19] While Romano identifies and addresses this concern (1998:

[18] I have argued above that various factors would impede the formation of an equilibrium.

[19] Choi states that '[t]he continuing absence of and subscription to international reporting standards should be a major concern of policy makers around the world. Even ardent opponents of governmental

2394–400), her remedial proposal is to suggest that states could accept centralized Financial Accounting Standards Board (FASB) standards, or that private firms would do so voluntarily. So, with one hand, Romano rejects centralized *governmental* regulation, but, with the other hand, she advocates centralized *quasi-private* regulation. As FASB standards, subject to indirect SEC supervision (Gore 1992: 18, 22; Securities and Exchange Commission 1938; 1973), are already the central feature of US federal disclosure regulation, and the source of the greatest difficulty to foreign issuers, this would render Romano's proposal far less dramatic than it might appear. While Romano would remove the FASB from SEC supervision, there are already serious concerns about the FASB's accountability (McEnroe and Martens 1998: 53), which would be accentuated if SEC supervision were terminated. If there is to be a monopolist—if our exit is to be blocked—many of us would prefer to have the voice available with a governmental monopolist.

Both rootless recognition and territoriality-based national treatment are decentralized models that do not reap economies of scale or advance the development of network externalities. However, under each of these alternative regimes, we would expect to see some possibility of capturing economies of scale or network externalities through autonomous cooperation, or conscious parallelism. These might be captured more quickly under territoriality-based national treatment, because the United States would maintain its 'market-leading' position. Furthermore, managed recognition, by virtue of its essential harmonization component, would be likely to capture economies of scale and network externalities the most.

XIX. EXTERNALIZATION AND COMMONS PROBLEMS

The possibility that benefits of regulation would be enjoyed by foreign states—by host states—would cause home states to underinvest in regulation unless the host state could pay or otherwise impel the home state to regulate at the desired level. Thus the reason why some states might have more lax regulation is simply that they do not enjoy the benefits of strict regulation. Under rootless recognition, the host state would have no way to 'make up' the difference, but under territoriality-based national treatment, it would be able to do so. Under managed recognition, this commons problem or prisoners' dilemma could be addressed by essential harmonization. Given accentuated competition, the 'winners'—those states that attract more issuers with their regulation—would experience increased costs of regulation. They could, like Delaware, charge for their regulation services, and could even make a profit, especially if they experience economies of scale.

Lax home state regulation may adversely affect other jurisdictions; it may cause negative externalities. For example, an issuer may commit international securities

intervention in the marketplace recognise that a fundamental obligation of public authority is to define property rights in order to support efficient exchange.'

fraud, defrauding foreign investors. Where the detriments affect others (and especially assuming there are local benefits concomitant with the foreign detriments), home states will have incentives to provide lax securities regulation. The measure of the negative externalities will depend upon: (1) the difference in regulation between the host state and the home state, as the host state regulation (assuming no public choice problems) may be assumed to be an expression of its preferences as to the appropriate level of regulation, and (2) the extent to which home state firms may offer securities in the host state, which in turn will depend upon two factors: (a) the attractiveness of host state securities markets as a source of financing, and (b) barriers to entry of home state firms in the host state, including national treatment-type choice of law rules that apply home state regulation to host state firms upon entry.

Thus again, territoriality-based national treatment, or managed recognition, would allow host states to forestall externalization by imposing their own regulation, thus creating a stable equilibrium. Furthermore, managed recognition would provide an opportunity for states to reveal their anti-externalization preferences in negotiation over essential harmonization. This process requires states to revisit—and perhaps to modify—their preferences for regulation. Thus democratic accountability for harmonization agreements becomes important.

XX. COSTS OF OVERLAPPING AND UNPREDICTABLE APPLICATION OF JURISDICTION

Private persons incur costs of compliance with, and utilization of, multiple regulatory systems. They often comply where they are uncertain about the application of regulation. National treatment based on territorial conduct or effects is the regime that maximizes these costs, as, of course, conduct and effects often take place in multiple territories. Rootless recognition seems the most predictable, and it eliminates all overlap. Managed recognition will also be relatively predictable but, if it contains exceptions to reduce risks of externalization, may give rise to some uncertainty.

XXI. FACILITATION OF TRANSACTIONS IN JURISDICTION, INCLUDING DEVELOPMENT OF ORGANIZATIONS, IN APPROPRIATE CASES

The work of Coase (1988), Williamson (1985; 1994), North (1986; 1987), and others suggests that the choice between property rights—greater decentralization—and organization—greater centralization—is determined by comparison of the transaction costs (including strategic costs) occasioned by the different structures. Thus, in order to choose, it would be necessary to assess the transaction costs involved in each proposed structure. Here, we are not assessing transaction costs in the private market, but transaction costs associated with transactions in jurisdiction between states.[20]

If we think of rules of horizontal jurisdiction as analogous to property rights, international organization is analogous to the firm (Trachtman 1996). Of course, it is necessary to analyse the firm in order to know what property it controls, what decisions are allocated to the international organization and how it is governed, and how the international organization makes decisions. International organizations may be intergovernmental, with each member retaining veto rights, or more transnational. Furthermore, international organizations may make new legal rules through quasi-legislative processes, or may delegate authority to adjudicative processes (Trachtman 1999).

It is important to recognize that, at least in theory, competition may occur within an international organization. That is, as competition in a market is planned, it is possible to establish a market-like institutional structure within the firm, or the international organization. Consider a firm like General Motors, with its Cadillac, Chevrolet, Pontiac, Oldsmobile, Opel, and other divisions. These divisions compete with one another, despite the fact that they are within the same firm. Thus the choice of international organization does not necessarily eliminate the possibility of regulatory competition. In other words, decentralization and centralization are not always the same as market and firm.

In this context, rootless recognition seems to deny the potential utility of organization or centralization. Rootless recognition seems also to take decisions to reallocate jurisdiction out of the hands of states and to place them in the hands of private individuals. This move could be supported by a public choice critique of the ability of the state to 'deal' effectively in jurisdiction on behalf of its citizens. However, if we consider the 'market' for jurisdiction as a market in which states are transactors, rootless recognition diminishes substantially the possibility for transactions. On the other hand, national treatment retains the possibility of transactions in jurisdiction to allow states to reallocate toward Pareto superior configurations. Managed recognition itself represents a 'transaction' in jurisdiction, and accepts more explicitly the choice between property rights (through recognition) and the firm (through harmonization or other centralization), and would allow the retention of national treatment in connection with particular rules.

XXII. AGGREGATING ANALYSIS

The above factors form the basis for policy analysis. We can try to assess the direction that a particular vector will take, and its magnitude, in one institutional structure as opposed to another. But we cannot do this formally, or with any informal

[20] Choi and Guzman (1997: 1891) seem reflexively to prefer the market: '[T]o the extent substantive agreements impose rules not honed from competitive pressures but rather imposed by expert bureaucrats, such rules may suffer from the same problems as regulatory regimes in isolated countries'.

precision. Moreover, much depends on the value of securities regulation or other regulation, which in turn depends on the quality of the regulation and its utility to particular individuals. There is a serious problem of interpersonal, and interjurisdictional, comparison of utility. Thus all that scholars or other analysts may do is present an analysis of these factors. Courts would have similar problems, but are sometimes delegated authority to make decisions such as these. Moreover, in order to provide more specific weights to these factors, a substantial research effort would be required to be mounted. This may be worthwhile, but it has not yet been carried out, and so no definitive positive analysis is possible.

XXIII. CONCLUSION

This chapter has sought to provide a taxonomy of factors that must be considered in connection with policy decisions regarding horizontal regulatory competition. It has argued that allocation of jurisdiction is the core decision, with regulatory competition serving as only one parameter in the decision regarding allocation of jurisdiction. Regulatory competition is appropriate to be used where it provides greater benefits than other institutional choices.[21] But scholars can only assist this type of cost–benefit analysis—they cannot substitute their determination for that of legitimate governmental organs. Legislative organs are the primary decision makers, although they may delegate components of the decision to judicial bodies.

This chapter has also highlighted deficiencies in arguments for a change to 'rootless recognition' in international securities regulation. Securities law is different from corporate law, and the international setting is different from the US federal setting. These differences must be considered together. From a dynamic perspective, it is worth considering the fact that the US federal system has had an opportunity to engage in a degree of regulatory competition, and regulatory management, during the past century. There has been a remarkable autonomous harmonization of corporate law. There has also been an almost complete federal harmonization of securities law through federal government legislative and administrative action. Who is to say that one of these processes has been more 'efficient' than the other? Could the federal legislative process be the mechanism by which US society has chosen where to have competition and where to have cooperation? Could the federal government be Breton's hegemon? Could the selection of securities law for centralization (and the dynamic definition by selection of the content of 'securities law') be designed to reduce the potential for externalization or promote a stable equilibrium and therefore provide an efficient competition in

[21] '[A] comparative cost–benefit analysis of regulatory competition and harmonization suggests that, where relevant, regulatory competition and harmonization should be seen as complements, rather than substitutes. The demarcation between the two is best determined on a case-by-case basis according to the principle of subsidiarity' (Sun and Pelkmans 1995: 67).

corporate law? If this were true, attempts to *analogize* between corporate law and securities law would be seriously misguided.

The international system is different from the federal system. The international system has less institutional capacity to enforce a stable equilibrium. As groups of states engage in cooperation, perhaps they will develop enhanced institutional mechanisms to do so, as the European Union has done. In the multilateral setting, however, it will be more difficult to engage in harmonization. Given concerns about externalization, equilibria, and other conditions of the Tiebout model, some level of prior centralization may be a prerequisite for the type of recognition that would greatly increase regulatory competition. Or to put it another way, it may be that a global mechanism, or set of mechanisms, to choose more deliberately between centralization or decentralization, and to select the type of centralization or decentralization, is desirable. These things exist in areas other than securities disclosure. The Basle Committee, Codex Alimentarius and the ISO interact in important ways with the legal rules of the WTO. The work of the IASC and IOSCO is similar. These organizations serve as fora for the negotiation of essential harmonization as a predicate for recognition.

In order to address the interconnected problems of unstable equilibria and externalities, it appears necessary to address more broadly the question of regulatory jurisdiction: what is the most efficient mechanism for internalizing externalities, and to what extent is it useful to do so? These questions cannot be answered by theory because they depend on different societies' regulatory preferences, which can only be revealed through competition or through political institutions. The problem of regulatory competition requires a political choice between these preference revelation devices. The political choice should be informed by the likely outcomes, in terms of local societal preferences, of the alternatives.

14

Regulatory Competition and the Global Coordination of Labour Standards

DAVID CHARNY*

This chapter develops a framework for analysing regulatory competition in labour standards. The analysis proceeds from two premises. First, assessment of regulatory competition in labour standards must be keyed to the economic impacts of the specific legal standard at issue. Although this is obvious enough stated abstractly, many economic analyses of labour standards model these standards generically as causing a per unit increase in the cost of labour. In fact, the characterization of the economic impact of a standard is rarely so simple. A more refined analysis generates a typology of labour regulations and suggests that many standards should not be problematic in the context of jurisdictional competition, because these standards reduce labour costs or, at least, do not increase them.

Once one eliminates standards that are unlikely to affect labour costs in a way which would induce regulatory competition, the standards that remain often aim substantially at redistribution or at affecting class or social structure or social norms, rather than simply aiming at efficiency in some narrower sense. The second premise of the analysis here, then, is the need for a set of specifically political criteria—beyond simple welfarism—for evaluating regulatory competition in labour standards. This chapter considers the role played by appeals to rights, democratic theory, cultural autonomy, and global equity in the political analysis of labour standards.

To clarify the analytic issues involved in interjurisdictional competition in labour standards, this chapter approaches the problem from a relatively abstract viewpoint. The analysis will consider a group of jurisdictions, each independently setting labour standards; to add a bit more concreteness to some of the analysis, it is sometimes helpful to contrast a set of 'North' countries, which are comparatively wealthy and technologically sophisticated, have more capital, and impose higher domestic labour standards, and 'South' jurisdictions, which are weaker in all these aspects. (These may be the Southern part of the United States, the southern tier of Europe, or the global 'South'.) Of course, this is extremely stylized, as some 'North' countries, such as the United States and Britain, may feature in the world

* For invaluable discussion and suggestions, I am grateful to John Coates, Dan Esty, Rob Howse, Alan Hyde, Christine Jolls, Brian Langille, Richard Steinberg, and George Triantis; to participants in the Conference on Regulatory Competition and Economic Integration, Yale University, 1999, organized in cooperation with the Institut d'Etudes Juridiques Européennes at the University of Liège, Belgium; and to participants in the faculty seminar at the UCLA Law School.

as having comparatively weak labour standards; and, further, within the United States, the European Union, and even the global arena, there are substantial institutions for influencing or imposing labour standards transjurisdictionally. The chapter turns to these in the conclusion. The main goal of this chapter is to provide an analytic basis for assessing the rationales for the regulatory activities of these transjurisdictional legal institutions, and for some proposed extensions of them.

Part I offers a basic discussion of the circumstances under which trade or capital mobility among jurisdictions might plausibly lead to a distortion in jurisdictions' labour standards. The models use a very simple conception in which a labour standard is modelled as a per unit increase in the cost of labour. Part II considers more precisely the types of cost impacts that would be observed for characteristic labour institutions. The discussion identifies five types of standards and traces out their main cost and distributive effects. Parts III and IV take up the question of political criteria for evaluating these impacts, and conclude by briefly considering the implications of these criteria for questions of institutional design.

A note on terminology: following the suggestions of a number of commentators (Bratton and McCahery 1997; Oates 1997), I shall avoid use of the term 'race to the bottom'. In the present context, as elsewhere, the term is a misnomer: whatever the regulatory decisions that are made, they virtually never land one at 'the bottom'. I shall, however, use the term 'jurisdictional (or regulatory) competition' somewhat loosely to refer to any situation in which one jurisdiction sets a labour standard because that standard gains an advantage *vis-à-vis* the economy of another jurisdiction either in the terms of trade or in attracting mobile investment capital. Similarly, I will use the term 'regulatory distortion' simply to mean that the outcomes from jurisdictional competition differ from those that would obtain in some specified baseline. The baseline, which will vary with the context of discussion, might be, for example, autarky; or the standard prior to trade liberalization; or the outcome from competition in an ideal Tiebout setting. Thus the terms 'jurisdictional competition' and 'regulatory distortion' are meant purely descriptively. From a normative point of view, the important question is whether the forces of regulatory competition or distortion induce the jurisdiction either to move away from an optimal standard or, more generally, to fail to adopt and enforce the optimum.[1]

I. FUNDAMENTALS

A natural way to view a labour standard is as a tax on labour; the funds from the tax are used to confer a public good. If one takes this view, the question of labour standards is readily assimilated into the more general framework that has developed for analysing fiscal regulatory (particularly environmental) distortions. Familiarly, if

[1] Esty (1996) provides a lucid formulation of this perspective in the environmental context.

the jurisdiction has access to a perfect set of fiscal instruments, faces no market imperfections, and is a price-taker on world markets, the jurisdiction gains nothing by attempting to manipulate its regulatory policies in order to attract resources to the jurisdiction (Oates and Schwab 1998; Revesz 1992). To discover circumstances in which regulatory distortions might occur, one must look for terms-of-trade effects, or fiscal or market imperfections.

For labour standards, then, as elsewhere, it is useful to distinguish several types of jurisdictional competition; the types differ in how they describe what the jurisdictions are actually competing about.[2] One type of jurisdictional competition occurs with jurisdictions set rules to affect terms of trade. To simplify, one can assume, in exploring this class of models, that the jurisdictions have a fixed capital endowment—that is, jurisdictions are vying for investment, as they are in many jurisdictional-competition models. Even in this situation, however, the jurisdictions may modify their rules if they can influence terms of trade by doing so. Consider an import-competing jurisdiction—that is, a jurisdiction that imports a good which it also produces domestically.[3] The levels of tariffs and of non-tariff trade barriers are fixed by a trade agreement, but the jurisdiction is free to set labour standards for the industry. The labour standard takes the form of a regulation that increases the cost per unit of labour, and the nation is economically large enough so that changes in its level of output affect world prices. In this situation, the jurisdiction may choose a labour standard in order to affect terms of trade. As the standard is tightened, the costs of the domestically produced good go up, and so the equilibrium price for the good in the home country (and so on the global markets) rises. In effect, some of the cost of the labour standard is passed on to the foreign exporters, who now sell less of their good at the higher price, or on to the foreign purchasers of the good.

The effect of trade on the import-competing country is to promote tighter labour standards, as some of the costs of those standards are, in effect, externalized to the exporting country.[4] From the point of view of advocates of tighter labour standards, the problem arises when trade is liberalized—for example, if, under the General Agreement on Tariffs and Trade (GATT) regime, the import-competing jurisdiction reduces tariffs. Considering terms-of-trade effects, the import-competing country now has an incentive to weaken its labour standards. On the new terms of trade under the liberalized trade regime, less of the cost of the labour standards can be externalized to the exporting country; and so the import-competing country perceives its labour standards as more costly than before

[2] Farber (1997a) provides a good general analysis of these categories.

[3] The text draws on the analysis of Bagwell and Staiger (1999a). A more informal presentation can be found in Bagwell and Staiger (1999b). Brown, Deardorff, and Stern (1996: 227) discuss terms-of-trade effects for this type of standard more briefly, but focus on the case of a standard that constricts the endowment of labour. For reasons discussed below, I will not consider this type of standard in detail here.

[4] Note, however, that the effect is the opposite on the exporting country, which will have an incentive to relax its labour standards in the presence of trade (Srinivasan forthcoming).

liberalization (that is, than under the previous terms of trade).[5] Of course, this is not really a 'race to the bottom' story. There is no convergence toward a single lower system, but simply a slackening of the extant pre-liberalization labour regime. Nonetheless, the argument illustrates that trade liberalization may induce a jurisdiction to relax its pre-liberalization labour standards when these standards influence the terms of trade.

A second type of regulatory distortion arises from the jurisdiction's incentives to influence investment rather than terms of trade. To sharpen the difference between the two types of models, one might begin by assuming that a jurisdiction engages in no trade at all, and has a fixed labour endowment. It can, however, attract capital investment from other jurisdictions. Will this influence its choice of labour standards, when one models the labour standard as producing a social good by increasing the unit costs of labour? In particular, given the standard chosen once foreign capital becomes available, does an increase in the mobility of capital—say, the emergence of a global financial regime, which facilitates foreign investment—affect the choice of labour standard? With perfect fiscal instruments, the simple answer is no. The jurisdiction may set its tax levels and the amounts of public goods either optimally or, in a Cournot–Nash equilibrium, suboptimally (Mintz and Tulkens 1986); but either way, it can accrue no further gain by manipulating its labour standards. Distortion might occur, however, with an imperfect set of fiscal instruments. For labour standards, note that it may not be feasible for the jurisdiction to design its taxes to obtain the optimal incidence of the labour standards' costs. Absent further government interventions, the incidence is determined by the elasticities of supply and demand for labour. Although it might be desirable for the government to alter the incidence of the implicit labour-standard tax, it may find itself unable to do so. For example, if the cost of the labour standard falls suboptimally on capital, the government might counteract this with a capital subvention—a programme that would be difficult to design and administer, and that might be politically unacceptable for public-choice reasons. The government instead may choose to relax the labour standard in order to diminish the fiscal distortions that the standard causes.

A third set of models for regulatory distortion appeals to imperfections in the markets for goods or factors of production. Again, these are readily adapted to the case of labour standards—most often with an additional stipulation as to limits on the range of fiscal instruments, since otherwise these instruments would suffice to respond to the imperfection, without any change in labour standards. For example, adjustment of labour standards might play a role in bargaining for 'lumpy' investments or in a jurisdictional policy to mitigate involuntary unemployment. But the question again arises why the jurisdiction would not use direct subsidies for these purposes. The most natural answer again reverts to the administrative or public-

[5] Trade has the opposite effect in the exporting country, which now has an incentive to tighten its labour standards. Bagwell and Staiger (1999b) suggest, however, that in the current 'North–South' situation there is an asymmetry here: because the 'South' exporters are severally too small to influence the terms of trade, they do not see a terms-of-trade advantage to tighter labour standards.

choice considerations that generate fiscal imperfections: most simply, the government may lack the information to design and implement the ideal tax; or it may prefer to place the costs of attracting capital on the poorer and politically less powerful, rather than on wealthier, more influential citizens; and find that the desired incidence is most readily achieved by adjusting labour standards rather than taxes.

II. A TYPOLOGY OF LABOUR STANDARDS

The simple models treat labour standards as a tax on labour that produces a pure public good. Evidently, this is too simple. What happens when we try to specify the effects of labour standards more precisely?

In this Part, I shall distinguish five types of labour standards: 'purely efficient' static labour standards, static redistributive labour standards, dynamic labour standards, social welfare standards, and empowerment standards. Interjurisdictional regulatory competition must be analysed differently for each type of standard.

Static labour standards: 'purely efficient' vs. redistributive

The most evident modification of the simple model of the standard-as-tax is to specify that labour standards confer a benefit directly on the employees of the affected firms, rather than creating a generic public good. Examples include labour standards that mandate work breaks, safety protections, and protections against arbitrary discharge or harassment. Once such a standard is instituted the equilibrium wage may decline: the workers are willing to work for a lower wage because they also now receive compensation in the form of the non-wage benefit; employers reduce the wage that they are willing to pay because of the added unit labour cost generated by the labour standard.

There is no simple prediction about the equilibrium outcome in this situation. In the simplest situation—the case of the 'purely efficient' standard—all workers value the benefit precisely at its cost to the employer. The benefit simply substitutes for a money wage payment, and so the money wage is correspondingly reduced by the value of the benefit; there is no effect on employment. For the purely efficient standard, then, a jurisdiction cannot gain an advantage—either in terms of trade or in terms of attracting investment—by adjusting its labour standard. Any adjustment simply accomplishes a corresponding change in wages, and the net effect confers no benefit on employers, either as capitalists or trading partners. Indeed, in some circumstances, workers may value the benefit at more than its cost to the employer; relaxation of these standards may actually increase labour costs, because deregulation would cause wages to go up more than employers would save from the relaxation of standards.[6] Note, finally, that if the workers value the

[6] In this situation, it might appear puzzling why it would be necessary for government to prescribe the benefit. Explanations in the literature include: adverse selection problems which deter firms from

benefit at less than cost, imposition of the standard reduces workers' total compensation. To the extent of the difference between the workers' gain and employers' cost, the mandate functions like a tax on employment, and we are returned to the simple standard-as-tax models of regulatory competition.

The most likely situation, however, is that workers are heterogeneous: some workers value the benefit at more than cost, others do not. Here, there is a distributive effect. Workers who find themselves paying (through a wage reduction) for a benefit that they do not value at that cost are worse off, and may at the margin drop out of the labour force if the equilibrium wage is not high enough to keep them in. Workers who value the benefit at more than cost gain from the distributive consequences of the rule; and some individuals may now choose to enter the workforce because the new benefit makes the available compensation package more valuable to them. Assessment of the welfare effects will depend on how one weights the welfare effects on these different subgroups of workers.[7]

This account helps to unpack some of the rhetoric about 'social dumping' and 'low labour standards', particularly in contexts such as the US states or the European Union in which the member states are not too far apart in terms of wealth and level of industrialization. In these debates, the implicit assumption is that the social welfare requirements imposed on firms function like a tax, as in the simple models discussed above. But this is evidently not the case for many of the social-welfare type benefits at issue: rather, these labour standards simply mandate non-wage benefits that would be traded off against wages, in the manner just discussed. In the simplest case, the net effect on employment costs (and equilibrium employment) is zero, so it is not clear that jurisdictions can gain any advantages from diluting these standards. Indeed, if the mandates deviate from the optimum, the only effect may be, as we have seen, to reduce employment by inducing some workers to leave the job market.

In the more complex cases, however, there may be an inducement towards relaxed labour standards. For example, workers may value the benefit at its average cost, but costs of compliance with the labour standard may vary among types of employers, so that for some employer-types the cost of the benefit exceeds its value to employees. Equivalently for the analysis here, some employer-types might be more likely to employ workers who did not value the benefit at cost: for example, some employer-types might tend to employ young workers who, if myopic or hyperbolically discounting, are less likely than older workers to see a net gain from mandated pension contributions or health insurance. If these employer-types were

offering benefits; drafting, bargaining, and information costs; status quo biases or myopia, which prevent workers from appreciating the value of the benefit before it is actually given to them by the mandate; and pure paternalism (Gruber 1994; Jolls, Sunstein, and Thaler 1998; Summers 1998).

[7] Charny (1996) provides further analysis of regulatory conflicts among subgroups of workers modelling standards in an economy where workers have heterogeneous preferences for safety. Brown, Deardorff, and Stern (1996) develop a model in which the safety standards prove suboptimal even when the analysis is purely domestic—a setting which, needless to say, hardly provides a fertile opportunity for considering the effects of jurisdictional competition.

concentrated in import-competing sectors, then the standard, operating like a tax, might be relaxed as trade was liberalized, along the lines of the terms-of-trade story discussed above. Similarly, in investment-competition models, jurisdictions would face an incentive to relax previously optimal labour standards if they were competing for employer-types who saw the mandate as a tax, particularly if employers who saw it as neutral or beneficial were fixedly domestic.

How plausible are these adjusted scenarios? The paradigmatic employer-type in many discussions of labour-standard competition is the large-scale manufacturer of relatively simple consumer or intermediate goods. The workers in these sectors are relatively young, unskilled, and low-paid, and so presumably likely to value many benefits at less than the average worker (particularly in wealthier countries, where labour standards appear particularly to benefit wealthier middle-aged or older workers over younger ones). A jurisdiction could attract such employers by adopting lower labour standards, because these employers would then be free to design optimal compensation packages for their workers. Jurisdictions which adhered to the higher standards—perhaps because of the demographic predominance or political power of older, wealthier workers—would experience themselves as having some employers 'competed away' to jurisdictions with laxer regulatory standards. What generates the appearance of 'social dumping' is the difficulty that jurisdictions apparently may have in tailoring their mandated benefits provisions to particular employer-types. Although adjustment of labour standards in these circumstances may have distributive impacts, it would be inaccurate to claim that there is a clear welfare loss from a social point of view. Assessment of the distributive impacts depends, again, upon how one weighs the welfare of particular subgroups of workers—or, more generally, on one's political conception of distributive justice, a question to which we return in Part III.

Dynamic labour standards

A further modification of the simple standard-as-tax model focuses on the dynamic rather than the static standards. Consider minimum wage laws. On the static view, minimum wage laws simply raise the cost of labour and increase unemployment.[8] Dynamically, however, the claim is that minimum wage laws induce a choice in a situation of multiple equilibria. Two possible equilibria are postulated: one in which production is accomplished by low-skill, low-wage workers using primitive technology ('sweatshops'); and another in which high-skill, high-wage workers use more sophisticated technology. The sector is currently at the sweatshop equilibrium. The dynamic conception is that minimum wage laws, by banning sweatshops, induce investment for the development of more sophisticated technology

[8] Of course, an important line of research suggests that the minimum wage may raise wages without having an impact on unemployment (Card and Krueger 1995). For the analysis in text, I set this case aside.

which is then deployed using the highly skilled, and so highly paid, workers that the new technology requires (Piore 1990; Rodrik 1996a).

Is this strategy for minimum wage laws threatened by jurisdictional competition? Consider the investment-competition model. The question is whether the move to the high-wage equilibrium can be effected in a situation in which capital may be invested in other jurisdictions. The fear would be that the anti-sweatshop strategy no longer works if the opportunity to invest in other, low-wage jurisdictions dissipates the technology- or capital investment-forcing effect of the minimum-wage sweatshop ban. When the minimum wage is imposed, capital moves abroad, and so the minimum wage merely causes unemployment; jurisdictional competition for capital thus would force the government to abandon its minimum-wage policy. In effect, this account postulates that the minimum-wage policy operated as a type of implicit tax on capital, which was induced by the policy to underwrite the development of the new forms of production. So, again, the account comes down to claims about fiscal or political distortion. Why cannot the government implement the anti-sweatshop policy with an explicit subsidy for the preferred alternative forms of technology or production? The answers at this point should be familiar: such a subsidy would be difficult to design and administer (how does the government identify appropriate candidates?); and taxes to raise money for the subsidy are unavailable politically or objectionable because they cause economic distortions as well.

Labour standards alternatively may aim at dynamic effects on human capital formation, rather than physical capital or technology. For example, gender discrimination laws may be aimed at fostering women's human capital investments. The prospect of gender discrimination in wage payments or promotions may discourage women from investing in human capital, as their investment will not receive the return which would be paid to male workers for the equivalent investment (Becker 1985). Child labour laws also are designed in part to foster a better educated workforce; on this view, children who spend their youth being educated rather than working will grow up to be more skilled and therefore more productive workers.[9]

Here, as with minimum wage laws, an initial judgement would be that dynamically justified labour standards are less likely to be threatened by jurisdictional competition than statically justified ones. Statically, both gender wage-equality norms and child labour laws raise labour costs: they can be analysed as a tax, as in the models in Part I. In the gender case, a wage-equality requirement functions analogously to a minimum wage: it raises the cost of employing women from its pre-regulation equilibrium up to the cost of employing men for comparable positions (however the law defines 'comparable'). In the new static equilibrium, labour costs rise and employment falls for both men and women. Dynamically, however, the effect of

[9] Of course, minimum wage, anti-discrimination, and child labour laws also sound in claims of 'rights' or moral duty. I take up some structural aspects of these claims below.

the law should be neutral or positive for employers: on the dynamic hypothesis, women are no longer deterred from human capital investment by the prospect of discrimination, and so will acquire human capital sufficient to justify their employment at the mandated higher wages. Consequently, from the point of view of jurisdictional competition there is no terms-of-trade effect, because the labour standard does not change labour costs; nor does the standard affect employers' investment decisions.[10]

The European experience with wage equity is suggestive (Sapir 1996).[11] Gender equity in wages was an aspect of social programmes that was incorporated into the EC treaties quite early on, at the insistence of France, whose standards in this regard were far more stringent than those of other European countries and who therefore feared that it would be placed at a competitive disadvantage (in sectors with a large proportion of women in the workforce). After substantial delays, the measure has been implemented quite rigorously, and apparently, at least in recent years, without the impediments and resistance that have so decisively attended other aspects of the attempt to implement a European social plan. Of course, in part this suggests a high-level consensus in support of the anti-discrimination norm; but it also suggests that gender discrimination in wages was not, contrary to the French fears, a long-term source of competitive advantage, because of the dynamic effects of laws that ban this discrimination.

Labour standards as social insurance

Labour standards may be used to implement a type of social insurance scheme that spreads risks among workers as a group. At times, these are government-managed insurance funds to which workers and employers pay premiums in the form of payroll taxes. More indirectly, labour standards often serve to insure workers against economic risk. Regulation of discharges and mass layoffs, plan closures, and general requirements for union negotiation or consultation impose costs on employers and workers in order to protect workers who lose their jobs because of economic fluctuations. Similarly, one might interpret the tendency of unions to compress wage differentials as having a social-insurance aspect: wage compression, over time, limits the degree of wage volatility in the face of changes in demands for different worker-types.

Arguably, jurisdictional competition for investment disrupts these schemes by increasing the volatility of capital investment in each jurisdiction, and correspondingly

[10] Of course, this assumes that employers do not experience hiring women of itself as generating costs, either because of an aversion to women workers or because of 'cultural' tensions in the workplace introduced by the presence of women in environments that had been predominantly male. The dynamic rationale works for statistical discrimination. However, one could also develop dynamic accounts for other types of discrimination, emphasizing that the law may change social preferences or attitudes about women at work.

[11] In other areas of social policy, the barriers to harmonization have proved steep, if not insuperable (Sapir 1996; Bercusson, Ch. 11).

increasing the cost of the social insurance provided by the labour standard (Rodrik 1997; Rodrik and van Ypersele 1991a). Faced with this increased cost, a jurisdiction may choose to reduce the level of social insurance protection. Capital cannot be taxed to pay for these schemes because it is more mobile; workers may be reluctant to pay the higher premiums in effect required by higher levels of risk. Note that, in theory, these risks could be eliminated by an insurance scheme that pooled workers across borders: as workers in one national sector lose because of capital mobility, workers in a sector in another nation presumably gain; faced with this risk ex ante, workers in both jurisdictions should be willing to pay a small premium to limit their subsequent losses, should dislocation occur. Viewed as an instance of jurisdictional distortion, then, the gravamen of the problem would have to be that there is a type of transnational contract failure: the optimal implicit labour-standard risk-sharing contract would spread risks not simply among workers who are citizens in a particular jurisdiction, but also among workers across borders.

Labour standards designed to empower groups of workers

A final type of labour standard aims explicitly at redistribution of bargaining power between workers and investors or among groups of workers. Evident examples are rules designed to facilitate cooperative action by workers in forming unions; rules which mandate disclosure to or consultation with groups of workers; and rules which designate worker representatives for corporate boards or other decision-making bodies within the firm.[12] I shall refer to these rules as 'empowerment rules'.

Empowerment rules combine features of each of the rule-types that we have already examined. On different characterizations, empowerment rules may be purely efficient; they may redistribute among subgroups or workers; or they may aim at dynamic or social-insurance goals. Correspondingly, analysis of those rule-types carries over directly to empowerment rules. First, the jurisdiction evidently gains no competitive advantage by relaxing empowerment rules that enhance the total efficiency of the employment relationship. Even if unions and other representational devices enhance efficiency, however, this is rarely their sole effect. They also generally enable workers to use market power to raise wages, by restricting supply or by extracting rents from the firm through negotiating tactics. Further, dealing with unions may raise the prospect of strikes, higher bargaining costs for contract negotiations, and higher ongoing administrative costs of dealing with union representatives. From this perspective, empowerment rules appear simply as rules that increase labour cost to employers; correspondingly, terms-of-trade or capital investment effects that would induce jurisdictions to seek lower labour costs would lead to laxer regulatory standards concerning unions.[13]

[12] In the most compelling account, empowerment by unions transforms the collective consciousness of workers and their relationship to the firm (Barenberg 1993).

[13] Of course, what are the actual effects of unionization is a complex and highly controversial area of inquiry. Without trying to arbitrate this controversy, I wish here simply to explore the implications for jurisdictional competition of some of the most influential claims.

On some interpretations of the activities of unions, these relaxed standards clearly lead to social loss. For example, in the Freeman and Medoff analysis (1984), unions generate gains from a social point of view, but use their bargaining power over rents to transfer all of these gains, and more, to workers. Implicitly, union-promoting labour standards impose a tax on capital. But, if the jurisdiction relaxes the rules in order to compete for capital investment, the weakening of unions incurs a social cost. Here, as always, the question is why the beneficent social arrangements cannot be preserved through appropriate fiscal measures. In this instance, the government might try to sustain stronger unions, in the face of jurisdictional competition, by devising a fiscal scheme that transferred rents from workers to investors: unions would continue to garner the efficiency advantages of 'voice', but capital would not disinvest because it would not face unions' rent-extraction activities. Evidently, the difficulty faced with the fiscal scheme is that unions can counteract its effects as long as they retain bargaining power; the scheme would have to involve a policy of government wage setting, which may be politically untenable and generally introduces rather drastic economic distortions of its own.

The impact of jurisdictional competition is even starker when the jurisdiction promotes unions not to achieve the efficiency advantages of worker voice but to accomplish purely redistributive goals. In effect, when foreign jurisdictions compete for investment by reducing their labour standards, they may disrupt the home country's arrangements for distributing rents between labour and capital. Indeed, in a simple uncoordinated equilibrium, both countries evidently may end up with standards that allocate less rent to workers than each country would choose in autarky, or that the countries would agree to do if they could coordinate labour standards. Aside from effects on the jurisdictions' choice of union-promoting rules, competition for investment and terms-of-trade effects may affect unions' own power and bargaining strategies. These effects are clearest in the limiting case of a single national union that represents all workers in negotiating with all employers to set contract terms for workers. This union would experience the interjurisdictional regulatory constraint that the government itself would experience in setting labour terms for workers, with the difference only that the government maximand includes considerations other than the welfare of current union workers. So, for example, this union might see that, as trade liberalized, less of the costs of generous contract terms were effectively externalized onto the foreign exporter (its workers would experience this in terms of higher prices for consumer goods) and so the union would moderate its contract demands. Similarly, in competition for investment, the single national union might see that it needed to reduce its contract demands in order to attract investment to the jurisdiction or prevent disinvestment from it. In short, while the union could still formally exercise the power delegated to it by national labour laws, its ability to negotiate contract terms favourable to workers would be substantially diminished.

As one moves from the abstract national-union to more realistic settings, the story is modified in several ways. First, it is not apparent that unions will always be extensive enough for their bargaining positions to influence the terms of trade. One comes closest to the national-union model in the 'corporatist' regimes of some Western European states, in which unions at times have participated in tripartite national bargaining or wage-setting institutions that have substantial macroeconomic effects. In the United States, where unions may predominate in wage setting in some import-competing sectors (most notably, perhaps, cars and formerly steel), terms-of-trade effects would appear in these sectors. Further, as unions became less inclusive, conflicts of interest between union members and the jurisdictions' citizens, taken as a group, are exacerbated. If terms-of-trade effects appear as changes in consumer prices, the unions may be willing to ignore or discount these in order to promote wage gains for their own members. In turn, this would provide an indirect inducement for the jurisdiction to loosen its labour-law standard, in order to reduce the power of unions and so avoid the welfare losses that the rest of the jurisdiction's citizens would suffer from the unions' exercise of their bargaining power. Hence trade liberalization exacerbates political conflicts between unions and non-unionized workers and citizens—certainly one of the most salient features of the recurrent political situation of the wealthy import-competing nations.

Competition for capital investment can be analysed similarly. The national union reduces contract demands to attract investment. The effect would also be present in sectoral terms, in import-competing sectors (Bertrand 1999). It is not clear that there is a conflict of interest between citizens and union workers; this depends on whether the citizens receive net benefits from capital investment, perhaps because the jurisdiction taxes capital, or because capital investment increases labour productivity and so increases wages. Again, unions' incentives may diverge from welfare to the jurisdiction's citizens as a group, and trade liberalization or increased capital mobility may exaggerate this divergence. The diminution of unions' bargaining ability may mean terms for their workers that are less generous than would be optimal if one considered only the welfare of the workers and investors; nonetheless, the impacts on non-union workers (through the diminution of 'insider–outsider' effects) or consumers may be such that the outcomes are still superior to those that would be obtained if one optimized considering only unionized workers and their employers.

Assessment

The rule-specific analysis of jurisdictional competition in labour standards suggests two generalizations. First, for many rules, jurisdictional competition is not a problem because the rules enhance the efficiency of the employment relationship; the jurisdiction gains no competitive (that is, cost) advantage by relaxing the rules. These competitive gains may derive either from static or dynamic effects of the standard.

Conversely, the rules to which jurisdictional competition poses a threat generally have strong distributive effects. Here, one can divide rules into three subtypes.

For some rules, redistribution is not the aim of the rule, but is the inevitable side-effect of the government's inability either to draft a more precise rule or devise a fiscal scheme that counteracts the rule's distributive impact. This is the case, for example, for mandated benefits rules where workers differentially valued the benefit, and for unions understood as gaining the efficiency advantages of worker voice. In other cases, the point of the labour standard is redistributive, and jurisdictional competition frustrates the redistributive policy. The most evident case is union rent extraction; 'dynamic' labour market policies like anti-sweatshop rules provided a less overt example. Finally, there is the case of labour standards which function as pure social insurance: although not redistributive in theory (because all workers gain ex ante from the provision of insurance), their implementation requires redistribution ex post in ways which may be blocked by jurisdictional competition.

Once labour standards are parsed in this way, regulatory distortion for some rule-types—relative to the regime prior to trade or investment liberalization—should come as no surprise. It is a familiar lesson from the tax literature that a jurisdiction pursues suboptimal redistributive policies when faced with competition from other jurisdictions: those subject to the redistributive exactions leave the jurisdiction, while those who benefit flock to it. Only the former effect has been significant to the analysis here, because the effect of immigration has been put aside; but even without that effect, it seems plausible that a jurisdiction's labour-based redistributive and fiscal policies will be impeded by the threat of jurisdictional competition.

III. POLITICS

The analysis of rule-types highlights the need for a set of political criteria to evaluate the outcomes of interjurisdictional regulatory effects. Conceptions of political theory—such as 'rights' or 'sovereignty' or 'distributive justice'—supply the gap that is created by the intractability of distributive issues when considered in purely economic terms. Hence it is not surprising that appeal to these political conceptions has been so prominent in debates about labour standards. Without purporting to offer a comprehensive assessment, the point of the discussion is simply to determine what the analysis of regulatory effects might tell us about the bearing of the political conceptions.

Rights

'Rights' are the characteristic language for laying claim to distributive entitlements of the type that might be threatened by jurisdictional competition over labour standards. The structure of the claim is that the entitlement should be evaluated not simply by the gain in welfare that it produces; rather, the values that the entitlement confers should be given a lexical priority over mere improvements in welfare. If workers have a right to avoid sweatshop conditions or to form unions, then they are entitled to a regime of labour standards that enforces these rights, even if the regime sacrifices gains from trade or capital mobility.

In the context of labour standards, two types of 'rights' claims should be distinguished (Howse and Trebilcock 1996). Consider, for concreteness, an import-competing country whose trading partner permits 'sweatshop' conditions—hazardous work at extremely low wages—and suppresses unions. The import-competing country may seek to make a rights claim on behalf of the oppressed workers in the exporting country, or, alternatively, it may be concerned about the 'rights' of its own workers. As a normative matter, the first claim does not depend on the effects of jurisdictional competition in labour standards. Presumably, the workers have a right to be exempt from oppressive labour conditions whether or not the goods they produce are exported. Of course, it may be that the enterprise is in business only because of the availability of a market for the goods abroad, but this fact would hardly be determinative of whether the workers' rights were violated.

In contrast, the second rights claim—that of workers in the import-competing jurisdiction—directly refers to the phenomenon of jurisdictional competition. The import-competing jurisdiction, and particularly workers in the affected sectors, suffer economic disadvantage because the exporting jurisdiction has inappropriately low labour standards. The theory has the structure of theories of 'unfair competition' in the common law, which on some readings permits a cause of action for economic harm done by any wrongful taking of economic advantage. In short, there is a general right to be free of the adverse consequences of another's wrongful act. Here, the harm may take the form of a reduction in wages or a deterioration of labour protections in the import-competing jurisdiction.

How should we assess this claim of right? Initially, let us set aside two arguments that often colour the practical force of the argument, but do not affect its validity in theory. First, the argument is marred by its frequent protectionist invocation in circumstances where the facts do not support it. Second, the argument does not depend on the notion that those claiming the right have some sincere or legitimate interest in the welfare of those abroad who are harmed by weak labour standards; the import-competing workers have an independent claim to be free from harm suffered as a result of wrongs abroad.

Even waiving these objections, it is difficult to conclude that conceptions of rights should exert substantial weight in evaluating possible regulatory distortions. As an empirical matter, the evidence that such violations of right garner economic advantages is equivocal: for example, it appears that low labour standards discourage foreign investment rather than attract it (Rodrik 1996b). No doubt this correlation reflects in part the fact that countries with low labour standards are likely to be unattractive in a host of ways—in particular, they are likely to be undemocratic, socially oppressive, and politically unstable. But labour standards which are so low as to permit routine violation of fundamental rights may be difficult to sustain politically in a democratic regime.

More fundamentally, labour standards must deteriorate significantly before a convincing claim can be made that rights are violated. The problem for institutional design is that there is little general consensus on what counts as the minimally adequate implementation of core labour rights (Leary 1996). In part, indeterminacy plagues the appeal to rights because rights claims in the labour context are easily 'flipped' by reference to values of autonomy: minimum wage laws interfere with workers' freedom to alienate their labour; pro-union closed shop rules impinge upon workers' rights of association; and so forth. In part, the difficulty is the cultural specificity of values about work: work by children, or a fair amount of deference to supervisors, may be an embedded feature of employment relations. One could repudiate any form of cultural relativism—and might even go fairly far in making welfarist judgements about cultural practices (Nussbaum 1999)—but still conclude that substantial interference with most extant labour practices on grounds of 'right' would be unduly intrusive, paternalistic, or imperialist.

Democratic theory

The critique of jurisdictional competition from democratic theory is simply that the outcomes of labour standards, in situations of jurisdictional distortion, are not produced 'democratically'. In setting labour standards (in a world without provision for international standard setting) each regime is simply playing a bargaining game with the others; the suggestion is that the outcome of such bargaining games does not have the imprimatur of democratic legitimacy (Langille 1996).

Evidently, the criterion for democratic legitimacy here is that affected groups have a reasonably direct institutional voice in the setting of legal standards that have an effect on them. In instances of regulatory distortion, standard determination fails to meet this criterion in one of several respects. First, jurisdictions set labour standards with regard to the external effects that their standards have on other jurisdictions: for example, in the terms-of-trade context, the standard is set so as to manipulate the degree of externalization of the costs of labour standards. The essence of regulatory distortion here, then, is that those outside the jurisdiction, who have no input on the setting of the standard, bear some of its effects. There is, in turn, a secondary distortion that also can be criticized from the point of view of democratic theory. Those who bear the external cost of the regulatory distortion may do so in the form of an effect on their freedom to set the standards that they would set in the situation of autarky.[14] The jurisdiction that relaxes its standards in response to the pressure of relaxed standards set by other jurisdictions finds, from the viewpoint of democratic theory, that its exercise of democratic will has been tainted by the external impacts of the decisions of other polities. The citizens of the home jurisdiction have no direct input into the decisions of these other polities. In

[14] Note that the dual effects here have the same structure as the dual effects in the case of rights claims.

that sense, not only the home jurisdiction's welfare but also its own democratic autonomy are affected by the decisions of other jurisdictions.

From one perspective, the implicitly Marxist paternity of this approach to legitimacy should be apparent. The root presupposition is that it is illegitimate for collective choices to reflect passively the outcome of 'blind' economic forces or market forces, when in fact these forces are the creations of collective choices and could be modified by deliberate institutional design. Clearly, this judgement does not enjoy any general favour. After all, in the classic Tiebout model, jurisdictional competition produces the social optimum; the outcome would not generally be considered illegitimate simply because the jurisdictions are embedded in a 'market' for numerous local providers of public goods (Tiebout 1956).

In the case of labour standards, however, the claims of democratic theory are substantially stronger. The interests at stake in regulatory competition—even if not characterizable as 'rights'—are at the core of those social values that ought to be subject to collective determination by democratic institutions: the standard for equitable division of wealth; the degree of differentiation among social classes; the integrity and power of civic associations (such as unions and works councils); and the extent to which economics risks are shared collectively rather than borne by individuals. In short, basic considerations of social structure and social solidarity are at stake. These are matters, it is proposed, that should be subject to active debate among affected citizens; that should be determined—to the extent that they are determined collectively—by democratic means; and that ought not to be forfeit to the vicissitudes of international markets or to the decisions of foreign sovereigns. It might also be suggested that jurisdictional competition does independent harm to goods of cultural autonomy, the recognition of the value of distinct cultural norms. On this view, the difficulty with the current regime is the threat that jurisdictional distortion poses to the maintenance of the distinctive cultural rules or norms by which nations have constituted the sphere of work.

The set of jurisdictional distortions would count as undemocratic, then, to the extent that there was a plausible mechanism for jurisdiction standard setting that gave due voice to the interests of all affected. At first cut, this may seem a somewhat paradoxical basis on which to make claims for global cooperation about labour standards, which, after all, is in a sense effective only by impeding the independent exercise of nations' sovereign power. It is now well understood, though, that the partial sacrifices of sovereignty involved in transnational coordination may prevent the more complete erosion that is caused by naked jurisdictional competition (Moravcsik 1998). Nonetheless, there is an evident tradeoff between the democratic advantages of centralized and decentralized modes of resolving these issues. It is much easier to design institutions that are locally democratic than globally democratic, particularly in terms of responsiveness to the 'cultural' aspects of what counts as democratic decision making; moreover, preferences and social circumstances are likely to be more homogeneous within localities than across a set of boundaries. Even putting aside the general difficulties with designing democratic institutions of global or supranational jurisdiction, the advantages of decentralized decision making are quite evident in the context of labour standards. Standards must be adapted to local circumstances, cultures of work, and structures of labour markets, which vary widely even among countries of roughly the same level of wealth. Ability to use voice effectively is partly endogenous to the structure of domestic labour standards, so this too will vary widely to the extent that citizens' groups seek to be influential at the global institutional level. Finally, transnational institutions may be subject to interest-group capture or to economic pressures in a way which may actually weaken standards of the constituent members (Paul 1996; Streeck 1997). Distortions particularly may occur when international institutions are designed—as under the current trade regime—to be responsive primarily to interests as expressed by sovereign states; a global labour regime should presumably be responsive to the array of non-state agents who have stakes in labour relations.

Global equity and economic development

Although the discussion has pinpointed the distributional goals of labour institutions, the focus so far has been on the implementation of these goals within the nation-state. What of the claims for a standard of global economic equity, or, at least, for programmes that would systematically reduce the vast disparities in global wealth by fostering development of poorer countries? It is evident that law probably has a relatively small role to play in this global project, but the analysis of labour standards suggests two ways in which these standards are implicated in questions of global equity.

First, regulatory competition may threaten the strategies of some national programmes for development. For example, this competition may make it difficult for poorer nations to pursue the 'high-wage option' or to reduce gender disparities in employment, because the transition costs imposed by these programmes could cause capital flight or disadvantage in international trade. Second, the analysis has suggested that social-insurance programmes implemented through labour standards would function best if they could incorporate some mechanism for pooling of risks across borders.

Developmental concerns, however, may counsel against attempts to mitigate the problems of jurisdictional competition by international measures. The fundamental difficulty is that economies at different stages of development may require very different labour institutions; the attempt to impose a uniform template by international standard setting would then impede rather than foster development. The irony becomes acute when wealthier countries attempt to announce, as universally valid standards, rules that they themselves routinely violated on the path to development (and sometimes still violate in some informal or poorly regulated sectors) (Bhagwati 1998). Thus the claims of democratic theory and global development, though pertinent, pose severe problems of institutional design.

IV. PARADOXES OF TRANSNATIONAL INSTITUTIONAL DESIGN

The analysis here underscores a pervasive mismatch between the distortions caused by regulatory competition and the governance capacities of international labour institutions. Global agencies such as the International Labour Organization (ILO) will be most effective at identifying severe violations of 'core' labour rights, that is, those on whose content there is a general consensus. But these will be only a small part of those regulatory problems that arise from jurisdictional competition, and, indeed, it is unclear that rights violations are characteristically linked to regulatory competition at all. International activity to promote core labour rights is perhaps better rationalized as the attempt of the international community to counteract the effects of rather severe 'public choice' problems in non-democratic states.

Conversely, the large-scale problems of shoring up the dynamic, redistributive, and social-insurance roles of labour regulation appear substantially resistant to solution by any set of 'global' standards, or indeed by centralized regional or transnational coordination. One barrier is the specificity of these arrangements to the cultures of work and politics in particular unions, or even particular regions or subdivisions in the nation-state. This specificity makes it difficult to construct consensus on a core set of transnational labour policies, aside from the very minimal basic rights set out in the commonly ratified ILO conventions. Second, the construction of redistributive and social-insurance schemes, in particular, would require substantial transfer payments between jurisdictions, even regular tax or premium payments to some international authority. It is hard to imagine a general acceptance of the large sacrifice in national sovereignty that such schemes would entail. Third, international coordination of labour standards is impeded by tight restrictions on immigration between jurisdictions. Movement of workers would be the natural way of smoothing out the large differences in labour endowments which now helps to create incentives for regulatory competition; large-scale migrations were crucial, of course, to the effective functioning of centralized regulation in the United States. But again, as with transfer payments, a substantial change in the current regime seems ruled out by the infringement on conceptions of national integrity that such large-scale movements now seem to imply. Finally, of course, there are the characteristic difficulties with international enforcement; for labour standards, the perversity of enforcement through trade sanctions has been widely discussed.

In this setting, strategies to preserve labour standards from regulatory distortion must proceed on a more piece-meal or *ad hoc* basis. On one account, the key is the emergence of 'networks' of actors committed to a set of labour policies—including unions, local and multinational business, non-governmental organizations (NGOs), national governments, and regional and international organizations—which act in situationally specific ways to address particular labour problems. Opportunities to act are created by numerous structural connections across borders, including the institutions set up by regional or global treaties (such as the North

American Free Trade Agreement (NAFTA) or the ILO conventions), cross-border ties among unions, and business susceptibility to pressure in various national markets and regulatory spheres (Trubek and Rothstein 1998).[15] The openness of these networks to various non-governmental actors serves as a corrective to the tendency of extant international organizations to be too exclusively attentive to national interests as defined by national sovereigns. To many observers, nonetheless, the emergent structure of *ad hoc* regulation will present itself as a public choice nightmare, in which powerful economic groups of dubious accountability use their regional or global leverage to aggrandize their own economic interests. Even presented as labour 'advocacy', it suffers the difficulty that less well-organized workers—those in informal sectors of agriculture, services, and small-scale manufacturing, to which the model of large-scale organizational mobilization is difficult to apply—will find their interests slighted or ignored.

An important corrective would be to move away from the predominantly 'legal' model of how global labour standards operate. In the legal model—the basis for the ILO and for most proposals to incorporate labour standards into the GATT—the international regime promulgates rules or standards, enforced by an adjudicatory body in specific cases of violation. An alternative would be to emphasize, at an international level, the development of a set of 'benchmarking' criteria for systematic evaluation of national or regional labour law regimes, along performance dimensions such as wage equity, job safety, skills developments, and so forth. This benchmarking would provide standards by which the 'network' participants could evaluate and criticize local labour institutions, while at the same time avoiding the mistake of attempting to impose a single labour template on diverse national institutional arrangements. The point would be to facilitate transnational coordination without intruding upon a core set of national prerogatives in labour policy making; the aspiration would be to foster transparent transnational forms of deliberation on the appropriate form of labour institutions (Dorf and Sabel 1998; Freeman 1997). The basic paradox of regulatory competition, however, would remain: that jurisdictional autonomy can be preserved only by the development of institutions that yield substantial elements of this autonomy to the imperative for interjurisdictional coordination.

[15] Stone (1996) provides a comprehensive description of the legal institutions that create the arenas for such transnational activity.

15

Environmental Regulation and Economic Integration

DAVID VOGEL

This chapter explores the relationship between economic integration and environmental regulation. Part I begins by observing that fears that economic competition would lead to a regulatory 'race toward the bottom' appear to have proven unwarranted: increased economic integration has proved compatible with the general strengthening of environmental standards. Part II then explains why economic interdependence has not led subnational, national, and regional governments to compete by lowering their environmental standards. Parts III, IV, V, and VI examine the ways in which economic integration has contributed to the strengthening of regulatory standards. Finally, Parts VII and VIII explore the shortcomings of existing mechanisms of global environmental governance and specify the circumstances under which regulatory coordination can promote more effective environmental governance.

I. THE IMPACT OF ECONOMIC INTERDEPENDENCE

Contrary to the fears of many environmentalists, increased economic interdependence has not led to a weakening of either product or process environmental standards (Nader *et al.* 1993). International trade as a proportion of Gross National Product (GNP) has significantly increased in every industrial nation since the late 1960s, yet during this same period environmental regulations have become progressively stricter in all industrial nations and a number of industrializing ones as well (Piore and Sabel 1984: 185). Virtually all nations now devote substantially more resources both in absolute and relative terms to environmental protection than they did in 1970.

Since the early 1970s few major economies have experienced a greater increase in their exposure to the global economy than the United States: between 1970 and 1980 both its imports and exports as a share of GNP more than doubled (Piore and Sabel 1984). At the same time, US regulatory standards have become substantially stronger during the last quarter-century. The proportion of the US GNP devoted to pollution control stood at 1.5 per cent in 1972; it has been higher every year since, averaging more than 1.7 per cent between 1980 and 1986 and increasing to 2.2 per cent in 1992 (Economist 1993; OECD 1989a). Annual expenditures on compliance with federal environmental regulations totalled US$ 90 billion in 1990 and increased by approximately US$ 30 billion following the passage of the 1990 Clean Air Act Amendments (Kopp, Portney, and Dewitt 1990).

In Europe, the goal of creating a single market was in large measure motivated by the interests of business managers and political leaders in making European industry more competitive in the global economy. Yet the Single European Act also authorized and has contributed to a significant strengthening of European environmental regulations. In recent years, the European Union has emerged as the world's pace-setter for environmental innovation, led by Germany, its largest and most important member state. Since the early 1970s Japan has been both a major exporter and has significantly increased its environmental expenditures (Pharr and Badaracio 1986).[1]

The strengthening of domestic environmental standards has not been confined to the world's richest nations. In recent years, Taiwan, South Korea, Israel, and Singapore—all major exporters—have committed substantially more resources to environmental protection (Nam 1997; Vogel 1999). The compatibility between increased exposure to the global economy and the strengthening of domestic regulatory efforts is also borne out by the experience of Mexico. Since 1986, Mexico has significantly opened its economy, while between 1988 and 1991, government spending on environmental protection increased ten fold (Husted and Logsdon 1997; Lash 1993).

The United States provides the clearest example of the compatibility of strict regulatory standards and economic interdependence (Revesz 1992). As a union of fifty states, the United States itself is a highly integrated market whose constitution permits few restrictions on interstate commerce, especially for traded goods. While many regulatory standards are set by the federal government, a number of federal regulatory statutes only set minimum standards. For example, within limits, states are permitted to enact stricter controls on automobile emissions than those required for the nation as a whole. States are also free to impose tougher standards on stationary sources of pollution and additional restrictions on land use. Additionally, recycling requirements are set by state and local governments.

While states do compete with one another to attract investment, many state standards are stricter than federal ones. A number of states have enacted more stringent controls over the use of pesticides and chlorofluorocarbons (CFCs) than the federal government. Several state and local governments have also established ambitious recycling programmes, bans on the use of specific materials in packaging, and strict standards for solid waste disposal and incineration. A number of states have also chosen to adopt stricter automotive emissions standards.

Nor is the United States unique. A number of subnational governments in other federal systems, including Canada and Australia, have enacted environmental regulations stricter than those of their central governments. Indeed, it was precisely the increasing propensity of local governments to establish their own tougher regulatory standards that led the drafters of the World Trade Organization (WTO)

[1] For a more recent discussion of Japanese environmental policies, see Vogel (1993) and Moore and Miller (1994).

Agreement on Technical Barriers to Trade to include a provision holding central governments responsible for the regulatory standards of subnational political units. Likewise, an ongoing source of conflict within the European Union comes from the efforts of the European Union's greener member states to impose stricter environmental standards than those required by the European Union.

Environmental standards are primarily determined by domestic political preferences and interests.[2] They tend to be stronger and better enforced in affluent nations with influential green pressure groups. They also tend to be strengthened during periods of economic prosperity and stabilized or weakened during periods of slower growth.[3] There is anecdotal evidence that some political jurisdictions have lowered their existing environmental standards or weakened their enforcement in order to increase the competitiveness of domestic producers. In other cases competitiveness concerns have reduced the rate at which regulations on domestic producers have been strengthened or enforced (Maddox 1994).[4] But, while it is impossible to determine how much stricter EU or US environmental regulations would be if the rest of the world posed no competitive threat to their domestic producers, it is highly unlikely that either would devote significantly more resources to environmental protection than they now do.

Strategic considerations are not the only reason why a government might hesitate to impose stricter environmental standards on domestic firms. Legitimate concerns about the impact of environmental regulation on firm growth, profitability, and employment exist even in the absence of pressures from foreign competitors.[5] What is clear is that on balance an increasingly integrated and competitive global economy has not interfered with the ability of many governments to enact both product and process regulations stricter than those of their trading partners as well as to devote substantial resources to environmental protection over the last three decades.

II. WHY NO RACE TOWARD THE BOTTOM?

Why has increased regional and international integration not led regions, nations, or subnational governments to compete with one another by enacting less stringent environmental regulations? How can we account for this phenomenon? For example, why did the Single European Act, which was primarily enacted to strengthen the competitiveness of European firms, also contain provisions facilitating the

[2] For a similar analysis of the limited impact of economic globalization on domestic economic policies, see Wade (1996).

[3] This argument is developed in detail for the United States by Vogel (1989).

[4] For anecdotal evidence that 'some degree of competitiveness induced lowering of environmental standards is taking place at the national and regional levels', see Maddox (1994: 18). However, as the author acknowledges, 'These examples do not tell us whether the lowering of standards is welfare enhancing or not' (18–19).

[5] For another perspective on this issue, see Esty and Geradin (1998).

strengthening of European environmental standards? Why have various member states sought to impose stricter environmental standards than those of other member states with whose products they compete? Why have many US states enacted more demanding environmental standards than those of other states? Why have those central European nations who have applied for membership in the European Union strengthened their environmental standards? Why did Mexico both strengthen its environmental standards and improve their enforcement prior to opening up its market to Canadian and US products?

Moreover, in light of recent trends in labour markets, it seems puzzling that regulatory policies in rich nations have not followed the same pattern as wages—which do appear to have been adversely affected by increased competition from developing nations. To take one example from an important industrial sector, why have real wages, fringe benefits, and employment security for US automobile workers declined, in part due to increased international competition, while over the same time period both emission and fuel economy standards have been strengthened?

One important reason is that, for all but a handful of industries, the costs of compliance with stricter regulatory standards have not been sufficient to force relatively affluent nations or subnational governments to choose between competitiveness and environmental protection. In marked contrast to labour costs, the overall costs of compliance with environmental regulations have to date been modest. According to Martin Houldin, the environmental director at the consulting firm KPMG Peat Marwick in London, 'The international differences in the cost of labour are generally so much more important that the environment pales into insignificance' (Maddox 1994: 8). This is not to say that such costs are non-existent: many expenditures to improve environmental quality do reduce output and lower the rate of productivity growth and employment and in particular sectors these burdens can be severe (Esty and Geradin 1998: 17–21). But in the aggregate, increases in national levels of pollution-control expenditures have had little effect on the growth of economic output (Cairncross 1991). Nor have US states with stronger environmental policies experienced inferior rates of economic growth and development (Meyer 1992).

While production standards obviously can and do affect corporate plant location decisions, for most industries the effects are not significant.[6] Within the United States, differences in environmental standards have not been a major factor in plant siting or expansion decisions (Bartik 1988a; 1988b). Studies of international corporate location decisions reach similar conclusions. For example, only a relatively few heavily polluting industries have relocated their production from the United

[6] For a summary of the literature on environmental regulation, trade, and corporate location decisions, see Dean (1992); Low and Yeats (1992); Lucas *et al.* (1992); Tobey (1990); Stewart (1993); and von Moltke (1993). For a sophisticated analysis of the conditions under which firms will seek to compete by investing in political jurisdictions with laxer environmental standards, see Spar and Yoffie (unpublished paper).

States to developing countries, 'mostly because pollution control expenses alone are generally not large enough a share of total costs to make it worth a company's while to relocate' (French 1993: 166). Significantly, environmental control costs comprise less than 2 per cent of total production cost for most US industries, even though US standards are relatively stringent (Stewart 1993: 2077). The Organization for Economic Cooperation and Development (OECD) reports that 'very little evidence exists of firms being transferred abroad in order to escape the more stringent environmental regulations at home' (1989b: 6). In short, there is little evidence of 'pollution havens'.

In addition, just as industrial production often imposes public costs, so do protective regulations produce public benefits. Thus expenditures on air pollution may increase agricultural output while improvements in water quality may result in better fishing yields or increased tourism. Equally importantly, improvements in environmental quality can improve the health, and thus the productivity, of a nation's workforce, in addition to reducing healthcare expenditures. This analysis cannot be pushed too far: nations are not free to impose whatever environmental regulations they wish. For while stricter environmental standards may not make a nation poorer, neither do they make it richer; greater wealth leads to a preference for strong regulatory standards, not the reverse (Koretz 1994: 20).[7] Thus, to the extent that many environmental regulations represent a form of collective consumption, we would expect citizens in relatively affluent countries to support public policies that increase their consumption of such goods, even at the price of some reduction in their levels of private consumption.

III. THE RACE TOWARD THE TOP

Not only has national, regional, and international competition not forced a weakening of environmental standards, but in some respects economic openness and capital mobility have actually encouraged nations to enact higher standards than they would have done in the absence of increased economic interdependency.

There are a number of ways in which open markets can strengthen regulatory standards. First, stricter domestic regulations can create market opportunities for the export of pollution-control equipment (Moore and Miller 1994; Porter 1990; US EPA 1993). These markets are not large: for example, pollution-control equipment accounts for less than one-half of 1 per cent of total US merchandise exports. But they can be important for particular sectors. For example, due to their strict emission standards for coal-burning power plants, both Germany and Japan dominate the world market in scrubbers, which remove sulphur dioxide from power plant smokestacks.

[7] According to the World Bank, pollution levels begin to decline once per capita income reaches $5,000.

There is a second, more subtle way in which stricter regulatory standards can strengthen the international competitiveness of domestic firms. Regulations rarely affect all producers equally: they usually advantage some firms and disadvantage others. Some regulations create a competitive advantage for domestic producers by making it more difficult for foreign producers to sell their products. In fact, knowing or anticipating that the burdens of compliance will fall disproportionately on their international competitors may make domestic producers more willing to support stricter regulations than they would have been in the absence of foreign competition.

Examples of 'alliances' between environmentalists and domestic producers abound.[8] For example, the recycling requirements enacted by Denmark and the Canadian province of Ontario have both disadvantaged foreign beer producers while improving environmental quality. The strict automobile emission controls requirements supported by German environmentalists during the 1980s protected the domestic market share of German automobile companies, since it was more difficult for French and Italian firms to comply with them. The US strict automotive fuel economy standards have helped both to improve US energy efficiency and raise the prices of European luxury car imports. The US ban on exports of logs from government-owned forests both reduced the cutting of old-growth forests in the Pacific Northwest and increased the market share of US lumber mills—satisfying the demands of US environmentalists and the interests of segments of the US forestry industry.

From this perspective, rather than pressing nations to lower their regulatory standards, more liberal trade policies may actually provide governments with an economic incentive for strengthening them. By contrast, since relatively closed economies can rely on tariffs and quotas to restrict imports, they have less need to adopt protective regulations that advantage domestic producers.

IV. THE CALIFORNIA EFFECT

A number of environmental regulations exhibit what I have described as the 'California effect': they have moved in the direction of political jurisdictions with stricter regulatory standards.[9] The California effect can be illustrated by the history of US automobile emission standards. The 1970 Clean Air Act Amendments specifically permitted California to enact stricter emissions standards than the rest of the United States, an option which California then exercised. Consequently its standards remained stricter than those of any other state. In 1990, Congress brought national emission standards up to those of California and once again permitted

[8] Unless otherwise noted, the cases discussed in this chapter are drawn from Vogel (1995).

[9] The concept of the California effect is developed by Vogel (1995: chs 1 and 8).

California to impose stricter standards. It also gave other states the option of choosing either national or California standards (Bryner 1993).

In 1994, twelve eastern states requested the federal government to permit them to adopt California's new standards (Wald 1994). These standards, in turn, are likely to become the basis for the next round of minimum federal requirements. California has now had the United States' strictest automotive pollution control standards for more than three decades. Thus, instead of states with weaker standards undermining those with stricter ones, in the case of automobile emissions precisely the opposite has occurred: California has helped to make US auto emissions standards steadily stronger. Automobile producers had a strong incentive to produce vehicles that complied with California's stricter standards so that they could continue to market their cars in such a large and important market.

The term 'California effect' is meant to suggest a much broader phenomenon than the impact of US federalism on state regulatory standards. The general pattern suggested by this term, namely the upward ratcheting of regulatory standards through market mechanisms, applies to many national regulations as well. Political jurisdictions which have developed stricter product standards often force foreign producers in nations with weaker domestic standards to design products that meet those standards, since otherwise the producers will be denied access to these markets. This, in turn, encourages those producers to make the investments required to produce the new products as efficiently as possible. Moreover, having made these initial investments, they now have a stake in encouraging their home markets to strengthen their standards, in part because their exports are already meeting them (Braithwaite 1993; Vogel 1995).

Thus the willingness of Germany's automobile manufacturers to support stricter EU standards was in part due to their previous experience in producing vehicles for the US market. It was precisely the firms supplying the largest, wealthiest automobile market in Europe which took the lead in pressuring the European Union to adopt the product standards already set by the world's largest, richest market, the United States. They made common cause with German environmentalists to demand that Europe adopt US standards. Significantly, half of German automobile sales in the United States are in California, the political jurisdiction with the world's strictest automotive emission standards.

Indeed, German producers stood to benefit from the European Union's adoption of US standards, since they could then produce similar vehicles for both markets at lower costs. For a similar reason, Japan chose to adopt the strict 1970 US automobile emission standards. Indeed they are referred to in Japan as 'the Muskie standards' in recognition of Senator Muskie's sponsorship of the automobile emission standards of the 1970 Clean Air Act Amendments (Pharr and Badaracco 1986). By requiring its auto makers to instal the same pollution-abatement device on cars sold in the domestic market as on exports, Korea has effectively upgraded its regulatory standards to match those of the United States, the European Union, and Japan (Lee 1993).

Similarly, the eventual willingness of the French and Italian manufacturers to support the stricter standards of the Small Car Directive stemmed in part from the experience they had gained in producing cars for export to greener markets in Europe and the United States as well as their fear of losing additional export markets to their greener competitors. The expansion of trade between the United States and Canada following the Free Trade Agreement between the two countries prompted Canada in 1993 to establish automobile emission requirements similar to those imposed on vehicles sold in the United States three years earlier.

As a result of the growth of Israeli agricultural exports to the European Union, Israel recently adopted EU pesticide standards. Moreover, because of its dependence on automobile imports from Japan, the United States, and the European Union, it has recently required all imported vehicles to run on unleaded petrol.[10] The United States has had a similar impact on the pesticide standards of those nations from whom it imports food (Pearson 1994: 52). A number of Latin American governments closely follow US pesticide regulations, often prohibiting or restricting the use of pesticides whose use has been cancelled or suspended by the US Environmental Protection Agency (EPA). And due to their dependence on exports of manufactured goods to Germany, Dutch producers have been forced to substantially change their own packaging policies as a result of Germany's *Verpackungsverordnung* (Packaging Law). Likewise, a German ban on leather and leather products containing pentachorophenol forced Indian firms to modify their own production processes (Jha 1998).

The pattern of chemical regulation also illustrates how concerns about market access can strengthen regulatory standards. The enactment of the Toxic Substances Control Act by the United States prompted the European Union to enact the Sixth Directive. The European Union feared that unless its standards were comparable to those of the United States, it would be deprived of access to one of the world's largest chemical markets. As a result, it established a much stricter system for the introduction and marketing of chemical products. Once again, stricter US standards drove those of its major trading partner upward.

The relationship between product standards that disadvantage importers and those that prompt exporters to strengthen their own standards in order to maintain market access must be understood in dynamic terms. The environmental regulatory agenda is a highly fluid one. Rich green nations are continually enacting new regulatory standards. In some cases these may create only a temporary source of competitive advantage until other nations have adopted them, while in other cases this advantage may prove more enduring. But the result is similar: economic integration can promote the ratcheting upward of regulatory standards.

[10] For a more detailed discussion of Israeli environmental policies and the impact of international pressures on them, see Vogel (1999).

V. PRODUCTION STANDARDS

The California effect primarily holds for product standards. But product standards constitute only one dimension of environmental regulation; many environmental harms stem from the way a product is produced or processed. But in some cases 'greener' nations have used similar restrictions, or the threat of restrictions, on access to their markets to force their trading partners to change their production standards—notwithstanding the fact that such practices may violate General Agreement on Tariffs and Trade (GATT)/WTO rules. Such restrictions have generally been enacted due to some combination of pressures from domestic firms that want to create a 'level playing field' by imposing additional costs on their international competitors, and environmental groups that want to use access to their domestic market as leverage to influence the environmental practices of other countries.

For example, the threat of the withdrawal of market access by the European Union forced Canada to end its killing of baby seals and has persuaded the United States, Canada, and Russia to phase out their use of leg-traps to catch fur-bearing animals.[11] The European Union's eco-labelling programme, because it is based on a 'life-cycle' analysis, explicitly covers the way imported products are made: many of its provisions are intended to force the European Union's trading partners to change the way forestry products, leather and footwear, and marine life are produced.[12] For example, European eco-labelling standards have pressured Brazil, a major exporter of shoes, to change the way its leather goods are produced. This in turn has affected processing standards for hides in Argentina and Uruguay, for whom Brazil is a major export market (Tussie and Vasquez 1997).[13] Likewise, a number of non-European firms have 'voluntarily' adopted ISO 14,000 in order to maintain their access to European markets.

Thirteen US laws authorize the use of unilateral sanctions to force the United States' trading partners to adopt US environmental production standards (De Sombre 1995). All involve efforts to protect animals and marine life outside the legal jurisdiction of the United States. These laws have had a significant impact on the conservation practices of a number of the United States' trading partners. For example, thanks to the US tuna embargo against Mexico, incidental dolphin deaths by non-US tuna fishing vessels significantly declined. The United States has also effectively used the leverage of its domestic market to protect whales and, more recently, turtles. In some cases, the impact of the threat of withdrawal of market access has gone beyond specific products. Israel has been effectively (if informally)

[11] The European Union's efforts to use trade policy to change the environmental practices of its trading partners is explored by Vogel (1998).

[12] For a good overview of the extensiveness of such market pressures, see Jha (1998).

[13] For a more general discussion of the impact of trade liberalization on Latin American environmental standards and practices, see Munoz and Rosenberg (1993).

pressured by both the United States and the European Union to impose production requirements on its new manufacturing plants that conform to US and European environmental standards—lest goods produced in these factories 'unfairly' compete with those produced under US and EU laws. A US threat to impose 'environmental countervailing duties' on goods from nations whose pollution control standards were laxer than those of the United States played a critical role in encouraging Korean policy-makers to upgrade their nation's environmental standards (Lee 1993: 659). In 1994, the European Union approved a proposal to modify its Generalized System of Preferences (GSP) to extend additional tariff benefits to 'recipient countries which are able to prove a commitment to international standards of social progress and environmental protection' (Hudnall 1996: 212).

In addition, the interest of some countries in increasing their access to rich, green country markets has also provided an incentive for the former to strengthen their environmental standards. While the North American Free Trade Agreement (NAFTA) does not formally govern national production standards, the environmental objections raised to NAFTA during the congressional debates over US approval of the trade agreement played a critical role in strengthening Mexican environmental controls during the early 1990s (Husted and Logsdon 1997; Jenkins and Branch 1996). Likewise, the possible extension of NAFTA to Chile has encouraged that nation to strengthen its domestic environmental standards (Silva 1996), and the prospect of membership of the European Union has provided an important incentive for a number of central European nations to bring their production as well as product standards closer to those of the European Union.

The use of market leverage also has an important non-governmental or political dimension. Environmental activists in rich countries have frequently targeted particular products that are produced in environmentally harmful ways. In some cases they have organized boycotts of these products, while in others they have applied pressure on multinational firms responsible for their production. A number of these pressures have been highly effective, particularly in the areas of forest and wildlife conservation. International environmental activists based in rich countries have also become an important source of influence on the environmental practices of multinational firms and their subcontractors in many less developed nations (Spar 1998).

Moreover, 'multinational companies are increasingly adopting the same environmental standards for their plants, regardless of the country in which they operate', thus helping to promote the export of green country standards to less green ones (Weiss 1993: 2135). The Chemical Manufacturers Association Responsible Care programme, established in response to widespread criticisms of the environmental impact of global chemical production, has contributed to a general improvement of health, safety, and environmental standards in this sector.[14]

[14] For a detailed discussion of the global environmental practices of this industry, see Gunningham and Grabosky (1999).

Thanks in part to pressure from activists, a number of other international industries, including pulp and paper, electronics, and forest products, have also adopted global environmental production standards similar to those of the world's greener countries (Sonnenfeld 1999).

VI. LEGAL MECHANISMS

International legal mechanisms have also played a role in strengthening regulatory standards for processes as well as products. The most important of these is the European Union. While primarily an economic agreement, the European Union has played a crucial role in both coordinating and strengthening environmental standards among its fifteen member states.[15]

The European Union has significantly magnified the external environmental impact of its six greener member states, namely Germany, the Netherlands, Denmark, Finland, Austria, and Sweden. Thanks to the increasing scope of EU environmental regulations and directives, environmental standards have been significantly strengthened throughout the Union, including in poorer member states in which environmental non-governmental organizations (NGOs) enjoy relatively little influence. For much of southern Europe, the European Union is the most important cause of any additional resources they have devoted to environmental protection.

Finally, there are also approximately 120 environmental treaties, the majority of which are regional in scope and some of which have been reasonably effective.[16] The Montreal Protocol has succeeded in reducing emissions of chemicals that harm the ozone layer, while the Long-Range Transboundary Air Pollution Convention has effectively addressed the problem of acid rain in Europe. Three related agreements—the (London) Convention for the Prevention of Marine Pollution by Dumping from Ships and Aircraft, the Convention on the Protection of the Marine Environment of the Baltic Sea Area along with the Oslo, Paris and Helsinki Commissions—have made substantial progress toward protecting water quality in the Baltic and North Atlantic, and the Mediterranean Action Plan has improved water quality in this sea (Haas 1990). Other environmental agreements have reduced cross-border flows of pollution between the United States and Canada and between the United States and Mexico, and have protected both the Arctic and Antarctic regions from pollution and commercial exploitation (Young 1994).

The impact of other more ambitious agreements, such as the Convention on International Trade in Endangered Species, various agreements to promote inter-

[15] There is an extensive literature on this topic. See, for example, Vogel (1995: ch. 3); Liefferink, Lowe, and Mol (1993); and Haigh (1987).

[16] The most comprehensive account of the effectiveness of environmental agreements is by Haas, Keohane, and Levy (1993). For a mixed picture of the effectiveness of international environmental agreements, see Carrol (1988; 1990); Jacobson and Weiss (1997).

national fisheries management, the International Tropical Timber Agreement, the Bonn Convention on Migratory Species, and the Rio Agreement on Biological Diversity, have been more limited.[17] But as in the case of the Montreal Protocol, the threat of rich countries to deny access to their markets has pressured less green countries to either agree to their terms or abide by them—in effect, an application of the California effect to both product and production standards through international law.[18]

VII. THE SHORTCOMINGS OF ENVIRONMENTAL GOVERNANCE

If the California effect is interpreted broadly to encompass the role of external economic, political, or legal pressures on political jurisdictions to raise or strengthen their environmental standards, then under what circumstances is it most likely to occur?[19] The California effect is most effective for product standards. More specifically, it is most likely to affect standards for products significant quantities of which are exported from nations with weaker environmental, health, safety, or product standards to nations with stricter ones. In the case of production standards, the California effect applies primarily under three circumstances: domestic political or economic pressures in a green country have targeted the environmental practices of a particular sector in a less green country, the country in which the production takes place aspires to enter into a free trade agreement with either the European Union or the United States (or is already a member of the European Union), or the production process is covered by an effectively enforced international environmental agreement.

This means, of course, that a significant share of global economic activity that has important environmental consequences is unlikely to be reached by the California effect. Most obviously, it does not apply to relatively closed economies. But even in relatively open ones, most products are either consumed domestically or are traded primarily among nations with relatively weak regulatory standards, thus rendering them unaffected by the product standards of green countries. Because most international trade is among rich countries, many of the countries whose product standards have been affected by the use of international market mechanisms had relatively high environmental standards to begin with: US product standards have had the greatest impact on its major trading partners, namely Canada, the European Union, and Japan.

In the case of production standards, multinational firms account for only a relatively small share of production in most developing countries. Moreover, relatively

[17] For a highly critical view of the effectiveness of international environmental agreements, see Latin (unpublished paper).

[18] For an excellent case, see Mofson (1997).

[19] For a critical analysis of the significance and limitations of the California effect, see Swire (1996). Another excellent analytical overview of this issue can be found in Kahler (unpublished paper).

few products produced in developing countries and exported to developed ones have become the focus of considerable public concern in the latter. Most of these are associated with natural resources. Few consumers or policy makers in rich countries know or care about the environmental consequences of how most manufactured goods are produced in developing countries. Citizen outrage in rich countries is highly selective, often focusing on developing country practices that have considerable symbolic value but may have limited environmental significance, such as wildlife protection. Significantly, the two most important environmental problems that affect citizens in developing nations, namely urban air pollution and the lack of access to safe drinking water, have been all but ignored by both environmentalists and policy makers in rich countries. Moreover, even if they were to become a focus of concern, the ability of rich country governments or consumers to use their economic leverage to ameliorate them is limited.

The experiences of countries such as Israel and Korea are atypical; most countries have faced relatively little scrutiny of the way their exports are produced. Significantly, neither the European Union nor the United States sought to use their market leverage to pressure China to change its environmental practices. To date, the use of economic leverage has been confined to the United States and the European Union. Japan has been reluctant to use access to its large domestic market to pressure other Asian countries to improve their environmental practices, even though Japan imports considerable quantities of raw materials and, more recently, manufactured goods from this region. (Japan is the world's largest importer of tropical timber, but has made no effort to encourage sustainable harvesting practices in Indonesia and Malaysia.) Recently, however, because China has begun to 'export' air pollution to Japan, Japanese policy makers have begun to assist China in upgrading its pollution control equipment.

Moreover, the WTO has also played a role in discouraging rich countries from using production standards to restrict imports from less developed ones on environmental grounds. The decision of the GATT dispute panel in the 1991 tuna/dolphin case, which held that GATT rules prohibited signatories from restricting the import of a product on the basis of how it was produced outside their legal jurisdiction, has promoted a lively and frequently heated debate about the environmental impact of trade rules (Zaelke, Orbuch, and Housman 1993). While this holding was modified in the 1998 shrimp/turtle decision, the GATT/WTO does appear to have had a chilling effect on the use of trade restrictions to strengthen extraterritorial regulatory standards.

The European Union remains a unique institution. No other regional trade agreement has played a comparable role in strengthening either product or production standards among its members. While a number of others, including MERCOSUR (Argentina, Brazil, Paraguay, and Uruguay), the Asia Pacific Economic Cooperation Forum (APEC), and NAFTA, do have provisions designed to promote the improvement of regulatory standards among their signatories, their impact to date has been modest (Tussie and Vasquez 1997; Zarsky and Hunter, working paper).[20] In the foreseeable future, a relatively small number of countries can realistically aspire to join the European Union or NAFTA.

Only a handful of international industries have established uniform production standards. More importantly, most economic activity occurs through domestic firms, not international ones. Finally, with the notable exception of the Mediterranean Action Plan, regional environmental agreements primarily impose costs and distribute benefits between or among rich countries. Virtually all are among countries in or adjacent to western Europe or North America. Effective regional environmental agreements are virtually non-existent in Asia, Latin America, or Africa—the regions in the world in which environmental problems are the most serious (Richards and Tucker 1988). And those international environmental agreements that do include poorer countries tend to be relatively limited in scope and poorly enforced.

This means that many of the most serious environmental problems in developing nations, such as the destruction of the coral reefs and overfishing in Asia, deforestation and the destruction of farmlands in Latin America and Asia, and air and water pollution everywhere, remain largely unaffected by the 'California effect' or any of its variants. Many developing nations, including the growing economies of China, India, and Indonesia, and the most important Latin American economy, Brazil, remain unwilling to curb trade in endangered species, protect the coral seas, reduce their cutting of hardwood trees, or maintain biodiversity. They might well change their behaviour in response to economic incentives from rich countries, as they did in the case of the Montreal Protocol. But the amount of resources that would be required to be transferred to make them do so is well beyond the political capacity of the European Union, the United States, and Japan.

As many developing nations become more affluent and their environmental problems more acute, they will develop both the economic capacity and the political willingness to devote more resources to address domestic environmental problems. Presumably, they will then enter into regional agreements to address cross-border pollution problems and comply with global treaties that address international ones. But such changes are likely to occur slowly. This is not because international competition is pressuring them to lower their regulatory standards; it is rather that in many cases their current level of economic development has made them unwilling to trade off economic growth for environmental quality—even in those cases where many of their own citizens are adversely affected by the environmental harms they cause. As Haas concludes:

> [T]he NICs [newly industrialized countries] pose a big environmental threat which may not be easily met through international governance mechanisms. Most of the NICs have weak environmental legislation and economic growth is driven by some of the world's most polluting intensive sectors . . . Loss of biodiversity, toxic wastes, heavy metals, sulfur dioxide, nitrogen oxide, and carbon dioxide emissions are likely to rise dramatically with increase in

[20] For Mexico, see Husted and Logsdon (1997) and Zagaris (1992).

economic growth in China, Taiwan, South Korea, Malaysia, India, Indonesia and Thailand. (1999: 125)

The most important shortcoming of global environmental governance is not that rich countries with relatively competent governments and influential green pressure groups are unable to establish environmental standards that adequately protect their own environment because of fears of foreign competition. It is rather that too many poorer countries have relatively ineffective governments and weak green pressure groups. They are therefore either unable or unwilling to establish environmental standards that adequately protect their own citizens and nation—let alone the global commons. The problem is not that poorer countries are driving richer country standards downward; it is that the regulatory standards and/or enforcement capacity of many poorer countries remain suboptimal. In other words, the problem is not so much the existence of a Delaware effect on the environmental policies of richer countries, but the relative weakness of the California effect on the environmental policies of poorer countries. Contrary to the claims of those who blame economic globalization for weakening the environmental standards of poorer countries, it is precisely the extent to which developing nation producers are *not* integrated into the global economy that retards their 'greening'.

In this context, the relevant issue is not whether there is a 'race to the bottom'. There is not. It is rather that some developing countries appear to be 'stuck at the bottom' (Porter 1998). The OECD argues that the fears that poorer countries would 'deliberately keep environmental standards lax in order to attract investment by becoming pollution havens have [not] materialized . . . mostly because pollution control expenditures are generally not a large enough share of total costs to make it worth a company's while to relocate' (French 1993: 166). Accordingly, it suggests that 'there is no reason to suppose that international competition for comparative advantage will lead nations to adopt inappropriately low environmental standards' (Stewart 1993: 2058). But this argument misses the point. The problem is not that poorer countries have or will become pollution havens for investments from rich countries; it is rather that they have suboptimal standards for domestic producers. For many locally owned developing nation firms, the relative costs of environmental regulation are substantial and imposing stricter regulatory standards does constitute a substantial economic burden, even if such measures might be optimal from the perspective of their society as a whole. To the extent that their products are domestically consumed or exported to other, equally less green countries, they have little market incentive to strengthen their environmental standards.

VIII. THE CASE FOR COORDINATION

To what extent does more effective environmental governance require the coordination of regulatory standards? The fact that there have been a number of efforts to coordinate regulatory standards—most notably the increased centralization of environmental policy making within the US federal system, the shift in the locus of standard setting from fifteen European national governments to the European Union, and numerous bilateral, regional, and international environmental agreements—suggests that there is a role for the coordination of environmental standards across political jurisdictions. What is this role?

First, by lowering transaction costs, coordinated standards can play a role in facilitating trade and cross-jurisdictional investment. This is particularly important in the case of product standards. To the extent that public welfare is enhanced by the lowering of barriers to trade, then more uniform standards, by reducing non-tariff barriers and otherwise lowering the costs of cross-border transactions, can confer important public benefits. The centralization of product standards has been critical to the creation and maintenance of a single market within the European Union, while the coordination of standards and approval procedures for a variety of products has facilitated trade between Europe and the United States (Vogel 1997). The economic case for coordination can also hold for production standards. An important motivation for establishing federal production standards for air and water pollution in the United States during the early 1970s was the interest of firms in having uniform standards, and many multinational firms prefer uniform international standards for a similar reason.

Second, coordinated standards are essential to address environmental problems that span political boundaries. This has been a particularly important motivation for international environmental agreements, whose central purpose is to address environmental problems that cannot be adequately ameliorated without policies that bind more than one political jurisdiction. It has also been an important motivation behind a number of federal environmental initiatives in the United States as well as for the coordination of some production standards within the European Union.

Third, coordination may be appropriate if the costs of pollution abatement are perceived as seriously burdening domestic producers *vis-à-vis* their competitors in other political jurisdictions with whose firms they compete. The problem is not so much that competitive pressures will force some political jurisdictions to lower their standards as that their fear of being competitively disadvantaged—regardless of whether that fear is warranted—may make some political jurisdictions unwilling to establish standards as strong as their citizens prefer. As Swire notes, 'the perception of a prisoner's dilemma may well be more important than whether one really exists' (1996: 104). Hence political jurisdictions with 'greener' preferences may establish less than optimal standards unless other jurisdictions are required to do likewise. This logic underlay much of the push for federal environmental standards during the early 1970s as well as a number of the European Union's production standards. It is also the basis for a number of environmental treaties. As Esty and Geradin observe: '[F]ears about cost disparities with other jurisdictions operates as a political drag making it difficult for governments to raise environmental standards

. . . even if more stringent requirements would demonstrably optimize net environmental welfare'(1998: 16).[21]

Finally, coordinated standards may be appropriate if a political jurisdiction is unable or unwilling to enact environmental policies that reflect the preferences of its citizens. Such a political market failure may stem from a variety of causes, such as inadequate information or uncertainty about the costs and benefits of new regulatory standards, inadequate information about citizen preferences on the part of policy makers, the lack of adequate citizen access to the policy-making process, the political power of producers, and/or administrative incapacity (Esty 1996; Kahler, unpublished paper; Swire 1996). In some cases, this rationale for coordination can be paternalistic: it assumes that absent some extrajurisdictional authority, political jurisdictions will not enact standards that are optimal for their citizens.

Of these four rationales for cross-border coordination, the one for cross-border or global externalities is the most compelling.[22] However, most environmental practices in developing countries, albeit they may outrage environmentalists in rich countries, primarily affect only their own citizens or those in neighbouring countries. The same is true for environmental practices in rich countries that affect their neighbours. Consequently, such cross-border standards will often be regional in scope. There is a limited category of environmental practices that do affect the global commons—CFC emissions, global climate change, and biodiversity are three important examples—and in such cases, global standards are essential.

Each of the other three rationales have more limited applicability. Just because coordinated process or product standards facilitate trade or lower the transaction costs for firms who produce in multiple jurisdictions does not mean that such standards are necessarily in the interests of the citizens in each of these jurisdictions. Such standards are particularly likely to be problematic if the citizens in one jurisdiction have different preferences or face different environmental conditions than those in another. Similarly, if citizens in two jurisdictions have comparable preferences for stricter regulatory standards, but neither will enact them unless it can be assured that the other will also do so, then coordination may well be welfare-enhancing for both. But if their preferences differ substantially, then having the 'greener' standards preferred by one jurisdiction extended to another with less green preferences or less adverse environmental conditions may not be welfare-enhancing for the latter.

These concerns apply with even greater weight for coordinated standards motivated by regulatory paternalism. If the harms caused by particular environmental practices are not irreversible and their effects are primarily local, why should a political jurisdiction be pressured to raise its standards just because some of its practices differ from those preferred by citizens in more powerful countries? A compelling case for regulatory paternalism requires substantial evidence that citizens in

[21] For a contrary view, see Revesz (1997e).

[22] See Butler and Macey (1996) for the position that this is the only compelling case for regulatory harmonization.

a particular jurisdiction actually prefer stricter standards but, due to political factors outside their control, such standards are unlikely to be adopted in the absence of extrajurisdictional coordination. It bears repeating that not all the world's citizens share similar environmental policy preferences.

Finally, regulatory coordination does not require identical standards. The latter may often be either too strict or lax or simply too inflexible to respond to the wide diversity of environmental and economic conditions that exist in different political jurisdictions, even within a particular country—a point which has been repeatedly made by critics of regulatory harmonization (Revesz 1992). Moreover, as the California effect illustrates, regulatory diversity has played a critical role in the ratcheting upwards of regulatory standards: in the long run it is welfare-enhancing for some political jurisdictions to have stricter regulations than others.

To the extent that there is a compelling case for regulatory coordination, this coordination should often take forms other than identical standards, such as the establishment of minimum standards, common disclosure requirements, uniform decision-making criteria, or the use of regulatory instruments which permit flexibility in response to local conditions. In some cases, it may be sufficient to make certain that governments are fully informed about the environmental and economic consequences of their policy choices or to help give local constituencies the resources they need to participate in the policy process.[23] In fact, much environmental coordination, even within the European Union and the United States, as well as at the global level through environmental treaties such as the Montreal Protocol, does not establish harmonized standards. In short, the choice is not necessarily between harmonization and regulatory diversity. There are a variety of strategies that can achieve many of the benefits of coordination while minimizing the shortcomings of uniform standards.

[23] For excellent discussion of the circumstances under which harmonization is and is not appropriate, see Klevorick (1996) and Esty and Geradin (1998).

16

Antitrust Law on a Global Scale: Races Up, Down, and Sideways

ELEANOR M. FOX*

Antitrust law is national. Markets—many of them—are global. Arguments have been made for internationalizing antitrust law or raising surveillance of anti-competitive restraints to a level higher than the nation. Analysis of these arguments is complicated by the fact that there are many versions of antitrust law and its goals, descriptively and normatively, and there are many possibilities for internationalization or cooperation on antitrust rules and their enforcement.

In this chapter, I explore the federalism of antitrust in view of global markets. First, to set the stage, I ask: What is antitrust law and what are its goals, and why are we observing the increasing adoption of antitrust laws by nations of the world? Second, I describe the state of play of internationalization of antitrust. Third, I ask: Is there regulatory competition among the antitrust regimes of nations, and is there a race toward the bottom or the top? Fourth, I inquire: How best can we preserve local autonomy while giving coherence to antitrust principles in a global economy and providing checks against nationalistic strategies and negative externalities?

I. WHAT IS ANTITRUST LAW AND WHY IS ITS PURVIEW EXPANDING?

It is necessary to ask the definitional question for two reasons. First, we need a foundation for the ensuing discussion, and second, the economists' usual conception—that antitrust law is a tool to produce efficiency through markets—is not necessarily a faithful description. In fact, antitrust (or competition law) is whatever legislators and judges of particular jurisdictions say it is, and it ranges from law to control business practices in order to protect or empower the underdog, to law to check and disperse business power and ensure a better distribution of opportunity and wealth to the non-established, to law to preserve the competitive process and its governance of markets, to law to advance efficiency through markets anchored (for example) by an aggregate wealth or by a consumer welfare paradigm.

* The author is grateful for the support of the Filomen D'Agostino and Max E. Greenberg Faculty Research Fund of New York University School of Law. The author thanks Barry Friedman, John Fingleton, Richard Revesz, Paul Stephan, and the participants at the Conference on Regulatory Competition and Economic Integration, Yale Law School, organized in cooperation with the Institut d'Etudes Juridiques Européennes at the University of Liège, Belgium, 1999.

Even within a particular national system, the goals of competition law may evolve and transmogrify, often depending on the state of industrialization of the economy, the strength of the political democracy, the power of the judiciary and of bureaucrats, and the exposure of domestic firms to global competition.

There is a large area of agreement among nations regarding certain types of restraints. This is particularly evident in the law against competitors' price fixing, market division, and bid rigging (cartels), and against naked monopolistic exclusions designed to block market entry or growth. But even in the realm of near-consensus rules, there are exceptions. For example, less developed countries may exempt from antitrust proscriptions cartels in strategic goods where they have a comparative advantage, especially raw materials and commodities. Moreover, there is often disagreement even within a single jurisdiction about what is a naked monopolistic exclusion, as evident in opinions and discussions about the *Microsoft* case (Antitrust 1999). When we leave the area of cartels, the margin of divergence among national laws increases. For example, many countries, following a European model, regulate unfair uses of market power, while the United States focuses more narrowly on the tendency of restraints to lower the output of goods and services.

For many years, US antitrust law (which itself has been the subject of political economy swings) was the only significantly enforced competition law in the world. Today, some eighty countries have competition laws. More than half of these laws were adopted in the last decade. Approximately twenty additional countries are currently working on draft competition laws.

Why is the adoption of competition law now so fashionable in the world? The adopting countries have mixed motives. Some central European countries that are hopeful members of the European Union have adopted competition laws, and indeed European-style competition laws, because they must do so under 'Europe Agreements' in order to be admitted to the waiting room for membership in the European Union (Jakob 1993). Indonesia adopted a competition law last year because the International Monetary Fund required it to do so as a part of the economic reforms on which rescue funds were conditioned. Many countries moving from statism or command-and-control economies to markets want rules in place to check the greed expected to attend free markets. Many nations are convinced (often by US or EU advocates) that competition law is good for them; that it will, in a Michael Porter sense (1985), make their businesses more robust and better able to compete while attracting investment and jobs, thus increasing economic opportunity and serving their people as entrepreneurs, consumers, and workers.

Most of the new statutes contain a healthy dose of protection against 'unfair' competition, 'unfair' contracts, or 'unfair' behaviour of suppliers (Fingleton *et al.* 1996). I write this chapter in view of the diversity of choices that nations make.

II. THE STATE OF PLAY OF INTERNATIONALIZATION IN ANTITRUST

In modern times, market conduct has nearly always had transnational dimensions. Trading nations have discussed the possibility of world disciplines against restrictive business practices since the mid- to late 1940s, when they contemplated and nearly adopted the Havana Charter. Thereafter, nations formulated voluntary codes and principles in the context of the United Nations Conference on Trade and Development (UNCTAD) and the Organization for Economic Cooperation and Development (OECD).

Until the end of the 1980s, diverse attitudes towards competition itself created animosities, especially towards US extraterritorial enforcement when it collided with other nations' decisions about how to organize their economies. Then came the failure and fall of communism and command-and-control, and the eastward expansion of European economic space. Nation after nation began to adopt a competition law, most often in the image of the European Community, which protects both competitors and consumers from abuses. Nations began to form a new consensus on the legitimacy of a nation's jurisdiction over actors and acts abroad that cause domestic harm. Most nations now recognize the applicability of their competition laws to conduct abroad that causes effects within their territories.

Meanwhile, the World Trade Organization (WTO) has become more aggressive in requiring lower tariffs and open markets, thus facilitating global competition and a more nearly integrated world. Globalization, in turn, has brought with it needs and incentives for cooperation among antitrust agencies. The consumers of various nations are targeted by offshore cartels. To enforce their antitrust laws, the competition agencies need evidence from the home state of the cartel members. Moreover, nations whose exporters are blocked from markets abroad have interests in inducing the sister agency to enforce its own law. These interests and incentives have produced new generation cooperation agreements, which now exist between the European Union and the United States, the European Union and Canada, and the United States and, respectively, Canada, Australia, Japan, and Brazil.

Officials of the European Union have put forward a vision and a work programme. In their proposals and thinking they have gone qualitatively further than effects-based enforcement and bilateral cooperation agreements. Since the mid-1990s, they have analysed the need for global minimum rules or core principles. As a result of their contemplations, the European Union proposed, and the WTO accepted, the creation of a Working Group on the Interaction Between Trade and Competition Policy. The Working Group has completed its initial work, and the question now posed is whether competition issues should be readied for a future WTO agenda.

Soft harmonization, meanwhile, is an evolving phenomenon. Numerous meetings and workshops, and *ad hoc* technical assistance to nations that are newly adopting competition laws, have led to much cross-fertilization and increasing convergence.

In the context of the WTO, the trading nations have adopted various agreements that include reference to or rules of competition law. For example, the General Agreement on Trade in Services (GATS), Article 9.1, and the Telecommunications Annex forbid discriminatory abuse of dominance and require reasonable access to networks, and an accompanying reference paper suggests that members commit to maintain adequate measures to prevent anti-competitive practices by major suppliers, including cross-subsidization, use of information obtained from competitors to compete against them, and withholding from competitors of technical or commercial information about essential facilities.

III. ARE ANTITRUST LAWS OF NATIONS TOOLS OF VIRTUOUS OR HARMFUL COMPETITION?

Regulatory competition

One reason suggested for internationalizing economic law stems from the hypothesis that, if left alone, nations will design or use their laws to attract trade, investment, or the establishment of business, and that, to seduce business away from their neighbours, nations will degrade their laws. International rules could restrain this perverse competition (Farber 1997a). Races—toward bottom or top—assume that there is regulatory competition; that is, the concept assumes that nations are competing against one another in the formulation or application of their laws to be more attractive to business than the neighbour's laws. The competition of laws to attract business hypothesis does not very well fit competition laws. There is, for example, no parallel to corporations law, wherein one and only one state will grant a firm's corporate charter. In matters of incorporation, it is natural that states will compete to be the one that 'wins'.

Competition law systems do not compete in that way. Competition laws of Nation A govern the conduct of firms within that jurisdiction *and* the conduct of firms outside the jurisdiction that harm competition within the jurisdiction. Thus, because of accepted principles of extraterritoriality, the host's law will not be the exclusive law. Moreover, firms will choose to enter many different markets to serve the people there (for example, Coca-Cola or McDonald's may establish themselves in Russia), knowing that they will be subject to the nation's entire system of laws. Competition law that is helpful or harmful (however it is seen by the firm) could possibly be a marginal incentive or disincentive, but the firm first chooses to serve the market, and probably will do so absent 'unlivable' law.

Thus, unlike the phenomenon of corporate charters, states or nations are not set into direct competition with one another to have the most desirable competition law from the viewpoint of a firm that is a target of opportunity.

Efficiency-based antitrust and race to the bottom

It is worth exploring, nonetheless, whether there is a margin for a race among nations that might tend to degrade national competition laws. The framing of the problem depends upon what is 'good' antitrust law. Currently, in the United States, 'good' antitrust law proscribes only conduct or transactions that lessen both rivalry and efficiency; if these effects are absent (according to many authorities and cases), the law has no basis for intervention. To the extent that a nation's antitrust law is based on such an efficiency principle, there is small purview for a convincing race-to-the-bottom argument in antitrust, for antitrust law would tend to attract, not repel, business. Stated differently, when the best law—best as seen by firms and investors—is law that removes costs and does not impose them, there is no scope for a race to the bottom.[1]

This narrow scope for a convincing race argument may become apparent from a contrast with environmental law, as to which the race argument is classically made (though debated) (Revesz 1992). Environmental regulation normally imposes costs on businesses, even efficient ones, and does so at the point of production. Firms may shift their production sites in response to local costs. Firms that must pay the costs of environmental regulation are worse off in competition with firms that operate production facilities in jurisdictions with less costly requirements. Therefore, nations might feel the competitive pressure to lower environmental standards and thereby make themselves a more attractive home to business.

Efficiency-style competition law, as compared with competitor-regarding competition law, does not handicap business; at least it is self-consciously intended to be not handicapping. Efficient, responsive firms do not have to pull punches or pay a tax. A business environment with an efficiency-based competition law should be attractive and inviting, at least to those business people who are betting that they will succeed on the merits.

But let us flip the paradigm, for, as indicated, in the world antitrust community there is no agreement on what is the top and what is the bottom. We have assumed above that the antitrust top is law designed to promote efficiency and to give firms freedom to do that which will lower their own costs. There is another conception. We take as an example the abuse of dominance law of the European Union (Fox 1986; Jebsen and Stevens 1996) and of the many countries of the world (most countries with antitrust law) that adopt the EU model. Firms abuse their dominance if they unfairly exclude or exploit smaller firms. We assume here that, if countries choose the EU model, it is, for them, 'the top'.[2] If so, US-style antitrust law *could* trigger a race toward the bottom.

[1] For convenience and theoretical clarity, this statement discounts the costs of administration and enforcement. In calling US law efficient law on the grounds that it is only proscribing market impediments, it also puts to one side the pre-merger notification and merger regulatory system. It discounts costs of error especially in regard to protectionist applications, including costs of class actions and treble damages in such cases. Therefore, one must relax the assumption that US antitrust law is efficient.

[2] It is not conceivable that the member nations of the European Community chose Article 86 (now

Here is the scenario, through the eyes of a hypothetical European: European Union abuse of dominance law is good for society. It maintains the right economic, human, and governance values, that are good for Europe and good for the world. But, given the globalization of markets, Europe cannot maintain this system unless the United States adopts it too. Otherwise European businesses will pay higher costs; US firms will out-compete European firms, and firms will gravitate to US shores. Europe might be forced to degrade its law to the US model—soulless aggregate efficiency. To the extent that Europe stands its ground, the competition it faces from lower-cost US firms is unfair competition.

Perhaps this perspective is not hypothetical. In its 1995 White Paper on Enlargement, the European Commission (1995) explained its policy to require hopeful EU members to approximate the major bodies of law of the European Community, prominently including competition law, into their *national* legal systems (Jakob 1993). The White Paper says, at point 2.13:

> Another reason for legislating at the Community level has been the need to create and maintain equal conditions for economic operators. Competition could be distorted if undertakings in one part of the Community had to bear much heavier costs than in another and there would be a risk of economic activity migrating to locations where costs were lower . . . The implementation of high common standards of protection is among the Union's objectives and at the same time helps to ensure this 'level playing field'.

Some officials of the European Union have indeed suggested that the end game of internationalization of competition policy is the adoption of common substantive principles of law for international transactions, and they commonly envision those principles as EC principles.

If, however, such a strategy were a gleam in European eyes, the gleam may have been extinguished by *realpolitik*. The United States will not accept EC abuse of dominance law as world law; and it has the power of veto.

Efficiency law that is not US-style

In the above version of 'high-standard' antitrust, we assumed that deviation from the US model was explained by non-efficiency goals; for example, fairness in protecting smaller firms from abusive domination. But the United States does not have a monopoly on 'what is efficiency'. Deviation from the US model might be attributable to nations' different requirements for creating and maintaining efficient markets. For example, as Polish, Hungarian, Indonesian, and South African officials have said: their country needs to 'grow' competition. They need to create a hospitable environment for building a system of competition on the merits. Especially, they need a hospitable environment for the entry and growth of small and

Article 82) of the Treaty establishing the European Community rather than the less regulatory US counterpart (Section 2 of the Sherman Act) in order to attract US businesses to the European Community or to prevent European businesses from migrating to the United States.

medium-sized firms. In these nations, capital may be hard to get, capital markets may lack efficiency, and the risk of an entrepreneur's failure or setback (including through cronyism, renationalization, or new grants of special privilege) in connection with new or renewed entry is likely to be higher than in mature, stable market economies. Thus the US *laissez-faire* price-predation or market foreclosure rules may not be the most efficient rules for non-US countries (Fingleton *et al.* 1996).

In this context, we may find a stronger claim of a race toward the bottom. If the forces of globalization put pressure on countries to adopt austere US-style antitrust law (a plaintiff virtually never wins a US price-predation case because low prices *are* competition and crushed competitors are not in themselves a concern of US antitrust), this pressure may undermine the ability of developing or reindustrializing nations to establish an efficient economy—especially an efficient economy that includes its citizens among the players.

No antitrust law as possibly efficient

Some countries choose to have no antitrust law. Why would they do this? One hypothesis is: to attract business and investment. How would the absence of antitrust law attract business and investment? Business might want freedom to do what antitrust usually prohibits (cartelize, monopolize, exclude rivals by unreasonably restrictive acts, merge to market power; perhaps price discriminate, tie, refuse to deal); and firms might value this freedom more than they value protection against rivals' predations.

A second hypothesis is: antitrust law and its enforcement is expensive; it takes resources. For practical and political reasons, it may be difficult to enforce the law effectively and especially to enforce the law where gains may be greatest—for example, where the state is involved. Antitrust proponents that have in mind efficient antitrust may fear that their nation's legislators will adopt an antitrust law that will spill over into overregulation and protectionism. Moreover, the marginal gains to economic welfare from antitrust may be small, and even below zero if antitrust is or becomes protectionist. The small-marginal-gains possibility would be true especially if the economy is small and open, so that most domestic markets will be protected by inbound foreign competition, and domestic anti-competitive conduct that spills over to the world may be prosecuted by mature antitrust jurisdictions.

The first hypothesis—freedom from antitrust will attract business—is relatively unlikely to be the case. If the attracted business sells abroad, its anti-competitive practices will be subject to scrutiny in the consumer jurisdictions (Stephan 1999); the firm cannot escape antitrust. If, on the other hand, the business invests in Country A because it wants to serve Country A's market, the attraction *is* Country A. Although excessively burdensome law of A could be a dissuasion, by definition, freedom from antitrust would not have been the attraction.

The second hypothesis could hold; for example, for Hong Kong or Singapore. If it does, pressure on the nation to adopt a competition law, as per EU aspirations for a WTO agenda, could be a pressure toward the bottom.[3]

Antitrust law for nationalistic ends

There are, to be sure, quite troublesome deviations from good antitrust law. For example, nations may offer anti-competitive incentives to particular firms to induce them to locate or invest in the nation. One form of inducement is law that lets firms restrain trade anti-competitively. Another is selective non-enforcement of law, letting firms restrain trade anti-competitively in return for their coveted establishment or investment. In these cases, there is no ambiguity between top and bottom, and there *is* a case for checking an inter-nation game that results in degraded law.

For example, nations' antitrust laws commonly do not cover or they exempt export cartels. Yet such cartels hurt foreigners, enforcement at the source of the wrong is usually most efficient, the targeted victims are often left with no practical remedy, and outbound cartels commonly also distort competition in the world and therefore hurt even the home country (though less immediately than they hurt foreigners). Export cartel exemptions are common even in nations such as the United States, where cartel conduct is considered so egregious when it hurts US consumers that cartelists go to jail.

Nations give excuses for blinking at export cartels. One explanation—a modest view of state authority to regulate acts that radiate beyond national borders—is plausible and, where authentic, is not attributable to bad world citizenship. The limits-of-sovereignty explanation is especially plausible if it does not co-exist with generous extraterritorial application of the national antitrust law when the application helps the nation's citizens against foreigners.

The United States cannot claim the limits-of-sovereignty explanation, and its example seems to fit the mutual-degradation hypothesis. The United States withdrew its antitrust coverage of export cartels in 1982. Congress gave as a major reason for this legislation that the law of our trading partners offers export exemptions and that therefore US antitrust law (which was ambiguous in its external coverage) was handicapping US business.

The hypothesis that nations may try to attract or retain business establishments by giving firms freedom to harm foreigners is not implausible. It is certainly not difficult to induce national legislatures to confer such largesse; foreigners do not vote.

Above, we have discussed export cartels, the immediate harmful effect of which is external. Now we turn to freedom from antitrust altogether, but on the supposition now (in contrast to the previous section) that the motivation is wholly

[3] The negative pressure, however, would have to be discounted, because a good part of the no-antitrust advantage depends on a free ride on other nations' competition law cultures, and because competition law itself almost always exerts useful forces towards openness, transparency, and meritocracy.

negative. A nation may decide to run a cartel haven as a strategy for attracting businesses to locate and remain in the nation. If the country is democratic and consumer-conscious, this strategy may be difficult to implement even for wholly local markets, for the citizens will be obliged to bear a good part of the costs of the private restraints. Further, few markets are wholly local today, and, as noted above, in a world of effects jurisdiction the walls of the citadel (such as Switzerland once may have been) have been breached.

Finally, nations may grant special privileges, either by not enforcing their law against nationals who anti-competitively exclude foreigners, or by giving special rights to nationals; for example, sole import licences or government procurement business. These privileges are not likely to be a means to *compete* for the investment or establishment of businesses (though they might sometimes be a means to keep their 'own' businesses at home). These are discriminatory, nationalistic, crony-like practices. Practices of this sort obstruct the world trading system, and they are in part, though weakly, controlled by the WTO.

Race to the top

Thus far, we have considered the possible competition of nations for business and investment. We might now observe a second form of competition. Fittingly for competition law, nations compete for buyers of the products and services offered within the nation or by firms located there. The competition for buyers means that nations, in their regulatory choices, have the incentive to seek ways and construct environments likely to make 'their' businesses responsive to buyers. This competition is a race toward the top.

Competition to be the law of the world

There is a third form of competition. This is a particular competition between the United States and the European Union for expanding the geographic scope of their law. The European Union and the United States use one common mode and two divergent modes in competing for this economic hegemony.

The common vehicle is advocacy in the course of advice and technical assistance. There are many buyers in this market. Some one hundred countries in the WTO do not (yet) have competition laws, and many forces and sources—the International Monetary Fund, the World Bank, the European Union, the United States—are priming these countries to want one. This is virtuous competition to the extent that the country 'buying' competition law is free to choose its competition law on the merits and is sufficiently well informed to make a rational choice. But these conditions are not normally present at today's margin.

The divergent routes are: for the United States, extraterritoriality; for the European Union, Europe Agreements and free trade agreements. As we have seen, hopeful future members of the European Union *must* adopt EC-like competition law into their national law. In addition, Europe Agreement partners must, and other free trade partners must normally, agree to apply EC principles to competition problems in the free trade area.

This competition may be either a race toward the bottom or toward the top if one characterizes the law of one of the contestants as inferior and the other as superior. In any event, the European Union is winning the competition.

This competition concerns exporting law, not importing law. The dominant exporter of its model will have the stronger position if and when, at a future advanced stage of globalization and world integration, businesses find it no longer tenable *not* to have one overarching set of rules for the game. The question will be, then, whether the United States will maintain its veto over world competition law, or whether it will, as it did in adopting the WTO Agreement on Trade-Related Intellectual Property, give up 'principle' (it gave up the 'first to invent' principle in TRIPs) for a greater gain.

In sum, there may be muted races toward the bottom in competition law. The dominant aspects in which such a race might occur involve nationalistic strategies and resulting externalities. Negative effects may be counteracted by races toward the top.

In the next Part, we observe the world from the other end of the telescope. Looking from 'above', we ask: Are there problems that can best be solved by some degree of internationalization? The race-toward-the-bottom problems of nationalistic strategies are subsumed by this second perspective.

IV. A CASE FOR INTERNATIONALIZATION OF COMPETITION LAW

Problems that can best be addressed by a borderless conception of the world

Race-toward-the-bottom analysis has a built-in perception limitation. By focusing on horizontal competition among the laws of nations, the paradigm steers the mind away from the global picture. Only by focusing on the global picture can we observe problems that can be solved and opportunities that can be seized to enhance world welfare (Christiansen 1994; Fox and Ordover 1995).

A 'borderless' conception implies the treatment of a market problem as if there were no national boundaries, or, conceived differently, as if all harms and benefits fell within the geographic bounds of the same polity. A borderless conception would have benefits in solving the following problems, some of which are overlapping:

The vision problem

Under national-only antitrust, one nation does not 'see' the full dimensions of a problem. A nation may see the proverbial elephant's front right leg but not the elephant. Thus, when the European Community sought to impose on IBM Europe the duty to disclose to competitors the interface changes of new products, it did not have the incentive to take account of the effects of predisclosure on IBM (international) and on inventiveness in general. When Ohio planned to rule on whether out-of-state Mobil Oil could complete its hostile takeover of Ohio's Marathon Oil (a major Ohio employer), the vision from Ohio surely looked different from the vision from the 'top' of the United States.

The proliferation problem

Some eighty nations now have competition laws. Approximately forty nations require pre-merger notification and vetting. The numbers are growing. Firms whose business or conduct crosses borders often must comply with numerous national laws at once. The laws are not identical, and even identical words in statutory law are often given different interpretations and applications. Even if we prefer not to override national choices, in some instances the problem of proliferation and overlap (against the background of accepted principles of extraterritoriality) may be so extreme as to call for a solution. This is so in the area of pre-merger control, where one small country (in terms of a merger's impact) can delay or abort an entire transnational merger that has passed through the clearance process in some twenty or thirty other jurisdictions.

The nationalism (externality) problem

At some margin, nations tend to make competition law decisions based on what is good for the nation even at the expense of the world. Europe supported Airbus in opposing Boeing's acquisition of McDonnell Douglas, and the United States supported Boeing in completing the acquisition. Japan's MITI has supported the Japanese glass industry against claims of a market-blocking cartel and Fuji Film against claims of monopolistic exclusion of Kodak, while US agencies or officials have supported the US glass industry and Kodak in connection with their claims of unlawful exclusion.

Moreover, possibly for nationalistic reasons, nations may refuse to prohibit their nationals from doing abroad acts that are prohibited, even criminally, at home. This is so even where the host nation also prohibits the conduct and would find enforcement practically impossible.

State trade-restraining measures, including exemptions and derogations, may stem from nationalistic impulses, or they may be patently excessive in view of legitimate goals. Some such measures are caught by the prohibitions of the WTO, but many, including blessings in the form of a state action defence, are not. There is no international understanding of what is or is not appropriate government intervention to limit trade. Examples of situations that would have profited from common understandings, or at least shared knowledge and clarity, are the uranium cartel matter of the 1970s and the Russian aluminium market-flooding problem of the early 1990s.

Easily triggered anti-dumping laws likewise present a problem of state restraints on trade and competition. Moreover, anti-dumping laws are a major facilitator of world cartels. The anti-dumping problem appears, appropriately, on many agendas for reform. In concept, it fits neatly into the list of competition-related state restraints of trade. As a concession to political pragmatism, however (the US opposition to reform), we may need to de-emphasize the problem or defer its solution.

The problem of systems clash

One nation may allow, and sometimes wish to facilitate, what another nation prohibits. Systems clash may lead to hostilities, possibly culminating in a trade war (as nearly occurred in the matter of Boeing/McDonnell Douglas) or in nationalistic measures (blocking and claw-back statutes, as in the British Protection of Trading Interests Act of 1980). There are no transnational or international rules or protocols to channel behaviour so as to alleviate such conflicts. For example, there are no rules of primary jurisdiction to grant or withhold an order to enjoin a merger (Fox 1999).

Discovery and enforcement: the information problem

There are some areas in which there is wide agreement in the world on important antitrust prohibitions (for example, the rule against hard core cartels in the absence of a nation-state exemption on one side). Even so, discovery by one nation regarding targets or defendants located in another nation is so difficult that world cartels remain undetected and trials against cartelists are lost for lack of evidence.

Extraterritoriality: problem or solution?

European Community officials have argued that internationalization is a means to cure a problem of excessive, if not imperialistic, extraterritorial application of competition law. They point, for example, to US threats to use its antitrust laws to prise open foreign markets closed by anti-competitive private restraints. If international rules would prohibit private market access restraints, it is thought, the United States may forego its claim of right to so use the Sherman Act. While excessive extraterritoriality may be seen as a problem that justifies internationalization, it may be seen, alternatively, as a means to address transnational problems in the absence of transnational law. The earliest use of extraterritoriality, and still its dominant use in antitrust, is catching offshore cartels targeted at the enforcing nation. This usage is widely accepted today; it is progressive, and is not a problem when no conflicting state policy is involved. Had such inbound extraterritoriality been ultimately condemned rather than increasingly embraced, the need for international antitrust would have been so pressing so long ago that we surely would already have adopted an international antitrust law.

The threatened use of antitrust to prise open foreign markets goes a large step further. It is self-help in a global world without global law. The underlying problem—foreign markets closed by anti-competitive private restraints—is real. It is a problem that can be solved in the context of the WTO.

Opportunities

When we open our eyes to the interdependent world, we see many opportunities. First, educational opportunities are waiting to be realized. To some extent, competition law is divergent merely as a result of lack of information and understanding. Law tends to achieve greater convergence through cross-fertilization. Also, as noted, numerous countries have recently adopted, or are contemplating adoption of, competition laws. Many of these are less developed countries. They need technical assistance and could profit from benchmarking and competition peer reviews. Formalization of educational and assistance projects could help solidify the infrastructure of competition law. A firmer world infrastructure with a body of common understanding could advance other objectives dealt with above. For example, as more nations' competition agencies provide credible threats against cartels, we can expect greater worldwide deterrence against, and detection of, cartels.

Second, also noted above, some WTO agreements now prohibit certain private or other commercial restraints, as do the GATS Agreement and the Telecoms Annex. They contain competition law vocabulary, such as 'essential facilities' and 'abuse of dominance', without definition of these terms. There is a particular need for nations either to adopt a choice of law principle (which could be added to the relevant WTO agreements), or to develop common understandings of the competition concepts on which trade panels may draw in the event of disputes. There is thus a need for nations to collaborate, at least to identify the core common ground of their laws, and possibly to work further on common definitions.

There are many projects and conversations that could be launched and that could be useful in facilitating the enterprise of better[4] and more nearly seamless competition policy for a world without artificial economic borders.

V. WHICH IS THE BEST FORUM?

We have identified a panoply of competition problems, solutions to which might minimize nationalism and conflicts, enhance the harmonious relationship of systems, and provide a more nearly seamless market economy. Most of these problems are not distinctly trade-related, except in the overbroad sense that eliminating artificial barriers helps to make markets work and better-functioning markets enhance trade.

The WTO is the most obvious and most frequently mentioned forum for addressing these problems. As to the wisdom of the WTO as a forum, there are two

[4] By 'better' I mean either enhancing world welfare or moving national systems into a more nearly frictionless relationship with one another, for political as well as economic ends.

schools of thought. First, the EU school, joined by Canada, Korea, and Japan, urges that the world competition issues be brought under the WTO umbrella. The WTO is an existing structure already committed to enhancing the world trading system. It incorporates basic accepted disciplines against nationalistic discrimination and in favour of transparency; it includes a broad constituency of developed and developing countries; it provides a forum for reaching agreement on rules; and it has put into place a system for rule-of-law adjudication. Second, the US school opposes negotiations in the WTO; in general, it opposes a multilateral or plurilateral alternative to national enforcement and voluntary bilateral cooperation.

Some less developed countries side with the United States, expressing fear that a regime forcing open markets will leave them and their cultures vulnerable to the on-rush of multinational corporations, or asserting the right to have no antitrust, or claiming the need for time to learn. Others side with the European Union, noting that they have no power to obtain cooperation agreements on their own, and they assert, with moral force, that they should have the benefits of whatever agreements are struck by the developed world (Jenny 1997).

There is a strong case for bringing focused trade and competition issues into the WTO. For example, a rule could and should require nations to prevent anti-competitive blockage of markets (E. Fox 1997a; 1997b; 1998; 1999).

As we have seen, there are many other larger-than-national competition law problems that are not trade problems except in the sense that higher prices lower output and thus tend to reduce trade. For these issues, there is no existing natural home; but there is a need for a home. Perhaps the need could be met by a free-standing forum or meeting place; a sustained opportunity for interchange, brainstorming, and cooperation on world competition problems, open to all nations in the world and to voices of business and consumers.

The forum could be hosted, successively, by competition agencies of the various nations. It could and should interact with the WTO and the OECD, and provide a resource for informing the competition issues embedded in the WTO. A positive momentum to identify and vet the world competition issues has developed in the WTO Working Group on the Interaction Between Trade and Competition Policy. In view, however, of the institutional limits of the WTO, its inherent trade perspective, and reverberations of Seattle scepticism (Friedman 2000), it may be wise and even necessary to shift energy to a complementary forum to develop perspectives on and possibly solutions to the non-trade world competition issues.

A number of possible missions would naturally fall within the aegis of a forum for world competition issues. These include consideration of:

1. The sharing of ideas and the development of awareness and common understandings, including deeper appreciation of: (a) the needs of less developed countries (LDCs) and the effect of competition policy on their development goals (Jenny 1997); (b) the importance of LDCs' development to the industrialized world and to the community of nations as a whole; and (c) the

significance of various nations' choices of goals in formulating and enforcing their national competition laws.

2. Multilateralizing cooperation agreements and positive comity among agencies.
3. Limiting beggar-thy-neighbour anti-competitive private action, excessive state trade-restraining action, and excessive state immunization of anti-competitive private action (Fox and Ordover 1995).
4. Requiring non-discriminatory treatment and transparency of rules of law and of methodology of analysis (E. Fox 1997a; 1997b; Slaughter 1997; 1999).
5. Developing rules for appropriate and inappropriate extraterritorial jurisdiction, and protocols in the event of clashes of jurisdiction regarding enforcement, liability, and relief.
6. Providing information and technical assistance for developing countries that may wish to adopt, or have recently adopted, competition laws.
7. Organizing peer review and benchmarking teams and visits, particularly to assist emerging systems or to respond to claims of underenforced or overenforced law.
8. Developing consensus where possible on substantive principles (Matsushita 1998; Pitofsky 1998; Shelton 1998), with obligations for transparency as to derogations.
9. Rationalizing multinational merger control, with respect to systems for notification, waiting periods, and clearance (Rowley and Campbell 1999).
10. Developing rules for the protection of confidential business information, and a common understanding of what is and is not confidential.
11. Coordinating activities with the WTO Working Group and the relevant OECD and UNCTAD committees.

A global competition forum could deepen convergence, cooperation, cross-fertilization, understanding, and respect, and could put into motion a programme for agreements to limit nationalistic action and to enhance a hospitable linking of systems.

CONCLUSION

A race-toward-the-bottom-or-top analysis enlightens consideration of global competition problems but, in the end, does not emerge as a rallying call for global competition. The competitive races among nations by way of competing antitrust laws are not intense; they are submerged in a larger dynamic.

The important point is that markets transcend national borders, yet nations see issues through nationalistic eyes. Some issues are at the intersection of trade and competition, and these issues can and should eventually be addressed in the context of the WTO. Other issues might find a home in an inclusive global forum for vetting competition law problems that are bigger than nations.

Whatever the forum, there are synergies to be realized and negative externalities to be eliminated by a vision that rises above national boundaries while preserving autonomous law formation in the nation-state. Forming the vision, forging the interrelationships, and creating a space in which they can grow are the challenges for competition law at the millennium.

17

The TRIPS Agreement: A Response to Global Regulatory Competition or an Exercise in Global Regulatory Coercion?

INGE GOVAERE AND PAUL DEMARET*

To the extent that intellectual property laws have already been harmonized worldwide by virtue of the Agreement on Trade-Related Aspects of Intellectual Property Rights (TRIPS), annexed to the World Trade Organization (WTO) Agreement, the most urgent question is, in reality, twofold.[1] First, one needs to consider whether there was a justification for the global regulation of intellectual property rights in the framework of the WTO. The second question is why this issue was raised and put on the agenda of the multilateral trade negotiations in the mid-1980s. Those questions do not necessarily entail the same, or even a similar, answer. Whereas it is rather easy to explain why the TRIPS Agreement came into being, it seems more difficult to find a satisfactory justification for the regulation of intellectual property rights at this level of governance.

In order to assess the need for worldwide regulation of intellectual property rights in the framework of the WTO, one must first determine whether there was a 'race to the bottom' of intellectual property legislation prior to the TRIPS Agreement. If not, one should ask whether there were perhaps 'interstate externalities' that might have justified the adoption of minimum standards of intellectual property protection worldwide. These matters are to be evaluated against the context of not only the increased globalization and world economic integration but also the technological revolution, with the emergence of the information society entailing an increased dependence on technology worldwide. It is apparent in this context that information, and intangible property in general, are increasingly considered to be indispensable trade assets (Govaere 1994).

* This chapter has been written within the framework of 'Interuniversity Poles of Attraction Programme—P4/04 Belgian State, Prime Minister's office—Federal Office for Scientific, Technical and Cultural Affairs', University of Liège (ULg), Univesity of Ghent (UG), and University of Brussels (ULB).

[1] For an overview of the most controversial issues and conceptual problems during the negotiations leading up to the TRIPS Agreement, see Cottier (1991).

I. REGULATORY SPECIFICITY OF INTELLECTUAL PROPERTY

Regulation of most issues covered in the framework of the WTO (or of issues informally discussed, such as environment, labour, and tax regulation) is essentially held to be in the public interest. The TRIPS Agreement is somewhat peculiar in this respect. The preamble unequivocally acknowledges that 'intellectual property rights are private rights'.[2] It is often forgotten that intellectual property rights are essentially and inherently a tradeoff between private and public interests. Legal protection is granted, in the form of exclusive rights based on the principle of territoriality, in order to disclose valuable information or inventions and to stimulate research and development. The latter is done by giving the possibility to obtain a return, thus providing an incentive to invest time and money in research and development. As such, it is generally considered necessary to tolerate a temporary restriction on competition by granting exclusive rights to the intellectual property holder, in order to enhance competition in the long run. Only trademark protection is not limited in time.[3] The objective is to guarantee the commercial origin of a product to consumers, so that goodwill may be created. The exclusivity entails that the proprietor of a trademark may prevent the affixing of his distinctive mark, or a confusingly similar trademark, to similar products. As similar products may be marketed under different brand names, trademarks are less likely to have a major impact on competition in the market, although well-known brands may confer a certain degree of market power (Baden Fuller 1981: 162; Parr and Hughes 1993: 157).

Private interest in obtaining intellectual property protection

The private interest of the intellectual property holder is immediately apparent. In the absence of legal protection, intangible property falls into the public domain and may thus be freely appropriated by others at little or no cost. He therefore clearly has an interest in obtaining exclusive rights. These allow the intellectual property holder to prohibit certain acts by others that would be legitimate in the absence of intellectual property protection, such as sale, production, and importation of intellectual property-based products or services.[4] It is also important that he obtains this

[2] Note that outside the intellectual property field, the GATT/WTO traditionally is not concerned with granting private rights (Fickentscher 1989: 121), except of a procedural nature, such as under the WTO Agreements on sanitary and phytosanitary measures, technical barriers to trade, anti-dumping duties, countervailing duties, pre-shipment inspection, or under the General Agreement on Trade in Services (GATS).

[3] For an overview of the main current economic theories with respect to patents, copyright, and trademarks, see Besen and Raskind (1991).

[4] Nothing prevents him from competing in the market in the absence of intellectual property protection, but he would not be able to obtain an exclusive position and charge higher prices by excluding imitators from the market.

exclusive right on the basis of the principle of territoriality and the principle of independence. These principles ensure that what happens to the exclusive rights in one country (for example, the refusal or revocation of the exclusive right, or the grant of compulsory licences) will not affect the status or enforcement of his exclusive rights in other countries. A major distinction with other types of regulation discussed here, such as environmental regulation, is that, with respect to intellectual property rights, it is essentially the technology-based industries, as well as those possessing well-known brands, in the industrialized countries that are demanding more and worldwide regulation.[5] As such, it is not to be feared that those industries would transfer production out if intellectual property regulation is adopted. Rather to the contrary, intellectual property protection is likely to attract business and investment.

Seen from this perspective, it is easily understandable why there was no 'race to the bottom' with respect to intellectual property regulation prior to the TRIPS Agreement.[6] It would be more logical to presume that there might have been a 'race to the top' regarding intellectual property regulation, although there does not appear to be any overwhelming evidence of this. For example, if a certain interaction was discerned between the US and EC initiatives in the field of databases and biotechnological interventions[7] prior to the TRIPS Agreement, there definitely was no real 'race to the top' that would, of itself, justify the conclusion of the latter agreement at the level of the WTO. The question nonetheless remains why the TRIPS Agreement does not impose maximum norms of intellectual property protection, thereby leaving it up to the WTO members to adopt a higher level of protection if they so wish.[8] The chosen option would be difficult to understand if one took into account only the private interest in obtaining intellectual property protection. If industry itself is the party demanding better and more intellectual property protection worldwide, then it would be logical to assume that all countries would wish to attract business and investment by adopting adequate protection of intellectual property at a national level. So why was it necessary to impose the adoption of appropriate intellectual property legislation by means of an agreement

[5] Calls for more worldwide regulation come in particular from industries in the industrialized countries, as intellectual property protection is only interesting to firms if they have intangible property (especially technology) worth protecting.

[6] However, in the late nineteenth century there appears to have been a race to the bottom of intellectual property legislation as intellectual property rights were considered to be important barriers, and thus deterrents, to trade (Machlup and Penrose 1950).

[7] For instance, the EC Commission held, in the explanatory memorandum of the first proposal on the legal protection of biotechnological inventions, that 'establishing a harmonized system of patent law in this area will facilitate the development of Community industry in biotechnology, trade in biotechnological products and the establishment of a common market in this field. Moreover, it will enable the Community industry to keep pace with the leading nations in biotechnology and to close or narrow existing gaps' (European Commission 1988b).

[8] Article 1 of TRIPS stipulates that 'Members may, but shall not be obliged to, implement in their law more extensive protection than is required by this Agreement, provided that such protection does not contravene the provisions of this Agreement'.

at the level of the WTO? Would the public interest then provide the justification for the TRIPS Agreement and the (high) minimum level of protection it seeks to achieve?

Public interest in granting intellectual property protection

It is a difficult exercise to define the public interest in granting intellectual property protection. One may not presume that the private and public interests will always merge, in the sense that the public interest would consist only of attracting technology-based industries. A cost–benefit analysis of granting intellectual property protection is a highly complex matter, the outcome of which is largely dependent on a factual and economic analysis of any given market. Improving technology and/or inducing technology transfer, which in turn should lead to economic progress, are, of course, among the criteria that will weigh heavily in favour of the benefit side. The crucial question is whether this is enough to outweigh the social and economic costs that also go hand-in-hand with the introduction of, or raising the level of, intellectual property protection.

A first important cost in terms of income and employment may arise from the fact that one firm will be able to exercise its temporary exclusive rights to exclude one or more competing firms from the market. For countries that do not have an important local technology-based industry this cost will be considerable, as it essentially means that local economic activity will be temporarily restrained by the grant of exclusive rights to foreign firms. A second important cost for those countries ensues from the higher prices that will most likely be charged as a result of the exercise of the exclusive right. It is the very essence of intellectual property rights to render a product scarce that might otherwise be freely available, so that higher prices may be charged.[9] Related to the purely economic costs are social costs, which are even more difficult to calculate. It might suffice here to point to the repercussions that increased prices on certain products, such as pharmaceutical products,[10] may have on public health policies of individual countries.

What is certain is that the outcome of the cost–benefit analysis is not necessarily the same for each country, as it is highly dependent on the level of economic development. It is also likely to change over time, keeping pace with the economic progress that individual countries achieve.

[9] Trademarks do not share this characteristic with the other intellectual property rights, but may be used to enforce differential pricing on different markets.

[10] Article 27(1) of TRIPS provides that 'patents shall be available for any inventions, whether products or processes, in all fields of technology', meaning that all WTO members are obliged to grant patent protection also to pharmaceutical products, in spite of the potential repercussions on their public health policies. See in this respect the case *India-Patent Protection for Pharmaceutical and Agricultural Chemical Products* (WTO 1997a; 1997b.). See also below at pp. 378–9.

Rationale of, instead of justification for, the TRIPS Agreement

The preceding sections indicate that it is difficult to find a straightforward justification for the TRIPS Agreement. The Agreement applies to developing and industrialized countries alike, allowing only for a longer transitional period for the developing countries but not for substantive derogation. The Agreement is structured as though it were based on the—false—presumption that the public interest of all WTO members in granting intellectual property protection is necessarily the same and, moreover, necessarily converges with the private interests of intellectual property holders in obtaining a high level of intellectual property protection. This approach is nonetheless easy to explain if one takes into account the reasons that have led to the TRIPS Agreement in the first place.

It is no secret that the TRIPS Agreement is essentially a market-stimulated regulation. Business in the United States (Gadbaw 1989; Kastenmeter and Beier 1989), later on followed by EC counterparts, pressed hard to obtain exclusive rights on third country markets, by spelling out the losses they allegedly incurred due to 'counterfeit' and 'piracy' worldwide.[11] These claims for better global intellectual property protection were subsequently taken over by the government of the industrialized countries.[12] In particular, the United States and the European Community started to use unilateral and bilateral measures to force reluctant third countries to adopt higher norms of intellectual property protection, in order to secure exclusivity on export markets for their respective industries. Section 301 special of the 1988 US Trade Act and the EC New Commercial Policy Instrument (now replaced by the trade barriers Regulation) proved to be useful unilateral tools in this respect, and also linked the grant of Generalized System of Preferences (GSP) status to the issue of adequate intellectual property protection. In bilateral trade agreements, clauses were gradually inserted that obliged the trading partner to raise the level of intellectual property protection and to accede to certain specified intellectual property conventions. The TRIPS Agreement was just one step further along this route, as it was annexed to and formed an integral part of the package deal of the WTO Agreement. This introduced the 'all or nothing approach' also in multilateral trade relations. Paradoxically enough, the use of a multilateral dispute settlement mechanism, which was to replace the unilateral and bilateral pressures by the industrialized countries, was now presented as the solution to the sometimes untenable situation of developing countries who faced different demands from the United States and the European Community.[13] The developing countries had previously consistently disagreed with the industrialized countries on the issue of the

[11] Quite substantial figures were advanced, such as an estimated economic loss of about 10 per cent of world trade or US$ 60–70 billion (Uchentagen 1990: 770).

[12] On the linkage of intellectual property rights to trade, see Govaere (1997a: 468–71).

[13] The case of Korea is illustrative. After the United States successfully used Section 301 to secure better intellectual property protection for US industry in the Korean market, Korea was suspended from the EC list of countries benefiting from GSP in retaliation for discriminating against EC industry, as compared to US industry, in the field of intellectual property protection.

need to render the existing intellectual property conventions more effective by virtue of specific enforcement mechanisms.

It is difficult to deny that the TRIPS Agreement is clearly the result of a public policy choice of the industrialized countries. They basically sought to secure exclusivity for their industries in as many third markets as possible to protect export and investment and, to this end, did not hesitate to coerce the developing countries into accepting their terms.

II. FROM NATIONAL TO INTERNATIONAL PROTECTION OF INTELLECTUAL PROPERTY: THE OPTIONS

It is important to stress that the question of whether or not the WTO is the appropriate forum to regulate intellectual property is not necessarily identical to the question of whether or not intellectual property protection should be subject at all to international rather than purely national regulation. The TRIPS Agreement is not the first occasion on which the issue of international protection of intellectual property rights has arisen. The so-called 'Great Intellectual Property Conventions'[14] were concerned precisely with the issue of extending intellectual property protection beyond national borders. The justification of the TRIPS Agreement should therefore also be assessed in the light of the achievements of the Great Intellectual Property Conventions (as discussed below).

International protection of intellectual property rights can be achieved on the basis of two basic options. A first option would consist of the introduction of truly 'international' intellectual property rights. This would imply an extension of the principle of territoriality to encompass the territory of all participating states. In practice, it would also require the establishment of international procedures to secure such rights. A second option, which is less far-reaching, is to facilitate the 'bundling' of various national intellectual property rights by one and the same intellectual property holder. This could be done with or without an international procedure to secure such rights.

Option 1: International intellectual property rights

International intellectual property rights would imply that one exclusive right is granted which is valid for the whole territory of the participating states, so that between those states the principles of territoriality and independence would no longer have a role to play. Such a situation would have both apparent advantages and disadvantages for intellectual property holders. A major advantage is that the regulatory framework would be much simplified and rendered more transparent.

[14] In particular, this refers to the Paris Convention of 1883 on the Protection of Industrial Property and the Bern Convention of 1886 on the Protection of Artistic and Literary Works.

However, the cost of obtaining and maintaining such an exclusive right, which is likely to increase in proportion to the number of participating states, could well prove to be a considerable disadvantage.[15] Even where this cost is equal to, or less than, the total cost for obtaining and maintaining intellectual property protection in all of those countries separately, there may be a financial burden for those who would not normally have sought protection in all of those markets.

Another major drawback of such a system is that it would only be logical if, when the intellectual property right is revoked in one participating country, it is also lost in all other participating countries. The elimination of the principles of territoriality and independence of international intellectual property rights raises the delicate problem of administration and justiciability/enforcement of such rights. Ideally, world intellectual property offices, and specialized world tribunals and courts, would need to be created. In the alternative, participating countries—and intellectual property holders—would need to place an unconditional mutual trust in one another's national intellectual property offices, as well as courts and tribunals, to duly uphold and enforce the exclusive rights. It is generally felt, therefore, that the introduction of international intellectual property rights is not very realistic in a world-wide context, be it in the framework of the Great Intellectual Property Conventions or in the framework of the WTO.[16]

The creation of international intellectual property rights is possible in a regional integration context, such as in the framework of the European Union, although this idea also leads to certain difficulties. The EC Trade Mark Regulation has indeed introduced the Community Trade Mark, which applies throughout the territory of the European Community, and has set up the Office for Harmonization in the Internal Market (Trade Marks and Industrial Designs) (OHIM) to administer this exclusive right (European Commission 1994a). National trademarks nonetheless continue to co-exist, and it may be expected that they will continue to be skilfully used by industry as long as the language rules of the OHIM, which bear directly on the cost of registration, are not simplified. A similar proposal to introduce a Community Industrial Design is still awaiting approval (European Commission 1994b). The Community Plant Variety Rights were introduced and a Community Plant Variety Office was set up in 1994 (European Commission 1994c).

Option 2: Bundling of national intellectual property rights

The 'bundling' of intellectual property rights implies the possibility for the same intellectual property holder to obtain national intellectual property rights in more than one country whilst leaving the principles of territoriality and independence untouched. The idea is simply to protect intellectual property internationally on

[15] This, of course, does not apply to copyrights as it is not subject to registration.

[16] With respect to the Great Intellectual Property Conventions, see Penrose (1951). With respect to the TRIPS Agreement, see Evans (1999: 710).

the basis of national exclusive rights without different states having to agree on the introduction of a single international intellectual property right with a unitary character. Different states may nonetheless wish to establish a single international procedure in order to facilitate the securing of exclusive rights in the different countries,[17] but this is not essential. With or without such a single procedure to secure exclusive rights, what happens with the exclusive right in one country will not affect the status or the enforcement of the national exclusive rights in the other countries. The latter is the approach taken under both the Great Intellectual Property Conventions and the TRIPS Agreement.

There is nonetheless a major difference to be discerned between the approach adopted under the Great Intellectual Property Conventions and the approach under the TRIPS Agreement. The former essentially introduces basic principles which aim at facilitating the bundling of existing national intellectual property rights,[18] whereas the latter goes a step further. Through imposing worldwide harmonization of intellectual property legislation, it makes it possible to obtain intellectual property rights also in countries where, prior to the TRIPS Agreement, no such protection was granted. The TRIPS Agreement thus seeks greater international protection for intellectual property holders by allowing them to bundle not only existing but also newly to be introduced national intellectual property rights (including new fields of technology, new types of intellectual property rights, and different countries). In addition, in stark contrast to the Paris and Bern Conventions, the TRIPS Agreement deals in considerable detail with the enforcement of intellectual property rights. It therefore needs to be examined whether or not the TRIPS Agreement is justifiable in view of the prior achievements of the Great Intellectual Property Conventions in this respect.

III. FROM NATIONAL TO INTERNATIONAL INTELLECTUAL PROPERTY PROTECTION: JUSTIFICATION OR NECESSITY?

Natural justice theory as a justification for international regulation

The natural justice theory is based on the presumption that men and women have a natural right in their ideas, so that any use of those ideas by others, without authorization, in reality amounts to theft.[19] At first sight, this is an appealing and easily accessible theory which is readily invoked, or at least alluded to, in order to justify

[17] See, for instance, the Munich Convention on the European Patent.

[18] Also, the Great Intellectual Property Conventions established minimum norms of protection, but not at such a high level as TRIPS (because all participating countries, including the developing countries, had to agree), and without providing for specific enforcement mechanisms. On this difference, see Govaere (1994) and O'Regan (1995: 13–14). As O'Regan points out, no dispute was ever brought before the International Court of Justice (ICJ) in this respect (1995: 13).

[19] For an account of the discussions when this theory was first invoked, see Machlup and Penrose (1950: 11–17).

the strive to extend intellectual property protection for technology-based industries worldwide. The argument goes, for instance, that it is only natural for developing countries either to have to pay for the use of inventions that were developed in industrialized countries or to stop profiting from such inventions altogether. Upon closer examination, however, it is immediately apparent that this is a popular fallacy. Intellectual property rights are not viewed as natural rights, either in the Great Intellectual Property Conventions or in the TRIPS Agreement, or under any national legislation currently in force. The clearest indicator of this is that intellectual property protection is limited in time, under both national laws and international forms of regulation. If it were considered a natural right, then it would, of course, not be limited either in time or in space (Penrose 1951: 24).

It is generally acknowledged that intellectual property falls into the public domain upon the expiry of the duration of protection and may be freely appropriated by others. Any other approach would have unacceptable social costs and hold up economic and social progress. Could one truly imagine the situation where important inventions, such as the wheel or the first motor, would forever belong exclusively to the inventor and his descendants? Or that copyright, which confers exclusive protection for at least fifty years after the death of the author, could cover mathematical concepts and ideas instead of only their original form of expression?[20] If not, then one should have no problem with accepting the fact that geographical limitations also may be placed on a temporary exclusive right by virtue of the fact that it concerns a legal right and a legal right only.

A legal right is naturally limited to the territory of the state granting the protection. This is generally acknowledged, although confusion is readily maintained, if not fostered, as a means of putting 'moral pressure' on states that are reluctant to adopt intellectual property protection.[21] The use of language in the current trade debate is significant in this respect. Arguments in the sense that 10 per cent of 'legitimate' world trade is lost, or that there are important market distortions due to 'piracy' and 'counterfeit', are, in reality, only expressing the wish to see one form of legitimate trade (imitation, which is legitimate in the absence of intellectual property protection) replaced by another (exclusivity). As such, contrary to what the choice of language may lead to believe, the mere existence of 'counterfeit' and 'pirate' products does not, in itself, constitute 'interstate externalities' that would justify worldwide harmonization of intellectual property rights in the framework of the WTO.

[20] The idea/expression dichotomy underlying copyright is expressly written into Article 9(2) of the TRIPS Agreement.

[21] A perfect illustration is the use by the European Community of the new commercial policy instrument against Indonesia for failure to respect the Bern Convention and the Universal Copyright Convention, to neither of which Indonesia had adhered (Govaere 1993: 201–2).

Need for international regulation to resolve practical problems?

Certain criteria posed by national intellectual property legislation may, of themselves, prevent the bundling of intellectual property rights and warrant regulation at the international level. The most important obstacles to international protection of intellectual property rights are the novelty and/or originality requirements and the principle of reciprocity.[22] Those problems were already identified at the time of the negotiation of the Great Intellectual Property Conventions, which sought precisely to offer solutions to the ensuing problems for the intellectual property holders.

It is apparent that the novelty and/or originality requirements constitute a first major obstacle to bundling national intellectual property rights. It is, of course, essential that inventions be new, and artistic and literary works original, in order to qualify for intellectual property protection in view of the functions that those exclusive rights fulfil. Such conditions may nonetheless prevent, for none other than practical reasons, the obtaining of exclusive protection by one and the same intellectual property holder in different countries. The disclosure to the public of an invention in one country normally entails the loss of novelty, so that the conditions are no longer fulfilled to qualify for patent protection in other countries where absolute novelty is required. In other words, when intellectual property is subject only to national regulation an inventor needs to choose carefully in which country he wants to benefit from patent protection, as his invention will fall into the public domain in all other countries. A groundbreaking solution to this problem was introduced early on by the Great Intellectual Property Conventions. The insertion of the right of priority, allowing an intellectual property holder to register for similar exclusive rights in several countries within a certain period from the first registration (usually up to one year) without losing novelty status, was considered to be the very *raison d'être* of those Conventions (Penrose 1951: 68). The TRIPS Agreement does not really bring anything new in this respect. This is different for the principle of reciprocity, which will be considered in the following Part.

[22] Another obstacle includes local working requirements, which apply specifically to patents and, until the 1980s, to printed works under US copyright law (Demaret 1987: 178–9). This obstacle to international protection of patents was remedied by the Great Intellectual Property Conventions. It was still considered important that a patent should be worked locally, albeit not necessarily by the patent holder himself. Compulsory licensing was therefore introduced as a sanction for infringement of the local manufacturing clause, instead of compulsory working with possible revocation of the right. According to some authors, the TRIPS Agreement brings a major modification in this respect. It would follow from Article 27(1) of TRIPS, which stipulates that 'patents shall be available and patents rights enjoyable without discrimination as to . . . whether products are imported or locally produced', that compulsory licences for failure to work the patent locally can no longer be imposed if the patented product is imported by the patentee (Einhorn 1998: 1090–1; Ullrich 1995: 176 n. 103). Another interpretation would be 'that the requirement of that provision is met if the compulsory licensing rules do not treat differently imported and locally produced products' (Correa 1994: 331).

IV. RECIPROCITY AND INDEPENDENCE OF INTELLECTUAL PROPERTY RIGHTS

The Great Intellectual Property Conventions

Besides the introduction of the right of priority, a main feature of the Great Intellectual Property Conventions is that the principle of national treatment is introduced in order to replace the principle of reciprocity, which was the usual practice under national law (Ullrich 1995: 161–8). At the same time, the principle of independence of rights is maintained, if not stressed. The rationale of the Great Intellectual Property Conventions is essentially to facilitate international protection of intellectual property rights to the fullest extent possible in the public interest. Regard is thereby given to the fact that the Conventions concern sovereign states at a different stage of economic development, which may call for a different level of protection of intellectual property rights. In particular, under the Great Intellectual Property Conventions it was thought that less developed countries should not be pressured into enacting intellectual property legislation against their own interests (Evans 1999: 715). As a direct consequence of the introduction of the principle of national treatment, alongside the existing principle of independence of rights, a foreign intellectual property holder should receive at least equal treatment to domestic intellectual property holders in each participating country.[23] As material reciprocity may no longer be required there may, however, be unequal treatment of one and the same intellectual property holder in different countries. This implies, for instance, that whereas EC pharmaceutical firms may not benefit from intellectual property protection in India due to lack of intellectual property protection for pharmaceutical products there, under the Great Intellectual Property Conventions Indian firms would nonetheless benefit from the same intellectual property protection as EC intellectual property holders in the European Community. Under this system there is no direct obligation to align intellectual property legislation to that of other signatory countries. However, in certain cases it appears that the situation whereby one's own nationals received exclusive rights in third countries, on a non-reciprocal basis, has acted as an indirect incentive to enact intellectual property legislation, even where the benefit to the home country of granting intellectual property protection is not totally clear.[24]

The TRIPS Agreement: back to square one

At first sight, it seems as though the TRIPS Agreement does not bring any truly innovative features in this respect either, other than the introduction of the prin-

[23] Note that the principle of national treatment in the Great Intellectual Property Conventions has always related to persons and not to goods.

[24] This was apparently the case when Swiss patent law was introduced (Machlup and Penrose 1950: 6).

ciple of most favoured nation treatment in relation to intellectual property rights (Article 4 of TRIPS). The principle of independence of intellectual property rights is maintained and the principle of national treatment (as well as the principle of most favoured nation treatment) is formulated as relating to persons, similarly as in the Great Intellectual Property Conventions, rather than relating to goods, as was traditionally the case under the General Agreement on Tariffs and Trade (GATT) (Articles 3 and 4 of TRIPS). A closer analysis nonetheless reveals an important move away from the philosophy of the Great Intellectual Property Conventions in the TRIPS Agreement. The latter de facto reintroduces the principle of material reciprocity by laying down rather high minimum standards of protection which need to be complied with effectively by all WTO members, including the developing countries. This follows from the fact that, contrary to normal GATT practice, there is no scope for substantive derogation for the developing countries but only for a longer transitional period (Ullrich 1989: 148–9). The *India-Patent Protection for Pharmaceutical and Agricultural Chemical Products* case of 1997 clearly points out that, in spite of the wording of the TRIPS Agreement, WTO members—including the developing countries—will not be *totally* 'free to determine the appropriate method of implementing the provisions of this Agreement within their own legal system and practice' (Article 1 of TRIPS) (WTO 1997a; 1997b). This once again clarifies that the aim of the TRIPS Agreement is to ensure that there will no longer be unequal treatment of one and the same intellectual property holder in different countries but, to the contrary, that the protection granted should be significantly similar, regardless of the country where protection is sought. The dispute settlement mechanism, which was negotiated after agreement had been reached on TRIPS, is crucial in this respect.

In the context of such an extensive harmonization of intellectual property legislation worldwide, it is apparent that the principle of national treatment loses much of its original meaning and importance (Ullrich 1995).[25] This raises the question of why such a departure from the approach of facilitating international protection of intellectual property rights, which was adopted under the Great Intellectual Property Conventions, can be justified. In the following Parts it will be considered whether there were perhaps interstate externalities prior to the TRIPS Agreement, or other imperative conditions, that warranted worldwide harmonization in the framework of the WTO.

[25] Ullrich points out that:

> [N]ational treatment has a different quality when it is supposed to work on the basis of largely harmonized national intellectual property law. It works within the context of substantive reciprocity rather than in the context of minimum protection, which leaves the formulation of intellectual property policies to the sovereign judgement of Member States. Under such circumstances, Member States no longer grant privileges to foreigners, regardless of their own domestic interest, but rather comply with the obligations of a quid pro quo deal. The Member States have entered into the deal presumably as legally and economically equal partners seeking to secure comparable advantages to their own nationals abroad. (1995: 180)

V. EXISTENCE OF 'INTERSTATE EXTERNALITIES' AS A JUSTIFICATION FOR THE TRIPS AGREEMENT?

In the absence of an identifiable 'race to the bottom' or 'race to the top' of national intellectual property legislation prior to the TRIPS Agreement (as discussed in Part I), it needs to be considered whether one can identify interstate externalities that could only be remedied by worldwide harmonization in the framework of the WTO. It was established above that any attempt to identify interstate externalities on the basis of the so-called natural justice theory is perhaps appealing but inherently fallacious (as discussed in Part III). A totally different and more serious argument invokes the new economic context which, since the technological revolution, gradually created new economic realities also for intellectual property holders. As such, it is argued that securing new export markets for intellectual property-based products is needed to stimulate increasingly costly investment in the research and development of products which, also due to technological progress, have become easier to copy. It is thus maintained that benefiting from exclusive protection and obtaining a return only on the home market is no longer sufficient. There would be interstate externalities because the ability to secure exclusive rights also on export markets, by virtue of worldwide harmonization of intellectual property legislation, has become essential in order to offset the costs and to provide an incentive for the creative effort (Esty and Geradin, Ch. 2).

It is a powerful economic argument to imply that, without worldwide harmonization of intellectual property legislation in the framework of the WTO, the whole process of inventive activity would necessarily come to a halt for lack of sufficient economic incentives. Furthermore, this argument apparently would be able to explain the different approach to international protection of intellectual property rights over time, as expressed in the TRIPS Agreement compared to the Great Intellectual Property Conventions, because it invokes the new economic situation that has arisen since the technological revolution. In view of the alleged novelty of the economic context, it may therefore seem surprising that similar economic arguments had already been raised and considered at the time of the negotiation of the Great Intellectual Property Conventions (Penrose 1951). It cannot be ignored that the implicit rejection of those arguments at that time has not prevented technological progress from taking place, even in the absence of worldwide harmonization of intellectual property legislation as envisaged by the TRIPS Agreement.

Until now it has not been proved that without the ability to secure exclusive rights in all WTO member countries, which is the objective of the TRIPS Agreement, investment in research and development would not take place. There are many other factors that would seem to weigh in favour of investing in research and development in any case. In particular, it appears that a sufficient incentive may be present if the home market is already large.[26] Additionally, it should not be for-

[26] It is ironic that the US market and the EC market most readily come to mind in this respect.

gotten that intellectual property protection could already be obtained, by virtue of the principle of national treatment as introduced in the Great Intellectual Property Conventions, in many third countries, so that the intellectual property holder could also obtain a return on those markets.[27] No proof has been given to suggest that there was less creative effort in the past, or that there would be less in the future, due to the absence of a prospect of obtaining intellectual property protection in virtually all the countries of the world.

The following counter-argument is even more important, as it relates to the public interest which is also inherent in granting intellectual property protection (as discussed in Part I, second section). So far, neither economists nor lawyers have proved that the social and economic costs of granting exclusive rights to mainly foreign firms may not become too great a burden for developing countries. A prime example concerns the obligation under the TRIPS Agreement to grant patent protection to pharmaceutical products (as discussed in Part I, second section).[28] It is immediately apparent that compliance with this obligation, which will entail an increase in the price of such essential products, will potentially have major implications for the public health policies of developing countries in particular.[29] Does the potential benefit to some industries, mainly of industrialized countries, really outweigh the sometimes considerable socio-economic costs to many countries? Any answer to this fundamental question would need to tackle the bold presumption that one can easily equate the interests of industries with those of states.

VI. A SINGLE GLOBAL MARKET AS A JUSTIFICATION FOR THE TRIPS AGREEMENT?

It is also interesting to consider whether or not there are differences to be discerned between the TRIPS Agreement and EC regulation of intellectual property rights. If so, this could lead to the conclusion that regulation of intellectual property rights may be warranted at EC level, but not necessarily at the level of the WTO. A first

[27] However, while trade by the intellectual property holder is possible on other markets where no intellectual property protection is granted, the property holder will not be able to obtain a monopoly return.

[28] On the social reasons that were invoked to oppose patent protection for drugs, see Saxena (1988). On the point of view of the industrialized countries, see Nogues (1990). For an analysis of the issue from the point of view of the United States, as well as the developing countries, see a most interesting article by Scherer (1993: 108–12). Scherer concludes succinctly that: 'Bargaining power carries more weight in resolving the conflict than equity considerations' (112).

[29] In such circumstances compulsory licences could probably be granted in the public interest, but a reasonable remuneration would still need to be given to the patent holder, which would drive up the cost (Article 31 of TRIPS). That the use of compulsory licensing in such matters is a practice which is not alien to industrialized countries is illustrated by Scherer. He points out that 'on at least six occasions during the 1950s and 1960s, the United States ordered compulsory licensing of more than 100 drug patents on its home turf under antitrust case settlements' (1993: 112). On the limitations and conditions which are now posed by the TRIPS Agreement on the possibility of granting compulsory licences on patents, see Ullrich (1995: 175–6).

difference lies in the fact that the EC Treaty does not mention the principle of national treatment, but lays down a general principle of non-discrimination based on nationality (Article 12 (ex Article 6) EC). The European Court of Justice held in the *Phil Collins* case of 1993 that this principle applies to all intellectual property holders who have a nationality of a member state (Joined Cases C–92 and 326/92, *Phil Collins* v. *Imtrat Handelsgesellschaff mbH and Patricia Imund Export Verwaltuhgsgesellschaft mbH* and *Leif Emanuel Kraul* v. *EMI Electrola GmbH*, 1993 ECR I–5145). This principle goes further than what is provided for under the TRIPS Agreement. The European Court of Justice clarified that it applies even where a reciprocity requirement would have been in conformity with intellectual property conventions which the member states have signed.[30]

A second distinction is that the EC Treaty does not of itself impose harmonization of intellectual property legislation, but merely allows for this to be done by virtue of secondary legislation. This implies that essentially a permissive approach is adopted, rather than the coercive approach in the TRIPS Agreement.[31] It is no secret that harmonization by means of EC measures is still far less extensive than the scope of harmonization achieved by the TRIPS agreement.[32]

A third major difference is that the European Court of Justice has held that, in the context of intra-Community trade, the principle of exhaustion necessarily applies (Case 78/70, *Deutsche Grammophon* v. *Metro*, 1971 ECR 487).[33] Surprisingly enough, the TRIPS Agreement does not introduce this trade-liberalizing principle, which would have seemed a logical corollary to the substantive harmonization of intellectual property rights at a worldwide level achieved by the TRIPS Agreement.[34] It merely provides that for the purpose of dispute settlement, subject to the principles of national treatment and most favoured nation treatment, 'nothing in this Agreement shall be used to address the issue of the exhaustion of intellectual property rights' (Article 6 of TRIPS).[35] This in itself is proof of the fact that the TRIPS Agreement is not meant to free trade in the usual sense.

[30] Compare to Article 3 of TRIPS, which allows for exceptions to the principle of national treatment which were already provided for in the most important intellectual property conventions. On the interrelation of the EC principle of non-discrimination with the principle of national treatment in the TRIPS Agreement, see Govaere (1997a: 488–9).

[31] On the origin and implications of this difference in approach, see Govaere (1994).

[32] As the European Court of Justice succinctly stated in Opinion 1/94: 'Suffice to say . . . that the harmonization achieved within the Community in certain areas covered by TRIPS is only partial and that, in other areas, no harmonization has been envisaged' (Opinion 1/94, Competence of the Community to Conclude International Agreements Concerning Services and the protection of Intellectual Property, 1994 ECR I–5267, para. 103). See also the factual circumstances of Case C–53/96 (*Hermes International* v. *FHT Marketing Choice, BV*, 1998 ECJ I–3603).

[33] This principle was later extended by the Agreement on the European Economic Area (EEA) to encompass all signatory countries.

[34] Moreover, this principle would most likely have benefited the developing countries. On this issue, see Von Hase (1992: 124).

[35] This implies that 'it should be permissible to apply the exhaustion of exclusive rights only to domestic trade and not to external trade, provided that the national and foreign holders of the exclusive right are treated in the same manner' (Demaret 1995: 168).

The most important difference, however, resides in the fact that harmonization of intellectual property legislation in the European Community finds a justification in the ultimate objective to create a Single Market.[36] This implies that the competitive conditions should necessarily be the same in all participating states. The problem with intellectual property rights is that they are true non-tariff barriers to trade, whereby the mere enforcement of intellectual property protection may of itself lead to the resurrection of barriers to intra-Community trade. Allowing for the regulation of intellectual property rights only on a national level would potentially jeopardize the fundamental objective of establishing free movement of goods and workable competition in the European Community. It is considered that the best way to avoid these prejudicial consequences for the Single Market is to regulate intellectual property rights at the highest, namely European Community, level by means of harmonization measures whenever necessary to safeguard the internal market objective. Concurrently, it is thought essential to apply complementary and uniform EC competition rules to the anti-competitive behaviour of intellectual property holders. Furthermore, it is to safeguard the Single Market to the fullest extent possible without doing away with the principle of territoriality inherent in intellectual property rights that the principle of Community exhaustion is applied, also in the absence of parallel intellectual property protection (Case 187/80, *Merck* v. *Stephar and Exler* (Merck I), 1981 ECR 2063; Joined Cases C–267/95 and C–268/95, *Merck & Co. Inc., Merck Sharp & Dohme Ltd and Merck Sharp & Dohme International Services BV* v. *Primecrown Ltd, Ketan Himatlal Mehta, Bharat Himatlal Mehta and Necessity Supplies Ltd* and *Beecham Group plc* v. *Europharm of Worthing Ltd.* (Merck II)).[37] To have the principle of exhaustion or not is extremely important, as it determines who may control parallel importations. In the European Community, intellectual property owners can no longer use intellectual property rights in order to resurrect barriers to intra-Community trade. As soon as they have consented to putting their products on the EC market, then it is the principle of free movement of goods and services that will prevail.[38] Without the principle of exhaustion, it is the intellectual property owners who determine, in each given case, whether or not it is in their best commercial interests to invoke their exclusive rights in the member state of importation to prohibit parallel importation.[39]

[36] See, in particular, the judgment by the European Court of Justice in Case C–350/92 (*Kingdom of Spain* v. *Council of the European Union*, 1995 ECR I–1985).

[37] The application of the principle of exhaustion in the absence of parallel exclusive protection is, however, subject to strong criticism (Demaret 1978: 59–76; 1987: 161; Govaere 1996: 158–68; Koch 1986: 605).

[38] The principle of exhaustion does not play in the relations with third countries, except for the EEA, in spite of far reaching association agreements such as the Europe Agreements with Central and Eastern European countries (Govaere 1997b).

[39] This is so in the relation between the European Community and third countries, as the European Court of Justice has always refrained from extending the principle of Community exhaustion to international exhaustion (and the only exception is the EEA Agreement). See the following cases: C–270/80, *Polydor Limited and RSO Records Inc.* v. *Harlequin Records Shops Limited and Simons Records Limited,* 1982 ECR 329; C–355/96, *Silhouette International Schmied GmbH & Co. KG* v. *Hartlauen Handelsgesellschaft*

Contrary to the EC Treaty, the TRIPS Agreement on its own cannot purport to give rise to, or to be necessitated by, a single global market. Edith Penrose pertinently wrote that 'no amount of talk about the economic unity of the world can hide the fact that some countries with little export trade in industrial goods and few, if any, inventions for sale have nothing to gain from granting patents on inventions worked and patented abroad except the avoidance of unpleasant foreign retaliation in other directions' (1951: 116–17). It has already been mentioned that the TRIPS Agreement does not unequivocally open up the global market by automatically and unconditionally introducing the trade-liberalizing principle of exhaustion of intellectual property rights. The TRIPS Agreement thus departs from traditional GATT practice, as it is concerned not with trade liberalization but only with trade regulation. The TRIPS Agreement imposes minimum standards of protection and enforcement of intellectual property, which should lead to a worldwide harmonization at a high level. This would prima facie seem to point to the objective of setting similar competitive conditions for intellectual property holders in all WTO members. Yet, if this were to be the justification for the TRIPS Agreement, then it is unclear, to say the least, why an agreement on competition, which then becomes the indispensable counterpart to the TRIPS Agreement, was not negotiated and concluded simultaneously.[40] Although the TRIPS Agreement indicates that anti-competitive behaviour by intellectual property holders may be curtailed (Articles 8(2) and 40 of TRIPS), it is apparent that the enactment and enforcement of competition rules are still considered to be a purely national matter (Fox, Ch. 16).

The creation of a single global market, similarly as the EC internal market, would, of course, necessitate more than the adoption of worldwide harmonization in the field of intellectual property rights. It would call not only for complementary competition rules but also for environmental rules, social legislation, as well as all other forms of regulation, so as to avoid competitive conditions from one state to another. In its current state, after the Marrakech Agreement, it seems that the WTO does not aim to, nor is it suited to, create a single global market in which the competitive conditions should necessarily be the same. Whether or not this should be the goal of the WTO in the future is a topical matter of discussion.

VII. CONCLUSION

It is apparent that in order to fully support regulation of intellectual property rights at the WTO level, regulation at such a level should be demonstrated unequivocally to be necessary, or at least potentially beneficial, to all participating countries. A global cost–benefit analysis would need to be undertaken which duly takes into

mbH, 1988 ECJ I–4799; C–173/98, *Sebago Inc. and Ancienne Maison Duboi and Fils* v. *G-B Unic SA*, 1999 ECJ CELEX LEXIS 2740.

[40] Such an agreement would, of course, raise complex and difficult issues (Fox, Ch. 16).

account the public interest in granting intellectual property protection and not just the private interests of the intellectual property holders. This has not been done convincingly so far by either economists or lawyers.

The extension of intellectual property protection to cover several countries certainly poses practical problems which are specific to intellectual property rights, such as those ensuing from the principles of novelty, originality, and reciprocity. To a large extent, these problems had already been resolved satisfactorily at the international level by the Great Intellectual Property Conventions.

It is not apparent what the advantages of the TRIPS Agreement are in terms of improving world trade, if one takes into account not only the benefits accruing to specific, especially technology-based, industries but also the concurrent losses incurred by the imitating, or so-called 'piracy', industries. What is certain is that the rationale of the TRIPS Agreement is not to eliminate competition between governments and states for business. Its *raison d'être* is rather to regulate competition between firms. The TRIPS Agreement uses global regulation in order to equalize the conditions under which firms producing and supplying goods and services based on new technology, incorporating new forms of expression or sets of data, or invested with high consumer appeal, do compete in both the developed and the developing worlds. It does so by increasing the effective content and by enlarging the territorial coverage of proprietary rights on new technology, new ideas, or brand names, which today are mostly held by firms from the developed world. The TRIPS Agreement is not about regulatory competition, regulatory cooperation, or *regulatory co-opetition* (Esty and Geradin, Ch. 2) for that matter. All three presuppose a respect of the sovereignty of those states participating in the regulatory process, as they remain free to choose their strategies. The TRIPS Agreement is, to the contrary, essentially an exercise in *regulatory coercion*, for which it is difficult to find a fully satisfactory justification in terms of world welfare.

Pessimists will stress the short-term costs that the TRIPS Agreement undeniably entails for many developing countries and that are not necessarily matched by social gains elsewhere. Optimists will hope that, in the medium or long run, the TRIPS Agreement will benefit developing countries in two ways: first, by attracting foreign investments to these countries; and second, by inducing domestic firms, in at least some developing countries, to play the intellectual property game both at home and abroad, as firms in developed countries do. The question remains whether the TRIPS Agreement would have come about at all if it were not part of a package deal.

Bibliography

Ackerman, Bruce and Hassler, William (1981). *Clean Coal/Dirty Air*. New Haven: Yale University Press.

Alesina, A. and Wacziarg, R. (1999). 'Is Europe Going Too Far?'. National Bureau of Economic Research, Working Paper No. 6883.

Alstott, Anne L. (1996). 'Federalism and U.S. Social Welfare Policy: Fundamental Change and New Uncertainties'. 2 Columbia Journal of European Law 441.

Alva, C. (1990). 'Delaware and the Market for Corporate Charters: History and Agency'. 15 Delaware Journal of Corporate Law 885.

Amihud, Y. and Mendelson, H. (1996). 'A New Approach to the Regulation of Trading across Securities Markets'. 71 New York University Law Review 1411–66.

Amihud, Y. and Miller, G. (1993). *Costly Policies: State Regulation and Antitrust Exemption in Insurance Markets*. AEI Press, 44.

Antitrust (1999). 'Browsing the Microsoft Case: The Trial of the Century?' Summer.

Appleborne, Peter (1993). 'South Raises Stakes in Fight for Jobs'. *New York Times*, 4 October, A-12, col. 4.

Armour, J. (1999). 'Share capital and creditor protection: efficient rules for a modern company law?'. Forthcoming, ESRC Centre for Business Research Working Paper series.

Armstrong, K. and Bulmer, S. (1998). *The Governance of the European Single Market*. Manchester: Manchester University Press.

Atkinson, Anthony J. and Stiglitz, Joseph E. (1976). 'The Design of Tax Structure: Direct Versus Indirect Taxation'. 6 Journal of Public Economics 55.

Atleson, James (1998). *Labor and the Wartime State: Labor Relations and Law During World War II*. Chicago: University of Illinois Press.

Auerbach, Alan (1996). 'Tax Reform, Capital Allocation, Efficiency, and Growth'. In Henry J. Aaron and William G. Gale (eds), *Economic Effects of Fundamental Tax Reform*. Brookings Institution Press, 29–73.

Auerbach, A. J. (1997). 'Measuring the Impact of Tax Reform'. 49 National Tax Journal 665–73.

Avi-Yonah, Reuven S. (2000). 'Globalization, Tax Competition, and the Fiscal Crisis of the Welfare State'. 113 Harvard Law Review 1573–676.

Ayres, Ian (1995). 'Supply-Side Inefficiencies in Corporate Charter Competition—Lessons from Patents, Yachting and Bluebooks'. 43 Kansas Law Review 541.

Ayres, I. and Gertner, R. (1989). 'Filling gaps in incomplete contracts: a theory of default rules'. 99 Yale Law Journal 87–130.

Backes, Chris and Betlem, Gerrit (eds) (1999). *Integrated Pollution and Control, The EC Directive From a Comparative Legal and Economic Perspective*.

Baden Fuller, C. (1981). 'Economic issues relating to property rights in trademarks: export bans, differential pricing, restrictions on resale and repackaging'. 6 European Law Review 162.

Bagwell, Kyle and Staiger, Robert W. (1999a). 'Domestic Policies, National Sovereignty and International Economic Institutions'. National Bureau of Economic Research, Working Paper No. 7293.

Bagwell, Kyle and Staiger, Robert W. (1999b). 'The Simple Economics of Labor Standards and the GATT'. In Alan V. Deardorff and Robert M. Stern (eds), *Social Dimensions of U.S. Trade Policy*.

Baldwin, R. and Cave, M. (1999). *Understanding Regulation. Theory, Strategy and Practice*. Oxford: Oxford University Press.

Baltensperger, E. and Dermine, J. (1990). 'European Banking: Prudential and Regulatory Issues'. In J. Dermine (ed.), *European Banking in the 1990s*. Oxford: Basil Blackwell Ltd, 17–36.

Barenberg, Mark (1993). 'The Political Economy of the Wagner Act: Power, Symbol, and Workplace Cooperation'. 106 Harvard Law Review 1379.

Barenberg, Mark (1991). 'Interview with Milton Handler, General Counsel to the National Labor Board of 1933–34—New York, Oct. 17, 1991'. Unpublished transcript.

Barenberg, Mark (1994). 'Democracy and Domination in the Law of Workplace Cooperation: From Bureaucratic to Flexible Production'. 94 Columbia Law Review 753.

Barnard, C. (1994). 'Sunday Trading: a Drama in Five Acts'. 57 Modern Law Review 449.

Bartik, Timothy (1988a). 'Business Location Decisions in the United States'. Growth and Change.

Bartik, Timothy (1988b). 'The Effects of Environmental Regulation on Business Location in the United States'. 19 Growth and Change 22.

Bartik, Timothy (1989). 'Small Business Start-Ups in the United States: Estimates of the Effects of Characteristics of States'. 55 South Economics Journal 1004.

Baudru, D. and Kechidi, M. (1998). 'Les investisseurs institutionnels étrangers: Vers la fin du capitalisme à la française?'. 48 Revue d'Economie Financière 93.

Baumol, William J. and Oates, Wallace E. (1988). *The Theory of Environmental Policy*. Cambridge: Cambridge University Press.

Bebchuk, Lucian (1985). 'Toward Undistorted Choice and Equal Treatment in Corporate Takeovers'. 98 Harvard Law Review 1695.

Bebchuk, Lucian (1987). 'The Pressure to Tender: An Analysis and Proposed Remedy'. 12 Delaware Journal of Corporation Law 911.

Bebchuk, Lucian (1992). 'Federalism and the Corporation: The Desirable Limits on State Competition in Corporate Law'. 105 Harvard Law Review 1435–1510.

Bebchuk, L. and Ferrell, A. (1999). 'Federalism and Takeover Law: The Race to Protect Managers from Takeovers'. 99 Columbia Law Review 1168–99.

Becker, Gary S. (1985). 'Human Capital, Effort, and the Sexual Division of Labor'. 3 Journal of Labor Economics S33.

Becker, Randy and Henderson, Vernon (1997). 'Effects of Air Quality Regulation on Decisions of Firms in Polluting Industries'. National Bureau of Economic Research, Working Paper No. 6160 (September).

Begg, P. F. (1991). *Corporate Acquisitions and Mergers*. London: Graham and Trotman.

Bendar, J., Ferejohn, J., and Garrett, G. (1996). 'The Politics of European Federalism'. 16 International Review of Law and Economics 279.

Bensel, Richard (1984). *Sectionalism and American Political Development: 1880–1980*. Madison: University of Wisconsin Press.

Benston, G. J. (1994). 'International Harmonization of Banking Regulations and Cooperation among National Regulators: An Assessment'. 8 Journal of Financial Services Research 205.

Bercusson, B. (1996). *European Labor Law*. London: Butterworths.

Bercusson, B. (1997). Trade Union Rights in the 15 Member States of the European Union, Research Study for the Committee on Social Affairs and Employment. European Parliament, Luxembourg: Office of Official Publications of the EC.

Bercusson, B. (1999). 'Democratic Legitimacy and European Labour Law'. Industrial Law Journal 153.

Bercusson, B. *et al.* (1996). *A Manifesto for Social Europe*. Brussels: European Trade Union Institute.

Bergstrom, C. *et al.* (1988). 'A Test for Efficiency in the Supply of Public Education'. 35 Journal of Public Economics 289.

Berman, Eli and Bui, Linda (1997). 'Environmental Regulation and Labor Demand: Evidence from the South Coast Air Basin'. National Bureau of Economic Research, Working Paper No. 6299 (December).

Berman, Eli and Bui, Linda (1998). 'Environmental Regulation and Productivity: Evidence from Oil Refineries' (manuscript) (September).

Bernard, Christopher B. (1996). 'Towards an International Market in Mutual Funds'. 36 Virginia Journal of International Law 467.

Bertrand, Marianne (1999). 'From the Invisible Handshake to the Invisible Hand? How Import Competition Changes the Employment Relationship'. National Bureau of Economic Research, Working Paper No. 6900 (January).

Besen, S. and Raskind, L. (1991). 'An Introduction to the Law and Economics of Intellectual Property'. 5 Journal of Economic Perspectives 3–27.

Besley, T. and Seabright, P. (1999). 'The Effects and Policy Implications of State Aids to Industry: An Economic Analysis'. Economic Policy 15–53.

Bhagwati, Jagdish (1998). *A Stream of Windows: Unsettling Reflections on Trade, Immigration, and Democracy*. Cambridge: MIT Press.

Bhagwati, Jagdish and Hudec, Robert E. (eds) (1996). *Fair Trade and Harmonization: Prerequisites for Free Trade?* Cambridge: MIT Press.

Bhandari, J. S. and Sykes, A. O. (eds) (1997). *Economic Dimensions in International Law. Comparative and Empirical Perspectives*. Cambridge: Cambridge University Press.

Bishop, M., Kay, J., and Mayer, C. (eds) (1995). *The Regulatory Challenge*. Oxford: Oxford University Press.

Black, Bernard S. (1999). 'The Legal and Institutional Preconditions for Strong Stock Markets: The Nontriviality of Securities Law'. Stanford Law School John M. Olin Program in Law and Economics, Working Paper No. 179 (September).

Black, J. (1997). *Rules and Regulators*. Oxford: Oxford University Press.

Blaustein, Saul, Cohen, William, and Haber, William (1993). *Unemployment Insurance in the United States: The First Half Century*. Kalamazoo: WE Upjohn Institute.

Boadway, R., Marchand, M., and Vigneault, M. (1998). 'The Consequences of Overlapping Tax Bases for Redistribution and Public Spending in a Federation'. 68 Journal of Public Economics 453–78.

Bok, Derek (1971). 'Reflections on the Distinctive Character of American Labor Laws'. 84 Harvard Law Review 1394.

Boot, A. W. A. and Thakor, A. V. (1993). 'Self-Interested Bank Regulation'. 83 American Economic Review 206–12.

Braithwaite, John (1993). 'Transnational Regulation of the Pharmaceutical Industry'. ANNALS, AAPSS, 525: 12–30.

Brand, R. A. (1997). 'Recognition of Foreign Judgments as a Trade Law Issue: The

Economics of Private International Law'. In J. S. Bhandari and A. O. Sykes (eds), *Economic Dimensions in International Law. Comparative and Empirical Perspectives*. Cambridge: Cambridge University Press, 592–641.

Brandenburg, Adam M. and Nalebuff, Barry J. (1996). *Co-opetition*. New York: Doubleday.

Branson, Douglas M. (1990). 'Indeterminacy: The Final Ingredient in an Interest Group Analysis of Corporate Law'. 43 Vanderbilt Law Review 85.

Bratton, W., McCahery, J., Picciotto, S., and Scott, C. (eds) (1996). *International Regulatory Competition and Coordination: Perspectives on Economic Regulation in Europe and the United States*. Oxford: Clarendon Press.

Bratton, William and McCahery, Joseph (1997). 'The New Economics of Jurisdictional Competition: Devolutionary Federalism in a Second-Best World'. 86 Georgetown Law Journal 201–78.

Bredahl, Maury E. and Forsythe, Kenneth W. (1989).'Harmonizing Phyto-sanitary and Sanitary Regulations'. 12 World Economy 189.

Brennan, G. and Buchanan, J. N. (1980). *The Power to Tax: Analytical Foundations of a Fiscal Constitution*. Cambridge: Cambridge University Press.

Breton, Albert (1991). 'The Existence and Stability of Interjurisdictional Competition'. In Daphne A. Kenyon and John Kincaid (eds), *Competition Among States and Local Governments*. Washington, DC: Urban Institute Press; Lanham, MD: Distributed by University Press of America.

Breton, Albert (1996). *Competitive Governments: An Economic Theory of Politics and Public Finance*. Cambridge: Cambridge University Press.

Brinkhorst, Laurens J. (1993).'Subsidiarity and EC Environmental Policy'. 8 European Environmental Law Review 20.

Bronckers, Marco and Larouche, Pierre (1997).'Telecommunications Services and the World Trade Organization'. 31 Journal of World Trade 5.

Brown, Drusilla K., Deardorff, Alan V., and Stern, Robert M. (1996). 'International Labor Standards and Trade: A Theoretical Analysis'. In Jagdish Bhagwati and Robert E. Hudec (eds), *Fair Trade and Harmonization: Prerequisites for Free Trade: Volume 1: Economic Analysis*. Cambridge: MIT Press, 227.

Brudney, Victor and Chirelstein, Marvin A. (1974). 'Fair Shares in Corporate Mergers and Takeovers'. 88 Harvard Law Review 297.

Brueckner, Jan K. (1998). *Welfare Reform and Interstate Welfare Competition: Theory and Evidence*. Washington, DC: Urban Institute.

Brussels Convention (1968). 1968 Brussels Convention on Jurisdiction and the Enforcement of Judgments in Civil and Commercial Matters, 1972 OJ (C 299) 32.

Bryner, Gary (1993). *Blue Skies, Green Politics*. Washington, DC: Congressional Quarterly Press, 149–50.

Bucovetsky, S. (1991). 'Asymmetric Tax Competition'. 30 Journal of Urban Economics 167–81.

Bucovetsky, S. (1998). 'Federalism, Equalization and Risk Aversion'. 67 Journal of Public Economics 301–28.

Bucovetsky, S. and Wilson, J. D. (1991). 'Tax Competition with Two Tax Instruments'. 21 Regional Science and Urban Economics 333–50.

Burton, George, and Schwab, Stewart. *Employment Law*. Prentice-Hall, 452.

Butler, Henry N. and Macey, Jonathan R. (1988). 'The Myth of Competition in the Dual Banking System'. 73 Cornell Law Review 677.

Butler, H. and Macey, J. (1996). 'Externalities and the Matching Principle: The Case for Reallocating Environmental Regulatory Authority'. Yale Law and Policy Review, and Yale Journal of Regulation, Special Symposium Issue, 25.

Buxbaum, R. M., Hertig, G., Hirsch, A., and Hopt, K. J. (eds) (1991). *European Business Law*. Berlin/New York: Walter de Gruyter.

Buxbaum, R. M., Hertig, G., Hirsch, A., and Hopt, K. J. (eds) (1996). *European Business and Economic Law*. Berlin/New York: Walter de Gruyter.

Cairncross, Frances (1991). *Costing the Earth*. Boston: Harvard Business School Press, 23.

Calabresi, Stephen G. (1995). 'A Government of Limited and Enumerated Powers: In Defense of United States v. Lopez'. 94 Michigan Law Review 752.

Calabresi, Steven G. (1998). 'The Era of Big Government is Over'. 50 Stanford Law Review 1015.

Caldwell, Lynton K. (1998). 'Beyond NEPA: Future Significance of the National Environmental Policy Act'. 22 Harvard Environmental Law Review 203.

Card, David and Krueger, Alan (1995). *Myth and Measurement: The New Economics of the Minimum Wage*. Princeton: Princeton University Press.

Carney, William J. (1998). 'The Production of Corporate Law'. 71 Southern California Law Review 715.

Carrol, John (ed.) (1988, 1990). *International Environmental Diplomacy*. Cambridge: Cambridge University Press.

Cary, William L. (1974). 'Federalism and Corporate Law: Reflections Upon Delaware'. 83 Yale Law Journal 663.

Casella, A. and Frey, Bruno (1992). 'Federalism and Clubs. Towards an Economic Theory of Overlapping Political Jurisdiction'. 36 European Economic Review 639–46.

Cashin, Sheryll D. (1999). 'Federalism, Welfare Reform, and the Minority Poor: Accounting for the Tyranny of State Majorities'. 99 Columbia Law Review 552.

Cass, D. (1992). 'The Word that Saves Maastricht: The Principle of Subsidiarity and the Division of Powers within the European Community'. 29 Common Market Law Review 1107–36.

Castaneda, Jorge (1996). *The Mexican Shock: Its Meaning for the U.S.* New York: New Press.

CEC (Commission of the European Communities) (1997a). Resolution of the Council and the Representatives of the Governments of the Member States, meeting with the Council of 1 December 1997 on a code of conduct for Business Taxation, 1998 OJ (C2) 2.

CEC (1990). Communication of 20 1990, SEC (90) final (Brussels).

CEC (1988). The Social Dimension of the Internal Market, Interim Report of the Interdepartmental Working Party of the Commission, Social Europe, Special Edition, Annex 10, Brussels.

CEC (1987, 1988). Social Europe, 1/87, 51; 1/88, 19.

CEC (1992). Ruding Report: Report of the Committee of Independent Experts on Company Taxation Official Publications of the European Communities (Luxembourg).

CEC (1996). Taxation in the European Union, Report on the Development of Tax Systems, COM (96) 546 (Brussels).

CEC (1997). A Package to Tackle Harmful Tax Competition in the European Union, COM (97) 564 final, 5 November 1997.

CEC (1967). Memorandum of the Council of 26 June 1967, Bulletin of the European Communities, supplement 8 of 1967 (Brussels).

Centeno, M. and Mello, A. S. (1999). 'How Integrated Are the Money Market and the

Bank Loans Market within the European Union?'. 18 Journal of International Money and Finance 75–106.

Chang, H. (1997). 'The Economics and Politics of Regulation'. 21 Cambridge Journal of Economics 703.

Charnovitz, Steve (1987). 'The Influence of International Labor Standards on the World Trade Regime: An Historical Overview'. 126 International Labor Review 565.

Charnovitz, Steve (1992). 'Environmental and Labor Standards in Trade'. 5(15) World Economy 335.

Charny, David (1991). 'Competition Among Jurisdictions in Formulating Corporate Rules: An American Perspective on the "Race to the Bottom" in the European Communities'. 32 Harvard International Law Journal 423.

Charny, D. (1994). 'Competition Among Jurisdictions in Formulating Corporate Law Rules: an American Perspective on the "Race to the Bottom" in the European Communities'. In S. Wheeler (ed.), *A Reader on the Law of the Business Enterprise*. Oxford: Oxford University Press.

Charny, David (1996). 'The Employee Welfare State in Transition'. 74 Texas Law Review 1601.

Cheffins, B. (1997). *Company Law: Theory, Structure and Operation*. Oxford: Oxford University Press.

Chen, Show-Mao (1992). 'U.S. Financial Reporting Requirements for Private Foreign Issuers: Policy Implications of Recent Empirical Studies'. NYSE, Working Paper 2-06.

Choi, Frederick D. S. (1998). 'Global Consequences of International Accounting Diversity'. Accounting & Business (http://www.iasc.org.uk/news/cen8_127.htm).

Choi, Frederick D. S. and Levich, Richard M. (1990). *The Capital Market Effects of International Accounting Diversity*. Homewood, IL: Dow Jones-Irwin.

Choi, Steven J. and Guzman, Andrew T. (1997). 'National Laws, International Money: Regulation in a Global Capital Market'. 65 Fordham Law Review 1855.

Choi, Stephen J. and Guzman, Andrew (1998). 'Portable Reciprocity: Rethinking the International Reach of Securities Regulation'. 71 Southern California Law Review 903.

Choper, Jesse H., Coffee, John C., and Gilson, Ronald J. (1995). *Cases and Materials on Corporations*. Boston: Little, Brown.

Christiansen, Thomas (1994). 'European Integration Between Political Science and International Relations Theory: The End of Sovereignty'. European University Institute, Working Paper RSC No. 94/4.

Christie, W. G. and Schultz, P. H. (1994). 'Why Do Nasdaq Market Makers Avoid Odd-Eighth Quotes?'. 49 Journal of Finance 1813.

Clark, Robert C. (1986). *Corporate Law* (4th edn). Boston: Little, Brown and Company.

Clarotti, P. (1994). 'The Implementation of the Second Banking Directive and its Aftermath'. In E. Wymeersch (ed.), *Further Perspectives in Financial Integration in Europe*. Berlin/New York: Walter de Gruyter, 43–56.

Coase, Ronald (1988). *The Firm, the Market, and the Law*. Chicago: University of Chicago Press.

Coates, John C. (1999). '"Fair Value" as an Avoidable Rule of Corporate Law: Minority Discounts in Conflict Transactions'. 147 University of Pennsylvania Law Review 1251.

Coffee, J. (1989). 'The Mandatory/Enabling Distinction in Corporate Law: an Essay on the Judicial Role'. 89 Columbia Law Review 1618.

Coffee, John C. Jr. (1984). 'Market Failure and the Economic Case for a Mandatory Disclosure System'. 70 Virginia Law Review 717.

Coffee, John C. Jr. (1999).'The Future as History: the Prospects for Global Convergence in Corporate Governance and its Implications'. 93 Northwestern University Law Review 641, 699.

Cohen, D. (1998). 'Theories of the Corporation and the Limited Liability Company: How Should Courts and Legislatures Articulate Rules for Piercing the Veil, Fiduciary Responsibility and Securities Regulation for the Limited Liability Company?'. 51 Oklahoma Law Review 428–93.

Cohen, Joshua and Sabel, Charles (1998). 'Directly-Deliberative Polyarchy'. In C. Joerges and O. Gerstenberg (eds), *Private Governance, Democratic Constitutionalism and Supranationalism*. Luxembourg: European Communities.

Cohen, Marc (1996).'Commentary'. In Eide Ehrling and Roger Van den Bergh (eds), *Law and Economics of the Environment*. 167–71.

Compa, Lance (1995). 'The First NAFTA Labor Cases: A New International Labor Rights Regime Takes Shape', 3 United States Mexico Law Journal 159.

Company Law Review Steering Group (1999). *Modern Company Law for a Competitive Economy: The Strategic Framework*. London: Department of Trade and Industry.

Complaint of Sydkraft AB for Itself as the Owner of Barsebäck Kraft AB, 20 August 1999.

Confédération Fiscale Européenne (1999). 'Draft Directive on Withholding'. European Taxation 229–31.

Correa, C. (1994). 'The GATT Agreement of Trade-Related Aspects of Intellectual Property Rights: New Standards for Patent Protection'. 16 European Intellectual Property Review, 16: 327.

Cottier, T. (1991). 'The Prospects for Intellectual Property in GATT'. CML Rev 383–414.

Crandall, Robert W. (1983). *Controlling Air Pollution: The Economics and Politics of the Clean Air Act*. Washington, DC: Brookings Institution.

Cremer, H. and Pestieau, P. (1996). 'Distributive Implications of European Integration'. 40 European Economic Review 747–57.

Culem, C. (1988). 'The Locational Determinants of Direct Investment among Industrialised Countries'. 32 European Economic Review 885–904.

Currie, David (1985). *The Constitution in the Supreme Court: The First Hundred Years 1789–1888*. Chicago: University of Chicago Press.

Czamanski, Daniel Z. and Fogel, Smadar (1985). 'Industrial Location and the Divorce of Management and Ownership'. 19 Annals of Regional Science 77.

Daines, Robert and Hanson, Jon (1992). 'The Corporate Law Paradox: The Case for Restructuring Corporate Law'. 108 Yale Law Journal 577.

Dalhuisen, J. H. (1999). 'Liberalization and Re-Regulation of Cross-Border Financial Services. The Situation in the EU and WTO/GATS (Part 1)'. 10 European Business Law Review 158–92.

Dana, David A. (1996). 'The Perverse Incentives of Environmental Audit Immunity'. 81 Iowa Law Review 969.

Danthine, J.-P., Giavazzi, F., Vives, X., and von Thadden, E.-L. (1999). *The Future of European Banking*. London: Centre for Economic Policy Research.

Dashwood, Alan (1983). 'Hastening Slowly: The Community's Path Towards Harmonization'. In H. Wallace *et al.* (eds), *Policy-Making in the European Communities*. London: Wiley.

Davies, P. (1995). 'Market Integration and Social Policy in the Court of Justice'. 24 Industrial Law Journal 49–77.

Davis, Charles E. and Lester, James P. (1989). 'Federalism and Environmental Policy'. In James P. Lester (ed.), *Environmental Politics and Policy: Theories and Evidence*. Durham: Duke University Press.

Davis, Mike (1986). *Prisoners of the American Dream*. London: Verso.

De Bandt, O. and Davis, E. P. (1999). 'A Cross-Country Comparison of Market Structures in European Banking'. European Central Bank, Working Paper No. 7.

De Sombre, Elizabeth R. (1995). 'Baptists and Bootleggers for the Environment: The Origins of United States Unilateral Sanctions'. 4(1) The Journal of Environment and Development 53–76.

De Witte, Bruno (2000). 'Carving out a Place for European Union Law in the Legal Universe'. Paper presented at the conference Ius Commune in a World Context, Maastricht, 15 April 1999, forthcoming in the Maastricht Journal of European and Comparative Law.

Deakin, S. (1996). 'Labour Law as Market Regulation: the Economic Foundations of European Social Policy'. In P. Davies, A. Lyon-Caen, S. Sciarra, and S. Simitis (eds), *European Community Labour Law: Principles and Perspectives*. Liber Amicorum Bill Wedderburn. Oxford: Oxford University Press.

Deakin, S., and Hughes, A. (1999). 'Economic Efficiency and the Proceduralisation of Company Law'. 3 Company, Financial and Insolvency Law Review 169–89.

Deakin, S., and Morris, G. (1998). *Labour Law* (2nd edn). London: Butterworths.

Deakin, S., and Pratten, S. (1999). 'Reinventing the Market? Competition and Regulatory Change in Broadcasting'. 26 Journal of Law and Society 323–50.

Deakin, S., and Slinger, G. (1997). 'Hostile takeovers, corporate law, and the theory of the firm'. 24 Journal of Law and Society 124–51.

Deakin, S., and Wilkinson, F. (1994). 'Rights versus efficiency? The economic case for transnational labour standards'. 23 Industrial Law Journal 289–310.

Dean, Judith (1992). 'Trade and the Environment: A Survey of the Literature'. In Patrick Low (ed.). *International Trade and the Environment*. Washington, DC: World Bank, 16–20.

Dehousse, R. (1994). 'Community Competences: Are there Limits to Growth?'. In R. Dehousse (ed.), *Europe After Maastricht: An Ever Closer Union*. 104–25.

Demaret, P. (1978). *Patents, Territorial Restrictions and EEC Law*. VCH.

Demaret, P. (1987). 'Industrial Property Rights, Compulsory Licenses, and the Free Movement of Goods under Community Law'. International Review of Industrial Property and Copyright Law 178.

Demaret, P. (1995). 'The Metamorphoses of the GATT: From the Havana Charter to the World Trade Organization'. 34 Columbia Journal of Transnational Law 123–71.

Demaret, P. (1996). 'A Short Walk in the Realm of Subsidiarity'. In R. Buxbaum *et al.* (eds), *European Economic and Business Law, Legal and Economic Analyses on Integration and Harmonization*, 13–31.

Demirguc-Kunt, Asli and Maksimovic, Vosislaz (1998). 'Law, Finance and Firm Growth'. 53 Journal of Finance 2107, 2134.

DeMott, Deborah A. (1983). 'Current Issues in Tender Offer Regulation: Lessons from the British'. 58 New York University Law Review 945.

Demsetz, Harold (1967). 'Toward a Theory of Property Rights'. 57 Am. Econ. Rev. Papers & Proc. 347.

Depaolo, Anthony (1995). 'Plastics Recycling Legislation: Not Just the Same Old Garbage'. 22 Boston College Environmental Affairs Law Review 873.

Dermine, J. (ed.) (1990). *European Banking in the 1990s*. Oxford: Basil Blackwell Ltd.

Dermine, J. (1999a). The Economics of Bank Mergers in the European Union, A Review of the Public Policy Issues, Final Draft (Fontainebleau, May 1999).

Dermine, J. (1999b). 'European Capital Markets: Does the Euro Matter?'. In J. Dermine and P. Hillion, *European Capital Markets with a Single Currency*. Oxford: Oxford University Press, 1–30.

Dermine, J. and Hillion, P. (eds) (1999). *European Capital Markets with a Single Currency*. Oxford: Oxford University Press.

Deudney, D. (1996). 'Binding Sovereigns: Authorities, Structures, and Geopolitics in Philadelphian Systems'. In T. Bierseteker and C. Weber (eds), *State Sovereignty as Social Construct*. Cambridge: Cambridge University Press.

Diamond, Peter and Mirrlees, James (1971). 'Optimal Taxation and Public Production'. 61 Am. Econ. Rev. 8–27, 261–78.

Dodd, Peter and Leftwich, Richard (1980). 'The Market for Corporate Charters: "Unhealthy Competition" versus Federal Regulation'. 53 Journal of Business 259.

Dolvik, J. E. (1997). 'Redrawing the Boundaries of Solidarity? ETUC, Social Dialogue and the Europeanisation of Trade Unions in the 1990s', ARENA Report No. 5/97, Fafo Report No. 238, Oslo.

Dorf, Michael and Sabel, Charles (1998). 'A Constitution of Democratic Experimentalism'. 98 Columbia Law Review 267.

Dowding, K., John, P., and Biggs, S. (1994). 'Tiebout: A Summary of the Empirical Literature'. 31 Urban Studies 767–97.

DTI (Department of Trade and Industry) (1999). *Modern Company Law for a Competitive Economy: The Strategic Framework*. London: Department of Trade and Industry.

Dua, André and Esty, Daniel C. (1997). *Sustaining the Asia Pacific Miracle: Environmental Protection and Economic Integration*. Washington: Institute for International Economics.

Duerksen, Christopher (1983). *Environmental Regulation of Industrial Plant Siting: How to Make It Work Better*. Washington, DC: Conservation Foundation.

Dwyer, John P. (1995). 'The Practice of Federalism Under the Clean Air Act'. 54 Maryland Law Review 1183.

Easterbrook, Frank H. (1983). 'Antitrust and the Economics of Federalism'. 26 Journal of Law and Economics 23.

Easterbrook, Frank H. (1984). 'Managers' Discretion and Investors' Welfare: Theories and Evidence'. 9 Delaware Journal of Corporation Law 540.

Easterbrook, Frank H. (1994). 'Federalism and European Business Law'. 14 International Review of Law and Economics 125–32.

Easterbrook, Frank H. and Fischel, Daniel R. (1981). 'The Proper Role of a Target's Management in Responding to a Tender Offer'. 94 Harvard Law Review 1161.

Easterbrook, Frank H. and Fischel, Daniel R. (1983). 'Voting in Corporate Law'. 26 Journal of Law and Economics 395.

Easterbrook, Frank H. and Fischel, Daniel R. (1984). 'Mandatory Disclosure and the Protection of Investors'. 70 Virginia Law Review 669.

Easterbrook, Frank H. and Fischel, Daniel R. (1991). *The Economic Structure of Corporate Law*. Cambridge, MA: Harvard University Press.

ECOFIN (Economy and Finance Council) (1998a). Conclusions of the ECOFIN Council Meeting on 1 December 1997 Concerning Taxation Policy, 1998 OJ (C 2) 1.

ECOFIN (1998b). Proposal for a Council Directive to Ensure a Minimum of Effective Taxation of Savings Income in the Form of Interest Payments Within the Community, COM(98)0295 draft.

Economist (1985). 'Nine for the Seesaw'. 2 March, 21.

Economist (1992). 'Let Them Eat Pollution'. 8 February, 66.

Economist (1993). 'When Green is Good'. 20 November, 19.

Economist (1999). 3 July, 25.

ECOSOC (Economic and Social Committee) (1994). Opinion of the Economic and Social Committee of 31 December 1994 on the Communication Concerning the Application of the Agreement on Social Policy Presented by the Commission to the Council and to the European Parliament, 1994 OJ (C 397) 17, 40.

Edwards, J. and Keen, M. (1996). 'Tax Competition and Leviathan'. 40 European Economic Review 113–34.

Edwards, V. (1999). *European Company Law*. Oxford: Oxford University Press.

Ehrenberg, Robert (1994). *Labor Markets and Integrating National Economies*. Washington, DC: Institute for International Economics.

Ehrlich, I. and Posner, Richard (1974). 'An Economic Analysis of Legal Rule Making'. Journal of Legal Studies 257–86.

Einhorn, T. (1998). 'The Impact of the WTO Agreement on TRIPS (Trade related aspects of intellectual property rights) on EC law: A Challenge to Regionalism'. C.M.L. Rev 1069–99.

Eisenberg, Melvin A. (1989). 'The Structure of Corporation Law'. 89 Columbia Law Review 1461.

Elliott, E. Donald, Ackerman, Bruce A., and Millian, John C. (1985). 'Toward a Theory of Statutory Evolution: The Federalization of Environmental Law'. 1 Journal of Law, Economics and Organization 313.

Ellis, M. (1999). 'Are Measures to Curb Harmful Tax Competition Necessary?'. European Taxation 8–10.

Ellison, G. and Glaeser, E. (1994). 'Geographic Concentration in U.S. Manufacturing Industries'. National Bureau of Economic Research, Working Paper Series, No. 4840 (August).

Engel, Kirsten (1997). 'State Environmental Standard-Setting: Is There a "Race" and Is It "To the Bottom"?'. 48 Hastings Law Journal 271.

Engel, Kirsten H. (1999). 'The Dormant Commerce Clause Threat to Market-Based Environmental Regulation: The Case of Electricity Deregulation'. 26 Ecology Law Quarterly, 243.

Engel, Kirsten and Saleska, Scott R. (1998).'Facts Are Stubborn Things: An Empirical Reality Check in the Theoretical Debate Over the Race-to-the-Bottom in State Environmental Standard-Setting'. 8 Cornell Journal of Law and Public Policy 55.

Environment Watch (1999).'France Imposes Emergency Bans on Phtalates in Baby Toys'. Vol. 8, No. 14, 16 July, p. 9.

Environmental Law Institute (1998). *An Analysis of State Superfund Programs: 50-State Study, 1998 Update*. Washington, DC: Environmental Law Institute.

Esty, Daniel C. (1994). *Greening the GATT: Trade, Environment and the Future*. Washington: Institute for International Economics.

Esty, Daniel C. (1996). 'Revitalizing Environmental Federalism'. 95 Michigan Law Review, 570.

Esty, Daniel C. (1998). 'Non-Governmental Organizations at the World Trade Organization: Cooperation, Competition, or Exclusion'. 1 Journal of International Economic Law 123.

Esty, Daniel (1999a). 'Economic Integration and the Environment'. In Norman Vig and Regina Axelrod (eds), *The Global Environment*, 190–209.

Esty, Daniel C. (1999b). 'Toward Optimal Environmental Governance'. 74(6) New York University Law Review 1495–574.

Esty, Daniel C. and Geradin, Damien (1997). 'Market Access, Competitiveness, and Harmonization: Environmental Protection in Regional Trade Agreements'. 21 Harvard Environmental Law Review 265.

Esty, Daniel C. and Geradin, Damien (1998). 'Environmental Protection and International Competitiveness: A Conceptual Framework'. 32 Journal of World Trade 5.

Eule, Julian N. (1982). 'Laying the Dormant Commerce Clause to Rest'. 91 Yale Law Journal 425, 426 n 2.

European Central Bank (1999). *Possible Effects of EMU on the EU Banking Systems in the Medium to Long Term*. Frankfurt am Main: European Central Bank.

European Commission (1976a). Convention 76/76/EEC of 15 December 1975 on the Convention for the European Patent for the Common Market (Community Patent Convention), 1976 OJ (L 17) 1; as amended by Agreement 89/695/EEC of 15 December 1989 on the Agreement Relating to Community Patents, 1989 OJ (L 401) 1.

European Commission (1976b). Council Directive 76/464 on the Discharge of Dangerous Substances into the Aquatic Environment, 1976 OJ (L 129) 23.

European Commission (1979). Council Directive 79/409/EEC of 2 April 1979 on the Conservation of Wild Birds, OJ (L 103) 1.

European Commission (1985a). Council Directive 85/374/EEC of 25 July 1985 on the Approximation of the Laws, Regulations and Administrative Provisions of the Member States Concerning Liability for Defective Products, 1985 OJ (L 210) 29.

European Commission (1985b). White Paper on Completing the Internal Market, Doc. COM(85)310, 14 June 1985.

European Commission (1987). 'Toward a Dynamic Economy—Green Paper on the Development of the Common Market for Telecommunications Services and Equipment', COM(87)290 final.

European Commission (1988a). Council Directive 88/361/EEC of 24 June 1988 for the Implementation of Article 67 of the Treaty, 1988 OJ (L 178) 5.

European Commission (1988b). Proposal for a Council Directive on the Legal Protection of Biotechnological Inventions, COM(88)496 final, 1988 OJ (C 10) 3.

European Commission (1990a). Council Directive 90/434/EEC of 23 July 1990 on the Common System of Taxation Applicable to Mergers, Divisions, Transfers of Assets and Exchanges of Shares Concerning Companies of Different Member States, 1990 OJ (L 225) 1.

European Commission (1990b). Council Directive 90/435/EEC of 23 July 1990 on the Common System of Taxation Applicable in the Case of Parent Companies and Subsidiaries of Different Member States, 1990 OJ (L 225) 6.

European Commission (1991). Proposal for a Council Directive Concerning Certain Aspects of the Organization of Working Time, COM(90)317 final, explanatory memorandum 2, paragraph 2.

European Commission (1992a). Council Directive 92/30/EEC of 6 April 1992 on the

Supervision of Credit Institutions on a Consolidated Basis, 1992 OJ (L 110) 52, amended by Council Directive 93/6/EEC, 1993 OJ (L 141) 1.

European Commission (1992b). Council Directive 92/43/EEC of 21 May 1992 on the Conservation of Natural Habitats and of Wild Fauna and Flora, 1992 OJ (L 206) 7.

European Commission (1993a). Communication of the Commission to the Council and the European Parliament Concerning the Implementation of the Protocol on Social Policy, COM(93)600 final, paragraph 6(c).

European Commission (1993b). Council Directive 93/104/EC of 23 November 1993 Concerning Certain Aspects of the Organization of Working Time, 1993 OJ (L 307) 18.

European Commission (1993c). Council Regulation 259/93 of 1 February 1993 on the Supervision and Control of Shipments of Waste within, into and out of the European Community, 1993 OJ (L 30) 1.

European Commission (1993d). Council Directive 93/22/EEC of 10 May 1993 on Investment Services in the Securities Field, 1993 OJ (L 141) 27.

European Commission (1994a). Council Regulation 40/94 of 20 December 1993 on the Community Trade Mark, 1994 OJ (L 11) 1; as amended by Council Regulation 3288/94 of 22 December 1994, 1994 OJ (L 349) 83.

European Commission (1994b). Proposal for a European Parliament and Council Regulation on the Community Design, COM(93)342 final, 1994 OJ (C 29) 20.

European Commission (1994c). Council Regulation 2100/94 of 27 July 1994 on Community Plant Variety Rights, 1994 OJ (L 227) 1; as amended by Council Regulation 2506/95 of 25 October 1995, 1995 OJ (L 258) 3.

European Commission (1994d). Council Directive 94/45/EC of 22 September 1994 on the Establishment of a European Works Council or a Procedure in Community-Scale Undertakings and Community-Scale Groups of Undertakings for the Purposes of Informing and Consulting Employees, 1994 OJ (L 254) 64.

European Commission (1995). White Paper of the Associated Countries of Central and Eastern Europe for Integration into the Internal Market of the Union, COM(95)163 final.

European Commission (1996a). Council Directive 96/34/EC of 3 June 1996 on the Framework Agreement on Parental Leave Concluded by UNICE, CCEP and the ETUC, 1996 OJ (L 145) 4.

European Commission (1996b). Council Directive 96/61/EC of 24 September 1996 on Integrated Pollution Prevention and Control, 1996 OJ (L 257) 26.

European Commission (1997a). Supplementary Pensions in the Single Market—A Green Paper, Doc. COM(97)283, 11 June 1997.

European Commission (1997b). Proposal for a Council Directive Establishing a Framework for Community Action in the Field of Water Policy, COM(97)49 final, 1997 OJ (C 184) 20.

European Commission (1998a). Commission Notice on the Application of the State Aid Rules to Measures Relating to Direct Business Taxation, 1998 OJ (C 384) 3.

European Commission (1998b). Communication of the Commission, COM(98)322 final, section 1.2, p. 5.

European Commission (1998c). Council Regulation 98/2679 of 7 December 1998 on the Functioning of the Internal Market in Relation to the Free Movement of Goods Among the Member States, 1998 OJ (L 337) 8, article 2.

European Commission (1998d). Council Directive 98/27/EC of the European Parliament and Council of 19 May 1998 on Injunctions for the Protection of Consumers' Interests, 1998 OJ (L 166) 51.

European Commission (1998e). Proposal for a Council Directive Concerning the Distance Marketing of Consumer Financial Services, COM(98)468 final.

European Commission (1999). Action Plan for a Single Financial Market, Doc. COM(99)232, 11 May 1999 (downloadable at http://www.europa.eu.int/comm/dg15/en/finances/general/actionen.pdf).

European Industrial Relations Review (1993). No. 230, 'The Hoover Affair and Social Dumping', 14.

European Works Councils Bulletin (1997). No. 11, 12–17 September/October 1997.

Evans, A. (1998). 'European Union Decision-Making, Third States and Comitology'. 47 International and Comparative Law Quarterly 257.

Evans, G. (1999). 'TRIPS and the Sufficiency of the Free Trade Principles'. 2 Journal of World Intellectual Property 707–25.

Farber, Daniel A. (1986). 'State Regulation and the Dormant Commerce Clause'. 3 Constitutional Commentary 395.

Farber, Daniel A. (1992). 'Politics and Procedure in Environmental Law'. 8 Journal of Law, Economics and Organization 59.

Farber, Daniel (1997a). 'Environmental Federalism in a Global Economy'. 83 Virginia Law Review 1283.

Farber, Daniel (1997b). 'Symposium: The Allocation of Government Authority: Environmental Federalism in a Global Economy'. 83 Virginia Law Review 1283.

Faure, Michael (1998). 'Harmonization of Environmental Law and Market Integration: Harmonizing for the Wrong Reasons ?'. European Environmental Law Review 169–75.

Faure, Michael and Lefevere, Jürgen (1994). 'Some Public Interest and Private Interest Aspects of Environmental Standard Setting in the European Community'. In D. G. Mayes (ed.), *The Evolution of Rules for a Single European Market, II, Rules, Democracy and the Environment*, 320–51.

Faure, Michael and Lefevere, Jürgen (1995). Protecting Drinking Water Quality Against Contamination by Pesticides: An Alternative Regulatory Framework. RECIEL, 321–6.

Faure, Michael and Lefevere, Jürgen (1996). 'The Draft Directive on Integrated Pollution Prevention and Control: an Economic Perspective'. European Environmental Law Review 112–22.

Faure, Michael and Lefevere, Jürgen (1999). 'Integrated Pollution Prevention and Control: an Economic Appraisal'. In Chris Backes and Gerrit Betlem (eds), *Integrated Pollution Prevention and Control, the EC Directive from a Comparative Legal and Economic Perspective*, 93–120.

Feldstein, Martin and Valliant, Marian (1994). 'Can State Taxes Redistribute Income?'. National Bureau of Economic Research, Working Paper No. 4785.

Feldstein, M. and Wrobel, M. (1998). 'Can States Redistribute Income?'. 69 Journal of Public Economics 369–96.

Ferejohn, F. and Weingast, B. R. (eds) (1997). *The New Federalism. Can the States be Trusted?* Stanford: Hoover Institution Press.

Fern, Danielle F. (1998). 'The Crafting of the National Low Emission Vehicle Program: A Private Contract Theory of Public Rulemaking'. 16 UCLA Journal of Environmental Law and Policy 227.

Fickentscher, W. (1989). 'GATT Principles and Intellectual Property Protection'. In Beier and Schricker, *GATT or WIPO?*. VCH: 99–126.

Financial Times (1997). 'Defending the Code', 4 November, 12.

Financial Times (1999). 13 September, 2.

Fine, Sidney (1969). *Sit-Down: The General Motors Strikes of 1936–1937*. Ann Arbor: University of Michigan Press.

Fingleton, John, Fox, Eleanor, Neven, Damien, and Seabright, Paul (1996). *Competition Policy and the Transformation of Central Europe*, chs 4 and 6. London: Centre for Economic Policy Research.

Fischel, Daniel R. (1982). 'The "Race to the Bottom" Revisited: Reflections on Recent Developments in Delaware's Corporation Law'. 76 Northwestern University Law Review 913.

Fischel, Daniel R., Rosenfield, Andrew M., and Stillman, Robert S. (1987). 'The Regulation of Banks and Bank Holding Companies'. 73 Virginia Law Review 301.

Fischel, William (1975). 'Fiscal and Environmental Considerations in the Location of Firms in Suburban Communities'. In Edwin S. Mills and Wallace E. Oates (eds), *Fiscal Zoning and Land Use Controls*. Lexington: Lexington Press.

Foerster, Stephen R. and Karolyi, G. Andrew (1993). 'International Listings of Stocks: The Case of Canada and the U.S.'. 24 Journal of International Business Studies 763.

Forbath, William (1991). *Law and the Shaping of the American Labor Movement*. Cambridge. MA: Harvard University Press.

Fox, Eleanor (1986). 'Monopolization and Dominance in the United States and the European Community—Efficiency, Opportunity, and Fairness '. 61 Notre Dame Law Review 981.

Fox, Eleanor (1997a). 'World Antitrust: A Principled Blueprint'. Festschrift for Professor Wolfgang Fikentscher.

Fox, Eleanor (1997b). 'Toward World Antitrust and Market Access'. 91 American Journal of International Law 1.

Fox, Eleanor (1998). 'International Antitrust: Against Minimum Rules; for Cosmopolitan Principles'. 43 Antitrust Bulletin 5.

Fox, Eleanor (1999). 'Competition Law and the Millennium Round'. 2 Journal of International Economic Law 665.

Fox, Eleanor and Ordover, Janusz (1995). 'The Harmonization of Competition and Trade Law: The Case for Modest Linkages of Law and Limits to Parochial State Action'. 19 World Competition Law & Economic Review 5.

Fox, Merritt B. (1997). 'Securities Disclosure in a Globalizing Market: Who Should Regulate Whom'. 95 Michigan Law Review 2498.

Fox, Merritt B. (1998). 'The Political Economy of Statutory Reach: U.S. Disclosure Rules in a Globalizing Market for Securities'. 97 Michigan Law Review 696.

Fox, Merritt B. 'Empowering Issuers to Choose Their Own Disclosure Regimes: A Misplaced Reform' (unpublished paper on file with the author).

Fredman, S. (1998). 'Social Law in the European Union: The Impact of the Lawmaking Process'. In P. Craig and C. Harlow (eds), *Lawmaking in the European Union*. Kluwer, 386.

Freedman, J. and Godwin, M. (1994). 'Incorporating the Micro-business: Perceptions and Misperceptions'. In D. Storey and A. Hughes (eds), *Finance and the Small Firm*. London: Routledge.

Freeman, Jody (1997). 'Collaborative Government in the Administrative State'. 45 UCLA Law Review 1.

Freeman, R. and Lazear, E. (1994). 'An economic analysis of works councils'. In J. Rogers and W. Streeck (eds), *Works Councils: Consultation, Representation, Cooperation*. Chicago: University of Chicago Press.

Freeman, Richard B. and Medoff, James L. (1984). *What Unions Do*. New York: Basic Books.

French, Hilary F. (1993). 'Reconciling Trade and the Environment'. In Linda Starke (ed.), *State of the World*, 166. New York: W. W. Norton & Company.

Frey, Bruno (1994). 'Direct Democracy: Politico-Economic Lessons from Switzerland'. 84 American Economic Review 338–42.

Frey, Bruno (1996). 'FOCJ: Competitive Governments for Europe'. 16 International Review of Law and Economics 315–27.

Frey, B. S. and Eichenberger, R. (1996). 'To Harmonize or to Compete? That's Not the Question'. 60 Journal of Public Economics 441–58.

Friedman, Joseph *et al.* (1992). 'What Attracts Foreign Multinational Corporations? Evidence from Branch Plant Locations in the United States'. 32 Journal of Regional Science 403.

Friedman, Thomas L. (2000). '1 Davos, 3 Seattles'. New York Times, 1 February, A21.

Fuerst, Oren (1998). 'A Theoretical Analysis of the Investor Protection Regulation Arguments for Global Listing of Stocks'. Working paper (dated 10 September 1998).

Gadbaw, R. (1989). 'Intellectual Property and International Trade: Merger or Marriage of Convenience?'. 22 Vanderbilt Journal of Transnational Law 223.

Garcia, Frank J. (1990). 'Protecting Nonshareholder Interest in the Market for Corporate Control: A Role for State Takeover Statutes'. 23 University of Michigan Law Review 507.

Gastel (1990). 'Financial and Market Conditions: Property/Casualty Insurance: American Council of Life Insurance'. 1990 Life Insurance Fact Book, 81.

GATT Secretariat (3 February 1992). 'Trade and Environment'. GATT/1529 in World Trade Materials, January 1992.

Geiger, Uri (1997). 'The Case for the Harmonization of Securities Disclosure Rules in the Global Market'. Columbia Business Law Review 241.

Geradin, Damien (1997a). 'Trade and Environmental Protection in the Context of World Trade Rules: A View from the European Union'. 2 European Foreign Affairs Review 33.

Geradin, Damien (1997b). *Trade and the Environment: A Comparative Study of EC and US Law*. Cambridge: Cambridge University Press.

Gey, Steven G. (1989–90). 'The Political Economy of the Dormant Commerce Clause'. 17 Review of Law and Social Change 1.

Giddy, I., Saunders, A., and Walter, I. (1996). 'Clearance and Settlement'. In B. Steil (ed.), *The European Equity Markets, The State of the Union and an Agenda for the Millennium*. London: The Royal Institute of International Affairs, 321–48.

Gilson, Ronald J. (1981). 'A Structural Approach to Corporations: The Case Against Defensive Tactics in Tender Offers'. 33 Stanford Law Review 819.

Gilson, Ronald J. (1982). 'The Case Against Shark Repellent Amendments: Structural Limitations on the Enabling Concept'. 34 Stanford Law Review 775.

Gilson, Ronald J. and Black, Bernard S. (1995). *The Law and Finance of Corporate Acquisitions*. Westburg: Foundation Press.

Gilson, Ronald J. and Kraakman, Reinier (1989). 'Delaware's Intermediate Standard for Defensive Tactics: Is There Substance to Proportionality Review?'. 44 Business Lawyer 247.

Gingrich, Newt (1985). *To Renew America*. New York: HarperCollins.

Golub, J. (1999). 'In the Shadow of the Vote? Decision Making in the European Community'. 53 International Organization 733–64.

Goetschy, Janine (1999). 'The European Employment Strategy: Genesis and Development'. 5 European Journal of Industrial Relations 117.

Goklany, Indur M. (1998a). 'Did Federalization Halt a Race to the Bottom for Air Quality?'. EM, June.

Goklany, Indur M. (1998b). 'Do We Need the Federal Government to Protect Air Quality?' Center for the Study of American Business Policy, Study No. 150.

Goldfield, Michael (1997). *The Color of Politics: Race and the Mainsprings of American Politics*. New York: New Press.

Gordon, R. H. (1985). 'An Optimal Taxation Approach to Fiscal Federalism'. 95 Quarterly Journal of Economics 567–86.

Gordon, R. H. and Bovenberg, L. (1996). 'Why is Capital So Immobile Internationally? Possible Explanations and Implications for Capital Income Taxation'. 86 American Economic Review 1057–75.

Gordon, Roger H. and Wilson, John D. (1986). 'An Examination of Multijurisdictional Corporate Income Taxation Under Formula Apportionment', 54 Econometrica 1357.

Gore, Al (1992). *Earth in the Balance*. Boston: Houghton Mifflin Company.

Gore, Pelham (1992). *The FASB Conceptual Framework Project 1973–1985*. New York: Manchester University Press, distributed by St Martin's Press, at 18, 22.

Gormley, Laurence W. (1985). *Prohibiting Restrictions on Trade Within the EEC*. Amsterdam: Elsevier.

Govaere, I. (1993). 'Intellectual Property Protection and Commercial Policy'. In M. Maresceau (ed.), *The European Community's Commercial Policy after 1992: The Legal Dimension*. Martinus Nijhoff Pub., 197–222.

Govaere, I. (1994). 'Trade-related Aspects of Intellectual Property Rights: The EC dichotomy uncovered'. In *La place de l'Europe dans le commerce mondial*. Institut Universitaire International Luxembourg, 161–215.

Govaere, I. (1996). *The Use and Abuse of Intellectual Property Rights in EC Law*. Sweet & Maxwell.

Govaere, I. (1997a). 'Convergence, Divergence and Interaction of Regional Trade Agreements and the Agreement on Trade Related Aspects of Intellectual Property Rights (TRIPS)'. In P. Demaret *et al.*, *Regionalism and Multilateralism after the Uruguay Round*. European Interuniversity Press, 465–194.

Govaere, I. (1997b). 'Trade-related Aspects of Intellectual Property Rights in the European Agreements: Stimulus or Limitation to Parallel Imports?'. In Maresceau (ed.), *Enlarging the European Union: Relations between the EU and Central and Eastern Europe*. Longman, 179–92.

Graetz, Michael J. and O'Hear, Michael M. (1997). 'The "Original Intent" of U.S. International Taxation'. 46 Duke Law Journal 1021.

Gramlich, Edward M. (1987). 'Cooperation and Competition in Public Welfare Policies'. 6 Journal of Policy Analysis & Management 417.

Grasso, Thomas V. (1996). 'Wetlands Permitting Programs in the Chesapeake Bay Area'. ALI-ABA Course of Study Materials.

Griffith, Barbara (1988). *The Crisis of American Labor: Operation Dixie and the Defeat of the CIO*.

Gross, James (1995). *Broken Promise: The Subversion of U.S. Labor Relations Policy, 1947–1994*. Ithaca: Cornell University Press.

Gruber, Jonathan (1994). 'The Incidence of Mandated Maternity Benefits'. 64 American Economic Review 622.

Grundfest, Joseph A. (1993). 'Just Vote No: A Minimalist Strategy for Dealing with Barbarians Inside the Gates'. 45 Stanford Law Review 857.

Guerrero, Peter F., Director, Environmental Protection Issues, Resources, Community, and Economic Development Division Before the Subcommittee on Finance and Hazardous Materials, Committee on Commerce, US House of Representatives (23 March 1999) 'Superfund: Progress, Problems, and Future Outlook'.

Gunningham, Neil and Grabosky, Peter (1999). *Smart Regulation*. New York: Oxford University Press.

Haagsma, Auke (1989). 'The European Community's Environmental Policy: A Case Study in Federalism'. 12 Fordham International Law Journal 311.

Haas, Peter M. (1990). *Saving the Mediterranean: The Politics of International Environmental Cooperation*. New York: Columbia University Press.

Haas, Peter (1999). 'Social Constructivism and the Evolution of Multilateral Environmental Governance'. In Aseem Prakash and Jeffery Hart (eds) *Globalization and Governance*. London: Routledge, 103–33.

Haas, Peter M., Keohane, Robert O., and Levy, Marc A. (eds) (1993). *Institutions for the Earth: Sources of Effective International Environmental Protection*. Cambridge: MIT Press.

Haddock, D. and Macey, J. (1987). 'Regulation on Demand: Special Interest Groups and Insider Trading Law'. 30 Journal of Law & Economics 311.

Haigh, Nigel (1987). *EEC Environmental Policy and Britain*. Harlow: Longman.

Halpern, Martin (1988). *UAW Politics in the Cold War Era*. Albany: State University of New York Press.

Hamilton, Bruce (1975). 'Zoning and Property Taxation in a System of Local Governments'. 12 Urban Studies 205.

Hammen, H. (1999). 'Zweigniederlassungsfreiheit europäischer Gesellschaften und Mitbestimmung der Arbeitnehmer auf Unternehmensebene'. 53 WM Zeitschrift für Wirtschafts- und Bankrecht 2487–95.

Handler, Milton (1974). 'Oral History'. Oral History Research Office: Columbia University.

Hanks, Sara and Nardini, Gregory G. (1999). 'International Accounting Standards in SEC Filings: Closer Than You Think?'. 13 Insights 25.

Hawley, E. (undated). 'The Great War and Organizational Innovation: The American Case'. Unpublished manuscript.

Hazard, Jr., Geoffrey C. and Orts, Eric W. (1999). 'Environmental Contracts in the United States'. Unpublished manuscript.

Head, C. K. *et al.* (1994). 'Investment and Agglomeration Economies'. National Bureau of Economic Research Working Paper Series, No. 4878 (October 1994).

Hellerstein, Walter (1986). 'Selected Issues in State Business Taxation'. 39 Vanderbilt Law Review 1033.

Henderson, J. Vernon (1996). 'Effects of Air Quality Regulation'. 86 American Economic Review 789.

Herring, R. J. and Litan, Robert E. (1995). *Financial Regulation in the Global Economy*. Washington, DC: The Brookings Institution.

Hertig, Gerard (1994). 'Imperfect Mutual Recognition for EC Financial Services'. 14 International Review of Law and Economics 177.

Hertig, G. (1996). 'Imperfect Mutual Recognition for EU Financial Services'. In R. M. Buxbaum, G. Hertig, A. Hirsch, and K. J. Hopt (eds), *European Business and Economic Law*. Berlin/New York: Walter de Gruyter, 218–29.

Heylen, F. (1995). 'Institutions and the Rise of Taxes on Labour in the OECD'. 131 Weltwirtschaftliches Archiv 623–54.

Hicks, A., Drury, R., and Smallcombe, J. (1995). Alternative Company Structures for the Small Business, ACCA Research Report 42 (London: Certified Accountants Educational Trust).

Hines, James R. and Rice, Eric (1994). 'Fiscal Paradise: Foreign Tax Havens and American Business'. 109 Quarterly Journal of Economics 149.

Hirsch, A. (1991). 'Worldwide Legal Harmonization of Banking Law and Securities Regulation'. In R. M. Buxbaum, G. Hertig, A. Hirsch, and K. J. Hopt (eds), *European Business Law*. Berlin/New York: Walter de Gruyter, 347–61.

Holahan, John *et al.* (1998). *Health Policy for the Low-Income Population: Major Findings from Assessing the New Federalism Case Studies*. Washington DC: Urban Institute.

Honey, Michael (1993). *Southern Labor and Black Civil Rights*. Chicago: University of Illinois Press.

Hoppmann, C. (1999). 'Europäische Börsenaufsicht'. 10 Europaïsches Wirtschafts- und Steuerrecht 204–12.

Horn, N. (1999). 'The Monetary Union and the Internal Market for Banking and Investment Services'. 10 European Business Law Review 150–7.

Hoschka, T. C. (1993). *Cross-Border Entry in European Retail Financial Services. Determinants, Regulation and the Impact on Competition*. New York: St Martin's Press.

Howse, Robert (1999). 'The World Trade Organization and the Protection of Workers' Rights'. 3 Journal of Small and Emerging Business Law 131.

Howse, Robert and Trebilcock, Michael J. (1996). 'The Fair Trade–Free Trade Debate: Trade, Labor, and the Environment'. 16 International Review of Law and Economics 61.

Hudec, Robert E. (1990). 'Thinking about the New Section 301: Beyond Good and Evil'. In Jagdish Bhagwati and Hugh T. Patrick (eds), *Aggressive Unilateralism: America's 301 Trade Policy and the World Trading System*. Ann Arbor: University of Michigan Press.

Hudnall, Shannon (1996). 'Towards a Greener International Trade System: Multilateral Environmental Agreements and the World Trade Organization'. 19(2) Columbia Journal of Law and Social Problems 212.

Husted, Bryan and Logsdon, Jeanne (1997). 'The Impact of NAFTA on Mexico's Environmental Policy'. Growth and Change, Vol. 28, 24–48 (Winter 1997).

IMF (1998). *Toward a Framework for Financial Stability*. Washington: IMF.

International Environment Reporter (1999). 'Environment Ministers to Revise EMAS Eco-label Program to Boost Participation'. Vol. 22, No. 14, 7 July, p. 570.

Inman, R. P. and Rubinfeld, D. (1994). 'The EMU and Fiscal Policy in the New European Community: An Issue for Economic Federalism'. 14 International Review of Law and Economics 147–61.

Inman, R. P. and Rubinfeld, D. (1996). 'Designing Tax Policy in Federalist Economies: An Overview'. 60 Journal of Public Economics 307–34.

Inman, R. P. and Rubinfeld, D. (1997a). 'The Political Economy of Federalism. In Dennis C. Mueller (ed.), *Perspectives on Public Choice: A Handbook*. New York: Cambridge University Press, 73, 85.

Inman, R. P. and Rubinfeld, D. (1997b). 'Rethinking Federalism'. 11 Journal of Economic Literature 43–64.

International Environment Reporter (1999). 'Thirty Firms Plan Pilot Scheme on Emissions Trading in Order to Head off Proposed Energy Tax'. Vol. 22, No. 14, 7 July, p. 580.

International Labour Organization (1998). 'ILO Declaration on Fundamental Principles and Rights at Work'. International Labour Conference, 86th Session, Geneva, June 1998.

IOSCO (International Organization of Securities Commissions) (1998). 'A Resolution of the Presidents' Committee on IOSCO Endorsement of Disclosure Standards to Facilitate Cross Border Offerings and Listings by Multinational Issuers' (http://209.41.134.29/resolutions/resolutions-document18.html).

Jachtenfuch, M. (1995). 'Theoretical Perspectives on European Governance'. 1 European Law Journal 115.

Jacobson, Harold K. and Brown Weiss, Edith (eds) (1997). *Engaging Countries: Strengthening Compliance with International Environmental Accords.* Cambridge: MIT Press.

Jacoby, Sanford (1990). 'Norms and Cycles: The Dynamics of Nonunion Industrial Relations in the United States'. In K. Abraham and R. McKersie (eds), *New Developments in the Labor Market.* Cambridge: MIT Press.

Jacoby, Sanford (1997). *Modern Manors: Welfare Capitalism Since the New Deal.* Princeton: Princeton University Press.

Jaffee, Adam, Peterson, S., Portney, S., and Stavins, Robert (1995). 'Environmental Regulation and the Competitiveness of US Manufacturing: What Does the Evidence Tell Us?'. 33 Journal of Economic Literature 132–63.

Jakob, Thinam (1993). 'EEA and Eastern European Agreements with the European Community'. In B. Hawk (ed.), *Annual Proceedings of the Fordham Corporate Law Institute.* Transnational Juris Publications, 403.

Janeba, E. and Peters, W. (1999). 'Tax Evasion, Tax Competition, and the Gains from Nondiscrimination: The Case of Interest Taxation in Europe'. 103 Economic Journal 93–101.

Jebsen, Per and Stevens, Robert (1996). 'Assumptions, Goals, and Dominant Undertakings: The Regulation of Competition Under Article 86 of the European Union'. 64 Antitrust Law Journal 443.

Jenkins, Rhys and Branch, Tammy (1996). 'NAFTA and the Mexican Environment: Facts and Fears'. Presented to the Canadian Association for Latin American and Caribbean Studies' XXVII Congress.

Jenkins, Robin R. *et al.* (May 1999). 'The Determinants of Household Recycling: A Material Specific Analysis of Unit Pricing and Recycling Program Attributes'. Resources for the Future Discussion Paper 99–41.

Jenny, Frédéric (1997). 'The Interface Between Competition Policy and Trade, Investment and Economic Development'. Paper presented for the Global Forum for Competition and Trade Policy at New Delhi, India, 17–18 March 1997.

Jensen, Michael C. and Murphy, Kevin J. (1990a). 'CEO Incentives—It's Not How Much You Pay, But How'. 1990 Harvard Business Review, May–June.

Jensen, Michael C. and Murphy, Kevin J. (1990b). 'Performance Pay and Top Management Incentives'. 98 Journal of Political Economy 225.

Jha, Veena (1998). 'Industry Concerns'. In Duncan Brack (ed.), *Trade and Environment: Conflict of Compatibility?* London: Royal Institute of International Affairs, 87.

Johnson, W. R. (1988). 'Income Redistribution in a Federal System'. 78 American Economic Review 570–3.

Joint Statement of US–EU Summit (1997). 'Regulatory Cooperation: Promoting Trade While Facilitating Consumer Protection'. 5 December, Washington, DC (document available at <http://www.state.gov/www.regions/eur/eu/971205_useu_regulatory_js.hmtl>).

Jolls, Christine, Sunstein, Cass, and Thaler, Richard (1998). 'A Behavioral Approach to Law and Economics'. 50 Stanford Law Review 1471, 1505–8.

Kahler, Miles. 'Modeling Races to the Top' (unpublished paper).

Kahn, Alfred (1970). *The Economics of Regulation*. Cambridge: MIT Press.

Kamar, Ehud (1998). 'A Regulatory Competition Theory of Indeterminacy in Corporate Law'. 98 Columbia Law Review 1908.

Kanbur, R. and Keen, M. (1993). 'Jeux Sans Frontière: Tax Competition and Tax Coordination When Countries Differ in Size'. 83 American Economic Review 877–92.

Kane, E. (1990). 'Principal–Agent Problems in S&L Salvage'. 45 Journal of Finance 755–64.

Kaouris, Demetrios G. (1995). 'Is Delaware Still a Haven for Incorporation?'. 20 Delaware Journal of Corporation Law 965.

Kaplow, L. (1996). 'Fiscal Federalism and the Deductibility of State and Local Taxes Under the Federal Income Tax'. 82 Virginia Law Review 413–92.

Kapstein, Ethan (1999). 'Distributive Justice as an International Public Good: A Historical Perspective'. In I. Kaul, I. Grunberg, and M. Stern (eds), *Global Public Goods: International Cooperation in the 21st Century*. New York: Oxford University Press.

Kastenmeter, R. and Beier, D. (1989). 'International Trade and Intellectual Property: Promise, Risks and Reality'. 22 Vanderbilt Journal of Transnational Law 298.

Katz, M. and Shapiro, C. (1994). 'Systems Competition and Network Effects'. 8 Journal of Economic Perspectives 133.

Keen, M. J. (1993). 'The Welfare Economics of Tax Co-ordination in the European Community: A Survey'. 14 Fiscal Studies 15–36.

Keen, M. J. (1998). 'Vertical Tax Externalities in the Theory of Fiscal Federalism'. 45 IMF Staff Papers 454–85.

Keohane, Nathaniel O., Revesz, Richard R., and Stavins, Robert N. (1998). 'The Choice of Regulatory Instruments in Environmental Policy'. 22 Harvard Environmental Law Review 313.

Kimber, Clíona (1995). 'A Comparison of Environmental Federalism in the United States and the European Union'. 54 Maryland Law Review.

Kirchgaessner, G. and Pomerehne, W. W. (1996). 'Tax Harmonization and Tax Competition in the European Union: Lessons from Switzerland'. 60 Journal of Public Economics 351–71.

Kitch, Edmund W. (1995). 'The Theory and Practice of Securities Disclosure'. 61 Brooklyn Law Review 763, 875.

Klabbers, J. (1994). 'Informal Instruments Before the European Court of Justice'. 31 Common Market Law Review 997.

Klevorick, Alvin K. (1996). 'The Race to the Bottom in a Federal System: Lessons from the World of Trade Policy'. 14 Yale Law and Policy Review 177.

Koch, N. (1986). 'Article 30 and the Exercise of Industrial Property Rights to Block Imports'. In Hawk (ed.), 1986 Fordham Corporate Law Institute: 605.

Kochan, Thomas, Katz, Harry, and McKersie, Robert (1986). *The Transformation of American Industrial Relations*. New York: Basic Books.

Kohl, Helmut (1996). 'Federalism and Corporate Law'. In I. Pernice (ed.), *Harmonization of Legislation in Federal Systems*. Baden-Baden: Nomos.

Kolstad, Charles (1987). 'Uniformity versus Differentiation in Regulating Externalities'. 14 Journal of Environmental Economics and Management 386–99.

Kopp, Raymond, Portney, Paul, and Dewitt, Diane (1990). *International Comparisons of Environmental Regulations*. Washington DC: Resources for the Future 3.

Koretz, Gene (1994). 'A Robust Economy Can Help Cure a Sick Environment'. Business Week, 23 May, p. 20.

Koskela, E. and Schob, R. (1998). 'Why Government Should Tax Mobile Capital in the Presence of Unemployment'. CES Working Paper, No. 175.

KPMG (1999). 'Tax Advisers Brief: European Taxation'. United Kingdom: New Commissioner for Taxation (http://www.mondaq.com).

Kraft, Michael E. and Vig, Norman J. (1990). 'Environmental Policy from the Seventies to the Nineties: Continuity and Change'. In N. J. Vig and M. E. Kraft (eds), *Environmental Policy in the 1990s*. Washington: CQ Press.

Kramer, Ludwig (1995). *E.C. Treaty and Environmental Law*, second edn. London: Sweet & Maxwell.

Krenzler, Horst G. and Schomaker, Astrid (1996). 'A New Transatlantic Agenda'. 1 European Foreign Affairs Review 9.

Kübler, Friedrich (1996). 'Legislative Competition and Corporate Law Reform: Some Questions from a European Perspective'. In I. Pernice (ed.), *Harmonization of Legislation in Federal Systems*. Baden-Baden: Nomos.

Kuehn, Robert R. (1996). 'The Limits of Devolving Enforcement of Federal Environmental Laws'. 70 Tulane Law Review 2373.

La Porta, Rafael *et al.* (1996). 'Law and Finance', National Bureau of Economic Research, Working Paper, 5661.

La Porta, Rafael *et al.* (1997). 'Legal Determinants of External Finance'. 52 Journal of Finance 1131.

Lando, O. (1993). 'Die Regeln des Europäischen Vertragsrecht'. In Peter-Christian Müller-Graf (ed.), *Gemeinsames Privatrecht in der Europäischen Gemeinschaft*. 473–4.

Langille, Brian A. (1996). 'Competing Conceptions of Regulatory Competition in Debates on Trade Liberalization and Labour Standards'. In William Bratton, Joseph McCahery, Sol Picciotto, and Colin Scott (eds), *International Regulatory Competition and Coordination: Perspectives on Economic Regulation in Europe and the United States*. Oxford University Press.

Langille, Brian (1997). 'Eight Ways to Think About International Labour Standards'. 31 Journal of World Trade 27.

Lash III, William (1993). *NAFTA and the Greening of International Trade Policy*, 11. St Louis: Center for the Study of American Business.

Latin, Howard. 'The Mirage of International Environmental Law' (unpublished paper).

Leary, Virginia A. (1996). 'Workers' Rights and International Trade: The Social Clause (GATT, ILO, NAFTA, US Laws)'. In Jagdish Bhagwati and Robert E. Hudec (eds), *Fair Trade and Harmonization: Prerequisites for Free Trade: Volume 1: Economic Analysis*. Cambridge: MIT Press, 177.

LeBeouf, Jacques (1994). 'The Economics of Federalism and the Proper Scope of the Federal Commerce Power'. 31 San Diego Law Review 555.

Lee, R. (1996). 'Supervising EU Capital Markets: Do We Need a European SEC?'. In

R. M. Buxbaum, G. Hertig, A. Hirsch, and K. J. Hopt (eds), *European Business and Economic Law*. Berlin/New York: Walter de Gruyter, 187–204.

Lee, R. (1998a). 'Regulation of Capital Markets in the European Union'. In P. Newman (ed.), *The New Palgrave Dictionary of Economics and the Law*, 3 vols. London: Macmillan Reference Ltd, Vol. 3, 228–32.

Lee, R. (1998b). *What is an Exchange? The Automation, Management, and Regulation of Financial Markets*. Oxford: Oxford University Press.

Lee, Sang Don (1993). 'The Effect of Environmental Regulations on Trade: Korea's New Environmental Laws'. The Georgetown International Law Review, 5.

Lefevere, Jürgen and Faure, Michael (1995). 'Introduction to European Environmental Law'. In T. Kegels (ed.), *Shipping Law faces Europe: European Policy Competition and Environment* 93–107.

Legal Service (1998). Note d'Information du Service Juridique: Affaire T–135/96, UEAPME contre Conseil, Brussels, 7 July 1998, Doc. 10218/98.

Legrand, B. (1997). 'The impossibility of "legal transplants"'. Maastricht Journal of European and Comparative Law 111 ff.

Lenaerts, Koen (1994). 'The Principle of Subsidiarity and the Environment in the European Union: Keeping the Balance of Federalism'. 17 Fordham International Law Journal 846.

Levich, R. M. (1990). 'The Euromarkets after 1992'. In J. Dermine (ed.), *European Banking in the 1990s*. Oxford: Basil Blackwell Ltd, 373–403.

Levinson, Arik (1996). 'Environmental Regulations and Manufacturers' Location Choices: Evidence from the Census of Manufacturers'. 62 Journal of Public Economics 5.

Licht, A. (1998). 'Regulatory Arbitrage for Real: International Securities Regulation in a World of Interacting Securities Markets'. 39 Virginia Journal of International Law 563–638.

Licht, A. N. (1999). 'Games Commissions Play: 2x2 Games of International Securities Regulation'. 24 Yale Journal of International Law 61–128.

Lichtenstein, Nelson (1982). *Labor's War at Home: The CIO in World War II*. Cambridge: Cambridge University Press.

Liefferink, J. D., Lowe, P. D., and Mol, A. P. J. (1993). *European Integration and Environmental Policy*. London: Belhaven Press.

Light, Alfred R. (1998). 'He Who Pays the Piper Should Call the Tune: Dual Sovereignty in U.S. Environmental Law'. 4 Environmental Law 779.

Lipton, Martin (1987). 'Corporate Governance in the Age of Financial Corporatism'. 136 University of Pennsylvania Law Review 1.

Lomas, Owen (1988). 'Environmental Protection, Economic Conflict and the European Community'. 33 McGill Law Journal 506.

Louis, J. V., Begg, I., Garcia de Enterria, E., Horn, N., de Lohoneux, E., Radicati di Brozolo, L. G., Smits, R., and Stoufflet, J. (1995). *Banking Supervision in the European Community: Institutional Aspects*. Brussels: Institut d'Etudes Européennes.

Low, Patrick and Yeats, A. (1992). 'Do "Dirty" Industries Migrate?'. In P. Low (ed.), *International Trade and the Environment*. Washington: World Bank.

Lucas, Robert, Wheeler, David, and Hettige, Hemamala (1992). 'Economic Development, Environmental Regulation and International Migration of Toxic Industrial Pollution: 1960–1988'. In P. Low and A. Yeats (eds), *International Trade and the Environment*. Washington: World Bank, 67–86.

Lugano Convention (1988). Lugano Convention on Jurisdiction and the Enforcement of Judgments in Civil and Commercial Matters, 1988 OJ (L 319) 9.

Macey, J. (1990). 'Federal Deference to Local Regulators and the Economic Theory of Regulation: Toward a Public-Choice Explanation of Federalism'. 76 Virginia Law Review 265.

Macey, J. and Miller, G. (1993). 'Costly Policies: State Regulation and Antitrust Exemption in Insurance Markets'. AEI Press, 44.

Macey, J. and Miller, G. (1995). 'Deposit Insurance, the Implicit Regulatory Contract, and the Mismatch in the Term Structure of Banks' Assets and Liabilities'. Yale Journal on Regulation 1.

Macey, J. and Miller, G. (1997). *Banking Law & Regulation*, 2nd edn. New York: Aspen Law & Business.

Macey, Jonathan R. and Miller, Geoffrey P. (1987). 'Toward an Interest-Group Theory of Delaware Corporate Law'. 65 Texas Law Review 469.

Machlup, F. and Penrose, E. (1950). 'The Patent Controversy in the Nineteenth Century'. 10 Journal of Economic History 1–29.

Maddox, Bronwen (1994). 'Black Skies, Red Tape, Green Fields, Grey Area'. Financial Times, 3 March, p. 8.

Maloney, Michael T. and McCormick, Robert E. (1982). 'A Positive Theory of Environmental Quality Regulation'. 25 Journal of Law, Economics and Organization 99.

Mani, Muthukumara and Wheeler, David (1999). 'In Search of Pollution Harms? Dirty Industry in the World Economy, 1960–1995'. In P. Fredriksson (ed.), *Trade, Global Policy, and the Environment*. Washington: World Bank.

Mansori, Kashif S. and Weichenrieder, Alfons J. (1999). *Tax Competition and Transfer Pricing Disputes*.

Markusen, James R., Morey, Edward R., and Olewiler, Nancy D. (1993). 'Environmental Policy when Market Structure and Plant Location are Endogenous'. 24 Journal of Environmental Economics and Management 69.

Markusen, James R., Morey, Edward R., and Olewiler, Nancy D. (1995). 'Competition in Regional Environmental Policies when Plant Locations are Endogenous'. 56 Journal of Public Economics 55.

Mashaw, Jerry and Calsyn, Dylan S. (1996). 'Block Grants, Entitlements, and Federalism: A Conceptual Map of Contested Terrain'. 14 Yale Law and Policy Review 297.

Mashaw, Jerry L. (1997). *Greed, Chaos, and Governance: Using Public Choice to Improve Public Law*. New Haven: Yale University Press.

Mashaw, Jerry L. and Rose-Ackerman, Susan (1984). 'Federalism and Regulation'. In George C. Eads and Michael Fix (eds), *The Reagan Regulatory Strategy: An Assessment*. Washington, DC: Urban Institute Press.

Matheson, John H. and Olson, Brent A. (1991). 'Shareholder Rights and Legislative Wrongs: Toward Balanced Takeover Legislation'. 59 George Washington Law Review 1425.

Matsushita, Mitsuo (1998). 'Reflections on Competition Policy/Law in the Framework of the WTO'. In B. Hawk (ed.), *Annual Proceedings of the Fordham Corporate Law Institute*. Transnational Jones Publications, 31.

Mattoo, Aaditya and Subramanian, Arvind (1997). 'Multilateral Rules on Competition Policy—A Possible Way Forward'. 31 Journal of World Trade 129.

Mayer, C. (1995). 'The Regulation of Financial Services: Lessons from the UK for 1992'. In M. Bishop, J. Kay, and C. Mayer (eds.), *The Regulatory Challenge*. Oxford: Oxford University Press, 138–59.

Mayer, C. (1997). 'Corporate Governance, Competition, and Performance'. 24 Journal of Law and Society 152–76.

McCahery *et al.* (1996). *International Regulatory Competition and Coordination—Perspectives on Economic Regulation in Europe and the United States.* Oxford: Oxford University Press.

McCartin, Joseph (1997). *Labor's Great War: The Struggle for Industrial Democracy and the Origins of Modern American Labor Relations, 1912–1921.* Chapel Hill: University of North Carolina Press.

McConnell, M. W. (1987). 'Federalism: Evaluating the Founders' Design'. 54 University of Chicago Law Review, 1486.

McConnell, Virginia D. and Schwab, Robert M. (1991). 'The Impact of Environmental Regulation on Industry Location Decisions: The Motor Vehicle Industry'. 66 Land Economics 67.

McCubbins *et al.* (1987). 'Administrative Procedures as Instruments of Political Control'. 3 Journal of Legal Economics and Organization 243.

McEnroe, John E. and Martens, Stanley (1998). 'Perceptions of Chief Financial Officers Concerning FASB; Financial Accounting Standards Board'. CPA Journal, December: 53.

McLure, C. E. (1986). 'Tax Competition: Is What's Good for the Private Goose Also Good for the Public Gander?'. 39 National Tax Journal 341–8.

Mead, W. (1990). *The Low-Wage Challenge to Global Growth.* Washington, DC: Economic Policy Institute.

Meek, Gary K. (1983). 'U.S. Securities Market Responses to Alternate Earnings Disclosures of Non-U.S. Multinational Corporations'. Acct. Rev., April 1983, 394.

Melamed, Douglas (1998). 'Antitrust Enforcement in a Global Economy'. 25th Annual Conference on International Antitrust Law and Policy, Fordham Corporate Law Institute (document available at < http://www.usdoj.gov/atr/public/speeches/2043.htm>).

Mendelsohn, R. (1986). 'Regulatory Heterogeneous Emission'. 13 Journal of Environmental Economics and Management 301.

Merrill, Thomas (1994). 'Symposium: The Environment and the Law, Panel III: International Law, Global Environmentalism, and the Future of American Environmental Policy'. 21 Ecology Law Quarterly 485.

Merrill, Thomas W. (1997). 'Golden Rules for Transboundary Pollution'. 46 Duke Law Journal 931.

Meyer, Stephen (1992). 'Environmentalism and Economic Prosperity: Testing the Environmental Impact Hypothesis'. MIT Project on Environmental Politics and Policy.

Miller, Geoffrey (1998). 'Political Structure and Corporate Governance: Some Points of Contrast between the United States and England'. 1998 Columbia Business Law Review 52.

Mintz, Jack and Tulkens, Henry (1986). 'Commodity Tax Competition Between Member States of a Federation: Equilibrium and Efficiency'. 29 Journal of Public Economics 133.

Modigliani, Franco and Perotti, Enrico (1998). 'Security versus Bank Finance: the Importance of a Proper Enforcement of Legal Rules' (working paper dated 12 February).

Moffitt, Robert (1992). 'Incentive Effects of the U.S. Welfare System: A Review'. 30 Journal of Economic Literature.

Mofson, Phyllis (1997). 'Zimbabwe and CITES: Illustrating the Reciprocal Relationship between the State and the International Regime'. In Miranda Schreurs and Elizabeth Economy (eds), *The Internationalization of Environmental Protection.* New York: Cambridge University Press, 162–87.

Molle, W. (1997). *The Economics of European Integration. Theory, Practice, Policy*, 3rd edn. Aldershot: Ashgate Publishing Ltd.

Moore, Curtis and Miller, Alan (1994). *Green Gold: Japan, Germany, and the United States, and the Race for Environmental Technology*. Boston: Beacon Press.

Morandi, Larry (1998). *State Environmental Audit Laws and Policies: An Evaluation*. Washington, DC: National Conference of State Legislatures.

Moravcsik, A. (1999). 'A New Statescraft, Supranational Entrepreneurs and International Cooperation'. 53 International Organization 267–306.

Moravcsik, Andrew (1998). *The Choice for Europe: Social Purpose and State Power from Messina to Maastricht*. Ithaca: Cornell University Press.

Mortimer, T. (1996). 'The Removal of Barriers to Corporate Mobility: an Analysis of Cases Pertinent to Articles 52 and 58'. In A. Craiger and D. Floudas (eds), *Onwards. Lowering the Barriers Further*. Chichester: Wiley.

Mott, Richard (1990). 'Federal–State Relations in US Environmental Law: Lessons from The American Experience'. European University Institute Working Paper, EPU, No 90/2.

Mueller, D. and Sirower, M. (1998). 'The Causes of Mergers: Tests Based on the Gains to Acquiring Firms'. ESRC Centre for Business Research, Working Paper No. 109, University of Cambridge.

Munoz, Heraldo and Rosenberg, Robin (eds) (1993). *Difficult Liaison: Trade and the Environment in the Americas*. New Brunswick: Transaction Publishers.

Nader, Ralph *et al.* (1993). *The Case Against Free Trade: GATT, NAFTA, and the Globalization of Corporate Power*. San Francisco: Earth Island Press.

Nam, Young-Suck (1997). 'Korea'. In M. Janicke and H. Weidner (eds), *National Environmental Policies: A Comparative Study of Capacity-Building*. Berlin: Springer: 119–212.

Netherlands Ministry of Finance (1999). Corporate Effective Tax Rates in the European Union (The Hague: Ministry of Finance, written by Maastricht Accounting and Auditing and Education Centre).

Newman, P. (ed.) (1998). *The New Palgrave Dictionary of Economics and the Law*, 3 vols. London: Macmillan Reference Ltd.

Nicolaïdis, Kalypso and Trachtman, Joel P. (2000). 'From Policed Regulation to Managed Recognition: Mapping the Boundary in GATS'. In Pierre Sauve and Robert Stern (eds), *GATS 2000*.

Niskanen, William A. (1971). *Bureaucracy and Representative Government*. Chicago: Aldine Atherton.

Nogues, J. (1990). 'Patents and Pharmaceutical Drugs: Understanding the Pressures on Developing Countries'. 24 Journal of World Trade 81–104.

North, Douglass (1987). 'Institutions, Transaction Costs and Economic Growth'. 25 Econ Inquiry 419.

North, Douglass (1986). 'The New Institutional Economics'. 142 J. Inst. & Theo Econ. 230.

Nussbaum, Martha (1999). *Sex and Social Justice*. Oxford: Oxford University Press.

Oates, W. E. (1996). 'Taxation in a Federal System: The Tax Assignment Problem'. 1 Public Economics Review 35–60.

Oates, W. E. (1999). 'An Essay on Fiscal Federalism'. 37 Journal of Economic Literature 1120–49.

Oates, Wallace E. (1997). 'On Environmental Federalism'. 83 Virginia Law Review 1321.

Oates, Wallace E. (1998). 'Thinking About Environmental Federalism'. 130 Resources 14.

Oates, W. E. (1972). *Fiscal Federalism*. New York: Harcourt Brace Jovanovich.

Oates, Wallace E. and Schwab, Robert M. (November 1987). Pricing Instruments for Environmental Protection: The Problem of Cross-Media Pollution, Interjurisdictional Competition and Interregional Effects (unpublished manuscript).

Oates, Wallace E. and Schwab, Robert M. (1988). 'Economic Competition Among Jurisdictions: Efficiency Enhancing or Distortion Inducing?' 35 Journal of Public Economics 333.

Obradovic, D. (1998). 'Accountability of Interest Groups in the Union Lawmaking Process'. In P. Craig and C. Harlow (eds), *Lawmaking in the European Union*. Kluwer, 354.

Obstfeld, M. (1999). 'The Global Capital Market: Benefactor or Menace?'. 13 Journal of Economic Perspectives 9–31.

OECD (Organization for Economic Cooperation and Development) (1989a). Pollution Control Expenditures in Selected OECD Countries 1972–1986, 39. Paris: OECD.

OECD (1989b). 'Trade and the Environment'. Draft prepared by the Trade Committee of OECD, 27 June 1989, 6.

OECD (1997). The OECD Report on Regulatory Reform, Vol. 1: Sectorial Studies. Paris: OECD.

OECD (1998a). Harmful Tax Competition: An Emerging Global Issue. Paris: OECD.

OECD (1998b). Institutional Investors in the New Landscape. Paris: OECD.

Ogus, Anthony (1994a). *Regulation, Legal Form and Economic Theory*.

Ogus, Anthony (1994b). 'Standard Setting for an Environmental Protection'. In Michael Faure, John Vervaele, and A. Weale (eds), *Environmental Standards in the European Union in an Interdisciplinary Framework*. 25–30.

Ogus, Anthony (1999). 'Competition Between National Legal Systems: A Contribution of Economic Analysis to Comparative Law'. 48 International and Comparative Law Quarterly 405–18.

Olson, Mancur (1965). *The Logic of Collective Action: Public Goods and the Theory of Groups*.

Olson, M. Jr. (1969). 'The Principle of Fiscal Equivalence: the Division of Responsibilities Among Different Levels of Government'. 59 American Economic Review 482.

O'Regan, M. (1995). 'The Protection of Intellectual Property, International Trade and the European Community: The Impact of the TRIPS Agreement on the Uruguay Round of Multilateral Trade Negotiations'. Legal Issues of European Integration, § 1: 1.

Osterman, Paul (1999). *Securing Prosperity: The American Labor Market: How It Has Changed and What to Do About It*. Princeton: Princeton University Press.

Owens, J. (1993). 'Globalisation: The Implications for Tax Policies'. 14 Fiscal Studies 21–44.

Padoa-Schioppa, T. (1999). 'EMU and Banking Supervision'. 2 International Finance 295–308.

Papendrou, Andreas A. (1994). *Externality and Institutions*. New York: Oxford University Press.

Pâques, Michel (1996). 'Effet direct du droit communautaire, interprétation conforme et responsabilité de l'Etat en général et en matière d'environment'. In J. Van Dunné (ed.), *Non-Point Source River Pollution: The Case of the River Meuse*, 89–139.

Parr, N. and Hughes, M. (1993). 'The Relevance of Consumer Brands and Advertising in Competition Inquiries'. ECLR 157.

Pashigian, B. Peter (1985). 'Environmental Regulation: Whose Self-Interests Are Being Protected?'. 23 Economic Inquiry 551.

Passell, Peter (1998). 'Economic Scene: Payoff on a Stadium is Uncertain'. *New York Times*, 30 April, Section D, p. 1, col. 5.

Paul, Joel (1996). 'Competitive and Non-Competitive Regulatory Markets: The Regulation of Packaging Waste in the European Union'. In William Bratton, Joseph McCahery, Sol Picciotto, and Colin Scott (eds), *International Regulatory Competition and Coordination: Perspectives on Economic Regulation in Europe and the United States*. Oxford University Press.

Pauly, M. V. (1973). 'Income Redistribution as a Local Public Good'. 2 Journal of Public Economics 35–58.

Payne, Cymie (1998). 'Local Regulation of Natural Resources: Efficiency, Effectiveness, and Fairness of Wetlands Permitting in Massachusetts'. 28 Environmental Law 519.

Pearson, Charles (1994). 'Trade and Environment: The United States Experience'. Prepared for a United Nations Conference on Trade and Development, revised January 1994, 52.

Pelkmans, J. (1997). *European Integration. Methods and Economic Analysis*. Heerlen: Open University of the Netherlands.

Peltzman, Sam (1976). 'Toward a More General Theory of Regulation'. 19 Journal of Law and Economics 211.

Peltzman, S. and Tideman, T. (1972). 'Local v. National Pollution Control: Note'. American Economic Review.

Penrose, E. (1951). *The Economics of the Patent System*. Johns Hopkins Press.

Persson, T. and Tabellini, G. (1991). 'The Politics of 1992: Fiscal Policy and European Integration'. 59 Review of Economic Studies 689–701.

Persson, T. and Tabellini, G. (1994). 'Representative Democracy and Capital Taxation'. 55 Journal of Public Economics 53–70.

Petersen, K. F. V. (1995). 'Step-by-Step into the Future: Three Decades of Social Dialogue'. Research Report for the Swedish Centre for Working Life, Stockholm (mimeo).

Petersmann, Ernst-Ulrich (1996). 'International Competition Rules for Governments and Private Business'. 30 Journal of World Trade 5.

Peterson, Paul E. (1995). *The Price of Federalism*. Washington, DC: Brookings Institution.

Pfander, J. (1996). 'Environmental Federalism in Europe, and the United States: A Comparative Assessment of Regulation through the Agency of Member States'. In J. Braden, H. Folmer, and T. Ulen (eds), *Environmental Policy with Political and Economic Integration, the European Union and the United States*, 62–75.

Pharr, Susan and Badaracco Jr., Joseph (1986). 'Coping with Crisis: Environmental Regulation'. In Thomas McCraw (ed.), *America versus Japan*. Boston: Harvard Business School Press, 229–60.

Phillips, S. M. and Zecher, R. (1981). *The SEC and the Public Interest*. Cambridge: MIT Press, 53–89.

Pigou, Arthur (1918). *The Economics of Welfare*. London: Macmillan.

Piketty, T. (1996). 'A Federal Voting Mechanism to Solve the Fiscal Externality Problem'. 40 European Economic Review 3–17.

Pinto, C. (1998a). 'EC State Aid Rules and Tax Incentives: A U-Turn in Commission Policy? (Part I)'. European Taxation 295–309.

Pinto, C. (1998). 'EU and OECD to Fight Harmful Tax Competition: Has the Right Path Been Undertaken'. 26 Intertax 386–410.

Piore, Michael J. (1990). 'Labor Standards and Business Strategies'. In Stephen A. Herzenberg and Jorge F. Perez-Lopez (eds), *Labor Standards and Development in the Global Economy*. US Department of Labor, Bureau of International Affairs.

Piore, Michael and Sabel, Charles (1984). *The Second Industrial Divide*. New York: Basic Books.

Pitofsky, Robert (1998). 'Competition Policy in a Global Economy—Today and Tomorrow'. Remarks at European Institute's Eighth Annual Transatlantic Seminar on Trade and Investment, Washington, DC.

Pomp, Richard D. (1987). 'Reforming a State Income Tax'. 51 Albany Law Review 375.

Porter, Gareth (1998). 'Trade Competition and Pollution Standards: "Race to the Bottom" or "Stuck at the Bottom"?'. Journal of Environment and Development 133–51.

Porter, Michael E. (1985). *Competitive Advantage: Creating and Sustaining Superior Performance*. Collier Macmillan.

Porter, Michael (1990). *The Competitive Advantage of Nations*. New York: Free Press.

Portney, Paul R. (1990). 'Air Pollution Policy'. In Paul R. Portney (ed.), *Public Policies for Environmental Protection*. Washington, DC: Resources for the Future.

Portney, Paul R. (1994). 'The Contingent Valuation Debate: Why Economists Should Care'. 8 Journal of Economic Perspectives.

Posner, R. (1976). 'The Rights of Creditors of Affiliated Corporations'. 43 University of Chicago Law Review 499.

Posner, Richard A. (1982). 'Economics, Politics, and the Reading of Statutes and the Constitution'. 49 University of Chicago Law Review (Spring) 263.

Posner, R. (1986). *Economic Analysis of Law*, 3rd edn. Boston: Little Brown.

Radaelli, C. M. (1996). 'Fiscal Federalism as a Catalyst for Policy Development? In Search of a Framework for European Tax Harmonization'. 3 Journal of European Public Policy 402–20.

Radaelli, C. M. (1997). *The Politics of Corporate Taxation in the European Union: Knowledge and International Policy Agendas*. London: Routledge.

Raff, H. and Wilson, J. D. (1997). 'Income Redistribution and Well-Informed Local Governments'. 4 International Tax and Public Finance 407–27.

Ramsey, Frank P. (1927). 'A Contribution to the Theory of Taxation', 37 Economic Journal 47.

Rawls, John (1999). *The Law of Peoples*. Cambridge: Harvard University Press.

Regan, Donald (1986). 'The Supreme Court and State Protectionism: Making Sense of the Dormant Commerce Clause'. 84 Michigan Law Review 1091.

Rehbinder, Eckard (1997). 'Environmental Agreements: A New Instrument of Environmental Policy'. Jean Monnet Chair Paper, RSC 97/45.

Repetto, R. (1994). Trade and Sustainable Development, UNEP, Environment and Trade Series.

Revesz, Richard L. (1992). 'Rehabilitating Interstate Competition: Rethinking the "Race to the Bottom" Rationale for Federal Environmental Regulation'. 67 New York University Law Review 1210–54.

Revesz, Richard L. (1996). 'Federalism and Interstate Environmental Externalities'. 144 University of Pennsylvania Law Review 2341–2416.

Revesz, Richard L. (1997a). 'Environmental Regulation, Ideology, and the D.C. Circuit'. 83 Virginia Law Review 1717.

Revesz, R. L. (1997b). 'Federalism and Environmental Regulation. A Normative Critique'. In F. Ferejohn and B. R. Weingast (eds), *The New Federalism. Can the States be Trusted?* Stanford: Hoover Institution Press, 97–127.

Revesz, Richard L. (1997c). 'Federalism and Environmental Regulation: Lessons for the European Union and the International Community'. 83 Virginia Law Review 1331, 1339–40.

Revesz, Richard L. (1997d). *Foundations of Environmental Law and Policy*. New York: Oxford University Press.

Revesz, Richard (1997e). 'The Race to the Bottom and Federal Environmental Regulation: A Response to Critics'. 82 Minnesota Law Review 535.

Revesz, R. (2000). 'Environmental Regulation in Federal Systems'. In *Yearbook of European Environmental Law*. New York: Oxford University Press, 50–1.

Rice, David A. (1985). 'Product Quality Laws and the Economics of Federalism'. 65 Boston University Law Review 1.

Richards, J. and Evans, M. (1999). 'The European Directive on Settlement Finality in Payment and Securities Settlement Systems—Is this the End of the Story or just the Beginning?'. Journal of International Financial Markets 41–50.

Richards, John and Tucker, Richard (1988). *World Reforestation in the Twentieth Century*. Durham: Duke University Press.

Riedinger, Susan A. (1999). *Income Support and Social Services for Low-Income People in New York*. Washington, DC: Urban Institute.

Riker, W. H. (1964). *Federalism, Origin, Operation, and Significance*. Boston: Little Brown.

Ringquist, Evan J. (1993). *Environmental Protection at the State Level: Politics and Progress in Controlling Pollution*. Armonk, N: Sharpe, 76.

Rodden, Jonathan and Rose-Ackerman, Susan (1997a). 'Does Federalism Preserve Markets?'. 83 Virginia Law Review 1521.

Rodden, Jonathan, and Rose-Ackerman, Susan (1997b).'The Allocation of Government Authority: Does Federalism Preserve Markets?'. 83 Virginia Law Review 1521, 1564.

Rodrik, Dani (1996a). 'Coordination Failures and Government Policy: A Model with Applications to East Asia and Eastern Europe'. 17 Journal of International Economics 393.

Rodrik, Dani (1996b). 'Labor Standards in International Trade'. In Robert Z. Lawrence, Dani Rodrik, and John Whalley (eds), *Emerging Agenda for Global Trade*. Overseas Development Council.

Rodrik, Dani (1997). *Has Globalization Gone Too Far?* Washington: Institute for International Economics.

Rodrik, Dani and van Ypersele, T. (1999a). 'Capital Mobility, Distributive Conflict and International Tax Coordination'. National Bureau of Economic Research, Working Paper No.7150.

Rodrik, D. and van Ypersele, T. (1999b). 'When Does International Capital Mobility Require Tax Coordination?'. Center for Economic Policy Research, Working Paper No. 9927.

Roe, M. (1993). 'Takeover Politics'. In M. Blair (ed.), *The Deal Decade*. Washington, DC: Brookings Institution.

Rogers, Joel (1990). 'Divide and Conquer: Further "Reflections on the Distinctive Character of American Labor Laws" '. Wisconsin Law Review 1.

Rogers, J. and Streeck, W. (1994). 'Workforce Representation Overseas: the Works Councils Story'. In R. Freeman (ed.), *Working under Different Rules*. New York: Russell Sage Foundation.

Rogoff, K. (1999). 'International Institutions for Reducing Global Financial Instability'. 13 Journal of Economic Perspectives 21–42.

Rogowski, R. and Wilthagen, T. (eds) (1994). *Reflexive Labor Law*. Deventer: Kluwer.

Roin, Julie (2000). 'Competition and Evasion: Another Perspective on International Tax Competition' (unpublished manuscript).

Romano, Roberta (1985). 'Law as a Product: Some Pieces of the Incorporation Puzzle'. 1 Journal of L. Econ. & Org. 225.

Romano, Roberta (1987a). 'The Political Economy of Takeover Statutes'. 73 Virginia Law Review 111.

Romano, Roberta (1987b). 'The State Competition Debate in Corporate Law'. 8 Cardozo Law Review 709.

Romano, Roberta (1992). 'A Guide to Takeovers: Theory, Evidence and Regulation'. 9 Yale Journal on Regulation 119.

Romano, Roberta (1993a). 'Competition for Corporate Charters and the Lesson of Takeover Statutes'. 61 Fordham Law Review 843.

Romano, Roberta (1993b). *The Genius of American Corporate Law*. Washington: AEI.

Romano, Roberta (1998). 'Empowering Investors: A Market Approach to Securities Regulation'. 107 Yale Law Journal 2359, 2365–6.

Rome Convention (1980). 1980 Rome Convention on the Law Applicable to Contractual Obligation (consolidated version), 1998 OJ (C 27) 34.

Rose-Ackerman, Susan (1980). 'Risk Taking and Reelection: Does Federalism Promote Innovation?'. 9 Journal of Legal Studies 593.

Rose-Ackerman, Susan (1992). *Rethinking the Progressive Agenda: The Reform of the American Regulatory State*. New York: Free Press, 166–70.

Rose-Ackerman, Susan (1994). 'Environmental Policy and Federal Structure: A Comparison of The United States and Germany'. 47 Vanderbilt Law Review 1587.

Rose-Ackerman, Susan (1995). *Controlling Environmental Pollution. The Limits of Public Law in Germany and the United States*, 37–54.

Rose-Ackerman, Susan (1999). *Corruption and Government: Causes, Consequences and Reform*. New York: Cambridge University Press.

Rosen, Harvey S. (1999). *Public Finance* (5th edn). Irwin/McGraw Hill: 474.

Rothstein, Richard (1996). *Developing Reasonable Standards for Judging Whether Minimum Wage Levels in Developing Nations Are Effective*. Washington, DC: Economic Policy Institute.

Rowley, J. W. and Campbell A. N. (eds) (1999). 'Policy Directions for Global Merger Review'. A Special Report by the Global Forum for Competition and Trade Policy (Global Competition Review).

Sabel, Charles (1995). 'Learning by Monitoring: The Institutions of Economic Development'. In N. Smelser and R. Swedberg (eds), *Handbook of Economic Sociology*. Princeton: Princeton University Press.

Sabel, Charles, O'Rourke, Dara, and Fung, Archon (1999). 'Open Labor Standards: Towards a System of Rolling Rule Regulation of Labor Practices'. Discussion paper presented at the Annual Meeting of the World Bank, Seminar on Labor Rights, 28 September.

Saleska, Scott R. and Engel, Kirsten H. (1998). '"Facts are Stubborn Things": An Empirical Reality Check in the Theoretical Debate over the Race-to-the-Bottom in State Environmental Standard-Setting'. 8 Cornell Journal of Law and Public Policy 55.

Samuelson, P. A. (1954). 'The Pure Theory of Public Expenditures'. 36 Review of Economics and Statistics 387–8.

Sandler, Todd and Tschirhart, John T. (1980). 'The Economic Theory of Clubs: An Evaluative Survey'. 18 Journal of Economic Literature 1481.

Sapir, Andre (1996). 'Trade Liberalization and the Harmonization of Social Policies: Lessons from European Integration'. In Jagdish Bhagwati and Robert E. Hudec (eds), *Fair Trade and Harmonization: Prerequisites for Free Trade: Volume 1: Economic Analysis.* MIT Press.

Sarnoff, Joshua D. (1997). 'The Continuing Imperative (But Only from a National Perspective) for Federal Environmental Protection'. 7 Duke Environmental Law and Policy Forum 225.

Saudagaran, Shahrokh M. and Biddle, Gary C. (1995). 'Foreign Listing Location: A Study of MNCs and Stock Exchanges in Eight Countries'. 26 Journal of International Business Studies 319.

Saxena, R. B. (1988). 'Trade-related Aspects of Intellectual Property Rights and the Indian Patent Act: A Negotiating Strategy'. World Competition 81–116.

Scharpf, F. W. (1997). *Games Real Actors Play, Agent-Centered Institutionalism in Policy Research.* New York: Westview Press.

Schaub, Alex (1998). 'International Co-operation in Antitrust Matters: Making the Point in the Wake of the Boeing/MDD Proceedings'. Competition Policy Newsletter 1, 3.

Scherer, F. (1993). 'Pricing, Profits, and Technological Progress in the Pharmaceutical Industry'. 7 Journal of Economic Perspectives 97–115.

Schmidt, R. H., Hackethal, A., and Tyrell, M. (1999). 'Disintermediation and the Role of Banks in Europe: An International Comparison'. 8 Journal of Financial Intermediation 68–89.

Schmitthoff, C. (1973). 'The Future of the European Company Law Scene'. In C. Schmitthoff (ed.), *The Harmonization of European Company Law.* London: UKNCCL.

Schnapf, David (1982). 'State Hazardous Waste Programs Under the Federal Resource Conservation and Recovery Act'. 12 Environmental Law 679.

Schoenbrod, D. (1996). 'Why States, not EPA, should set Pollution Standards', 4 Regulation.

Schoettle, Ferdinand P. (1993). 'Facts, Law, and Economics in Commerce Clause Challenges to State Taxes'. 50 Tax Notes 1149 (11 March 1991).

Schuster, G. (1996). *Die internationale Anwendung des Börsenrechts. Völkerrechtlichen Rahmen und kollisionsrechtliche Praxis in Deutschland, England und den USA.* Berlin/Heidelberg/New York: Springer-Verlag.

Scotchmer, S. (1994). 'Public Goods and the Invisible Hand'. In J. M. Quigley and E. Smolensky (eds), *Modern Public Finance.* Cambridge: Harvard University Press, 93–119.

Scott, Kenneth (1977). 'The Dual Banking System: A Model of Competition in Regulation'. 30 Stanford Law Review 1.

Securities and Exchange Commission (1938). Accounting Series Release 4. 25 April.

Securities and Exchange Commission (1973). Accounting Series Release 150. 20 December.

Securities and Exchange Commission (1990). Offshore Offers and Sales, Securities Act Release No. 6893 [1989–90 Transfer Binder] Fed. Sec. L. Rep. (CCH) 84, 524, (24 April 1990) at 15–16, 80, 665.

Securities and Exchange Commission, Office of the Chief Economist (1986). The Effects of Poison Pills on the Wealth of Target Shareholders (23 October 1986).

Seligman, Joel (1993). 'The Historical Need for a Mandatory Corporate Disclosure System'. 9 J. Corp. L. 1, 10.

Sen, Amartya (1999). 'Global Justice: Beyond International Equity'. In I. Kaul, I. Grunberg, and M. Stern (eds), *Global Public Goods: International Cooperation in the 21st Century.* New York: Oxford University Press.

Shapiro, Fred R. (1991). 'The Most-Cited Articles from the Yale Law Journal'. 100 Yale Law Journal 1449.

Shaviro, Daniel (1993). *Federalism in Taxation: The Case for Greater Uniformity*. AEI Press.

Shaviro, Daniel (1997). 'The Minimum Wage, the Earned Income Tax Credit, and Optimal Subsidy Policy'. 64 University of Chicago Law Review 405, 411–14.

Shaviro, Daniel (2000a). 'Endowment and Inequality'. In Joseph Thorndike and Dennis Ventry (eds), *Tax Justice Reconsidered: New Looks at a Forgotten Concept*. Urban Institute Press.

Shaviro, Daniel (2000b). *Making Sense of Social Security Reform*. University of Chicago Press.

Shaviro, Daniel (2000c). *When Rules Change: An Economic and Political Analysis of Retroactivity and Transition Relief*. University of Chicago Press, 93–7.

Shelton, Joanna R. (1998). 'Competition Policy: What Chance for International Rules?'. Remarks made at Wilton Park, UK.

Silva, Eduardo (1996). 'Democracy, Market Economies and Environmental Policy in Chile'. 38(4) Journal of International Studies and World Affairs, Winter 1996, 1–33.

Sinn, H. W. (1998). 'European Integration and the Future of the Welfare State'. Center for Economic Policy, Working Paper No. 153.

Skowrenek, Stephen (1982). *Building a New American State*. Cambridge: Cambridge University Press.

Slaughter, Anne-Marie (1997). 'The Real New World Order'. 76 Foreign Affairs 183.

Slaughter, Anne-Marie (1999). 'Governing the Global Economy through Government Networks'. In *The Role of Law in International Politics* (in publication).

Slinger, G. and Deakin, S. (1999). 'Company Law as an Instrument of Inclusion: Re-regulating Stakeholder Relations'. ESRC Centre for Business Research, Working Paper No. 145, University of Cambridge.

Slot, Piet Jan (1996). 'Harmonization'. 21 European Law Review 378.

Smith, Katherine and Sofianos, George (1997). 'The Impact of an NYSE Listing on the Global Trading of Non-U.S. Stocks'. Working Paper 97-02 (NYSE).

Snyder, F. (1994). 'EMU—Metaphor for Monetary Union? Institutions, Rules and Types of Regulation'. In Renaud Dehousse (ed.), *Europe After Maastricht, An Ever Closer Union*. Munich: Law Books in Europe, 63–99.

Smith, R. C. and Walter, I. (1997). *Global Banking*. Oxford: Oxford University Press.

Smith, R. C. (1999). 'The European Securities Industry under a Single Currency'. In J. Dermine and P. Hillion (eds), *European Capital Markets with a Single Currency*. Oxford: Oxford University Press, 310–49.

Sonnenfeld, David (1999). 'Social Movements and Ecological Modernization; the Transformation of Pulp and Paper Manufacturing'. Presented at the annual meeting of the American Sociological Association, Chicago, Illinois, August 1999.

Spar, Debora (1998). 'The Spotlight and the Bottom Line: How Multinationals Export Human Rights'. 77(2) Foreign Affairs, March/April 1998, 7–12.

Spar, Debora and Yoffie, David (unpublished paper). 'A Race to the Bottom or Governance from the Top'.

Special Issue (1999). 'Grenzüberschreitende Sitzverlegung von Gesellschaften in Europa'. 28 Zeitschrift für Unternehmens- und Gesellschaftsrecht, 1–156.

Spindler, Charles J. and Forrester, John P. (1993). 'Economic Development Policy: Explaining Policy Among Competing Models'. 29 Urban Affairs Quarterly 28.

Srinivasan, T. N. (1999). 'Comment on Bagwell and Staiger'. In Alan V. Deardorff and Robert M. Stern (eds), *Social Dimensions of U.S. Trade Policy*.

Steil, B. (ed.) (1994). *International Financial Market Regulation.* Chichester: John Wiley and Sons.

Steil, B. (1996a). 'Equity Trading IV: The ISD and the Regulation of European Market Structure'. In B. Steil (ed.), *The European Equity Markets, The State of the Union and an Agenda for the Millennium.* London: The Royal Institute of International Affairs, 113–45.

Steil, B. (ed.) (1996b). *The European Equity Markets, The State of the Union and an Agenda for the Millennium.* London: The Royal Institute of International Affairs.

Steiner, Josephine (1994). 'Subsidiarity under the Maastricht Treaty'. In David O'Keefe (ed.), *Legal Issues of the Maastricht Treaty.* London: Chancery Law Publishers.

Steinzor, Rena (1999). 'Reinventing Environmental Regulation Through the Government Performance and Results Act: Are the States Ready for the Devolution?'. 29 Environmental Law Reporter 10074.

Stephan, Paul B. (1999). 'Regulatory Cooperation and Competition — The Search for Virtue'. In G. Bermann and P. Lindseth (eds), *Transatlantic Regulatory Cooperation.* Columbia conference book, in publication.

Stern, Arthur C. (1982). 'History of Air Pollution Legislation in the United States'. 32 Journal of Air Pollution Control Association 44.

Stern, Paula (1997). 'The Transatlantic Business Dialogue: A New Model for Trade Expansion and Regulatory Harmonization' (document available at <http:www.tabd.org/resources/content/stern2.html>).

Stewart, Richard B. (1977). 'Pyramids of Sacrifice? Problems of Federalism in Mandating State Implementation of National Environmental Policy'. 86 Yale Law Journal 1196–1272.

Stewart, Richard B. (1992). 'Environmental Law in the United States and the European Community: Spillovers, Cooperation, Rivalry, Institutions'. 1992 University of Chicago Legal Forum 41.

Stewart, Richard B. (1993). 'Environmental Regulation and International Competitiveness'. 102 Yale Law Journal 2039.

Stigler, George J. (1971). 'The Theory of Economic Regulation'. 2 Bell Journal of Economics 3.

Stiglitz, J. E. (1988, 2nd edn). *Economics of the Public Sector.* New York: Norton.

Stone, Katherine (1996). 'Labor in the Global Economy: Four Approaches to Transnational Labour Regulation'. In William Bratton, Joseph McCahery, Sol Picciotto, and Colin Scott (eds), *International Regulatory Competition and Coordination: Perspectives on Economic Regulation in Europe and the United States.* Oxford University Press.

Streeck, W. (1990). 'La dimensione sociale del mercato unico europeo: verso un economia non regolato?'. 28 Stato e Mercato 29.

Streeck, W. (1999). 'Comparative Solidarity: Rethinking the "European social model"'. MPIfG Working Paper 99/8, Max Planck Institut für Gesellschaftsforschung, Cologne.

Streeck, Wolfgang (1997). 'Citizenship Under Regime Competition: The Case of the "European Works Councils"'. Working Paper 97/3, Max Planck Institut für Gesellschaftsforschung.

Summers, Lawrence H. (1998). 'Some Simple Economics of Mandated Benefits'. 79 American Economic Review, May 1988, Papers and Proceedings 177.

Sun, Jeanne-Mey and Pelkmans, Jacques (1995). 'Regulatory Competition in the Single Market'. 33 Journal of Common Market Studies 67, 82–8.

Sundaram, Anant K. and Logue, Dennis E. (1996). 'Valuation Effects of Foreign Company Listings on U.S. Exchanges'. 27 Journal of International Business Studies 67.

Swire, Peter P. (1996). 'The Race to Laxity and the Race to Undesirability: Explaining Failures in Competition Among Jurisdictions in Environmental Law'. 14 Yale Journal on Regulation 67.

Sykes, Alan O. (1995). *Product Standards for Internationally Integrated Goods and Markets.* Washington: Brookings Institution.

Sykes, Alan O. (1999). 'The (Limited) Role of Regulatory Harmonization in International Goods and Services Markets'. 2 Journal of International Economic Law 49.

Symposium (1998). 'Symposium on Second-Best Theory and Law & Economics'. Chicago-Kent Law Review 73.

Terra, B. and Wattel, P. (1997, 2nd edn). *European Tax Law.* Deventer: Kluwer.

Teubner, G. (1993). *Law as an Autopoietic System.* Oxford: Blackwell.

Teubner, G. (1994). 'Company Interest. The Public Interest of the Enterprise in Itself'. In R. Rogowski and T. Wilthagen (eds), *Reflexive Labor Law.* Deventer: Kluwer.

Thieffry, G. (1999). 'Towards a European Securities Commission'. October 1999 International Financial Law Review 14–18.

Tiebout, C. (1956). 'A Pure Theory of Local Expenditures'. 64 Journal of Political Economy 416–24.

Tirez, D. (1997). 'Easdaq Benefits from European Framework'. International Financial Law Review, November: 11–15.

Tobey, James A. (1990). 'The Effects of Domestic Environmental Policies on Patterns of World Trade: An Empirical Test'. 43 Kyklos 191–209.

Toth, A. G. (1994). 'A Legal Analysis of Subsidiarity'. In David O'Keefe (ed.), *Legal Issues of the Maastricht Treaty.* London: Chancery Law Publishers.

Trachtman, Joel (1992). 'L'Etat, C'est Nous: Sovereignty, Economic Integration and Subsidiarity'. 33 Harvard International Law Journal 459.

Trachtman, Joel P. (1993). 'International Regulatory Competition, Externalization and Jurisdiction'. 34 Harvard International Law Journal 47.

Trachtman, Joel P. (1994). 'Conflict of Laws and Accuracy in the Allocation of Government Responsibility'. 26 Vanderbilt Journal of Transnational Law 975.

Trachtman, Joel P. (1996). 'The Theory of the Firm and the Theory of the International Economic Organization: Toward Comparative Institutional Analysis'. 17 Northwestern Journal of International Law & Business 470.

Trachtman, Joel P. (1997). 'Externalities and Extraterritoriality: The Law and Economics of Prescriptive Jurisdiction'. In Jagdeep Bhandari and Alan O. Sykes (eds), *Economic Dimensions in International Law: Comparative And Empirical Perspectives.* New York: Cambridge University Press.

Trachtman, Joel P. (1998). 'Cyberspace, Sovereignty, Jurisdiction and Modernism'. 5 Indiana Journal of Global Legal Studies 5: 561.

Trachtman, Joel P. (1999). 'The Domain of WTO Dispute Resolution'. 40 Harvard International Law Journal 333.

Trebilcock, Michael and Howse, Robert (1998). 'Trade Liberalization and Regulatory Diversity: Reconciling Competitive Markets with Competitive Politics'. 6 European Journal of Law and Economics 5–37.

Trubek, David M. and Rothstein, Jeffrey S. (1998). 'Transnational Regimes and Advocacy in Industrial Relations: A "Cure" for Globalization?'. Working Paper Series on Political Economy of Legal Change No. 4.

Tucker, E. (1999). 'New Commissioner Opposes Harmonizing Taxes'. Financial Times (7 September).

Tullock (1969). 'Federalism: Problems of Scale'. 6 Public Choice 19.

Tussie, Diana and Vasquez, Patricia (1997). 'The FTAA, Mercosur and the Environment'. Prepared for a Round Table on Trade and the Environment, UCLA, April.

US EPA (US Environmental Protection Agency) (1993). International Trade in Environmental Protection Equipment.

US EPA (1997a). Semiannual Report to the Congress 1 October 1996–31 March 1997.

US EPA (1997b). Semiannual Report to the Congress, 1 October 1997–31 March 1997.

US EPA (1998a). Audit Report: Consolidated Report on OECA's Oversight of Regional and State Air Enforcement Programs, Report No. E1GAE7-03-0045-8100244.

US EPA (1998b). Semiannual Report to the Congress, 1 October 1997–31 March 1998.

US EPA (1998c). Semiannual Report to the Congress, 1 April 1998–30 September 1998.

US EPA (1999a). Semiannual Report to the Congress, 1 October 1998–31 March 1999.

US EPA (1999b). Audit Report: Identification and Enforcement of RCRA significant Non-Compliers by EPA Region III and the Virginia Department of Environmental Quality, Report No. 1999-P-00215.

US Environmental Protection Agency Partnership (1998). 1998/99 Environmental Performance Partnership Agreement Between the Florida Department of Environmental Protection and Region IV of the U.S. Environmental Protection Agency (document available at: http://www.epa.gov/region04/oeapages/intergov/ppappg.htm).

US General Accounting Office (1995). 'EPA and the States: Environmental Challenges Require a Better Working Relationship'. Report No. GAO/RCED-95-64.

US General Accounting Office (1996). 'Water Pollution: Differences Among the States in Issuing Permits Limiting the Discharge of Pollutants'. Letter Report, GAO/RCED-96-42.

US General Accounting Office (1998). Hazardous Waste Sites: State Cleanup Practices. GAO/RCED (December).

Uchentagen, U. (1990). 'The GATT Negotiations Concerning Copyright and Intellectual Property Protection'. 21 International Review of Industrial Property Law & Copyright 765–82.

Ulen, Thomas S. (1998a). 'Courts, Legislatures, and the General Theory of Second Best in Law and Economics'. 73 Chicago-Kent Law Review189.

Ulen, Thomas (1998b). 'Economic and Public Choice Forces in Federalism'. 6 George Mason Law Review 921.

Ullrich, H. (1989). 'GATT: Industrial Property Protection, Fair Trade and Development'. In Beier and Schricker (eds), *GATT or WTO?* VCH: 127–59.

Ullrich, Hans (1995). 'TRIPS: Adequate Protection, Inadequate Trade, Adequate Competition Policy'. 1 Pacific Law and Policy Journal 153.

Unger, Roberto and Cui, Zhiyuan (1994). 'China in the Russian Mirror'. New Left Review, November/December: 79–87.

Van Alstyne, W.W. (1985). 'The Second Death of Federalism'. 83 Michigan Law Review 1709.

Van Beers, C. and Van den Bergh, C. J. M. (1997). 'An Empirical Multi-Country Analysis of the Impact of Environmental Regulations on Trade Flows'. 50 Kyklos 25.

Van den Bergh, R. (1994a). Subsidiariteit rechtseconomisch bekeken. Adieu Bruxelles.

Van den Bergh, Roger (1994b). 'The Subsidiarity Principle in European Economic Law:

Some Insights from Law and Economics'. 1 Maastricht Journal of European and Comparative Law 337.

Van den Bergh, R. (1996). 'Economic Criteria for Applying the Subsidiarity Principle in the European Community'. 16 International Review of Law and Economics 363–83.

Van den Bergh, Roger (1998). 'Subsidiarity as an Economic Demarcation Principle and the Emergence of European Private Law'. 5 Maastricht Journal of European and Comparative Law 129–52.

Van den Bergh, Roger (1999). Economics in a legal strait-jacket: the difficult reception of economic analysis in European Law (paper presented at the workshop Empirical Research and Legal Realism. Setting the Agenda, Haifa, 6–9 June 1999).

Van den Bergh, Roger, Faure, Michael, and Lefevere, Jürgen (1996). 'The Subsidiarity Principle in European Environmental Law: An Economic Analysis'. In Erling Eide and Roger Van den Bergh (eds), *Law and Economics of the Environment*. Oslo: Juridisk Forlag.

Van Dunné, J. (1991). Transboundary Pollution and Liability: the Case of the River Rhine.

Viandier, A. (1998). 'Free Movement and Mobility of Companies'. 9 European Business Law Review 301–6.

Viénot, M. (1995). 'Rapport sur le Conseil d'Administration des Sociétés cotées'. 8 Revue de Droit des Affaires Internationales, 372.

Villiers, C. (1998). *European Company Law: Towards Democracy?* Aldershot: Dartmouth.

Vitols, S., Casper, S., Soskice, D., and Woolcock, S. (1997). *Corporate Governance in Large British and German Companies*. London: Anglo-German Foundation for the Study of Industrial Society.

Vogel, David (1989). *Fluctuating Fortunes: The Political Power of Business in America*. New York: Basic Books.

Vogel, David (1993). 'Representing Diffuse Interests in Environmental Policy-making'. In R. Kent Weaver and Bert K. Rockman (eds), *Do Institutions Matter?*. Washington DC: Brookings Institution.

Vogel, David (1995). *Trading Up: Consumer and Environmental Regulation in the Global Economy*. Cambridge, MA: Harvard University Press.

Vogel, David (1997). *Barriers or Benefits: Regulation in Transatlantic Trade*. Washington DC: Brookings Institution Press.

Vogel, David (1998). 'EU Environmental Policy and the GATT/WTO'. In J. Golub (ed.), *Regulatory Reform and EU Environmental Agreements*. London: Routledge, 142–60.

Vogel, David (1999). 'Israeli Environmental Policy in Comparative Perspective'. Israel Affairs, 5 Winter–Spring, 246–65.

Von Hase, Y. and M. (1992). 'Intellectual Property Protection and International Trade: Exhaustion of Rights Revisited'. World Competition: 1115–31.

von Moltke, Konrad (1993). 'Environmental Protection and its Effects on Competitiveness'. In Haraldo Munoz and Robin Rosenberg (eds), *Difficult Liaison: Trade and the Environment in the Americas*. New Brunswick: Transaction Publishers, 5–20.

Wade, Robert (1996). 'Globalization and its Limits: Reports of the Death of the National Economy are Greatly Exaggerated'. In Suzanne Berger and Ronald Dore (eds), *National Diversity and Global Capitalism*. Ithaca: Cornell University Press, 60–88.

Wald, Matthew (1994). 'Harder Auto Emission Rules Agreed to by Eastern States'. New York Times, 2 February, p. 1, A6.

Wall Street Journal (1999). 'Bitter Rivals Jointly Seek Major Changes in the Markets'. 1 October, c11.

Walter, I. (1988). *Global Competition in Financial Services*. Cambridge, MA: Harvard University Press.

Walter, I. (1999). 'Financial Services Strategies in the Euro-Zone'. 17 European Management Journal 447–65.

Weiler, Paul (1983). 'Promises to Keep: Securing Workers' Rights to Self-Organization Under the NLRA'. 96 Harvard Law Review 1769.

Weiler, Paul (1990). *Governing the Workplace*. Cambridge, MA: Harvard University Press.

Weingast, Barry (1995). 'The Economic Role of Political Institutions: Market Preserving Federalism and Economic Development'. 11 Journal of Law, Economics and Organization 1.

Weir, Margaret (1992). *Politics and Jobs: The Boundaries of Employment Policy in the United States*. Princeton: Princeton University Press.

Weiss, Edith Brown (1993). 'Environmentally Sustainable Competitiveness: A Comment'. 102 Yale Law Journal 2123.

Weiss, Elliot J. and White, Lawrence J. (1987). 'Of Econometrics and Indeterminacy: A Study of Investors' Reactions to "Changes" in Corporate Law'. 75 California Law Review 551.

Wellens, K. C. and Borchardt, G. M. (1989). 'Soft Law in European Community Law'. 14 European Law Review 267–321.

Wernicke, T. (1996). *Privates Bankvertragsrecht im EG-Binnenmarkt*. Baden-Baden: Nomos Verlagsgesellschaft.

Wheeler, S. (1997). 'Works Councils: Towards Stakeholding?'. 24 Journal of Law and Society 44–64.

White, Lawrence J. (1996). 'Competition versus Harmonization—An Overview of International Regulation of Financial Services'. In Claude Barfield (ed.), *International Financial Markets: Harmonization versus Competition*. Washington DC: AEI Press, 5, 39.

Wildasin, D. E. (1991). 'Income Redistribution in a Common Labor Market'. 81 American Economic Review 757–75.

Williamson, Oliver E. (1985). 22 The Economic Institutions of Capitalism.

Williamson, Oliver (1994). 'Comparative Economic Organization: the Analysis of Discrete Structural Alternatives'. 36 Admin. Sci. Q. 219.

Wils, Wouter (1994). 'Subsidiarity and EC Environmental Policy: Taking People's Concerns Seriously'. 6 Journal of Environmental Law 85–90.

Wilson, J. D. (1985). 'Optimal Property Taxation in the Presence of Inter-Regional Capital Mobility'. 18 Journal of Regional Economics 73–89.

Wilson, J. D. (1996). 'Capital Mobility and Environmental Standards: Is there a Theoretical Basis for a Race to the Bottom?'. In J. Bhagwati and R. E. Hudec (eds), *Fair Trade and Harmonization: Prerequisites for Free Trade? Volume I: Economic Analysis*. Cambridge, MA: MIT Press, 393–427.

Winter, Ralph (1989). 'The "Race to the Top" Revisited: A Comment on Eisenberg'. 89 Columbia Law Review 1526.

Winter, Ralph K. (1977). 'State Law, Shareholder Protection, and the Theory of the Corporation'. 6 Journal of Legal Studies 251.

Wolff, G. (1993). 'The Commission's Programme for European Company Law Harmonisation: the Winding Road to a Uniform European Company Law?'. In M. Andenas and S. Kenyon-Slade (eds), *EC Financial Market Regulation and Company Law*. London: Sweet & Maxwell.

Wolkoff, Michael J. (1992). 'Is Economic Development Decision Making Rational?'. 27 Urban Affairs 340.

Wolman, Harold (1988). 'Local Economic Development Policy: What Explains the Divergence Between Policy Analysis and Political Behavior?'. 10 Journal of Urban Affairs 19.

Woolcock, S. (1996). 'Competition among Rules in the Single European Market'. In W. Bratton, J. McCahery, S. Picciotto, and C. Scott (eds), *International Regulatory Competition and Coordination. Perspectives on Economic Regulation in Europe and the United States*. Oxford: Clarendon Press, 289–321.

World Trade Organization (1997a). India—Patent Protection for Pharmaceutical and Agricultural Chemical Products, 5 September 1997, WTO Doc. WT/DS50/R (report of the panel), available in 1997 WL 556224.

World Trade Organization (1997b). Report of the Appellate Body on India-Patent Protection for Pharmaceutical and Agricultural Chemical Products, 19 December 1997, WTO Doc. WT/DS50/AB/R.

World Trade Organization (1998). United States: Import Restrictions of Certain Shrimp and Shrimp Products. 1998 WL 720123 (report of the Appellate Body).

World Trade Organization Secretariat (14 November 1996). Report of the WTO Committee on Trade and Environment. PRESS/TE 014.

Wymeersch, E. (ed.) (1994). *Further Perspectives in Financial Integration in Europe*. Berlin/New York: Walter de Gruyter.

Xanthaki, H. (1999). 'The Secondary Establishment of Companies within the EU: Challenge or Missed Opportunity?'. 10 European Business Law Review 120–39.

Xing, Y. and Kolstad, Charles (1995). Do Lax Environmental Regulations Attract Foreign Investment? (working paper in economics, University of California).

Yandle, G. (1999). 'Public Choice at the Intersection of Environmental Law and Economics'. 8 European Journal of Law and Economics 5–27.

Young, Ian (1999). 'Corporation Tax: 12.5% or 19%'. TaxMonitor (visited July 1999) <http://www.kpmg.ie./taxmon/1999/corptax.htm>.

Young, Oran R. (1994). *International Governance: Protecting the Environment in a Stateless Society*. Ithaca: Cornell University Press.

Zaelke, Durwood, Orbuch, Paul, and Housman, Robert (eds) (1993). *Trade and the Environment: Law, Economics and Policy*. Washington DC: Island Press.

Zagaris, Bruce (1992). 'The Transformation of Environmental Enforcement Cooperation Between Mexico and the United States in the Wake of NAFTA'. 18 North Carolina Journal of International Law and Commercial Regulation 61–132.

Zarsky, Lyuba and Hunter, Jason (working paper). 'Environmental Cooperation at APEC: The First Five Years'. Nautilus Institute for Security and Sustainable Development, Working Paper 6.

Zeiger, R. (1995). *The CIO: 1935–1955*. Chapel Hill: University of North Carolina Press.

Zodrow, G. R. and Mieszkowski, P. (1986). 'Pigou, Tiebout, Property Taxation and the Underprovision of Local Public Goods'. 19 Journal of Urban Economics 356–70.

Zurstrassen, P. (1998). 'The European Investment Funds Industry in 1997'. In OECD, *Institutional Investors in the New Landscape*. Paris: OECD, 207–31.

Index

ACEA *see* Association of European Automobile Manufacturers
acid rain 34–5
Ackerman, Bruce A. 12, 273
AFL *see* American Federation of Labor
agglomeration effects 132–3
Agreement on Social Policy 247
Agreement on Trade-Related Aspects of Intellectual Property Rights xix, 366–7, 368, 371, 374–5, 378–80, 381
air pollution 8, 12
Alesina, A. 187
Alstott, Anne L. 27
Alva, C. 209
ambient quality standards 278
American Federation of Labor 117, 123
Amihud, Y. 107, 204
anti-takeover statutes 76
antitrust law *see* competition law
Appleborne, Peter 64
apportionment 56–7
area of effect, environmental problems 135
Armour, J. 203
ASP *see* Agreement on Social Policy
Association of European Automobile Manufacturers 45–6
association, right of 112, 125–8
Atleson, James 117
Auerbach, Alan 61, 180
automatic teller machines 102–3
automobile emission standards 335–6
automobile pollution 13
Avi-Yonah, Reven S. 61, 64, 67
Ayres, Ian 25, 212

Backes, Chris 264
Badaracco Jr., Joseph 331, 336
Baden Fuller, C. 365
Bagwell, Style 313 (n. 3), 314 (n. 5)
Baltensperger, E. 230
Bank of Credit and Commerce International 230
Banking Advisory Committee 233
banking charters 25–6, 96, 101
banking regulation 101–3
Barenberg, Mark xv–xvi, 111–34, 320 (n. 12)
Barnard, C. 199
Bartik, Timothy 6, 334
Basle Committee on Banking Supervision 229
Baudru, D. 233
Baumol, William J. x, 34
BCCI *see* Bank of Credit and Commerce International
Bebchuk, Lucian Arye xii, xv, 68–94, 206–7, 209, 219, 293 (n. 6)
Becker, Gary S. 6
Becker, Randy 318
Begg, P.F. 87–8
Beier, D. 368
benchmarking 329
Bendar, J. 168
Bensel, Richard 123, 126
Benston, G.J. 234
Bercusson, Brian xvii, 113, 127, 241–62, 319 (n. 11)
Bergstrom, C. 185
Berman, Eli 6
Bertrand, Marianne 322
Besen, S. 365
Besley, T. 174
Betlem, Chris 264
Bhagwati, Jagdish vii, 31
bidders, rules restricting 75–6, 78–80
Biddle, Gary C. 299 (n. 10)
Biggs, S. 183
Black, J. 79, 80, 211, 299
Boadway, R. 163, 165
Bok, Derek 119 (n. 5), 121
bonds 175
Boot, A.W.A. 233
Borchardt, G.M. 174
Bovenberg, L. 57
Braithwaite, John 336
Branch, Tammy 14
Brand, R.A. 235
Branson, Douglas M. 87
Bratton, W. xii, xvi, 31, 157–89, 291 (n. 2), 293, 293 (n. 8), 294, 296, 312
Bratton, W. *et al.* 241
Bredahl, Maury E. 42
Brennan, G. 158, 185–6
Breton, Albert 39, 43, 291 (n. 2), 294, 295
Brinkhorst, L. 19 (n. 3)
British City Code *see* City Code
Bronkers, Marco 41
Brown, Drusila K. 313 (n. 3)
brownfield sites 13–14
Bryner, Gary 336
Buchanan, J.N. 158, 185–6
Bucovetsky, S. 167, 168
Bui, Linda 6
'bundling' effect:
  capital markets 292
  intellectual property 370–1
business combination statutes 80

Butler, Henry N. xii, 25, 26, 35, 95, 99, 101, 135, 346 (n. 22)

Cairncross, Frances 333
Calabresi, Stephen G. 27, 33
Caldwell, Lynton K. 15
'California effect' 335–8
Calsyn, Dylan S. 27
Campbell, A.N. 362
capital import/export neutrality 64–5
capital income tax 61–2
capital mobility ix
capital tax 166–7, 174–9, 185–6
capital/labour rate distortion 181–2
capture 142–3, 282
Card, David 317 (n. 8)
Carney, William J. 74, 76, 85 (n. 23)
Carrol, John 340 (n. 16)
Cary, William L. xii, 68–9, 193
Casella, A. 266
Cashin, Sheryll G. 27
Cass, D. 158
Cassis de Dijon jurisprudence 44
Castaneda, Jorge 125
Cave, M. 233
CEC *see* Commission of the European Communities
centralization vii–xi
Centros case 190–1, 198–203
Chang, H. 242
Charnovitz, Steve 38, 42
Charny, David xviii, 36, 130 (n. 13), 209, 311–29, 316 (n. 7)
charter amendments 83–4
Cheffins, Brian 203–6, 208
Chen, Show-Mao 305
Chirelstein, Marvin A. 79
Choi, Steven 69 (n. 2), 205 (n. 1), 289 (n. 1), 294, 305, 308 (n. 20)
choice of law 290–1
Choper, Jesse H. 80
Christiansen, Thomas 357
CIO *see* Congress of Industrial Organization
City Code on Takeovers and Mergers 70, 87–9
City Panel on Takeovers and Mergers 87–8, 214
Clark, Robert C. 71 (n. 4)
Clean Air Act 8–9, 12, 13, 139 (nn. 9–10), 146 (n. 21)
co-evolution 210
co-operation:
- federal-state 42
- government-NGOs 44–6
- US-EU 41

co-opetition *see* regulatory co-opetition
Coase, Ronald 50, 307
Coase's theory of the firm 50, 130
Coates, John C. 87
Code of Conduct on Business Taxation:
- assessment 176–9
- drafting 159
- fiscal federalism 176–9, 179–82
- potentially harmful tax measures 172–4, 178–9, 180–2, 184
- status 159, 169, 172–4, 178–9
- subsidiarity 157, 179–82
- tax competition 182–3

Codex Alimentarius 42
Coffee, John C. Jr. 209, 299, 300, 305
Cohen, Joshua 115 (n. 4)
Cohen, Marc 268, 268–9, 276
collective bargaining 112, 121, 254
collective representativity 257–8
command-and-control regulation 141–2
Commerce Clause 58–9, 150–1, 152 (n. 36)
Commission of the European Communities 171–2, 177, 179–80, 246 (n. 2), 247 (n. 3)
Community Trade Mark 370
Compa, Lance 125
company law:
- EU: company, concept 195, 197; conclusions 216–17; convergence 209; corporate governance 194–8, 208–9; Directives 194; harmonization 191–5; insider/outsider systems 196–7; public choice issues 216; reflexive harmonization 209–13; regulatory competition issues 191; *siège réel* doctrine 190, 200–3; stakeholder 194–8; treaty basis 192–3
- UK 205–6
- US 209

comparative advantage 54, 130–1, 335
competition law:
- abscence 354–5
- borderless conception 356–9
- competition EU–US 352–3
- convergence 356–7, 360
- corporate law analogy 351
- definition 348–9
- developing countries 353–4
- diversity 349, 360
- efficiency 352–5
- enforcement 359
- environmental law analogy 352
- EU 350
- export cartels 355
- externalities 358–9
- extraterritoriality 359–60
- forums 360–2
- global, case for 357–9
- hegemony, global 356–7
- history 350
- international perspective 357–9, 362–3

national interest 353–6
proliferation 358
race to the bottom 352, 353–4, 362
trade issues 361
US, efficiency 352 (n. 2)
World Trade Organization 350–1, 360–1
competitiveness:
environmental regulation vii, 6–7, 18–19, 30, 41, 270–4, 332–5
labour regulation 122
product standards ix–x, 336–40
Congress of Industrial Organization 117, 123
consumer protection 236
contractual framework, EU 235–6
coordinating mechanisms, effect 122–5
corporate charters 24–5, 68–9
corporate control market 215
see also takeovers
corporate governance 194–8, 208–9
corporate law, state competition 68–71, 90–3
Correa, C. 373 (n. 22)
Cosean bargaining 176–7, 268–9
Cottier, Thomas 364 (n. 1)
Court of First Instance of the EC 256–9
Crandall, Robert W. 12
Cremer, H. 164, 166, 178
cross-listing 299–300
Cui, Zhiyuan 125
Currie, David 58

Dalhuisen, J.H. 237
Danthine, J.-P. 223, 224, 225, 232
Dashwood, Alan 30
Davis, Charles E. 137
Davis, Mike 117, 123–4, 126
De Witte, Bruno 285
Deakin, Simon xvi, 190–217, 198, 204, 207, 210, 211, 212, 213, 214, 215
Dean, Judith 333 (n. 6)
Deardorff, Alan V. 313 (n. 3), 316 (n. 7)
decentralization:
cooperative 42
coordinated 122–8
enforcement 147–50
environmental regulation 145–50
presumption viii, 32–3, 158–9, 267
securities regulation 105–9
see also centralization; subsidiarity
defensive tactics 76–8, 80–6, 88
Delaware:
incorporation effect 36
takeover law: Cary, William 68–9; defensive tactics 76–7, 81–3, 88; legislative protections 84–5; managers preferences 71–2; uncertainty 70, 86–7
tax revenue 204
theoretical perspectives 191

Demaret, Paul xix, 158, 364–81, 373 (n. 22), 378 (n. 35), 379 (n. 37)
democratic deficit 255–9
democratic theory, labour regulation 125–8, 130, 325–7
DeMott, Debora A. 88
Demsetz, Harold 295
Depaolo, Anthony 14
deposit insurance, federal 102, 105
deregulation 103
Dermine, J. 224, 230
destination principle 170
developing countries:
competition law 368–9
intellectual property 368–9, 377, 380, 381
devolution, environmental regulation 145–50
Dewitt, Diane 331
Diamond, P. 55
direct taxes 170–1
distortionary effects 162, 164, 180–2, 185–6
distortions of competition xvii
Dolvik, J.E. 248
Dorf, Michael 112, 128, 329
Dowding, J. 183
Drury, R. 206
Dua, André 37
Dwyer, John P. 136
dynamic of regulatory competition 121

Easterbrook, Frank H. 33, 68, 72, 81, 91–2, 191, 203, 208, 210, 228, 299
ECB *see* European Central Bank
ECOFIN *see* Economy and Finance Council
Economic and Social Committee 251
economies of scale:
environmental regulation 136–7
financial regulation 229
regulating xiii
securities regulation 305–6
Economy and Finance Council 172, 174
Economy and Finance Council *see* Code of Conduct
ECOSOC *see* Economic and Social Committee
Edwards and Keen model 187–9
Edwards, V. 181, 187, 188, 193
Ehrenberg, Robert 132
Ehrlich, I. 278
Eichenberger, R. 162, 266
Einhorn, T. 373 (n. 22)
Eisenberg, Melvin 73 (n. 6)
Elliott, E. Donald 12, 273
Ellis, M. 180
Ellison, G. 132
emission limit values 278–81
employee representation 195
employment *see* labour
endogeneity of interest groups 113, 121

enforcement 147–8
Engel, Kirsten xii, xvi, 7, 135–55, 136, 137, 138, 139, 140, 143, 144, 145
environmental groups:
free-rider problems 9–10
level of operation 10
Environmental Law Institute 14
Environmental Protection Act 14
Environmental Protection Agency 13–14, 146–7, 149–50, 334
environmental regulation:
California effect 335–8, 341
comparative advantage 335
constitutional law 150–2
cost of compliance 6, 18, 272, 333
delegated enforcement 147–50
developing countries 341–4
devolution 145–50
domestic firms 335
economic integration 330–2
economies of scale 16, 136–7
emissions standards viii
empirical studies 5–7, 139–40
enforcement 140–2, 147–50
EU 18–20; bureaucracy 284; enforcement 280; environmental heritage 275–7; harmonization 279–81; legal mechanisms 340–1; 'levelling the playing field' approach 273–4; lobbying 282; minimum standards 277–81; overview 331; policy justification 264–5, 267–77; public choice issues 281–3; race to the bottom 270–4; rhetoric 285; single market 274, 281–3, 285
externalities xiii, 7–9, 33–5, 46, 267–70
federal, policy justification vii, xi, 15–17
global economy 341–4
human rights 20–2, 131, 276–7
integration 344
international perspective 20–4
legal mechanisms 340–1
market conditions 4–5
minimum standards 276–80, 280–1
national interest 269
Newly Industrialized Countries 343–4
prisoners' dilemma 137–8, 270, 273
psychic spillovers 275
public benefits 334
public choice issues 9–12, 142–5
public goods 136–7
public health 17
race to the bottom 3–7, 7, 137–40, 270–4
race to the top 334–40
trade measures 21–4, 338
transaction costs 274–5
transboundary pollution 267–70
treaties 340–1
under/over valuation 9
uniformity 16–17
US; delegation 145–52; enforcement 147–50; history 11–15; overview 330; state liability 150–2
variation standards 23–4
EPA *see* Environmental Protection Agency
Esty, Daniel C. xii, xiv, 9, 27, 30–47, 114, 137, 267 (n. 12), 268, 271–2, 272 (n. 22), 274 (n. 26), 275 (n. 31), 276 (n. 37), 277–9, 279 (n. 43, 46), 281–5, 312 (n. 1), 332–3, 345–7, 381
Eule, Julian N. 58
Eurobonds 175–6
European Central Bank 223, 234
European Commission 41, 221, 224, 229, 254, 258, 264, 268, 278 (n. 42), 284, 353, 366 (n. 7)
European Court of Justice:
mandatory requirements 199
negative harmonization 198–203
proportionality test 199, 201–3
subsidiarity 19 (n. 4)
European (financial) passport 218–19, 221, 225–7
European Industrial Relations Review 243
European Securities and Exchange Commission, call for 238–9
European Works Councils 195, 211–12, 252–4
Evans, A. 112
Evans, G. 370 (n. 16), 374
exchange:
regulation 105–9
SEC definition 106–7
exhaustion, principle 378–9
export cartels 355
exports *see* trade measures
externalities:
economic x, xiv, 33–45, 46, 158, 163–4, 230–1, 358–9
environmental 7–9, 267–70, 281–3
interstate 3, 7–9, 16, 267–70
securities regulation 306–7
transboundary xvii
types 34

fair price statutes 76
Farber, Daniel 11, 138, 351
FASB *see* Financial Accounting Standards Board
Faure, Michael xvii–xviii, 17, 19, 263–86
Federal Deposit Insurance Corporation 101
federalism:
allocation of power 42, 98–9
definition 95
normative perspective 99, 103–4
structure of 39
US 96–9

federalization x, 38
Feldstein, Martin 63, 165, 166
Fern, Danielle F. 13
Ferrell, Allen xv, 68–94, 206, 210, 219, 293 (n. 6)
FESCO *see* Forum of European Securities Commissions
Financial Accounting Standards Board 306
financial regulation:
EU; burden 228–30; competition 222; contractual framework 235–6; economies of scale 229; effectiveness 238; financial intermediaries 236–8; free-riding 230–1; incorporation 236–7; market access 222–5; minimum standards 228–9; mutual recognition 221–2, 227; overregulation 227; overview 218–20; political aspects 103–5, 110; private interests 228–30; public choice issues 231–4; regulators 233–4, 238; securities 237; single market 220–1; supervisory authority 234
European passport 218–19, 221, 225–7
global 240
race to the bottom 225–7
US 100–3, 109
Fine, Sydney 123
Fingleton *et al.* 349, 354
fiscal federalism xiv, xvi, 158–61, 167–8
Code of Conduct on Business Taxation 176, 179–82, 182–3
redistribution 164–7
Fischel, Daniel R. 68, 72, 81, 91–2, 191, 203, 208, 210, 299
Flatt 140
Forrester, John P. 137 (n. 5)
Forsythe, Kenneth W. 42
Forum of European Securities Commissions 233
Fox, Eleanor M. xi, 69 (n. 2), 348–63
Fox, Merritt B. 300
fraud 230
free-riding 9–10, 231
Freedman, J. 206
freedom of establishment 192–3, 202
Freeman, Jody 40, 208, 321, 329
French, Hilary F. 334, 344
Frey, Bruno 162, 266, 273
Friedman, Joseph *et al.* 6
Friedman, Sandra 261–2 (n. 23)
Friedman, Thomas L. 361
Fuerst, Oren 227

Gadbaw, R. 368
GATS *see* General Agreement on Trade in Services
GATT *see* World Trade Organisation
Geiger, Uri 305
gender discrimination legislation 318
General Accounting Office 140, 146, 150 (n. 31)
General Agreement on Tarriffs and Trade *see* World Trade Organisation
General Agreement on Trade in Services 351
Geradin, Damien 30–47, 268, 270–2, 272 (n. 22), 277–9, 279 (n. 43, 46), 281–3, 285, 332–3, 345–6, 376, 381
Gertner, R. 212
Gey, Steven G. 138
Gilson, Ronald J. 79–81, 84
Gingrich, Newt vii
Glaeser, E. 132
Godwin, M. 206
Goetschy 113
Goklany, Indur M. 12
Goldfield, Michael 117
Golub, J. 168
Gordon, Roger H. 57, 163, 166, 186
Gore, Al 23
Gormley, Laurence W. 44
Govaere, Inge xix, 364–81, 397 (n. 37)
Grabosky, Peter 339 (n. 14)
Graetz, Michael J. 59
Gramlich, Edward M 294
Grasso, Thomas V. 15
Great Intellectual Property Conventions 374
Griffith, Barbara 117
Gross, James 111, 121
Gruber, Jonathan 315–16 (n. 6)
Grundfest, Joseph A. 81
guaranty schemes 101–3
Guerrero, Peter F. 13
Guyon, J. 223 (n. 4)
Guzman, Andrew T. 69 (n. 2), 205 (n. 1), 289 (n. 1), 294, 308 (n. 20)

Haagsma, Auke 18
Haas, Peter 340, 340 (n. 16), 341–2
Hackethal, A. 223
Haddock, D. 108
Haigh, Nigel 340 (n. 15)
Halpern, Martin 117
Hamilton, Bruce 53
Hammen, H. 237
Handler, Milton 119 (n. 5)
harmonization:
company law 191–5
environmental regulation: EU policy 279–81; policy justification 267–77; types vii, 278–9
EU 17–20
financial services 220–2
labour 116–18
level playing field xiv
mandatory 58–9
product standards 17–18, 273–4, 337–40

harmonization (*cont.*):
- regulatory vii, viii, x
- reflexive xvii, 191–2, 209–16
- tax 49, 51–3, 54–6
- uniformity 37 (n. 7)
- voluntary 51

Havana Charter 350
hazardous waste regulation 13–14
Head, C.K. et al. 132–3
heavily polluting industries 6–7
Hellerstein, Walter 137 (n. 5)
Henderson, J. Vernon 6
Herring, R.J. 42
Hertig, Gérard xvii, 218–40
Heylen, F. 181
Hicks, A. 206
Hines, James R. 66
Hirsch, A. 237
Honey, Micheal 123, 124, 126, 132
Hoppmann, C. 232
horizontal co-opetition 40–2
horizontal subsidiarity 251–2
Horn, N. 225
Hoschka, T.C. 223
hostile takeovers 196, 213–16
Housman, Robert 342
Howse, Robert 43, 131 (n. 14), 272 (n. 23), 324
Hudec, Robert vii, 31, 39
Hudnall, Shannon 339
Hughes, A. 207, 210, 212, 365
human rights *see* rights
Hunter, Jason 342
Husted, Bryan 331, 339, 343 (n. 20)

ILO *see* International Labor Organization
IMF 240
imperfect information 35
imports *see* trade measures
incorporation 69, 236–7
- market 203–9
- territorial regulations 204–6, 207

indirect taxes 170
industrial relations *see* labour regulation
Inman, R.P. 158, 162, 164, 177, 186, 266, 291 (n. 3), 293 (n. 8)
insurance regulation 100–1
Integration of Pollution Prevention and Control, Directive 264, 282–3
intellectual property protection
- Agreement on Trade-Related Aspects of Intellectual Property Rights 366–7, 371, 374–5, 378–80, 381
- assessment 367
- coercion 368–9
- cost–benefit analysis 367
- developing countries 368–9, 377, 380–1
- EC 378–80
- exhaustion 379
- externalities 368, 372, 376
- global, mechanisms 369
- global market 380
- Great Intellectual Property Conventions 374
- investment 376–7
- market variation 367
- maximum standards 366
- national treatment 374–5
- natural justice 371–2
- natural treatment 374–5
- private interest 365–7
- public choice 368–9
- public interest 367
- race to the bottom 366
- reciprocity 374–5
- rights: compliance with 32; international 369–70; national 370–1; priority 373–4
- socio-economic costs 377
- trade measures 368–9
- trademarks 365
- World Trade Organization 375, 380–1

interest groups, endogeneity 113, 121
International Accounting Standards Committee 292
International Labor Organization 130, 328–9
International Organization of Securities Commissions 292
International Pollution Deterrence Act 23
International Securities Commissions Organization 229
internet 224–5
Investment Services Directive 225
investment-competition model 318
IOSCO *see* International Securities Commissions Organization
IPPC Directive *see* Integration of Pollution Prevention and Control
ISD *see* Investment Services Directive
issuers 108–9

Jachtenfuch, M. 177
Jacobson, Harold K. 340 (n. 16)
Jacoby, Sanford 118, 120
Jaffee *et al.* 6, 38, 272
Jakob, Thinam 349, 353
Janeba, E. 170
Jebsen, Per 352
Jenkins, Rhys 339
Jenkins, Robin R. *et al.* 14
Jenny, Frédéric 361
Jensen, Michael C. 73 (n. 5)
Jha, Veena 337, 338 (n. 12)
John, P. 183
Johnson, W.R. 164
Joint Statement of US–EU Summit 41
Jolls, Christine 315–16 (n. 6)

judicial review 256–61
jurisdiction, market 266–7, 308
jurisdictional competition 158–64
  assumptions 161–2
  Code of Conduct on Business Taxation 182
  empirical verification 183–6
  EU company law 205–9, 215
  government size 185
  labour regulation 322–3
  types 313–14
jurisdictional structures:
  assessment 303–8
  types 302–3

Kahler, Miles 341 (n. 19), 346
Kamar, Ehud 87
Kaouris, Demetrios G. 71 (n. 4)
Kaplow, L. 162, 166
Kapstein, Ethan 131
Kastenmeter, R. 368
Katz, Harry 118, 120
Katz, M. 132
Kechidi, M. 233
Keen, M.J. 164, 166, 168, 171, 179, 181, 187, 188
Keohane, Nathaniel O. 11
Keohane, Robert O. 340 (n. 16)
Kimber, Clíona 268, 277 (n. 39), 280, 280 (n. 49), 286 (n. 58)
Kirchgaessner, G. 160, 183–4, 266
Kitch, Edmund 299, 301
Klabbers, J. 174
Klevorick, Alvin K. xii, 38, 347
Koch, N. 379 (n. 37)
Kochan, Thomas 118, 120
Kohl, Helmut 36
Kolstad, Charles 272
Kopp, Raymond 331
Koretz, Gene 334
Koskela, E. 167
Kraakman, Reinier 81
Kraft, Michael E. 42
Kramer, Ludvig 19
Krenzler, Horst G. 41
Krueger, Alan 317 (n. 8)
Kübler, Friedrich 36
Kuehn, Robert R. 147

Labor Relations Act *see* National Labor Relations Act
labour costs 242–6
labour regulation:
  benchmarking 329
  comparative advantage 245
  democratic legitimacy 255–9
  democratic theory 325–7
  EU 261–2; collective bargaining 254; costs 241–6; democratic legitimacy 255–9; history 241–2; subsidiarity 249–54; UK stance 246; working time 254
  global equity 327
  goals 114
  international effects 313–14
  investment–competition model 318
  jurisdictional competition 322–3
  market imperfections 314–15
  market for mobile industry 324
  migration 328
  normative aspects 131
  poorer nations 327
  redistribution 320–2
  rights 323–5
  social values 326
  sovereignty 326–7
  US; history 112, 116–25, 126–7 (n. 10); supranational status 111–12, 122
  see also labour standards; social dialogue
Labour Relations Board *see* National Labor Relations Board
labour standards:
  consensus 328
  dynamic 317–19
  efficiency 322–3
  empowerment rules 320–2
  social insurance 319–20
  static 315–17
  valuation 315–16
Lando, O. 274 (n. 23)
Languille, Brian 325
Larouche, Pierre 41
Lash III, William 331
Lazear, E. 208
Leary, Virginia A. 325
LeBeouf, Jaques 27
Lee, R. 225, 232, 238–9
Lee, Sang Don 336–7, 339
Lefevere, Jürgen 17, 19, 264, 272, 277 (n. 41), 278 (n. 42), 282, 285
legal systems market 266–7, 308
Legrand, B. 274
Lester, James P. 137
'level playing field' approach xiv, xviii, 273–4, 281–2, 338–9
levels of competition 40
Leviathan state 158–9
Levich, R.M. 228, 305
Levinson, Arik 6
Levy, Marc A. 340 (n. 16)
Licht, A. 205, 219, 226
Liefferink, J.D. 340 (n. 15)
Light, Alfred R. 146
Lipton, Martin 81
listings 299–301

Litchenstein, Nelson 117
lobbying *see* public choice issues
locational neutrality 52–3
  tax havens/holidays 64–5
locational rights market
  effect of regulation 4–5, 7
  imperfections 33–40; competitors 38–40; economies of scale 36–7; externalities 33–5; information limitations 35; lack of mobility 35; market failure 33; prisoners dilemma 37–8; public choice 37
logic of collective action 9–11
Logsdon, Jeanne 331, 339, 343 (n. 20)
Logue, Dennis E. 299
Lomas, Owen 18, 34
Louis, J.V. *et al.* 238
Low, Patrick 38, 333 (n. 6)
Lowe, P.D. 340 (n. 15)
Lucas, Robert *et al.* 333 (n. 6)
Luce, E. 224 (n. 6)

Maastricht summit 248
Maastricht Treaty on European Union 255
McCahery *et al.* 31, 32, 166, 184, 291 (n. 2), 293, 293 (n. 8), 294, 296, 312
McCahery, Joseph xii, xvi, 157–89
McConnell, M.W. 6, 99
McCormick, Robert E. 11
McCubbins *et al.* 33
McEnroe, John E. 306
Macey, Jonathan xii, xv, 25, 26, 35, 87, 95–110, 135, 191, 346 (n. 22)
Machlup, F. 366 (n. 6), 371 (n. 19), 374 (n. 24)
McKersie, Robert 118, 120
McLure, C.E. 162, 165
Maddox, Bronwen 332, 332 (n. 4), 333
Maloney, Michael T. 11
mandatory requirements doctrine 199
Mani, Muthukumara 38
Mansori, Kashif S. 57
Marchand, M. 163, 165
market access:
  banking 223
  investment management 224
  securities 224–5
market for locational rights *see* locational rights market
market for mobile industry 140, 333–4, 354–6, 366
Markusen, James R. 5, 139
Marshaw, Jerry L. 33
Martens, Stanley 306
Mashaw, Jerry L. 27, 137 (n. 4), 138
Matsushita, Mitsuo 362
Mattoo, Aaditya 41
Mayer, C. 196, 219
Mead, W. 133
mechanisms of coordination 113
Medoff 321
Meek, Gary K. 301
Melamed, Douglas 41
Mello, A.S. 223
Mendelsohn, R. 204, 274
Mendelson, H. 107
Merrill, Thomas 135, 136, 136 (n. 1)
Meyer, Stephen 333
Mieszkowski, P. 167
Miller, Geoffrey 87, 96, 99, 105, 191, 331 (n. 1), 334
Millian, John C. 12, 273
minimum capital requirements 201–3, 207–8
Minimum Effective Taxation of Interest Income, Draft Directive 174–9
minimum standards, EU 228–9
minimum wage 318
Mintz, Jack 314
Mirrlees, James 55
MITE case 76, 91
mobile industry market 140, 333–4, 354–6, 366
mobility:
  capital 61–4, 161–2, 166–7, 171, 185
  jurisdictional 292
  labour 328
  taxpayer 59–63
  technical 292
Modigliani, Franco 301
Moffitt, Robert 63
Mofson, Phylliss 341 (n. 18)
Mol, A.P.J. 340 (n. 15)
Molle, W. 221
Monti Report 172, 180–1
Moore, Curtis 331 (n. 1), 334
Moravcsik, A. 176, 326
Morey, Edward R. 5, 139
Morris, G. 215
Mott, Richard 42
Mueller, D. 213
multinationals, environmental standards 339
Munoz, Heraldo 338 (n. 13)
Murphy, Kevin J. 73 (n. 5)
mutual recognition 41, 221–2, 227

Nader, Ralph *et al.* 330
NAFTA *see* North American Free Trade Agreement
Nam, Young-Suck 331
National Labor Relations Act 119–20
National Labor Relations Board 116, 119
national treatment 374–5
negative harmonization 198–203
neocorporatism 127–8
Netherlands Ministry of Finance 171, 178
New Deal 116–18
New Growth theory 132–3

New York Stock Exchange 97
Newly Industrialized Countries 343–4
Nicolaïdis, Kalypso 291
Niskanen, William A. 100
NLRA *see* National Labor Relations Act
NLRB *see* National Labor Relations Board
Nogues, J. 377 (n. 28)
non-hazardous waste regulation 14
North American Free Trade Agreement 339
North, Douglass 307
nuclear power regulation 104–5
Nuclear Regulatory Commission 104–5
Nussbaum, Martha 325
NYSE *see* New York Stock Exchange

Oates, Wallace E. viii, x, xi, 4, 30, 34, 95, 135, 138, 141, 158, 167, 183, 185, 266, 312, 313
Obrdovic, D. 261 (n. 22)
Obstfeld, M. 185
OECD *see* Organization for Economic Cooperation and Development
Ogus, Anthony 266, 266 (nn. 8–9), 268, 271, 272 (n. 23), 275, 275 (n. 32), 276 (n. 38), 278, 280–1, 280 (n. 49)
O'Hear, Michael M. 59
Olewiler, Nancy D. 5, 139
Olson, Mancur viii, x, 10, 143
optimal provision of public goods *see* Tiebout model
optimal tariffs 54
Orbuch, Paul 342
Ordover, Janusz 357, 362
O'Regan, M. 371 (n. 18)
Organization for Economic Cooperation and Development 39, 64, 67, 330
O'Rourke, Dara 132
Osterman, Paul 118
overregulation xiv
Owens, J. 169

Padoa-Schioppa, T. 223, 228–9, 238
Panel on Takeovers and Mergers *see* City Panel
Papendrou, Andreas A. 295
Pâques, Michel 269
Parental Leave Directive 255
Parr, N. 365
Passell, Peter 64
passport, financial 218–19, 221, 225–7
Paul, Joel 327
Pauly, M.V. 165
Payne, Cymie 15
Pearson, Charles 337
Pelkmans, J. 221, 303, 309 (n. 21)
Peltzman, Sam 10, 273
penalty default rule 212
Penrose, E. 366 (n. 6), 370 (n. 16), 371 (n. 19), 372, 373, 374 (n. 24), 376, 380
Perotti, Enrico 301
Persson, T. 186
pesticide standards 337
Pestieau, P. 164, 166, 178
Peters, W. 170
Petersen, K.F.V. 27
Petersmann, Ernst-Elrich 41
Pfander, J. 280 (n. 49)
Pharr, Susan 331, 336
Phillips, S.M. 106
PHTMs *see* potentially harmful tax measures
Pigou, Arthur 34
Pigovian taxes 186
Piketty, T. 186–7
Pinto, C. 173, 180
Piore, Michael 117, 317–18, 330
Pitofsky, Robert 362
poison pill defence 76–7, 81, 85–6
pollution havens *see* race to the bottom
Pomerehne, W.W. 160, 183–4, 266
Pomp, Richard D. 137 (n. 5)
portable reciprocity 302
Portanger, E. 223 (n. 5)
Porter, Michael 334, 344, 349
Portney, Paul R. 12, 22, 331
Posner, R. 100, 208, 287
potentially harmful tax measures 172–4, 178–9, 180–2, 184
preemption 16
pressure-to-tender problem 79, 81
presumption of decentralization 158–9, 267
prisoners' dilemma 37–8, 270, 273
product standards ix, 17–18, 273–4, 337–40
production processes *see* process standards
proportionality test 199, 201–3, 222
public choice:
  capture 142–3
  definition 3–4
  election motives 143
  environmental regulation 9–12, 142–5, 281–3
  federal governments 144–5
  financial regulation 231–4
  logic of collective action 9–11
public goods 32–3, 50, 53, 60, 136–7, 163–4, 188

qualified majority voting 168–9, 248

race to the bottom:
  aspects vi, xiv, xix, 27, 38
  bank charters 25–6
  common market, distinguished 271–2
  company law 193, 211–13
  competition law 352, 353–4
  corporate charters 24–5

race to the bottom (*cont.*):
  definition x, 3, 30
  desirability 50–1
  economic redistribution 26–7
  environmental regulation 30, 137–40, 270–4; empirical studies 5–7, 272; models 3–5
  externalities, distinguished 26–7
  financial regulation 225–7
  imperfect competition 5
  intellectual property 366
  labour rights 133
  market conditions 4–5, 28, 138–9
  perfect competition 4–5
  taxation 62, 62–3, 63
race to the top 68, 272–3
  company law 210
  competition law 353, 356
  financial regulation 227
  intellectual property 366
race towards the bottom *see* race to the bottom
Radaelli, C.M. 169, 170, 179
Raff, H. 165, 187
Raskind, L. 365 (n. 3)
Rawls, John 131
real seat doctrine see *siège réel* doctrine
redemption rights 76, 79
redistribution 26–7, 63–4, 162–3, 164–7
reference to standards approach 194
reflexive harmonization 191–2, 209–16
Regan, Donald 58, 143
regulation:
  level 95, 100, 103, 109–10
  self-definition effect 100, 104–5
  subsidiarity 157–8
Regulation of Takeover Bids, draft Thirteenth Directive 213–16
regulator self-interest 233–4, 238
regulatory authority vii
regulatory co-opetition:
  aspects 32
  extragovernmental 44–6
  horizontal 40–2
  intergovernmental 40–3
  intragovernmental 43–4
  model xiv
  utility 46
  vertical 42–3
regulatory competition theory
  application xii, xix, 30–1
  coordinated action 114–16
  cost–benefit analysis 296
  criticism 31–2
  jurisdictional structures 302–8
  labour law 114–15
  limitations 33–40
  literature xiii
  market conditions xiv, 4–5
  merits 51
  models 115
  policy implications viii–ix
  social welfare xiii
  Tiebout model xii, 32–40
regulatory ecology 46
regulatory harmonization, *see* harmonization
regulatory jurisdiction 290–1
regulatory mismatch 15–17
Rehbinder, Eckard 46
reincorporations 203–6, 236–7
relative sufficiency test 250–1
representativity 257–9
Revesz, Richard viii, xii, xiv, 3–29, 30, 34, 37–8, 135, 137–8, 137–8 (nn. 6–7), 228, 270–1, 272 (n. 21), 273, 279 (n. 44), 313, 331, 347, 352
Rice, Eric 66
Richards, John 343
rights:
  association 112, 125–8
  environmental regulation 20–2, 131, 276–7
  intellectual property 369–71, 373–4
  labour 323–5
risk management 238
Rodden, Jonathan 145
Rodrik, Dani 18, 38, 167, 182, 317–18, 319–20, 324
Roe, M. 191, 205, 216
Rogers, Joel 119 (n. 5), 120, 121, 208
Rogoff, K. 240
Rogowski, R. 210
Roin, Julie 64, 65
Romano, Roberta xii, 30, 35, 71 (n. 4), 72, 74, 81, 84, 85 (n. 22), 86, 92, 96, 99, 104, 106, 191, 205 (n. 1), 209, 211, 215, 237, 289 (n. 1), 290, 291 (n. 4), 293, 293 (n. 7), 301, 305–6
rootless recognition 302
Rose-Ackerman, Susan xvi, 135–53, 265, 267, 267 (n. 12), 268, 270, 274 (n. 25), 274 (n. 25, 27, 30), 274 (n. 30), 275 (n. 33), 276 (n. 36), 279 (n. 45), 281, 283 (n. 55), 284, 284 (n. 57)
Rosen, Harvey S. 60
Rosenburg, Robin 338 (n. 13)
Rothstein, Richard 133, 329
Rowley, J.W. 362
Rubinfeld, D. 158, 162, 164, 177, 186, 266, 291 (n. 3), 293 (n. 8)

Sabel, Charles 112, 115 (n. 4), 117, 128, 132, 329, 330
Saleska, Scott 7, 137, 143, 144
Samuelson condition 161
Samuelson, P.A. 161
sanctions *see* trade measures

Sapir, Andre 319, 319 (n. 11)
Sarnoff, Joshua D. 137
Saudagaran, Shahrokh M. 299 (n. 10)
Saunders, A. 225
Scharpf, F.W. 176
Schaub, Alex 41
Scherer, F. 377 (nn. 28–9)
Schmidt, R.H. 223
Schmitthoff, Clive 193
Schob, R. 167
Schoenbrod, D. 276
Schoettle, Ferdinand P. 58
Schomaker, Astrid 41
Schuster, G. 237
Schwab, Robert M. xi, 4, 6, 30, 138 (n. 7), 141, 266, 313
Scotchmer, S. 163
Scott, Kenneth 101
Seabright, P. 174
SEC *see* Securities and Exchange Commission, US
Securities and Exchange Commission, US 96–8, 106–8, 301
securities regulation:
  capital allocation 300–1
  corporate law analogy 298–9, 309–10
  empirical evidence 308–9
  enforcement 108–9
  EU: mechanisms 302–3; mutual recognition 237
  externalities 295–6
  international system 297–8, 310
  jurisdictional structures 302–8
  listing value 299–300
  regulatory jurisdiction 295–6
  social welfare 299–301
  stability 294–5
  territoriality 297–8
  US 105–10, 299–300
Seligman, Joel 301
Sen, Amartya 131
Sesit, M. 224 (n. 6)
Shapiro, Fred R. 68, 132
share value 72–3
Shaviro, Daniel xiv–xv, 49–50, 49–67, 52, 56, 57–9, 62
Shelton, Joanna R. 362
Sherman Act 359
Shrimp-Turtle case 21, 45, 342
siège réel doctrine xvi–xvii, 190, 200–4, 236
Silva, Eduardo 339
single market 220–1
  intellectual property rights 379
Sinn, H.W. 167
Sirower, M. 213
Slaughter, Anne-Marie 362
Slinger, G. 207, 213–14
Small Car Directive 337
Smallcombe, J. 206
Smith, R.C. 224, 228
Snyder, F. 172
social dialogue:
  autonomy 259–61
  democratic legitimacy 256–9
  modelling 261–2 (n. 23)
  origin 247–8
  representativity 257–9
  scrutiny 260
  treaty basis 255
social dumping xvii, 242–6, 316–17
social insurance 319–20
Societas Europea 195
Sonnenfeld, David 340
sovereignty 326–7
Spar, Debora 333 (n. 6), 339
Special Issue 236
Special Negotiating Body 253
spillovers vii, 54–5, 65–6, 230–1
Spindler, Charles J. 137 (n. 5)
stability 294
Staiger 313 (n. 3), 314 (n. 5)
stakeholders 194–6, 214–15
state aid 174
Stavins, Robert N. 11
Steinzor, Rena 145
Stephan, Paul B. 222
Stern, Arthur C. 12, 46, 313 (n. 3), 316 (n. 7)
Stevens, Robert 352
Stewart, Richard viii, 17, 20, 30, 34, 38, 41, 135, 137, 267 (n. 12), 276 (n. 38), 333 (n. 6), 334, 344
Stigler, George K. 10
Stiglitz, J.E. 162, 165
stock exchange *see* exchange
Stone, Katherine 329 (n. 15)
Streeck, Wolfgang 208, 212 (n. 2), 243, 327
Subramanian, Arvind 41
subsidiarity:
  aspects viii, 249–51
  Code of Conduct on Business Conduct 179–82
  criteria 252
  debate over viii
  fiscal federalism 157–8
  justiciability 19
  labour regulation 251–4
  overview 19–20
  presumption of decentralization 19–20
  tax competition 160
  types 251–2
Summers, Lawrence H. 315–16 (n. 6)
Sun, Jeanne-Mey 303, 309 (n. 21)
Sundaram, Anant 299
Sunstein, Cass 315–16 (n. 6)

Swire, Peter P. 137, 341 (n. 19), 345, 346
Sykes, Alan ix, 37, 222

TABD *see* Transatlantic Business Dialogue
Tabellini, G. 167, 186
Takeover Bids, Thirteenth Directive 194
Takeover Code, UK 213–14
takeover law:
  bidders, rules restricting 75–6, 78–80
  certainty 70, 86–7, 88–9
  constitutionality 76, 78–9
  defensive tactics 76–8, 80–4, 85–6, 88
  hostile takeovers 223
  legislative protections 84–5
  managers' interests 69–70, 71–4
  poison pill defence 76–7, 81, 85–6
  policy basis 78
  shareholders' interests 72
  state competition 92–4
  UK 87–9, 213–14
takeovers, hostile 196, 213–14
tariffs *see* trade measures
tax:
  competition xiv
  havens 64–7
  locational neutrality 50, 52–3
  monopsony power 54–5
  transfer pricing 57 (n. 14), 66
  types 61–3, 163, 170–1
  uniformity 52 (n. 3)
tax regulation:
  Code of Conduct on Business Taxation 182–3
  conclusions 67
  coordination 187–9
  distortative effects 162, 164, 167, 180–2, 185–6
  distortion 168
  efficiency 51–2, 61–3, 162
  EU 168–72; asymmetric information 186–7; Code of Conduct 172–4; coordination 168; Draft Directive 174–6; harmonization 169; pre-1997 171–2; qualified majority voting 168–9; state interest 177–8; strategies 176–9; subsidiarity 189
  harmonization 53, 58–9
  Ireland 183
  overview 49–51
  redistribution 63–4, 162–3, 164–6
  subsidiarity principle 157
  tax havens 64–7
  taxpayer mobility 59–60, 59–61
  theory 163
  trade barriers 54–9, 55, 57
taxpayer mobility 59–63
Terra, B. 169, 171
Teubner, B. 210
Thakor, A.V. 233
Thaler, Richard 315–16 (n. 6)
theory of the firm 50
Thieffry, G. 232
Thirteenth Directive *see* Regulation of Takeover Bids
Tiebout, Charles xi, 32–3, 42, 50, 95, 158, 265, 293, 326
Tiebout model:
  criticism 33–40
  locational neutrality 50, 52–3
  presumption of decentralization 267
  securities regulation 293–4
  tax regulation 52–3, 60–1
  theory 32–3
Tiedman, T. 273
Tirez, D. 232
Tobey, James A. 333 (n. 6)
Trachtman, Joel P. xviii, 289–310
Trade Act 368
trade barriers *see* trade measures
Trade Mark Regulation, EC 370
trade measures:
  customs duties 56
  environmental regulation 21–3, 29, 338
  intellectual property protection 368–9
  tariff equivalents 56–7, 65
  tariffs 54–6
  tax harmonisation 55–6, 57
  unilateral sanctions 338
trademarks 365
trading systems *see* exchange
transaction costs 274, 307–8
Transatlantic Business Dialogue 46
transboundary pollution 267–70
transfer pricing 57 (n. 14), 66
Treaty on European Union 157
Trebilcock, Michael 43, 272 (n. 23), 324
TRIPS *see* Agreement on Trade-Related Aspects of Intellectual Property Rights
Trubek, David M. 329
Tucker, E. 169, 343
Tulkens, Henry 314
Tullock 100
Tuna-Dolphin case 20–1
Tussie, Diana 342
Tyrell, M. 223

UK Takeover Code 213–14
Ullrich 41, 373 (n. 22), 374, 375, 375 (n. 25), 377 (n. 29)
underregulation xiv
Unger, Roberto 125
Union Européenne de l'Artisan et des Petites et Moyennes Entreprises 255–6, 260
unions 120–1, 320–2
US Clean Air Act 8–9, 12, 13, 335–6

US Environmental Protection Agency 147
US Trade Act 368

Valliant, Marian 63
Van Alstyne, W.W. 96
Van den Bergh, Roger 17, 19, 36, 264, 266, 268–9, 273–4, 274 (n. 29), 278 (n. 42), 279 (n. 48), 284 (n. 56), 285
van Ypersele, T. 167, 320
Vasquez, Patricia 342
vertical co-opetition 42–3
vertical subsidiarity 251–2
Viander, A. 236
Vig, Norman J. 42
Vigneault, M. 163, 165
Villiers, C. 193, 194, 216
Villiers, Charlotte 194
Vitols, S. *et al.* 208
Vogel, David ix, xix, 272 (n. 23), 274, 330–47
voluntary agreements 45–6
voluntary harmonization 51
Von Hase, Y. 378 (n. 34)
von Moltke, Konrad 333 (n. 6)

Wacziarg, R. 187
Wade, Robert 332 (n. 2)
Wald, Matthew 336
Walter, I. 223–5, 228
water pollution 8, 140 (n. 12)
Wattel, P. 169, 171
Weichenrieder, Alfons J. 57
Weiler, Paul 118, 120
Weingast, Barry 95, 144
Weiss, Edith Brown 339, 340 (n. 16)
Wellens, K.C. 174
Wernicke, T. 236
wetlands protection 15
Wheeler, David 38
White, Lawrence J. 305
Wildasin, D.E. 165–6
Wilkinson, F. 210–11
Williamson, Oliver 307
Wils, Wouter 34, 275
Wilson, John D. xii, 57, 161, 165, 167, 187
Wilthagen, T. 210
Winter, Ralph xii, 68, 72, 90–1
withholding tax 175
Wolkoff, Michael J. 137 (n. 5)
Wolman, Harold 143
worker association *see* rights
Working Group on the Interaction Between Trade and Competition Policy 350, 361
working time 254
World Trade Organization xiii, 20–1, 39, 45, 342
  competition law 350, 360–1
  intellectual property 375, 380–1
Wrobel, M. 165, 166

Xanthaki, H. 236
Xing, Yuqing 272

Yandle, G. 282
Yeats, A. 38, 333 (n. 6)
Yoffie, David 333 (n. 6)
Young, Oran R. 183, 340

Zaelke, Durwood 342
Zagaris, Bruce 343 (n. 20)
Zarsky, Lyuba 342
Zecher, R. 106
Zeiger, R. 124
Zodrow, G.R. 167
Zurstrassen, P. 224

The manufacturer's authorised representative in the EU for product safety is Oxford University Press España S.A. of el Parque Empresarial San Fernando de Henares, Avenida de Castilla, 2 – 28830 Madrid (www.oup.es/en or product.safety@oup.com). OUP España S.A. also acts as importer into Spain of products made by the manufacturer.

www.ingramcontent.com/pod-product-compliance
Lightning Source LLC
LaVergne TN
LVHW011901200926
848484LV00002B/500

* 9 7 8 0 1 9 8 2 9 9 0 5 9 *